MASTERPLOTS II

AMERICAN FICTION SERIES, REVISED EDITION

MASTERPLOTS II

AMERICAN FICTION SERIES, REVISED EDITION

6

Ten - Z
Indexes

Edited by
STEVEN G. KELLMAN
The University of Texas at San Antonio

SALEM PRESS

Pasadena, California   Hackensack, New Jersey

Editor in Chief: Dawn P. Dawson
Managing Editor: Christina J. Moose
Project Editor: Robert A. McClenaghan   *Research Editor:* Jeffrey Jensen
Acquisitions Editor: Mark Rehn   *Research Assistant:* Jun Ohnuki

Library of Congress Cataloging-in-Publication Data
Masterplots II. American fiction series / edited by Steven G.
Kellman.—Rev. ed.
    p.   cm.
Includes bibliographical references and index.
    ISBN 0-89356-871-6 (set) — ISBN 0-89356-872-4 (v. 1) —
ISBN 0-89356-873-2 (v. 2) — ISBN 0-89356-874-0 (v. 3) —
ISBN 0-89356-875-9 (v. 4) — ISBN 0-89356-876-7 (v. 5) —
ISBN 0-89356-877-5 (v. 6)
    1. American fiction—Stories, plots, etc. I. Title: Masterplots
2. II. Title: Masterplots two. III. Title: American fiction series.
IV. Kellman, Steven G., 1947-   .
PS373 .M37   2000
809.3'0097—dc21   99-053295

First Printing

PRINTED IN THE UNITED STATES OF AMERICA

LIST OF TITLES IN VOLUME 6

LIST OF TITLES IN VOLUME 6

MASTERPLOTS II

AMERICAN FICTION SERIES, REVISED EDITION

TEN NORTH FREDERICK

Author: John O'Hara (1905-1970)
Type of plot: Deterministic realism
Time of plot: 1945
Locale: Gibbsville, Pennsylvania, and New York City
First published: 1955

Principal characters:
> JOE CHAPIN, a lawyer and a member of the Gibbsville aristocracy, with ambitions for the presidency of the United States
> EDITH CHAPIN, his wife
> ANN CHAPIN, his daughter
> JOBY CHAPIN, his son
> MIKE SLATTERY, an Irish state senator in Gibbsville and chairman of the city's Republican county committee
> ARTHUR MCHENRY, Joe Chapin's law partner and best friend

The Novel

  Ten North Frederick begins with the death of Joe Chapin, the novel's main character. The date is April, 1945; Joe Chapin has died and his wife, Edith, has begun to receive sympathetic calls from her husband's close friends, business acquaintances, and political associates. From this starting point the novel begins to review Joe Chapin's life and all the people who were a part of it, shifting back in time as far as 1881, to the marriage of Joe's parents. O'Hara's goal in using this technique is to construct a composite portrait of life in Gibbsville, Pennsylvania (an imaginary city based on O'Hara's actual experiences in Pottsville, Pennsylvania), and it is not until the very end of *Ten North Frederick* that readers can fully understand that portrait. It is only at the end of the novel, for example, that O'Hara reveals that Joe has died of cirrhosis of the liver. By the novel's end, readers learn how Joe's political ambitions have been totally ruined; his marriage is a basically unhappy one; his two children, especially his daughter, Ann, have failed to establish any clear direction in their lives. Reacting to all of this, Joe drinks himself to death.

  On this level, *Ten North Frederick* presents a study of the futility of one man's life, as O'Hara shows that wealth and aristocratic social status cannot shield individuals from personal misery. On a deeper level, however, *Ten North Frederick* presents O'Hara's general view of American life in 1945. The street on which the Chapin family lives, Frederick Street, once represented the most desirable residential area in Gibbsville. As O'Hara describes it, however, in 1945 Frederick Street is no longer fashionable; the homes on North Frederick (including the Chapins') are quickly becoming monuments to a passing way of life (as the moneyed classes of Gibbsville move to a different section of town, Lantenengo Street). This kind of progress is not portrayed as positive in *Ten North Frederick*. In tracing the fortunes of the Chapin family, O'Hara presents a view of an evolving American society that is, at the bottom, tawdry. The people in Joe's class enjoy material wealth, but such comfort provides an insufficient buffer against life-styles that involve distant marriages (like that of Joe and Edith Chapin), pointless sexual affairs (both Joe and Edith have adulterous encounters; their daughter, Ann, sleeps with a number of men), political chicanery (Mike Slattery controls Gibbsville politics, and undoes Joe's political chances), and many instances of social hypocrisy. O'Hara is sympathetic to Joe, who tries to hang on to the values of a gentleman, but O'Hara is careful to show how such values are inadequate in 1945 America.

Essentially, O'Hara uses North Frederick Street as a microcosm of American society. A certain upper-class life-style that is symbolized by Joe and his family is passed by on this street; replacing that style of life is a younger, almost wholly materialistic world. At the novel's end, Joe gives up because he is, in O'Hara's words, both unable and unwilling to adapt to this new world. In *Ten North Frederick*, characters are not crushed by the changes that O'Hara portrays, but they all are forced to compromise (in one way or another), accepting a style of living that becomes increasingly sordid.

The Characters

Joe Chapin is clearly the main character in *Ten North Frederick*, yet O'Hara gives almost equal time and attention to the people who figure prominently in Joe's life. O'Hara's method of examining his characters is always the same: In one part of the novel he devotes several pages to a full description of Edith in order to illustrate her extremely cold, rational, and calculating desire to control all the people around her (she marries Joe because she believes she will literally own him by doing so, for example). In another part of *Ten North Frederick*, O'Hara gives five pages to a contemplation of Mike Slattery's life and political career, which blends impersonal or vindictive acts with those of unselfish generosity (he is a consummate politician). O'Hara regularly shifts into paragraph-long meditations that are designed to reveal a fundamental quality of each of his main characters. Joe's best friend, Arthur McHenry, is perhaps the only purely good person in Gibbsville; yet his total dedication to Joe is powerless to prevent his best friend's self-destruction. Ann, Joe's favorite child (thirty-four years old in 1945), can sustain only physical relationships with men, which do not last very long. Joby, her brother, age thirty, gradually adopts a cynical attitude that barely disguises his inability to find any real direction in his life.

The portrait of Gibbsville life that emerges from such character descriptions is a detailed and complex one, especially as O'Hara weaves a large number of minor characters throughout the fabric of the Chapin world. One problem is that O'Hara rarely shows his main (or minor) characters in action; he tries to explain them instead. Thus, Joe is never shown actually practicing law, nor is Mike observed in the midst of a back-room political deal. O'Hara relies on exposition to delineate his characters; his tendency is to explain rather than illustrate a character through a series of portrayed actions.

Another prominent feature of O'Hara's characterization, and one that has brought him much criticism, involves the fairly graphic sexual content of *Ten North Frederick*. The relationships between the main characters inevitably result in some form of sexual attraction or conduct. For example, as the novel unfolds, O'Hara reveals how both Edith and Joe had sexual affairs prior to their marriage. Edith's was a lesbian affair at a girl's school; Joe's liaison was with a girl who later died of an abortion. Neither admits this truth to the other. Mike admits a sexual desire for Edith, early in the novel, but the desire is never fulfilled. At the same time that Edith and Joe become involved in adulterous affairs (Edith with Lloyd Williams, a minor character, and Joe with Kate Drummond, his daughter's roommate in New York), Ann's approach to sex evolves into a form of casual promiscuity.

This kind of content, along with the graphic language O'Hara uses in describing the sexuality of his characters, lends an air of realism to *Ten North Frederick*. At the same time, however, O'Hara's descriptions lead to a number of instances of gratuitous sensationalism. At one point in the novel O'Hara describes the sexual intercourse between Joe and his wife during the latter months of her pregnancy; at another, Ann's adolescent activities with the driver of a butcher's delivery truck are portrayed. Such content certainly adds to the realism of the social portrait of *Ten North Frederick*, yet these episodes have (at best) a tangential connection to the novel's main ideas. Still, in no way is O'Hara presenting pornography in this novel. While his sexual content may at times become excessive—and sometimes, indeed, unnecessary—such content is an important part of characterization in *Ten North Frederick*, as any realistic assessment of life in the twentieth century must include some ideas of the complex force that sexuality exerts upon the lives of such characters as O'Hara portrays.

Themes and Meanings

There are two main themes in *Ten North Frederick*. One involves O'Hara's perceptions about the relationships between American men and women during the first half of the twentieth century; the second and equally important theme concerns O'Hara's ideas about American society itself.

At the end of the novel, O'Hara presents a bleak portrait of the Chapin family. Edith, from an established and cold distance, watches her husband drink himself to death. She cleans up his first hemorrhage herself, telling no one about it, and simply waits for the coma that finally overtakes him. Her son, Joby, sees a part of this when he visits his home, and the sight forces him out of the house in disgust. He is not present at his father's death, nor is Ann. Except for Edith, the only close friend at Joe's deathbed is Arthur.

On one level, this conclusion is a very dark one. Yet the key to a full understanding of O'Hara's final ideas can be found in the relationship that is established between Joe and Edith at the novel's end. Edith, who has always sought to control her husband, eventually realizes that there is more to Joe's life and personality than she could ever control. This realization leads to her final respect, however distant it is, for her husband as a complex, flawed, but basically decent human being. Mike arrives at a simi-

lar assessment of Joe; though Mike is responsible for ruining Joe's political ambitions, at Joe's death Mike admits that his perceptions of Joe were incomplete, even
stupid. At the end of *Ten North Frederick* O'Hara presents a view of Joe's life that can
be applied, generally, to all the main characters in the novel. His point is that each person's life can be remembered only in fragments: Some parts provide pleasure, others
sadness. O'Hara does not attempt to create pure sympathy, or hatred, for any of his
characters in *Ten North Frederick* (even though Joe is clearly a figure whom O'Hara
admires above the others). Instead, his idea is to evoke an understanding of the complex, unpredictable, and often unpleasant realities people must confront in their everyday interactions with one another. The irony of the novel, which contributes to its
dark vision, is that such an understanding (which Edith and Mike obtain) often comes
too late in our lives.

O'Hara's social theme is considerably harsher. It is important to remember that, at
the novel's end, all of the Chapin family members are affluent; at the reading of Joe's
will, Ann and Joby receive $100,000 (a considerable sum in 1945), and Edith over-
sees a trust fund of $1,250,000 to be divided between her children at her death. Yet
none of these characters is happy or personally satisfied. In fact, few characters in *Ten
North Frederick* seem content with their lives, which points up O'Hara's basic assessment of the evolving directions of American life. Social change is a part of that life, as
indicated by Gibbsville's shifting of high-class society from North Frederick Street to
Lantenengo Street. Accompanying that shift is the possibility, and the frequent reality,
of material comfort; yet the consistent view in *Ten North Frederick* is that material
comforts—and the values that accompany them—only partially satisfy the needs of
Americans such as the Chapins. At bottom, O'Hara is expressing a deep dissatisfaction with a society that, in turning away from the values of a character such as Joe, rewards its members materially while at the same time imbuing them with desires that
extend beyond material satisfaction. The social problem is that even a family unit cannot satisfy nonmaterial desires, and so the unhappiness of the Chapin family at the
novel's end symbolizes the discontent that O'Hara sees as part of the American way
of life at mid-twentieth century.

Critical Context

Ten North Frederick was both a critical and a popular success for John O'Hara. After its appearance in 1955, it sold 65,703 copies in its first two weeks and remained on
the best-seller list for thirty-two weeks. In 1956, *Ten North Frederick* received the National Book Award for fiction, and a film version of the novel was eventually produced.

John O'Hara wanted to be ranked with the greatest American writers of his time,
such as Ernest Hemingway and F. Scott Fitzgerald, and he believed that he deserved
such stature. O'Hara was, in fact, able to manipulate several of the literary techniques
that characterize the novels of the great modernists, and one of the strengths of *Ten
North Frederick* is its presentation of modernist techniques (stripped-down dialogue,
nonlinear shifts of time and focus) in a context that is accessible to a wide popular au-

dience. The basically negative perception of progress that is presented in *Ten North Frederick* also associates O'Hara with the bleak modernist themes of his contemporaries.

Unlike the established masters of American literature, though, O'Hara was never able to develop a genuinely individual style. All of the literary techniques that can be found in *Ten North Frederick*—its realistic details, its naturalistic portrait of individuals coping with forces they cannot fully control, its modernist techniques and themes—had been developed by writers before O'Hara. The often sensational and gratuitous sexual content of a novel such as *Ten North Frederick* also precludes O'Hara's fiction from a first ranking in American literature. Yet John O'Hara did make his own special contribution to American literature through his explorations of the complex interactions of human sexuality and psychology, set against realistic backgrounds such as the Gibbsville environment in *Ten North Frederick*. By continuing in the twentieth century, O'Hara established himself as an important, if not a great, American writer.

Bibliography

Bruccoli, Matthew. *John O'Hara: A Descriptive Bibliography.* Pittsburgh: University of Pittsburgh Press, 1978. A thorough, scholarly bibliography on all aspects of O'Hara's work. A must for the serious student.

_____. *The O'Hara Concern: A Biography of John O'Hara.* New York: Random House, 1975. The expertise of Bruccoli is evident here in this comprehensive biography of O'Hara. Contains valuable background, critical references to his works, and a useful bibliography.

Eppard, Philip B., ed. *Critical Essays on John O'Hara.* New York: G. K. Hall, 1994. Divided into sections on reviews and essays. All of O'Hara's major fiction is discussed, as well as his relationship to naturalism, his view of society, his short stories, and his view of politics, the family, and small towns. Includes a comprehensive introductory chapter on O'Hara's career and the reception of his novels, but no bibliography.

Grebstein, Sheldon Norman. *John O'Hara.* New York: Twayne, 1966. This critical study both interprets and assesses O'Hara's work. Grebstein is mostly sympathetic toward O'Hara, but has some reservations about his writings. Also assesses other criticism on O'Hara.

MacShane, Frank. *The Life of John O'Hara.* New York: E. P. Dutton, 1980. Looks at O'Hara's life through his work. A thorough study well worth reading for its valuable insights.

Shannon, William V. *The American Irish.* New York: Macmillan, 1963. Deals with O'Hara's work from the point of view of his Irish ancestry and his desire to escape from it.

Christopher J. Forbes

THE TENANTS

Author: Bernard Malamud (1914-1986)
Type of plot: Absurdist
Time of plot: The 1960's
Locale: New York City
First published: 1971

Principal characters:

HARRY LESSER, a white writer, tenant of an abandoned tenement, who is trying to finish a novel

WILLIE SPEARMINT, a black writer, a daytime squatter in the same tenement

LEVENSPIEL, a Jewish landlord who wants to demolish the building and rebuild

IRENE BELL, Willie's white Jewish girlfriend, an Off-Broadway actress

MARY KETTLESMITH, a black woman, a friend of Irene and Willie

The Novel

In *The Tenants*, Malamud blends gritty realism, absurd comedy, and fantasy to deal with both social issues and the nature of the creative writing process. The setting of the novel is an abandoned apartment house in New York City in the 1960's, a time of racial strife affecting both the book's Jewish and black characters. The point of view is that of Harry Lesser, rendered in third-person-limited narration. All experience, even when the narration appears omniscient, is filtered through Harry's mind and voice.

The tenement, on East Thirty-first Street, reeks of human excrement, urine, and garbage. Harry and the rats are the only tenants, Harry holding out against a landlord, Levenspiel, who wants to demolish the rent-controlled building and construct a new building with shops at the street level and five floors of apartments above. Levenspiel continues to offer Lesser more and more money to move out, but Lesser will not move until the novel he has been writing for ten years is completed.

Harry Lesser's isolation is shattered one day when he finds Willie Spearmint, a daytime squatter and a self-taught black writer, who types his novel in a deserted apartment next to Lesser's. These two men are wary of each other; they form a tenuous friendship but never real trust. While Harry's novel, *The Promised End*, is about love (a subject about which Lesser knows little), Willie's work focuses on a narrative of black experience. Lesser is so obsessed with the nature of art that he does not experience life. Spearmint is torn between being a black activist and being a writer. Thus, each is an incomplete writer: Spearmint lacks form, and Lesser lacks experience.

As the men continue writing and intellectual sparring, Willie invites Harry to socialize, first at Harry's apartment and later at the apartment of a black friend, Mary Kettlesmith. Harry becomes acquainted with both Willie's white Jewish girlfriend, Irene Bell who is an Off-Broadway actress, and Mary. Harry has sexual relations with both of the women during the course of the novel. Harry begins an affair with Irene. After several months of secret liaisons with Irene, Harry finally tells Willie that they are in love and intend to be married. Willie strikes back at Harry by destroying his manuscript. Harry then destroys Willie's typewriter, each depriving the other of something important to the artist-writer.

Trying to save his novel, Harry makes a desperate attempt to reconstruct his work. He hopes to write a better book than the earlier draft. He is so caught up in the attempt that he ignores Irene more each day. One morning, he finds in the rubbish container a barrelful of crumpled yellow pages, indicating that Willie is back and also trying to write. Harry never actually sees Willie, but each day he reads the discarded crumpled paper so that he can keep track of Willie's attempts at writing. He then learns that Willie is keeping track of Harry's progress also. Neither writer is able to perform his art in the way he wants.

Malamud combines reality and fantasy in the final climactic scene of confrontation between the two men, which occurs in a dark hallway of the tenement building. Harry imagines it as a jungle in which they are locked in a final bloody struggle. They use racial epithets to illustrate their hatred; Harry attacks Willie's skull with an ax, while Willie castrates Harry with a sharp saber, thus reversing the racial stereotypes. The last words of the novel are spoken by Levenspiel, who discovers the two men's bodies and prays for mercy for them and for himself.

The Characters

The characters in Malamud's novel function both as individuals and as stereotypes. Even though the characters of the two men are quite well developed, the writer clearly intends them to be types; the other characters are less developed.

Malamud uses names to suggest the character of people—an old technique used effectively, for example, in eighteenth century Restoration comedy. Willie Spearmint is possibly the most obvious, with its echoes of William Shakespeare; Harry Lesser is perhaps the "lesser man." Mary Kettlesmith seems to tie in to the old adage about "the pot calling the kettle black." Levenspiel is certainly a stereotype of the moneymaking Jew. None of the characters is particularly sympathetic. The Jewish writer who should represent a humanistic tradition is obsessed with "form" in art, while the black writer seems to represent raw talent and "experience" as the necessary component of art.

Harry is working on his third novel. He mentions a first one, good, and a second one, bad, which was bought for a film, and Harry is living from the royalties. His current book has been ten years in the process. He refuses to move because he wants to finish his book where it was born; the irony is that he cannot finish his book in his condition of self-imposed isolation from life.

Harry lives in fear of the jungle outside his apartment. His apartment is an island in New York City, a place of withdrawal. Harry's fantasies are populated by islands— stereotyped romantic ones, mysterious and beautiful, with crashing waves, trees, flowers, and native dancing girls, specifically one beautiful Mary Kettlesmith. Harry also lives in fear of fire, a real enough fear in a deserted tenement. At one point, he cries, "Where can I run with my paper manuscript?" He carefully puts a carbon copy of his current writing in a bank-deposit vault. Ironically, all the copies of his manuscript are burned by Willie and his friends. Doubly ironic is the probability that they may have been doing him a favor. Unwilling to participate in life, Harry also fears death. He feels that each book nudges him closer to death and absurdly tries to hold it off, reflecting that "one thing about writing a book" is that one can "keep death in place."

Willie Spearmint comes into Harry's carefully ordered sterile retreat, another writer poaching on Harry's territory with his ancient typewriter. Willie might be the means of engaging Harry in life, but that process turns sour when they compete for a woman as well as for creativity. Willie is viewed through Harry's consciousness. Willie, however, does have a life beyond the tenement. He comes during the day to work on his writing. He lives with a girlfriend, Irene Bell, but leaves her place in order to write. He is an unskilled raw talent trying to use his writing as a means of black activism. He asks Harry to read his manuscript and possibly help him with the formal aspects of writing.

The two women characters function as objects of competition for the men. Mary Kettlesmith is little more than a symbol so that Harry can sleep with a black woman. Irene Bell is more important to the novel in that she is central to the essential conflict between commitment to humanity and commitment to art. She could have become the way back to life for Harry, or earlier for Willie, although neither of the men is ever aware of it; she ends up being used and ignored. Harry's initial attachment to Irene is sexual, then romantic. He professes love for her, but his only real commitment is to his work. During the relationship with her, he is engaging in life and thus freed to write: "It helped him write freely and well after having had to press for a while." The irony is that he never realizes that commitment in a human relationship might be his own salvation as well as hers, and he refuses to discuss marriage until the book is finished.

Irene is the only one of the triangle who shows concern for others as human beings. Although no longer in love with Willie, she continues to show concern for him as a man and for his writing. She comes to realize that both men are married only to their work. She ultimately is rejected by both; their writing takes first priority always. She leaves New York for San Francisco.

Levenspiel is never more than a type. His character is not developed, and he lives on the fringes of Harry's life, his only concern being materialism. He does conclude the novel with a plea for mercy for all of them, but the reader has no indication of his motive for doing so.

Themes and Meanings

Malamud presents his major theme of the novel, the conflict between art and life, through the two male writers of different races. He presents them in direct polarity: Harry is a form-and-structure man, Willie has raw experience and no form; Harry writes for immortality, Willie for money; Harry insists on the universality of art, Willie insists that black art cannot be universal because black experience is beyond white apprehension. Malamud is not saying that either man is right or wrong but that both are both right and wrong. The author treats them with a complex kind of irony that is sympathetic while it satirizes.

Each writer is incomplete as an artist as he is incomplete as a human being. They are both egocentric in their concerns. Harry is obsessed with his writing, and Willie is obsessed with his own blackness as well as his writing. Malamud also satirizes Hollywood and the film industry that bought Harry's bad book. Ironically, the bad book is supplying the funds that enable him to survive financially, isolated from life, so that he can finish his third novel.

In the final death scene, both writers are annihilated. Malamud undercuts the violence with subtle irony; the reader is never sure whether the scene is fantasy or reality. Harry and Willie are armed with stock weapons, an ax for the white man, a razor for the black. The black is traditionally feared for his virility and the white for his brain, but in this novel, Harry destroys Willie's brain, and Willie castrates Harry.

Critical Context

No matter how one reads the ending, as fantasy or as reality, this novel ends differently from Malamud's earlier novels. The Malamud hero, from Roy Hobbs in *The Natural* (1952) to Yakov Bok in *The Fixer* (1966), is generally left with suggested regeneration and affirmation. In *The Tenants*, Harry Lesser and Willie Spearmint are dead, with only the last line of comfort, and cold comfort it is to know that "each feels the anguish of the other." The ending is negative, and if there is affirmation, it is in that negation. The negativist presents truth in that he renders the absurdity of life. The void that Malamud is affirming in this novel is what happens when two potentially creative men become so obsessed with art that they refuse human commitment. The result is sterility in both life and art. Malamud presents them both with a qualifying irony that loves as it condemns in offering them as part of the human condition.

Bibliography

Abramson, Edward A. *Bernard Malamud Revisited*. New York: Twayne, 1993. Provides an evaluation of Malamud's literary vision in relation to the entire body of his work, both novels and short stories. A chapter is devoted to *The Tenants*.

Allen, John Alexander. "The Promised End: Bernard Malamud's *The Tenants*." In *Bernard Malamud: A Collection of Critical Essays*, edited by Leslie A Field and Joyce W. Field. Englewood Cliffs, N.J.: Prentice-Hall, 1975. A short but clear analysis of the novel. The collected essays are useful for a broader view of Malamud's work.

Astro, Richard, and Jackson J. Benson, eds. *The Fiction of Bernard Malamud*. Corvallis: Oregon State University Press, 1977. A collection of key essays presented by scholars at a conference featuring Malamud's work.

Helterman, Jeffrey. *Understanding Bernard Malamud*. Columbia: University of South Carolina Press, 1985. Focuses on Malamud's characters in terms of individual morality.

Hershinow, Sheldon J. *Bernard Malamud.* New York: Ungar, 1980. Useful overview and analysis of literary works treating the writer as moral activist.

Salzberg, Joel. *Critical Essays on Bernard Malamud.* Boston: G. K. Hall, 1987. Useful collection of essays with a foreword by Salzberg.

Betty Alldredge

TENT OF MIRACLES

Author: Jorge Amado (1912-   )
Type of plot: Magical Realism
Time of plot: From 1968 to 1969, with flashbacks to the years from 1868 to 1943
Locale: Salvador, in the state of Bahia, Brazil
First published: Tenda dos milagres, 1969 (English translation, 1971)

> *Principal characters:*
>> PEDRO ARCHANJO (OJUOBÁ, EYES, or XANGÔ), the mulatto, bon vivant
>> protagonist, a self-taught anthropologist, champion of
>> miscegenation, and jack-of-all-trades, including writer, cult priest
>> and runner/messenger at Bahia's School of Medicine, a bastion of
>> tradition
>> FAUSTO PENA, the dramatized narrator, poet, and journalist, Pedro
>> Archanjo's 1968 biographer
>> NILO D'ÁVILA ARGOLO DE ARAÚJO, the antagonist, a professor of
>> forensic medicine and a racist defender of white supremacy
>> LÍDIO CORRÓ, Archanjo's intimate friend and cohort, a canvas miracle
>> painter and printer/owner of the shop the Tent of Miracles
>> ANA MERCEDES, a brazen mulatta, poetess, reporter, and Fausto Pena's
>> unfaithful girlfriend
>> ROSA DE OXALÁ, Lídio Corró's mistress and Archanjo's secret and
>> unrequited love

The Novel

Most of the story takes place during different time periods in the old neighborhood of Pelourinho, where a type of a free university of Afro-Brazilian culture holds sway, owing to the practices of popular mestizo poets, artists, storytellers, musicians, craftsmen, singers, *capoeiristas* (dancers of a self-defense sport), black magicians, cult priests, and folk healers. This natural campus, actually situated near the state's official school of medicine, has as its main building a shop called the Tent of Miracles where Master Lídio Corró runs his printing press and paints miracle pictures for those who wish to acknowledge their gratitude for having had their prayers answered.

The chancellor of this unofficial university is the protagonist, Pedro Archanjo, a mestizo whose knowledge, books (published by Corró), camaraderie, honor, generosity, and sexual feats command the respect of this community. Pedro Archanjo's story is told in 1968, one hundred years after his birth, by Fausto Pena, an unappreciated poet, hired by the handsome and blond American scholar, winner of the Nobel Prize, and professor at Columbia University, Dr. James D. Levenson, to do research on Pedro Archanjo for an introduction to the professor's English translation of the mulatto's works. Unknown to the rest of Brazil's literati until Levenson's discovery, Pedro Archanjo's works are praised and consecrated by the famous American's recognition of their overall ethnological merit. Considered to be indispensable reading for understanding the racial problem in Brazil, these acclaimed works spark a local and national campaign for institutionalizing Pedro Archanjo as a Brazilian hero. In counterpoint to the fanfare and ultimate fictionalization of Archanjo as a national hero in 1968, a factual historical account, narrated by an omniscient voice, traces the hero's humble beginnings from 1868, when his father was killed in Brazil's devastating war with Paraguay, up to his position as messenger in the school of medicine in 1900, and during the time of his main publications (1904-1928) which cause a reactionary debate by the racist professor Nilo d'Ávila Argolo de Araújo with his theories of Aryan superiority.

Eventually discredited when Archanjo's research reveals Argolo to be his distant relative, the pedant epitomizes the prejudice and hatred engendered by a black/white dichotomy inciting racial, economic, social, and political divisiveness. Archanjo's defense of miscegenation leads to his imprisonment and to the destruction of the Tent of Miracles by the vigilante police chief, Pedrito Gordo. While Fausto Pena's narrative closes with the protagonist in prison, the omniscient narrator resumes the rest of the story, paralleling the indigent mulatto's death in 1943 with allusions to Nazism and the impact on the world of its belief of Aryan supremacy. Before dying, Archanjo, always the crusader, reminisces over his lifelong battle against the evil forces of bigotry and exhorts those who are to come after him to close the "gates" of division between the races by making the mixture of blood complete.

As the narrative draws to a close with the hypocritical pomp surrounding the centennial celebration of Archanjo's birth, promoted by Bahia's politicians, businessmen, and pseudointellectuals, the novel ends with the carnival of 1969, where Archanjo's glory is celebrated. More festive and authentic, this popular tribute, in the form of a samba school's musical theme, symbolizes Archanjo's humane, real-life mulatto existence in the colorful streets of Bahia.

The Characters

Pedro Archanjo, the quintessential self-made man, who, despite all racial and socioeconomic odds, fights for the rights of blacks and mestizos via his actions and publications, is one of Jorge Amado's most vibrant, sympathetic, and humane male protagonists. In true Amado fashion, Archanjo personifies the mobilizing force of good and truthfulness over evil and falsity, an antinomy in concert with Brazil's popular oral poetics as well as with the Marxist dialectic of the struggle of the oppressed against the oppressors. As a staunch advocate of miscegenation, individual freedom, popular culture, a natural code of honor, spontaneity, carnivalesque customs and habits, as well as the fantasy and magic inherent in African ritual and legend, Archanjo practices what he preaches. Thus, he contrasts markedly with the authoritarian and chauvinist figures of Professor Argolo and Police Chief Gordo, who represent self-aggrandizement and, respectively, bigotry and violence.

An authentic folk hero, Archanjo is portrayed as fallible at times, but in most instances he is larger than life, given his relentless commitment to racial equality and the expressed need for individual freedom, love, humanity, and truth. For these reasons, other characters serve to highlight Archanjo's qualities and beliefs. Tadeu Canhoto, for example, Archanjo's light-skinned illegitimate son, reflects the struggle for upward social mobility, while Rosa de Oxalá, Archanjo's undying but never-realized love (because of his respect for his brotherly friend Lídio Corró, Rosa's lover) attests his sense of honor. In another example, Major Damião de Souza, a mulatto self-made lawyer, represents the crusading force on behalf of the poor and the downtrodden blacks. While several characters are developed more than others in order to mirror Archanjo's struggle, it is clear that Jorge Amado wants the reader to sympathize mostly with the protagonist since he champions the author's thesis for racial democracy in Brazil.

Themes and Meanings

The novel's central theme focuses on this struggle for racial equality within a society manifesting insidious prejudice and practicing covert and overt discrimination which at times becomes unexpectedly violent. Plagued by the turn-of-the-century spurious theories of Joseph-Arthur comte de Gobineau on the inferiority of the black race, Brazil is portrayed here as a country striving to eradicate an image that might label it as a backward nation. Ironically, it is an American, bestowing a foreigner's approval of Archanjo's worth, who ignites Brazilian interest in its own racial history and resources. So concerned about projecting the right national image, Brazil is mocked and satirized by Amado as a society and a government dependent upon foreign influence.

The issues of image, racial bigotry, and socioeconomic inequities surface via Amado's deft treatment of shifting points of view, rich symbolism stressing the spontaneous mixture implicit in carnival and miscegenation, and contrastive narrative techniques. For example, the true account of Archanjo's humble beginnings, life, and death are told by an omniscient narrator in direct contrast to the first-person version developed, almost uncontrollably by the naive, well-intentioned, but unreliable narrator Fausto Pena, a middle-class poet used in 1968 by local politicians, businessmen, and the state to create a profitable and "safe" myth out of Archanjo's bawdy but noble life.

The preoccupation with a "correct and proper image" leads to the question about the actual interpretation of social history and the relativity of points of view. The reader questions this process as he views how the pernicious powers of the media and the state reinterpret history for their own aims. The Archanjo and Pena stories mirror, respectively, the fact and fiction dilemma or, in other words, the reality/image dialectic. This problem has more subtle implications when the reader considers the hidden realities of the violent 1868 and 1968 periods in Brazilian history and their "official" images as promoted by the government. Added to this sense of history and "image-making" are allusions to the rampant presence of Nazism and its racial campaign within Brazil and abroad in the 1930's and 1940's, during Archanjo's time. The historical parallels here are more than coincidental. Thus, by underscoring a local incident, Amado, with the use of contrastive techniques and a historical framework, undermines the inhumanity of racism and violence, thereby raising important questions which accord his novel true universal meaning.

Critical Context

Tent of Miracles, Jorge Amado's sixteenth novel and twenty-sixth book, has been printed in more than twenty editions and translated into every major language, including English and Russian. This novel, considered to be one of Amado's most technically sophisticated creations, is representative of his second literary phase, which is commonly recognized as beginning with the critically acclaimed *Gabriela, cravo e canela* (1958; *Gabriela, Clove and Cinnamon*, 1962), a novel which announces Amado's closer attention to character development, narrative techniques, and lyric prose, while de-emphasizing the overt thesis formula of his earlier social realist works. This phase is also marked by Amado's allegiance to Brazil's rich literary oral tradition, the *literatura de cordel*, poetry composed and sung by popular balladeers of the Northeast, stressing the time-honored values of the common folk. *Tent of Miracles* illustrates many of these themes and techniques in Amado's development as a novelist, including a panoramic depiction of numerous Afro-Brazilian rituals and practices in which spiritual events magically play upon the destinies of his characters.

Known primarily as a popular, best-selling novelist, Amado proves himself to be a skillful craftsman in *Tent of Miracles*, frequently referred to as one of his masterpieces. In 1977, a feature-length Brazilian film based on this novel was made by the famous Brazilian director Nelson Pereira dos Santos.

Always a first-rate storyteller, Amado infuses his social criticism with humor, irony, and sex. Praised as well as criticized for his portraits of "sensual mulattas" and for alluding to Brazil as a racial democracy, Amado in *Tent of Miracles* provides through symbol and characterization an implicit explanation of his stand on these issues. Moreover, *Tent of Miracles* also constitutes one of the first examples of Amado's allegorical documentation of violence, bigotry, and repression in Brazil, in the past and the late 1960's. Ultimately, this novel accentuates Amado's overriding theme of individual freedom while proving the author to be one of Brazil's masterful novelists of the twentieth century.

Bibliography

Chamberlain, Bobby J. *Jorge Amado*. Boston: Twayne, 1990. Useful, informative, and readable, this critical analysis of Amado's work covers all periods of the novelist's output while focusing on a few of the author's most important works. A biographical chapter is included, as well as an extensive bibliography.

Hinchberger, Bill. "Jorge Amado Writes from Heart, Home." *Variety* 366 (March 31, 1997): 56. Hinchberger explores the inspirations that shape Amado's work, the filming of Amado's novels, and Amado's reaction to the critical acclaim he has received. Offers interesting insight into the influences that shaped Amado's work.

Pontiero, Giovanni. "Brazilian Backwater: Jorge Amado's Bahia." *Third World Quarterly* 12 (January, 1990): 208-214. Reviews several books by Amado, including *Tent of Miracles*. Praises *Tent of Miracles*, noting that it is "loquacious and pensive, in turn, irrepressibly driven on by life and its enigmas, at once whimsical and wise, biting and compassionate."

Robitaille, L. B. "These Men of Letters Speak for the Powerless." *World Press Review* 38 (December, 1991): 26-27. An intriguing profile of Amado, covering his political activity, his life in Paris, and his feelings for his native Brazil. Presents background that sheds considerable light on his writings.

Nelson H. Vieira

THE TENTS OF WICKEDNESS

Author: Peter De Vries (1910-1993)
Type of plot: Comedy of manners
Time of plot: The late 1950's
Locale: Decency, Connecticut
First published: 1959

   Principal characters:
       CHARLES (CHICK) SWALLOW, the protagonist, a newspaperman in his
           forties
       CRYSTAL SWALLOW, his wife
       ELIZABETH (SWEETIE) APPLEYARD, Swallow's onetime girlfriend
       CHARLES APPLEYARD, her father
       MME PIQUEPUSS, Elizabeth Appleyard's rich maternal grandmother
       NICKIE SHERMAN, Swallow's brother-in-law, a self-styled detective and
           boulevardier
       LILA SHERMAN, Swallow's sister and Nickie's wife

The Novel

   Toward the end of the second section of the book, Charles Swallow recounts a vision: "With that odd unreality we experience in dreams, I seemed unable to do anything right, but bungled whatever I put my hand to." Though the events of the dream are indeed unreal, the incompetence that they expose is not.

   As the *Picayune Blade*'s "Lamplighter," Swallow advises those who write to him in distress. He takes this role of Dutch uncle seriously and so cannot refuse Charles Appleyard's plea for help with his daughter. Years earlier, Swallow and Elizabeth had been discovered together in a coal bin, and this traumatic experience had arrested her sexual and intellectual development.

   Swallow attempts to repair the damage by exposing her to F. Scott Fitzgerald, and he succeeds all too well. Soon Elizabeth runs away to Greenwich Village to live with Danny Dolan; she decides to have a child without the nuisance of a husband, imitating the uninhibited Isadora Duncan. She chooses Swallow as the father; even though he initially refuses, he later consents when he sees her getting into a taxicab with his brother-in-law, Nickie Sherman, his other botched case.

   To persuade Nickie to abandon his unremunerative detective work for a regular job, Swallow arranges a supposed murder that reveals exactly how inept Sherman can be. Instead of curing Nickie, though, the exposure induces schizophrenia: Half of Nickie remains a mediocre sleuth, but the other half becomes Johnny Velours, master thief.

   It is to save his sister's marriage from further strain that Swallow agrees to father Beth Appleyard's child. After she becomes pregnant, she has second thoughts. When her father and grandmother are killed in a plane crash, she reverts to her adolescent inability to cope with life.

Swallow thus fails to help the two people he has tried so hard to aid, watching them drift off into insanity. Frustrated, he, too, takes refuge in temporary madness. All ends happily, though, as Nickie recovers his sanity and prepares for a teaching job, Elizabeth moves to California and marries well, and Swallow emerges from his experiences a wiser man.

The Characters

Charles Swallow's life imitates art. At the beginning of the novel, he imagines himself a Marquandian hero, and when confronted with difficulties in life, he translates them into scenes from William Faulkner, Theodore Dreiser, and Ernest Hemingway. To cure Elizabeth Appleyard, he naturally turns to a novelist—believing that fiction teaches people how to live, absorbed as he himself is in the world of the books he has read.

Though Swallow's views are clearly derivative, he is capable of clever observations, and it is through his eyes that the reader sees the others in the novel. Naturally, he likens them to literary characters: Madame Piquepuss resembles Miss Havisham in Charles Dickens's *Great Expectations* (1860-1861); Nickie Sherman is a latter-day Oscar Wilde. Beyond these stereotypes, though, Swallow notes minute, revealing details. Madame Piquepuss's long fingers resemble fried bananas. Later, when he feels more sympathetic toward her, he likens them to chocolate eclairs.

Clothes are significant in showing character. Beth Appleyard's initial reluctance to wear shoes and her preference for long, white gowns suggest the child playing at being an adult. Having become a liberated woman, she dresses—and undresses—like a flapper. Upon reverting to childishness, she again appears in white and barefooted.

Language, too, serves to reveal states of mind. Relaxed at the start of the book, Swallow talks like a character in a J. P. Marquand novel. As he becomes increasingly tormented, his voice becomes Faulkneresque; eventually, he will sound like Gregor Samsa in Franz Kafka's *Metamorphosis* (1915). Only at the end of the novel does he find his own voice. Nickie Sherman is a master of the epigram; one can tell when he imagines himself to be Johnny Velours by his more natural speech. Beth Appleyard converses largely through her poetry, which is initially as juvenile as her attitude. As she matures so does her verse, though it remains parodic, just as she parodies the women in Fitzgerald's fiction. At the end of the novel, she is able to achieve a voice of her own, one still ironic and amusing but also original and sensitive.

Swallow is a keen observer of mannerisms. The Greek who runs the Samothrace cafe is notable for his hypochondria and his reluctance to serve his would-be customers; the druggist Hickett "always looked as though he were trying to swallow his eyeballs." In her youth, Beth Appleyard sits in trees and showers passersby with pages of poetry torn from library books. Bulwinkle, Swallow's boss, keeps "black coffee, aspirin, and stale pie" on his desk in an effort to cultivate his image as editor of a large metropolitan daily; he also sports curious pictorial ties. While a few of the minor characters are interchangeable, most possess these quirks that render them both humorous and memorable.

Themes and Meanings

The novel is a literary pastiche, echoing and parodying most of the major writers of the late nineteenth and twentieth centuries. This technique, a virtuoso performance in which De Vries always delights, contributes to the book's humor, but it has a deeper significance as well, for the novel reveals the danger of taking literature too seriously as a guide to life. Swallow, Beth Appleyard, and Nickie Sherman all base their lives on literary models, and all are betrayed by their texts. The parodies thus warn the reader not to take even serious literature too seriously.

Modern literature is an inadequate guide to life because it is the product of the imagination unrooted in reality. In its distrust of the unbridled imagination, *The Tents of Wickedness* is reminiscent of Samuel Johnson. Swallow persuades himself that he has been transformed into a pig and offers extended psychological explanations for the change. In fact, he suffers from an acute case of trichinosis. Nevertheless, he cannot recognize the nature of his malady: When he looks in the mirror he does not see reality. Beth Appleyard and Nickie Sherman cannot cope with life as long as they hide behind literary personas.

De Vries himself revels in bizarre coincidences and unusual lives, but he warns that such singularity leads to unhappiness. He distinguishes between pleasure, which one may obtain momentarily by violating society's norms, and happiness, which is less intense but more enduring, and is obtainable only by living conventionally. Such adherence to societal norms is for De Vries not confining but the reverse. As he writes, "Conformity is after all the broad highway—it's the way of the transgressor that's strait and narrow."

He thus quarrels with modern literature for its rejection of conformity and conformists. Coming as it did at the end of the "beat" generation, *The Tents of Wickedness* rejects the Bohemian existence. It parodies the literary idols of Greenwich Village as well as those who worship them. The brief segment of the novel set in New York, closely modeled as it is on *The Great Gatsby* (1925), reveals the fatal lunacy of those who fail to conform. The nonconformist is not more but less imaginative; his way of life is not a sign of genius but of mediocrity.

Critical Context

The Tents of Wickedness is an extraordinary novel that praises the ordinary. Like De Vries's three earlier novels it was popular; the Book-of-the-Month Club offered it as part of its dual summer selection in 1959. Critical response was more mixed. Some reviewers praised it as highly as his earlier work, but others sensed a decline. The same ingredients were present—the clever wordplay, the witty allusions, the faithful echoes of other writers. Yet these elements do not always cohere, and in seeking to point a moral, De Vries mars his tale.

In part, *The Tents of Wickedness* is a reworking of earlier material: Some of the book was originally intended for *Comfort Me with Apples* (1956), where the Swallows and Shermans first appear, and some of the incidents are derived from *The Tunnel of Love* (1954). The narration shifts uncertainly between first and third person, and the pun "Legal Tender is the Night" is repeated. Despite these minor flaws, however, the novel is among the most memorable (and the most amusing) of the many modern fictions which center on the relationship between literature and life.

Bibliography

Bowden, Edwin T. *Peter De Vries*. Boston: Twayne, 1983. A concise critical biography that provides a useful overview of De Vries's life and works. After an introductory biographical chapter, Bowden discusses each of De Vries's major novels. The text is supplemented by a chronology, notes, and a selected bibliography of primary and secondary works.

Campion, Dan. *Peter De Vries and Surrealism*. Lewisburg, Pa.: Bucknell University Press, 1995. Provides chapters on De Vries's literary life, his encounter with Surrealism in the 1930's, his novel *But Who Wakes the Bugler*, and his use of humor. Includes very detailed notes and bibliography.

David, Douglas M. "An Interview with Peter De Vries." *College English* 28 (April, 1967): 524-530. A lively interview in which the author raises some interesting questions about De Vries's style of humor. De Vries discusses his use of suburban settings, his character types, and his humorous attitude toward sexuality.

Higgins, William R. "Peter De Vries." In *American Novelists Since World War II*. Vol. 6 in *Dictionary of Literary Biography*. Detroit, Mich.: Gale, 1980. A standard author entry that provides a useful profile of De Vries's life and works. It includes a list of primary and secondary sources.

Jellema, Roderick. *Peter De Vries: A Critical Essay*. Grand Rapids, Mich.: William B. Eerdmans, 1966. This monograph in the Contemporary Writers in Christian Perspective series includes a critical study of De Vries's first eight novels. This study points to the religious issues that are often overlooked in discussions of De Vries as a humorist.

Sale, Richard B. "An Interview in New York with Peter De Vries." *Studies in the Novel* 1 (1969): 364-369. This interview touches on De Vries's writing habits and includes questions about the type of humor in his novels and his view of the world. De Vries discusses the question of whether he is a black humorist.

Yagoda, Ben. "Being Seriously Funny." *The New York Times Magazine*, June 12, 1983, 42-44. A feature article that presents a portrait of De Vries and an overview of his literary career. Yagoda's article offers a good introduction to the writer and his work.

Joseph Rosenblum

TERMS OF ENDEARMENT

Author: Larry McMurtry (1936-   )
Type of plot: Domestic/seriocomic realism
Time of plot: The 1960's and the 1970's
Locale: Houston, Texas; Des Moines, Iowa; and Kearney and Omaha, Nebraska
First published: 1975

> *Principal characters:*
> AURORA GREENWAY, an affluent, middle-aged widow
> EMMA HORTON, Aurora's daughter
> ROSIE DUNLUP, Aurora's maid
> VERNON DALHART, a Texas oilman, one of Aurora's suitors
> GENERAL HECTOR SCOTT, a retired military man who is later Aurora's
>   principal suitor
> THOMAS "FLAP" HORTON, Emma's husband, a young academic

The Novel

Aurora Greenway, a selfish, fanciful widow, spends much of her rather empty life talking on the telephone to her daughter, Emma. They talk nearly every morning at seven-thirty (often to Emma's chagrin—unlike her mother, she is not an early riser), and it is around their problematic relationship that the novel is built. *Terms of Endearment* is divided into two books of unequal length: The first, longer book covers a single year (1962) in the life of Aurora Greenway; the second book, a fraction the length of the first, is devoted to the last five years (1971-1976) of Emma's short life. This disproportionate division reflects the central tragedy of the novel: Emma has always lived in her mother's shadow, has never lived up to the older woman's expectations. The brief final section of the novel is as stunted and formless as Emma's self-esteem.

Since she has been left financially independent by a shadowy, seldom-mentioned husband, Aurora Greenway has little to do with her days except receive and reject her various suitors, and much of the first part of the novel is devoted to her seriocomic relationships with men. She is proud of the fact that most men are terrified of her exacting standards and her erratic behavior. She plays one beau off against another, juggling luncheon and dinner dates with great virtuosity and actively encouraging jealousy among her suitors. When one man is deemed too dull or too overbearing, he is dropped and soon replaced by a new, more pliant subject. This rather reckless game is Aurora's method of coping with widowhood; her indolent though well-mannered husband, Rudyard, has been dead for three years when the novel opens. Her elegant house in the River Oaks section of Houston is filled with beautiful objects, her closets with expensive clothes. Her existence is diverting and leisurely but ultimately unfulfilling.

In stark contrast to her mother's frivolous, self-absorbed life is Emma's own. When the novel opens, Emma has been married for two years to "Flap" Horton, a college English major who can provide her with no better a residence than a garage apartment. The marriage is unsatisfying on every level: The couple's sex life is perfunctory and unimaginative, and their conversations frequently end in violent but comic confrontations. Aurora is probably correct in her assessment that Emma has married badly. Only two years into the marriage, Flap's interest in his wife is waning, and they are expecting their first child (it is born at the close of the first book). Emma spends her days reading the newspaper classified ads, seeing her beautiful and self-assured friend Patsy Clark, and talking on the telephone with her alternately judgmental and solipsistic mother.

Since the novel has no consistent point of view, McMurtry is able to move easily in and out of his characters' consciousnesses; thus, what would pass for subplots in other novels will receive much attention in *Terms of Endearment*. Much of the first book, for example, is devoted to Rosie Dunlup, Aurora's hapless maid of twenty-two years, whose unexciting marriage parallels both Aurora's and Emma's lack of fulfillment. Royce, Rosie's truck-driver husband and the father of her seven children, is a philanderer with a fondness for low-life bars and disreputable women. During the course of the first book, Rosie finds out about her husband's secret life. Their tragicomic separations and reconciliations are conducted in the lower-middle-class world of country and western dance halls and drive-ins, a world far removed from Aurora's River Oaks domain. Rosie is more than a servant, and the bond between the Greenway women and their maid is strong, though mostly unarticulated.

Toward the end of the first book, Aurora experiences a mid-life crisis of sorts. Now a grandmother (Emma's first child, Thomas, has been born), she sets about acclimating her chosen mate, sixty-seven-year-old General Hector Scott, to her other suitors, having no intention of dropping them altogether. Unable to find the perfect man, Aurora decides to make do with many, and by the end of the first book she has somewhat come to terms with the compromises with which she must live out her days.

Emma's sad story comprises the brief second book, which opens in 1971 in Des Moines, where Flap has taken a job as a college English instructor. Flap, doomed to a life of academic mediocrity, has long since lost interest in his wife, and both of them have started having affairs. They are responsible, if lackluster, parents to their two sons, Tommy and Teddy; a third child, Melanie, is born soon after the family moves to Kearney, Nebraska, where Flap becomes a department head.

Emma's life as a faculty wife is bleak. She has few friends, and what time she has away from her children she spends with a string of unremarkable lovers. Unlike her mother's, Emma's romantic involvements are highly physical but essentially unrewarding. Never prey to the romantic self-delusion that sustains Aurora, Emma has long since given up on happiness. She is hard-pressed to find even momentary diversion in her joyless and aimless life.

The novel's climax occurs when it is discovered that Emma has an incurable form of cancer. Her impending death transforms her into the kind of catalyst she has never been in life: Aurora, Rosie, General Scott, and Aurora's failed suitor Vernon Dalhart arrive from Houston to be at Emma's bedside in Omaha; her friend Patsy leaves her fairy-tale life in Hollywood to watch Emma die. Heavily sedated, Emma lies dying for months, experiencing a sort of death-in-life that is really no more than an intensification of the life that she has led for years. She accepts death with few regrets, having long given up on life. Aurora's reaction to her daughter's death is notably unsentimental. Standing dry-eyed at Emma's graveside, she turns to Patsy and says, "There's no point in us standing here like bookends, my dear," thus having, as usual, the last word.

The Characters

The characterization of Aurora Greenway is strong enough to make every other character in the novel seem like a mere foil. With the possible exception of the strong-willed Rosie, everyone who comes into even momentary contact with Aurora is dominated by her, and she has kept many of the novel's characters in tow for decades. At least three of her suitors (a term she insists upon with characteristic Victorian propriety) have been kept waiting for thirty years. Aurora Greenway is a woman who, despite her strong need for love and attention, keeps other people at a distance. Her perfectionism and her lack of self-criticism prevent her from becoming too close to anyone—including, sadly, her only child.

In many ways, Aurora is an anachronistic character, out of place in post-World War II America. A stickler for gracious manners and seemly behavior, Aurora values form over content. She is fanatically concerned with physical appearance, her own and that of her suitors: She will forgive a man much if he is well dressed. Aurora Greenway is in many ways reminiscent of the coquettes of nineteenth century British fiction. She is a self-absorbed romantic who has never questioned her right to everything and everyone she desires. A sensualist who loves to feel the wet grass beneath her bare feet and who delights above all else in good food and drink, she is also capable of surprising coldness and insensitivity. Her relationships with her suitors are for the most part old-fashionedly chaste and formal. Physical love is both a weapon for and a threat to Aurora, and it is not surprising that her comfortable but passionless marriage to the attractive Rudyard Greenway produced only one child.

Unfortunately, Aurora is the only fully developed major character in the novel. The other characters seem too obviously calculated to highlight various aspects of Aurora's character, a fault which extends to the characterization of Emma. The reader is told little of Emma's childhood and must intuit from Emma's and her mother's characters how Emma developed into such a markedly defeated adult. Still, this incomplete characterization is somewhat justified by the extent to which Aurora's life has overshadowed her daughter's. Emma serves both as a contrast to Aurora and as an embodiment of the shortcomings of Aurora's methods of dealing with people. Dumpy, badly dressed, and careless of her appearance, Emma has never measured up to her mother's expectations. She has made a bad marriage largely, one suspects, to escape Aurora's domination, but Aurora will not relinquish control, and continues to criticize her daughter almost daily with her early morning telephone calls. Nor does Emma receive support from the other people in her life. To the constantly distracted Flap, she is little more than a cook and a bed partner. Her attractive and poised friend Patsy, while genuinely devoted to Emma, is in some ways a younger version of Aurora and almost certainly the kind of woman that Aurora wanted her daughter to become. Emma Horton is surrounded by reminders of her own inadequacies. Her death from cancer is the symbolically appropriate end to a life totally lacking in self-esteem.

The novel's minor characters, especially Aurora's numerous suitors, are among the most interesting and successful elements of the novel. Vernon Dalhart, a fifty-year-old oil millionaire who has never before been in love, is a colorful and eccentric Texas character, capable of running a business empire, but helpless in the presence of the domineering Aurora. General Hector Scott, an aging military man who lives down the street from Aurora, shares with Vernon an easy authority in the masculine world and a complete bewilderment at Aurora's maddeningly feminine character. Completing the group of Aurora's most devoted suitors are Alberto, a retired operatic tenor, and Trevor Waugh, a suave and sophisticated yachtsman, both of whom bring an element of the bittersweet to Aurora's saga.

Rosie Dunlup, Aurora's long-suffering maid, occupies a central position in *Terms of Endearment* as the hardworking, realistic foil to Aurora's solipsism and indolence. Her relationship with the Greenway women is successfully executed, but the plot involving her perennial marital troubles is too often handled with condescension and a certain vulgarity. The lower-middle-class world of Rosie's Lyons Avenue home does not add very much to the reader's understanding of Aurora Greenway and Emma Horton, although it does function thematically to emphasize the universality of unhappy love relationships.

Themes and Meanings

Terms of Endearment is a book about the failure of human relationships. None of the love relationships described in the novel, whether familial or romantic, is quite satisfactory, but the characters involved cling to them in order to stave off loneliness. Aurora Greenway's frenzied love life masks a profound fear of being left alone. When at length she settles on General Scott as her principal suitor, she is fully aware of the compromises involved but equally aware that her lofty expectations will never be fulfilled by any one man. Bereft of the illusions that sustain her mother's, Emma's love life is a joyless cycle of thwarted extramarital affairs. The secondary characters mirror this pervasive lack of fulfillment: Rosie Dunlup's disastrous marriage and Vernon Dalhart's perpetual virginity are representative of the novel's bleak view of romantic love.

Ultimately more tragic, however, is the failure of the mother-daughter relationship that lies at the heart of *Terms of Endearment*. Aurora has, through her incessant criticism and her overwhelming insensitivity, produced a daughter whose sense of self-worth is almost nil. Emma has known unconditional love only from Rosie, who has served as a surrogate mother from Emma's infancy. In like manner, the well-dressed and well-bred Patsy, Emma's closest friend, is clearly the daughter that Aurora believes that she deserves, though the two remain suspicious of each other. This fractured family dynamic seems destined to repeat itself in the next generation:

Though Flap is alive and well, Aurora becomes her grandchildren's guardian at Emma's death. The middle child, Teddy, has a sensitive nature much like Emma's, and his need for affection is unlikely to be fulfilled in his mother's absence. Only Emma's little daughter, Melanie, provides hope that the damage of the past may be repaired. Unpredictable, volatile, and utterly charming, the child is the image of Aurora, and in her her grandmother has clearly met her match.

At the end of the book, Aurora says of her dead daughter, "She often made me feel I was faintly ridiculous. . . . Somehow she just had that effect. Perhaps that was why I remained so unremittingly critical of her." In this rare moment of self-awareness, Aurora articulates the subtle antagonism that separated mother and daughter. It is characteristic of their relationship that this admission occurs too late.

Critical Context

In the 1960's, Larry McMurtry established his reputation with a series of novels that dealt realistically with rural and small-town Texas. In *Horseman, Pass By* (1961), *Leaving Cheyenne* (1963), and *The Last Picture Show* (1966), McMurtry gave a new twist to the time-honored American genre of the Western. These novels all treat a Texas in a state of flux, still deeply captivated by the myth of the cowboy but increasingly confronted with the realities of industrial America. The mythology of the American West has gone stale: The ranch has been replaced by the oil field, the frontiersman by the bureaucrat. The fictional town of Thalia becomes the locus of the confrontation between past and present.

Terms of Endearment is the third of a sequence of novels set in the changing urban Southwest of the 1960's and 1970's. The first two novels in this loose trilogy, *Moving On* (1970) and *All My Friends Are Going to Be Strangers* (1972), deal with characters at least tangentially related to Emma Horton. Danny Deck, for example, the young writer who figures in both *Moving On* and *Terms of Endearment*, is the protagonist of *All My Friends Are Going to Be Strangers*. Though these later novels take place in the urban rather than the rural Southwest of McMurtry's novels of the 1960's, they share some of the regionalism of the earlier books. *Terms of Endearment* is a book strongly influenced by its setting: Aurora Greenway is intensely proud of her New England heritage and clings to Yankee culture in her Spanish home in Houston; a character such as Vernon Dalhart is virtually unthinkable outside Texas.

The film version of *Terms of Endearment* received the Academy Award for Best Picture of 1983. Earlier, all three of the 1960's novels were adapted to the screen, the best known being the 1971 film version of *The Last Picture Show*. The popularity of Larry McMurtry's novels and of their film adaptations is hardly surprising in an era in which much of the focus of American society has been moving from the industrial centers of the North to the rapidly developing South and Southwest.

Bibliography

Busby, Mark and Tom Pilkington. *Larry McMurtry and the West: An Ambivalent Relationship*. Denton, Tex.: University of North Texas Press, 1995. Offers a comprehensive overview of McMurtry's fiction, including insights on film versions of his novels. Also includes bibliographical references and an index.

Cawelti, John G. "What Rough Beast—-New Westerns?" *ANQ* 9 (Summer, 1996): 4-15. Cawelti addresses the revival of the Western in print, film, and on television. He notes that the new genre reflects the loss of the mythic West of the past and shows how the contemporary Western, instead of glorifying the American spirit, now criticizes America's shortcomings. Although this essay does not directly address *Terms of Endearment*, it offers an illuminating perspective on McMurtry's fiction.

Jones, Malcolm. "The Poet Lariat." *Newsweek* (January 11, 1999): 62. Briefly discusses the film versions of McMurtry's novels, including *Terms of Endearment*. Offers an interesting profile on McMurtry's life and work.

Jones, Roger Walton. *Larry McMurtry and the Victorian Novel*. College Station: Texas A & M University Press, 1994. Jones explores McMurtry's lifelong love of Victorian authors and explores three Victorian themes that are prominent in all of McMurtry's fiction: the individual's importance in society, the conflict between society and nature, and the search for a coherent spirituality in an age that does not believe in God.

James D. Daubs

TERRA NOSTRA

Author: Carlos Fuentes (1928-   )
Type of plot: Historical allegory
Time of plot: From the first century to New Year's Eve, 1999
Locale: Rome, Paris, Mexico, and Spain
First published: 1975 (English translation, 1976)

> *Principal characters:*
> POLLO PHOIBEE, the protagonist of the Parisian section of the novel
> CELESTINA, a female pimp who also appears as a young woman with tattooed lips
> FELIPE (also called EL SEÑOR), Philip II, King of Spain from 1556 to 1598
> ISABEL (ELIZABETH TUDOR, also called LA SEÑORA), Queen Elizabeth I of England, married to Philip II
> FELIPE THE FAIR, Philip I, King of Spain in 1506, son of the Emperor Maximilian I
> JOANNA REGINA, the Mad Lady, wife of Felipe the Fair
> GUZMÁN, the secretary to El Señor
> THE THREE BASTARDS, half brothers of Felipe
> TIBERIUS CAESAR, the Emperor of Rome

The Novel

Although the narrative of this complex novel begins on July 14, 1999, in Paris, and ends on New Year's Eve of the same year in the same city, the historical time frame of the events spans many centuries. In Paris, Pollo Phoibee meets Celestina, a naïve young woman with tattooed lips, who asks him to explain to her the mysteries of chaotic modern civilization. As Pollo slips and falls into the river Seine, the time of the narrative shifts to the first century and the assassination of Tiberius Caesar, and to the sixteenth century of Felipe, King Philip II (also called El Señor), who is engaged in building the Escorial, the massive palace and mausoleum near Madrid. Pollo, transformed into one of the three mysterious, illegitimate sons of El Señor's father, Felipe the Fair (Philip I), becomes the lover of Isabel, Felipe's wife (Queen Elizabeth I). Another of the sons washes up on a beach in the New World and is welcomed by the Aztecs as the promised redeemer. When he returns to the court of Philip II with news of the discovery of America, the king refuses to accept the possibility of a world beyond the confines of the known Old World, all of which he has sought to reproduce and preserve in the Escorial.

Meanwhile, Joanna Regina has had the body of Felipe the Fair embalmed and preserved against the ravages of time. She then takes as her lover the third illegitimate son of her dead husband. Felipe continues to build the Escorial, in an attempt to enclose within the enormous structure all times and all spaces and thereby defeat the forces of change and preserve his ultimate power. His wife, Isabel, remains secluded in her room, in which she has re-created a Moorish pleasure palace furnished with white sand, blue water, and a bed of total sexual abandon. As she cultivates physical pleasure, she seeks in vain to escape her nightmare of lying prone in the courtyard at the mercy of a mouse which incessantly gnaws at her genitals and "knows the truth."

Toward the end of the novel, Felipe climbs the endless stairs of his mausoleum. On every step, he encounters the opportunity to make new choices and change the course of his past life. Instead, he reinforces his refusal to accept the possibility of a New World that would disrupt the totality of his hermetic space. The last chapter of the novel portrays a return to Paris at the end of the twentieth century. In the ruins of the city, devastated by riots and famine and the collapse of Western civilization, Pollo and Celestina unite in an ecstatic act of love and become one hermaphroditic creature who gives birth to a new creature, the New World of the twenty-first century.

The Characters

Most of the characters of *Terra Nostra* are historical in the sense that they have analogues either in the history of Hispanic civilization or in the fictional characters of Hispanic literature. In many cases, the fictional narrative alters the factual relationships of the historical and literary personages. Felipe the Fair and his wife, Joanna, the daughter of the Catholic Monarchs, Ferdinand II and Isabella I, are portrayed in the novel as the parents of Philip II, though they were in fact the parents of Charles V, the Emperor of the Holy Roman Empire, who was the father of Philip II. Although Philip II did try to marry Queen Elizabeth I of England after the death of his second wife, Mary Tudor, Elizabeth refused. In the novel, Isabel has spent her childhood in the Spanish court and, married to Felipe, exemplifies the lascivious alternative to Felipe's frustrated attempts at enforcing an absolute asceticism in the world contained in the Escorial.

Celestina is the female procuress from the Renaissance play by Fernándo de Rojas, and the Chronicler who is engaged in writing the history of a gentleman of La Mancha is Miguel de Cervantes, the author of *Don Quixote de la Mancha* (1605, 1615; English translation, 1612-1620). The mysterious bastard pilgrim who washes up on the beach reflects the protagonist of Luis de Góngora y Argote's *Soledades* (1613; *The Solitudes*), and the scribe Guzmán is reminiscent of the main character in Mateo Alemán's *La vida de Guzmán de Alfarache, atalaya de la vida humana* (1599, 1604; *The Rogue: Or, The Life of Guzmán de Alfarache*, 1622). In the final scene of Parisian destruction, there is a game of cards played by characters from modern Spanish American fiction—Oliveira, of Julio Cortázar's *Rayuela* (1963; *Hopscotch*, 1966); Cuba Venegas, of Guillermo Cabrera Infante's *Tres tristes tigres* (1967; *Three Trapped Tigers*, 1971); Humberto Peñalosa, of José Donoso's *El obsceno pájaro de la noche* (1970; *The Obscene Bird of Night*, 1973), and Pierre Menard, of Jorge Luis Borges's "Pierre Menard, autor del Quijote" ("Pierre Menard, Author of the Quixote"). In addition, there are numerous extended references to characters created in various cultural manifestations of Spain and the Spanish Empire—the paintings of

Francisco Goya, Hieronymus Bosch, and Pieter Bruegel, the films of Luis Buñuel, the novels of Cervantes, and the Don Juan dramas.

The four central characters of *Terra Nostra* are Felipe, his secretary Guzmán, his wife, Isabel, and his mother, Joanna, the Mad Lady. The other characters tend to be archetypical or symbolic, functioning as representations of various specific roles played by the despotic Felipe and by those who threaten his existing order. Thus, most of the minor characters are reflections of the struggle between the absolutism of Felipe and the forces of freedom and multiplicity led by the sensuous Isabel, the bureaucratic, opportunistic Guzmán, and the insane, deposed Mad Lady. The minor characters are not well developed, precisely because they are both references to historical persons or literary personages and reincarnations of the four characters who form the central power conflict of the novel.

Themes and Meanings

Through the fictional manipulation of history and the Hispanic literary tradition, Carlos Fuentes creates an allegorical interpretation of the Iberian experience from the time of the Roman Empire to the end of the twentieth century.

The episode that dominates the novel is a narrative of building of the Escorial. As the novel moves in a complex temporal mosaic through the periods of the Roman Empire, the destruction of the Aztec civilization in pre-Columbian Mexico, the sixteenth century Spanish Empire, and the apocalyptic Paris of 1999, the Escorial becomes a symbol of the denial of both worldly pleasure and the passage of time. Felipe attempts to contain all historical experience in his monument to the ascetic ideal, duplicating within its walls everything that exists and gathering together all knowledge, thus creating a space that contains all spaces and a time which embodies all time. Meanwhile, Felipe's wife cultivates her hedonism, seeking in vain to ward off the devastating effects of the passage of time.

The Escorial represents Felipe's attempts to solidify and protect his power in the face of threats from all sides. Within the central narrative are many other narratives, all concerning the eternal struggle for power. The Roman emperor Tiberius Caesar dies at the hands of the reincarnated Agrippa, the ruler that he himself had assassinated. In pre-Columbian Mexico, the struggle for power is played out in human sacrifices and assassinations. In the time of Felipe, the mythical sons of Agrippa are reincarnated in the three mysterious bastard sons, each with the mark of the cross on his back and six toes on each foot, whose individual identity can be established only by the manuscript contained in each of three green bottles floating in the ocean.

Terra Nostra is an interpretation of Iberian civilization as a quest for supreme power, exemplified in Felipe, who is portrayed as the quintessential despot. Knowledge is power, and the King's desire to create a repository of all things and all times is a desire to gain ultimate knowledge, which implies ultimate control. His denial of the possibility of a New World is an attempt to negate the existence of anything beyond the limits of his own ordering of the universe. The truth contained in the manuscripts and the truth held by the mouse in Isabel's nightmare are threats to the king's ordered world.

Critical Context

Mexican novelist Carlos Fuentes is one of Latin America's leading writers. His most successful novel, *La muerte de Artemio Cruz* (1962; *The Death of Artemio Cruz*, 1964), is a stylistically complex revelation of the life of a twentieth century Mexican who helped shape the image of his country. In *Terra Nostra*, Fuentes turns to sixteenth century Spain as the historical moment in which the whole of Hispanic cultural and political history can be revealed. Just as *The Death of Artemio Cruz* is directly related to the ideas developed by the Mexican essayist Octavio Paz in *El laberinto de la soledad: vida y pensamiento de Mexico* (1959; *The Labyrinth of Solitude*, 1961), *Terra Nostra* is a fictive narrative of the ideas developed by Fuentes in his essay, *Cervantes: O, La crítica de la lectura* (1976; *Cervantes: Or, The Critique of Reading*, 1976). As Fuentes says, his novel reveals an attempt to reconcile the dual history of liberal Spain and reactionary Spain, a concept also explored by Paz in *The Labyrinth of Solitude*.

Terra Nostra attempts to be a "total novel" not only in its interpretation of the whole of Hispanic history, but also in its stylistic complexity. In *Terra Nostra*, Fuentes treats "memory as total knowledge of a total past," not only what actually happened but also "what could have been and was not." To convey this complex vision, he employs a dazzling array of narrative devices, so that, in the words of Milan Kundera, the novel becomes "an immense dream in which history is performed by endlessly reincarnated characters who say to us: it is always us, we are the same who go on playing the game of history."

Bibliography

Duran, Victor Manuel. *A Marxist Reading of Fuentes, Vargas Llosa, and Puig.* Lanham, Md.: University Press of America, 1994. An interesting study comparing the politics in the writings of these three important Latin American authors. Many of Fuentes's works are examined in detail.

Helmuth, Chalene. *The Postmodern Fuentes.* Lewisburg, Penn.: Bucknell University Press, 1997. A solid overview of Fuentes's work from a postmodernist point of view. Several individual works are discussed, focusing on the issues of identity, national and narrative control, and reconsiderations of the past.

Ibsen, Kristine. *Author, Text, and Reader in the Novels of Carlos Fuentes.* New York: Peter Lang, 1993. Concentrating on four novels, including *Terra Nostra*, Ibsen offers valuable insight into the problem of communication, which remains one of the central preoccupations throughout the work of Fuentes. Her analysis focuses on the means of textualization by which Fuentes activates his reader and how this coincides with his notions of the role of literature in society.

Pollard, Scott. "Canonizing Revision: Literary History and the Postmodern Latin American Writer." *College Literature* 20 (October, 1993): 133-147. Scott analyzes the impact of Latin American narrative on Western literary history after World War II. Focusing on authors Alejo Carpentier, Carlos Fuentes, and Lezama Lima, Scott discusses narratives of conquest and exploration, international modernism, the fashioning of cultural identity, and the primacy of European culture. Offers valuable insight into several of Fuentes's works.

Van Delden, Maarten. *Carlos Fuentes, Mexico, and Modernity.* Nashville, Tenn.: Vanderbilt University Press, 1998. Using Fuentes's writings as a springboard for his discussion, Van Delden presents a comprehensive analysis of Fuentes's intellectual development in the context of modern Mexican political and cultural life. Includes extensive notes and a helpful bibliography.

Gilbert G. Smith

TEXACO

Author: Patrick Chamoiseau (1953-   )
Type of plot: Impressionistic realism
Time of plot: The 1820's to the present
Locale: Rural Martinique and the capital, Fort-de-France
First published: 1992 (English translation, 1997)

> *Principal characters:*
> MARIE-SOPHIE LABORIEUX, the narrator, an old woman who founded the shanty town of Texaco
> ESTERNOME, Marie-Sophie's father, a former slave
> IDOMÉNÉE, Marie-Sophie's mother, a blind woman
> THE URBAN PLANNER, an educated bureaucrat given the task of razing Texaco
> THE "WORD SCRATCHER," Chamoiseau himself, who writes down Marie-Sophie's story

The Novel

   Texaco is an epic narrative that traces the history of the island of Martinique from the time it was a slaveholding French colony to its present status as a part of France under the sway of powerful cultural and economic outside forces. The historical perspective is provided by an account of Marie-Sophie's family beginning in the 1820's, well before the French abolition of slavery in 1848, and of her own life, which covers most of the twentieth century.

   The novel is presented as a myth. Like the life of Christ, it begins with "The Annunciation," or the arrival of the Urban Planner who is sent to "rationalize" and "sanitize" (that is, destroy) the slum, which was called "Texaco" because of its proximity to large oil tanks. It ends with "The Resurrection," in which Chamoiseau tells of his meeting with Marie-Sophie for the first time, of the story that she and he managed to save from oblivion (just like Texaco was ultimately saved from destruction), and of her death, which supposedly occurred a short time before he wrote his final version of her account.

   The bulk of the narrative recounts Marie-Sophie's origins, telling of her grandparents, of her father's long life as a slave, freed slave, and witness to the major events of Martinican history, and of her own life. Orphaned at a young age, she was old enough to learn history and the art of storytelling from her dying father, and then she had to survive on her own in the hostile environment of the "In-City," the word used to describe the center of Fort-de-France. Forced to rely on others, she is taken in by a series of employers, one of whom teaches her the joys of French literature. After several negative experiences with men, she falls in love with Félicité Nelta, a restless dreamer who leaves her when she cannot give him a child, probably because self-performed abortions had made her sterile. The return of her loneliness makes her want to build a house. With inspiration provided by a "Mentoh" (a type of powerful spirit) who takes on the human form of an old man named Papa Totone, she creates her home on property owned by the Texaco oil company, and an entire community of poor, displaced former peasants is born on the outskirts of the city. In spite of the efforts of the oil company and the government to destroy it (culminating in the arrival of the Urban Planner), Texaco continues to grow.

The Characters

Texaco is populated by a series of eccentric individuals, most of whom would be considered insane, criminal, or at least marginal by European standards. The focus is on Marie-Sophie's family, beginning with her grandfather, who as a form of revolt used to poison cattle on the plantation where he worked as a slave, and her grandmother, who was of mixed Indian and African blood, providing a genetic link to the Arawak Indians who inhabited the island before they became extinct as a people.

Esternome, Marie-Sophie's father, is the second most important character in terms of the amount of space his story takes. After being granted his freedom for having saved his master's life, he continues to live in poverty and servitude. The role of magic is especially apparent in his life: He is surrounded by spirits, including the zombie of his wife Ninon, who was killed in the eruption of Mount Pelée in 1902. Saint Pierre, the city where they lived, was completely destroyed in the eruption, and Esternome moved in with Adrienne Carmélite Lapidaille, a woman of Fort-de-France whom he followed home one day because he knew she would give him some food. Adrienne turns out to be a witch, and she casts a spell over Esternome that is broken only when he makes Adrienne's blind sister Idoménée pregnant. This is where Marie-Sophie's story begins.

Marie-Sophie is born some time before World War I, a conflict that unexpectedly brings out Esternome's French patriotism. From this point, the narrative focus switches from Esternome to Marie-Sophie, as she recounts her childhood, her apprenticeship with a milliner, and her flight from abusive families and men. Her life takes a turn when she lives in the home of Alcibiade, a pro-colonialist civil servant. When Aimé Césaire, the well-known poet and anticolonial activist, wins election as mayor of Fort-de-France in 1946, Alcibiade becomes insane and rapes Marie-Sophie. She is saved from this desperate situation by Félicité Nelta, her one true love.

Although he receives very little space in the narrative, the character of the Urban Planner is very important. He represents the assimilated Creole who has absorbed the speech patterns and values of the colonial power. When he arrives in Texaco to begin its demise, he is knocked unconscious by a rock thrown by one of its inhabitants. Marie-Sophie takes care of him, and she realizes that she must tell him her story in order to save the community. The Urban Planner becomes a convert to the community, and his scholarly sounding statements on the need to preserve the identity of Texaco appear as inserts in the narrative.

Finally, there is the "Word Scratcher," the character of Patrick Chamoiseau himself, whose presence as the transcriber of the narrative is implied throughout. Marie-Sophie refers to him sometimes as "Oiseau de Cham," a play on the author's name meaning "bird of Shem" (Shem is one of Noah's sons) or, possibly, "bird of the field" (*champ*). He speaks in his own voice in the final section ("Resurrection"), in which he claims to have interviewed Marie-Sophie up until her death and also to have used her diaries as the content of his novel.

Themes and Meanings

Thematically, the novel develops a basic duality: the European belief in logic and order on one hand, represented by the French language and government bureaucracy, and the Creole sensibility, with its emphasis on magic, allusion, and a nonchronological concept of time on the other. It is important to realize that this duality is far from simple or absolute. The Creole worldview is itself largely composed of French language and values. Marie-Sophie's enthusiasm for the writing of François Rabelais, which reminds her of her father's Creole speech, and Esternome's sudden enthusiasm for France during World War I are merely two examples of the positive contribution of France to the identity of the novel's characters. At the same time, many aspects of French culture are portrayed as extremely hostile to the individuals who inhabit the novel: the institution of slavery, of course, but also the social hierarchy of Martinique, in which *Blancs français* (French whites) are at the top, followed by *békés* (white Creoles), brown Creoles, blacks, and every nuance in between. Finally, the title itself evokes the American as well as global impact of capitalism on the Third World, a force even more powerful than colonialism because it is more impersonal. Capitalism is an abstract enemy that looms over the novel and, more than the French government, is the reason why the community is doomed, even if Chamoiseau—the "Word Scratcher"—and the Urban Planner are able to save it temporarily.

In spite of the use of messianic imagery, the theme of the novel is not optimistic. Even though the community of Texaco was saved from the bulldozer, its oldest inhabitants, who are also the depositories of its history and its spiritual strength, are dying one by one. Soon, readers feel, Chamoiseau's novel and other works like it will be the only remnants of the powerful culture from which they arose and the fleeting existence of which they record.

Texaco purports to be a mostly oral narrative, and its greatest achievement is in its mixture of "standard" French, West Indian (or Antillean) French dialect, and Creole to reflect the multiplicity of points of view as well as the cultural richness of the mixed-race population. Chamoiseau translates the actual phrases of Creole into standard French, indicating that Creole is really an entirely separate language (though composed partly of French words and syntax). His use of Creole words, Martinican slang, and a typically Antillean rhythm and syntax in his narrative, however, makes the book somewhat hard to read for anyone who is not familiar with the languages spoken in that part of the world. As one progresses in the narrative, one undergoes a learning process, so that by the end, one has become comfortable with Marie-Sophie's language. In this way, the novel succeeds in initiating the reader into its highly idiosyncratic language, thereby "converting" the reader to its own worldview.

Critical Context

Chamoiseau first gained attention as a Martinican writer whose main interest is in interpreting and promoting Creole language and culture in essays, fiction, drama, autobiography, and folk tales. *Texaco*, his most ambitious work, earned for him France's most prestigious literary award for a novel, the Prix Goncourt, upon its publication. In addition to making him known to a wider audience, *Texaco* confirmed his status as one of the foremost contemporary authors of the French Antilles, alongside his mentor Edouard Glissant, Maryse Condé, and others. Among its many accomplishments, *Texaco* is notable for having brought the native languages of Martinique into the mainstream of French and Francophone literature. Whereas the great Martinican poet Aimé Césaire (who appears briefly in the novel) championed the notion of a pan-African cultural identity expressed via the French language, Chamoiseau tries instead to represent specific, local cultural identities by mixing French and non-French linguistic elements. Francophone literature generally has shied away from using as much indigenous language and dialect as Chamoiseau incorporates into his novel, which therefore sets a new standard for the literary representation of cultures of which the spoken languages rarely appear in print.

Chamoiseau does more than create a linguistic mix that is relatively new to literature. The synthesis of lyricism and realism, exemplified by the vivid depiction of the interior lives and magical beliefs of his main characters, juxtaposed with a harsh analysis of their poverty and of the economic exploitation of the Martinican population, presents a major literary achievement. The character of the Urban Planner is symbolic of the novel as a whole. A simple bureaucrat who was sent by the government to sanitize and thereby destroy the shanty town of Texaco, he is mistaken by the inhabitants to be Christ himself come to save them. Under the strange spell exerted by this hybrid, decaying, yet dynamic world, he indeed becomes converted into a would-be savior. From a faceless agent of power, he metamorphoses into a human being who identifies with the marginal population he had previously deemed insignificant. In this way, he symbolizes the mix of French and Antillean, master and slave, future and past that the novel achieves on such a large scale.

Bibliography

Burton, Richard D. E. "Débrouya pa peché, or Il y a toujours moyen de moyenner: Patterns of Opposition in the Fiction of Patrick Chamoiseau." *Callaloo: A Journal of African-American and African Arts and Letters* 16, no. 2 (Spring, 1993): 466-481. Appearing shortly after the publication of *Texaco*, this article does not actually include any detailed analysis of it, concentrating instead on Chamoiseau's earlier works. However, it constitutes the best introduction to Chamoiseau and to many of the themes he would explore in *Texaco*.

Glissant, Edouard. *Caribbean Discourse*, translated by J. Michael Dash. Charlottesville: University Press of Virginia, 1989. Written before *Texaco*, but worth mentioning as one of the best books written on French Caribbean literature, and therefore essential to anyone wanting to do further research on Chamoiseau.

M. Martin Guiney

THE THANATOS SYNDROME

Author: Walker Percy (1916-1990)
Type of plot: Science fiction
Time of plot: The 1990's
Locale: Feliciana Parish, Louisiana
First published: 1987

> *Principal characters:*
> TOM MORE, a psychiatrist who has just been released from federal
> prison
> LUCY LIPSCOMB, More's cousin, an epidemiologist who becomes
> involved in his investigation
> BOB COMEAUX, More's parole officer on the medical ethics committee,
> an instigator of the plot that More uncovers
> ELLEN MORE, Tom More's second wife, who has suddenly become a
> bridge expert
> JOHN VAN DORN, Ellen More's bridge partner and operator of the Belle
> Ame Academy
> FATHER SIMON RINALDO SMITH, a friend of Tom More who runs a
> hospice

The Novel

The Thanatos Syndrome is in some ways an extension of Walker Percy's *Love in the Ruins: The Adventures of a Bad Catholic at a Time Near the End of the World* (1971), also narrated by Tom More. In *The Thanatos Syndrome*, More confronts a plot to adulterate the drinking water for his area with heavy sodium. Although the chemical has the desirable effects of reducing crime rates and teenage pregnancy, it causes people to revert to childlike thinking and speaking patterns and also changes women's bodies from a menstrual to an estrous cycle. The novel's characters debate the issues involved in programs of social control in this primary plot as well as in a secondary plot involving a hospice.

As the novel opens, More has just returned to his home in Feliciana, Louisiana, after spending two years in federal prison for selling prescription drugs illegally. More, a psychiatrist, is asked by Bob Comeaux, his parole officer on the medical ethics committee, to examine a patient. More notices that Mickey LaFaye, formerly one of his patients, no longer demonstrates her former symptoms of agoraphobia and anxiety but now speaks in simple sentences and jumps from topic to topic. She also shows somewhat aggressive sexuality and an ability to recall obscure facts.

When More meets other former patients and acquaintances, he notices the same types of behavior and absence of former psychiatric symptoms. Even his wife, Ellen, is affected. She manifests her increased memory in her newfound skill at bridge, a game at which she has become an expert and won tournaments with her partner, John

Van Dorn. More suspects that something unusual is going on but receives no support in his investigation from Comeaux, who appears to want More to stop investigating. He offers More a lucrative government consulting job while simultaneously threatening to alter the conditions of his parole if he does not take the job.

Lucy Lipscomb, an epidemiologist and More's cousin, tells him that she thinks something peculiar is going on. She taps into government data banks and discovers that all the people in whom More saw changed behavior showed high levels of heavy sodium. More thinks that the behavioral changes result from cortical deficits caused by the chemical. Lipscomb and More quickly trace the sodium to a water intake valve coming from the local power plant.

When More, Lipscomb's uncle, and one of her friends investigate the intake valve, they are arrested for trespassing. Bob Comeaux bails them out and, in private, tells More that the heavy sodium is part of a government experiment to reduce crime. He reiterates his job offer, stating that More will be able to monitor the program from inside the system if he takes the job. In the meantime, Lipscomb discovers that no government agency formally acknowledges the heavy sodium program.

John Van Dorn, Ellen's bridge partner, also works at the power plant and runs the Belle Ame Academy, which More's children attend. More discovers that Van Dorn knows about the diversion of heavy sodium into the water supply and agrees with the short-term goals of the program. Lipscomb examines some of the children at the Belle Ame Academy, observing signs of sexual abuse and noticing that the children appear to expect sexual behavior from her toward them.

At this point, the primary plot is interrupted by a section entitled "Father Smith's Confession." More had known Father Simon Rinaldo Smith as a parish priest and had talked with him while Father Smith was in a counseling program for alcoholics near the prison where More was serving his sentence. Father Smith had abandoned his duties at the local parish and moved into a fire tower, refusing to come down, when government budget cuts forced the closing of his hospice. Comeaux wanted to convert the hospice into a center for euthanasia. In his confession, Father Smith discusses his time spent in Germany and confesses that if he had been German he would have joined the Schutzstaffel (SS), the Nazi secret police. This confession ties into the main story line by reiterating questions of the morality of social control through medical means and by reinforcing Comeaux's heavy-handedness in promoting his programs.

The climax of the novel comes when More, Lipscomb's uncle, and her friend return to the Belle Ame Academy and discover photographic evidence of sexual molestation of the children there. Knowing that this evidence may be dismissed in court and that some of the adults involved have already had charges of sexual abuse dismissed, More devises a plan to incriminate them. He forces them to drink water with an extremely high concentration of heavy sodium. He summons the sheriff, who witnesses their regression to primate sexual behavior caused by drinking the treated water. Arrests of all the adults who run the academy lead to its closure. More bargains with Comeaux to end the experiment and reopen Father Smith's hospice, with increased government funding.

The Characters

More is introduced as a character alienated from his society. He wonders, when he comes back to Feliciana, whether something really has changed or if he has simply misremembered life outside prison. Throughout the novel, he questions his beliefs in the way the world operates, wondering about the propriety of running the heavy sodium experiment on unknowing subjects, including the children at the Belle Ame Academy. His is the voice of a social conscience.

More's character is presented sympathetically. Even his conviction for selling prescription drugs is cast positively: He sold the drugs because he needed the money, but he also thought that they would help truckers to adjust to their schedules of long hauls without sufficient breaks to sleep. Readers will sympathize with the facts that his practice has all but disappeared and his wife no longer stays home, even though both are largely results of his own actions. His narration is friendly and informal, encouraging readers to like him.

The villains in this story do not appear in stereotype form. Their behavior appears to stem from humanitarian goals of reducing crime and, in Van Dorn's case, increasing abilities. He uses water treated with heavy sodium to improve the mathematical skills of children at the Belle Ame Academy. Comeaux thinks like a stereotypical government bureaucrat, concerned with outcomes but not bothered by the moral questions involved in his actions. His threats to More come in subtle forms, and he appears to be genuinely interested in getting More involved in his program.

More's patients are mostly one-dimensional. Percy uses them primarily as examples of unusual behavior that put More on the track of Comeaux and Van Dorn. Each, however, also has a small story of his or her own. Through these minor characters, Walker discusses religious communes, couples counseling and counselors, politics in El Salvador, people's desires to behave correctly (as defined in part by the false reality of television characters), and race relations.

Apart from More, Father Smith is the most developed character. Prior to Father Smith's confession, More establishes that he is mentally unsound. Percy uses Father Smith to question some of society's beliefs, asking whether it is Father Smith or instead the rest of society that is crazy. Father Smith believes that language has failed to "signify," that words no longer carry meaning, with the exception of the word "Jew." Ironically, More is unable to comprehend much of Father Smith's side of their conversations.

Father Smith's confession to More, coming just prior to the climax, highlights the issues raised in the novel. Father Smith chose the priesthood rather than a career in medicine because, as he says, one must choose between life and death. While in Germany, he witnessed doctors experimenting on and killing children in the name of helping humanity. He concludes that he would have joined the SS, as he saw sense in the German commitment to the state. The confession is the most direct statement of the idea that the world has entered what More calls "the age of thanatos," in which society collectively has a death wish.

Themes and Meanings

Percy's primary intent in *The Thanatos Syndrome* is to question the thinking behind programs of social control. He asks whether controlling socially undesirable behavior and killing children with genetic defects will destroy society. He presents his side convincingly, arguing through More and Father Smith that people should be left to behave according to their own free will and that all people are entitled to life. Percy allows his version of good to triumph over evil. The heavy sodium experiment is abandoned by the end of the novel, and Father Smith's hospice is receiving government funding and taking in patients who formerly would have been sent to the Qualitarian centers promoted by Comeaux, with euthanasia as their fate.

The theme of alienation is important in this work. More returns from federal prison unsure if society has changed or if, instead, he has lost touch as a result of his years in prison. His alienation and status as an outsider allow him to ask questions that no one else cares to. Father Smith, declared mentally unsound by More, appears to have a firmer grasp on morality than does society, as represented by Comeaux and Van Dorn.

Although the novel is in some ways structured as a thriller, the reader never gets the impression that More is in serious danger. The threats against him are subtle: implied loss of his favored parole status, arrests for trespassing, and a cable television van that appears to be following him. The subtlety of the threats underscores the idea that society as a whole can be attacked nonviolently, with damage done before anyone realizes the danger.

After its climax, the novel slips into comic moments, suggesting that all has ended well. Percy uses irony and satire to make some minor points. Van Dorn, for example, takes several months to recover from his dose of heavy sodium and retains primate characteristics during his recovery. More convinces the director of the Tulane Primate Center to take Van Dorn in and pair him with Eve, a gorilla who had learned sign language but no longer uses it. With Van Dorn as her companion, she again begins to use sign language and teaches it to him. Once he recovers, Van Dorn returns to human society and is convicted for his crimes. He is sentenced to ten years in prison, where he writes a book entitled *My Life and Love with Eve*. That episode ends with Van Dorn a celebrity, the director of the primate center appointed as a professor of semiotics at twice his former salary, and Eve returned to Zaire, where she is shunned by other mountain gorillas. Percy makes it very clear who benefits in contacts between humans and their supposed lessers.

The people of Feliciana recover from their treatment with heavy sodium, exhibiting their former psychiatric symptoms and increasing More's practice. The novel ends with More counseling Mickey LaFaye, who once again is anxious and has disturbing dreams in which a stranger is trying to tell her something. Percy appears to believe that this is a desirable state of affairs, that people should have doubts and questions.

Critical Context

Comparisons of *The Thanatos Syndrome* to George Orwell's classic *Nineteen Eighty-four* (1948) and Aldous Huxley's *Brave New World* (1932) are unavoidable.

All three novels discuss the morality of social control through medical means, each pointing out the dangers of going too far in trying to improve society. Percy's book adds religious content to the discussion and updates the social problems supposedly being solved.

The Thanatos Syndrome is Percy's last novel. It illustrates many of the themes common in both his fiction and his essays, themes of religious belief, racial relations, social control, and personal identity. Percy earned his M.D., but his practice was interrupted by an episode of tuberculosis, during which he began an intense study of philosophy that manifests itself in each of his novels. He turned his attention to writing and earned the National Book Award for his first novel, *The Moviegoer* (1961). That novel introduced the idea of people identifying more with films than with real life, a theme touched on in *The Thanatos Syndrome*.

The Thanatos Syndrome brings back the character of Tom More from *Love in the Ruins*. In the earlier book, More was declared crazy, and his first wife left him to join a religious cult, much as Ellen is attracted by the Pentecostals at the end of *The Thanatos Syndrome*. More waited for the end of the world and became an alcoholic in the earlier book; here, he appears to have conquered alcoholism, though he is still prone to knocking back a shot of Jack Daniels, and he takes positive action to save the world from itself.

Bibliography
Allen, William Rodney. *Walker Percy: A Southern Wayfarer.* Jackson: University Press of Mississippi, 1986. Allen reads Percy as a distinctly American, particularly southern writer, claiming that the formative event in Percy's life was his father's suicide, not his reading of existentialist writers or conversion to Roman Catholicism. Allen's readings of individual novels emphasize the presence of weak fathers and rejection of the southern stoic heritage on the part of Percy's protagonists.
Coles, Robert. *Walker Percy: An American Search.* Boston: Little, Brown, 1978. An early but always intelligent and certainly sensitive reading of Percy's essays and novels by a leading psychiatrist whose main contention is that Percy's work speaks directly to modern humanity. In Coles's words, Percy "has balanced a contemporary Christian existentialism with the pragmatism and empiricism of an American physician."
Desmond, John F. *At the Crossroads: Ethical and Religious Themes in the Writings of Walker Percy.* Troy, N.Y.: Whitston, 1997. Chapters on Percy and T. S. Eliot; on Percy's treatment of suicide; on Percy and Flannery O'Connor; on his treatment of myth, history, and religion; and his philosophical debt to pragmatism and Charles Sanders Pierce. A useful, accessible introduction to Percy's background in theology and philosophy.
Hardy, John Edward. *The Fiction of Walker Percy.* Urbana: University of Illinois Press, 1987. The originality of this book, comprising an introduction and six chapters (one for each of the novels, including *The Thanatos Syndrome*), derives from Hardy's choosing to read the novels in terms of internal formal matters rather than

(as is usually the case) Percy's essays, existentialism, Catholicism, or southern background. Hardy sees Percy as a novelist, not a prophet.

Lawson, Lewis A. *Following Percy: Essays on Walker Percy's Work*. Troy, N.Y.: Whitston, 1988. Collects essays originally published between 1969 and 1984 by one of Percy's most dedicated, prolific, and knowledgeable commentators. Discussions of *The Moviegoer* and *Lancelot* predominate.

Percy, Walker. *Conversations with Walker Percy*, edited by Lewis A. Lawson and Victor A. Kramer. Jackson: University Press of Mississippi, 1985. This indispensable volume collects all the most important interviews with Percy, including one (with the editors) previously unpublished. The volume is especially important for biographical background, influences, discussion of writing habits, and the author's comments on individual works through *Lost in the Cosmos*.

Quinlan, Kieran. *Walker Percy: The Last Catholic Novelist*. Baton Rouge: Louisiana State University Press, 1996. Chapters on Percy as novelist and philosopher, existentialist, explorer of modern science. Recommended for the advanced student who has already read Desmond. Includes notes and bibliography.

Tharpe, Jac. *Walker Percy*. Boston: Twayne, 1983. Reading Percy as a Roman Catholic novelist concerned chiefly with eschatological matters, Tharpe divides his study into ten chapters: "Biography, Background, and Influences," "Theory of Art," "Christendom," "Techniques," one chapter on each of the five novels through *The Second Coming*, and conclusion. The annotated secondary bibliography is especially good.

_____, ed. *Walker Percy: Art and Ethics*. Jackson: University Press of Mississippi, 1980. Ten essays by diverse hands, plus a bibliography. The essays focus on settings, existential sources, Martin Heidegger, Percy's theory of language, the semiotician Charles Saunders Peirce, Percy's politics, and *Lancelot* (in terms of his essays, Roman Catholicism, medieval sources, and semiotics).

A. J. Sobczak

THEM

Author: Joyce Carol Oates (1938-   )
Type of plot: Neonaturalism
Time of plot: 1937-1967
Locale: The Midwest and Detroit
First published: 1969

>   *Principal characters:*
>   LORETTA WENDALL (nee BOTSFORD), the mother of Jules and Maureen,
>   who originates the conflicting desires that tear her children apart
>   HOWARD WENDALL, Loretta's husband and the father of Jules and
>   Maureen, a stolid man who rescues and marries Loretta after the
>   murder of her boyfriend Bernie
>   JULES WENDALL, a firebrand confronting the cycle of violence inherent
>   in his family's and his culture's history
>   MAUREEN WENDALL, Jules's sister, who is terrified by brutality and
>   tries to withdraw from the reality in which her brother participates

The Novel

Joyce Carol Oates's *them* begins with Loretta Botsford: "One warm evening in August 1937 a girl in love stood before a mirror." She is enchanted with her own reflection, and she dreams about the future. She is less pleased with her last name because it has "no melody." She creates a kind of fairy-tale setting for herself that has been deeply influenced by her fascination with the movies. The reality is that she lives a cramped existence in a "fair-sized city on a Midwestern canal," and her unstable brother, Brock, brutally ends her fantasies by murdering her boyfriend Bernie when he discovers them sleeping together.

Loretta is "saved" by Howard Wendall, a cop who takes her away from the scene of the crime. With him she starts a family, giving birth to Jules, Maureen, and Betty. Howard is an uncommunicative dolt who nearly destroys Loretta's romantic view of herself. His silence depresses the whole family, which is also terrorized by his mother, Mama Wendall, until the day when Betty viciously fights back and knocks down her grandmother. Jules reacts to this tyranny by leaving home, and Maureen tries to evade it by withdrawing into herself. When Howard is killed in a factory accident, Loretta marries Furlong, a crude man who nearly beats Maureen to death.

Loretta's behavior, the way she fosters illusions about her beauty and independence while marrying and succumbing to precisely the kinds of men who will crush her, is repeated in the lives of her children. As in the naturalistic novels of Theodore Dreiser (1871-1945), Oates's characters have the illusion that they are free to choose, and yet their choices apparently confirm societal patterns that they are powerless to ameliorate. Jules, for example, is attracted to a wealthy Grosse Pointe girl, Nadine, who shoots and nearly kills him. In spite of her fears of mistreatment, Maureen becomes a prostitute in order to acquire the money to escape from her home.

Oates uses time and place, Detroit from the late 1930's to the race riot of 1967, as a context for her characters' violent progress. An earlier Detroit race riot in 1943, the assassination of John F. Kennedy, and the student protests of the 1960's are interwoven into the lives of these characters in order to show how individuals are part of a society, a world, that is in virtually constant ferment. Periods of peace, as Jules tells his sister at the end of the novel, are the exception, not the rule, and she will not be able to hide from that hideous truth—which, to the astonishment of many readers, liberates rather than depresses Jules.

The Characters

Loretta is the character who sets the story in motion, yet she is the least conscious of her connections to the world that she represents and engenders, a world glamorized by films and magazines. She concentrates, rather, on her own body, her own concerns—the way she looks in the mirror, the way her hair is styled. Although she is constantly pushed around, she swears that she lets no one boss her. She is a brilliant creation that allows the author to explore the efforts of a second generation to deal with conflicts and contradictions that Loretta cannot contemplate. She is, in a sense, so close to the culture which shapes her that she cannot differentiate herself from it.

Jules, on the other hand, fights his father and his society. As a child he is fascinated by the destructive power of fire and burns down a barn; years later he will be in the forefront of rioters planning the conflagration of a whole society. Jules has all the violent tendencies of Loretta's brother, Brock, and like his uncle, Jules murders a man, a policeman who is meant, no doubt, to be reminiscent of his father, Howard. Yet Jules is also capable of tender love, not only for Nadine—the rich girl he meets while delivering flowers in Grosse Pointe—but also for his mother and sister, to whom he writes moving letters.

Maureen, who has passively shared much of her mother's degradation, sees in Jules the hope of her life. Yet her aspirations, unlike his, are essentially middle-class. She thinks that she would be content with the status quo as long as she found a refuge from its hurtful elements. Unlike her mother, she is tormented by the differences between literature and life, between films and reality. How could anything be more real than her life, she wonders, in her attack on the way that novels intensify life and make readers care about characters that do not exist. In one of the most remarkable passages of the novel, she vents these feelings in letters to her college literature instructor, Joyce Carol Oates.

Oates is, indeed, a major character, even though she appears only in Maureen's letters and in the "Author's Note," where she claims that *them* is "a work of history in fictional form," a story told to her by the character who appears as Maureen in the novel. Oates's humor, her ease with men, her attentive but somewhat removed attitude toward her students fascinate and, to a certain extent, repel Maureen. She wonders how her teacher can appear to be so self-contained, yet she also admires that independence, that seeming lack of illusions about the world. Oates, in short, is the antithesis of what Maureen knows about her family and society. In her experience, individuals cannot have that much control over themselves. On the contrary, they are usually the victims of forces that they are not strong enough to defeat.

Themes and Meanings

Maureen's letters to Joyce Carol Oates are the author's way of commenting on the novel's naturalistic theme. As in Dreiser's novels, human character is shaped by nature, by forces beyond the individual's control. Unlike Dreiser's creations, however, at least some of Oates's characters are aware that they have real choices that can change the course of history. Education, for example, can alert one to certain tendencies in life. Books, as one of Jules's mentors points out, encapsulate experience and can explain it in a way that cannot be understood by simply living. The mentor is implicitly providing an argument for *them* itself, for the novel that is of life but outside it as well. This is exactly what bothers Maureen about Oates, that her teacher can be both aloof and intimate with her students and colleagues.

Although Oates states that *them* is a story told to her, it is just as likely that the characters are projections of her imagination. The letters to her imply as much when Maureen observes that she sees aspects of herself and of her brother Jules in Oates. Many authors like to think of characters coming to them in their imagination. Oates has given a literal twist to this conceit by alleging in the "author's note" that one of the characters did approach her, and that another one, Jules, may some day "be writing his own version of this novel."

Oates is implying that she is as much a part of these characters as they are of her. Similarly, these characters stand in the same relation to society as she does to her characters. In other words, society creates human character—this is clear from Loretta's modeling herself after what film and magazines and friends have to tell her. Yet human beings, individuals, also create society—Loretta, after all, never relents before the crushing forces incarnated in the figures of her two husbands. No matter how downtrodden she becomes, she persists in believing that she has an ideal self that is not the sum of her corrupt environment. So it is that Oates's characters have an existence separate from her own, from her creation of them, entitling her to speak of Maureen as if Maureen were telling her the story of her life. Maureen and the others are the "them" of the novel's title, the "them" to which other characters refer when they want to distinguish themselves from the society by which they are encumbered.

Critical Context

Both a critical and a popular success, *them* was the recipient of the National Book Award in 1970. Already the author of three highly regarded novels—*With Shuddering Fall* (1964), *A Garden of Earthly Delights* (1967), and *Expensive People* (1968)—and several volumes of short stories and poetry, Oates was hailed as one of the most promising and prolific writers of her generation. She has continued her enormous output, publishing several volumes of literary criticism as well as a steady stream of novels and stories.

Many readers have been disturbed by the prominence of violence in Oates's fiction. Joanne Creighton, for example, cites discussions with college students who find it difficult to accept Jules's rebirth through violence. Oates has made it clear, however, that certain kinds of violence—individual and collective—may be therapeutic and lead to important changes in human character and in society. The Detroit riot, at the end of the novel, reflects an energy that is not condemned, since it at least holds out the hope of shaping a world that is different and perhaps better than the one the rioters are destroying.

In much of her work, Oates takes a philosophical tack, trying to blend her interest in Eastern religious ideas about the unity of human beings with the traditional Western concept of individuality. Violence enters into her concerns because she cannot envision a change in human consciousness without radical action being taken. Thus Jules excitedly responds to the Indian author Vinoba Bhave: "We are all members of a single human family. . . . My object is to transform the whole of society. Fire merely burns. . . . Fire burns and does its duty. It is for others to do theirs." Jules echoes these last words while putting a part of Detroit to the torch during the riot.

"History isn't a natural sequence, it's made by man. We create it. Man does and undoes everything." This statement, made by one of her characters on the eve of the Detroit riot, is neither endorsed nor disowned by Oates, but it remains as part of the equation of change. The other part of the equation is nature, the rhythms of repetition that make it difficult for a person to be himself or herself. In all of Oates's novels, people struggle to express themselves in a culture that would coerce them into becoming an extension of itself.

Bibliography

Creighton, Joanne V. *Joyce Carol Oates: Novels of the Middle Years*. New York: Twayne, 1992. Creighton presents the first critical study of the novels Oates published between 1977 and 1990, including the mystery novels published under the name of Rosamund Smith.

Daly, Brenda. *Lavish Self-Divisions: The Novels of Joyce Carol Oates*. Jackson: University of Mississippi Press, 1996. An excellent study that argues that the "father-identified daughters in her early novels have become, in the novels of the 1980's, self-authoring women who seek alliances with their culturally devalued mothers." Offers a perceptive reading of the evolution of feminist elements in Oates's work.

Johnson, Greg. *Invisible Writer: A Biography of Joyce Carol Oates*. New York: Dutton, 1998. An illuminating look at the novelist once dubbed "the dark lady of American letters." Drawing on Oates's private letters and journals, as well as interviews with family, friends, and colleagues, Johnson offers a definitive study of one of America's most gifted novelists.

Wesley, Marilyn C. *Refusal and Transgression in Joyce Carol Oates' Fiction.* Westport, Conn.: Greenwood Press, 1993. An interesting study spanning the spectrum
of Oates's work. Includes a helpful bibliography and index.

Carl Rollyson

THEOPHILUS NORTH

Author: Thornton Wilder (1897-1975)
Type of plot: Social chronicle/fictional memoir
Time of plot: From June to August, 1926
Locale: Newport, Rhode Island
First published: 1973

Principal characters:
> T. THEOPHILUS NORTH, the narrator, a former schoolmaster
> DR. JAMES BOSWORTH, a scholar and retired statesman
> PERSIS TENNYSON, Bosworth's granddaughter, a widow
> BARON BODO VON STAMS, an Austrian diplomat
> FLORA DELAND, a gossip columnist
> HENRY SIMMONS, a British manservant
> EDWEENA WILLS, Henry's fiancee
> COLONEL NICHOLAS VANWINKLE, a World War I flying ace
> AMELIA CRANSTON, the owner of a servants' boardinghouse

The Novel

Ostensibly a memoir written from the perspective of nearly fifty years later, *Theophilus North* is the last of Wilder's works to have been published during his lifetime. It is also, despite a deceptive simplicity, one of the more puzzling items in Wilder's varied literary canon.

Writing in the first person for the first time since his first published novel, *The Cabala* (1926), Wilder in *Theophilus North* creates a narrative persona so close to his own that at times the two voices merge: North, indeed, shares with his creator the accidents of birth (Madison, Wisconsin, 1897), early residence (China, California), education (Yale, class of 1920), military service in the Coast Guard during World War I, graduate study in Rome, and a teaching stint at a New Jersey preparatory school; not much more than the name has been changed. The older brother and younger sisters to whom North refers are clearly Wilder's own, as are certain real-life acquaintances. It would be erroneous, however, to read the novel as if it were an autobiography, or even a fragment of one: Wilder, among the most private of persons despite the celebrity thrust upon him from his early thirties onward, was far too canny a writer thus to expose himself after years of remaining concealed behind his plays, essays, and often experimental novels. Still, the autobiographical content is too strong and too pervasive to be dismissed out-of-hand. On balance, it seems most likely that Wilder intended *Theophilus North* as a memoir of the mind, the fictionally transposed record of his life in art.

"Memory and imagination combined," writes Wilder in the novel's closing sentence, "can stage a servant's ball or even write a book, if that's what they want to do." With that statement as guide, it is possible to view *Theophilus North* as a skillful, if flawed, blend of recollection and invention, and its often irksome narrator-protagonist as a retrospective projection of Wilder the successful literary artist. Like the Stage Manager in *Our Town* (1938), Wilder's best-known play, the twenty-nine-year-old Theophilus is ubiquitous and meddlesome, assuming a variety of postures and disguises in his effort to repair the botched or impaired lives of those around him. Taken together, Theophilus's adventures and accomplishments might well be seen as a summary of Wilder's career in letters as he himself perceived it, the Nunc Dimittis of an aging writer who, in fact, survived the novel's publication by barely two years.

Theophilus North recalls the narrator's experiences as academic tutor, tennis coach, and general-purpose meddler in Newport, Rhode Island, during the summer of 1926. Unmarried, having just resigned his schoolmaster's post, North feels somehow on loan from his own life, hence free to straighten out the lives of others. Getting about on a secondhand bicycle, declining social invitations, North moves with equal ease among servants and employers; soon he is notorious throughout Newport for his skill at mending flawed marriages, liberating housebound wives or henpecked husbands, adjusting maladjusted adolescents, and dispelling the frequent ill effects of gossip and bad company. At one point, he reluctantly finds himself advertised by word of mouth as a kind of faith healer. Enlisting, or at least assuming, the reader's tacit complicity, the elderly narrator remains as sure of himself as he was at twenty-nine, offering no apology for having poked his intrusive nose into other people's business, or for his often outrageous behavior in pursuit of his generally beneficent short-term goals. At certain moments, North the character can be profoundly irritating to the reader, seeming as he does a cross between Mary Poppins and a superannuated Eagle Scout. Notwithstanding, he continues to represent throughout his narrative the disinterested voice of common sense, tempered by gentle wisdom and sensitive tenderness.

As an outsider, North is perhaps uniquely able to perceive the root causes of abuses that have been going on for years, taken for granted by the sufferers and often resulting in apparent physical illness. The octogenarian scholar and statesman James Bosworth, for example, honestly and falsely believes himself to be terminally ill, having in fact accepted the wishful thinking of the younger relatives who hold him a virtual prisoner within the spacious grounds of his estate; similarly afflicted is young Elspeth Skeel, whose debilitating headaches derive uniquely from her Danish father's iron-fisted discipline. A related case is that of Myra Granberry, whose husband George is so intimidated by her love that he has turned Myra into a near invalid, thus freeing himself to enjoy without guilt the less demanding favors of a French mistress. In each case, young Ted North plunges straight to the root of the problem, restoring each "victim" to a position of control over his or her own life, often at great risk to North himself; one of Bosworth's sons-in-law, for example, feels sufficiently threatened by the old man's sudden "recovery" that he plans and nearly implements an attempt on North's life.

Like Dolly Levi, the title character of Wilder's play *The Matchmaker* (1955), North frequently intervenes in other people's amatory lives as well. Early in his stay, he prevents the potentially disastrous elopement of the bored heiress Diana Bell with the public-school athletic coach Hill Jones; although hired by Diana's father, North soon finds that he is really acting on behalf of Hill Jones, whose marriage can still be repaired and who in fact has more to lose than the Bells from the possible scandal of elopement. Thereafter, North will happily arrange to marry off two young widows, both of whom have been "under a cloud" owing to the circumstances of their husbands' deaths: One of them is Bosworth's granddaughter Persis Tennyson, secretly in love with North's friend and frequent accomplice Baron Bodo von Stams. Bodo, hopelessly drawn to Persis, does not believe his love to be reciprocated until North informs him otherwise, proceeding thereafter to dispel the vicious rumors occasioned by Archer Tennyson's violent death.

One of North's more frequent tactics is to fight bad publicity with good, whether in the case of Persis Tennyson or in that of the supposedly haunted Wyckoff house. To that end, he enlists the assistance of such allies as the popular Bodo, the local police, and the gossip columnist known by her pen name, "Flora Deland." Born to one of Newport's finer families, "Flora" has long since become an outcast because of her riotous living and multiple marriages; as a journalist, she uses the unique perspective and connections of her background to "expose" the society that has rejected her. Cultivated, even "used" by the enterprising North, "Flora" becomes his unwitting accomplice in righting the wrongs wrought by other, less prominent gossips.

Although frequently serious in tone, as befits the nature of North's undertakings, *Theophilus North* is just as often highly entertaining, even broadly humorous, owing mainly to North's inveterate, often outrageous gift for playing roles and striking poses. North does not suffer fools gladly, and he is especially skilled at defusing pompous bureaucrats and butlers. Among the novel's most humorous scenes is the one in which North pseudonymously confronts the pompous, parsimonious wife of Nicholas "Rip" Vanwinkle, a Yale acquaintance of North who later became a world-famous military aviator but has since lapsed into uxorious servitude. At times North becomes so absorbed in his assumed roles as to disappear almost completely behind them, even before the reader's forewarned eyes.

The Characters

Considerably different in tone and content from Wilder's previous novels, *Theophilus North* may to some extent be seen as an attempted novel of manners, describing customs and manners in the homes of the very rich, both above stairs and below. The fictional moment, located between World War I and the Great Depression, is indeed well chosen for the purpose, showing a society in transition yet not quite fully transformed. As narrator, North frequently mentions the names of Henry James and Edith Wharton, both of whom had spent some time at Newport while composing their well-known novels of manners; also noted in passing is F. Scott Fitzgerald's *The Great Gatsby*, published during the year 1925. Coming from an author as self-conscious and deliberate as Wilder, such references are not to be ignored.

In preparing the sketches that comprise *Theophilus North*, Wilder remained well aware of his most evident models, particularly in the delineation of character. If North himself appears by turns irritating and implausible as a character unless and until he is viewed as an extension of Wilder the literary artist, the various inhabitants of Newport are presented from a distinctly Jamesian or Whartonian perspective; any number of the episodes, moreover, might well have been expanded into full-fledged novels of manners, had the author chosen to do so. James Bosworth, a self-absorbed New England eccentric worthy of James or John P. Marquand, surrounded by a houseful of grasping parasites even more deluded than himself, could surely have served as the central figure in a different novel; his granddaughter Persis, an intelligent woman of rare beauty condemned by malicious gossip to a premature middle age, might even deserve a novel of her own. Colonel Vanwinkle, emerging from the heady experiences of aerial combat to find that his family has lost all its money, married thereafter to an eccentric heiress who forbids him even to look for a job, might well have furnished the subject matter for a novel by Fitzgerald. To Wilder's credit, however, the scope of *Theophilus North* is sufficiently broad to include characters and groups normally omitted from novels of the James and Wharton periods: Thanks in part to his (and Wilder's) archaeological training in Rome, North is interested in people from all walks of life; moreover, as a middle-class midwesterner transplanted to the East, he feels more at home among servants and tradespeople than among the idle rich.

Early in his visit to Newport, North befriends Henry Simmons, a British-born "gentleman's gentleman" whose employer, an explorer, travels frequently without him. Henry, whose gifts for reading human character closely rival North's own, frequently serves as North's adviser and consultant. Henry's fiancee, Edweena, with whom North has had some unrevealed prior acquaintance, is with Persis Tennyson one of the novel's true heroines; formerly a servant, Edweena has prospered as a clothing merchandiser, all the while maintaining her ties to the servant class; at the time of the novel she is a kind of supervisory maid, in effect a prototypical fashion consultant, charged with coordinating ladies' attire at parties. She is also a beneficent meddler after Theophilus's own heart, and often a willing accomplice.

Also featured in the novel are the Materas, Italian immigrants, proprietors of the newsstand and stationery store that North frequents. Of particular interest is the son Mino, a self-taught genius crippled for life by a childhood accident. Under North's tutelage, the young man begins to perceive the scope and potential of his intelligence, proceeding also to discover love in the person of the widowed Agnese O'Brien. Here as elsewhere, Wilder shows a considerable gift for credible characterization, all the more remarkable for its economy.

Themes and Meanings

Curiously, the number nine looms large in the substructure of *Theophilus North*: At the start of the novel, the narrator lists his nine boyhood ambitions; not long thereafter, he will divide Newport into nine distinct but sometimes intersecting "cities," following Theodor Schliemann's division of ancient Troy. Later, he will present his remarkable theory of the "constellations" in human friendship; each human life, he maintains, should be complemented by two sets of nine friends, evenly divided by sex and further divided by age: three older, three contemporary, and three younger. Such classifications, at first rather bewildering, begin to make sense as they are used to explain or elucidate the action: As North moves freely among the nine cities, he will act out one after another of his nine boyhood ambitions, frequently two or more at once, functioning as detective, anthropologist, actor, magician, and picaro, to name only a few of his roles. In the process, he will also acquire new friends to add to his "constellations."

Significantly, North's early choices of possible professions included both anthropology and archaeology, distinct if closely related fields. Newport fascinates him both for its past and for its present, as a kind of living artifact, and it is Newport's people, whether dead or alive, that are the most interesting of all. As a student of human nature, North appears to have few peers, yet his talents and methods are those of the archaeologist: Reading human character as Schliemann read Troy, he penetrates layers of accumulated sediment in search of the reality beneath. In order to bring that truth back to the surface, he employs his own variation of Jean-Jacques Rousseau's pedagogy, restoring in each of the oppressed—and sometimes in the oppressors as well—a long-lost capacity for wonder. Like Wilder himself, who once described *Our Town* as "an attempt to find a value above all price for the smallest events in our daily lives," North endeavors to restore people to contact with their own lives and with the lives of others; although irritating at times, his therapy succeeds more often than it fails.

Not far below the surface, *Theophilus North* thus begins to show forth as a subtle exposition of Wilder's life in art. The methods of North the busybody are demonstrably those of Wilder the novelist and playwright, and a quick review of Wilder's works will reveal one or another of North's ambitions realized, forcing the reader or spectator to view experience through refreshed, unjaundiced eyes. So great, indeed, is the identification of author with narrator that *Theophilus North* is perhaps most readily accessible to those already familiar with Wilder's earlier works.

Critical Context

Although he began his career as a novelist, earning worldwide acclaim at thirty with his second novel, *The Bridge of San Luis Rey* (1927), Wilder is perhaps better remembered as a playwright, who, in addition to his famous *Our Town*, wrote *The Skin of Our Teeth* (1942) and *The Matchmaker* (1955; later adapted for the musical stage as *Hello, Dolly!*). His novels, however, remain worthy of attention and may, in fact, constitute the greater part of his accomplishment. Unfortunately, they are considerably less easily understood than his plays, and often lend themselves to misinterpretation.

As a novelist, Wilder tends toward the restrained, the understated, even the oblique, with a preference for timeless themes over topical ones. *The Woman of Andros*, set in ancient Greece and published during 1930 at the depth of the Depression, provoked a spate of hostile criticism from the political Left. *Heaven's My Destination* (1934), although set in the 1930's in America, is so heavily ironic in tone that few contemporary readers appear to have understood it. In 1948, after service in Europe during World War II, Wilder paid homage to Sartrean existentialism in *The Ides of March*, an epistolary novel covering the last days of Julius Caesar; predictably, the topicality of his thought was generally obscured by the novel's historical setting, and nearly twenty years elapsed before Wilder returned to long fiction. *The Eighth Day*, published in 1967, was a generally well-received philosophical and historical meditation cast more or less within the mystery genre.

In voice, tone, and style, *Theophilus North* harks back to Wilder's very first novel, *The Cabala*, inspired by the author's recent residence and study in Rome. The narrator of *The Cabala*, an American known only as Samuele, is an insatiably curious young man quite similar to North, with a similar penchant for archaeological classifications. In both cases, the autobiographical resonances are strong and not to be overlooked, offering useful clues to Wilder's own perceptions of the interrelation between his life and his art.

Bibliography

Castronovo, David. *Thornton Wilder.* New York: Ungar, 1986. Two chapters on Wilder's early and later novels. A useful introductory study, including chronology, notes, and bibliography.

Goldstein, Malcolm. *The Art of Thornton Wilder.* Lincoln: University of Nebraska Press, 1965. An early and still useful introduction to Wilder's novels and plays. A short biographical sketch is followed by an in-depth look at his work through the one-act play *Childhood* (1962). Includes bibliographical notes and an index.

Goldstone, Richard H. *Thornton Wilder: An Intimate Portrait.* New York: Saturday Review Press, 1975. An intimate portrait of Wilder by a close friend who had written previous studies on the subject, had access to personal documents, and interviewed family and friends. Includes notes, a selected bibliography, and an index.

Harrison, Gilbert A. *The Enthusiast: A Life of Thornton Wilder.* New York: Ticknor & Fields, 1983. A chatty biographical study of Wilder by a biographer who was provided access to Wilder's notes, letters, and photographs. Harrison successfully re-creates Wilder's life and the influences, both good and bad, that shaped him.

Simon, Linda. *Thornton Wilder: His World.* Garden City, N.Y.: Doubleday, 1979. A solid biographical study of Wilder that includes examinations of his published works and photographs, notes, a bibliography, and an index.

Wilder, Amos Niven. *Thornton Wilder and His Public.* Philadelphia: Fortress Press, 1980. A short critical study of Wilder by his older brother, who offers an inside family look at the writer. A supplement includes Wilder's "Culture in a Democracy" address and a selected German bibliography.

David B. Parsell

THERE IS A TREE MORE ANCIENT THAN EDEN

Author: Leon Forrest (1937-1997)
Type of plot: Stream of consciousness
Time of plot: Primarily the 1920's through the 1960's
Locale: Indeterminate; New Orleans, Memphis, but primarily the minds of the characters
First published: 1973

> *Principal characters:*
> NATHANIEL (TURNER) WITHERSPOON, the boy whose mother's funeral is a major theme in the book
> JAMESTOWN FISHBOND, an artist, criminal, and friend of Nathaniel
> MADGE ANN FISHBOND, Jamestown's older sister
> HILDA MAE FISHBOND, their mother
> JERICHO WITHERSPOON, Nathaniel's grandfather, once a slave, the son of a white father
> TAYLOR (WARM-GRAVY) JAMES,
> MAXWELL (BLACK-BALL) SALTPORT, and
> GOODWIN (STALE-BREAD) WINTERS, friends of Nathaniel
> AUNT HATTIE BREEDLOVE WORDLAW, Nathaniel's aunt

The Novel

There Is a Tree More Ancient than Eden is a novel which explores the consciousness of a number of characters. From the record of those explorations, one comes to understand not only the characters but also some of the events which shaped them. There is no traditional plot line which proceeds in an orderly fashion throughout the novel. There are, however, a number of incidents which were important enough to influence the characters.

One of those incidents, referred to in the initial description of Nathaniel Witherspoon and repeated in the final chapter of the book, is the funeral procession of Nathaniel's mother. Another has to do with Nathaniel's grandfather, Jericho Witherspoon. Born into slavery, his father a white man, Jericho once attempted to escape, and the pursuit by bloodhounds has become a part of the family memory. So that he would "know his place," the white man branded his black son, and that memory, too, has come down through the generations. Jericho hated his white father; Jericho's son hates his white grandfather.

The lives of the Fishbond family also become important in the novel. Hilda Mae Fishbond becomes the head of the family when her husband walks out, leaving seven children and a pregnant wife. For a time she manages, working for rich people for almost nothing. Finally, one cold night, without heat, almost without food, she snaps, tears up her apartment and sets it on fire, leading her brood down the fire escape.

In his progress through jails and mental institutions, Jamestown Fishbond is taunted and abused. At one time he is beaten and fears damage to his genitals; at another he is plunged into water in a straitjacket and fears that he is being drowned. Yet his most humiliating experience occurs when he is a small boy: At a party of Nathaniel's color-proud mulatto kin, Jamestown has the door slammed in his face.

Finally, the funeral train of Abraham Lincoln, winding through the countryside and through the novel, fusing with the funeral procession of Nathaniel's mother, is an important plot element and a major motif in what is a thematically constructed work.

The Characters

Forrest's list of characters in the first section of the book, "The Lives," includes purely fictional characters along with real ones—Louis Armstrong, Frederick Douglass, Harriet Tubman, and Abraham Lincoln. Among Nathaniel Witherspoon's childhood friends, Goodwin "Stale-Bread" Winters is disposed of in two phrases—he was the class valedictorian, he overdosed and died. The lives of Taylor "Warm-Gravy" James and Maxwell ("Black-Ball") Saltport are related fairly objectively, though Forrest does become more poetic when he speaks of Saltport's religious change. For M. C. (or Master-of-Ceremonies) Browne, who was killed by his father, Forrest changes technique, simply recording his dying words. Madge Ann Fishbond is characterized through the dramatic monologue, addressed to Nathan (Nathaniel Witherspoon). Hattie Breedlove Wordlaw, whose religious views are expressed frequently throughout the novel, is described in "The Lives" merely by the use of one word, "honor," which is both the key to her character and the mode in which Nathaniel must treat her.

The two most important characters in "The Lives," and the major characters in the novel as a whole, Nathaniel Witherspoon and Jamestown Fishbond, are treated in extremely complex ways. The book begins with Nathaniel's description of himself and his increasingly poetic evocation of the images of his life, as he moves backward and forward through the years, ending with his friendship with Jamestown. Several pages later, when Forrest comes to Jamestown, he begins in the third person with limited omniscience, later moves to a journalistic listing of jobs, dates, and talents, in the manner of notes for a biographical entry, and finally returns to the third-person mode, broken by a first-person fragmentary birthday entry in diary form. Most of the later sections of the book record Nathaniel's thoughts or dreams, but Jamestown's own horrors have penetrated the mind of his friend Nathaniel.

It is obvious that the characters differ in the extent to which their minds are penetrated by the author. The historical characters, Jericho Witherspoon, and all of Nathaniel's friends except Jamestown are dealt with externally. Madge Ann Fishbond tells her own story in one section of the first chapter. Only Nathaniel and Jamestown reveal their inner experience to the reader—their fears and dreams and nightmares.

Themes and Meanings

The themes of *There Is a Tree More Ancient than Eden* are suggested through contrasting elements which are repeated in varying motifs and symbols throughout the novel. First there is the contrast between white and black, emphasizing the white society's assumption that pure whiteness is the norm. Thus, Jericho's white father must brand his illegitimate son so that he will "know his place," know that he is less than he would have been without his black blood. Nathaniel's mulatto uncle turns away the black boy Jamestown as if, says Nathaniel's aunt, the black would rub off on the yellow. Insultingly, Uncle Dupont accuses her of liking black men. The relative values of color as perceived by most of Nathaniel's family are clear in this incident. Symbolically, in a passage of "The Nightmare," white angels dance and pray, while the black angels are described as "skeletons" which have been chopped down from a tree in Eden, punished for their very blackness.

A second theme is that of broken relationships between fathers and sons, particularly between white fathers and part-black sons. Thus, Nathaniel thinks of fathers (or of great-grandfathers) as lynching their dark sons. Like William Faulkner, Forrest draws on the story of Absalom, but he also refers to Oedipus. Absalom rebelled against his father, but was loved by him; Absalom's death was not willed by his father. On the other hand, Oedipus's father ordered a servant to leave the infant Oedipus on a hillside where he would die; only the servant's disobedience saved him. Both black and white fathers in this novel are responsible for the physical or spiritual deaths of their sons. Thus, Jericho's father rejects him because he has black blood, brands him as inferior, leaves him with a confusion of identity which persists throughout the generations of mixed blood. Hilda Mae Fishbond's husband rejects all of his children, including one unborn, and the church singer M. C. Browne is beaten to death by his own father. Significantly, Browne becomes a Christ figure when he forgives his father from his deathbed.

Searching for meaningful lives, searching for identities, Forrest's blacks take different paths. The class valedictorian escapes into heroin and into death at twenty. For others, the answer is one or another form of religion. Two of Nathaniel's friends eventually turn to Islam; he himself is torn between the Roman Catholicism in which he is reared and the passionate tabernacle emotionalism of his aunt, Hattie Breedlove Wordlaw. At one point, Nathaniel thinks that by attending both church and tabernacle, he is hedging his bets.

One reason that religion is so important to the blacks who can embrace it is that it assures them of their identity as human beings. The animal imagery throughout the novel emphasizes the level to which black humanity has been reduced by white society. Black people are forced to live with rats; they are pursued by bloodhounds; they are herded into cattle cars.

Yet finally, in "The Vision," the crucifying crowd discovers that Christ is black. Although His wooden cross then turns into the tree of the book's title, from which He is lynched, it is clear that in His suffering, He is triumphing over death; that in His humiliation, He is more royal than those who scorn Him; that in His death, He wins through to life. Not everyone can choose his situation, Hattie Breedlove Wordlaw says. Often the only control man has over his own life comes from his own will to make it a celebration, to force others to honor him. Like Nathaniel at the end of the book, one must come out from under the bed and face life, face one's own nakedness. For some people, such as Jamestown, talented, fatherless, finally a criminal, finally mad, or Hilda, overburdened with poverty, the task may be too difficult. Then there is a crucifixion without an ascent.

Critical Context

In technique and in material, Leon Forrest is clearly in the tradition of Faulkner. Even the emphasis on history, whether national, familial, or personal, reminds one of Faulkner. Also like Faulkner, Forrest is preoccupied with the problem of identity in a society which begot sons and then rejected them because their mothers were of a subject race.

The background of Forrest's work is complex. He calls upon gospel rhythms and jazz beats, upon Christian and classical symbolism, and upon historical events. In his visionary passages, the grim facts of black history are seen as part of a people's memory: the slave boats, the bloodhounds, the lynchings, the castrations. In the juxtaposition of allusions from so many sources, there is a great richness of texture and of suggestion; in the variety of styles, from matter-of-fact to poetic, from elegiac to gospel, there is almost a symphonic effect.

Forrest's complexity has drawn varied reactions from critics. Some have found him incomprehensible or undisciplined, indulging in private symbolism. Others—among them, Saul Bellow—admire the integrity and originality of his vision and argue that his difficulty results from the scope of his allusions and from the fineness of his thought. It is significant that Ralph Ellison, himself a difficult but a rewarding writer, praised Forrest in the introduction to the novel, suggesting that only a complex style such as that of Forrest (and such as that of Ellison himself) can do justice to a complex world.

Bibliography

Forrest, Leon. "Beyond the Hard Work and Discipline: An Interview with Leon Forrest." Interview by Charles Rowell. *Callaloo* 20 (Spring, 1997): 342-356. Forrest talks about the importance of poetic elements in his fiction and voices his preference for books that employ lyrical language. He attributes his inclination toward the lyric to his early exposure to famous black singers.

_____. "The Mythic City: An Interview with Leon Forrest." Interview by Kenneth Warren. *Callaloo* 16 (Spring, 1993): 392-408. Forrest talks about the influence of his family on his writing, especially his aunt, who instilled a love of storytelling and reading in Forrest in his formative years.

_____. "The Yeast of Chaos: An Interview with Leon Forrest." Interview by Molly McQuade. *Chicago Review* 41 (Spring/Summer, 1995): 43-51. Focuses on Forrest's life and his views on the writer's craft. McQuade edited the interview, so it reads as an autobiographical essay by Forrest.

Warren, Kenneth. "Thinking Beyond Catastrophe: Leon Forrest's *There Is a Tree More Ancient than Eden.*" *Callaloo* 16 (Spring, 1993): 409-418. Warren discusses the narrative and form of Forrest's novel and comments on the author's cinematic technique. Warren sees the central theme of the novel as the necessity for African American writers to approach narrative of the past as a means of bringing about transformation by "thinking through and against history."

Wideman, John Edgar. "In Memoriam: Leon Forrest, 1937-1997." *Callaloo* 21 (Winter, 1998): 7-9. Wideman's tribute to and appreciation of Leon Forrest provides insights into some characteristics of Forrest's writings.

Williams, Dana A. "Leon Forrest." In *Contemporary African American Novelists: A Bio-Bibliographical Critical Sourcebook*, edited by Emmanuel S. Nelson. Westport, Conn.: Greenwood Press, 1999. Williams provides a biographical and critical assessment of Forrest's works as well as a primary and secondary bibliography for further study.

Rosemary M. Canfield Reisman

THESE THOUSAND HILLS

Author: A. B. Guthrie, Jr. (1901-1991)
Type of plot: Historical realism
Time of plot: The 1880's
Locale: Oregon and Montana
First published: 1956

> *Principal characters:*
> LAT EVANS, the protagonist, the son of a poor Oregon farmer-rancher
> CALLIE KASH, a prostitute, the niece of a madam
> JOYCE SHERIDAN, a schoolteacher from Indiana, the niece of a
> storekeeper
> TOM PING, a young cowboy
> MIKE CARMICHAEL, an older cowboy

The Novel

These Thousand Hills traces the rise of Lat Evans from penniless cowboy to well-to-do rancher, civic leader, and political candidate. In order to attain the success that he craves, in order to reach a financial and social level which his pioneer father merely dreamed about, Evans must struggle with nature, with society, and with his own impulses.

Courage, skill, and luck are essential if a poor boy and raw hand such as Evans is to succeed. Because he can break horses, he earns top wages on the drive to Fort Benton, Montana, and there wins the wild horse Sugar in a bronco-riding exploit. A hard winter of wolfing and capture by Indians also test his stamina, but luck plays a part in the medical feat which wins his release from captivity and even in the race on Sugar, which gives him a stake.

As Evans moves up the ladder, he becomes more concerned with guarding his reputation than he is with guarding his life. Although he continues to be generous to his dirt-poor parents and his old companions, he becomes more and more concerned about his associations, more and more vulnerable in his new social role. The conflict of loyalties intensifies, and in the last section of the book, his ambitions are threatened by the desperate acts of his friend Tom Ping, the appearance of his scoundrelly grandfather Hank McBee, and the suspicion of murder which falls upon Callie, the prostitute who has helped to make him a success.

It is at this point that Evans must recognize the price which he and those who love him must pay for his success. The choice which he must make is heartbreaking; he expects to lose his status, his family, his ranch, and his political future. He realizes, however, that being worthy in his own eyes is more important than any other consideration, and he chooses to be loyal and honest. At that point, Guthrie permits him to be reprieved through the loving choices of his friends and of the two women in his life. The lesson has been learned, but the ultimate price has not been demanded of Evans. Although he can never forget those times when he turned his back on his family and his friends, above all on Callie, there will be no price except memory. His luck has held.

The Characters

In Lat Evans, Guthrie has a protagonist who is far less noble than the mountain men of his earlier novels or Lat's own grandfather, Lije, the protagonist of *The Way West* (1949). Lat does not seek freedom, adventure, or challenge. He wants status in the community, financial success, a wife who is a lady, and a family which will make him proud. Even his seeming rebellion—he leaves his poor, moralistic family, and swears, drinks, whores, and gambles—is belied by the fact that from the first he saves his money for the ranch he desires. Guthrie seems to realize that he risks losing the reader's sympathy for Lat. Therefore he must stress the fact that Lat sends money to his parents, though he does not write to them or visit them, and that, as his old friend Mike Carmichael points out, he buys drinks and aids the poor. His marriage to the Indiana schoolteacher Joyce Sheridan, however, seems as much dictated by his mind as by his heart, and the fact that the marriage works is a result of Joyce's fitting the pattern of respectability, as well as of her charm and goodness.

Lat's cowboy friends are carefully differentiated. Mike Carmichael, the middle-aged little man whom Lat meets when he hires on to a cattle drive, understands the conflicts in Lat, perhaps because he came from a good family, as he confides late in the novel. Tom Ping, who ran away from home when he was ten, cannot understand Lat's desertion of him when Ping marries a prostitute, nor can he forgive Lat's protection when Ping is caught with a gang of rustlers. In his poverty, he snarls at Lat, reminding the town that Lat's prosperity came from one horse and one race, forgetting Lat's frugality and seriousness through the years. Lat does provide for several of his cowboy friends, concealing their sexual ventures from his straitlaced wife and keeping them from the bottle, which she detests. As they grow older, men such as Carmichael are willing to exchange their freedom for the security which they have on the Evans ranch, and therefore Carmichael in particular can understand Lat's choice of respectability.

Callie Kash and Joyce Sheridan more closely approach stock characters than do Guthrie's cowboys. Callie, the good-hearted prostitute, was betrayed by a lover and sent by her father to the aunt who runs a "boarding house." When she falls in love with Lat, she remains faithful to him by detaching herself mentally from her carnal activities. She loans him money, nurses him, and bakes for him, only to be thrown over after Lat meets Joyce and decides to move into a world which likes picket fences and uses the word "vice" with frequency. Callie is most alive in the scene when she inveighs against men—all men, brutal or idealistic. Joyce Sheridan, the proper schoolmistress, comes alive when she speaks or thinks of the fear which the big sky produces in her; a nester by nature, she is terrified by the grandeur of Montana, which her God seems too small to govern. Despite the tenderness Joyce has shown to the injured Carmichael, her forgiveness of Lat's involvement with Callie seems rather easy, given her narrow-mindedness.

Themes and Meanings

The pioneers sought freedom, but they also sought material betterment. In *These Thousand Hills*, Guthrie dramatizes the conflict between the two goals. Those men who cherish freedom, like the mountain men of Guthrie's earlier books, become the wandering cowhands of *These Thousand Hills*, free to indulge in "vice" and to avoid commitment. Those men, like Lat, who choose material betterment find themselves also choosing respectability, the church, the school, the symbolic picket fence. In Montana, with its big sky and distant mountains, choosing to limit oneself physically and intellectually seems an even greater loss than where nature is itself less awesome. Perhaps, Guthrie suggests, civilization will always win over the primitive. This is the theme of history.

The second theme in *These Thousand Hills* also involves the dream of material betterment. In *The Way West*, Lat's grandparents and parents had made the overland journey to Oregon in a wagon train. In *These Thousand Hills*, the reader learns that their dreams of prosperity were never realized. His parents' poverty is one motivation of Lat Evans and yet is probably one reason that as he rises, he rarely communicates with them except to make it clear that he is succeeding by sending them money. Thus, the deferred dream of the settlers in Oregon becomes the dream of a rancher in Montana. Unlike his grandfather, however, still confusedly warning him to beware of the British, still thinking of building the nation, Lat has a purely personal dream, and thus a somewhat diminished one.

However selfish Lat's motivation, he becomes worthy of his mountains when he must choose between his dream and that which he knows is the right action. Despite the dwindling of horizons as Guthrie's multivolume chronicle of the West continues, there can be the triumph of a moral action which refuses to be denied by the threat of gossip or hemmed in by the picket fences of narrow respectability.

Critical Context

These Thousand Hills was the third in a series of Western chronicles by A. B. Guthrie, Jr., following *The Way West*, which had won the Pulitzer Prize in 1950. Critically, it has been less well regarded than *The Way West* or Guthrie's first major novel, *The Big Sky* (1947), but sympathetic readers have argued that the lack of force or lack of unity which they observe is the result of the subject, an increasingly more complicated society, rather than any technical defect. As Guthrie's chronicle moves into the twentieth century with the books that follow *These Thousand Hills*, the lack of color and of epic scope are even more evident.

Although the trappings of the Western novel are familiar to everyone—the saloon, the prostitutes, the Indians, the rustlers—Guthrie's details are better researched than many another writer's. He can re-create a river scene in spring or tell the reader how to save on strychnine in wolf-poisoning. What finally elevates him above many other writers of the Western historical novel, however, is his emphasis on the complex and difficult decisions which are forced upon his characters in a wilderness which is becoming civilized. In *These Thousand Hills*, the decisions are still being made in a society which has not lost its memory of the time when men dared the impossible, when the best of them stretched toward the big sky. Yet in this book midpoint in Guthrie's Western series, the dream of freedom is already in retreat.

Bibliography
Chatterton, Wayne. "A. B. Guthrie, Jr." In *A Literary History of the American West.* Western Literature Association. Fort Worth: Texas Christian University Press, 1987. Chatterton gives an overview of Guthrie's career.
Erisman, Fred. "Coming of Age in Montana: The Legacy of A. B. Guthrie, Jr." *Montana: The Magazine of Western History* 43 (Summer, 1993): 69-74. Erisman evaluates Guthrie's legacy and contributions to the literature of the West.
Ford, Thomas W. *A. B. Guthrie, Jr.* Boston: Twayne, 1981. Ford provides a critical and interpretive study of Guthrie, with a close reading of his major works, a solid bibliography, and complete notes and references.
Guthrie, A. B. *The Blue Hen's Chick: An Autobiography.* New York: McGraw-Hill, 1963. Reprint. Lincoln: University of Nebraska Press, 1993. Guthrie's autobiography illuminates the themes of his novels and the autobiographical direction his later fiction would take.
Kich, Martin. *Western American Novelists.* Vol. 1. New York: Garland, 1995. Part of a multi-volume annotated bibliography of prominent western writers of the 1930's and 1940's, including Guthrie. Primary and secondary resources, including first reviews of Guthrie's novels, are included.
Petersen, David. "A. B. Guthrie: A Remembrance." In *Updating the Literary West.* Fort Worth, Tex.: Texas Christian University Press, 1997. An overview of Guthrie's life and career.

Rosemary M. Canfield Reisman

THEY SHOOT HORSES, DON'T THEY?

Author: Horace McCoy (1897-1955)
Type of plot: Social realism
Time of plot: 1935
Locale: Los Angeles, California
First published: 1935

> *Principal characters:*
>> GLORIA BEATTY, a suicidally depressed woman involved in a dance
>> marathon
>> ROBERT SYVERTEN, Gloria's dance partner and the novel's first person
>> narrator
>> MRS. LAYDEN, an elderly dance marathon enthusiast
>> ROCKY GRAVO, the master of ceremonies of the dance marathon
>> VINCENT "SOCKS" DONALD, the promoter of the dance marathon
>> MRS. J. FRANKLIN HIGBY, the president of the Mother's League for
>> Good Morals
>> MRS. WILLIAM WALLACE WITCHER, the vice-president of the league

The Novel

Originally titled "Marathon Dance," *They Shoot Horses, Don't They?* grew out of Horace McCoy's harsh experiences in Hollywood during the worst days of the Great Depression, when some twenty thousand extras were reportedly unemployed. McCoy centers his narrative on Robert Syverten and Gloria Beatty, two Hollywood hopefuls who are forced by poverty to become partners in a grueling marathon dance contest held in a dance hall on a Santa Monica pier.

As is typical of most 1930's *noir* fiction, the novel employs a flashback structure, with narrator Robert Syverten recounting the events that led up to his murdering Gloria Beatty, an act for which he is in the process of being sentenced to death. As Syverten recalls, he and Beatty met by accident when he mistook her waving for a bus as a greeting directed at him. Beatty suggests that the two of them enter a marathon dance contest, which provides free food and sleeping accomodations to contestants and a thousand dollars if they win. The contest also affords valuable public exposure, as dance marathons are often attended by Hollywood producers and directors. Though he is still weak from intestinal flu, Syverten agrees to join the contest as Beatty's partner. Ironically, he proves the stronger of the two, especially during the derbies: nightly races held to generate excitement and eliminate contestants more efficiently than the marathon itself (the couple finishing last every night is disqualified). A month into the marathon, Syverten and Beatty have not only managed to survive but also attracted the attention of Mrs. Layden, a wealthy, eccentric dance-marathon enthusiast who finds them a clothing sponsor. Yet, all the while, Gloria Beatty complains bitterly about life, relentlessly taunts fellow contestants, and makes things miserable for Syverten, who is trying his best to cope with the physical and psychological stresses of the contest. Obnoxious though it is, Gloria's intense pessimism is personally empowering—at least on an ideological level—as it enables her to understand the corrupt nature of the dance contest with a clarity that Syverten utterly lacks. Gloria's negativity also lends her the insight to deconstruct bourgeois moralism as fatuous nonsense. When two meddling old ladies from the Mother's League for Good Morals come to the dance contest to protest its supposed indecency, Gloria lashes out at them in an obscene and withering tirade that constitutes the dramatic climax of the novel.

In the end, though, Syverten's hopefulness and Gloria's nihilism are both rendered moot when a shooting in the dance hall accidentally takes the life of Mrs. Layden and brings the marathon to a sudden, scandalous end. Bereft now even of the tawdry hope of winning the dance contest, Gloria is more suicidal than ever. She draws a small pistol from her purse and asks Syverten to shoot her in the head. He obliges, rationalizing, "They shoot horses, don't they?" With Gloria dead, Robert Syverten has no convincing means of explaining the mitigating circumstances surrounding the shooting. He is convicted of murder and sentenced to death. In the end, Gloria's darkness has consumed him as well.

The Characters

There is little real character development in Horace McCoy's novel. It might be said, however, that the characters become more deeply and essentially themselves, especially Gloria Beatty. From the outset, McCoy characterizes Gloria as a woman in the throes of extreme alienation. Brought up in West Texas by a sexually abusive uncle and a bickering aunt, Gloria has never known love, security, or happiness. Her experiences in Los Angeles in the depths of the Depression have only strengthened and reconfirmed her sense of life as desolate, absurd, and entirely unrewarding. Already having survived one suicide attempt, Gloria is increasingly obsessed with finding the courage and means to kill herself. A woman without any of the comforting illusions that allow people to function in the modern world, Gloria is a figure both monstrous and fascinating. Her nihilism is paradoxical. Though it is socially offensive and self-destructive, there is something to be said for the unflinching honesty and truthfulness that such nihilism exemplifies. In a world of sham, delusion, and hypocrisy, Gloria, to her credit, is having none of it. On the other hand, Gloria Beatty errs in equating a senile capitalist America with life itself. Her negativity is too radical and all-encompassing—it misses a greater truth about life.

Compared to Gloria, Robert Syverten is a rather weak and insipid figure through much of the novel. If Gloria remains stuck in disillusionment, Robert is mired in a more primitive stage of awareness. Despite ample evidence to the contrary, he still subscribes to the American Dream, thus inhabiting an ideological fantasy world where penniless Hollywood extras can miraculously become wealthy and powerful directors. If there is any character development in the novel, it is Robert's subtle drift toward Gloria's nihilism. In their final conversation before the shooting, Robert admits to Gloria that she has had a decisive effect on his outlook: "Before I met you I didn't see how I could miss succeeding. I never even thought of failing. And now—" Robert's willingness to shoot Gloria at her request most dramatically confirms the fact that he has become something of a nihilist in his own right. If not an outright nihilist, Robert is now at least a de facto existentialist, a man whose ethics are flexible and situationally determined, who no longer adheres to conventional notions of right and wrong, or the near-universal shibboleth that merely being alive is always good in and of itself.

While Gloria embodies the dark side, pulling Robert toward death and destruction, Mrs. Layden represents, at first blush, something akin to the fairy godmother figure of folklore. She adopts Robert and Gloria as her favorite couple on the dance floor but reveals, in chapter 11, that Robert is the one she was really interested in all along. She pulls him aside and warns him that Gloria "is not the right kind of girl" for him, that she is "an evil person and she'll wreck your life." Mrs. Layden's accurate assessment of Gloria's true nature is then immediately tainted by the hint of an offer of patronage to Robert in exchange for sexual favors. Yet Mrs. Layden's character is suspect from the outset by virtue of her naïve admiration for the grotesque ritual of the dance marathon. That her death by a stray bullet also destroys the dance contest conclusively invalidates her as a redemptive force in the novel, suggesting that her brand of affirmation was specious, perhaps also suggesting the irrelevance of fairy godmothers to Depression-era America.

Themes and Meanings

On a basic level, *They Shoot Horses, Don't They?* is a fictive exposé of the dance marathon, a short-lived Depression-era fad that Horace McCoy saw as a particularly grotesque example of what American popular culture can spew up in moments of economic crisis.

On a deeper level, McCoy's novel is a sweeping indictment of American civilization. It takes little imagination to understand that the marathon dance contest serves as a metaphor for life in 1930's America. What is supposed to be fun (dance or life) has become hard, competitive work, really a Darwinian endurance contest with no other object than survival. In keeping with the pyramidal nature of capitalist society, only one couple will win the big prize. Yet the promise of the prize, the ideology of the American Dream, is held out to all contestants, most of whom will find only meager sustenance before they fall by the wayside. Grueling, monotonous, physically and psychologically punishing, the marathon also happens to be crooked. (Promoters Socks Donald and Rocky Gravo concoct a phony wedding ceremony to stir up publicity and ticket sales and then unjustly disqualify a couple to preserve the scam.) Furthermore, the contest is held indoors, in a large hall situated on an ocean pier. For the thirty-seven days of the marathon, the contestants are imprisoned in the building, shut off from nature, from the sun and sea that is all around them, from life in its widest context—a literal metaphor for an industrial civilization that keeps people trapped in buildings most of their waking hours and a more figurative metaphor for entrapment in a rigidly structured economic and political system. Finally, perhaps most tellingly, the contest is patently absurd. It serves no useful purpose other than to exhaust and humiliate contestants for the sadistic amusement of spectators—a spectacle not all that different from the circuses and gladiatorial contests that distracted the ancient Romans. McCoy seems to suggest that an inane popular culture reflects a generally vacuous society (and vice versa).

On a deeper level still, *They Shoot Horses, Don't They?* is something of a philosophical novel. McCoy poses some profound questions: How does one sustain faith in life when one's own life is miserable and one's prospects dim? What is there to believe in once one discovers that society is bankrupt in every imaginable sense of the term? Are suicide and euthanasia sometimes morally justifiable acts? McCoy supplies no easy answers to these kinds of questions, but the fact that he asks them at all is remarkable, especially for an author writing a decade before the emergence of existentialism in Europe.

Critical Context

Contemporary reviews of *They Shoot Horses, Don't They?* were mixed. Some reviewers pronounced the novel a small masterpiece, while others chastised McCoy for supposedly imitating James M. Cain or compared him unfavorably—and unfairly—to Nathanael West, a writer working in a parallel but distinctly different idiom. Though not widely read anymore, McCoy's novel is still generally regarded as one of the finest literary representations of the Great Depression.

Interest in *They Shoot Horses, Don't They?* was revived in 1969, when director Sydney Pollack released a much-admired film version of the novel starring Jane Fonda as Gloria and Michael Sarrazin as Robert. (Actor Gig Young won an Academy Award for his portrayal of the Rocky Gravo character.)

Bibliography

Durham, Philip. "The Black Mask School." In *The Mystery Writer's Art*, edited by Francis M. Nevins. Bowling Green, Ohio: Bowling Green University Popular Press, 1970. Focuses on McCoy's stylistic similarities to other writers who contributed to H. L. Menken's *Black Mask* magazine.

Kutt, Inge. "Horace McCoy." In *Dictionary of Literary Biography: American Novelists, 1910-1945*. Vol. 9. Detroit: Gale Research, 1981. A survey of McCoy's life and work, focusing almost exclusively on McCoy's five novels (McCoy also wrote or cowrote thirty-two Hollywood screenplays between 1936 and 1955).

Sturak, Thomas. "Horace McCoy's Objective Lyricism." In *Tough Guy Writers of the Thirties*, edited by David Madden. Carbondale: Southern Illinois University Press, 1979. A stylistic analysis of McCoy's fiction, with particular attention paid to *They Shoot Horses, Don't They?*

Robert Niemi

A THIEF OF TIME

Author: Tony Hillerman (1925-   )
Type of plot: Detective and mystery
Time of plot: 1980's
Locale: New Mexico, Arizona, and Utah
First published: 1988

> *Principal characters:*
> JOE LEAPHORN, a member of the Navajo Tribal Police who is
> attempting to find a missing woman anthropologist
> JIM CHEE, a younger member of the Navajo Tribal Police who
> investigates mysterious and violent incidents involving pot hunters
> ELEANOR FRIEDMAN-BERNAL, an anthropologist tracing Anasazi pots
> who has mysteriously vanished
> RANDALL ELLIOT, an aristocratic anthropologist who violates protected
> sites and resorts to murder to protect his reputation
> JANET PETE, a lawyer with the Navajo Tribal legal services and friend
> of Jim Chee
> SLICK NAKAI, a likeable Navajo fundamentalist Christian evangelist
> involved in selling Anasazi pots
> HARRISON HOUK, a prominent Utah rancher who sells Anasazi pots
> BRIGHAM HOUK, Harrison's son, an insane recluse who lives in a
> remote canyon

The Novel

Set amid the Anasazi ruins of the American Southwest, *A Thief of Time* is an anthropological mystery in which Joe Leaphorn and Jim Chee, two members of the Navajo Tribal Police, work together to locate a missing anthropologist and to solve the murders of two pot hunters, "thieves of time" who ransack Anasazi graves to steal artifacts, thereby damaging the sites for researchers trying to understand the past. Narrated from the omniscient third-person point of view, most of the novel's chapters alternate between Leaphorn and Chee as they conduct parallel investigations, using their intimate familiarity with Navajo culture and the Southwestern landscape. Although solving the mystery provides the major physical action, both characters also deal with personal problems that add significant emotional tension to their investigations.

The novel opens with Dr. Eleanor Friedman-Bernal's nighttime arrival at an unexplored Anasazi ruin in southern Utah. Friedman-Bernal is looking for potsherds bearing the pattern of Kokopelli, the humpbacked fertility god of Indian myth. The pots are apparently the work of a single artist whose pottery was first unearthed at the Chaco Canyon site in New Mexico. Friedman-Bernal believes that this potter's work may help to explain the migratory patterns and mysterious disappearance of the Anasazi people seven centuries ago. Injured in a fall, the anthropologist discovers someone has already ransacked the graves, and the only episode featuring this character ends shrouded in mystery and suspense.

Leaphorn, depressed and grieving over the death of his wife Emma, agrees to help find the anthropologist, whose disappearance has puzzled and alarmed her coworkers at the Chaco Canyon site. On terminal leave and initially apathetic, Leaphorn finds his curiosity returning as he pieces together the puzzle of Friedman-Bernal's disappearance, beginning his search with clues from her appointment calendar. Learning of her research on the Anasazi pots with the Kokopelli design, he starts his hunt for the missing woman at a fundamentalist Christian revival conducted by the Navajo evangelist Slick Nakai, who tells Leaphorn he has an arrangement with Friedman-Bernal to show her and verify the origins of Anasazi pots with the peculiar pattern.

In trouble with Captain Largo for failing to guard a backhoe (stolen from a tribal storage yard while Chee helped a drunken relative), Chee links a suspect to Slick Nakai's revival, where he meets Leaphorn. Chee eventually discovers that the backhoe was stolen by Joe Nails, a white man, and Jimmy Etcitty, another Navajo who follows the "Jesus Way." Chee tracks the backhoe to a remote Anasazi ruin, where he finds that both men have been murdered while vandalizing graves. Since both pot hunters have ties to Nakai, Friedman-Bernal, and the Chaco Canyon anthropologists, Leaphorn and Chee agree to work together.

Harrison Houk, a Utah rancher, tells Leaphorn about an Anasazi pot with the Kokopelli design that he had sold to an art dealer in New York City. After tracing Friedman-Bernal's visit to the dealer and the collector in New York, Leaphorn returns to find Houk murdered, and he trails Friedman-Bernal to the Anasazi site near Houk's ranch. Meanwhile, Janet Pete, Chee's Navajo lawyer friend, helps him to discover Friedman-Bernal and Randall Elliot's mutual interest in the unexplored site in Utah.

At the site, Leaphorn finds the injured anthropologist in the care of Brigham Houk, Harrison's deranged son. Elliot also arrives, and Leaphorn learns the motives that drove the anthropologist to violence. Elliot has been digging up gravesites in search of genetically marked lower jawbones, documenting his finds until he could later get permits to explore the sites officially. Nails and Etcitty, his helpers, had been selling pots from the gravesites, thus attracting Friedman-Bernal's attention. To prevent her from destroying his reputation, Elliot killed his helpers and Harrison Houk and intends to murder Friedman-Bernal, but he is himself killed by Brigham. Chee, who had followed Elliot to the site, helps Leaphorn to rescue the anthropologist, while Brigham disappears into the canyon. The mystery solved and order restored, Leaphorn decides not to retire, and he asks Chee to sing a healing ceremony.

The Characters

Although *A Thief of Time* is built on the framework of the detective story, it is essentially a novel of characterization, a portrayal of the values and complex development of two Navajo tribal policemen, Joe Leaphorn and Jim Chee. The remaining cast of characters is subordinate to the portrayal of the two major characters, underscoring the fact that the novel's action derives from character.

Joe Leaphorn is a modern Navajo who functions as a mediator between cultures—comfortable with the ways of the dominant white culture, pragmatic, a bit skeptical and cynical about taboos (he does not believe in witches or evil ghosts), yet steeped in tribal traditions and at home in the Southwestern landscape. He accepts the basic metaphysical thrust of Navajo culture: *hozho*, the Beautyway, which implies harmony, cosmic orderliness, and the interdependency of nature and the Navajo people. Crime, therefore, is disharmony, disorder, a social and spiritual aberration. Keenly analytical, Leaphorn seeks the underlying pattern of events. His quest to solve the mystery of Friedman-Bernal's disappearance by connecting intricate links becomes a complex metaphor for his need to restore social and spiritual order, not only to his jurisdiction but also to himself as he recovers from his grief over his wife Emma's death. Leaphorn's movement from despondent apathy to a reawakened curiosity and an appetite for life forms part of a pattern that includes his own healing and acceptance of Emma's death and the reaffirmation of his self-identity and Navajo roots. The ethnographic material that gives the novel its rich density of texture and emotional power is revealed through characterization, and Leaphorn emerges as a complex, fully developed, and heroic person.

Jim Chee is effectively juxtaposed to Leaphorn. A younger, more traditional Navajo (he is a *hatathali*, a singer of the Blessed Way), Chee initially does not particularly like the legendary Leaphorn, but he respects him, wants his approval, and finds himself quoting Leaphorn. Leaphorn regards Chee as smart and alert, but "bent," a romantic and a dreamer, yet he comes to admire Chee's detective skills and spiritual calling. Thus the two complement each other well; Chee is an intuitive, somewhat impulsive foil to Leaphorn's rational distrust of hunches and coincidences. Chee's adherence to traditional values serves to emphasize Leaphorn's skepticism. For example, when Chee discovers two murdered pot hunters, one a Navajo, he is deeply affected by his belief in *chindi*, the ghost representing all that was evil in the dead Navajo's being, and Chee must restore inner harmony through the cleansing ritual of a sweat bath. With the help of Janet Pete, his lawyer friend who is also recovering from a romantic entanglement with a white, Chee comes to terms with his loss of Mary Langdon, a white woman for whom he had once contemplated forsaking his Navajo culture. Chee's Navajo beliefs permeate his thoughts and actions, allowing Hillerman subtly to introduce tribal lore and anthropological material through characterization rather than through authorial comment.

Themes and Meanings

An absorbing and entertaining mystery story suffused with Navajo culture, the novel becomes a telling social commentary on the consequences of crosscultural relationships. Leaphorn and Chee, members of a racial minority whose self-identities are perpetually at risk in their exposure to the dominant white culture, dramatize in their thoughts, actions, and quest for harmony the importance of sustaining cultural tradition with cohesive meaning. Of the two, Leaphorn more easily compromises with the hard, practical reality of modern life, regarding Chee as a romantic trying to live by the Old Way in a competitive world. The novel's subtext is Leaphorn's need to reaffirm traditional values. This is conveyed in the pervasive symbolism of the fertility god Kokopelli, the flute-playing, humpbacked bearer of seeds. When Leaphorn paddles down the San Juan River in search of Friedman-Bernal, he is identified with Kokopelli, and his quest becomes an affirmation of life and the continual renewal of the present by the past.

The crosscultural theme is mainly objectified in the tension between the organic, interrelated beauty and harmony of the Navajo way, with its emphasis on family relationships, balance, and sense of the spiritual infusing all of life, in contrast to the moral expediency of a materialistic white culture based on competition, professional rivalry, and greed for prestige and fortune. The beliefs, taboos, rituals, and intricacies of clan structure provide Chee and Leaphorn with interior rules by which to live. In contrast, deracinated Navajos who are indifferent to taboos vandalize graves, and Randall Elliot, thwarted by the tangled bureaucratic laws and regulations protecting unexplored sites, resorts to violent crime. According to Leaphorn's moral code, justice is a higher principle than bureaucratic law enforcement. He has no compunction about letting Brigham Houk disappear after the deranged man kills Elliot, for Houk's action illustrates the Navajo wisdom that things even up: Those who practice evil are self-destructive.

Those characters responsible for crime and "evil" are not judged but are understood as reflecting the distortion of cultural values. Indeed, the white lust for riches and reputation is the moral equivalent of the origin of evil in Navajo myth. Thus Randall Elliot is as much a victim of his wealthy background and professional aspirations as he is a murderous villain. Even the tragedy that befalls the Houk family illustrates the consequences of the acquisitive life, which can lead to derangement and death. Deracinated Navajos such as Slick Nakai and Jimmy Etcitty, who forsake their heritage to embrace the "Jesus Way," are portrayed with sympathy. Their surrender to the temptation to trade the precious Indian artifacts of the past for material gain is only a symptom of the disorder that attends the crosscultural loss of identity and the failure to see the life-affirming value of the past for the present.

Critical Context

A Thief of Time, the eighth novel in Hillerman's series of eleven mysteries set on the vast Navajo Reservation, represents a significant artistic achievement in the depth and complexity of the author's portrayal of Navajo culture. Always a masterful storyteller, Hillerman has uniquely infused the classic novel of detection, which emphasizes the linear thrust of action, with the psychological and spiritual complexity of holistic Navajo beliefs, creating through the consciousnesses of Leaphorn and Chee a rich texture of interlinking details and events. The structure becomes almost nonlinear (like the Native American oral tale), as apparently disparate threads from past and present and from remote distances are woven together into a single, unified pattern of meaning, discoverable only through the Navajo perspective of Leaphorn and Chee.

The first three of Hillerman's mysteries, *The Blessing Way* (1970), *Dance Hall of the Dead* (1973), and *Listening Woman* (1978), feature Leaphorn, the modern, older, cynical detective. Jim Chee, a younger, more traditional detective who reconciles his vocation as a tribal policeman with his avocation as a *yataali*, a Navajo singer, is the main character of the next three novels, *The People of Darkness* (1980), *The Dark Wind* (1982), and *The Ghostway* (1984). Leaphorn and Chee are finally brought together in *Skinwalkers* (1986) and are reunited in *A Thief of Time* (1988). Hillerman continued to pair the two in *Talking God* (1989), *Coyote Waits* (1990), and *Sacred Clowns* (1993), but it is in *A Thief of Time* that he most effectively provides a balanced portrayal of characters whose own personal growth and interaction are central to the conflict and its resolution.

Although Hillerman disclaims writing "mainstream" novels and calls his work "category fiction," he successfully engages the reader in a compelling anthropological mystery with social and moral significance. It is a tribute to Hillerman's mastery of his craft that the reader never bumps into the author with his arms full of ethnographic materials; Hillerman's substantial anthropological knowledge is conveyed artfully through the interaction of setting, plot, and characterization.

Bibliography
Bakerman, Jane S. "Tony Hillerman's Joe Leaphorn and Jim Chee." In *Cops and Constables: American and British Fictional Policemen*, edited by Earl F. Bargainnier and George N. Dove. Bowling Green, Ohio: Bowling Green State University Popular Press, 1986. Shows how Hillerman's novels address the realistic complications peculiar to fictional law-enforcement officers in a vast setting where jurisdictions overlap. Considers how Leaphorn and Chee maintain independence, resourcefulness, and a sense of justice in a cynical milieu of crime and violence. Focuses on the way ethnicity informs characterization.
Engel, Leonard. "Landscape and Place in Tony Hillerman's Mysteries." *Western American Literature* 28 (Summer, 1993): 111-122. Insightful analysis of Leaphorn's search for pattern in crime as a way of reestablishing his relationship to the Earth. Landscape imagery and sense of place are seen as at the core of Hillerman's narrative method.
Erisman, Fred. *Tony Hillerman*. Boise, Idaho: Boise State University, 1989. Extensive treatment of Hillerman's work. Useful consideration of the theme of time—personal, professional, and cultural—in *A Thief of Time*, the "most regionally and humanly evocative of all the Navajo police stories."
Greenberg, Martin, ed. *The Tony Hillerman Companion: A Comprehensive Guide to His Life and Work*. New York: HarperCollins, 1994. A well-researched guide to Hillerman's life and works. Presents a chronology highlighting events in Hillerman's life, a never-before-published interview with Hillerman, critical essays, a short essay on Navajo culture, and excerpts from Hillerman's most popular fiction and nonfiction work.
Laughlin, Rosemary. "Hillerman's Harmony." *English Journal* 82 (February, 1993): 63-65. Laughlin discusses the use of Hillerman's novel as reading material in a col-

lege English course. She demonstrates that students learned that the Navajo way of walking in beauty could be used to assess their own behavior and attitudes.

Reilly, John M. *Tony Hillerman: A Critical Companion.* Westport, Conn.: Greenwood Press, 1996. Provides a brief biography of Hillerman, along with an overview of his fiction. Discusses themes, plot, and characterization of many of Hillerman's novels, and offers a critical perspective on several books. Includes a comprehensive bibliography and index.

Roush, Jan. "The Developing Art of Tony Hillerman." *Western American Literature* 28 (Summer, 1993): 99-110. Argues convincingly that Hillerman has created a new genre; the anthropological mystery. Shows how Hillerman's fiction has shifted from romance to the novel.

Schneider, Jack W. "Crime and Navajo Punishment: Tony Hillerman's Novels of Detection." *Southwest Review* 67 (Spring, 1982): 151-160. An analysis of how Hillerman adapts the classical detective novel to the vast Southwestern landscape. Schneider sees the books' setting as not a passive background but as playing "an active role in the novels."

Clifford Edwards

THE THIN RED LINE

Author: James Jones (1921-1977)
Type of plot: Psychological realism
Time of plot: 1942-1943
Locale: Guadalcanal, in the Solomon Islands, and the west Pacific Ocean
First published: 1962

> *Principal characters:*
> JOHN BELL, a private, later a sergeant and a first lieutenant, and a
>   member of C-for-Charlie Company
> JAMES STEIN, the captain of C-for-Charlie Company, who is removed
>   from command
> GEORGE BAND, the first lieutenant who replaces Stein and who is also
>   removed
> EDWARD WELSH, the first sergeant in C-for-Charlie Company
> DOLL, a private first class in C-for-Charlie Company
> FIFE, a corporal in C-for-Charlie Company
> WITT, a private in Cannon Company
> QUEEN, a corporal
> STORM, a mess sergeant
> GORDON TALL, a lieutenant colonel and battalion commander
> JOHN GAFF, a captain and Tall's aide

The Novel

The true protagonist of *The Thin Red Line* is not a single individual but an entire group, C-for-Charlie Company. No one character provides a point of view that unifies the narrative; instead, a sixty-man group, its fortunes and misfortunes, provides the dominant focus. In keeping with this, James Jones provides a list of all the members of the company at the beginning of the book. Although each is referred to at least once in the course of the novel, some individuals are more important than others, and Jones skillfully follows the action from the points of view of a variety of members of the company. At the novel's beginning, C-for-Charlie is about to go into combat for the first time. The battle for Guadalcanal was one of the bloodiest campaigns in the entire battle with Japan, and the reader enters this combat sharing the fears and anticipations of the soldiers. By novel's end, the company has participated in two major engagements of the protracted battle, the Japanese are finally defeated, and the United States Army, and C-for-Charlie with it, prepares to move on to the next island held by the Japanese, New Georgia. At this point, C-for-Charlie is almost entirely different from the company described at the beginning of the novel. There has been great attrition among its members, the commanding captain has changed twice, the lieutenant colonel commanding the battalion has been promoted and transferred, and those who happen to remain in the company—who have not been evacuated or killed—have become almost totally different personalities from what they were when the reader first encountered them.

The novel's action is subtle. The soldiers in the unit have common interests and concerns, yet because of differences in their personalities, they act in very different ways. In addition, they evolve incrementally as the novel progresses. Many things happen; a large variety of events surrounds the two major battles on the parts of the Guadalcanal mountain referred to as the Dancing Elephant and the Giant Boiled Shrimp. Military historians agree that the battle for Guadalcanal represented a turning point in the Pacific Theater of World War II, and Jones's description of the turning points in the lives of individual soldiers coincides with a turning point of the war. The drama, however, occurs not on the level of a major event but on that of detail. The reader is as interested as the soldiers in who will win the battle and the war, yet this becomes subordinate to the more immediate concerns of the soldiers: Will I be killed tomorrow? Will I be able to master my fear or not? Do the company commander and battalion commander know what they are doing? How willing are they to risk the lives of American enlisted men for a risky victory and promotion? *The Thin Red Line* is above all a psychological novel, and a superb one. The title is explained in an epigraph, said to be an old midwestern saying: "There's only a thin red line between the sane and the mad." This thin line, mentioned only in the title and epigraph, is present by implication throughout the novel in the exploration of the actions and motives of the members of C-for-Charlie Company. As Jones demonstrates, sanity and madness coexist constantly, from day to day, hour to hour, even minute to minute.

The Characters

Jones is particularly good at describing enlisted men. This virtuosity, prominent in his earlier novel, *From Here to Eternity* (1951), can be seen throughout *The Thin Red Line*. In fact, these two books form the first two parts of a trilogy about World War II, despite their publication eleven years apart; the third book in the trilogy, *Whistle*, was not published until 1978. Jones's fame as a writer will probably ultimately rest upon these three books—they are his major achievement. Jones knew his recruits very well, and few other writers about World War II can match him in probing their psychology. Jones is also quite good with his officers, although he tends to view them from the enlisted man's point of view. Captain Stein, Captain Gaff, and Lieutenant Colonel Tall are complex characters, their motivations subtly, probingly investigated. It is natural to compare Jones's novel to Norman Mailer's *The Naked and the Dead* (1948): Mailer's fictitious Pacific island, Anopopei, and Jones's Guadalcanal closely resemble each other, Mailer's Colonel Cummings and Jones's Tall perform very similar functions, and the two authors share an animus against the battalion commanders. Although Tall lacks the paraphernalia of a "Time Machine" to fill in his background, he is just as sharply drawn, vivid, and complex as Cummings. The portrait of Captain Stein is fuller still, and one of the most sensitive depictions of a company commander in World War II literature.

Jones's recruits, as noted above, are drawn with even more exactness and a surer knowledge or experience. Most of the members of C-for-Charlie Company are recruits. The realism of these portraits is open to no doubt—the pertinent question to ask, instead, is, How interesting are they? Though lifelike and vivid, do they have the articulated drama of personality that a reader expects in great literature? These enlisted men are shown with their fears, banalities, irrational impulses, and vulgarities intact, sometimes without traditional literary heightening. A few readers would be willing to forego certain realistic touches in the book, for example, those dealing with masturbation, excretory functions, cruelty, possibly cowardice. There are literary critics who are repelled by some of Jones's characters, preferring World War II recruits like those in Mailer's *The Naked and the Dead*: picturesque, exaggerated, and seen through the sociological prism of American regional folklore. Jones's recruits depend less on an analysis of sociological background and more on purely individual, observed personality traits. These recruits are complex, probably more so than Mailer's, and certainly the probing of their relationships and motives, as well as their gradual evolution in the course of the novel, are remarkably thorough and nuanced, close psychological observation taking the place of sociological schemata. Is the reader interested in the kind of characters described by Jones in the first place? Perhaps they are realistically portrayed, but are they interesting—would the reader care to meet Fife or Doll or Storm in real life? Perhaps not, but by no means is *The Thin Red Line* a book that appeals to the reader's sense of fantasy, his desire for fictionalized flat characters, for cliches or slogans. Sometimes the reader wonders if the book is fiction at all—it seems so close to observed life. One of the foremost contemporary military historians, John Keegan of Sandhurst, has singled out *The Thin Red Line* as a book of remarkable depth and one of the few American or British novels of World War II able to stand comparison with the best written about World War I. It is a book of astonishing insight—above all in its characterization.

A major paradox of the novel is that while the probing of psychological motivation and relationships is of great sophistication, Jones's style is often clumsy, and he seems closer in psychological outlook to ordinary or lower-class characters than to those who are educated, literary, or middle class. Jones was relatively uninfluenced by literary modernism, and he is certainly no Marcel Proust—at least not in his style. Yet he has much of Proust's psychological perspicacity. This is the paradox of Jones that explains, at least in part, why some critics think *The Thin Red Line* is one of the best American novels—possibly the best—about World War II, while others neglect to mention it at all. On one point, almost all critics are agreed: Jones's characterization is sensitive, complex, and often superb.

Themes and Meanings

Although the novel has multiple meanings, most bearing upon psychological motivation, one stands out above the others—the relation of madness and sanity. This theme is indicated by the title and present throughout the novel. Jones accepts war as a defensive necessity, hence as a historical institution. This attitude is essentially commonsensical and matter-of-fact; it is entirely different from that of Mailer. It is a truism that war and the army as an institution are highly problematic in democratic societies. John Keegan has observed how much of British and American war literature is critical of the army as such, of its disciplined hierarchy and authoritarian chain of command. Many have observed that civilians from a democratic society do not easily adapt to the military—commentators on this problematic relationship go at least as far back as Alexis de Tocqueville, who entitled one of the chapters in his *Democracy in America* (1835-1840) "Causes Which Render Democratic Armies Weaker than Other Armies at the Outset of a Campaign, and More Formidable in Protracted Warfare." Jones, however, was tempted at one point by a permanent career in the military. In his World War II trilogy, the institution of the army is not put into doubt, and *The Thin Red Line* correctly emphasizes many aspects of the war in the Pacific that have been forgotten: the Japanese policy of selling ground dearly and their use of suicide crews, their preference for dying over capture, and their belief that death while fighting meant going to Heaven. Americans had the widespread notion that the war could go on forever; the saying "See you at the Golden Gate in '48" was considered optimistic. Many characters in *The Thin Red Line*, such as John Bell, fear that they will never return to their former civilian functions and relationships. These conditions help to explain the particular strain upon the soldiers and informs Jones's particular notion of "madness." All the actions that he describes pushed individuals to the breaking point and beyond—yet they were seen as necessary at the same time. His notion of madness is not apart from sanity, removed or remote from it. On the contrary, it overlaps with it and is almost a precondition for it. For a critic opposed to warfare as an institution, the attrition of recruits was wasteful, meaningless, absurd, but for Jones it was truly tragic, the narrow line—the thin red line—between sanity and madness often disappearing among the conflicting claims of battle.

In the second half of the novel, Jones describes how the recruits come to resemble in their cruelty the Japanese when they are fighting. Combat numbness and animal brutality come to be a permanent state, and when those feelings wear off, debilitating fear increases to take their place. Caught between their own glory- and promotion-hunting superiors and the suicidal Japanese, whose one goal is to inflict as much destruction as possible, the soldiers are forced into a situation so lethal that madness becomes a constant state, and Jones's thin red line becomes an utterly tragic concept.

Critical Context

James Jones was lucky—his first novel, *From Here to Eternity*, was an enormous success, it was made into a film in 1953, and thereafter he was able to devote himself to writing. Critics largely agree that his war trilogy stands above all of his other books. When Ernest Hemingway read *From Here to Eternity*, he thought that Jones's talent was possibly greater than his own. The question now is just how high these war novels rank: Are they among the half dozen best American novels about World War II, or further down the list? Is *The Thin Red Line* as good as or even better than *The Naked and the Dead*, a famous but fatally flawed novel whose final third is an artistic disaster?

Critics who admire the modernists, above all T. S. Eliot and Ezra Pound in poetry, James Joyce in fiction, are hard on Jones. Frequently, his style is awkward—it is not literary or "high," and he often uses words that college graduates do not admit into their lexicons. Those critics, however, who are not advocates of Anglo-American modernism, tend to rate Jones much higher. This plain stylist, who is certainly not a philosophical novelist, treats almost every theme that can be found in Mailer's *The Naked and the Dead* and other war novels—the motivation of the soldier and the officer, the nature of fear and bravery, of leadership, free will, and authority in the varied situations of war—with more depth and with more probing, psychological breadth of understanding than anyone else.

Bibliography
Aldrich, Nelson W., ed. *Writers at Work: The Paris Review Interviews*. 3d ser. New York: Viking Press, 1967. Jones talks about his methods of composition and defends his novels and his own brand of realistic writing against critical attacks. He also believes that an academic education can hurt a writer. Although he was living in Europe at the time of the interview, he considers himself to be an American.

Carter, Steven R. *James Jones: An American Literary Orientalist Master*. Urbana: University of Illinois Press, 1998. A deeply probing study of Jones's spiritual evolution and philosophy and his concern with individual salvation and growth. Includes bibliography.

Giles, James R. *James Jones*. Boston: Twayne, 1981. Examines each of Jones's novels in detail and gives a brief biography of the novelist. Sees a central division between the he-man and the sophisticate in Jones's life and art. Contains an excellent bibliography.

Hassan, Ihab. *Radical Innocence*. Princeton, N.J.: Princeton University Press, 1961. Describes the hero of *From Here to Eternity*, Pruitt, as a passive sufferer and compares his alienation to that of the Negro. Hassan likes the novel but not the subliterary psychology in which Jones indulges.

Jones, Peter G. *War and the Novelist*. Columbia: University of Missouri Press, 1976. Praises James Jones's *From Here to Eternity* and *The Thin Red Line* highly, describing them as accurate portrayals of Army life and combat and as possessing psychological insights.

Morris, Willie. *James Jones: A Friendship*. Garden City, N.Y.: Doubleday, 1978. The friendship between these two writers occurred late in Jones's life. They both lived on Long Island and were drawn into conversations about life and art. Jones reveals much about his early military career.

John Carpenter

THE THIRD LIFE OF GRANGE COPELAND

Author: Alice Walker (1944-   )
Type of plot: Family chronicle
Time of plot: 1920 to the early 1960's
Locale: Georgia and New York City
First published: 1970

Principal characters:

>GRANGE COPELAND, the protagonist, a black sharecropper, later an independent cotton farmer
>MARGARET COPELAND, his wife
>BROWNFIELD COPELAND, their son
>MEM COPELAND, Brownfield's wife
>RUTH COPELAND, their youngest daughter
>JOSIE, a prostitute, owner of the Dew Drop Inn, mistress of both Grange and Brownfield, and later Grange's wife

The Novel

George Copeland's life stretches from before 1900 to the early 1960's. It covers roughly three generations of blacks in the state of Georgia, and his three lives roughly correspond to the generations. Alice Walker, however, does not focus exclusively on George Copeland to characterize the three generations. She devotes the first half of the novel to Grange's son, Brownfield, to reveal what Grange was as a young man; to capture the essence of Grange's "third life," she tells the story of Ruth, Grange's granddaughter. Only the account of the middle period of Grange's life, his ten-year experience in the North, relies totally on Grange's own experiences; those are told in flashback, and remain a secret even to Ruth, to whom Grange confides almost everything else. They are the crucial events that make him different from his son and allow him to go beyond a tainted past to cope creatively with the future. Grange's new attitude toward blacks and American society derives both from his own experience and reflection and from his granddaughter's fresh, instinctive responses to her world. What begins as a novel of overwhelming depression, of seemingly absolute entrapment, ends as an encouraging tribute to the human spirit.

Brownfield's life is a repetition of his father's—up to the crucial moment of change. A visit by his uncle, aunt, and cousins from the North creates for him the illusion that somewhere outside the South exists a world where blacks are, like whites, rich and free. In dreams contentment is confused with whiteness; he never develops a pride in his race. His own family is disintegrating, as his father, Grange, inextricably in debt to a white boss, Shipley, decides there is no hope of a future for him and his wife and children. He takes out his frustrations in wife-beating and unfaithfulness, especially (one learns later) with Josie, a prostitute in Baker County, just to the north. When Grange finally decides to escape to the North, his wife, Margaret, poisons herself and her new baby (not Grange's but a white man's). In a symbolic series of moves, Brownfield follows in his father's footsteps, going only as far as Josie's Dew Drop Inn. Suggesting a genetic and environmental determinism, Walker has him take up with Josie, as his father had done. After two years of being Josie's and her daughter's lover, and being kept by them, Brownfield meets Mem, Josie's niece, eventually marries her, and repeats his father's experience as a sharecropper, gradually falling into debt to a white boss. In the early years of their marriage, Brownfield is loving to Mem, but once again he falls into the pattern established by his father, beating Mem and being unfaithful to her. Mem's response, however, is different from that of Brownfield's mother. Trained as a teacher, Mem has a measure of independence and a strong sense of self-respect. At one point, she forces Brownfield at gunpoint to move into town, live in a modern home, and get a job in a factory while she teaches in a black school. She forces him to break the pattern and thus offers him a chance to be a new man. His pride, however, will not allow him to accept a new life from her hand. He forces the family back onto the land and resumes his life as a tenant farmer. Continuing to resist, however, and refusing to abandon her self-respect as a black woman, she finds another job. Again following his father's destructive example, Brownfield gets what he thinks is his final revenge by shooting her head off with a shotgun. Although both men are responsible for the death of their wives, their fates are not the same: While Grange went North for ten years, Brownfield goes to prison for ten years.

The second half of the novel shifts focus from Brownfield to Ruth, his daughter. When Grange reappears, he is not the young man that Brownfield represents but a man tempered by realities outside the South, and by one particular experience that he recalls in detail—the death of a pregnant white woman in Central Park. She had chosen to drown rather than grab his hand, the hand of a black man. If whites could not understand tolerance, love, and forgiveness, they will have to understand hate. It is this lesson that Grange teaches to Ruth. After Mem's death, Ruth moves in with him. He prepares her for a life of independence, pride in the black race, and hatred of the enemy—the whites. Grange has returned South and has married Josie in order to get her money to buy a farm. As an independent farmer with his own land and his own income, he can compete with whites on their terms. For a while, Josie continues to live with Grange and Ruth, but when it becomes clear that she is not really a member of the family, she turns to Brownfield in prison. Grange and Ruth have a home. As he introduces her to every imaginable experience and prepares her to face the realities of adult life, the two of them gain notoriety within the black community as rebels. Unfortunately, Grange must die for Ruth to live. After being released from prison, Brownfield gains custody of her. Knowing that Brownfield would sadistically destroy Ruth as he had his own wife, Grange shoots him in the courtroom in front of the judge, and then goes to his woods to die. Grange's third incarnation is not only the new man who returns from exile in the North; it is also Ruth, who carries in her his spirit and all he had taught her about joy and survival.

The Characters

Walker's purpose in this novel is to provoke an empathetic as well as critical response to the race problem in America. She writes primarily for readers who do not understand racism and its effects on personality—hence her strategy to create black characters that feel intensely the pressures of the situation, characters that are agonizingly human. She gives her characters a real setting, the American South that she knows so well. In fact, when she leaves the cotton fields, the dusty clay roads and quiet woods, the drafty tenant shacks, and travels north to Central Park, she loses the touch of immediacy. Walker is also successful with dialogue; she knows the dialect of her people. Nothing captures better the color, the humor, and the pain of the black experience than her manipulations of nonstandard English, and her vivid and often raunchy metaphors. In order to reveal the motivation behind the characters' behavior, Walker assumes an omniscient point of view and moves the center of consciousness from one character to another. First one sees the world through Brownfield's eyes, understands why he develops such hatred for his wife, his father, and his daughter. From his own perspective, his father never loved him. Grange's abandonment is, for him, a selfish, unfeeling act. From Brownfield, Walker transfers the reader to Josie's mind, where the keys to her weakness and her prostitution still dwell in her unconscious, in her dreams. In many scenes, Walker assumes total omniscience, reporting not only observable events but also the thoughts of various characters. In the second half of the novel, she mainly reports the thoughts of Grange and Ruth. One comes to understand that Grange's abandonment of his family was the result of extraordinary sensitivity and frustration, that Grange and Ruth, whom the society regards as crazy, are isolated examples of sanity, and that Ruth's dogged independence and defensiveness derive from the horrible experience of seeing her murdered mother's body.

Walker's purpose goes beyond identification with individual characters. She tries to survey the racial situation in the South (and to some extent in the rest of America) over the past hundred years, and perhaps by implication even earlier, during the era of slavery. The characters are thus not only individuals but also representations of black consciousness. Grange, the title character, contains in himself the history of the black race in America. In tracing the changes in his own racial consciousness, he identifies changes in black attitudes. In the first stage, he says, the white society hated him, and he, adopting their judgment, hated himself. In the second stage, he began to hate whites and love himself. The third stage is a movement outward from the self; Grange directs his love toward another. At the end of the novel, Ruth and others may be on the verge of a fourth stage, friendship and equality with whites, but Grange himself dies in the third.

As Alice Walker is a black woman writer, one might anticipate bias against whites and perhaps against men. Yet the novel is remarkably free of bias. Whites as individuals have little place in the action. When they do appear, Walker seems almost consciously trying to balance them out. The stereotyped white boss, Shipley, superficially well-meaning but patronizing and insensitive to blacks as human beings, is replaced by a white couple at the end participating in civil rights marches and voter registration. Walker does not try to make any of the white characters fully motivated human beings—there are enough white novels around to do that. She concentrates on black society. One sees a similar balance in the depiction of men and women. The strong wife (Margaret) eventually worn down by the man, the stronger wife (Mem) who is invincible and therefore murdered by the man, the strong-willed young woman with a future (Ruth), and the wise juju woman (Sister Madelaine) share the stage with Josie, defeated early in life by her own intolerant father, and Mrs. Grayson, Ruth's teacher, who has entirely lost her black consciousness. While Walker with some sympathy paints Brownfield as the most dangerous destructive force in black society—making him by the end a hateful devil that deserves killing—she insists that men are capable of change—Grange is the proof—and finally makes Grange a powerful force for good, not because he has attained the level of love and acceptance that characterize Quincey at the end, but because he, more than anyone, understands the hell of racism and yet survives with his personality intact. All that having been said, Walker clearly has the greatest respect for black women who have maintained racial pride in defiance of the oppressive slavery that both white and black males have imposed on them.

Themes and Meanings

Alice Walker offers at the same time an intimate portrait and a panoramic survey of racism in America from the black point of view. The success of the novel derives from her ability to convince her readers that the terrible conditions of blacks are absolutely inescapable—the despair of this vision recalls Richard Wright's *Native Son* (1940) and makes the reading almost unbearable—and then to suggest that escape is, after all, possible. The theme of the novel is the answer, or rather the complex of answers, to the question: How does one escape? Grange Copeland's three lives provide the clues. The first answer is to step outside conditions that appear to be universal but in fact are only indigenous to one's own local setting. This can be accomplished through education, which frees the mind of environmental determinism. For Grange, education comes first from experience in a different setting, then from reading. It provides a second environment that demonstrates the first to be local and limited. The resulting double consciousness reveals the apparently inescapable condition to be a syndrome that has a cure.

Walker emphasizes the importance of both consciousness and aggressiveness in the transformation. Past experiences must not remain repressed in the unconscious. They must be faced; the crimes one has committed in the name of despair must be acknowledged, and one's public behavior must witness to the new faith. Grange takes all the crucial steps. He names white society as the enemy, aggressively takes charge of his own life to combat that society, but also accepts responsibility for his own worst acts—he should never have permitted the enemy to take away all his manhood. He redefines himself as a man by never again violating his essential responsibilities, never again acting according to the will of the enemy.

Before the escape is complete, one must establish contact, through love, with another human being. For Walker, the place to begin is within the family, for Grange, the person is his granddaughter, Ruth. The obsessive concern of the male slave mentality was to keep one's fellows even lower than oneself; the enlightened concern of the new black is to open up the world, to give others the freedom to feel, think, and act. This is Grange's philosophy of life when he dies.

Critical Context

This first novel by Alice Walker is in some respects more ambitious and more satisfying than a later novel, *The Color Purple* (1982), which many have called her best work and which won for Walker the American Book Award and a Pulitzer Prize. The two books have much in common. They both reveal a preoccupation with the Southern black family; the problem and the solution for individual blacks are inseparable from the homes that nurture or fail to nurture love and self-respect. She studies especially the cause of deterioration in the family—the black male who (understandably, perhaps) cannot withstand racist pressures and sadistically takes out his frustrations on his wife and children. Hence, neither book offers a close look at a fulfilling sexual relationship within marriage. The male with no identity of his own resorts to oppression and violence. *The Color Purple* has two males on the edge of definition and, far away in Africa, a third who has already found it, yet in *The Third Life of Grange Copeland*, Walker has already created an epic figure of a black man, an exception to be sure, who attains spiritual and intellectual strength that does not require physical violence to assert itself. He discovers the identity too late to be a husband but not too late to be a father.

To emphasize the difficulty of transformation, both novels stretch over the entire lifetime of the protagonist. In both, the pattern is the same, a depressing, even hopeless beginning and eventual salvation through enlightenment, emotional honesty, and love. What is impressive about *The Third Life of Grange Copeland* is that Walker traces the transformation in a man and does it convincingly. What is especially satisfying is the unobtrusiveness of its moral. One cannot say the same for *The Color Purple*, yet Walker's imagination and narrative skill, even there, make palatable a heavy didactic strain—her gratuitous lessons on African culture and her promise of success to those who find themselves.

Bibliography

Appiah, K. A., and Henry Louis Gates, eds. *Alice Walker: Critical Perspectives Past and Present*. New York, Amistad, 1993. This volume features critical essays and reviews of Walker's fiction, as well as interviews. An article on *The Third Life of Grange Copeland* is included.

Bloom, Harold, ed. *Alice Walker*. New York: Chelsea House, 1989. A collection of essays that covers the spectrum of Walker's work. Includes an essay on *The Third Life of Grange Copeland*.

Butler, Robert James. "Alice Walker's Vision of the South in *The Third Life of Grange Copeland*." *African American Review* 27 (Summer, 1993): 195-204. Butler discusses the ways in which the characters Brownfield, Ruth, and Grange reveal

Walker's ambivalent vision of the South. He argues that Brownfield represents the cruel and destructive side of the South; Ruth's love for life and adventurous spirit causes her to move to the North; and Grange's ability to thrive in an atmosphere charged with injustice and hatred represents Walker's realistic optimism.

Smith, Felipe. "Alice Walker's Redemptive Art." *African American Review* 26 (Fall, 1992): 437-451. Smith addresses both the secular and spiritual redemption in Walker's work. Focusing on the Christological model, Smith discusses the character of Grange Copeland, Grange's killing of his son, and his own death at the hands of the police.

Winchell, Donna H. *Alice Walker.* New York: Twayne, 1992. An excellent introductory treatment of Alice Walker's writing career. Presents a detailed discussion of Walker's life, poetry, nonfiction, and novels, including an essay devoted to *The Third Life of Grange Copeland.* Also includes a selected bibliography and helpful index.

Thomas Banks

THIS SIDE OF PARADISE

Author: F. Scott Fitzgerald (1896-1940)
Type of plot: Novel of manners
Time of plot: From 1896 to 1919
Locale: New York City, New Jersey, Philadelphia, Maryland, and Minneapolis
First published: 1920

> *Principal characters:*
> AMORY BLAINE, the protagonist, a youth seeking his place in society
> BEATRICE O'HARA BLAINE, Amory's beautiful mother
> ISABELLE BORGE, Amory's first love
> CLARA PAGE, Amory's third cousin, with whom he falls in love briefly
> ROSALIND CONNAGE, the great love of Amory's life
> ELEANOR SAVAGE, an impetuous eighteen-year-old with whom Amory
> has a summer romance
> THAYER DARCY, a Catholic monsignor, Amory's confidant and mentor
> THOMAS PARKE D'INVILLIERS, one of Amory's literary classmates at
> Princeton
> ALEC CONNAGE, Rosalind's brother, whom Amory meets at Princeton
> BURNE HOLIDAY, Amory's reforming friend at Princeton

The Novel

The son of Stephen Blaine and Beatrice O'Hara Blaine, Amory grows up with money. He spends his early years traveling around the United States and Mexico in his father's private railroad car. At fifteen, he leaves his Midwestern home to attend St. Regis, a preparatory school in New Jersey, where he concentrates on football and popularity. Shortly after enrolling, he meets Monsignor Darcy, with whom he has a number of intellectual conversations and with whom he corresponds on important issues. Darcy serves as both confidant and mentor to the maturing youth, who is thirty years his junior.

From St. Regis, Amory goes on to Princeton; his first two years there, like those at St. Regis, are devoted to making friends rather than to studying. Amory is successful in his effort, which culminates in his election to the prestigious Cottage Club. He does, however, begin to write for the *Daily Princetonian*. In his sophomore year, he easily wins a competition in the newspaper, and he is the most likely candidate for the editorship until his poor grades make him ineligible.

Among the friends he makes at Princeton is Thomas Parke D'Invilliers, whom Amory admires for his poetry in the *Nassau Lit*. D'Invilliers introduces Amory to many modern writers, among them William Butler Yeats, Oscar Wilde, and Algernon Charles Swinburne. Under D'Invilliers's influence, Amory begins writing poetry. Thus, at Princeton he begins his love affair with literature.

He also begins his love affair with love. First he has a largely epistolary romance with Isabelle Borge, whom he meets in Minneapolis during the Christmas holiday of his sophomore year. Next he becomes infatuated with his widowed third cousin, Clara Page, but both realize that marriage would be impossible. After he has returned from military service in France in World War I, he meets Rosalind Connage, the sister of his rich Princeton friend Alec. Although they are deeply in love, Rosalind finally rejects marriage because Amory is too poor: The family fortune has been squandered in bad investments, and Amory earns little from his advertising job.

Distraught over the loss of Rosalind, Amory stays drunk for three weeks, then quits his job and heads for Washington, D.C., to talk with Monsignor Darcy. They fail to meet, and Amory drifts to Maryland to visit an uncle. There he meets the eighteen-year-old Eleanor Savage, who is as wild as her name suggests. Together they ride through the countryside and write poetry; for six summer weeks they are in love. One night Eleanor tries to kill herself, though, and their romance ends.

Unemployed and poor, Amory haunts the scenes of his earlier life: Atlantic City (where he rescues Alec from an embarrassing situation with a girl in a hotel), New York, and Princeton. Monsignor Darcy dies; Rosalind becomes engaged to the rich J. Dawson Ryder. Despite all these losses and failures, however, Amory believes that he has learned about himself and thus can face the future with hope.

The Characters

Through Amory Blaine, Fitzgerald tried to understand his own past. In certain superficial ways Amory and Fitzgerald differ: Amory is taller; Fitzgerald did not spend six years traveling around the country—though his family did move frequently; Fitzgerald's family never lost all their money; and Fitzgerald's military service in World War I did not take him to France. Nevertheless, Amory's experiences in preparatory school and college are Fitzgerald's, and his quest to find himself and his calling are the novelist's. When Fitzgerald was finishing *This Side of Paradise* in St. Paul, he, like Amory, had failed to take his degree at Princeton, had failed in the advertising business, and had apparently failed to win the hand of Zelda Sayre, the great love of his life. Still he could say of Amory, and so of himself, that "he was where Goethe was when he began 'Faust'; he was where Conrad was when he wrote 'Almayer's Folly.'" As Fitzgerald's subsequent career demonstrated, he was right to have Amory face the future optimistically, proclaiming in the last line, "I know myself."

Just as Amory Blaine is a thinly veiled Fitzgerald, so, too, most of the other characters derive from the novelist's acquaintances. Thayer Darcy, who as a wild youth was once in love with Beatrice O'Hara, is modeled on Sigourney Fay, the monsignor to whom Fitzgerald dedicated the novel. Just as Monsignor Darcy served as Amory's spiritual and intellectual guide, so Sigourney Fay was Fitzgerald's; it was Fay who told him of the girl who became Eleanor Savage in the novel, one of the few characters not based on Fitzgerald's own experience.

Isabelle Borge is a thinly disguised Ginevra King, whom Fitzgerald, like Amory, met during the Christmas holiday in January, 1915. Their romance, carried on largely through lengthy letters, ended in 1917. The kind Clara is a romanticized portrait of Cecelia Taylor, a first cousin whom Fitzgerald admired. Unlike Clara, though, who is the same age as Amory, Cecelia was sixteen years older than the author; in 1917, when they met, she was a widow with four children rather than two. Rosalind is Ginevra King again, combined with Zelda Sayre, whom Fitzgerald met while stationed at Camp Sheridan, Alabama.

Amory's Princeton friends are Fitzgerald's, too. Thomas D'Invilliers is John Peale Bishop, an editor of the *Nassau Lit*. Like D'Invilliers, Bishop was a faithful and astute literary guide. Burne Holiday is Henry Slater, who, like Holiday, led the movement to abolish the elitist Princeton clubs. Holiday later becomes a pacifist, a stance that Amory initially rejects. Later, however, he tends toward the radical politics that Holiday had espoused.

Themes and Meanings

Reflecting on his past, Amory refers to "the scrap-book of his life." *This Side of Paradise* is a verbal scrapbook of Fitzgerald's early experiences, yet the episodic nature of the work does not result merely from Fitzgerald's lack of distance from the events he is relating. True, he did not have the perspective necessary to select what is important, what trivial, in the development of the artist. Yet this loose structure also expresses Fitzgerald's belief at the time that the novel should be discursive, a theory that he adopted from H. G. Wells.

While Fitzgerald later rejected this view, he continued to espouse many of the other ideas present in his first novel. This work launched his career as spokesman for the Jazz Age. He chronicles the changing mores of the children of Victorian parents, children who indulge in petting parties, flirt shamelessly, and kiss promiscuously. He shows the freeing effects of the automobile and evokes America's college life on the eve of World War I. He also demonstrates the demoralizing effects of that war and Prohibition. These moral crusades had not made the world better. Before Gertrude Stein made her pronouncement about the "Lost Generation," Fitzgerald presciently wrote in the most famous passage of the novel, "Here was a new generation, . . . dedicated more than the last to the fear of poverty and the worship of success, grown up to find all Gods dead, all wars fought, all faiths in man shaken."

Fitzgerald shows the hollowness of this new world. Even though he loved Zelda Sayre and Ginevra King, he realized that they could not fully return his feelings; they were too materialistic to form strong emotional bonds. In the novel, Rosalind wants money, which can insulate her from the world, so she marries J. Dawson Ryder, whose wealth will leave her no concerns more serious than whether her "legs will get slick and brown" in the summertime.

At the same time that Fitzgerald attacks the emotional and intellectual wasteland of twentieth century America, he expresses a yearning for financial success. Amory is poor but loathes poverty. He advocates socialism not because he seeks a more just social order but because he hopes that a revolution might advance him. He attacks ownership of property while clinging desperately to the family estate. In his contradictions as in his college experiences, Amory is Fitzgerald, who wrote the novel to achieve the financial success which he criticized in order to win the girl he recognized as unworthy of him.

Hence his tone is not critical but elegiac; he is the Jazz Age prophet not of jeremiads but of lamentations, of nostalgia. The best writers of the 1920's believed that they and their world had lost something precious. F. Scott Fitzgerald seems already to stand at the end of the decade just beginning, as though he were surveying it from the perspective of the Great Crash and the ensuing Depression, shaking his head sadly and saying, "How vain, but how beautiful."

Fitzgerald suggests that one's first age is the best, that one is happiest in youth and innocence. He echoes William Wordsworth's "Ode: Intimations of Immortality"; he also seems to follow Wordsworth's *The Prelude* (1850) in tracing the growth of the writer's mind. Through Amory, Fitzgerald tries to understand not only his own development but also the development of any writer. His conclusion, too, is Wordsworthian, extolling the egotistical sublime: The writer must know himself.

Critical Context

The composition of *This Side of Paradise* was a quest for self-knowledge. Consequently, ideas sometimes remain inchoate, especially toward the end of the novel, which degenerates into lengthy, rambling monologues. Nevertheless, the novel helped Fitzgerald to clarify for himself a number of issues. He accepted his alienation from the Catholicism into which he was born. He developed the stance he would take toward his generation, a position both within and without, at once critical and admiring. He found his subject—the lives of the rich—and his style, always graceful and often lyric, sensuous and evocative.

He also came to an understanding, however tentative, of his own life, which he would retell repeatedly in his fiction. Amory and Rosalind resurface as Anthony Patch and Gloria Gilbert (*The Beautiful and Damned*, 1922), as Gatsby and Daisy (*The Great Gatsby*, 1925), and as Dick and Nicole (*Tender Is the Night*, 1934). Fitzgerald was also moving toward a grasp of the historical forces that had shaped the present. Only one scene in this novel explicitly invokes the past—Amory's brief visit to a Union cemetery in New Jersey. This episode may have been the germ, however, of the panoramic survey of the American past that informs *The Great Gatsby*.

Fitzgerald hoped not only to clarify his ideas but also to make a large amount of money with this novel, and in this regard, too, he succeeded. He later remarked, "The presses were pounding out *This Side of Paradise* like they pound out extras in the movies." Between its publication in March, 1920, and October, 1921, it sold forty-nine thousand copies. For all its flaws, it spoke to the generation of the 1920's; Glenway Wescott said that it "haunted the decade like a song." Fitzgerald was to write better novels, but none more popular.

It remains the best, as it was the first, record of the music, speech, dress, dances, and literary enthusiasms of the period. Yet it transcends the mere period piece in its depiction of the struggle of a youth to find himself and his place in society. Like all good writing, it is rooted within its time; like the best of writing, it presents characters and issues that are timeless.

Bibliography
Bloom, Harold, ed. *F. Scott Fitzgerald*. New York: Chelsea House, 1985. A short but important collection of critical essays, this book provides an introductory overview of Fitzgerald scholarship, plus readings from a variety of perspectives on his fiction.
Bruccoli, Matthew J., ed. *New Essays on "The Great Gatsby."* Cambridge, England: Cambridge University Press, 1985. This short but important collection includes an introductory overview of scholarship, plus interpretive essays on Fitzgerald's best-known novel.
_____. *Some Sort of Epic Grandeur*. New York: Harcourt Brace Jovanovich, 1981. In this outstanding biography, a major Fitzgerald scholar argues that Fitzgerald's divided spirit, not his lifestyle, distracted him from writing. Claims that Fitzgerald both loved and hated the privileged class that was the subject of his fiction.
Eble, Kenneth. *F. Scott Fitzgerald*. New York: Twayne, 1963. A clearly written critical biography, this book traces Fitzgerald's development from youth through a "Final Assessment," which surveys scholarship on his texts.
Kuehl, John. *F. Scott Fitzgerald: A Study of the Short Fiction*. Boston: Twayne, 1991. Part 1 discusses Fitzgerald's major stories and story collections; part 2 studies his critical opinions; part 3 includes selections from Fitzgerald critics. Includes chronology and bibliography.
Lee, A. Robert, ed. *Scott Fitzgerald: The Promises of Life*. New York: St. Martin's Press, 1989. Includes essays on Fitzgerald's major novels, his *Saturday Evening Post* stories, his treatment of women characters, and his understanding of ethics and history.

Joseph Rosenblum

THIS SUNDAY

Author: José Donoso (1924-1996)
Type of plot: Critical realism
Time of plot: The late 1950's
Locale: Santiago, Chile
First published: Este domingo, 1966 (English translation, 1967)

Principal characters:
JOSEFINA ROSAS DE VIVES (CHEPA), a wealthy woman with a
possessive personality
ALVARO VIVES, her husband, who finds refuge from his failed marriage
by isolating himself in his own world
MAYA, a convicted murderer, who exercises a dark attraction over
Chepa
VIOLETA, the former maid of the Vives family and the former lover of
Alvaro

The Novel

The plot of *This Sunday* is divided into five parts, presented through two different narrative voices. The first narrator, one of the grandchildren of Chepa, remembers, many years later, the weekends spent as a child at the house of his grandparents. His narrative includes the parts entitled "In the Fishbowl," "Legitimate Games," and "Sunday Night." The second voice is that of a third-person narrator who presents certain aspects of the life of Alvaro and Chepa unknown to the grandchild, and who relates the chapters entitled "Part One" and "Part Two."

This section of the story starts when Alvaro is a high school student. While his family is vacationing at a nearby resort, he must stay at home to prepare for exams. In the solitude of the house, sexual relations develop between Alvaro and Violeta, the maid in charge of taking care of him. Years later, Alvaro marries Chepa, but the marriage fails very soon because of temperamental incompatibilities. Both Alvaro and Chepa immerse themselves in selfish existences, isolated from each other, each of them solely concerned with his or her own interests. Alvaro takes refuge in himself, and Chepa hides her sexual frustrations behind charitable concerns for others. As the years pass, their marriage is reduced to a routine governed by the rules imposed by Chepa.

In a visit to the penitentiary, Chepa meets Maya, a brutal murderer. From the very first moment, she experiences a dark and irresistible attraction toward the convict and decides to obtain his freedom. Once she has achieved her goal, Chepa projects on Maya all her secret frustrations, hoping to exert absolute dominion over him, as she does with all those who surround her. Maya cannot cope with this type of life, and after a turbulent relationship of deceit and falsehood, he disappears.

The novel begins on a Sunday morning (its title alludes to this particular day) when Maya reappears several years later, seeking help from Chepa. Alvaro, however, impedes their meeting and, in doing so, sets in motion a fatal sequence of events.

The bulk of the novel concentrates on the torturous relationship between Chepa and Maya. Expanding from this point, the novel illuminates the distorted world of human relations that envelops all the characters, and its unavoidable breakdown.

The Characters

Chepa is a character-type frequently encountered in Donoso's fiction. She is the incarnation of the matriarch—in this case, a frigid and frustrated woman whose life is governed by the urge to dominate others, whether they be members of her own family or those she considers in need of her insatiable willingness to help.

In Alvaro, Donoso presents the counterpart of the dictatorial matriarch: the pitifully weak man. Heir of a wealthy middle-class family, Alvaro is a man whose selfishness grows mainly out of his inability to face "real" life. When aging, he becomes a stranger to his own family, and even more of a stranger to his grandchildren, who call him "the doll." At the beginning of the novel, the reader finds Alvaro in a panic facing the possibility of skin cancer. Nobody seems to believe him, but at the end his terrors will turn into reality.

Maya incarnates the unexpected element that destroys the artificial world built up by the Viveses. From their very first meeting, Maya exerts an animal attraction over Chepa, bringing to life her repressed sexuality. Tortured by the conflict between gratitude and hatred toward the woman who has obtained his freedom but is turning him into a toy, Maya—Alvaro's macho counterpart—rebels against the complacent, self-contained world represented by Chepa, the world of bourgeois society.

Like Maya, the maid Violeta, the fourth major character, represents the world outside the sanctuary of the bourgeois household; she is Chepa's counterpart, as Maya is Alvaro's. At the end, Violeta will also be involved in the torturous relationship between Chepa and Maya, eventually becoming the main victim of its dire consequences.

Themes and Meanings

This Sunday offers a powerful treatment of the theme that has obsessed Donoso throughout his career: the conflict between the dominant and visible order of society and the marginal, the repressed. The way of life of Alvaro and Chepa, as well as that of those who surround them, reflects the former. For them, everything has been established once and forever. Chepa, for example, submerged in her own reality, is incapable of understanding that society does not conform to her personal will. The same occurs not only with the rest of her relatives, but also with Violeta, who considers herself a member of the Vives family.

Isolation, lack of communication, and ambiguity are some of the literary motifs introduced by Donoso to bring to light the existential condition of the Viveses. As is usual in his novels, Donoso concentrates on the moment when a disruptive element suddenly appears to violate the dominant order, revealing the presence of another reality.

Critical Context

José Donoso belongs to the tradition of critical realism characteristic of most Chilean authors, for whom revealing the fragility of the dominant social order has been a constant, significant achievement. The fictitious world presented in most of Donoso's novels is predicated on conflict between upper and lower levels of society.

Nevertheless, Donoso's ultimate concerns are not with class struggle or any other kind of social conflict, but rather with a metaphysical conflict between two different modes of consciousness: that of human beings who do not wish to face reality and who seek to impose their own order on it, and that of those who meet reality without such artificial constructs. Donoso shows that, sooner or later, the former will always pay painfully for their hubris.

Bibliography

Finnegan, Pamela May. *The Tension of Paradox: José Donoso's "The Obscene Bird of Night" as Spiritual Exercises.* Athens: Ohio University Press, 1992. Finnegan examines the novel as an expression of man's estrangement from the world. The novel's two alter-egos, Humberto/Mudito, perceive and receive stimuli, yet they regard the world differently, even though they are interdependent. In a series of chapters, Finnegan follows Donoso's intricate treatment of this idea, showing how the world composes and discomposes itself. A difficult but rewarding study for advanced students. Includes a bibliography.

McMurray, George R. *Authorizing Fictions: José Donoso's "Casa De Campo."* London: Tamesis Books, 1992. Chapters on Donoso's handling of voice and time, his narrative strategies (re-presenting characters), and his use of interior duplication and distortion. Includes a bibliography.

_____. *José Donoso.* Boston: Twayne, 1979. An excellent introductory study, with chapters on Donoso's biography, his short stories, *The Obscene Bird of Night*, and *Sacred Families.* Includes chronology, detailed notes, and annotated bibliography.

Magnarelli, Sharon. *Understanding José Donoso.* Columbia: University of South Carolina Press, 1993. See especially chapter 1: "How to Read José Donoso." Subsequent chapters cover his short stories and major novels. Includes a bibliography.

Mandri, Flora. *José Donoso's House of Fiction: A Dramatic Construction of Time and Place.* Detroit, Mich.: Wayne State University Press, 1995. Chapters on all of Donoso's major fiction, exploring his treatment of history and of place. Includes detailed notes and extensive bibliography.

Jose Promis

A THOUSAND ACRES

Author: Jane Smiley (1949-   )
Type of plot: Family
Time of plot: 1979 through the early 1980's
Locale: Iowa
First published: 1991

> *Principal characters:*
> VIRGINIA (GINNY) COOK SMITH, the daughter and wife of farmers, the novel's narrator
> ROSE COOK LEWIS, Ginny's sister and the mother of two daughters
> CAROLINE COOK, Ginny and Rose's younger sister, an attorney
> LAURENCE (LARRY) COOK, the sisters' father, a strong-willed, domineering man
> TY SMITH, Ginny's husband
> PETE LEWIS, Rose's husband
> HAROLD CLARK, Cook's friend and the owner of a neighboring farm
> JESS CLARK, Harold's long-absent son, who becomes both Ginny and Rose's lover upon his return
> LOREN CLARK, Jess's brother, who has remained on the family farm with his father

The Novel

Set on a farm in Iowa, *A Thousand Acres* draws on William Shakespeare's *King Lear* (c.1605) in its story of an aging farmer who decides to divide his land among his three daughters. His decision alters the family's life forever and forces his oldest daughter, Ginny, the book's narrator, to confront her past.

The story opens in 1979 in Zebulon County, Iowa, as Larry Cook announces his decision to split his land among his children. Cook's married daughters and their husbands agree to the plan, but his youngest daughter, Caroline, who has left the farm and is now an attorney, voices her disapproval and is cut out of the arrangement by her father. The plan unfolds quickly, and though Ginny herself has misgivings about it, Cook is a domineering man whose family rarely challenges him.

For Ginny's husband, Ty Smith, a hardworking man who has treated his father-in-law with respect and patience, the agreement offers a chance to undertake a hog-farming project of which he has long dreamed. Ginny and Ty have been unable to have children—Ginny has suffered five miscarriages, only three of which she has revealed to her husband—yet their marriage is placid, steady, and comfortable. Rose and Pete's relation is less successful—he drinks and is sometimes abusive—but they have two daughters, Pammy and Linda.

Larry Cook's decision coincides with the return of Jess Clark, the son of Cook's neighbor and friend, Harold Clark. Jess has not been home since he fled to Canada during the Vietnam War, and his return is an event in the small community. His brother, Loren, has remained at home with his father on the family farm. Ginny is immediately drawn to Jess, who has lived the unsettled life of a drifter and returned with unfamiliar habits and ideas. The two eventually become lovers, as Ginny begins to grow dissatisfied with Ty.

Soon after his land has been divided between Ginny and Rose, Larry's actions become increasingly erratic and give rise to considerable tension within the family. The two sisters decide to be firm with their father and set rules for his behavior, which leads him to seek out Caroline and repair his rift with her. During a violent thunderstorm, Larry refuses to come indoors and later tells Harold Clark that his daughters turned him out of the house. As the storm rages, Rose confronts Ginny with the truth about their childhood, truth that Ginny has long since repressed; following their mother's death when they were teenagers, their father had sexually abused both girls.

At a church dinner, Harold Clark denounces Ginny and Rose and what he perceives as their mistreatment of their father, who is now living with the Clarks. He also turns on Jess, whom he had seemed to favor over Loren, claiming that Jess is plotting to gain control of the farm. Several days later, Harold is blinded while treating his fields with anhydrous ammonia. Ginny and Rose also learn that Caroline is suing them on behalf of their father in an attempt to regain control of the farm, and Ginny discovers that Ty has provided Caroline with information about the night of the storm. Ty also learns the truth about Ginny's miscarriages, and the gulf between them widens.

Following a drunken quarrel with Harold, Rose's husband Pete drowns in the local quarry, a possible suicide, and Rose confesses to Ginny that she, too, is having an affair with Jess. When Ginny learns that it is Rose whom Jess loves and that her sister knows of their affair, she conceives a plan to poison Rose with a jar of homemade sausages, which Rose puts aside and never eats. The lawsuit brought by Caroline is settled in favor of Ginny and Rose, and Ginny takes a thousand dollars from Ty and leaves the farm.

She settles in St. Paul, where she finds work as a waitress. When she at last contacts Rose several months later, she learns that their father died of a heart attack shortly after the lawsuit was concluded. Several years pass before Ty appears suddenly one day with the news that his portion of the farm has failed; he announces that he is moving to Texas and would like a divorce. The following spring, Rose, who has since broken up with Jess, suffers a recurrence of breast cancer, from which she will not recover, and she asks Ginny to take her daughters. While sorting through items in the farmhouse with Caroline before it is auctioned off, Ginny considers confronting her sister with their father's sexual abuse, but ultimately says nothing. She returns to St. Paul and builds a life with her nieces.

The Characters

Ginny, the book's narrator, is also its central figure. A quiet farmwife who dislikes confrontations and remains emotionally dominated by her father, she is living with repressed memories of abuse and incest that have unknowingly shaped her adult life. Although she is outwardly content in her marriage, she longs for children and has spent most of her life accommodating herself to other people's wishes. When memories of her father's abuse resurface, her emotional world is shattered. The situation is exacerbated by her pain over the outcome of her affair with Jess. Her attempt to poison her sister is an outgrowth of her despair and long-suppressed anger; afterward, she is able to regain her emotional balance and begin a new life.

Rose has not repressed her memories of incest, and she is filled with rage and hatred for her father. Her own marriage is often unhappy and sometimes abusive, yet she is in many ways freer that Ginny. Rose is able to express herself openly and is unafraid of her own feelings. Yet, she too remains under her father's thumb, spending her life as a farmer's wife and giving in to Larry Cook's demanding, domineering ways. Her determination to safeguard her own daughters gives a focus to Rose's life, and she faces her death with courage, tying up loose ends and arranging for her children's care.

Larry Cook remains largely an enigma as seen through the eyes of the daughters he has abused and molested. A hard, powerful, often deliberately cruel man, he appears throughout the novel to be suffering from the onset of senility. His erratic behavior is at first suspected by Ginny and Rose to be a ploy, but it eventually becomes clear that he is not acting. He has trouble distinguishing between his daugters, and he comes to believe that Caroline is dead. His decision to divide his land is perhaps a result of his weakening mental powers, although his behavior remains as consistently difficult and selfish in his decline as it has been throughout his life.

Jess Clark, lover to both Ginny and Rose, is ultimately selfish as well. A tantalizingly foreign presence in the community, he arrives at a moment when upheaval within the Cook family leaves both women vulnerable to his charms. A vegetarian with an interest in Eastern philosophy and organic farming, he believes he is rebuilding his relationship with his father, and he is stunned when Harold denounces him. Unable to sustain a serious commitment, he leaves Rose and returns to the West Coast.

Ty Smith, Ginny's husband, is a decent, hardworking man whose dreams extend only as far as expanding the farm's hog-raising capabilities. Following the division of Larry's land, however, Ginny's perception of Ty undergoes a shift. She begins to see that his amiable, placating manner, while genuine, also makes it possible for him to manipulate those around him. Unaware of his wife's history of incest, he is unable to understand the feelings that color her relationship with her father.

Caroline Cook, like her father, remains largely a mystery to her two sisters. Although they have reared her and have attempted to shield her from the behavior they received from their father, their efforts are misunderstood by Caroline, who sees them as cold and manipulative. Caroline is also not unmotivated by self-interest, exulting in her position as her father's favorite.

Themes and Meanings

A Thousand Acres is not only a modern-day retelling of the *King Lear* story, it is a rethinking of the story as well. Each of the major characters in the novel corresponds to a character from the play, often sharing the same first letter of their names:

Ginny/Goneril, Rose/Regan, Larry/Lear, Caroline/Cordelia. Jane Smiley's purpose, however, is to reexamine the dynamics of the play's relationships and work against the reader's expectations in her portrayal of the novel's characters.

In its portrait of an aging king who decides to divide his kingdom among his three daughters and soon finds himself displaced and ill-treated by the elder two after he has cast out their sister for her honesty, *King Lear* demonstrates clearly that its sympathies lie with Lear and his youngest daughter, Cordelia. Smiley, however, refuses to accept the play at face value. She has remarked, "I never bought the conventional interpretation that Goneril and Regan were completely evil," adding that Shakespeare's version "is not the whole story." In her retelling of the story, Larry Cook has been as ruthless and controlling in his treatment of his daughters as he is in his acquisition of land; in his eyes, both are his property.

In the case of Ginny and Rose, this extends to incest, an act that has more to do with power than with sexual desire. Its effect on the two sisters has shaped their adult lives and is the underlying factor in their uneasy relationship with their father. Caroline remains unaware of her father's abusive behavior, having been protected throughout her childhood by Ginny and Rose, and she is now unable to understand her sister's anger and fear. The division of Larry Cook's farm raises powerful emotional issues for everyone involved, eventually shattering the family completely.

The parallels to *King Lear* also extend to the neighboring Clark family. Like Lear's friend and adviser the Duke of Gloucester, Harold Clark has two very different sons and is blinded during the course of the story. Unlike Gloucester, however, who is tricked and betrayed by one of his sons, Harold plays his sons against each other, letting them believe that he may alter his will in favor of Jess. The principal factor influencing relationships within both families is the father's manipulative and controlling behavior.

Indeed, the central theme of *A Thousand Acres* is the layers of complex emotional issues that inform the lives of all families. Actions by grown children that, taken out of context, may seem heartless or ungrateful are often the result of behavior years earlier on the part of their parents, whose respected positions within their community serve as a shield for their true natures. When the truth is finally acknowledged, the structure of the family crumbles, revealing a foundation built on deception and cruelty rather than love.

In keeping with its theme of hidden causes, the book also features a secondary storyline involving the damage done by unseen chemicals that have drained from the fields into the family's drinking water. Rose has developed cancer, and Ginny has suffered five miscarriages; although no conclusive link is ever proven, the implications are clear. For the Cooks, a family history filled with hidden dangers—both physical and psychological—has resulted in a legacy of irreparable harm.

Critical Context

The complexities of human relationships are at the heart of Jane Smiley's work, and intimate portraits of families make up the majority of her novels, novellas, and short stories. Even her historical saga *The Greenlanders* (1988), an epic novel set in the fourteenth century, focuses on families and relationships that help bring the era she has re-created to life.

Most of Smiley's work involves portraits of contemporary life, as is the case with her short-story collection *The Age of Grief* (1987), which was nominated for the National Book Critics Circle Award. The book's title story is told from the point of view of a man whose marriage is failing; her 1989 novellas *Ordinary Love and Good Will*, published together, also feature strong narrative voices from characters whose family lives have taken unexpected and unhappy turnings. This narrative device is one that Smiley uses to extraordinary effect in *A Thousand Acres*, as the reader experiences the unfolding events from Ginny's point of view. Like Smiley's earlier work, the novel places families and their interactions at the heart of its story and uses them as a means of exploring the universal aspects of the human experience.

A Thousand Acres is Smiley's best known and most acclaimed novel, although she has been the subject of much critical praise throughout her career. In addition to its favorable critical reception, the book received both the National Book Critics Circle Award and the Pulitzer Prize.

Bibliography

Carlson, Ron. "King Lear in Zebulon County." *The New York Times Book Review* 96 (November 3, 1991): 12. Carlson offers a thoughtful critical look at the novel and Smiley's use of the *King Lear* story within it.

Duffy, Martha. "The Case for Goneril and Regan." *Time* 138 (November 11, 1991): 92. Offers comments from Smiley on her work as well as background on her life.

Fisher, Ann H. Review of *A Thousand Acres*, by Jane Smiley. *Library Journal* 116 (October 1, 1991): 142. Brief but very favorable review.

Kellman, Steven G. "Food Fights in Iowa: The Vegetarian Stranger in Recent Midwest Fiction." *Virginia Quarterly Review* 71 (Summer, 1995): 435-437. Kellman examines how food and gastronomy are woven into Smiley's novel, as well as Robert James Waller's *Bridges of Madison County*. Kellman discusses the plots, food as language through which the characters communicate, and the novel's self-congratulatory reverence for abstract vegetarianism.

Leslie, Marina. "Incest, Incorporation, and 'King Lear' in Jane Smiley's *A Thousand Acres*." *College English* 60 (January, 1998): 31-50. Leslie argues that Smiley's novel represents a faithful yet subversive revision of William Shakespeare's story of King Lear. Although the story takes place in Zebulon County in Iowa of 1979, Smiley's novel echoes the universal themes of Shakespeare's classic.

Olson, Catherine C. "You Are What You Eat: Food and Power in Jane Smiley's *A Thousand Acres*." *Midwest Quarterly* 40 (Autumn, 1998): 21-33. Cowen discusses how characters in the novel reflect United States midwestern asceticism, offers Smiley's thoughts on feminism, and explores the connection of food to the level of political power in the United States.

Schiff, James A. "Contemporary Retellings: *A Thousand Acres* as the Latest Lear."

Critique 39 (Summer, 1998): 367-382. Explores the retelling of myths in many contemporary novels and examines the factors that led to a resurgence of incorporating myths into modern stories. Schiff compares the similarities and differences between Smiley's novel and Shakespeare's play, "King Lear."

Smiley, Jane. "My Own Private Iowa." *Mirabella* 85 (September/October, 1997): 68-70. Smiley presents a fascinating discussion on the conversion of her novel into a movie. She discusses what inspired her to write this book, the process by which the book was transformed into a motion picture, and the common themes shared by the novel and the film.

Janet Lorenz

THE THREE MARIAS

Author: Rachel de Queiroz (1910-   )
Type of plot: Realism
Time of plot: The 1930's
Locale: Fortaleza and Rio de Janeiro, Brazil
First published: As três Marias, 1939 (English translation, 1963)

Principal characters:
    MARIA AUGUSTA (GUTA), the narrator, as a student in a Girls' boarding
        school, and as a young woman following graduation
    MARIA JOSE (JOSE), Guta's closest friend and companion
    MARIA DA GLORIA (GLORIA), Guta's other close friend and companion
    ALUISIO, a young poet in love with Guta
    RAUL, a painter with whom Guta fell in love
    ISAAC, an immigrant Jew from Rio with whom Guta fell in love

The Novel
    The novel consists of a retrospective view of the lives of the narrator, Maria Augusta (Guta), her two close friends, Maria Jose and Maria da Gloria, and other boarding school companions. After recounting with great sensitivity their first encounter at boarding school, Guta goes on to tell about their school adventures and about the choices they have to make about their lives. In the crucial years before and after graduation from high school, each of the schoolgirls searches for a direction to give her life. Each of the girls makes a very different choice. The three Marias epitomize this difference of choice. Maria da Gloria becomes "a happy wife and mother," Maria Jose becomes a schoolteacher, and the narrator herself remains "a frustrated seeker of satisfying values."
    As the novel begins, Maria Augusta makes a fearful entry into the institution run by nuns. Frightened and insecure, she wants to hold on to the sister who escorted her in, especially when she discovers that all the commotion and excitement which she observes on arrival is not caused as much by the arrival of a "new" girl as by her silly-sounding name, Guta.
    As the girls torment and tease her mercilessly, Guta bashfully responds to their barrage of questions, timidly explaining the facts of her life, such as her age, her hometown, her parents, and the origin of her nickname. "Guta" is simply a degeneration of "Augusta," a name that Guta was unable to pronounce as a small child; the baby-talk substitute, "Guta," stuck with her for life.
    Gradually all the girls lose interest and stop questioning her. Only one, Maria Jose, remains at her side, obviously interested in Guta's well-being. Advising Guta not to pay attention to such mistreatment, she persuades the reluctant newcomer that she is not like the other girls and that she can be trusted. As Guta aptly observes, her newly found friend has taken "charge." As they walk through the schoolyard, Maria Jose

points out her main enemies while singling out her "only" friend, Maria da Gloria, whom she introduces to Guta. Thus, the three girls begin their life together.

To the homogeneous milieu of the school each Maria brought with her the baggage of her past life, which in turn conditioned how each girl responded to circumstances in school and after school. Following graduation, each girl searched for and found a different life. Each choice was influenced by each girl's own life and by the lives of the other girls. Thus the novel focuses on the growth and development of each of the three Marias through the critical years of her life.

The Characters

Among all of Rachel de Queiroz's characters, Guta stands out as the one who is totally incapable of making a choice regarding her life. As she watches her two close friends and other school companions make decisions about their lives, she slowly realizes that none of them is for her.

Her companions' choices of marriage, concubinage, prostitution, the theater, or nunhood as a way of life were not meant for her. Guta had hoped to find life's meaning in something very special, but that something was very elusive. While Guta envies Gloria's fairy-tale marriage and happiness, she feels sorry for the repressed, guilt-ridden Maria Jose, who will spend her life as a spinster schoolteacher.

In search of something special, Guta gets a job as a typist. Bored out of her mind by the monotony of the typing job, she continues her search. She thinks she has found her life's purpose when she falls madly in love with a famous, distinguished-looking painter, many years her senior. To sacrifice her life in the service of this great man seems like a noble mission to her.

The great painter, however, is interested only in bedroom scenes, for which Guta is not ready. While pursuing the painter, however, she fails to see the great love that Maria Jose's cousin Aluisio has for her. Aluisio's suicide and his family's consequent reprimands drive Guta to seek her fortune in Rio de Janeiro.

The author presents very skillfully the fears and loneliness experienced by a young small-town girl in the midst of the big impersonal metropolis. Contrary to Guta's expectations, the big city only aggravates her problem. The something special does not materialize in Rio, and Isaac, the man with whom she falls in love, because of personal problems rooted in his immigrant status, is incapable of offering her the lasting love and support for which she has hoped. Following a painful miscarriage, which may have been a purposely induced abortion, Guta returns to the family home, disillusioned and disappointed, without any idea of what to do with her life.

To the very end Guta remains a character in crisis. All of the options available to other women have failed her. Because the conclusion is left open, the reader has two options: to decide either that Guta will work things out after all or that, because of the limited number of options available to her, she will never find a satisfactory way to live her life.

Because the novel focuses essentially on the life and choices of Guta, none of the other characters is fully developed. They simply have the narrow function of illustrating the options available to Guta and are portrayed only within the parameters relevant to that function. The portrayal of Gloria presents Guta with the blissfulness of marriage and motherhood. Holding on to Gloria's child, Guta "felt calm and happy, full of hope and affection, oblivious of all my worries, as though I were being solaced before my time." Maria Jose illustrates the option of religiousness based on repression. She explains to Guta her reasons for turning to religion. "People instinctively desire evil. And furthermore, everything around us is so filthy. I don't know what would become of me if it weren't for religion holding me in check. I think I'd be lost, that I'd start sinning like mad. I'm full of desire and terribly afraid."

The male characters, beyond presenting love options available to Guta, also help illuminate the fact that Guta is really not ready for love. Aluisio, the young poet possessed by romantic and metaphysical rapture, is unable to inspire Guta with a great love emotion. Raul, the older and famous painter, frightens Guta completely with his carnal desire. She was not quite ready to face her own sexuality and hence was unable to accept the physical fulfillment Raul offered her. Finally, Isaac offered her both, the emotional romance of Aluisio and the physical relationship of Raul, but on a very subdued scale. Yet even with him she was unable to form a lasting relationship because she was unable to convert his interest in the present into plans for the future. "It was evident that Isaac was in love with me, but he had never spoken to me of love. He made no plans, sought no promises, took no mortgages on the future. . . . And I, who did my dreaming and planning all by myself, never dared to ask for a thing, imitating his neglect."

Viewed in the context of the novel, each of the characters above allows the reader to perceive another aspect of Guta. Had Queiroz carried out an in-depth study of each of these characters, it would detract from the presentation of the novel's main theme, the life and choices of Guta, to which theme all other characters and all other action are subordinate.

Themes and Meanings

Through Guta, Queiroz poses the fundamental question of what is a woman to do with her life in the traditional Brazilian society of the Northeast, where the only honorable options are engaging in a marriage or joining a religious order. It is particularly relevant that Queiroz asked this question in the 1930's when a career was not available as a choice to women in that society. The novel attempts to create awareness of the fact that not all women can be satisfied with marriage or nunhood, and that other honest options should become available to women. A choice of life as a single schoolteacher should be as legitimate and fulfilling as any other, and other choices must be made available for those women who are not cut out to be schoolteachers.

In effect the novel is one of the first works to pioneer the cause of women in Brazil. By focusing on a woman who cannot be either a satisfied wife and mother or a successful teacher, Queiroz calls attention to the fact that there are women who do not fit the traditional pattern, that they should not be ridiculed for that, and that just because they desire to be different, their lives should not be wasted as Maria Augusta's is bound to be. Rachel de Queiroz joins the voice of her fellow contemporary writer Graciliano Ramos in deploring the options available for women in the Brazil of the 1930's.

Critical Context

While until 1976 *The Three Marias* was Rachel de Queiroz's best work, it never received the appropriate critical acclaim. The lack of a decisive ending left the critics confused with regard to its main purpose and hence they failed to include it among the great works of that period. Yet it was not until the 1950's and 1960's that the novels of Jorge Amado, Clarice Lispector, and Lygia Fagundes Telles depicted with equal depth the problematic condition of growing up female in traditional Brazilian society. Fred Ellison's excellent translation of Queiroz's novel and the 1985 paperback edition by the University of Texas Press constitute appropriate if somewhat tardy recognition of the author's achievement.

Bibliography

Courteau, Joanna. "The Problematic Heroines in the Novels of Rachel de Queiroz." *Luso Brazilian Review* 22 (Winter, 1985): 123-144. An excellent analysis of the women characters and the female problematic in Queiroz's novels.

Ellison, Fred P. "Rachel de Queiroz." In *Brazil's New Novel: Four Northeastern Masters*. Berkeley, University of California Press, 1954. Offers a good starting point for a study of Queiroz's early work, particularly in the context of the Brazilian social novel of the 1930's.

_____. "Rachel de Queiroz." In *Latin American Writers*, edited by Carlos A. Solé and Maria I. Abreau. Vol 3. New York: Charles Scribner's Sons, 1989. Offers a comprehensive and critical discussion of Queiroz's life and works. Provides a selected bibliography for further reading.

Joanna Courteau

THREE TRAPPED TIGERS

Author: Guillermo Cabrera Infante (1929-   )
Type of plot: Comic realism
Time of plot: Summer of 1958
Locale: Havana, Cuba
First published: Tres tristes tigres, 1967 (English translation, 1971)

> *Principal characters:*
> BUSTRÓFEDON, an inveterate punster and the focus of the group of
>   principal male characters
> SILVESTRE, a writer deeply interested in film
> ARSENIO CUÉ, a television star and close friend of Silvestre
> CÓDAC, a photographer, first of celebrities and later of scenes of street
>   violence
> ERIBÓ, a mulatto bongo drummer and would-be social climber
> LA ESTRELLA, a huge black singer of boleros
> CUBA VENEGAS, a nightclub singer

The Novel

The plot of *Three Trapped Tigers* is conceived as a nightclub show, introduced by the frenetic multilingual wordplay of the emcee of the famous Tropicana cabaret in Havana. His first word is "Showtime!"; his last ones are "Curtains up!" At this point a number of characters, some of them present in the club and introduced by the emcee, narrate sections of the text, with no further introduction or explanation. There is a one-sided telephone conversation, a letter, a story appearing as a series of fragments placed at various points in the text, and another story in two translations (only in the Spanish original) and complete with "corrections" by the author's wife, who turns out to be a fictional creation of her husband. There are even fragments of a woman's sessions with a psychiatrist. The author has said that the text consists of a series of "voices," and that voices have no biography, which means that the only possible coherence results from the reader's ability to assemble the fragments into a more or less meaningful whole.

There is a certain symmetry to the fragments, in that several characters, stories, and themes introduced in the first half are mirrored in the second, in some cases approximately the same distance from the end as their initial appearance is from the beginning. Thus, a story of Silvestre in which he and his brother witness a murder on the way to the cinema is related by him to his friend Arsenio Cué near the conclusion with some significant details reversed. Silvestre then vows that he will one day write the incident as a story. Presumably, the result is the version that appears earlier in the text. A character named Beba Longoria, whose rise in the society world has led to a serious "confusion of tongues" in her manner of speaking, is called "Babel" near the book's conclusion. Also, Arsenio Cué completes a story near the book's end that he has narrated in unfinished form near the beginning.

The incidents related generally have to do with false appearances and the resultant disillusionment. Relations between the sexes are not functioning in a normal manner, and significant persons in the lives of the principal characters are dying. There is a definite theme of what Mikhail Bakhtin calls "carnivalization," which brings about a reversal of values. One of the most important models for the novel is the work of Lewis Carroll, so that mirrors, both literal and figurative, play an important role in effecting such a reversal. The transition between the two halves of the book is a segment entitled "Headcracker," in which Bustrófedon is viewed as a sort of Antichrist figure, or mirror image of Christ. Whereas the latter is presented as "the Word become flesh," Bustrófedon is the man who "tried to be language." He dies, and the text, which begins with an outburst of linguistic activity, ends in a manifold repetition of the word "silently." The text too has reversed itself.

The Characters

In one of the segments narrated by Silvestre, he mentions that the five principal male characters are engaged in a search for total wisdom and that they desire to achieve immortality "by uniting the end with the beginning." Each of them carries out that quest in his own way. Arsenio Cué races his convertible madly down the streets of Havana in what strikes Silvestre as an attempt to convert space into time. Códac seems to wish that he could unite sexually with all women at the same time, and Eribó transcends his mundane circumstances by means of sound and rhythm. For his part, Silvestre, who is a writer, desires to remember everything, while, as mentioned above, Bustrófedon has "tried to be language." All of them suffer from a vague uneasiness as they witness the progressive disintegration of the Havana nightlife that they have known and loved, with the result that they become preoccupied with their personal mortality.

The social disintegration around them, the description of which is often couched in apocalyptic terms, reflects the precarious situation of Cuba in mid-1958, a few months before Fidel Castro's revolution triumphed and Cuba's national life was utterly transformed. The epigraph to the text, drawn from Carroll's work *Alice's Adventures in Wonderland* (1865), reads, "And she tried to fancy what the flame of a candle looks like after the candle is blown out." Cabrera Infante has stated that his novels represent, in part, an attempt to re-create a Havana that no longer exists outside his works.

Each of the principal male characters reflects the move away from visual imagery and toward sound and language that characterizes much of twentieth century literature. Silvestre has been deeply involved with the cinema all his life, but is now a writer. Arsenio Cué has been a television actor, but he is no longer working at the studio and is increasingly interested in wordplay. The photographer Códac narrates the "I Heard Her Sing" segments, concerning La Estrella, whose essence, he says, is her voice. Códac also states that one of Bustrófedon's words is worth a thousand pictures. Eribó has left a career as an illustrator to become a drummer again. Bustrófedon has abandoned even his ordinary name to assume one that identifies him with a rhetorical device expressive of language's ability to reverse itself, just as he would like to be able to return from his inevitable death.

The major female characters also illustrate the play of visual and auditory phenomena. Cuba Venegas is a nightclub singer whose career is built largely on her superficial beauty. Her somewhat deficient singing must be accompanied by instrumental music. In total contrast is La Estrella, whose huge size and repulsive appearance are overcome in the public's estimation by her rich, unaccompanied voice. It becomes clear that she represents the intrusion of genuine, primordial, creative sound into an artificial environment. She is tricked into signing a contract requiring her to sing with accompaniment, which is a devastating blow to her. Not long after, she eats a massive meal in the rarefied atmosphere of Mexico City and dies of heart failure.

Themes and Meanings

Although politics might be expected to take on considerable importance in a novel concerning the months immediately prior to Castro's takeover of Cuba, such is not the case with *Three Trapped Tigers*, which the author himself has described as "the least political book ever written in Latin America." This is probably a reflection of the fact that Cabrera Infante had worked fairly closely with the Castro government for a time, but then became disillusioned, not only with it, but with political ideologies in general.

Instead, one of his major concerns in this work is the way in which the essence of a society can be re-created through that society's popular language. He insists that the novel is not written in Spanish but in "Cuban," as spoken in 1958 by the "voices" that now make up the text. Thus, the work's language is preoccupied mainly with itself as a creative phenomenon. The text consists largely of puns and other types of wordplay, which has caused some readers to conclude—very wrongly—that the novel is frivolous and not to be taken seriously. While it is consistently humorous, it is no more frivolous than Miguel de Cervantes's *Don Quixote de la Mancha* (1605, 1615). In both *Don Quixote de la Mancha* and *Three Trapped Tigers*, humor becomes a tool for the attainment of some very serious ends. The joke, according to both Aristotle and Immanuel Kant, operates by presenting the hearer with something unexpected, and it would appear that the creative possibilities inherent in that situation are not lost on the characters of this novel, who are in search of some viable new reality as the old reality seems about to disappear.

Reality is presented as a fundamentally linguistic phenomenon, so that, as both language and the other phenomena of daily life are perceived as breaking down, the characters appear to be searching for creative new combinations among the fragments, just as one might go on turning a kaleidoscope, fascinated by the endless procession of new symmetrical patterns formed by the shards inside.

Related to the linguistic quest is a rejection of the artificiality that characterized Havana nightlife in 1958. The combination of cosmetic techniques and creative lighting were able to produce illusions very disturbing to those in search of the essential. At times the principal male characters are troubled by the fact that, while relationships between the sexes appear to be increasingly sterile, homosexuality seems to be on the increase among both men and women. For Cabrera Infante's characters, a return to creative language represents their only hope of escape from a world they perceive as having been turned upside down.

Critical Context

In his book *La nueva novela hispanoamericana* (1969; the new Spanish-American novel), Carlos Fuentes first mentions *Three Trapped Tigers* in connection with its use of humor, which he considers "one of the notable features of the creation of the true Latin American language." He goes on to say that Cabrera Infante's novel "allows us to carry out the verbal transition from the past to the future," in that "Cabrera's savage intent to demolish goes to the roots of a Latin American problem: our language has been the product of uninterrupted conquest and colonization—a conquest and colonization whose language betrayed an oppressive hierarchical order." Such a statement is perhaps typical of the thinking of authors and critics in evaluating this author's contribution to Latin American prose fiction. During the years following its publication, it has gradually come to occupy an important place among the trendsetting novels of Latin America, especially where language and humor are concerned.

One of the major forces at work within the novel is the Cuban *choteo* tradition, which has been described as the tendency to mock everything that represents any form of authority. In this case, if Fuentes is correct, much of the text is concerned with an unrelenting attack on the Spanish language because that language is expressive of certain structures that Latin America must leave behind in her quest for a modern identity. Still, the author has repeatedly stated that the novel should not be taken too seriously, since it is nothing more than a joke that got out of hand. This is also in the *choteo* tradition, to attack even one's own work if one fears that it may be considered in an overly serious manner.

Bibliography

Cabrera Infante, Guillermo. "Wit and Wile with Guillermo Cabrera Infante." Interview by Suzanne Jill Levine. *Americas (English Edition)* 47 (July-August, 1995): 24-29. In this interview, the Cuban-born author discusses his career and the influences that have shaped it. He talks about his Cuban and British roots, his love of puns, and his interest in film and music. A good source of background information.

Firmat, G. P. Review of *Guillermo Cabrera Infante and the Cinema*. *Hispanic Review* 59 (Summer, 1991): 370-371. Firmat asserts that Hall's book "fails to produce new or interesting insights into the work of the author of *Arcadia sodas las noches*." However, Firmat does contend that Hall makes some interesting comparisons between the film version of *Tres tristes tigres* and *Some Like It Hot* starring Tony Curtis and Jack Lemmon. Also notes that Hall's book contains an excellent bibliography.

Siemens, William. Review of *Guillermo Cabrera Infante and the Cinema*, by Kenneth E. Hall. *Symposium* 44 (Fall, 1990): 225-227. Offers an in-depth discussion of the place of film in the work of Cabrera Infante. Siemens mentions that Hall traces the evolution of Cabrera Infante's thought concerning modern theories of film criticism, but notes that Cabrera Infante "may have undergone the same kind of transformation that Silvestre experiences in *Tres tristes tigres*, between an obsession with film and an equally strong preoccupation with the text."

Souza, Raymond D. *Guillermo Cabrera Infante: Two Islands, Many Worlds*. Austin, Tex.: University of Texas, 1996. An informative and lively biography of one of the most prominent contemporary Cuban writers. Souza's work offers intriguing insight into Cabrera Infante's family history as well as his literary career.

Vargas Llosa, Mario. "Touchstone." *The Nation* 266 (May 11, 1998): 56-57. Vargas Llosa offers a tribute to Cabrera Infante, noting that even when Cabrera Infante was nearly destitute in London, "from the typewriter of this harassed man . . . instead of insults there poured a stream of belly laughs, puns, brilliant nonsense and fantastic tricks of rhetorical illusion."

William L. Siemens

THROUGH THE IVORY GATE

Author: Rita Dove (1952-   )
Type of plot: Bildungsroman
Time of plot: The 1950's through the early 1970's
Locale: Ohio, Wisconsin, and Arizona
First published: 1992

> *Principal characters:*
> VIRGINIA KING, a puppeteer and an aspiring actress
> BELLE EVANS, her mother, withdrawn and genteel
> ERNIE EVANS, her father, who opened vistas to her
> ERNIE EVANS, JR., her brother
> CLAUDIA EVANS, her rebellious younger sister
> GRANDMA EVANS, her grandmother
> AUNT CARRIE, her father's sister
> CLAYTON EVERETT, Virginia's first and most intense love
> TERRY MURRAY, a single father who falls in love with Virginia
> RENEE BUTLER, a student who admires Virginia
> GINA, a puppet created by Virginia, her mask or other self

The Novel

Rita Dove's *Through the Ivory Gate* is a tale of a young African American woman's growing up, learning to use her varied artistic abilities despite obstacles, and beginning her career.

The frame action is set in Akron, Ohio, at the end of the Vietnam War era, with flashbacks to the 1950's and early 1960's and to events that took place in Wisconsin and Arizona. The third-person limited-omniscient narrative provides a full portrait of the main character, Virginia King, and an insight into what the coming-of-age must have been like for a talented African American woman of her era.

The "Prelude" to the story catches a glimpse of the child Virginia rejecting a black doll for a white one, then neglecting dolls, and finally finding the white doll not only outgrown but also ruined and decayed. The grownup Virginia has substituted puppets for dolls. The first chapter begins the present action, which takes Virginia back to her hometown of Akron, where she will begin a season as an artist-in-residence, teaching puppetry in a public grade school.

The time is the unsettled 1970's, and Virginia's life is at a standstill. In college, she has trained to be an actress, but at this time there are few calls for African American actresses. The question she must answer for herself is this: What can she and should she do with her abilities, which include mime, music, and puppetry as well as straightforward acting? The artist-in-residence program provides her with some breathing space, but she will shortly need to make irrevocable decisions. Defining her goals is difficult because her sense of self is uncertain, partly owing to the prejudices she has encountered in growing up in the 1950's, but also because of her family life. She has never understood why her family suddenly moved from Ohio to Arizona and why they seemed personally changed after this move; her young adulthood has been obscured by this mystery. She believes that her return to her former home will help her to solve it, and she thinks that learning more about her family will make her better able to plan her future.

Upon her return to Akron, Virginia learns to be more self-possessed when dealing with groups, and her expertise impresses many. Children with psychic wounds and their equally hurting parents reach out to the artist for healing. The puppets help the children to explain their problems, and this is the first step toward regaining health.

Virginia begins a love affair with the father of one of her students, and speaking more frankly through Gina, the puppet she has created, she makes strides in self-expression. Yet the direction of her life is still undecided. Skillful use of flashbacks show what factors led to her lack of decision: her pleasant childhood's interruption by the unexplained move, her first real love affair with a fellow musician (who finally left her for a man) and her satisfying experiences with Puppets and People, a talented troupe that went bankrupt. Her life has also been punctuated by indications that African Americans are not encouraged to pursue her kind of goals—especially that of being an actress.

Amid her teaching experiences, she visits her father's mother, now in a rest home, and her aunt, and she finally learns the family secret from Aunt Carrie. In adolescence, her father had had an incestuous relationship with his sister. When her mother learned about this, long afterward, she made the family move away from Akron to Arizona, although she never got used to the hot, arid climate and always hated Arizona. The father, however, soon made the desert his home, and he taught his children its wonders and dangers. With the gaps in the family history filled in and the success of her assignment in the grade school, Virginia is ready to move on to her next assignment when she receives a call from Nigel, an old colleague who is now a play director. He is now an Off-Broadway director, and he has a part for Virginia if she can drop what she is doing (after her next brief assignment) and go to New York. She is now mature enough to take this gamble.

There are some subplots as well: Virginia is so involved in all of her activities that she does not notice the intensity of one hurting child, Renee, who then injures herself in an attempt to win Virginia's attention; this incident teaches Virginia humility. How she deals with the challenges of getting ordinary, non-intellectual people interested in art is another slight diversion. A third is the preparation for and final presentation of the children's puppet play. At the end of the story, Virginia is ready to leave Akron, having swept away the shadows from her life and having been reconciled with both her grandmother, who had known the story, and her aunt. Her coming-of-age completed, she is ready to face the challenges of the uncertain life of the stage.

The Characters

Virginia's development and point of view are at the center of the novel. She believably changes from a tentative although enthusiastic young puppeteer to a woman in control of her life. Her discovery of the family secret really plays a minor part in her development, which comes mostly from her practice of her art and the observation of the effect of her art on others. She comes across as a sympathetic young artist who must deal with racial prejudice as well as the general indifference to art and culture that was part of the era.

Belle, her mother, flees from life, and it seems to Virginia that her childhood has been punctuated by her mother's inexplicable warnings. These make more sense after Virginia discovers the family secret. Belle's sense of personal outrage has prevented her from full participation in her family and has created barriers between herself and her children. She is hyper-respectable, perhaps partly in reaction to the shock of her husband's adolescent incestuous relationship. Although she loves her children, she seems to be constantly warning them not to expose themselves to any risks—in effect, not to live.

Ernie King has always made his children's education his prime interest. He has done most of the parenting, especially after the move, and has instilled in his children a love for history and culture. He carries a mysterious sense of sadness, which is accounted for by Aunt Carrie's revelation. He has been partly responsible for his daughter's artistic and cultural interests.

Aunt Carrie is in many ways the opposite of Belle. A woman who has had a hard life with much hard work and pain, she is accepting of the grittier side of human experience, and her openness is helpful to Virginia. Virginia finds that she has an element of Aunt Carrie in her.

Grandma Evans has been part of the family mystery. It always seemed to the child Virginia that the well-loved grandmother had suddenly withdrawn from the family, to appear again only when the youngest child, Claudia, was born. When Virginia learns that knowledge of the incest story and its repercussions had caused her grandmother's behavior, she feels close to her grandmother again.

Besides Virginia, perhaps the most fully developed character is Clayton, who is drawn into a love affair with Virginia by their mutual love of music. His homosexuality proves to be stronger than his love for her, however, and he finally leaves her. His defection is a blow to her developing self-esteem and makes her doubt the possibility of a lasting love relationship. When she compares her present feelings for Terry Murray with her past feelings for Everett, however, she concludes that she is not really in love with Terry.

Terry himself is a straightforward, quintessentially normal middle-class African American whose love and concern help Virginia grow. Her attachment to him, however, will clearly not be sufficient to keep her from pursuing her career as a dramatic artist.

Themes and Meanings

One major theme of the novel is that disguises and masks may facilitate truth and healing. Another is that growing up is difficult, especially for an African American girl born in the 1950's, particularly if she wishes to be an artist.

The title of this novel comes from Homer's *Odyssey* (c. 800 B.C.). Homer's epic contains a passage that describes two gates from which dreams issue, the gate of horn and the gate of ivory. Those dreams that come through the gate of ivory are deceptive, but those that issue from the gate of horn are truthful. It is Virginia's job to distinguish truth from falsehood in understanding her family's past. On the other hand, she is also a puppeteer, a dealer in illusion, but this kind of illusion is a healing fiction that helps those who become involved in it to learn to accept themselves and others. Memories as well as dreams are deceptive in this narrative, which interweaves imagination and reality, illusion and truth, to create a fable of healing through art.

The puppets themselves are a strong presence in the story. Through their apparent artificiality and their pose as amusement, they allow their creators to speak otherwise hidden truths. Virginia speaks through Gina, and the children speak through the characters they have created. Through these masks, they arrive at genuine communication. Masks, puppets, acting, and other ways in which meaning is communicated indirectly play a major part in the novel; the scenes that describe puppet shows and puppet play suggest the magic of the art. Not only do the puppets and other disguises of art help individuals to face their problems, but they also help to facilitate understanding among people of different backgrounds and races. At the end of the novel, it is Halloween, and masks, laughter, and a sense of general good feeling dominate the scene.

The book is also a women's coming-of-age novel that shows both the typical problems of an adolescent and also the special difficulties of African Americans. The adolescent's ordinary conflicts—the desire to excel versus the desire to be accepted, the need to resist parental pressure—are portrayed in vivid detail. The problems caused by being the only African American in various groups are described with humor, and yet the reader still gets a sense of the kind of isolation such a situation would produce. The precise and evocative details in the flashbacks give a strong impression of the 1950's and early 1960's, with that era's narrowness and its innocence. The limited options of that time for women are realistically presented. So is the heroine's rejection of these limitations as she enters the more promising 1970's with understanding and courage. As a coming-of-age novel, *Through the Ivory Gate* is an unusually friendly and upbeat book.

Critical Context

Rita Dove is better known as a poet than as a novelist. Her third poetry collection, *Thomas and Beulah* (1986), received a Pulitzer Prize, and she was named poet laureate of the United States. *Through the Ivory Gate* is clearly a poet's novel—it is lyrical, it contains patches of near-poetry, and its plot, despite the suspense, is secondary to its other elements. Passages of the novel would be well suited to oral presentation, as it is clear that attention has been paid to sound as well as to meaning.

The book may be read for the sheer lyricism of it, for its description and demonstration of the healing power of art. It also provides a good example of a relaxed and relaxing coming-of-age novel, or *Bildungsroman*. Virginia King is an appealing protagonist whose experiences may be matched or approximated by readers of varied ages and races. The novel also provides a strong sense of the time periods it represents; the subtle changes in background provide a sense of the differences between these time periods, especially as these differences relate to race relations. The book is also a *Kunstlerroman*, or novel about the development of an artist, and those factors that directed the heroine toward her art are painstakingly detailed.

Bibliography
Brody, Jennifer. "Genre Fixing: An Interview with Rita Dove." *Poetry Flash* 238 (January, 1993): 1, 9-11, 22-23. Dove discusses how writing her novel was different from writing poems. She also discusses factors that influenced her work.
Callaloo 14 (Spring, 1991). This special issue contains several articles on Rita Dove's poetry and an interview with her. Articles by Bonnie Costello, Ekaterini Georgoudaki, and Mohammed-B Teleb-Khyer help to place Dove's poetry in context with that of other African American women writers. These articles also define themes and concerns that are present also in her novel.
Dove, Rita. Interview by Grace Cavalieri. *The American Poetry Review* 24 (March/April, 1995): 11-14. A revealing interview where Dove talks about her childhood, her parents and grandparents, and her work. Although Dove does not specifically mention *Through the Ivory Gate*, this conversation is helpful in pinpointing common themes that run throughout her work.
Georgoudaki, Ekaterini. *Race, Gender, and Class Perspectives in the Works of Maya Angelou, Gwendolyn Brooks, Rita Dove, Nikki Giovanni, and Audre Lorde*. Thessaloniki, Greece: Aristotle University of Thessaloniki, 1991. Although this book considers poetry, its reflections on Dove's poetry may be applied to her novel. The book provides a solid background for studying current African American women's poetry. Its analysis of the societal elements in these women's work is clear and direct.
Muske, Carol. "Breaking Out of the Genre Ghetto." *Parnassus: Poetry in Review* 20 (Spring/Fall, 1995): 409-423. Describes Dove as a "genre-bender," equally adept at poetry or prose. Praises *Selected Poems* where Dove's lyric narrative blends plot and music. Also explores *Through the Ivory Gate*, which treats narrative as a continuation of poetic rhythm.
Neilen, Dierdre. Review of *Through the Ivory Gate*. *World Literature Today* 68 (Winter, 1994): 126-127. An enthusiastic review of Dove's first novel that focuses on the strength and honesty of the main character, Virginia. Praises the novel for its lyricism, precision, and use of irony.
Schneider, Steven. "Coming Home: An Interview with Rita Dove." *The Iowa Review* 19 (Fall, 1989): 112-123. This extended interview gives a sense of the writer's personality and commitment to her craft. Dove's comments show how much she is concerned with language as an arrangement of sounds. Although the novel had not yet been written at the time of the interview, the information she gives here about herself gives insight into the sources of Virginia.

Seaman, Donna. Review of *Through the Ivory Gate*, by Rita Dove. *Booklist*, September 15, 1992, 122. This review concentrates on plot, but it gives some sense of the writer's style, calling Dove "a melodious and meticulous writer."

Janet McCann

TIETA, THE GOAT GIRL
Or, The Return of the Prodigal Daughter

Author: Jorge Amado (1912-   )
Type of plot: Comic melodrama
Time of plot: 1965
Locale: The fictitious town of Sant'Ana do Agreste in the north of Bahia, Salvador, and São Paulo, Brazil
First published: Tiêta do Agreste, 1977 (English translation, 1979)

> *Principal characters:*
>
> ANTONIETA ESTEVES CANTARELLI (TIETA), the heroine, a former prostitute, now the owner of a high-class São Paulo bordello
> PERPÉTUA ESTEVES BATISTA, Tieta's older sister, a pious and mean-spirited widow
> ELISA ESTEVES SIMAS, Tieta's naïve and frustrated younger sister
> ASTÉRIO SIMAS, Elisa's unimaginative husband
> RICARDO (CARDO) and PETO BATISTA, Perpétua's sons, aged seventeen and thirteen, respectively
> ASCÂNIO TRINDADE, Agreste's county clerk and the local cat's-paw of an international industrial scheme
> DR. MIRKO STEFANO (MIRKO THE MAGNIFICENT), an unscrupulous São Paulo industrialist and chief architect of the industrial scheme
> SKIPPER DÁRIO QUELUZ, a retired seaman, perhaps even an officer, and local antipollution activist
> LEONORA CANTARELLI, a prostitute posing as Tieta's step-daughter
> DONA CARMOSINA SLUIZER DA CONSOLAÇÃO, the town postmistress and self-appointed arbiter of gossip

The Novel

The action of the novel (its full title is *Tieta, the Goat Girl: Or, The Return of the Prodigal Daughter, Melodramatic Serial Novel in Five Sensational Episodes, with a Touching Epilogue, Thrills and Suspense!*) takes place largely in the fictitious northern Bahian backwater of Sant'Ana do Agreste, a tiny and politically insignificant community whose backwardness is exemplified by its reliance on a none-too-reliable generator as its sole source of electric power. At the opening of the story, Tieta's sisters Perpétua and Elisa, accompanied by the ubiquitous Dona Carmosina, are worried because the monthly allowance generously sent to them by their wealthy sibling has for the first time failed to arrive on time. They depend on this largess not only for a few small luxuries but also for subsistence, and anxiety over the absent check provokes a relapse of Astério's chronic gastritis and a succession of prayers from the young seminarian Ricardo. Reluctantly concluding the worst, the family holds a funeral for their beloved sister and prepare to hire a lawyer to ensure the proper disposal of whatever inheritance might be forthcoming, whereupon they receive a letter informing them that Tieta has been in mourning for her husband and will soon make her first visit to Agreste in twenty-six years.

The town is electrified by the news of the visit of the benefactress, and practically paralyzed when the gorgeous widow shows up not in black but in a sexy blouse and sexier jeans and in the company of the irresistible Leonora. Perpétua contrives to persuade her wealthy sister to adopt one or both of her sons, but the heroine's interest in her nephews is anything but auntly, and she soon seduces Ricardo, an event which so delights the priest-to-be that it brings about a crisis of faith. Meanwhile, the benighted town clerk Ascânio, already madly in love with Leonora, is attempting to electrify the town in the literal sense, by having lines brought into town from a government hydro-electric project. When his efforts fail, the well-connected Tieta dashes off a single telegram and gets the power company to reverse its decision.

Tieta is not really a widow but the former kept woman of a wealthy businessman, under whose tutelage she has become owner of the elegant bordello, whose clients are the good connections. In Agreste, however, she poses as the owner of a chic boutique and discourages visits to São Paulo on the basis of a rather different kind of propriety than the town imagines.

Another novelty for Agreste is the appearance of two creatures of such outlandish appearance that they are first thought to be Martians. These visitors turn out to be merely two more people from São Paulo, albeit on a somewhat more sinister mission than that of Tieta and her ward. Mirko Stefano, one of the "Martians," is attempting to suborn selected government officials into allowing him and his company, Brastânio, to open a titanium dioxide plant in Brazil, and Agreste turns out to be one of the possible sites. He investigates the town's power structure and concludes that if Ascânio becomes mayor, the lovely dunes of Mangue Seco could be expropriated for his purposes under the law of eminent domain. Only he and a few other insiders know that titanium dioxide is one of the most toxic industries in the world. The only initial opposition to the factory comes from Skipper Dário, who reluctantly becomes an opposition candidate for mayor. Mirko takes the impressionable Ascânio to the state capital, Salvador, and treats him to the pleasures of fine food, good wine, and pliant females, all of which help convince Ascânio of Mirko's good intentions. The mayoral election heats up when Tieta convinces Ascânio's patron to sit out the contest, and a legal battle starts brewing over title to the dunes of Mangue Seco.

Tieta tardily discovers that Ricardo has become an ardent practitioner of the arts of love which she thought he was studying only with her. As a result, she throws him into the street, nude, and when the ruckus awakens her astonished sister Perpétua, she pays, in cash, for having taken the seminarian's virginity. The anticlimax of the Brastânio episode occurs when the company gets another, even better site approved. Demoralized by the whole process, Ascânio nevertheless proposes marriage to Leonora, who finally admits to her own and Tieta's sordid past and then attempts suicide. His pride mortally wounded, Ascânio denounces the two women for what they

are, and Tieta, Leonora, and the neophyte Maria Imaculada (one of Ricardo's conquests) depart for São Paulo.

The paved street, originally named after an obscure congressman, is rebaptized by
the townsfolk as "The Street of Tieta's Light."

The Characters

The characters of *Tieta, the Goat Girl* are, if not predictable, at least vaguely familiar to loyal Amadophiles. Since the publication of *Gabriela, cravo e canela* (1958;
Gabriela, Clove and Cinnamon, 1962), Amado has been producing novels peopled by
a motley array of protagonists, including drunks, bums, womanizers, charlatans,
whores, and assorted ne'er-do-wells, all of whom seem to share a single salient characteristic of indifference or even outright hostility to society's norms. Tieta is part of
the long literary tradition of whores-with-a-heart-of-gold, but she is also representative of protagonists in a very Amadian canon. Her sexual awareness comes at an early
age, when, as a goatherd, she witnesses the billy goat Inácio introducing the initially
reluctant nanny goats into adulthood. At the age of thirteen, she is chased across the
dunes by a randy itinerant vendor and caught rather too easily after which she is sexually insatiable. Her father beats her and runs her out of the house because of this pro-
clivity, but she continues to be sexually active and is delighted to learn the "sauces and
spices" of the operation with one of her early lovers. She goes from full-time prostitution to a rather more sedate but nevertheless illicit relationship with Felipe, whose
death precipitates her visit to Agreste. Through it all, she has sent her family money,
and she never mentions to her father the source of her large income. Tieta's seduction
of Ricardo is typical Amado as well: She is at the moment without a man, and even if
Ricardo is a nephew and a seminarian as well, he is a man and he wants her, although
it takes him a while to realize it.

The characterization of Ricardo is also consistent with the usual Amadian style. He
is tormented by sexual feelings even before the arrival of his comely aunt, and his tor-
ment becomes an agony when he sees her in a bathing suit, especially when his perverse little brother Peto notes that he can see pubic hair peeping out of her skimpy bi-
kini bottom. The seduction itself is an epiphany for him, though he is unable to resolve
the dilemma of sex and religion until he talks to his confessor, Frei Thimóteo. The ge-
nial friar, relentlessly beatific, understands the ways of the world and is thus able not
only to provide justification for the pleasures of the flesh but also to point out the evils
of industrial pollution.

The other side of the coin is provided by characters as apparently diverse as
Perpétua and Mirko Stefano. Perpétua's delight at her sister's visit is rooted fundamentally in greed, and her moral outrage on discovering that her son has been deflow-
ered by her own sister is a kind of knee-jerk reaction of the perpetually unimaginative,
the product of a forlorn and threadbare petit bourgeois mentality. Mirko's badness is
much more clearly a matter of turpitude than of small-mindedness, but he is nevertheless similar to her. The difference is that he is intelligent and has the wherewithal to be
a capitalist—it is likely that if she were smarter and richer she would be like him.

Mirko bribes politicians, large and small, and does anything else which seems to be necessary to produce the desired result: to make money.

The dichotomy is one familiar to Amado's readers. The basic character conflict in all of his later novels is between the crassness and triviality of bourgeois values and the healthy sensuality and irrepressible vitality of the common folk's worldview. It does not matter to his characters, nor apparently to his readers, that much of what goes on in such a scenario, even if it is good, dirty fun, is not exactly the kind of thing on which parent-teacher organizations look fondly.

Themes and Meanings

Amado is not a writer who attempts to approach transcendent truths. In addition to the bourgeoisie-folk tension mentioned above, most of his later works have some other central hook on which the narrative is hung. In *Tieta, the Goat Girl* that hook is obviously the potential which rapid industrialization has to destroy all that is right and good in a community. Since rapid industrialization is more corrosive in less-developed communities, the message is perhaps more immediate to Brazilians than to Americans, since many Brazilian towns are, like Agreste, not only preindustrial but also precapitalist. Another thread of this theme is the chronic venality of government officials, here depicted as either self-serving egotists of no redeeming ethical importance or mindless bureaucrats who merely follow the rules, however witless the rules may be.

Yet *Tieta, the Goat Girl* is not so much an indictment of evil as a celebration of life. True to form, Amado's narrator makes two of the most important parts of that celebration sex and cuisine, a pairing that he explored even more elaborately in his delicious *Dona Flor e seus dois maridos* (1966; *Dona Flor and Her Two Husbands*, 1969). The biological imperatives of food and sex are counterpointed by a society in which social control is carried out principally by means of gossip, and the sudden appearance of a recipe for green cashew stew in the midst of an inquiry into who is sleeping with whom is intentionally comic and not a little ironic.

Critical Context

Amado published his first novel in 1931; *Tieta, the Goat Girl* was his nineteenth. He became a best-selling author in the first decade of his career, but not until the 1960's was he generally recognized as a writer at the peak of his form, master of an inimitable style. Critics have chided him for being too facile or too ideological, and some have even called him racist or sexist, but such criticism seems irrelevant to novels in which the reading experience is something akin to listening to a witty and engaging blabbermouth recount a convoluted yarn about a town in which he might once have lived. Much of the negative criticism of his works is based on the fact that he was for many years a member of the Communist Party and that some of his early novels make that affiliation transparent. Yet he has never been an ideologue, and even if his novels consistently belittle the Brazilian bourgeoisie for its flaws, his faithful readers are not deterred, though most are members of that class.

There are no competitors to his commercial success in Brazil, and his works have been translated into more than forty languages, enjoying sometimes spectacular sales abroad. Since he has won practically every literary prize worth winning in Brazil, his massive and enthusiastic public has made him a perennial candidate for the Nobel Prize, and every new novel is a best-seller within days of release.

Part of Jorge Amado's popularity stems from his ability to portray Brazilians as they would like to think they are—at once lusty, courageous, charming, and, above all, unfettered. Some of the appeal of the works in translation may lie in this same exotic appeal of tropical eroticism and adventure. What really makes a novel such as *Tieta, the Goat Girl* work is its perverse narrator, with his leisurely and digressive story, genuinely amusing, concerning people who are either what the reader suspects his next-door neighbor may truly be or people who are just sufficiently larger than life to charm and beguile.

Bibliography
Chamberlain, Bobby J. *Jorge Amado*. Boston: Twayne, 1990. Useful, informative, and readable, this critical analysis of Amado's work covers all periods of the novelist's output while focusing on a few of the author's most important works. A biographical chapter is included, as well as an extensive bibliography.
Hinchberger, Bill. "Jorge Amado Writes from Heart, Home." *Variety* 366 (March 31, 1997): 56. Hinchberger explores the inspirations that shape Amado's work, the filming of Amado's novels, and Amado's reaction to the critical acclaim he has received. Offers interesting insight into the influences that shaped Amado's work.
Robitaille, L. B. "These Men of Letters Speak for the Powerless." *World Press Review* 38 (December, 1991): 26-27. An intriguing profile of Amado, covering his political activity, his life in Paris, and his feelings for his native Brazil. Presents background that sheds considerable light on his writings.

Jon S. Vincent

THE TIME OF THE HERO

Author: Mario Vargas Llosa (1936-   )
Type of plot: Rites of passage
Time of plot: The 1950's
Locale: The military academy Leoncio Prado in Lima, Peru
First published: La ciudad y los perros, 1963 (English translation, 1966)

    Principal characters:
        ALBERTO (THE POET), the bourgeois intellectual of the group
        JAGUAR, the leader of "the Circle," a tough boy of lower-class origins
        RICARDO ARANA (THE SLAVE), the group's whipping boy
        BOA, the sexual role model of the Circle
        LIEUTENANT GAMBOA, the dutiful officer in charge of discipline in the
           school
        TERESA, a young woman loved by Alberto, Ricardo, and Jaguar who
           finally marries Jaguar

The Novel

Based in part on Vargas Llosa's experience as a cadet in the Leoncio Prado Military Academy in Lima, Peru, from 1950 to 1952, *The Time of the Hero* is a fictionalized portrayal of a group of adolescent boys at the school during a three-year period which coincides, roughly, with the author's own stay there.

The Time of the Hero is divided into two parts, of eight chapters each, and an epilogue. It has four narrators: an omniscient third-person narrator; two first-person narrators, Jaguar and Boa, whose identity is discovered only in the last part of the book; and a fourth voice, that of Alberto, who communicates with the reader through several internal monologues.

The book begins during the boys' third and last year at the school. They are there for various reasons. Alberto's father, a middle-class dandy, somewhat dismayed at his son's interest in books, decides that what the young man needs is an education that will prepare him for adult life in the real world; the Leoncio Prado, the father believes, will do precisely that. Ricardo Arana is there because his absentee father considers him effeminate; the boy has been reared by a devoted mother and an aunt, and the father insists that he is in need of the discipline and toughening that a military education can provide. Jaguar, who comes from a family of thieves and is a budding juvenile delinquent, ends up in the academy as an alternative to reform school after he is caught stealing. As the novel begins, an omniscient third-person narrator relates how several boys are about to carry out a carefully planned maneuver designed by Jaguar, the undisputed leader of the school's student gang known as "the Circle." Their aim is to steal an important chemistry exam. They succeed in getting the exam but break a window in the process, thus exposing the theft. Pending the discovery or confession of the guilty parties, school authorities suspend all leaves.

The severing of the lifeline with the outside world becomes the catalyst for the novel; it tests the partnerships, relationships, and loyalties that had been established and upon which the Circle was built and impels the characters to act in ways which express their true nature. Ricardo Arana, "the Slave," so called because of his lack of aggressiveness and courage as defined by the other boys, cannot bear giving up his plan to get away from the school and the boys whom he detests and visit his beloved Teresa. He informs and thus breaks the honor code of the Circle. He is subsequently wounded by a bullet during the school's military exercises. He dies shortly thereafter. Following a superficial investigation of the incident, school authorities conclude, wrongly, that the Slave's death was caused by the accidental firing of the victim's own gun.

Alberto, "the Poet," Ricardo's only friend among the cadets, is certain that Ricardo's death was not an accident but rather Jaguar's revenge against the Slave for informing. The Poet, in turn, informs Lieutenant Gamboa of his suspicions about Jaguar and takes advantage of the opportunity to expose all the petty infractions and violations of the regulations carried out by the group: the gambling, drinking, illegal furloughs, and contraband. While Gamboa believes Alberto, he is unable to persuade his superiors to reopen the case. They are concerned about the good name of the school and the bad publicity that a full investigation might attract. They urge Alberto to withdraw his accusations, threatening to expose him as a pornographer, a reference to Alberto's sideline as a writer of erotic tales. Alberto succumbs and withdraws his charges. The lieutenant, in turn, is transferred to a distant post, a plan that causes him and his beloved family great hardship. He accepts the transfer with true dignity, which serves to highlight the contrast between the corruption of the upper echelons of the military hierarchy and the naive honesty of its more humble ranks. Alberto himself also becomes an informer when he tells Gamboa the truth about Jaguar. As for the leader of the Circle, his own comrades turn on him, give him a severe beating, and accuse him, falsely, of having revealed the details of their illegal rackets.

The epilogue of the work serves to tie lose ends. Alberto, feeling no guilt over his retreat from responsibility, plans to pursue technical studies in the United States and will eventually marry a suitable middle-class young woman. Jaguar confesses about the shooting to Gamboa before the lieutenant leaves the school; the latter decides not to expose him. Jaguar also becomes "respectable." He works at a bank and marries his childhood sweetheart Teresa, the same Teresa who had moved Ricardo to inform, setting off the chain of events described above, and who, at the same time, had been romanticaly ensnarled in a relationship with Alberto behind the Slave's back.

The Characters

Alberto the Poet captures the sympathy of the reader at the beginning of the book. A thinker rather than a doer, he must survive through his intelligence and wit in the rough school environment. He nevertheless proves disappointing in the end. He reveals the Circle's secrets presumably to avenge his friend Ricardo's death; he then, however, withdraws all charges—making it possible for school officials to close the investigation—revealing a selfish and cowardly nature. Alberto also disenchants the reader when he befriends and romances Teresa, whom he visits to deliver a message from her boyfriend, the Slave, who is unable to make the rendezvous in person because he has been grounded. The role of the bourgeois intellectual, the novel suggests, is to take the easy way out even if it means, as in this case, to be a traitor.

Jaguar, a petty thief and delinquent, impresses the reader with his strength, and with his control and leadership over the other boys. When he kills the Slave, he does so to protect the honor code of the Circle; yet, ironically, he is punished in the end not by the system itself but by his fellow cadets. Jaguar emerges as the only cadet with a firm set of laudable values and a willingness to suffer for the sake of a principle. At the end of the novel he rehabilitates himself, marries, and begins a life of middle-class respectability.

Ricardo the Slave is the professional victim, serving as prey even to his best friend, Alberto. His reactions, and even his fate, are somewhat predictable, insofar as he serves as the scapegoat for all that is wrong or goes wrong within the school. He is not, however, without some redeeming nobility. He informs, not because he is a coward and wants revenge against his abusers but because he wants to be away from the school, even for a short time, to see Teresa, who has shown him tenderness and humanity.

Gamboa, the rigid disciplinarian and stoic good soldier is, deep down, a decent, just, and loving individual, devoted to his family and to the best ideals of a military life. The book reveals, nevertheless, that there is no room for such individuals in the army, except in some remote region of the country where they cannot threaten the system or, even inadvertently, expose the corruption within it.

Teresa, the only developed female character of the novel, has no distinct personality and is not a very believable human being. In fact, she seems to exist, in part, to join and perhaps equalize emotionally the three principal characters of the novel, Alberto, Jaguar, and the Slave, and to serve as the desirable "nice girl" counterpoint in the otherwise rather raunchy sexual fantasies of the adolescent boys.

Themes and Meanings

The novel is a scathing critique of the hypocrisy and corruption of Peruvian society in general, of which the Leoncio Prado is a microcosm, and of its military establishment in particular. The events of the book transpire during the real dictatorship of General Manuel Odría, who ruled Peru for eight years beginning in 1948, after a military coup. Although the novel appeared several years after the Odría regime, its publication touched a raw nerve; the novel was attacked as antipatriotic and, presumably, several copies of it were burned in the courtyard of the Leoncio Prado.

The novel is also about growing up; about honor, loyalty, bravery, and love. The group of adolescent boys whose stay at the school the book chronicles, is a cross section of Peruvian—and Latin American—society, from a sociological and political perspective. The boys will grow up, which in the novel means that they will fulfill the roles that society has designed for them. There will be no surprises, and not one of the boys will ever overcome his assigned task. This sense of fatalism pervades the novel; growing up means coming to terms with this reality, conforming to one's fate. The first-year recruits, the "dogs" of the novel's original Spanish title (literally the city and the dogs), receive from Jaguar the impetus to challenge their script; he offers to protect them from the system that seeks to humiliate those at the bottom of an inevitably cruel hierarchical structure. The boys accept his leadership and its benefits only when he is strong; the moment he needs their help and support, they turn on him and break their dependence—in preparation for life outside the school—on what is, after all, a lower-class boy.

Critical Context

The Time of the Hero, Vargas Llosa's first full-length novel, was also his first commercial success. The book was published when the author was not yet thirty, yet its favorable reception by critics and public alike placed Vargas Llosa—along with Julio Cortázar and Carlos Fuentes—in the mainstream of the exciting wave of Latin American fiction of the 1960's and 1970's known as the "Boom." In this novel the author experiments, rather successfully, with a number of literary techniques; he uses multiple narrators, flashbacks, fragmented time sequences, introspective monologues, breaks in the structure of the narration, all of which contribute to make this book a complex work of literature whose story line is that of a rather simple *Bildungsroman*. Although the figure of the writer appears in this novel, represented by the Poet, Vargas Llosa has not yet begun to explore the role of the writer in the creation of reality and the relationship between reality and fiction, themes that will become central to some of his future celebrated novels, such as *La tía Julia y el escribidor* (1977; *Aunt Julia and the Scriptwriter*, 1982) and *La guerra del fin del mundo* (1981; *The War of the End of the World*, 1984).

Vargas Llosa has also been a prolific writer outside the area of fiction. He has established a reputation as an erudite and respected literary critic and has been a frequent contributor to important news and cultural publications throughout the world. He has become one of the most important novelists, in any language, of the last quarter of the twentieth century and a most likely recipient of the Nobel Prize in Literature.

Bibliography

Booker, M. Keith. *Vargas Llosa Among the Postmodernists*. Gainesville: University Press of Florida, 1994. A thorough examination of Vargas Llosa's works from a postmodern point of view. Includes a comparison of modernism and postmodernism, as well as extensive notes.

Castro-Klarén, Sara. "Mario Vargas Llosa." In *Latin American Writers*, edited by Carlos A. Solé and Maria I. Abreau. Vol 3. New York: Charles Scribner's Sons, 1989. Offers a comprehensive and critical discussion of Vargas Llosa's life and works. Provides a selected bibliography for further reading.

Gerdes, Dick. "Mario Vargas Llosa." In *Spanish American Authors: The Twentieth Century*, edited by Angel Flores. New York: H. W. Wilson, 1992. Profiles Vargas

Llosa and includes an extensive bibliography of works by and about the author.
Kristal, Efrain. *Temptation of the Word: The Novels of Mario Vargas Llosa.* Nashville,
Tenn.: Vanderbilt University Press, 1998. A collection of perceptive essays on
Vargas Llosa's novels written from the 1960s through the 1980s. A helpful bibliog-
raphy for further reading is also included.

Clara Estow

TO HAVE AND HAVE NOT

Author: Ernest Hemingway (1899-1961)
Type of plot: Social realism
Time of plot: The mid-1930's, during the Great Depression
Locale: Florida and the Caribbean
First published: 1937

Principal characters:

HARRY MORGAN, the protagonist, the roughneck owner of a charter
fishing boat in Florida
MARIE MORGAN, his wife, a former prostitute
RICHARD GORDON, a successful novelist
HELEN GORDON, his wife
ALBERT TRACY, Morgan's mate
EDDY, a "rummy" who sometimes works for Morgan

The Novel

Hemingway's most episodic novel, *To Have and Have Not* is arguably his one book in which the sum of the parts does not equal the individual fragments. It certainly is his one novel that does not maintain artistic unity. Although filled with vivid writing and peopled with memorable characters, the book is weak as a novel. In fact, Hemingway was on record as saying that it was conceived as separate short stories although eventually published as a novel.

The first chapters of the novel focus on Harry Morgan's efforts to support himself and his family. His tools for accomplishing this are his fishing boat, his wits, and his strength. He must depend on the rich, whom he often despises, to charter his boat, and then he must deal with their erratic, often destructive natures. He is not an immoral man, but he is willing to make compromises to achieve his principal goal: clothing and feeding his wife and three daughters. This leads him to progress from fishing trips for rich "sportsmen" to smuggling liquor, ferrying illegal immigrants, and, finally, providing a getaway for gangsters. He is one of the "have nots" and sympathizes with the other "have nots," but he lives off the "haves." This means that he must be willing, when necessary, to sacrifice other "have nots" such as the Chinese immigrants, whom he is paid to double-cross.

The episodic chapters reveal Harry Morgan driven closer and closer to the edge, forced to rely more and more on animal cunning and strength. Increasingly, the distance between himself and the "haves" is made clear. In fact, it is the rich who destroy Morgan's options, so that he must go outside the law and eventually become caught in the violence that ends in his death. A rich tourist, Johnson, sneaks away without paying Morgan for the charter of his boat or the loss of his equipment. Then, when Morgan is smuggling whiskey, he is seen and reported by a pompous rich official, losing the boat that is his only source of income.

The rich, however, exist only in the background of the book, until near the end, when Hemingway focuses on the writer Richard Gordon, his wife, and some of their lovers and acquaintances. Hemingway leaves no doubt in the reader's mind what he thinks of these characters, but they have nothing to do with the story of Harry Morgan and seem to have been dragged in merely so that their corruption would contrast with the animal power and essential honesty of Morgan.

The episodes of the novel propel Harry Morgan with relentless energy from one situation to another, until he is cornered with no hope of escape. He hates dealing with Johnson, the crooked lawyer Bee-lips Simmons, Mr. Sing (who pays him to double-cross his Chinese passengers), and the Cuban thugs. His distaste and scorn for these people is always evident. He may feel superior to his drunk, part-time helper, Eddy, and to Wesley, the black man who assists with bait, but he respects them more as human beings than he does the slimy characters for whom he must work.

When Morgan loses his own boat, he rents his friend Freddy's boat so that he can take out the four Cubans. The Cubans rob a bank before boarding the boat, and then kill Morgan's mate, Albert, because he saw them escaping the bank. Morgan has no time to feel regret, or even fear. When Albert's body is tossed over the side, Morgan manages to kick over the Cubans' machine gun. Eventually, he also manages to kill the Cubans, but in doing so he is mortally wounded. The boat drifts until finally it is found by the Coast Guard. They are amazed that he was able to kill the four Cuban thugs. These last moments of Harry Morgan are sharply contrasted with chapters exposing the pettiness of Richard Gordon and others like him, the rich and perverse who think that they are moral and socially aware but who actually are totally selfish and oblivious to true human feeling and morality.

The Characters

Harry Morgan is, in many respects, the most existential of Hemingway's male protagonists. At forty-two, he is a noble savage, battered but unbowed—at least, in the eyes of Helen Gordon, the novelist's wife. Actually, there is some truth to this view, but, beyond this superficial picture, he is the tough guy made hero, the survivor who is too much of a loner for his own good. He has a wife and children, he has friends and acquaintances, and he has known many women in the past, yet he is so ingrained with the essential aloneness of the human condition that he achieves his truest moments of being when he is battling alone.

Above all, Harry Morgan is a pragmatist, subordinating everything else to survival. The irony is that, in the end, he does not even survive. Yet he does not feel sorry for himself. It almost does not matter that he dies a brutal and painful death. What else could he expect? He has no illusions about the cards dealt by life. He takes what he gets and does the best he can. His mate, Albert, comments: "Since he was a boy, he never had no pity for nobody. But he never had no pity for himself either." When Morgan dies, he tries to explain to the Coast Guard men, "A man . . . ain't got no . . . hasn't got can't really . . . isn't any way out."

The women in this novel are portrayed as either "whores" or "earth mothers." Although Marie Morgan has in her past been a prostitute, she is pictured as a sympathetic and profound character. Married to Harry Morgan for many years, with three daughters, she has gone to fat, but she is seen as a pure, decent human being, a woman filled with love, who nurtures and takes care of her man. The novel concludes with her Molly Bloom-like interior monologue, as she tries to figure out how she will endure without Harry. She, too, faces the trials in her life with an existential stoicism. Somehow, she tells herself, she will get through the pain, and live through the days. There is no choice.

Contrasting to Marie Morgan is Helen Gordon, who, although beautiful and rich, is seen as a neurotic slut who delights in treating her husband viciously. Although on the surface highly civilized, under this glossy veneer, she has no more morals than the lowest prostitute.

Richard Gordon, the successful novelist who represents the "haves" of the world, was based on Hemingway's onetime friend John Dos Passos. Gordon is portrayed as a second-rate writer whose success is based on having the currently popular social convictions. He is shown as being blind to the real world, eagerly warping reality to fit his preconceived notions. He is so weak that he is vulnerable to Helen's taunting, yet he is lionized as a great man by tourists who discover him in the bars where he regularly gets drunk.

Morgan's mate, Albert Tracy, Albert's wife with her loose dentures, and poor old Eddy, the rummy who sometimes works for Morgan, are representative of the poor but honest "have nots" of the world. They are sketched somewhat more completely than most of the "haves," who are hardly more than outlines, but they, too, fall short of the full characterizations that Hemingway usually created in his books. Albert and Eddy merely want to get by, to earn a little cash, and live to see another day. They want so little, but cannot even have that.

Themes and Meanings

Although *To Have and Have Not* aspires to be a proletarian novel, it does not succeed on that level. It has been called one of the earliest examples of the "tough guy" school of fiction, but it does not succeed entirely on that level either. The theme that dominates *To Have and Have Not* is the moral superiority of existential stoicism. Harry Morgan demonstrates this throughout the book, and his wife, Marie, reveals that she, too, instinctively finds it in herself as she struggles to cope with his death.

The book clearly differentiates between Harry Morgan, who fights and kills to survive, and the others who kill either for profit, politics, or out of blood lust. Yet he has an amazing capacity to withstand physical punishment and pain. Hemingway may have meant for Morgan's courage, independence, and masculinity to contrast with the decadence of the two segments of the upper class depicted late in the novel: the idle rich and the intellectuals who use social conflict to show how clever they are. In fact, Morgan's toughness becomes part of the expression of his existential attitude toward life.

Similarly, Morgan—like Hemingway—admires skill for its own sake. This may be fishing skill, the skill of putting bait on well—as Wesley can—or fighting and killing well. The doing is its own reward. This is something that the rich can never understand. They buy and sell, but they do not "do." Society is so dominated by crime and injustice that law and order are hypocritical terms. Only power, money, and individual action lead to survival, and if one must survive at the expense of other human beings, so be it. The poor, through necessity, have skills, however, and they take pride in these skills. Often, this pride is the only reward that they can expect. Nevertheless, they do not despair. They endure, stoically facing the next day and the next, until, at last, they cease to exist altogether.

If the novel was meant to convey the usual proletarian novel's message of "cooperation" or of the power of the poor, it fails in this. The book's message is more that the individual man has no chance any more. The tone throughout the book is one of desperation, and despair. Morgan may share some of the gutty, self-reliant characteristics of the American pioneers, but these elements in his personality are mixed with a bitter realism. Harry sees no more hope in socialism or Communism than in capitalism. He assumes that everyone is equally alone.

Critical Context

During the 1930's, Hemingway was severely criticized for not demonstrating a social conscience in his writing. Other writers of the time, such as Dos Passos, John Steinbeck, and Erskine Caldwell, were highly regarded for their commitment to changing a society that had allowed a worldwide economic depression—with all of the attendant hardship for millions of people—to occur. This novel was meant to be Hemingway's answer to his critics, as is clear from the title.

The novel, however, is severely off-kilter, with the majority of the book devoted to the "have nots," and the "haves" (from the point of view of material wealth) represented at any length only at the end. There are several reasons for this lack of balance; a major reason is that at the last minute, before publication, Hemingway was required to make significant deletions because of legal pressures on his publisher. Apparently, his portraits of the corrupt "haves" were all too recognizable.

To Have and Have Not unquestionably possesses a socioeconomic dimension not found in most of Hemingway's other fiction, although this is not necessarily to the benefit of the work. Generally skilled at describing a social milieu when it serves as the background for his story, Hemingway here becomes laborious in his rather transparent setup of the different social classes, and how they are perceived by the characters.

A minor novel in the Hemingway canon, *To Have and Have Not* nevertheless was successful in its day. Although it never has been as highly regarded critically as his well-known masterpieces, it has remained popular, serving as the basis for the memorable Humphrey Bogart-Lauren Bacall film of 1945. In the 1940's, it was considered a forerunner of the "tough guy" school of fiction, but it has come to be seen more as a unique work, reflecting Hemingway's own personal devils. Uneven though it is, it is a fascinating and vivid achievement wedged between Hemingway's great works of the 1920's and the 1940's.

Bibliography

Benson, Jackson J., ed. *New Critical Approaches to the Short Stories of Ernest Hemingway.* Durham, N.C.: Duke University Press, 1990. Section 1 covers critical approaches to Hemingway's most important long fiction; section 2 concentrates on story techniques and themes; section 3 focuses on critical interpretations of the most important stories; section 4 provides an overview of Hemingway criticism; section 5 contains a comprehensive checklist of Hemingway short fiction criticism from 1975 to 1989.

Bloom, Harold, ed. *Ernest Hemingway: Modern Critical Views.* New York: Chelsea House, 1985. After an introduction that considers Hemingway in relation to later criticism and to earlier American writers, includes articles by a variety of critics who treat topics such as Hemingway's style, unifying devices, and visual techniques.

Lynn, Kenneth S. *Hemingway.* New York: Simon and Schuster, 1987. A shrewd, critical look at Hemingway's life and art, relying somewhat controversially on psychological theory.

Mellow, James R. *Hemingway: A Life Without Consequences.* Boston: Houghton Mifflin, 1992. A well-informed, sensitive handling of the life and work by a seasoned biographer.

Meyers, Jeffrey. *Hemingway: A Biography.* New York: Harper & Row, 1985. Meyers is especially good at explaining the biographical sources of Hemingway's fiction.

Reynolds, Michael. *The Young Hemingway.* Oxford, England: Blackwell, 1986. The first volume of a painstaking biography devoted to the evolution of Hemingway's life and writing. Includes chronology and notes.

_____. *Hemingway: The Paris Years.* Volume 2. Oxford, England: Blackwell, 1989. Includes chronology and maps.

_____. *Hemingway: The American Homecoming.* Volume 3. Oxford, England: Blackwell, 1992. Includes chronology, maps, and notes.

_____. *Hemingway: The 1930s.* Oxford, England: Blackwell, 1997. Volume 4 of Reynolds's biography.

Bruce D. Reeves

TO HAVE AND TO HOLD

Author: Mary Johnston (1870-1936)
Type of plot: Historical romance
Time of plot: 1621-1622
Locale: Jamestown, Virginia, and vicinity, and the West Indies
First published: 1900

Principal characters:
>> CAPTAIN RALPH PERCY, a Virginia planter and veteran of European wars
>> JOCELYN LEIGH, a ward of King James I
>> LORD CARNAL, the king's favorite, in pursuit of Jocelyn Leigh
>> JEREMY SPARROW, Percy's friend, a minister and adventurer, formerly a London actor
>> DICCON, Percy's indentured servant
>> JOHN ROLFE, the widower of Pocahontas and Percy's friend
>> NICOLO, Lord Carnal's sinister Italian doctor

The Novel

Ralph Percy's first-person narrative begins in 1621, only fourteen years after the founding of the Jamestown colony, where he has settled as a tobacco farmer after serving in the European wars. His friend John Rolfe urges him to marry one of the brides for sale who have just arrived from England. Idly casting dice, Percy vows that if he throws ambsace, he will go buy a bride—and ambsace he throws. Among the milkmaids, he sees a dark-eyed and dazzling beauty who returns his look with scorn. After Percy rescues her from the forceful advances of Edward Sharpless, however, and asks her to marry him, she agrees. They are married by Jeremy Sparrow, a picaresque minister who befriends Percy. When Percy takes his bride, Jocelyn Leigh, upriver to his farm, she informs him that to escape persecution in England, she disguised herself as her waiting woman and came to America, where she married him only as a last resort. Respecting her appeal to his generosity, Percy does not press his connubial rights. She in turn remains wary, aloof, and aristocratic.

Shortly thereafter, there arrives from England Lord Carnal, an arrogant favorite of King James, who dotes upon such exquisitely handsome young men. It was to escape marriage to him that Jocelyn, the king's ward, fled England. In Virginia, Carnal expects everyone to give him his way and to have the marriage annulled, and he is enraged when Percy defies him.

As her husband continues to defend her honor and her person, disregarding the risk to himself, Jocelyn develops a grudging respect for him. He disarms Carnal at rapier play, defeats him at wrestling, and saves her from abduction. When orders come from England for Jocelyn to be returned and her husband arrested, they escape by boat, and when Lord Carnal tries to stop them, they take him prisoner.

At sea they are driven south by a tempest until they are wrecked on an island. There, they encounter pirates burying their dead captain. Walking boldly into their midst, Percy claims the vacant captaincy and forces them to accept him by defeating the three leading contenders in swordplay. As reluctant captain of a pirate ship, he captures numerous vessels in the Spanish Main but compels his crew not to slaughter prisoners. When he refuses to fight an English ship, the men mutiny, whereupon he deliberately runs his ship onto a reef. Percy's party is rescued by the British, but he is tried for piracy. When Jocelyn speaks as his advocate and shames Lord Carnal into telling the truth, Percy is freed. At last he realizes that his wife has come to love him, as he has come to love her. Lord Carnal, however, still burns with evil passion.

Back in Virginia, news comes that the Duke of Buckingham has replaced Lord Carnal in the royal favor. Desperate, Carnal lures Percy into a trap with a forged letter from Jocelyn; at the supposed rendezvous, Percy and Diccon, Percy's indentured servant, are captured by Indians, whose panther springs upon the king's minion and rips open his beautiful face.

The Indians take their prisoners to their village and are about to torture them when Percy's friend Nantauquas, the son of Powhatan, rescues them. Learning that the Indians plan to massacre the colonists, Percy escapes and brings warning to Jamestown, where he has been thought dead. To his dismay, he learns that his wife has gone searching for him in the forest, which is full of marauding Indians. Thinking Jocelyn dead, Percy goes to kill Lord Carnal, only to find that Carnal—feeling damned, his face ruined—has taken poison, together with his Italian doctor, and is already dying.

When the Indians attack Jamestown, they are driven off, but there has been extensive slaughter throughout the colony. Believing his wife dead, Percy goes home grieving but finds that Jeremy Sparrow has brought her back safely. They have a blissful reunion, realizing that the marriage that began as a wager on his part and a loveless act of desperation on hers has become true and enduring.

The Characters

Though the bold hero, beautiful heroine, and picaresque sidekick are somewhat standard for historical romance, Johnston has made hers more interesting than usual. Ralph Percy, thirty-six years old, is a seasoned veteran, the best swordsman in Virginia, and a man to be reckoned with. Johnston makes Percy's first-person narrative believably masculine, with some fine repartee, and the relationship to his at first reluctant wife has more complexity than does the usual costume romance.

Jocelyn Leigh is perhaps more stereotypical—the proud, haughty beauty—but as her disdain turns to love, she too becomes more complex as well as more appealing. Her high-spirited courage is contagious.

The most complex characterization is that of Lord Carnal. A beautiful, arrogant minion of the king, he resembles those real favorites of King James, the Earl of Somerset and the Duke of Buckingham, but he becomes a fascinating study in damnation. Both his Italian doctor and the king seem to have a homosexual fascination with him, but his own passion for Jocelyn Leigh, carried to the point of an obsession, seems genuine, though utterly selfish, and his end is genuinely tragic. Though ruthless and unscrupulous, he has courage and is capable of gallantry.

There is a colorful cast of supporting characters, notably Jeremy Sparrow, former actor and crony of Ben Jonson, now an ordained minister but also an immensely strong fighting man; Diccon, the loyal retainer, who tries to kill his master in response to a blow given in anger; John Rolfe, still mourning his dead Pocahontas; and Nicolo, the treacherous Italian doctor, together with leading members of the Jamestown community, Indians, and pirates.

Themes and Meanings

Though some of Johnston's later novels advance the claims of pacifism, socialism, and mysticism, *To Have and to Hold* is neither a philosophical novel, nor, despite its colorful characters, a psychological novel. Its strength lies in a compelling, action-packed narrative, strong scenes, dramatic if sometimes archaic dialogue, a sense of irony, and a poetic style. Johnston skillfully evokes the beauty and the menace of nature in the raw frontier, with wilderness surrounding the infant colony. Combining old-fashioned romance with new realism, *To Have and to Hold* gives a vivid picture of life in Jamestown and is the best portrait in fiction of the earliest English colony in America. Its chief theme is the value of loyalty, integrity, love, and courage. The struggle of the lovers against pirates and an Indian war correlate with the survival of the colony, and their conflict with the king's minion foreshadows the later colonial struggle for independence from royal autocracy.

Critical Context

Though realism and naturalism are usually taught as the dominant mode of the novel in the late nineteenth and early twentieth centuries, much of the most popular and highly esteemed fiction of the time consisted of historical romances by such novelists as Robert Louis Stevenson and Arthur Conan Doyle in England, and by Lew Wallace, Winston Churchill, Francis Marion Crawford, S. Weir Mitchell, Charles Major, Paul Leicester Ford, Maurice Thompson, and others in the United States. Considered classics in their day, most of the American works are now forgotten, or at least neglected. Perhaps the most substantial American historical novelist of the time, both in style and content, is Mary Johnston, to whom Edward Wagenknecht dedicated his *Cavalcade of the American Novel*. Twenty of her twenty-three novels are historical. Seven of them are set in colonial Virginia, and of these, the most famous is *To Have and to Hold*. Johnston is notable for combining romantic plots with historical accuracy. Instead of providing mere costume escapism, she offers an interpretation of history, particularly in her Civil War novels *The Long Roll* (1911) and *Cease Firing* (1912). Chronicling the history of Virginia, Johnston is the first important novelist from that state and remains, with Ellen Glasgow and William Styron, one of Virginia's three leading novelists.

Bibliography
Cella, C. Ronald. *Mary Johnston*. Boston: Twayne, 1981. Cella provides a critical and interpretive study of Johnston with a close reading of her major works, a solid bibliography and complete notes and references.

Jones, Anne G. *Tomorrow Is Another Day: The Woman Writer in the South, 1859-1936*. Baton Rouge: Louisiana State University Press, 1991. Contains an assessment and critical interpretation of Johnston's novels.

Longest, George C. *Three Virginia Writers—Mary Johnston, Thomas Nelson Page, and Amelie Rives Troubetzkoy: A Reference Guide*. Boston: G. K. Hall, 1978. An extensive bibliography and useful reference guide, one section of which is devoted to the works of Mary Johnston.

Nelson, Lawrence G. "Mary Johnston and the Historic Imagination." In *Southern Writers: Appraisals in Our Time*, edited by R. C. Simonini, Jr. Charlottesville: University Press of Virginia, 1964. A discussion of Johnston's skills as a historical novelist.

Robert E. Morsberger

TO THE WHITE SEA

Author: James Dickey (1923-1997)
Type of plot: War
Time of plot: 1945
Locale: Japan
First published: 1993

Principal characters:

SERGEANT MULDROW, an American tail gunner on a B-29 in the
Pacific, whose unit is sent to bomb Japan in the latter days of World
War II

THE AMERICAN MONK, a member of a Zen monastery in Northern
Japan

THE FALCONER, an old hermit living in a shack on the island of
Hokkaido

The Novel

To the White Sea recounts the journey of Sergeant Muldrow from Tokyo to the
northern island of Hokkaido. Muldrow bails out of his plane, an American B-29
bomber, when it is shot down on a raid over Tokyo. He is the crew's only survivor.

Muldrow's journey begins in a sewer, where he hides while awaiting the next day's
bombing raid by the Americans. Amid the panic and chaos it causes, he joins the
crowds streaming through the burning city, shoots a man for his clothing, stabs a
woman who recognizes that he is foreign, and stabs another man for his shoes. Safely
out of the city, he heads north, sleeping along the road, hiding in fields, his only
weapon a small bread knife, carefully honed and polished. One night, outside a house
where a small family is at dinner, he lets the candlelight glint off the knife blade, then
moves on, thrilled that he has left his mark.

Along the way, he feels as though he enters the tree, the stone, the lake. Wrapping
himself in animal hides gives him the power of that animal. In his element, in control
of his fate, he has seldom been happier, eating the raw flesh of a swan, using its feathers for a mattress, and preying on humans. He stabs an old man for his winter clothing.
Near an airfield, Muldrow sees Japanese soldiers decapitate a captured American
prisoner. The scene lowers even further his respect for enemy life. Shortly after, he
stabs a woman and puts her severed head in a waterwheel bucket. This grisly episode
is followed by a touching encounter with two small children. Patiently, he makes a
string design for them, then sends them safely back to their house.

Hiding on a logging train heading north, he feels a spiritual oneness with the wind,
snow, and clouds. He spends several days by a secluded waterfall, resting and fishing.
Resuming his trek north, he slips into the house of an old samurai soldier and a
woman. The two men fight, sword to knife. He kills the man, then the woman. Calmly
shattering the man's arm, he makes a needle of the splintered bone and stitches to-

gether a garment for his northern journey. Encountering an American monk in a field, Muldrow accepts his offer of food and shelter at the Zen monastery nearby. In the night, however, Japanese soldiers take him prisoner, beating him with their rifle butts. In transit to their base, he kills the four guards and speeds north in the military truck. Finally reaching a fishing village opposite Hokkaido island, he steals a boat and paddles to the island. Ashore, he comes upon a herd of large goats attacking a native hunter, whom he rescues. Gored in the leg by one of the goats, he is taken to a village and cared for by the grateful natives. During the weeks of his recovery, he learns that they are chiefly bear hunters, and their cruel taunting and shooting of captured bears appall him. As he leaves the village for the wilderness, he stabs the native guarding a bear cub and frees the creature.

Several days later, he comes upon a shack of an old falconer. Fascinated by the giant hawks the old man has trained to hunt, Muldrow decides to stay. As he learns to hunt with the birds, he feels his soul transferring to them. They possess what he has been seeking all along: the power of flight. His journey has brought him to spiritual fulfillment. On the day he discovers the old falconer has died, the shack is surrounded by Japanese soldiers. He feels ready for the final stage of his journey, spiritual transformation. Covering himself with swan feathers, his own blood, and the blood of the old man, he steps in front of the soldiers. As they riddle him with bullets, his spirit takes flight, and he is transformed into a fiery wall, then into the wind, snow, cold. Now, he is everywhere.

The Characters

The world of the novel is the mind of Muldrow, so the importance of any character is determined by his or her relation to Muldrow's journey and thoughts. Each is used to define Muldrow's character. A newcomer to his flight crew, for example, prompts Muldrow to explain the need for careful preparation. Readers see how skilled he is in survival techniques, how methodical and focused he is. The encounter with the old samurai warrior reveals Muldrow's superior instincts and skill with a knife. The native hunters in Hokkaido demonstrate the universality of human depravity, especially in their treatment of animals. Each character reveals something important about Muldrow.

Muldrow was reared in Alaska and as a child was taught by his father to hunt and shoot a gun; his favorite survival tools are a knife and a piece of flint for making fire. He has the instincts and skills of a ruthless, methodical killer who feels spiritually akin not only to the lynx, wolverine, and fisher marten but also to trees, rocks, wind, and clouds. His journey through Japan is more than a flight to safety; it is a spiritual quest for fulfillment. The farther north he goes, the closer he comes to his physical death and spiritual birth, or transformation. The mystical experiences he encounters in his journey sometimes appear to be the hallucinations of a madman, but the final portrait is that of a loner who has escaped not only Japan but also human existence, merging with the forces of nature.

The American monk epitomizes the kind of human Muldrow despises and, presumably, flees. Muldrow dismisses the monk and his treachery with the thought, "He had to be like he was—for the rest of his life, too, and that was bad enough." The monk's is an understated presence in the novel but forceful nevertheless. He says that he came to Japan to lose himself, meaning the materialist that America had made of him. Readers come to realize, however, that the man has indeed lost himself, for in betraying Muldrow, he has betrayed the principles of truth and humanity. Ironically, he lauds the benefits of meditation and a life that contemplates the spirit in the stone. The life of meditation offers a purity of mind and spirit, but his own life has become corrupted by self-interest. His palaver about the spiritual life throws into relief the depth and intensity of Muldrow's.

The old falconer is a hunter who lives alone in the Japanese wilderness. Despite his inability to communicate with Muldrow in words, he teaches Muldrow how to hunt with the hawks and shows that Muldrow does not completely withdraw from all human contact.

Themes and Meanings

To the White Sea follows one man's lone quest for survival through hostile territory. Every moment threatens Muldrow with capture, torture, and death. To survive, he must use extraordinary skills and must have instincts that the ordinary person lacks. His instincts are those of the fiercest, most skilled predatory animals. He comes to respect animals more than humans. Toward the end, however, his thoughts are taken with the flight of the hunting hawk, which symbolizes for him the supreme predatory power and deliverance from a world he no longer wishes to inhabit. The hawk also has the power of natural flight. Muldrow seeks this mystical power for himself, for it offers lightness, expansiveness, and endless freedom. At the beginning, Muldrow seeks only to escape Japan, heading north to Alaska. Along the way, he loses all affection for humanity, wanting ultimately to be alone in the wilderness, on the white sea of snow, which symbolizes for him freedom from the sweltering confusion and destruction of war. For him, killing is necessary to survival. War—an outcrop of civilization—has corrupted killing, however, making it random, malicious, and unnecessarily brutal. It is humane to kill swiftly, skillfully, and necessarily. By torturing and mutilating, humans have corrupted killing.

On Japanese soil, all of his resources are challenged. The land contains the elements that give him most pleasure: trees, animals, and water. These are the points at which the spirit and the flesh merge. For Dickey, only the wilderness seems worth inhabiting. There, human instincts find their greatest challenge and expression. There, the physical being can merge with the spiritual. Civilization depraves humans and interferes with and ultimately destroys their ability to connect spiritually with the outward forms of the spirit—wind, tree, field, and lake.

Critical Context

Although Dickey's reputation as a poet overshadows his novelistic achievements, he enjoyed considerable popular success as a novelist with the publication of his first novel *Deliverance* (1970), in which wilderness survival and deliverance from modern conditions are major themes. In his poetry and his fiction alike, Dickey is concerned with humankind's relation to the natural environment. The way Muldrow speaks of the spirit of trees, rocks, and other natural objects reflects Dickey's belief that a common spirit informs all things and that one is, like Muldrow, enriched and empowered by becoming one with these natural objects. Muldrow wears the skins of animals not only for warmth but also for the almost magical power he derives from them. Smearing himself with the old falconer's blood has ritualistic overtones and suggests that Muldrow gains power from it as well as from the swan feathers.

The novel also explores ways of fusing the inner and outer states of consciousness. Although outer events are usually clearly distinct from Muldrow's thoughts and emotions, he often tries to bring the reader into his perceptions, as when he speaks of the sunlight in the lake, the blueness of the iceberg, and the nature of cold. In the end, the fusion of inner and outer states is complete, at least in Muldrow's experience.

The novel reflects Dickey's belief that civilization undercuts skills necessary to survive extreme situations. Muldrow is an ideal portrait of man's return to nature. He is the quintessential survivor, relying on primitive instincts and skills to survive. The role of violence in that survival is a major part of the novel and has attracted negative critical attention. Dickey himself may have encouraged this unfavorable reaction by referring to Muldrow as a sociopath. Pathological tendencies may be detected in Muldrow's graphic descriptions of his killings, in the way he mutilates some victims, and in his pleasure in the way his knife sinks into his victims. Even his final transformation, though it suggests spiritual triumph, comes amid much blood and physical mutilation. By ending with an emphatic image of man escaping the physical world through fire into pure air and spirit, Dickey seems to be saying that only violence can wrest the spirit from a world gone mad.

Bibliography
Baughman, Ronald. *Understanding James Dickey.* Columbia: University of South Carolina Press, 1985. Chapter 1 offers a useful overview of Dickey's poetry and prose, including subjects, themes, and techniques. The chapters are brief, and the discussions are accessible to the general reader.
Calhoun, Richard J., and Robert W. Hill. *James Dickey.* Boston: Twayne, 1983. A chapter on Dickey's prose sheds light on *To the White Sea*, discussing such subjects as primitivism, the hunter and the hunted, and others.
Kirschten, Robert, ed. *"Struggling for Wings": The Art of James Dickey.* Columbia: University of South Carolina Press, 1997. Published just after Dickey's death, this book collects reviews, interviews, and essays that cover the whole of Dickey's work, including *Deliverance* and *To the White Sea*.
Lieberman, Laurence. "Warrior, Visionary, Natural Philosopher: James Dickey's *To the White Sea*." *The Southern Review* 33 (Winter, 1997): 164-180. Traces connections between *To the White Sea* and Dickey's poetry, showing how the novel represents a fictional expression of Dickey's themes.

Suarez, Ernest. *James Dickey and the Politics of Canon: Assessing the Savage Ideal.* Columbia: University of Missouri Press, 1993. What Suarez says of the savage ideal in Dickey's second novel, *Alnilam* (1987), illuminates this theme in *To the White Sea*. Suarez's substantial bibliography includes titles of works on poetry and fiction in general that are relevant to Dickey's work.

Bernard E. Morris

THE TORRENTS OF SPRING

Author: Ernest Hemingway (1899-1961)
Type of plot: Farcical parody
Time of plot: The early 1920's
Locale: Rural Michigan
First published: 1926

> *Principal characters:*
> YOGI JOHNSON, a World War I veteran working in a Petoskey,
>   Michigan, "pump-factory"
> SCRIPPS O'NEIL, an alleged short-story writer who wanders to Petoskey
>   and finds work in the pump-factory
> DIANA, an "elderly" English waitress in a Petoskey beanery who
>   marries Scripps
> MANDY, a younger waitress in the beanery who steals Scripps from
>   Diana
> TWO INDIANS, acquaintances of Yogi who live outside Petoskey

The Novel

The Torrents of Spring is a short parody of Sherwood Anderson's novel *Dark Laughter* (1925) and a satire of literary manners and morals in the 1920's. As such, it is not an extremely important work, but as the second published book—after the stories of *In Our Time* (1924, 1925)—by a major American writer, the novella has biographical and historical interest. To be enjoyed, however, it must be read first for its nonsense and humor.

For such a short work, *The Torrents of Spring* is surprisingly complex—an indication of its parodic purpose. Subtitled "A Romantic Novel in Honor of the Passing of a Great Race," the book is divided into four parts, each with its own grandiose subtitle and each prefaced by an epigraph from the eighteenth century English novelist Henry Fielding. In the tradition of Fielding (who in *Joseph Andrews* was himself parodying his predecessor Samuel Richardson), Hemingway also conducts a humorous dialogue with his imaginary readers, explaining his novel—or urging them to get their friends to buy the book.

The structure of the work is equally elaborate, and to retell the story is to highlight its nonsense. Part 1 ("Red and Black Laughter") opens with Yogi Johnson and Scripps O'Neil staring out the window of the pump-factory where they work at the empty yard where snow covers the crated pumps. (*Dark Laughter* opens with two characters named Bruce Dudley and Sponge Martin looking out a factory window at "a more or less littered factory yard.")

The narrative now splits, and Hemingway picks up the absurd story of how Scripps got to Petoskey. A year earlier, he lived in the town of Mancelona, with his wife and daughter Lucy—or Lousy, as he calls her. (In *Dark Laughter*, Sponge Martin's daughter is named Bugs—and the parody goes on.) One night, Scripps and his wife went out drinking, and he lost her—or, he came home one night and she was gone. It does not matter which is true. (In the same way, Scripps's mother was either a poor Italian immigrant—or the wife of a Confederate general.)

Scripps wanders into Petoskey, meets Diana in Brown's Beanery ("The Best by Test"), finds work in the pump-factory, and returns to marry the waitress. Just as quickly, however, he meets Mandy, the junior waitress in the beanery, and falls in love with her "picturesque" language and her endless store of literary anecdotes: "Did I ever tell you about the last words of Henry James?" she asks Scripps when they first meet. Given this competition, Diana realizes that she "can't hold" Scripps—although she subscribes to every literary review and journal she can find in an attempt to keep her short-story writer (who claims to have sold stories to the *Saturday Evening Post* and *The Dial*). Part 2 ("The Struggle for Life") ends with Scripps and Diana, after a year of marriage, trudging down to the beanery for still another night of Mandy's literary gossip and small talk.

"In case the reader is becoming confused," Hemingway interjects with his first author's note, "we are now up to where the story opened," although it is quite difficult writing this way, he complains, "beginning things backwards," and he hopes that his readers will understand. "If any of the readers would care to send me anything they ever wrote, for criticism or advice, I am always at the Cafe du Dome any afternoon talking about Art with Harold Stearns and Sinclair Lewis." Such absurdities not only parody Fielding and Anderson but also satirize the Parisian literary life of which Hemingway himself was such a vital part.

In part 3 ("Men in War and the Death of Society"), Hemingway takes up the story of Yogi Johnson, who is worried that "he did not want a woman" and who spends the evening with two Petoskey Indians talking about the war (unpleasant but exciting, Yogi argues) and shooting pool (which the Indian with four artificial limbs wins). They go to an Indian speakeasy, but Yogi, in one of the most amusing scenes in the novella, is expelled because he is Swedish. ("In case it may have any historical value," Hemingway adds in another note, "I wrote the foregoing chapter in two hours directly on the typewriter, and then went out to lunch with John Dos Passos"—and then he proceeds to give a detailed description of the meal.)

In part 4 ("The Passing of a Great Race and the Making and Marring of Americans"), all the characters end up in the beanery, where, Hemingway notes, "there are no red women. Are there no squaws anymore?" At which point "a squaw came into the room," naked, but with a papoose on her back and a husky by her side. Yogi is seized by "a new feeling. A feeling he thought had been lost for ever," and, when the naked Indian woman is thrown out of the beanery, he hurries out into the winter night after her.

"At the other end of the counter of the beanery a marriage was coming to an end." Diana leaves; Scripps says to Mandy, "You are my woman" (even though his mind keeps straying to the naked woman); and Mandy launches into another long literary anecdote, this one about the time Knut Hamsun, the Norwegian novelist, worked as a streetcar conductor in Chicago.

The reader last sees Yogi walking down the railroad tracks beside the naked Indian woman, stripping off his own clothes—which are being picked up one by one by the two Indians following the pair, who then head into town to sell Yogi's clothes to the Salvation Army. "White chief snappy dresser," one of the Indians comments. In his "Final Note to the Reader," Hemingway himself exits: "I will just say a simple farewell and Godspeed, reader, and leave you now to your own devices."

The Characters

Characters in a parody such as *The Torrents of Spring* are necessarily stiff and stereotypical in order for the satire to work. The speech of Scripps and Yogi is full of literary allusions (to Willa Cather, H. G. Wells, et al.), as their thoughts are crowded with historical figures (Igor Stravinsky, the Haymarket anarchists). Yet their behavior is actually quite stupid: When Scripps first enters the pump-factory, for example, he is met by a sign that reads: "KEEP OUT THIS MEANS YOU. Can that mean me? Scripps wondered." Through the Fielding epigraphs, Hemingway implies that he is satirizing the ridiculous affectations of people, and especially literary affectations among his contemporaries. Characters here are always dropping literary names— Huysmans, Ruth Suckow—and quoting, or misquoting, other writers. ("What is it that old writing fellow Shakespeare says: 'Might makes right'?" Scripps misremembers at one point.)

In Scripps and Yogi, Hemingway is also parodying the particular kind of primitives for which Sherwood Anderson was famous. Anderson was one of the first American writers to apply Freudian theory to literary creation, and, in his most famous work, the stories of *Winesburg, Ohio* (1919), one can see Sigmund Freud's influence clearly in the rendering of internal thought and feeling. In such later works as *Dark Laughter*, however, Anderson's obsession with the inner lives of his characters verges on self-parody, and it is easy to see the source of Hemingway's humor. Characters in *The Torrents of Spring* are either free-associating or pondering cosmic questions. (Scripps watches a passenger train and wonders, "Were they . . . members of a worn-out civilization world-weary from the war?)

Finally, Hemingway's characterization is a slap at Anderson and other 1920's writers—such as Eugene O'Neill in *The Emperor Jones* (1920) and *The Hairy Ape* (1922)—who saw in the lives of blacks and Native Americans a healthy, primitive antidote to the increasing industrialization (and thus deadening) of white, middle-class life. The "Indian war-whoops" and "dark laughter" of the black characters that run through the novella are satiric motifs, as are the subtitle and scenes such as the one where Yogi "felt touched. Here among the simple aborigines, the only real Americans, he had found that true communion."

Besides being parodies of Anderson or satiric portraits of literary figures of the 1920's, the characters in *The Torrents of Spring* are simply comic—like Diana, for example, who reads and orders pork and beans as "a pig and the noisy ones."

Themes and Meanings

Dark Laughter was published in September, 1925, and was an immediate popular success: By December of that year, it had gone through seven printings. Hemingway's first book of stories, *In Our Time*, was published in October, and the generally kind reviewers noted Hemingway's debt to Anderson. (The story "My Old Man," for example, is very close in subject and tone to Anderson's stories "I Want to Know Why" or "I'm a Fool.") Throughout his career, Hemingway made a point to attack publicly other writers who had been helpful to him: In the posthumous *A Moveable Feast* (1964), for example, written about Hemingway's Paris years of the early 1920's, there are particularly biting portraits of Gertrude Stein and F. Scott Fitzgerald. Hemingway finished the first draft of *The Sun Also Rises* in the fall of 1925 (a novel whose hero, Jake Barnes, by the way, has a war wound, making it impossible for him to love), and he then spent the week of Thanksgiving writing this parody of Anderson and thus purging himself of his mentor's influence. (Later, Hemingway would write to Anderson and describe *The Torrents of Spring* as a "lousy, snotty book.")

Hemingway also used the novella to free himself from his publisher and to gain a more lucrative contract. *In Our Time* had been published by Boni and Liveright, thanks in part to the recommendation of Anderson, whom that firm also published. Boni and Liveright had contracted for Hemingway's next two books, but when he sent them the manuscript of *The Torrents of Spring*, Horace Liveright, who had just published *Dark Laughter* a few months earlier, was forced to refuse this parody of one of the firm's most famous writers. Thus, Hemingway was free to move to Scribner's, to begin his long and fruitful relationship with the editor Maxwell Perkins.

Dark Laughter is a fairly silly and sentimental novel by contemporary standards, and it probably deserved the parody, especially of Anderson's uncritical veneration of primitive emotional life. What is more important, however, now that *Dark Laughter* is no longer a part of the American literary canon, is Hemingway's satire of literary manners and social morals in the 1920's. There are numerous literary allusions in the novel—from James Joyce and H. L. Mencken to the drummer whose "nerves were on edge tonight" (a reference to a line in T. S. Eliot's *The Waste Land*, 1922). Other literary characters simply walk into the book: "It was at this point in the story, reader," says Hemingway in still another note, "that Mr. F. Scott Fitzgerald came to our home one afternoon, and after remaining for quite a while suddenly sat down in the fireplace and would not (or was it could not, reader?) get up and let the fire burn something else so as to keep the room warm." In the wonderful Indian bar scene, pictures of D. H. Lawrence, General Custer, and "a full-length oil painting of Henry Wadsworth Longfellow" line the walls where "town" Indians (some of them in tuxedos) are busy ostracizing "woods" Indians—clearly a satire on class distinctions and snobbery at all levels of American life.

Anderson's prose style is really very close to Hemingway's own—which is one reason why the parody works so well. It is easy to hear the voices of *In Our Time* and *The Sun Also Rises* in *The Torrents of Spring*. Anderson was an important American writer in the 1920's, not only because he deepened literature with psychology but also because he was one of the first American writers to develop a prose style that approached the idiom of ordinary Americans. Like Gertrude Stein, who also influenced Hemingway (and whom he also chides here: "Where were her experiments in words leading her?" Yogi asks), Anderson was trying to develop an indigenous American prose style. That style strikes contemporary readers as rather impressionistic, if occasionally poetic, but in the 1920's it was fresh and even revolutionary. Hemingway's parody of the dumb thought and clipped speech of Anderson's characters is also a backhanded tribute to the writer who as much as anyone had helped Hemingway find his own lean and sinewy prose. If imitation is the sincerest form of flattery, parody is a clear acknowledgment of literary power and accomplishment—and of a style that can be parodied.

Critical Context

The interest in *The Torrents of Spring* since its publication has been mainly historical. Certainly, the novella adds little to an overall appraisal of Hemingway's talent, except, perhaps, for the recognition of his capacity for such broad slapstick humor. In this regard, *The Torrents of Spring* resembles the nonsense plays that Ring Lardner was writing at about the same time.

The work may be most interesting for presenting a Hemingway with whom few readers are familiar. The typical Hemingway hero—from Jake Barnes to Frederic Henry (in *A Farewell to Arms*, 1929) to Robert Jordan (in *For Whom the Bell Tolls*, 1940)—is a rather unliterary "tough guy." Hemingway himself, especially in his later years, took on the characteristics of his own heroes, for he liked to leave the impression, in interview or essay, of the hardy, macho sportsman who had little time or inclination for the niceties of the literary life. Yet *The Torrents of Spring* reveals a Hemingway with a wide and deep literary background: The title comes from a short novel by the nineteenth century Russian writer Ivan Turgenev; the subtitle to part 4 is a veiled reference to Stein's *The Making of Americans*: *Being a History of a Family's Progress* (1925); there are numerous other allusions and references to writers both older (Percy Bysshe Shelley) and contemporary (Mencken, Ford Madox Ford, Joyce).

The 1920's in Paris was one of the most exciting periods in literary history, especially for expatriate American writers. Rarely in American literature has there been a period of such rich literary experiment and productivity, and Hemingway was at the center of it all. *The Torrents of Spring* is a minor literary work but a major revelation of Hemingway's immersion in the literary life swirling around him.

Bibliography

Benson, Jackson J., ed. *New Critical Approaches to the Short Stories of Ernest Hemingway*. Durham, N.C.: Duke University Press, 1990. Section 1 covers critical approaches to Hemingway's most important long fiction; section 2 concentrates on story techniques and themes; section 3 focuses on critical interpretations of the most important stories; section 4 provides an overview of Hemingway criticism;

section 5 contains a comprehensive checklist of Hemingway short fiction criticism from 1975 to 1989.

Bloom, Harold, ed. *Ernest Hemingway: Modern Critical Views*. New York: Chelsea House, 1985. After an introduction that considers Hemingway in relation to later criticism and to earlier American writers, includes articles by a variety of critics who treat topics such as Hemingway's style, unifying devices, and visual techniques.

Lynn, Kenneth S. *Hemingway*. New York: Simon and Schuster, 1987. A shrewd, critical look at Hemingway's life and art, relying somewhat controversially on psychological theory.

Mellow, James R. *Hemingway: A Life Without Consequences*. Boston: Houghton Mifflin, 1992. A well-informed, sensitive handling of the life and work by a seasoned biographer.

Meyers, Jeffrey. *Hemingway: A Biography*. New York: Harper & Row, 1985. Meyers is especially good at explaining the biographical sources of Hemingway's fiction.

Reynolds, Michael. *The Young Hemingway*. Oxford, England: Blackwell, 1986. The first volume of a painstaking biography devoted to the evolution of Hemingway's life and writing. Includes chronology and notes.

_____. *Hemingway: The Paris Years*. Volume 2. Oxford, England: Blackwell, 1989. Includes chronology and maps.

_____. *Hemingway: The American Homecoming*. Volume 3. Oxford, England: Blackwell, 1992. Includes chronology, maps, and notes.

_____. *Hemingway: The 1930s*. Oxford, England: Blackwell, 1997. Volume 4 of Reynolds's biography.

David Peck

TRACKS

Author: Louise Erdrich (1954-   )
Type of plot: Family
Time of plot: Winter, 1912-spring, 1924
Locale: Matchimanito, a fictional reservation in North Dakota
First published: 1988

Principal characters:

NANAPUSH, an Anishinabe elder who tells Fleur's story of survival to
    Lulu, his adopted granddaughter
PAULINE PUYAT, the other narrator, a fanatical nun
FLEUR PILLAGER, a survivor of epidemics and deprivations thought to
    possess supernatural powers

The Novel

Tracks deals with the devastation of the Anishinabe (also known as Chippewa or Objiway) people between the winter of 1912 and the spring of 1924 in Matchimanito, North Dakota. The novel focuses on the life of Fleur Pillager and those with whom she comes into contact, dramatizing their struggle for survival as well as their many-faceted conflicts. In alternating chapters, the story is narrated by Nanapush, a tribal elder, and Pauline Puyat, a fanatic nun of mixed heritage. The two narrators complement but at times also contradict and undermine each other.

At the age of seventeen, Fleur is rescued by Nanapush during a severe winter when inhabitants of Matchimanito are found dead from consumption and starvation. After recovery, she goes to Argus to work at a butcher shop. There, she meets a younger girl, Pauline, who has known her as a survivor of two drownings and hence is convinced that Fleur is the chosen one of Misshepeshu, the lake monster. Pauline reports how Fleur, having aroused the desires of three male workers and beaten them at the card table, is sexually assaulted. Russell, Pauline's nephew, tries to stop it but to no avail. Later, a tornado strikes the town, and the three men take refuge inside a meat locker, refusing to let Pauline and Russell in. Russell shuts them in from the outside, freezing two of them to death. After the incident, Pauline returns to the reservation, where she learns that Fleur is pregnant. It is uncertain how Fleur becomes pregnant, but according to Nanapush, through personal insights and love medicines, he has helped Eli Kashpaw, a hunter, win her passionate love. Fleur's childbirth proves to be so difficult that she almost dies. The baby, given the name of Lulu Nanapush, is in fact the person Nanapush addresses throughout his narrative.

Meanwhile, Pauline becomes a helper in Argus at a farm belonging to Bernadette Morrisey. Awakening to her sexuality, Pauline experiments with Napoleon, Bernadette's brother, but finds herself attracted to Eli instead. Spurned by him, she retaliates with the love potions, thus causing Eli to have sex with Sophie, Bernadette's daughter. Sophie is punished by her mother, who sends her away. She goes to Fleur's cabin and kneels in her yard for days on end, jeopardizing the relationship between Fleur and Eli. To avenge Sophie, Clarence, Bernadette's son, attacks Margaret, Eli's mother, by tying her up and shaving her bald. The insult leads Margaret, Nanapush, and Fleur to retaliate.

The sexual relationship between Pauline and Napoleon has led to her pregnancy. After giving birth to Marie, whom she turns over to Bernadette, Pauline joins Sister Anne's convent, where she sees visions of Christ. Determined to remove the devil from Indian country, she returns to the reservation. Fleur, who is again pregnant, gives birth prematurely one day when Pauline comes to visit. Pauline is too clumsy to help Fleur stop the bleeding. Fleur loses consciousness, and the baby dies.

The winter begins to get harsh again, and food is running out. Furthermore, Father Damien, the Catholic priest, brings news that the land allotted to the Pillager, Kashpaw, and Nanapush families would be foreclosed unless they pay their taxes. Faced with the crisis, Fleur is affected by a mysterious illness. She undertakes a healing ceremony, which Pauline disrupts ruthlessly. Eventually, the Kashpaws, Nanapush, and Fleur manage to pool their resources to pay the taxes. Nector Kashpaw (Eli's brother), entrusted to take the money to pay the taxes, betrays Nanapush and Fleur by making the payment toward Kashpaw land. The betrayal agonizes Fleur, alienates her from Eli, and causes her to attempt suicide by drowning.

Pauline, increasingly determined to become a martyr of her new faith, attempts to confront the lake monster—her idea of Satan. In her delusion, she runs into Napoleon and strangles him instead. Afterward, she takes her vow and becomes Sister Leopolda.

The lumber company has started cutting down the trees near Fleur's cabin. Desperate, Fleur sends Lulu to the government school for the sake of safety and plots her revenge. Secretly, she has sawed the trees around her cabin at the base, so that they remain lightly held. When the lumber company's men come to move her by force, the trees tumble down, crushing men and wagons beneath them. Finally, Fleur leaves her home ground. Having witnessed the way influence is exercised by bureaucratic means, Nanapush runs for tribal chairmanship in order to help the Indians. He is elected and, after many attempts, manages to retrieve Lulu from the government school.

The Characters

Although Fleur is the central figure of the novel, the reader's understanding of her character is mediated by Nanapush and Pauline, who also serve as the narrators of the novel.

From the perspective of Nanapush, Fleur is a real victim, like many others including himself, of harsh winters, diseases, starvation, government policies, and the scheming of outsiders such as lumber companies and even mixed-blood Indians. A bond exists between Nanapush and Fleur, who warmly calls him "uncle" and treats him as such. For Nanapush, however, Fleur is not only human and daughterly, but also symbolic of the historical predicament of the Anishinabe. As a young woman, Fleur has won his recognition by holding on to the traditional way of life, thus making her an ideal companion for a young man like Eli, who also lives by traditional ways. Thanks to her spiritual and moral strength, which surpasses her passion for Eli, she has turned into a woman warrior in the end, though paying the high price of losing her daughter and husband for her refusal to compromise.

The charming and eerie qualities of Fleur as a character are largely derived from Pauline's narration, unreliable as it is because of Pauline's delusions. From her perspective, Fleur is both a peer and a legend. As a peer, she is a model and a rival for Pauline, who is fascinated and overshadowed by her magnetic attraction, especially her sexuality, which Pauline tries to emulate, or else jeopardize. As a legend in the eyes of Pauline, Fleur is not only a miraculous survivor of drownings and hardships, but also a powerful sorceress endowed by the lake monster with the ability to wreak havoc. Yet as Pauline's religious fanaticism increases, for her Fleur begins to lose her individuality; instead, she has come to stand for the kind of Satanic paganism that Pauline must deter and oppose. Willfully, Pauline has turned Fleur into a flat character by obliterating the latter's genuine personality, an important part of which is Fleur's humane treatment of her and her nephew.

Because of her delusions, Pauline is an eccentric character. She is given more character development and psychological depth than the others, and her own experiences are rather extraordinary. Not unlike Fleur, she is a victim of the times; being a mixed-blood, however, allows her to imagine and to test the possibility of being non-Indian. Her confusions about herself as a woman and as an Indian have led to blunders of calamitous proportions, as for example her sexual liaison with Napoleon and her scheme on Sophie and Eli. Overcompensating for her guilt as well as her sense of insecurity, Pauline becomes a devious megalomaniac who, in the name of white religion, sanctifies herself and demonizes the others, in effect becoming an instrument of oppression with a martyr complex. From a literary point of view, however, Pauline's psychological problem is also the source of the many magically dramatic episodes in the novel.

By contrast, in the case of Nanapush, the cultural model for his character is not Christian saints but the Native American trickster. Not only is his name reminiscent of the trickster figure Naanabozho, his wit, resourcefulness, and trickery in both speech and action also qualify him as a trickster. More important, just as the trickster can be a cultural hero, Nanapush has indeed become a hero of his tribe in his struggle, as an elder and later on as the tribal chairman, to regain control of the tribe's destiny. Being the foster parent of Lulu, whom he teaches to respect her mother and appreciate her origin, Nanapush embodies the vitality and resilience of the native culture.

Intricately related to one another in life but diametrically opposed in their perspectives, Nanapush and Pauline together provide a fantastic and yet realistic portrayal of Fleur as a stubborn survivor of her clan. In the process of their narration, they also characterize themselves and each other as representatives of two ways of life emanating from a single tragedy.

Themes and Meanings

The struggle for survival is one of the most obvious themes in *Tracks*. All the major characters in the novel are survivors of not only the environment, famines, and epidemics, but also the historical reality of genocide, dispossession, and deprivation. Despite the sense of doom overshadowing the entire Matchimanito reservation upon the encroachment of outside interests, however, upholders of the tribe's cultural tradition have fought in the best way they can: Fleur by crushing the lumber crew and Nanapush by campaigning for the position of tribal chairman.

The struggle for survival, which reaches tragic proportions, is closely related to the theme of cultural conflict. Ostensibly, the Christianity of Pauline, though half-baked, is pitted against the traditional wisdom of Nanapush, who is nevertheless conversant with white culture. The native way of life, together with its tribal kinship system and symbiotic relationship with the environment, is challenged by the white way of life, including its nuclear family, exploitation of natural resources, greed for land, and oppression by legal codes. The mixed-bloods, caught between the two ways of life, lean toward one pole or the other, but while adapting to the cultural change, they also exhibit symptoms of dysfunctionality and confusion. Their predicament, which is epitomized by the conversion of Pauline, pervasive alcoholism, incestuous marriages aimed at amassing land, the subsequent loss of land due to swindling, the disintegration of family ties, and so forth, is also a kind of tragedy bordering on pathos.

Out of the entropic and fragmentary chaos created by cultural conflict, however, in *Tracks* there are also prospects of a cultural synthesis, which conceivably could begin from the mutual "contamination" of the white and the native cultural conditions. Pauline's Christianity, for example, is rife with indigenous beliefs and visions, whereas Nanapush, despite his traditionalism, is conditionally receptive to the white practices that hold promises for the revival of the tribe. These mutual "contaminations" suggest the possibility of certain cultural exchanges that might lead to a new consciousness for the community.

The drive toward a new consciousness is in fact the motivating force behind the seemingly dichotomized perspectives of Nanapush and Pauline, whose narratives are dialogic rather than mutually exclusive, though in the competition for credibility and authority it is Nanapush's narrative that succeeds in reestablishing a sense of order. Significantly, the implied audience of Nanapush, Lulu, can be regarded as the receptacle of the new consciousness. Growing up in the middle of her mother's struggles but educated at the government school, where she is segregated from her traditional heritage, Lulu is not unlike the mixed-bloods trapped between two worlds. Nanapush exhorts her to seek out Fleur, and despite her resistance to his narrative (she stops her ears), she is inevitably reintroduced to her roots and the destiny of her people. Although the formation of the new consciousness hinges on Lulu's willingness and ability to integrate the two cultures in her future life, Nanapush has left enough tracks for the pursuit through his artful storytelling.

Critical Context

   Tracks (1988) is designed, chronologically, as the first in a tetralogy about the lives of a group of Anishinabe originating from Matchimanito, a fictional locale based on the White Earth Reservation in North Dakota. The action started in *Tracks* is extended and expanded in *The Beet Queen* (1986) and *Love Medicine* (1984). Because the characters in the novels are intricately related through marriages and liaisons, they constitute a huge, extended family; as such, the cycle can be seen broadly as a family saga. Since the novels share in common the technique of multiple narrators who have stories of their own to tell, the polyphonic saga as a whole is an archive of a cross-section of Native Americans whose destinies intersect and diverge.

   The creation of Matchimanito as a world populated by characters steeped in the myths and legends of the Anishinabe is by no means just an aesthetic diversion. Rivaling William Faulkner's Yoknapatawpha County, Mississippi, in the magnitude of social significance, the world of Matchimanito is also a space for history to be rediscovered, imagined, explored, clarified, and interpreted.

   Tracks is a literary text charged with such a historical mission, the focal concern of which is the dispossession of native land and its aftermath. As Louise Erdrich and Michael Dorris explained in a 1988 article, "Who Owns the Land?," by that time only 53,100 out of 830,000 acres originally promised to the Anishinabe remained in the tribe's possession. The grim conditions on the White Earth Reservation, on which Matchimanito is based, epitomize the historical injustices imposed upon the Anishinabe and exemplify the intercultural and internal conflicts as well as the social problems created by the legal instruments of the United States government. Although Erdrich as an artist has always resisted moralizations, the collective memory by which her novel is informed leaves conspicuous tracks to be traced.

Bibliography

Brogan, Kathleen. "Haunted by History: Louise Erdrich's *Tracks*." *Prospects* 21 (Annual, 1996): 169-192. Brogan focuses on the themes of death and preoccupation with the past. She views Erdrich's novel as a "contemporary Ghost Dance," suggests that translation is necessary to the survival of Native American culture, and shows how Nanpush and Pauline try to establish history by reconstructing the past.

Burdick, Debra. "Louise Erdrich's *Love Medicine, The Beet Queen*, and *Tracks*: An Annotated Survey of Criticism Through 1994." *American Indian Culture and Research Journal* 20 (Summer, 1996): 137-166. Discusses the cyclical nature of time, diversity of narratives, lyrical prose style, tragicomic appeals of characters (including the trickster figure), and the cultural significance of three of Erdrich's novels.

Larson, Sidner. "The Fragmentation of a Tribal People in Louise Erdrich's *Tracks*." *American Indian Culture and Research Journal* 17 (Spring, 1993): 1-13. A review of the novel, with special focus on the impact of the General Allotment Act of 1887, which was to divide tribally allotted lands among individual Native Americans.

Peterson, Nancy J. "History, Postmodernism, and Louise Erdrich's *Tracks*." *PLMA* 109 (October, 1994): 982-994. Peterson argues that *Tracks* is neither historical realism nor postmodern historical fiction. Instead it lays the foundation for a new historicity and reform history, which has been destroyed by poststructuralists. An interesting analysis of the novel.

Rainwater, Catherine. "Reading Between Worlds: Narrativity in the Fiction of Louise Erdrich." *American Literature* 62 (September, 1990): 405-422. A semiotic reading of *Tracks*, focusing on narrative codes that contribute to its thematization of liminality, fragmentation, and cultural conflict.

Tanrisal, Meldan. "Mother and Child Relationships in the Novels of Louise Erdrich." *American Studies International* 35 (October, 1997): 67-79. Tanrisal examines key mother figures in Erdrich's work, including Marie Kashpaw in *Love Medicine*; and Pauline Puyat, the "anti-mother," and Fleur Pillager, the "mythic mother," in *Tracks*.

Towery, Margie. "Continuity and Connection: Characters in Louise Erdrich's Fiction." *American Indian Culture and Research Journal* 16 (Fall, 1992): 99-122. An overview article that maps out the intricate—fragmented but connected—relationships among the characters in Tracks, *The Beet Queen*, *Love Medicine*, and episodes possibly intended for the fourth volume of the family saga.

Balance Chow

THE TREASURE OF THE SIERRA MADRE

Author: B. Traven (Berick Traven Torsvan, 1890-1969)
Type of plot: Adventure
Time of plot: The 1920's
Locale: Mexico
First published: Der Schatz der Sierra Madre, 1927 (English translation, 1934)

> *Principal characters:*
> DOBBS, a penniless American struggling to survive in Mexico
> CURTIN, another American who joins Dobbs after they are both cheated
> by an unscrupulous employer
> HOWARD, an old prospector who understands both the lure and danger
> of the search for gold
> LACAUD, a prospector who has dedicated his life to finding one of the
> fabled mines of the Aztecs

The Novel

    The Treasure of the Sierra Madre describes three down-on-their-luck adventurers as they seek their fortunes mining for gold in the mountains of Mexico. It not only details the physical hardships the men face but also vividly portrays their mental deterioration as the lust for gold overwhelms them.

    The opening of the novel focuses on Dobbs, penniless and out of work, speculating about various methods to get some money. After successfully begging for a peso, he rents a cot at a slum hotel, indulges in a meal, succumbs to a beggar child who sells him a lottery ticket, and attempts to find more money. He makes an unsuccessful search for work in the oil fields and then is briefly employed by an exploitative contractor who refuses to pay his workers. Curtin, another American also cheated by this unscrupulous boss, teams up with Dobbs, and together they force the contractor to give them their full pay.

    Later, the two men encounter an old prospector, Howard, who entertains them with a description of La Mina Agua Verde, source of many of the treasures of the Aztec kings. The tale, dating back to the Spanish conquest, illustrates how the lust for gold drove both conquistadores and monks to exploit the people and environment they encountered. Eventually, the Spaniards were massacred, and the mine disappeared until a college student discovered an old map showing its location. He gathered a group of explorers, including Howard, who found and then lost the mine once again because of selfishness and greed. Tragedy, not wealth, has been the outcome for those who sought its riches.

    Although Dobbs finds himself shaken by the story, he and Curtin quickly conclude that gold could provide an escape from their present impoverished existence. They persuade Howard to join them, and the three set off for the Sierra Madre. It quickly becomes obvious that they would have little chance of survival without Howard. In spite of this, Dobbs repeatedly questions Howard's decisions.

Once they set up camp, the conditions are brutal: extremes of heat and cold, insects, deadly animals, back-breaking labor and no rest. When they begin to extract gold, the situation worsens. The men soon become wary of one another. Howard warns the puzzled Curtin that this is just the first sign of gold fever and that none of them is immune to its symptoms. Disputes become more regular and more severe. Only Howard manages to keep Dobbs and Curtin from seriously harming each other. He also convinces them to break camp and sell their gold in six to eight weeks, a decision that brings them a sense of peace, almost of friendship since they begin planning ahead instead of dwelling on their fears.

One day, Curtin is followed back to camp by another American prospector, Lacaud. His arrival is followed by the appearance of Mexican bandits. Lacaud, recognizing their leader, realizes they recently committed a particularly brutal train robbery, murdering women and children in the name of Christ. The prospectors are almost killed, but Mexican troops arrive and capture the bandits. The three allow Lacaud to stay with them while they break down their camp, realizing he poses no threat since he is totally committed to the search for his own illusory mine. Before they leave, Howard tells another cautionary story about the devastation the lust for gold can bring.

The men are very cautious on their return journey, wishing to avoid the notice of thieves. However, one night while they are eating, some Indians appear, pleading for help for an injured child. Howard leaves with them and treats the boy, who recovers. Because the Indians insist that Howard remain with them so that they can demonstrate their gratitude, Dobbs and Curtin plan to proceed to Durango, where Howard can meet them later. Dobbs even persuades Howard to let the two carry his gold.

Once Howard is gone, Dobbs's increasingly erratic behavior upsets Curtin, who begins to realize that Dobbs plans to kill him if he refuses to steal Howard's share of the gold. Protesting his innocent intentions, Dobbs shoots Curtin. Left alone, Dobbs disintegrates even further. On the outskirts of Durango, he is murdered by three bandits. Howard, now healer to the Indians, is brought to Curtin who is recovering from his wounds. They discover not only that Dobbs was murdered but also that the bandits threw away all but two bags of the gold, thinking it was sand. Howard convinces Curtin to join in his laughter at this ultimate joke of fate.

The Characters

Traven uses his characters, Dobbs, Curtin, Howard, and even Lacaud, to represent different aspects of the human reaction to gold. He presents gold as a chimera that eventually destroys most who follow its lure. The first chapters of the novel present the world from Dobbs's perspective. Although the reader initially views him as a sympathetic figure struggling to survive in an alien environment, Traven also presents many of his less admirable but very human characteristics, as he bullies waiters and other beggars, exerting fully the power that he gets from the money he has been given. He is not the noble worker of much proletarian fiction. While he may be, in fact, a victim of society, he is also a victim of his own behavior. Further evidence of his negative side appears when he first hears the story of La Mina Agua Verde; he suddenly feels the presence of a darker personality that had until this moment remained hidden. Although he is self-aware enough to recognize this warning, he is not self-controlled enough to heed it later. Once the three men set out on their quest, Dobbs becomes the most obviously influenced by fear and greed. When Howard and Curtin save his life, he quickly turns from gratitude to anger because he realizes that his death would have enriched them. Unable to accept their actions at face level, he suspects they too are acting on their greed, hatching some plot he does not yet understand. Dobbs projects his own feeling on those around him. In fact, Dobbs becomes increasingly overwhelmed by this negative emotion until it consumes him.

Initially, Curtin and Dobbs seem very similar. Traven describes them both as men who are filled with grand ideas but who give up easily, finding it more convenient to dream than act. Curtin remains in Dobb's shadow until the end of the novel, when he demonstrates an inner strength and integrity that Dobbs does not possess. Curtin never fully surrenders to his darker side. He refuses to steal Howard's gold, finding it unthinkable. He is unable to kill Dobbs, even when he realizes that this will probably cost him his life. He is like Dobbs was at the novel's opening, before his second self took control: a flawed but sympathetic human being.

Howard from the beginning is presented as more forceful, wiser, more tolerant, and more experienced. Although he also craves gold, he seems as fascinated by the quest and the lore of the hunt as by the gold itself. His perception of humankind and the world around him is ironic yet sympathetic. He continually warns that no individual is immune to temptation. At the novel's end, he can laugh at the loss of the gold, since he has already decided that there seems to be little lasting profit from it. By convincing Curtin to join his laughter rather that succumb to Dobbs's view, he provides some salvation for both of them.

Themes and Meanings

The Treasure of the Sierra Madre is more than a simple adventure story. It is a complex psychological study of how greed may corrupt and eventually destroy not only individuals but also larger groups, even a society. Traven juxtaposes the action of the novel, in which Dobbs degenerates into fear and madness, eventually paying with his life, with stories that indict the greed of the Spanish conquistadores and the complicity of the monks who accompany them. Even modern Mexican and American societies where workers are exploited are shown as flawed.

On the most basic level, the novel vividly demonstrates the devastating effect of greed on each of the three main characters. When Dobbs first hears Howard's story, he feels as if another self has suddenly appeared within him. This darker side of his personality eventually dominates him. Curtin and Howard are shown as men who somehow find the strength to resist evil, more by luck than by superior moral strength. Howard emphasizes this point, refusing to condemn Dobbs, even after he has stolen and attempted to murder Curtin. Throughout the novel, Howard restates that all men are weak enough to succumb if the circumstances are right.

Another theme, one that is present in much of Traven's fiction, is the search for self, for an identity in a society where one's position is determined by wealth and class structure. In the opening chapter, Dobbs describes the paucity of roles open to him, a poverty-stricken American in Mexico. Gold, initially, would seem to provide entry to the world of power, but the novel shows the dangers of clinging to that illusion. Traven portrays a closed society where the poor are forced into limited roles. The murderous bandits become simply a modern version of the monks and conquistadores who slaughtered the Aztecs, a more ruthless version of the capitalists who exploit the working class. They murder and steal in the name of Christ because these are their only opportunities to share in the two greatest sources of power they can imagine, gold and God.

The Indians provide a counterpoint to the ruthlessness of Western civilization. Although they are presented as extremely naïve, in a manner that might appear condescending or patronizing to a modern reader, Traven finds their way of life far superior to that which exists in the world around them.

Critical Context

B. Traven is still one of literature's most mysterious writers. Although he claimed to have been born in Chicago, his first novels were written in German, and he spent much of his life in Mexico. During the course of his career, he is reported to have used as many as twenty-seven different aliases. Traven published several short stories and novels in Germany during the 1920's. *The Treasure of the Sierra Madre*, his third novel, was published in 1927.

Traven's fiction centers on proletarian or working-class protagonists. In his first novel, *Death Ship* (1926), he vividly portrays the evils of both nationalism and capitalism. However, Traven is not a political writer; he does not advocate an alternate system of government. Instead, Traven's characters, often victims of the system, tend to withdraw from it—like Howard, who considers pursuing a life as a medicine man to the Indians. With them, he may find peace and security in a world that is not caught up in greed. Even in characters such as Dobbs, Traven treats his workers with sympathy, viewing them as individuals caught in a society where the trap of capitalism allows them little importance.

Bibliography

Baumann, Michael L. *B. Traven: An Introduction*. Albuquerque: University of New Mexico Press, 1976. Discusses Traven as a proletarian writer, focusing on his attitudes toward nationalism and capitalism. Discusses the novel's tone, vision, and proletarian point of view.

Chankin, Donald O. *Anonymity and Death: The Fiction of B. Traven*. University Park: Pennsylvania State University Press, 1975. Clear, insightful psychoanalytic analysis of character and theme in *The Treasure of the Sierra Madre*. Discusses literary parallels with Geoffrey Chaucer's "Pardoner's Tale" and Edgar Allan Poe's "The Gold Bug."

Mezo, Richard E. *A Study of B. Traven's Fiction: The Journey to Solipaz.* San Francisco: Mellon Research University Press, 1993. A comprehensive critical analysis of theme, character, style, and structure in Traven's fiction. Provides detailed comparisons of the four main characters. Extensive bibliography. A very good introduction to Traven and his fiction.

Schurer, Ernst, and Philip Jenkins, eds. *B. Traven: Life and Work.* University Park: Pennsylvania University Press, 1987. Comprehensive collection of essays analyzing Traven's life as well as major themes, ideas, and motifs in his writing. Provides a historical and political context for Traven's work. Includes several analyses of *The Treasure of the Sierra Madre.*

Stone, Judy. *The Mystery of B. Traven.* Los Altos, Calif.: William Kaufmann, 1977. Includes excerpts from the only extended series of interviews with Traven, including Traven's recollections of the filming of *The Treasure of the Sierra Madre.* Reveals his complex social philosophy. An important source for analyzing Traven's fiction.

Mary E. Mahony

TRIPMASTER MONKEY
His Fake Book

Author: Maxine Hong Kingston (1940-   )
Type of plot: Bildungsroman
Time of plot: The 1960's
Locale: San Francisco and Sacramento, California
First published: 1989

> *Principal characters:*
> WITTMAN AH SING, a Chinese American antiwar activist
> NANCI LEE, the most beautiful Chinese American girl of Wittman's
>   college days, an aspiring actress
> TAÑA DE WEESE, an insurance adjuster who marries Wittman

The Novel

Tripmaster Monkey is Maxine Hong Kingston's portrait of the artist as a Chinese American who attempts to assert his identity by blending together the two sides of his heritage. Using the Vietnam War as the backdrop, Kingston has also captured the exuberant antiestablishment sensibility of the Bay Area, immortalizing the flower-power counterculture of the psychedelic 1960's. Whereas the "tripmaster monkey" in the title alludes to the hero of a Chinese folktale and the hippies of American subculture, the "fake book" refers to the novel's similarity to "music fake books," which, according to Kingston, may contain many basic melodies or plots other people can develop.

The action begins with the depression of Wittman, a fifth-generation native Californian who is contemplating suicide every day after graduating with a bachelor's degree in English from the University of California at Berkeley. Working part-time as a toy salesman at a department store in San Francisco, Wittman, who aspires to be a writer, often feels alienated much the same way as the young poet in Rainer Maria Rilke's *The Notebooks of Malte Laurids Brigge* (1910), passages of which he recites as he goes about his daily business. Conscious of his Chineseness as well as his Americanness and conceited about his intellectual prowess, he looks for others of his kind. His first candidate is Nanci Lee, who aspires to be an actress. He dates her, shows her his trunk of poems, and declares his intention to write a play for her. Offended by her lack of sensitivity to his talents and identity crisis, however, he scares her away by acting crudely.

As the action progresses, Wittman encounters, in his workplace, a "stocking guy," a beatnik-hermit who happens to have been published as a Yale Younger Poet. Though encouraged by him, Wittman finds his own job frustrating; after making clockwork toy monkeys perform simulated copulation on Barbie dolls in front of his customers, he fires himself. Unemployed, he goes to the wedding party of Lance Kamiyama, a Japanese American friend and rival with a successful career. On the way, he runs into Judy Louis, a Chinese American who so bores him to death with her nosiness and snobbishness that he pretends to be Japanese in order to evade her stereotyping. At the party, he engages in round after round of verbal combat and intellectual wrestling, abusing and abused by his friends, with whom he has developed a love-hate relationship. Among the group is Yoshi Ogasawara, a smart pretty woman whom he takes as a nemesis because of her tireless discourse, replete with demonstrations, on the "epicanthic fold" typical of the eyelids of many Asians. Later on at the party, after anecdotal and satirical conversations about films, race, lifestyle, Nazism, nuclear war, and other topics of interest to him, Wittman discover Taña De Weese, a beautiful blonde who descends upon him like an angel. She gets along with him so well that the next morning they start having a serious but unromantic sexual relationship, which shortly afterward leads to their being declared husband and wife by a conscientious objector who claims to be a priest of the Universal Life Church.

Having found the personal and intellectual companionship of Taña, Wittman begins to act purposefully. He takes Taña to Sacramento to visit his mother, Ruby Long Legs (formerly an opera star), and his father, Zeppelin Ah Sing (a retiree who publishes a newsletter advocating the art of living on minimal means). Taña is also introduced to more than a dozen former "Flora Dora girls" who contributed to China's and America's cause during World War II. Their presence inspires Wittman to involve them in his forthcoming play.

During the visit, Wittman learns that his parents have taken PoPo (his grandmother of uncertain origins) out to the Sierra Mountains and abandoned her there. Horrified, he and Taña try to find her but to no avail (as Wittman discovers later, she has gone to San Francisco with a man, Lincoln Fong, her newfound hero and love). Going back to San Francisco, Wittman files for unemployment benefits, lives like a pig with Taña, and concentrates on the writing of his play, which is a formidable melange of folktales derived from classical Chinese novels, with the Monkey King as the main character. With the help of friends, relatives, and the residents of Chinatown, the play is launched in due course at a community center and proves to be a phenomenal success. Upon the triumphant close of the play, the action of which takes several days to complete, Wittman improvises a one-man show. Interacting with the audience, he gives a lengthy but critical monologue about cultural identity, war, love, and lifestyle. The completion of Wittman's apprenticeship as an artist is signaled by the audience's enthusiasm and approval.

The Characters

Although the novel contains several delightful characters, it is Wittman who is the focus throughout; all the others are seen through his eyes. Hence, the entire novel can be regarded as an extended character study of Wittman, with the other characters shedding light on his life and illustrating his philosophy. In characterizing Wittman, Kingston not only captures Wittman in action, but also relies heavily on the prolific verbalization of his inner consciousness.

On the social level, Wittman is characterized as both a misfit and a gadfly with a cause. Unlike his fellow Asian Americans such as Lance, Nanci Lee, and Judy Louis, he is ill prepared, both intellectually and academically, for a stereotypical career (such as engineering) that would readily earn him success and recognition from his peers, parents, relatives, and the mainstream society. This apparent failure is partly responsible for his inferiority complex (and megalomania), which he often exploits by adopting a hostile stance toward the people he comes across, including the new Chinese immigrants in the streets, the customers at the department store, and even his friends at Lance's party. Yet although his life is a shambles, like many other Americans of his generation who defy the draft in order not to fight an unacceptable war in Vietnam, Wittman also stands on a moral high ground, which makes his cynicism an act of courageous rebellion. While his witty diatribes against the stereotyping of Chinese Americans at times sound vindictive and self-contradictory, his outbursts against wars, atomic bombs, Nazism, and modern life bespeak the pacifism of his generation. His concluding monologue is a culmination of this sensibility.

On the cultural level, Wittman is portrayed as a juggler of cultures who, caught between two heritages that he both claims and disclaims, attempts to arrive at a synthesis. On the one hand, as a fifth-generation native Californian, he asserts his American identity by distancing himself from the "F.O.B.'s" (Chinese immigrants "fresh off the boats"). On the other hand, aware of the racial prejudices leveled against Chinese Americans, he also defends the Chineseness of his heritage and berates the insensitivity of those who either subscribe to stereotypes or refuse to recognize Chinese Americans as Americans. On balance, although Wittman is equally obsessed with certain aspects of both cultures (such as films and Cantonese operas), for him, Chineseness—in the way he defines it—weighs a little more than Americanness, because it is by Chineseness that he hopes to redefine his American identity. This is best symbolized by his relationships with two young women. He loses Nanci Lee, a Chinese American, but wins Taña, a Caucasian, essentially for the same reason: his insistence on being an American of Chinese descent, warts and all. His success as an artist would not have been possible without such a commitment.

Themes and Meanings

The themes and meanings of *Tripmaster Monkey* are derived from the character of Wittman as an artist and a Chinese American. As an apprentice to the art of writing, Wittman is sufficiently prepared—even tediously erudite—for his calling, but he has yet to find a voice to win recognition. Kingston's constant reference to *The Notebooks of Malte Laurids Brigge* is a reminder of this lonely struggle. This struggle is set back, early in the novel, by Wittman's failure to impress Nanci Lee with his poetry and by the realization that even a published Yale Younger Poet is going nowhere and has abandoned poetry altogether. With his sense of alienation compounded by such loneliness, his identity crisis as a writer intensifies. Fortunately, however, Wittman's artistic career is saved by his own cultural heritage and family upbringing, the common denominator of which is the folk tradition. The Cantonese opera, the cultural fabric that sustained generations of Chinese Americans (who in turn have helped to shape America into the country it is), contains materials from Chinese novels that can somehow be used to address the issues of the times; the form, however, has fallen into oblivion. Wittman's genius lies in the realization that he is the artist who could rebuild the Pear Garden (the Chinese theater) in the West and give a new life to this theater. Creating order out of the chaos of his life and his world, he has launched a communal play with a pacifist vision, winning instant approval and blessing from the community. In this sense, the one-man show in the last chapter is not a manic monologue but rather a celebration of his newfound voice as an artist who has come of age.

Closely connected with Wittman's struggle as an artist and a draft-dodging hippie is his campaign against the notion that the Chinese people are inscrutable and cannot be American. Wittman is exasperated by the fact that, wherever he turns—in films, readings, and daily life—Chinese Americans have been mistreated, misunderstood, misrepresented, and above all excluded from the definition of "American" despite the fact that they have created part of America. Because the American self as he knows it is defined by ethnicity, he is provoked into obnoxious harangues whenever people fail to acknowledge the validity of this uncompromisable definition. Even Chinese Americans are legitimate targets of his attacks when they subscribe to Caucasian views. This theme of Wittman's self-definition is recapitulated throughout the novel. Invariably angry whenever he thinks about it, Wittman cannot resist sarcastic tirades that seem never to end—hence the Rabelaisian verbosity of the novel. Concomitant with the theme of self-definition are Wittman's efforts to rediscover, reclaim, and celebrate his Chinese heritage and share it with his community, by preaching if necessary. Such an affirmation of his Chineseness does not contradict his position that he is an American, but it does complicate his self-definition somewhat; his challenge hence hinges on how he can grapple with both his American and Chinese identities at the same time without compromising either one. Ultimately, it is both heritages on which he wishes to lay his hands as a "Chinese no hyphen American."

Critical Context

Tripmaster Monkey is Kingston's answer to critics who, unable to decide whether her earlier book-length narratives (*The Woman Warrior: Memoirs of a Girlhood Among Ghosts*, 1976 and *China Men*, 1980) are factual or fictional, hesitate to give full credit for her work. Kingston writes *Tripmaster Monkey* as a testimony of her abilities and as a proof of her belief that fiction is by no means more difficult to write than memoirs and family histories. More important, having told the story of her parents' generation in two separate narratives, Kingston finds it appropriate to shift attention to her own generation, who have come of age as biculturals with problems, solutions, imaginations, and visions of their own. *Tripmaster Monkey* is only the beginning of an ongoing statement about such a generation, with Wittman as its impressive spokesman.

What Wittman has achieved in the novel has great symbolic significance for many Chinese Americans. Combining two kinds of wisdoms culled from two cultures, Wittman has put the history of America into the perspective of the Cantonese operas that once sustained the communities of Chinese pioneers who helped to develop the frontiers of the United States. By involving the community in reviving the Chinese theater, Wittman has fulfilled his personal quest as well as given a new life to an old tradition. Above all, through Wittman, Kingston has added an indelible historical dimension to the myth of the American Dream.

Wittman also addresses issues that concern the United States as a whole. As Kingston suggests, nothing in modern life is immune to Wittman's cornucopian if cynical commentaries. Impulsive as he is, Wittman is actually quite systematic in his protest against the dehumanizing condition of modern society, which at its worst moments has given rise to the Holocaust, nuclear weapons, and the Vietnam War. Through his cross-cultural and trans-temporal play, Wittman is stating that war and its propaganda ought to stop, that history has proven how even the best of warriors with the best tactics and the best weapons have invariably lost, and that peace, not war, is the real revolution of the modern world.

Bibliography

Chang, Hsiao-hing. "Gender Crossing in Maxine Hong Kingston's *Tripmaster Monkey.*" *MELUS* 22 (Spring, 1997): 15-34. Chang explores the ways in which Kingston intertwines two kinds of gender crossing: masculine gender anxiety and feminine blurring of gender boundaries. Within this context, Chang discusses Kingston's use of psychic and linguistic dislocations to destablize fact/fiction, history/myth, and Chinese/American polarities.

Furth, Isabella. "Bee-e-een! Nation, Transformation, and the Hyphen of Ethnicity in Kingston's *Tripmaster Monkey.*" *Modern Fiction Studies* 40 (Spring, 1994): 33-49. Furth explores the continuous transformations and complex relations between nation, ethnicity, and wounds caused by separation in the world Kingston has created. She focuses on the hyphen, a symbol of both the blending and distinctiveness of the Chinese and American cultures.

Ling, Amy. *Between Worlds: Women Writers of Chinese Ancestry.* New York: Pergamon Press, 1990. Contains an informative section on *Tripmaster Monkey.* The book is also an excellent introduction to the tradition behind Kingston.

Lowe, John. "Monkey Kings and Mojo: Postmodern Ethnic Humor in Kingston, Reed, and Vizenor." *MELUS* 21 (Winter, 1996): 103-126. Lowe's examination reveals Kingston, Vizenor, and Reed's novels as examples of ethnic humor from a postmodern perspective. Focusing on the trickster character in each novel, he demonstrates that the works owe much to the folklore tradition of Chinese, Native American, and African cultures.

Schueller, Malini J. "Theorizing Ethnicity and Subjectivity: Maxine Hong Kingston's *Tripmaster Monkey* and Amy Tan's *Joy Luck Club.*" *Genders* (Winter, 1992): 72-85. Schueller presents an analysis of Kingston and Tan's novels, focusing on the common theme of discovering a feminine identity that does not marginalize racial or ethnic orientations.

Tanner, James T. F. "Walt Whitman's Presence in Maxine Hong Kingston's *Tripmaster Monkey: His Fake Book.*" *MELUS* 20 (Winter, 1995): 61-74. Tanner explores the numerous references to Walt Whitman in Kingston's novel. He particularly focuses on the main character, Whitman Ah Sing, and demonstrates how the character's mottos follow the poet's own ideas for America.

Balance Chow

TRITON

Author: Samuel R. Delany (1942-   )
Type of plot: Science fiction
Time of plot: A.D. 2112, after humankind has colonized Mars and several moons of planets in the solar system
Locale: Triton, a moon of Neptune, and Earth
First published: 1976

Principal characters:

BRON HELSTROM, the protagonist, a metalogician checking computer outcomes, who becomes a woman

GENE TRIMBELL, an actress, playwright, director, producer, and teacher whom Bron loves and whose working name is The Spike

LAWRENCE, an old homosexual friend to Bron, intelligent and kindly

SAM, brilliant black diplomat, formerly a blonde waitress; Bron is attracted to him but envies him

AUDRI, Bron's boss and a lesbian mother of three children who falls in love with Bron when Bron is a woman

MIRIAMNE, a lesbian Bron rejects for a job after attempting to start a relationship with her

BRIAN, Bron's therapist after Bron's sex change

The Novel

Much of the action of *Triton* appears to take place in the mind of Bron Helstrom, the protagonist. Helstrom, unhappy in the seemingly Utopian society of an urban dome on Triton, seeks others to love him, to define him. He makes an appeal to The Spike, the woman he loves: "Help me. Take me. Make me whole." Much later in the novel, after his sex change, Bron makes a similar appeal to Sam, another person whom he admires, "Take me to another world . . . I don't care. I don't know if I can move on my own anymore. . . ." Bron's problem is that he does not know what he wants from a culture of groups, co-ops, and communes largely based on religious and sexual preferences. If he knew what he wanted, Bron could connect to the subcultures of Triton to obtain the pleasure, community, and respect he wants and needs.

Bron's failings, in part, make satellite culture *An Ambiguous Heterotopia* (the novel's subtitle). If Michel Foucault's heterotopia in *The Order of Things* (1966) challenges the idea of Utopia, Delany's ambiguous heterotopia goes even further. How can Utopian society aid someone such as Bron who does not know what he truly wants?

Bron, at the beginning of the novel, wonders whether he is happy. His uncertainty turns to doubt when he encounters a microtheater production written, directed, and produced by The Spike. Love for The Spike unsettles Bron's narcissism, especially because Bron is only a needing, not a giving, self. Unlike his friends Sam and Lawrence, Bron cannot be empathetic to the needs of others. Feeling his hollowness, Bron's potential and real lovers flee from him, although each tries to treat him/her kindly. To satisfy his own aimlessness and loneliness, Bron changes his sex to become the kind of woman the male Bron would desire: This solves nothing.

Bron is so wrapped up in his own needs that he repeatedly fails to see and respond to the needs of those about him. He expects others to feel his need when he temporarily loses his job as a metalogician, but he is unsympathetic to the plight of Miriamne, a lesbian whom he refuses to hire as an assistant, even though she is able, because she spurns his sexual advances. Bron is ignorant of the potential of war with Earth until, as a traveler with a satellite diplomatic delegation, he is incarcerated for a short time and questioned. Even the plight of the dead and dying on Lux and the near total devastation of Earth's population fail to attract Bron's notice. While Bron's selfishness makes him a largely unsympathetic character, his needs do elicit some sympathy, which Delany uses to challenge the structure of the society he creates on Triton and the behavior of the many men resembling Bron in our own society.

The Characters

Born on Mars, the youngest of five children of unsuccessful Martian colonists from Earth, Bron left home at fifteen to become a male prostitute catering to older women, and it is thus that he first learns to respond according to the type and power of the person he encounters. This thinking in types leads to Bron's occupation on Triton as a metalogician checking computer outcomes; it also leads to Bron's weaknesses as a person—he is continually pinning labels on people, making them his inferiors: The Spike is a woman, sometimes a "bitch"; Lawrence is an old homosexual or queer; Sam is a black. In this life of types, Bron is either dominating someone or that someone is dominating him. Types exercise a tyranny over Bron, as he continually worries about correct behavior in society, whether in space travel, eating at a restaurant, or meeting a potential lover. Desperate to know the type of a person, Bron has no knowledge of the individual within the type, no sympathy for others. A devoted fan of ice operas, Bron is forever separating his fellowman into the ice-opera equivalent of the cowboys and the Indians, or the good guys and the bad guys.

The Spike, or Gene Trimbell, is described by Bron as the wholesome, healthy brat of Ganymede ice-farmers "living the romantic life as a theatrical producer in the swinging, unlicensed sector of the city." This description, however, fails to account for The Spike's theatrical creativity in directing and producing her own plays designed for audiences of one, nor does it account for her honesty and integrity in her emotional interactions with people, her sympathy for the suffering of others, or the joy with which she meets new experiences. Although Bron tries to type The Spike, she always transcends the limits that Bron perceives and masters her experiences by acknowledging ignorance and asking questions.

Lawrence, too, is much more than the old homosexual Bron thinks him to be. A native of South Africa, Lawrence immigrated to Triton as a protest against the injustices he saw in South Africa. After a gravity wave destroys much of Triton's urban development, it is Lawrence who attempts to rescue others, since he, unlike Bron, can imagine and empathize with the difficulties that others face. Despite Bron's many slights, Lawrence is able to be kind to Bron when Bron needs kindness. An intelligent man and a master of strategic thinking, Lawrence, at the novel's end, joins a music commune, continuing his development.

Sam, according to Bron, is a stereotype of black virility. Sam began as a sallow, blonde waitress with too much intelligence for her job, but through the medical and psychological technology on Triton, he changes his sex, personality, and race. Around the co-op home which Lawrence, Bron, and Sam share with several others, Sam helps the group and the individuals within it with grace and without apparent effort. Aware of how others think and feel, Sam is able to act wisely and well, whether for the good of Serpent House, the unaligned male co-op that he shares with Bron, or for the good of Triton and the other satellites.

Themes and Meanings

While *Triton* is a Utopian novel testing the degree of happiness possible in a society characterized by sex-based communal living arrangements and a welfare state without a policing bureaucracy, with Sam, Lawrence, and The Spike its most successful citizens and Bron and the maladjusted Prynn and Alfred its least successful, the novel is more than that. Bron as a central character not only measures the success of the social arrangements and government but also provides the largely male reading audience of science fiction with a window through which to see the white traditional male of American society, the "majority configuration"—which is really a minority on Triton.

One of the problems of the traditional male, as Bron's counselor explains prior to Bron's sex change, is that his logic tells only about "possible relations of elements that are already known." It gives no tools to analyze more basic knowns or unknowns, nor can it deal effectively with changing processes. This higher reasoning skill is possessed by the creative people in *Triton*, particularly by the women, such as The Spike, who knows and escapes the tyranny of types.

This higher reasoning is described by Delany outside the novel in two appendices that accompany the text: "From the Triton Journal," an essay defining science fiction with two rejected pieces from the novel, and "Ashima Slade and the Harbin-Y Lectures." Although both appendices treat this new reasoning process, the second is more significant. Here, Delany appropriates a time-honored fictional device: An editor has put together notes of students and Colleagues of Ashima Slade and lecture notes and citations from Slade's previous books to describe a new theory of knowledge based on reflected-wave models, where any sensory input results in a change in the randomness of neural impulses. What Slade, a character who changed sex twice in his lifetime, suggests in the learning theory is that knowledge is a modular calculus description characterized by harmonies challenging randomness. This thinking is closer to music, to Susanne Langer's feeling as form, than it is to conventional logic of the sort that

Bron knows. To Delany in this novel, feminine intuition scores higher as a learning tool than does conventional male logic. The novel thus makes a strong feminist statement.

Critical Context

Most critics of Delany believe that the work he did in the middle 1960's is his best—*Babel-17* (1966), *The Einstein Intersection* (1967), and *Nova* (1968). *Dhalgren* (1975), published a year before *Triton*, is considered wordy and self-indulgent by many critics, especially when compared with the artistic compression of Delany's early works. *Triton* is more like the early work than *Dhalgren*, and it concerns itself with the same issues as Delany's great novels.

Delany's interests in psychology, language, communication, knowledge, and sexuality, as seen in an early novel such as *Babel-17*, are here in *Triton* as well. There is less verbal economy in *Triton* than in the novels of the middle 1960's, in part as a result of the type of protagonist that Delany uses. Bron is both the central character and an object of satire; consequently, the novel is more expansive than it would be if the brilliant poetess-heroine of *Babel-17* were solving the fictive problems. Bron does not simply act; he exhibits behavior of the traditional male which Delany mocks. Dramatizing Bron's bad behavior for the purpose of satire takes time. In the case of *Triton*, which is best described as a philosophical feminist novel, time is well used.

Bibliography

Blackford, Russell. "Jewels in Junk City: To Read *Triton.*" *The Review of Contemporary Fiction* 16 (Fall, 1996): 142-147. Blackford examines the inconsistencies in Delany's novel, noting that readers are sometimes jarred by Delany's rapid shifts of scene, internal interruptions in plot, and characters who depend on unreliable information. However, Blackford asserts that the reader can overcome these distractions by focusing on the playful tone of the novel.

Delany, Samuel. "On *Triton* and Other Matters: An Interview with Samuel R. Delany." Interview by Robert M. Philmus, Renee Lallier, and Robert Copp. *Science-Fiction Studies* 17 (November, 1990): 295-324. A wide-ranging interview in which Delany discusses a variety of topics, including the influence of the theory of quantum uncertainty on contemporary literature; the ways in which American science fiction shaped the Vietnam War; the search for the literary origins of science fiction; and the writing of his novel, *Triton*.

Massé, Michelle. "'All You Have to Do Is Know What You Want': Individual Expectations in *Triton.*" In *Coordinates: Placing Science Fiction and Fantasy*, edited by Eric S. Rabkin, Robert Scholes, and George E. Slusser. Carbondale: Southern Illinois University Press, 1983. Examines the role of desire in Delany's novel *Triton* (1976), which like many of Delany's novels has a strong sexual theme. *Triton* is similar to *Stars in My Pocket Like Grains of Sand* in use of technology to adapt people's thinking; in *Triton*, people can voluntarily change their sexual preferences as well as their sexuality.

Sallis, James, ed. *Ash of Stars: On the Writing of Samuel R. Delany.* Jackson: University Press of Mississippi, 1996. An interesting collection of critical essays by various scholars that address specific aspects of Delany's fiction. Includes an essay on *Triton*, as well as a selected bibliography.

_____. "Samuel R. Delany: An Introduction." *The Review of Contemporary Fiction* 16 (Fall, 1996): 90-96. Offers brief background information on Delany's life and career. Discusses Delany's reputation as a major critical voice in science fiction, as well as the unifying factors in his work, including central characters as storytellers, revolutions with real consequences, and sexual concerns. Sallis also takes note of Delany's thoughts on the points Blackford makes in the essay cited above.

Craig Barrow

TRUE CONFESSIONS

Author: John Gregory Dunne (1932-   )
Type of plot: Detective and mystery
Time of plot: The 1940's and the 1970's
Locale: Southern California
First published: 1977

> *Principal characters:*
> FRANK CROTTY, a Los Angeles Police Department (LAPD) detective
> LORENZO JONES, a black police detective who becomes mayor
> BINGO MCINERNEY, Jones's racist white partner
> LOIS FAZENDA, a murder victim whose body is cut in half
> TOM SPELLACY, an LAPD detective, the novel's narrator
> DESMOND (DES) SPELLACY, Tom's brother and a monsignor in the
>   Catholic Church
> MARY MARGARET SPELLACY, Tom's wife
> CORINNE, Tom's mistress
> BRENDA SAMUELS, a madam connected to Jack Amsterdam and Tom
>   Spellacy
> FRED FUQUA, Tom's ambitious boss
> DAN T. CAMPION, an attorney who does business for the Catholic
>   archdiocese
> SONNY MCDONOUGH, a contractor who does jobs for the archdiocese
> JACK AMSTERDAM, the chairman of the archdiocese building fund
> CARDINAL DANAHER, Des's superior

The Novel

True Confessions is the story of two brothers, Tom and Des Spellacy. The novel begins and ends in the 1970's, when Tom has retired from the police department and Des, an ambitious Catholic clergyman, is spending the last of his thirty years of exile in a small, neglected parish. Somehow Tom's actions have led to his brother's downfall, and the heart of the novel, "Then" (set in the 1940's), tells the story that leads to "Now," the first and last chapters.

The first "Now" section centers on Des's call to Tom. Why, Tom wonders, is he being summoned to Des's parish in the desert? The brothers have been intensely preoccupied with each other and yet estranged. Although one has chosen a career in the police department and the other the church, they are both worldly men. Tom cannot seem to live down his corrupt period on the vice squad, when he was "on the take," acting as a bagman for Jack Amsterdam, a pillar of the church and a supposedly legitimate contractor who is in fact a thug with numerous illicit enterprises. Amsterdam is the link between the careers of the two brothers, since Des has relied on Amsterdam to construct many of the church's most impressive buildings, even though Des knows that Amsterdam has padded his payroll and physically intimidated other contractors so that they have not put in bids for church construction projects. Des has also functioned as a kind of enforcer for Cardinal Danaher, who is trying to centralize power by depriving parish priests of their autonomy.

When the two brothers meet in the opening section of the novel, Des tells Tom that he is dying. It is this announcement that precipitates the action of the novel, as Tom remembers the events that have led to his brother's dramatic announcement.

"Then" begins as a traditional murder mystery. A woman is found with her body hacked in two. There is no blood, which suggests that the body has been moved from another location. The cut is clean, indicating that a very sharp, professional instrument was used. Tom Spellacy, Frank Crotty, Bingo McInerney, and Lorenzo Jones show up at the crime scene. There is much humor and character development in this episode. Although Bingo is quite stupid, he ridicules his black partner Lorenzo Jones, who takes meticulous notes (eventually, these will become important in Tom's solution of the crime). Jones ignores McInerney and does his job with a painstaking professionalism and desire to succeed that foretell his future as mayor. Crotty, an old hand, remains unmoved by the gory scene, worried only about a "hook," a catchy phrase for the murder that will play well in the press. The tag that finally satisfies him is "The Virgin Tramp," a ridiculous epithet for a young woman who came to Hollywood looking to become a star but who had to settle for whoredom instead.

Tom Spellacy is goaded into action by his boss, Fred Fuqua, who is bucking to become chief of police. Fuqua is a systems man. He claims to be able to find patterns in crime, though he has little sense of street life or of how crime is committed. He is an excellent politician, though, and following Frank Crotty's advice, Tom controls his contempt for a superior who is less a policeman than a politician. What also goads Tom, though, is his intuition that larger forces—namely Jack Amsterdam—are somehow connected with the mutilated body, which is eventually identified as that of Lois Fazenda. Because he cannot live down the period when he succumbed to corruption and collected money for Amsterdam, Tom is determined to root out the crooked cause of Fazenda's murder.

How Tom is led to the true murderer—which involves framing Amsterdam—should not be revealed, for it would spoil the superb plotting of this taut novel, but suffice it to say that by gunning for Amsterdam, Tom is also setting in motion the forces that expose his brother Des's complicity in evil and lead to his banishment from the center of power.

The Characters

One of the hallmarks of the detective novel is the use of suspense and of stereotyped characters. Dunne deftly delays the denouement of his novel by giving Tom more and more leads to follow, even as Jack Amsterdam carefully conceals himself by multiple masks of respectability. So frustrated is Tom that, in a key scene, he embarrasses Des and Armstrong at lunch by reminding Armstrong that he was once his bagman. As expected in the detective-story genre, Tom as detective is relentless. He is a deeply flawed character, and perhaps that is why he cannot abide others such as Amsterdam and his brother who profess to be pious. Tom recognizes the difference between his brother and Amsterdam, and Tom does go out of his way to help Des. Yet the hostility between the brothers remains.

Des is a fully rounded character. He realizes that his ambitions make him almost inhuman and mock his religious scruples. He wants to do good things for the church, but he is willing to cut corners and make compromises in order to satisfy the ruthless cardinal, who will support Des only so long as Des produces results. The cardinal and Des serve each other. Des will get his promotion so long as he does the cardinal's bidding and does not embarrass him. Yet the embarrassment seems inevitable with a brother who will not quit an investigation that becomes inconvenient, and then humiliating, for the archdiocese.

Dunne's handling of female characters is humorous and sophisticated. Tom's wife, Mary Margaret, is in a mental institution; she believes that she has conversations with a saint. She is a tormented woman, since it is clear that the man she has always really loved is Des. Tom was the consolation prize. Tom knows of Mary Margaret's preference, and he has turned to other women. His current mistress, Corinne, he once saved by persuading the man who abducted her that she was a lesbian. The police were ready the storm the hostage-taker, but Tom was able to talk him out of a shootout. Yet Tom cannot love Corinne, for he cannot get over her sexually active past. If he cannot condone his own corruption, he certainly cannot absolve her. For Tom, there is no pardon, which is what makes his pursuit of Jack Amsterdam and the downfall of his brother inevitable.

Dunne's handling of minor characters—Fuqua and Cardinal Danaher, for example—is impressive. Although Fuqua is a fool from Tom's perspective, the narrative does full justice to his bureaucratic maneuvering and his go-getter personality. Similarly, while Danaher is in the plot to help motivate Des's swim-or-sink mentality, he is also a person in his own right, recognizing that his powers are failing, disliking Des for his obvious relish of power, but willing to profit form his protégé's manipulative personality.

Themes and Meanings

As with so many detective stories, the principal theme of *True Confessions* is human corruption. The irony is that it is Tom, not Des, who is fixated on a flawed world. He has sinned, and he is determined to root out other sinners. Des, who hears confessions, does little more than dole out conventional penances. Yet Tom is so hard on himself and others that he allows no room for restitution. He isolates himself, and he exposes others in his single-minded quest to solve crimes. His motivations are hardly pure. Frank Crotty resists Tom's plan to frame Amsterdam, for he has figured out—as has Tom—who really murdered Lois Fazenda. Tom, it seems, is really out to bring down Amsterdam, no matter what happens to others.

True Confessions presents a world of corrupt institutions—whether it is the police department or the church. The novel seems to argue that corruption as such can never be exterminated. Tom's tragedy is that, unlike most people, he cannot live with some corruption while doing his best to minimize his participation in it. He is an absolutist; it is all or nothing, pure or impure. In this respect, he resembles Mary Margaret, who withdraws from the world rather than confront her own implication in its evils. The character who presents a middle way, so to speak, is Corinne. Like Tom, she has a shady past, but unlike him, she believes in redemption, in love. She will take Tom as he is, recognizing his effort to do the best he can, yet he cannot accept her terms. His deterministic bent, his sense of original sin, prevents him from getting on with his life and from forgiving his brother's hypocrisies.

Dunne uses the genre of the detective story to present a compelling drama about a world of difficult choices, of human personalities faced with the same fundamental choices no matter whether the realm is the political, the personal, or the religious. Crime—its causes, solutions, and consequences—becomes a metaphor for the human condition itself.

Critical Context

John Gregory Dunne is noted for his stories and essays about Irish-American life and popular culture. *True Confessions* was both a popular and a critical success when it first was published, and it was later turned into a movie starring Robert DeNiro and Sean Penn. The novel has remained one of Dunne's key works, complementing his screenwriting and essays about the culture of Hollywood and Southern California. His fine ear for dialogue, and his fast-paced narrative account in part for his popularity. Yet it is his moral concerns that provide his stories with depth. He is not didactic—that is, he is not preaching lessons. Rather, the messages or morals of his stories arise naturally out of plot and character. He demonstrates the consequences of human actions in scenes that seem to appear spontaneously and inevitably.

True Confessions also charts the changes in American life from the 1940's to the 1970's. In the 1940's, it seems unthinkable that Lorenzo Jones, a ridiculed African American detective, should not only be successful on the police force but also one day become mayor of Los Angeles. Here the novel mimics American history, since Tom Bradley, a veteran African American LAPD officer, did in fact become the city's mayor. However, even in the 1970's, in the "Now" sections of the novel, racism persists in Frank Crotty's reference to Jones as a "pickaninny mayor." The irony is that Crotty, a devotee of Chinese food, had Chinese business partners upon whom he relied and who deserted him; Des's most loyal lieutenant in his desert parish is the Hispanic Father Duarte, who believes that Des is as sincere as he is.

From an ethnic perspective, then, *True Confessions* tells the complex story of several immigrant groups—including Poles and Italians—and how they evolved over several decades. In terms of both style and content, Dunne has created a both profoundly accessible and deeply penetrating work of literature.

Bibliography

Dunne, John Gregory. "The Art of Screenwriting II: John Gregory Dunne." Interview by George Plimpton. *Paris Revue* 38 (Spring, 1996): 282-308. In spite of the title, this interview concerns Dunne's fiction as well, concentrating especially on problems with plotting his novels.

_____. *Harp*. New York: Simon & Schuster, 1989. This autobiography explores the roots of Dunne's Irishness and his use of it in his fiction.

_____. Interview by Dermot McEvoy. *Publishers Weekly* 241 (August 22, 1994): 30-31. Focuses on Dunne's Hollywood novel *Playland*. Dunne also discusses his handling of Catholicism, the Irish, and Southern California.

Fine, David, ed. *Los Angeles in Fiction*. Albuquerque: University of New Mexico Press, 1984. Contains one chapter on Dunne's treatment of the city.

Winchell, Mark Royden. *John Gregory Dunne*. Boise, Idaho: Boise State University Press, 1986. An informative introductory study that includes a useful bibliography.

Carl Rollyson

TRUE GRIT

Author: Charles Portis (1933-   )
Type of plot: Western
Time of plot: 1878-1903 (narrated in the 1920's)
Locale: Arkansas and Choctaw Nation territory in Oklahoma
First published: 1968

Principal characters:

MATTIE ROSS, the fourteen-year-old daughter of Frank Ross, whose murder by Tom Chaney she sets out to avenge

REUBEN J. "ROOSTER" COGBURN, a deputy U.S. marshall who, both in his official capacity and in Mattie's pay, assists her in the pursuit of Chaney

SERGEANT LABOEUF, a Texas Ranger who, in pursuit of Chaney for the murder of a Texas state senator, accompanies Cogburn and Mattie

TOM CHANEY, alias CHAMBERS, a robber and murderer whose real name is Theron Chelmsford

LUCKY NED PEPPER, the leader of the robber gang that Chaney joins

YARNELL POINDEXTER, a freeborn black man hired by Frank Ross and devoted to the Ross family

COLONEL G. STONEHILL, an auctioneer

J. NOBLE DAGGETT, Mattie's lawyer

MRS. FLOYD, a boardinghouse landlady from whom Mattie rents a room

The Novel

True Grit is a study of the indomitable spirit of three representative Americans: a hard-living, heavy-drinking lawman, Rooster Cogburn; young Mattie Ross, who hires Cogburn because of his reputation for grit and who proves herself to possess the same quality; and Sergeant LaBoeuf, a disciplined, clean-living lawman who is mercenary enough to contemplate maximum reward money. In varying degrees, all the characters in the novel, including the outlaws, either have "true grit" or show respect for it.

In seven unnumbered chapters, this short novel re-creates the idiom, melodrama, and morality of nineteenth century adventure fiction, particularly the dime-novel Western adventure stories. The events are related by Mattie Ross, who, in her late fifties or early sixties, looks back from her current situation as an unmarried, one-armed banker caring for her invalid mother, to the second year of the Rutherford B. Hayes Administration. Back then, her father, Frank Ross, had ridden from his home near Dardanelle in Yell County, Arkansas, to Fort Smith to purchase horses and had been shot to death and robbed by his companion, Tom Chaney. She recalls the details of her determined and ultimately successful mission, as a fourteen-year-old, to make Chaney pay for his crime.

She is first accompanied, traveling from her home to Fort Smith, by Yarnell Poindexter, a freeborn black man from Illinois, whom her father had hired to look after the Ross family and farm until his return from Fort Smith. Mattie shows her spunk early by winning a battle of wills with Colonel Stonehill, the fort's auctioneer: He is intimidated by her threat of legal action and repurchases horses he had sold to her father. As she sets out in pursuit of Chaney, her companions are the fortyish Cogburn, for whose services she has agreed to pay one hundred dollars, and a thirtyish Texas Ranger sergeant with the gender-bent name of LaBoeuf who, intent upon both justice and a large reward, is pursuing Chaney for a murder that Chaney had committed in Texas.

Cogburn and LaBoeuf constitute an odd couple. Although they are separated in age by only a decade, LaBoeuf is of a new order and Cogburn is of the old. LaBoeuf is well-groomed, wears large shining spurs, goes by the book, and has acquired skills and judgment from training and discipline. Cogburn, resembling President Grover Cleveland in mien, girth, and moustache, is something of an outlaw turned lawman. He has only one eye, is slovenly in dress, drinks self-indulgently, and makes more errors in judgment than he cares to acknowledge.

Much of the narrative develops the respect that each of the three pursuers comes to have for the other two. Mattie holds her own in the rigors of outdoor living and keeps up with the two seasoned lawmen; Cogburn and LaBoeuf grow to respect and, often grudgingly, to rely upon each other.

There is mutual respect also between the lawmen and their outlaw quarry. Lucky Ned Pepper is admired for his leadership quality and his fortuitous elusiveness, his cohorts for their unwillingness to betray their kind, and even Chaney for the consistency and durability of his deceitfulness. The lawmen and outlaws address one another sometimes as equals to whom matters of law are divisive incidentals, but more often as competitors in a contest that provides life with meaning.

The climactic showdown is filled with rough-riding, exchanges of pistol and rifle fire, wounds, fatalities, falls, snakebites, and the triumph of justice. Lucky Ned Pepper and Tom Chaney are killed by, respectively, LaBoeuf and Cogburn. Mattie falls into a cavern pit and breaks her left arm, which is then bitten by a rattlesnake. The wounded Cogburn descends into the pit to rescue her, and both must be extricated by LaBoeuf, who engineers the feat by tying the rescue rope to Mattie's indomitably spirited pony, Blackie. Blackie will be ridden to death, carrying both Mattie and Cogburn at an unrelentingly furious gallop toward medical aid. Mattie's life is saved, but her arm must be amputated just above the elbow.

In the epilogue to the revenge story, LaBoeuf, who carried the corpse of Theron Chelmsford, alias Tom Chaney, back to Texas in fulfillment of his mission, is not heard from again. Cogburn reverts to activities that will cost him his marshalship and will lead him, as part of the evidentiary legend of the Old West, into "Wild West" shows, where he appears on exhibit with Frank James and Cole Younger. After Cogburn's death in 1903, Mattie transfers his remains to her family burial plot. Mattie herself permits her younger siblings, Victoria and Little Frank, to live their lives away from home while she commits herself to the care of their mother and to spinsterhood. She brings her proven ability in money matters into a successful banking career.

Although they enter into no formal marriage, Mattie and Cogburn become married in spirit, that indomitable spirit that is true grit. Mattie makes no effort to maintain contact with LaBoeuf after his return to Texas, but she diligently follows the subsequent doings, both actual and legendary, of Rooster Cogburn. Little Frank will often tease his sister Mattie about Cogburn's being her "secret sweetheart"; and Mattie's satisfaction in living with the memory and near the remains of her hired protector bear out the substance of the epithet.

The Characters

Mattie Ross is a devout Presbyterian who supports her sincere beliefs and principles with pertinent references to the New Testament. She is honest and will not persist in a falsehood even in an effort to deceive the murderer Tom Chaney. She is as forthright with outlaws as she is with law-abiding citizens. Her strength is shown in her ability both to get men to act in accordance with her wishes and to resist the commands of men. Her political persuasion is that of postbellum Southerners: She is a confirmed Democrat. She is outspoken and does not mince or waste words. Her narration shows that she clearly adheres in later life to the principles and values that she presents herself as having adhered to during her fourteenth year.

Rooster Cogburn is an embodiment of the Old West, with its code of personal, as opposed to legislative, justice. When he is enlisted by Mattie at the age of forty-three, his way of life is already on the way out. He participates in the advent of legal justice by becoming a marshal, after the manner of Wyatt Earp, and he does his best to help the new order, embodied in LaBoeuf, to displace his own. As a Southerner, he had seen his civilization collapse in the Civil War, during which he had served not in the regulation Confederate Army but with William Quantrill and his outlaw raiders. The end of his age is commemorated by his becoming a living exhibition piece.

Sergeant LaBoeuf is duty bound and dedicated to his job as a Texas Ranger. Some of his orthodox methods of police work test the patience of Cogburn and strike the reader as verging on the comic; in almost every instance, however, they happen to be more effective than the old ways of enforcing the law. Well-trained, trim, and with a youthful cowlick, he is in dramatic contrast to the overweight, heavy-drinking Cogburn, who once falls off his horse in drunkenness and at another time is pinned under his horse; he is then spared death at the hands of Lucky Ned only by the crack shooting of LaBoeuf.

As a freeborn black man, Yarnell Poindexter is also representative of a new order. The status of blacks had changed with the defeat of the Confederacy, but the contempt that many whites had for them would linger. Yarnell, dignified and intelligent in his services as Mattie's protector, must on one occasion settle for Mattie's scolding of a train conductor she calls "nigger."

Lucky Ned Pepper is a small, agile, and opportunistic outlaw. Cogburn not quite grudgingly admires his talents in crime and his practicality, which in one incident strikes Mattie as cruel and incomprehensible; Ned deserts a dying young gang member who has saved his life. The understanding and respect that Cogburn and Lucky Ned have for each other lends dimension to the novel.

Tom Chaney, also known as Chambers, born Theron Chelmsford, is the closest of the characters to pure villainy. Despite his lack of talents and dignity, however, he is, in his self-pitying whining and his clumsy criminality, not inhuman and not incomprehensible to the reader. As LaBoeuf is Cogburn's antithesis, so Chaney is Ned Pepper's.

Themes and Meanings

Employing humor and impeccably crisp and credible dialogue to preclude any trace of sentimentality, Portis celebrates in his setting and characters his native Arkansas and the values and virtues of an America resilient enough to continue to live by the mythic dream of integrity and independence from which it is constantly awakened. Portis affirms a noble and heroic America even as he exposes the base accoutrements of nobility and heroism. The noble LaBoeuf is merely an efficient and somewhat narrow-minded policeman. The heroic Cogburn is something of a stubborn vigilante. Nevertheless, LaBoeuf's noble actions save Cogburn's life and complement Cogburn's heroic actions in saving Mattie's.

Nobility and heroism are tested in a crucible of transition during the two decades that follow the Civil War, and Portis shows them to undergo change without suffering annihilation. The old century moves toward the new century, and Mattie, as an encapsulation of pragmatic and God-fearing America, is as much at home in the new as she had been in the old. The Old South and the Old West, which meet in Arkansas, refashion their ways of living but not their indomitable spirit. Reconstruction will end in 1877 by order of the narrowly elected Republican president Rutherford B. Hayes, in keeping his pledge to the insistent South; the mission of strong-willed and self-confident Mattie begins in the wake of this event.

Moreover, Mattie, with her resoluteness and her facility for moving men into her field of purpose, anticipates the women's suffrage movement that will culminate in the Nineteenth Amendment to the Constitution in 1920, well within her own lifetime. Yarnell Poindexter, standing firm in his freedom and in his work, likewise anticipates the Civil Rights movement, which will begin in the 1940's and will progress in tandem with a new feminist movement in the 1960's.

As a celebration of America, with all of its faults and all of its promise, *True Grit* offers a tentative corrective to Herman Melville's brilliantly cynical *The Confidence Man: His Masquerade* (1857). The book also provides a contrast to negativistic countercultural movements of the 1960's that often sought to disparage the American archetypes that *True Grit* embraces.

Critical Context

That *True Grit* is Portis's masterpiece is the result at least in part of its celebratory scope and its thematic depth. It surpassed his exceptionally well-received first novel,

Norwood (1966), in critical praise, which continues to identify it as a classic. None of his later novels—*The Dog of the South* (1979), *Masters of Atlantis* (1985), and *Gringos* (1991)—matched his second novel in reception and acclaim. Initial comparisons of Mattie Ross to Huckleberry Finn came to be recognized as superficial and strained. What invites *True Grit* into the company of American regionalist classics is not coincidental and partial resemblances, but the genuine regionalist's deeply subjective identification of self with his or her regional roots in a stylistic objectification of that identity.

The style of Portis, a career journalist, is understandably journalistic, but only in that it effects a translation of the merits of good journalism—brevity, concision, lucid exposition, and rapid pace—into fictional narrative. The journalistic element does not account for Portis's humor, which informs each of his novels from *Norwood* through *Gringos* and which neither veers toward the bitter or the sardonic, as Mark Twain's can, nor intimates social protest, as Erskine Caldwell's often does. Portis's humor is usually an appeal, not against injustice, but in favor of the good sense and pragmatic morality that promote justice.

Bibliography

Garfield, Brian. "Song and Swagger of the Old West." *Saturday Review* 51 (June 29, 1968): 25-26. Garfield differentiates the quality and scholarly accuracy of *True Grit* from those of hackwork Western novels. He sees Portis's novel as one that raises the standards of the Western genre and as one that is imbued with truth instead of being rife with cliché and half-truth. He neglects, however, to mention the element of Southern honor that complements the integrity of the Old West.

Rosenbaum, Ron. "Our Least-known Great Novelist." *Esquire* 129 (January, 1998): 30-32. An admiring profile of Portis that discusses his stature in modern American literture, as well as some of his books. Useful as an introduction to Portis's work.

Shuman, R. Baird. "Portis' *True Grit*: Adventure Story or *Entwicklungsroman*." *English Journal* 59 (March, 1970): 367-370. Shuman argues that *True Grit* is a "developmental novel" that traces the coming of age and psychological maturation of Mattie Ross and that its Western trappings are merely its format. Shuman insists that the most moving and important passage in the novel is not the achievement of revenge with the death of Chaney, but the description of Mattie's falling into the "cave" and being rescued therefrom. With going so far as to see in this a version of the classical journey to the underworld, symbolic of conversion or rebirth to maturity, Shuman classifies it as an event of initiation.

Wolfe, Tom. "The Feature Game." In *The New Journalism*. New York: Harper & Row, 1973: This chapter concludes with reference to Portis as a feature writer who realized the dream of achieving literary status. Wolfe surmises that the success of journalists as novelists may presage novelistic journalism's superseding the novel as literature's "main event."

Roy Arthur Swanson

THE TUNNEL

Author: William H. Gass (1924-   )
Type of plot: Modernism
Time of plot: 1967
Locale: A college town in Indiana
First published: 1995

Principal characters:

WILLIAM FREDERICK KOHLER, a history professor at a midwestern
    university
MARTHA KOHLER, Kohler's disappointed wife
MARGARET KOHLER, Kohler's alcoholic mother
FREDERICK KOHLER, Kohler's ineffectual father
LOU, Kohler's former student and lover
MAGUS TABOR, a former history professor of Kohler in Germany
PLANMATEE,
CULP,
GOVERNALI, and
HERSCHEL, colleagues in Kohler's history department

The Novel

The Tunnel is told in the first person by a middle-aged history professor who has
just completed his major work, *Guilt and Innocence in Hitler's Germany.* He now
wishes to conclude the project by writing the introduction, but he is seized by some
paralysis of the soul and writes, instead, the contorted story of his own embittered life
and a meditation on history and the writing of history. The story loops backward and
forward to the recent end of his affair with Lou, his family tree, his childhood, his student days in prewar Germany, his loveless marriage, and his present woes.

As Kohler ruminates about his life, he is obsessed with his experiences in Germany
during the 1930's and with the book he has just written. He rereads the manuscript,
noting that he has neatly analyzed, explained, tabulated, and encapsulated the history
of the Holocaust. He has even "justified" Adolf Hitler. Yet doubts assail him. Perhaps
he has completed only half his task; he meditates on his German name and finds nothing German about himself, because he is a fourth-generation American; he taunts
Herschel, a Jewish colleague, about Nazi motives. He jokes with Martha about Jewish
suffering and enjoys a colleague's limericks on the subject. He searches within for
what he wants from his life, his book, and his current writings, and he muses about his
own relationship to history. He decides he wants to feel "a little less uneasy."

He finally realizes that he is engulfed with rage, and he is determined to mine his
past in an attempt to expiate it. Kohler is the only child of a disappointed mother
whose dreams center on her sulky, obstinate son and an angry, bigoted father. Vivid
scenes from his childhood and student days come back to Kohler, leading to the
novel's autobiographical set pieces. In the midst of this psychological tunnel, Kohler,

whose name means "miner" in German, begins to dig a tunnel in his basement, clearing dirt, rust, and coal, and finally assaulting the mortar with a pick. He is strangely exhilarated by this activity, particularly since it provokes his unloved wife, whom he has no desire to placate. A long interior monologue called "The Quarrel" ensues, detailing his failed relationship with Martha and leading to a meditation on the quarrels that erupted into World War II, the Vietnam War, and other conflicts.

As further childhood injustices occur to Kohler, more grievances against his wife surface. A visit to an abandoned country farm with Martha and their two sons segues into memories of country drives of his childhood, particularly one that ended in the family's witnessing a horrible car crash that narrowly avoided missing them. Memories of his disapproving father bring back his student days in Germany and his relationship with Magus Tabor, called "Mad Meg," the charismatic professor who is Kohler's idol. Tabor is interested in the glorious sweep and force of history, but individual deaths mean nothing to him. He demeans his students, encourages them to falsify historical facts, adores the German fatherland, despises truth and Jews, and loves conquest. Kohler remembers tossing bricks during the infamous *Kristallnacht* of November, 1938, when he joined some of his fellow students in wandering the streets and smashing the windows of shops inscribed with the names of their Jewish owners. Kohler's thoughts drift to the failure of his marriage, his father's death, and his own young-adult children, who disappoint when they do not disgust him. He finds his colleagues contemptible. Because of a student's harassment charges, his colleagues convene a faculty meeting to discuss Kohler's lechery. They bicker peevishly while Kohler alternately lies and confesses. At home, he adds a long defense of Hitler to his biographical writing and goes back to excavating his tunnel, the dirt of which he now deposits into Martha's collection of sideboards and bureaus that she hopes to turn into an antique business.

Kohler continues to dig and pick at his life, unearthing more grotesque scenes of his childhood, including the placing his own mother in an asylum when he was fifteen. A climax of sorts occurs at the end of the novel, when Martha, having just discovered where he was putting the dirt, barges into his study with a drawer full and dumps it over the desk on which his manuscript lies. The novel, Kohler's inquiry, and the tunnel find no resolution.

The Characters

Although they are always seen through the narrator's eyes, William H. Gass's characters are fully developed, and the author uses different techniques to bring them to life. For the first hundred pages of the novel, Kohler mentions only snippets and fleeting impressions of other characters, which start to build in the reader's mind. Initially, he circles around his former student and lover, Lou, the great love of his life, who leaves him when he tells her of his loathing for humankind. Tabor also appears early, and Kohler's wife, Martha, is introduced with several pages of invective.

The circle widens to include Kohler's family with a ten-page story about his Uncle Balt's farm. Uncle Balt is carefully described, from the shape of his knuckles to his eating habits, and speaks in his own words. This sets the pattern for the novel; long sections of stream-of-consciousness narration interspersed with stories of the characters told by the narrator from a more detached viewpoint. The novel is not broken up into chapters, but the stories often have titles, such as "Learning to Drive," about his father, "Aunts," and the beautifully lyrical "Do Mountains," about his love affair with Lou. Each of his colleagues has a section of his own. These individual sections are highly realistic and richly detailed, with physical descriptions of the characters and their distinctive patterns of speech. Although the reader learns not to trust the narrator's view of others, the dialogue is so brilliant throughout the novel that each time a character speaks, he or she reveals much.

The most problematic character in the book is Kohler himself. Although he tells the story, it is obvious how others feel about him from their reactions. His mother, drifting further and further into fantasy and alcoholism, dotes on her only child, but it is clear she has no one else. His father considers young Kohler stupid, unmanly, incompetent, and dishonest. While this may not be the whole truth, it is apparent that the child makes no attempt to please. Kohler's wife, Martha, turns against him during the first year of their union. He goes to great lengths to describe the unfortunate housing conditions that caused her disaffection, but now, after years of marriage in a lovely home, they thoroughly detest each other and stay together only for malice. He always disliked his two sons, one of whose name he cannot bear to utter. Kohler's colleagues find him a problem, both for his sexual proclivities and for his earlier book, *Nuremberg Notes*. In his own words, Kohler is a misanthrope, a bigot, and a Hitler sympathizer. William Gass writes such dazzling, energetic prose that the reader sometimes falls under the spell of this bitter antihero, but Kohler's hatred bubbles up so often that the spell is soon broken.

Themes and Meanings

William Gass spent almost thirty years writing *The Tunnel*. The most obvious theme is an exploration of the antihero's life, much of it written so masterfully that every vignette from his early years completely engages the reader. While the focus is on the narrator, a subtle family portrait emerges that traces the lives of the family members and the ways they react to each other's strengths and weaknesses in both obvious and hidden ways. The use of the tunnel as the overarching metaphor of the novel is a symbol of Kohler's digging into his life and into history, although it takes on humorous overtones as a sexual metaphor. By depositing the dirt in Martha's massive and beloved bureau drawers, Kohler performs a symbolic act, as she does when she empties a drawer of dirt on his manuscript.

The tunnel points to a much larger theme as well. In his youth, Kohler gave up his ambition to be a poet because he believed truth could be found only in history. Yet he finds written history is not reliable. At the beginning of the novel, the distinguished historian has finished his magnum opus only to question if it is true, or even if it is possible to dig through the ambiguity and chaos of the past to arrive at the truth. His subsequent ramblings on the rise of Hitler and the Holocaust indicate that his personal history and biases have had a stronger influence on his book than any objective research. One critic describes the book's theme as "fascism of the soul." With all its contradictions and confusions and deliberate darkness, *The Tunnel* is a long meditation on the difficulty of determining historical truth and the impossibility of representing such truth in language.

Critical Context

The American experimental writing that began in the 1960's and 1970's was driven by the violence and upheaval of the Civil Rights movement and the Vietnam War. For Gass and others such as Thomas Pynchon, Robert Coover, John Barth, and Gilbert Sorrentino, realistic fiction seemed no longer adequate. Just as protests and demonstrations sought to overturn the conventions of society, these writers aggressively attacked literary conventions such as linear plot line, "lifelike" characters, and language used merely to convey the story. Instead, they wrote stories and novels about writing stories and novels, parodied standard forms, and used language in truly innovative ways. Some of the devices of the modernist writers are allusion, puzzle, fragmented chronology, circular plots, and style as subject. In addition to this arsenal, Gass, who did graduate study at Cornell University in philosophy and became interested in aesthetic theory, also uses drawings, slogans, banners, different font styles, and cartoons to embellish *The Tunnel*.

Gass taught for fifteen years at Purdue University, where he completed his first novel, *Omensetter's Luck*. Published in 1966, it was acclaimed as the most important work of fiction by an American of that generation and placed Gass as the undisputed leader of his literary contemporaries. His second novel, *Willie Master's Lonesome Wife* (1968), exhibited even stronger influences of modernist tendencies in its narration. *The Tunnel*, a compelling example of modernist literature, is a direct descendent of these books and proceeds still further in its use of modernist devices. The language of the novel takes on a meaning of its own. It is full of puns, alliteration, concrete arrangements, and wordplay and leads the narrator toward digressions and dead ends. Gass's novel, while brilliant, makes heavy demands upon the reader.

Bibliography

Gass, William. "Language and Conscience: An Interview with William Gass." Interview by Arthur M. Salzman. *Review of Contemporary Fiction* 7, no. 3 (Fall, 1991): 15-31. Gass reveals the difficulties of using words, which filter and adulterate perception, as a useful tool for objectively comprehending the world.

Holloway, Watson L. *William Gass*. Boston: Twayne, 1990. An introductory study of Gass's work that offers a close reading necessary to appreciate the novelist. Includes a chapter entitled "The Tunnel," although it was written five years before *The Tunnel* was published.

Kelly, Robert. "A Repulsively Lonely Man." Review of *The Tunnel*, by William Gass. *The New York Times Book Review*, February 26, 1995. A five-page review that gives a fairly complete overview of *The Tunnel* and includes some comments by Gass.

Klein, Marcus. "Postmodernising the Holocaust: William Gass in *The Tunnel*." *New England Review* 18, no. 2 (Summer, 1997): 79-88. Klein analyzes the success and failures of treating one of the major events of the twentieth century in a modernist style.

Salzman, Arthur M. *The Fiction of William Gass: The Consolation of Language*. Carbondale: Southern Illinois University Press, 1986. A brilliant analysis of Gass's fiction, with a provocative chapter entitled "The Tunnel: Recent Excavations," written when Gass had been working on *The Tunnel* for fifteen years.

Sheila Golburgh Johnson

TYPICAL AMERICAN

Author: Gish Jen (1956-   )
Type of plot: Social realism
Time of plot: The 1940's to the 1980's
Locale: China and New York City
First published: 1991

> *Principal characters:*
> RALPH CHANG, a Chinese American mechanical engineer
> THERESA CHANG, Ralph's older sister, a Chinese American doctor
> HELEN CHANG, Theresa's best friend from China, Ralph's wife
> OLD CHAO, Ralph's superior at the university, a friend of the Changs
> GROVER DING, a third-generation Chinese American businessman and
> entrepreneur

The Novel

Typical American is a novel about three Chinese immigrants and how they are inspired, seduced, and betrayed by the promise of the American Dream. The book is divided into five parts: "Sweet Rebellion," "The House Holds," "This New Life," "Structural Weakening," and "A Man to Sit at Supper and Never Eat." The titles roughly sketch the protagonists' journey through the novel, from rebellion to prosperity to deterioration and alienation. The parts are further divided into short chapters with cleverly appropriate titles such as "A Boy with His Hands Over His Ears," "Love Animates," and "A Brand of Alchemy, Indeed."

In "Sweet Rebellion," Jen follows Yifeng Chang from his native village in China to the United States, detailing his immigration difficulties, his choice of the American name Ralph, and his entry into American academia as a mechanical engineer. Ralph struggles to learn the nuances of English and has his first brushes with romance. His newly arrived sister, now called Theresa, joins him in New York, and Ralph marries her best friend, Helen, another Chinese immigrant.

In "The House Holds," the three set up house together. Ralph continues to ascend the academic ladder, under the tutelage of a fellow immigrant nicknamed Old Chao, and Helen begins her medical studies. Relations in the little family shift under the strains of life in America, but advances are made: Theresa becomes a doctor, Ralph completes his Ph.D., and Helen gives birth to two daughters. Meanwhile, Ralph begins reading and dreaming about wealth and success. One night, while dining at Old Chao's, the Changs meet Grover Ding, a self-made American businessman of Chinese descent who captures Ralph's imagination.

"This New Life" brings more changes. Ralph, after much worry, receives tenure at the university, and with that security the family buys a suburban home. Theresa, devoted to her work and essentially quite lonely, starts having an affair with Old Chao. When Ralph and Helen find out about Theresa's affair, their censure creates unbearable tension in the little family.

In "Structural Weakening," the tension breaks the family apart, as Theresa moves into an apartment of her own. Meanwhile, Ralph's aspirations lead him to seek out Grover Ding, and he impulsively accepts an opportunity from Grover, giving up his university position to invest in a fast-food chicken restaurant. At first, all goes well, but eventually structural weaknesses in the building show it to be much less of a bargain than it seemed. In an emotional parallel to the business developments, Grover and Helen have a passionate affair, protected by Ralph's single-minded focus on the business. Grover soon disappears, however, and the Changs realize that they have been victims of shady dealing. As the restaurant deteriorates into uselessness, the Changs face economic and emotional disaster.

The novel's last part, "A Man to Sit at Supper and Never Eat," fulfills the dire promise in a surprising climactic sequence of events. The house is offered for sale, even as Theresa rejoins the troubled family. Ralph learns of Helen's infidelity, and the tension between them reaches violent proportions. Ralph's blind fury eventually leads to a bizarre accident that leaves Theresa in a coma, and the family is battered with grief. In the end, the Changs move into an apartment in the city, Theresa emerges from her coma, and the family begins to rebuild.

The novel is told in a third-person voice that establishes a swift, playful rapport with the reader. Jen moves freely among the characters' viewpoints and shifts tempos and time frames to fill in necessary details, only loosely anchoring the story in a specific geographic or temporal context. The narrative is full of references to Chinese culture and history: italics indicate the Chang's bilingual domestic life, and Chinese phrases are transliterated and explained. The breezy, almost cartoonish style of the earlier parts gradually gives way to a brooding, dramatic sobriety as the story winds toward its conclusion.

The Characters

Ralph is the first protagonist Jen introduces. He is a likeable, innocent young man who, in striving for success and an American identity, becomes ambitious, irresponsible, moody, and insensitive. He is a dreamer whose imagination often runs unfettered, but he lacks the circumspection and caution that will keep him and his family out of trouble. It is his fascination with success formulas and his adulation of Grover that wreak havoc on the family.

Theresa is a foil to Ralph, a large, straitlaced woman who survives on reserve and caution. Her story "curls from this sad truth: that as much as Ralph, growing up, should have been her, she should have been him." Innately a leader, she is relegated to third-wheel status in the family. She represents the traditional Chinese value of family devotion, a value that she abandons but to which she ultimately returns. At the same time, she is American, and her puzzled and illicit love for Old Chao is a source of liberation and identity.

Helen, conversely, is a slight, delicate woman with a surprising resourcefulness and knack for adaptation. At first, she is the grounded force that anchors Ralph's moods and dreams. Yet if she begins her life in America with images from fashion magazines and dreams of suburbia, she ends with an alienation and hopelessness that lead to her corruption. For Helen, marrying Ralph meant "officially accepting what seemed already true—that she had indeed crossed a violent, black ocean; and that it was time to make herself as at home in her exile as she could." The task turns out to be more difficult than imagined.

Old Chao is portrayed as a generous and well-meaning friend to the family whose involvement in their troubles comes from very human, if not wholly honorable, impulses. Grover Ding, on the other hand, is never fully revealed, to either the Changs or the reader, beyond the fact that he is the charming "imagineer" he appears to be. The other characters, such as Chao's long-suffering wife Janis, are treated with respect and distance, and the Changs' daughters Callie and Mona are ever-present reminders of the innocence that their parents are slowly, unwittingly losing.

Themes and Meanings

Typical American is a novel about migration: across the globe, across four decades, and across an expansive moral and emotional landscape. Unlike many earlier European immigrants to the United States who came fleeing poverty or hunger, Chinese American immigrants such as Ralph come in search of educational opportunities in advanced scientific fields. Ralph would have been a member of the elite in China, and in the beginning of the novel, he and other such immigrants become small pawns in the ideological battles of the Cold War.

The first adaptation to life in America is the choice of a name, which comes in Ralph's case rather haphazardly, and the mastery of the English language, the source of many comic moments. In a delightful twist of language, the Changs adopt a family nickname—the Chinese Yankees, or "Chang-Kees" for short. The term encapsulates their struggle: They are Americanized but are still inwardly Chinese. Ralph, Theresa, and Helen strive for assimilation, wearing American clothes, speaking American slang, and living in an American home. Jen writes, "In China, one lived in one's family's house. In America, one could always name whose house one was in; and to live in a house not one's own was to be less than a man."

Family is a theme that permeates the novel. It is the link that connects Ralph and Theresa and Helen, more even than romantic love. For Ralph and Helen, marrying is the right thing to do, a choice their Chinese parents would applaud. Similarly, Ralph's later rejection of Theresa, her shamed exile from the home, and her return in time of duress, are all rooted in family cohesion. Yet the traditional Chinese dedication to family is pitted against, and eventually lost to, the classical American devotion to independence and individualism, and the confrontation results in contradictions: Ralph has no difficulty underreporting his income, a "typically" American practice embodied in the ringing of the cash register, but he nevertheless cannot adopt the equally Western and modern attitude that would tolerate his sister's affair.

The structure of the family and the role of women are transformed as tradition confronts liberal attitudes in contemporary America. The family focuses on Ralph's career even as Theresa struggles as arduously to become a doctor. Theresa's independence and Helen's resourcefulness, and later their courage to have extramarital affairs, go beyond the traditional and accepted female roles. Such disruptive departures from tradition result from the positive yearnings for assimilation and belonging: Indeed, if Ralph had not accepted Grover as a role model for success, Grover never would have seduced Helen.

Love is not absent from the novel, but it is only rarely seen in a pure or innocent form. The romantic and sexual relationships are all imperfect, volatile, and dependent on dishonesty and accommodation. Impure love ultimately leads to alienation and the loss of all feeling, the insensate state made manifest in Theresa's comatose condition.

Partly to blame for the failure is the difficulty of translation, of learning to communicate in a new language. In moving from one world to another, the Changs have to learn not only what the new words mean but also what the new concepts and practices signify. Ralph fails miserably at truly understanding Grover Ding's counsels. Early in their relationship, Grover advises Ralph to "know who you're dealing with," and Ralph affirms, imperfectly, "Know who I'm deal with." The tragedy, of course, is that he cannot even begin to recognize the base nature of the man whose advice he so eagerly accepts.

Communication and understanding are key, and one of the lessons that Helen teaches Callie and Mona about talking is the importance, sometimes, of "not continuing." The American way of talking, it seems, is continuous and inexhaustible, whereas members of the Chang family, especially the women, often let the silence make their points. Implicit in this view of communication is a metaphor for the dangers of ambition and materialism. The Changs become assimilated in their focus on external status symbols: Their lives revolve around their job titles, their house, their car, their future opportunities for wealth and power. They begin to take what they have for granted, and look instead beyond it into the far realms of their imaginations. Rather than depend on the knowable, Ralph begins to believe in some mystical American deity composed of sheer arrogance and willpower. "Risk was the key to success. Clothes made the man." He covers his office walls with capitalistic catchphrases and fully believes them. Like talk that continues beyond the point when silence would serve better, so can aspiration overshoot reality. Playing with business terms and concepts, Jen makes the point clearly: Rather than keep his overhead to a minimum, Ralph decides to build a second floor to his restaurant, but the added weight creates too heavy a burden for the weak foundation, and eventually the whole building comes crashing down.

Early in the novel, in commenting ruefully on the foibles of the strange society that surrounds them, the Changs develop the habit of calling things "typical American": "typical American don't-know-how-to-get-along" and "typical American just-want-to-be-the-center-of-things." The phrase becomes a refrain in their lives as they grow to recognize and identify prevailing values. Yet the Changs eventually become blind to "typical American" qualities, and ultimately, in spite of themselves, end up embodying them.

Critical Context

Jen is an American-born writer of Chinese descent who traveled to China to explore her cultural heritage. A graduate of Harvard University, she attended business school briefly but soon turned to creative writing. Her reading of the immigration experience as portrayed by Jewish American writers is one of the major influences in her work. For her writing, Jen has received fellowships from the National Endowment for the Arts and the Bunting Institute at Radcliffe College.

Typical American is Jen's debut novel, preceded only by the publication of several short stories in *The New Yorker* and *The Atlantic*. Upon its appearance in 1991, *Typical American* was immediately acclaimed for its original voice and viewpoint, its use of humor and pathos, its insights into the Chinese American immigrant experience, and its deep indictment of typically American values.

With *Typical American*, Jen has been heralded as a member of a new generation of Chinese American writers. Modern Chinese American writing began to emerge in 1950 with the publication of Jade Snow Wong's *Fifth Chinese Daughter*, an autobiographical novel about assimilation into American culture. Other books that built the tradition include Maxine Hong Kingston's *The Woman Warrior: Memoirs of a Girlhood Among Ghosts* (1976), a collection of autobiographical stories and traditional tales; Bette Bao Lord's *Eighth Moon: The Story of a Young Girl's Life in Communist China* (1964); and Wong's autobiographical novel *The Immigrant Experience* (1971). Among Jen's contemporaries in the 1980's and 1990's are Amy Tan, known for her novels *The Joy Luck Club* (1989) and *The Kitchen God's Wife* (1991), and Playwright David Henry Hwang, whose *M. Butterfly* (1988) earned him Tony and Drama Desk Awards.

Bibliography

Jen, Gish. "Gish Jen Talks with Scarlet Cheng." Interview by Scarlet Cheng. *Belles Lettres: A Review of Books by Women* 7 (Winter, 1992): 20-21. Jen reveals her disappointment at the way the critics have treated her novel. She believes that the ethnic identity of a novel should not be used as the sole basis for judging a work. She also points out that she is careful in her use of humor because of the effect it may have on how people view the Chinese.

_____. Interview by Yuko Matsukawa. *MELUS* 18 (Winter, 1993): 111-120. Jen discusses various authors who influenced her writing, including Jane Austen, Alice Munro, and Jamaica Kincaid. Although Jen sees her writing as humorous as well as somewhat indeterminate in its final message, she attributes these characteristics to be a result of her Chinese upbringing.

_____. "Writing About the Things That Are Dangerous: A Conversation with Gish Jen." *Southwest Review* 78 (Winter, 1993): 132-140. Jen talks about the biographical elements in her novel, including the pursuit of the American dream and the conflict with the elders of the Chinese community. While she appreciates the multicultural approach to literature, she realizes that it also could result in narrowed expectations for writers.

Mojtabai, A. G. "The Complete Other Side of the World." *The New York Times Book Review*, March 31, 1991, 9-10. Mojtabai examines *Typical American* in terms of the themes of migration and mutation, the intelligence of Jen's prose, and the questions posed by the book. The favorable review is accompanied by an interview with Jen by Laurel Graeber.

Simpson, Janice C. "Fresh Voices Above the Noisy Din." *Time* 137 (June 3, 1991): 66-67. An article profiling four Chinese American novelists that places Jen alongside Amy Tan, David Wong Louie, and Gus Lee. Simpson briefly discusses each novel, quotes the authors, and attempts to link them to one another and to the context of Chinese American writing.

Snell, Marilyn Berlin. "The Intimate Outsider." *New Perspectives Quarterly* 8 (Summer, 1991): 56-60. A thoughtful and extensive interview with Jen exploring the sociopolitical implications of *Typical American*. Jen discusses American values, the tradition of American literature, and her role as an immigrant writer.

Storace, Patricia. "Seeing Double." *The New York Review of Books* 38 (August 15, 1991): 9. A review of *Typical American* focusing on the novel's theme of duality. Includes a synopsis and an exploration of duality in both the joining of opposites and the coexistence of parallels.

Zia, Helen. "A Chinese Banquet of Secrets." *Ms.* 12 (November-December, 1991): 76-77. A review of nine novels by Chinese American women writers, with major focus on Jen, Amy Tan, Sky Lee, and Carol Tsukiyama. In discussing *Typical American*, Zia looks primarily at Theresa and Helen. The article effectively places Jen's women beside other comparable female protagonists.

Barry Mann

THE UNDERGROUND MAN

Author: Ross Macdonald (Kenneth Millar; 1915-1983)
Type of plot: Mystery
Time of plot: The 1960's
Locale: California
First published: 1971

> *Principal characters:*
> LEW ARCHER, the narrator, a private detective
> JEAN BROADHURST, his client, whose son is kidnaped
> RONNY BROADHURST, her six-year-old son
> STANLEY BROADHURST, her estranged husband, Ronny's father
> ELIZABETH BROADHURST, the wife of Leo Broadhurst, mother of
>   Stanley, and grandmother of Ronny
> EDNA SNOW, her former housekeeper
> FREDERICK (FRITZ) SNOW, Edna Snow's son
> BRIAN KILPATRICK, a real-estate man, the partner of Mrs. Broadhurst in
>   Canyon Estates development
> ELLEN STROME, his former wife and the mistress of Leo Broadhurst
> SUSAN CRANDALL, the illegitimate daughter of Leo Broadhurst

The Novel

The Underground Man, like many of Ross Macdonald's novels, is set in the ficti-tious community of Santa Teresa, which bears more than a passing resemblance to Santa Barbara, where Macdonald (in real life, Kenneth Millar) lived from the late 1940's until his death in 1983. As is typical of Macdonald's Lew Archer novels, how-ever, the action also ranges widely to other locales up and down the state of California.

While feeding peanuts to squabbling jays outside his apartment in West Los An-geles, private detective Lew Archer becomes caught up in the entangled affairs of the Broadhursts, a well-to-do Santa Teresa family that is split by marital disputes. Leo Broadhurst, scion of the clan, vanished fifteen years earlier, supposedly leaving his wife for Ellen Strome Kilpatrick, but then deserting his mistress as well. Stanley Broadhurst, consumed by his desire to find his father, places an advertisement in a San Francisco newspaper, succeeding in dredging up the past but failing to locate his fa-ther. Among the reward seekers is Albert Sweetner, an escaped convict who once was a foster child of Edna Snow, formerly a housekeeper for the Broadhursts. Sweetner's return revives a long-buried scandal in which he and Fritz Snow, then teenagers, were accused of getting Marty Nickerson, also a teenager, pregnant. She is now Mrs. Lester Crandall and mother of Susan, a college girl who becomes involved first with Stanley Broadhurst and then with Jerry Kilpatrick, the rebellious son of Brian Kilpatrick and his former wife. Jerry and Susan steal a boat and then a car as they flee parents and all other authority figures in a frantic odyssey with six-year-old Ronny Broadhurst in tow.

While the past of the Broadhursts and the others is starting to close in on them all and threatening their present, there is also a raging forest fire that endangers their lives and property and gives an even greater sense of urgency to Archer's need to resolve the developing mystery, since the flames could destroy vital evidence. The fire, which Stanley carelessly started with a cigarette while digging to find his father's body, becomes a subplot and symbolizes nature's outrage at man's self-serving destruction of society and the environment. In this regard, when speaking of Jerry Kilpatrick, Archer comments: "He belonged to a generation whose elders had been poisoned, like the pelicans, with a kind of moral DDT that damaged the lives of their young."

In the course of the few days that the action of the novel covers, Archer learns that Leo Broadhurst was a womanizer who raped as well as seduced, but who finally was shot by his wife when she caught him with the girl Marty, whose daughter he had fathered three years earlier. While unconscious, Broadhurst was actually killed by Edna Snow, who finished him off with a knife as an act of vengeance for his having let Albert and Fritz be charged unfairly with a crime. Justifying her action fifteen years later, she tells Archer: "You can't call it murder. He deserved to die. He got Marty Nickerson pregnant and let my boy take the blame. Frederick has never been the same since then."

The three-year-old Susan witnessed the fatal tryst between her mother and Broadhurst and the shooting of Broadhurst by his wife—events that have haunted her ever since. At the start of the novel, she is with Leo's son, Stanley, who is trying to piece together the story of his father's fate through her recollections and those of others. Stanley's quest leads him back to his parents' mountain retreat, where he believes his father is buried. When he borrows a pick and shovel from Fritz Snow, the thirty-five-year-old boy-man reports to his mother, for fifteen years earlier he and Sweetner had buried Leo for her. Fearful of the consequences of Stanley's discovery, she dons a disguise, goes to the mountain, kills him, and then dumps him in the hole that he had begun to dig.

By the close of the novel, then, events have moved full circle. The mystery of Leo Broadhurst's disappearance has been solved, but his son has died in the process. Albert Sweetner's lust for Stanley's reward money has led the escaped convict to his death. (Mrs. Snow, afraid that he will reveal how he helped bury Leo, kills him.) Brian Kilpatrick commits suicide rather than risk exposure as an unscrupulous wheeler-dealer who had cheated his unwitting partner, Elizabeth Broadhurst. Yet there also are some positive aspects to the outcome: Ellen Strome is reunited with her son Jerry; Susan, after undergoing psychotherapy for her recurring nightmare, presumably will be able to lead a normal life, as will her parents, no longer hiding behind a lie; and Stanley's widow, Jean, and son Ronny are freed to go on with their lives. Of all the characters in the novel, only Lew Archer is unchanged, not even having made much money from his efforts.

The Characters

In all the novels in which he appears, Lew Archer is an atypical private eye, for money seems incidental to him, being little more than a means of paying the rent, and he inevitably is emotionally drawn to one or more of his clients, not necessarily sexually, but rather in a sense of kinship with fellow sufferers, for Archer believes that he "sometimes served as a catalyst for trouble, not unwillingly." A loner who has not fully recovered from the trauma of a long-ago divorce, he looks in his bathroom mirror and comments that "all I could read was my own past, in the marks of erosion under my eyes." Though he is not obsessed with the past in the way that the others are, it is a living presence and leads him to empathize with those who are its prisoners. Different as he is in this regard from the Dashiell Hammett and Raymond Chandler private eyes that are his predecessors in the genre, Archer is like them in his courting of physical danger, and in this novel he endures the obligatory attack (by Jerry Kilpatrick, with the butt of a gun). He is like them, too, in that women find him attractive: Jean Broadhurst, Ellen Strome, even Elegant, Albert Sweetner's prostitute. Yet almost everyone in the novel is drawn to Archer, who seemingly solves his case because he learns so much from those who eventually talk freely to him. Above all else Lew Archer is a good listener. When Ellen Strome—soon after they meet for the first time—tells him the story of her affair with Leo years earlier, he comments (as narrator of the novel), "we seemed to be held together by a feeling impersonal but almost as strong as a friendship or a passion. . . . The past was unwinding and rewinding like yarn which the two of us held between us." The closest relationship that develops, however, is between Lew and Ronny: One of them finds (if only temporarily) the son he never had, and the other gets a surrogate father for a time. For Ronny, at the end, Archer wishes "a benign failure of memory."

The other characters could profit from the same gift, because they have "all the years of their lives dragging behind them." Even Archer, nearing the resolution of the case, feels "shipwrecked on the shores of the past." Yet whereas everyone else has tried to forget the past, or at least keep it as thoroughly hidden as Leo in his red-Porsche tomb, his son Stanley's life for fifteen years "has been a kind of breakdown" and (as his wife Jean tells it) "He's been looking for his father in the hope that it would put him back together. . . . When his father ran out on him, it robbed his life of its meaning." Stanley is on the verge of finding Leo when he is killed and ironically is hastily buried just above his father's grotesque tomb.

Though most of the women in the book seem to be as much in thrall to the past and as dominated by a strong man as Stanley is, they are by and large survivors, including even Susan Crandall and her mother. Elizabeth Broadhurst also suffers at Leo's hand, but she finally shoots him; and though she falls prey to Brian Kilpatrick's financial chicanery, she lives to see him commit suicide rather than confront exposure and ruin. Though bereft of her son, she has her grandson Ronny and her daughter-in-law Jean; in addition, there is still a past for her to shape and control, through her memoir-in-progress of her father, whom she has idealized as "a god come down to earth in human guise." Ellen Strome, also mistreated by Leo and Brian, survives both, leading a solitary but productive life as an artist in her grandfather's home.

Edna Snow and her son also are survivors, to a point. A domineering, overprotective mother, she has clung to Fritz as the single stable and unchanging element in her life, even killing one man in revenge for Fritz and murdering two more men years later in a futile attempt to keep secret the first crime. When Archer confronts her with the truth, she takes a butcher knife to him, too, but despite "the kind of exploding strength that insane anger releases," she fails. According to Archer, she "was one of those paranoid souls who kept her conscience clear by blaming everything on other people. Her violence and malice appeared to her as emanations from the external world."

Themes and Meanings

The quest and Oedipal motifs are central to his novel, and they are most poignantly delineated in the character of Stanley, whose love-hate relationship with Leo is the motivating force of his life. Jean explains that "he's angry at his father for abandoning him; at the same time he misses him and loves him." This omnipresence of the past is the primary theme of the work, and Macdonald's attitude toward it is expressed in a letter from a minister to Stanley: "The past can do very little for us—no more than it has already done, for good or ill—except in the end to release us. We must seek and accept release, and give release." Archer thinks that the Reverend Riceyman "had given Stanley good advice" and regrets that the young man had failed to take it. Perhaps Stanley simply did not live long enough.

The forest fire that rages in the background of much of the action is a leitmotif that also functions as a metaphor for man's alienation from his fellows, from himself, and from nature. It consumes everything in its path in the same wantonly destructive manner as the characters in pursuit of their dreams or in rebellion against their nightmares. Archer's initial reaction to the blaze invokes war, the ultimate destructive act of alienated man: "Under and through the smoke I caught glimpses of fire like the flashes of guns too far away to be heard. The illusion of war was completed by an old two-engine bomber, which flew in low over the mountain's shoulder." Later, when he reaches the Broadhurst ranch, Archer notices that the darkening fruit "hung down from their branches like green hand grenades."

Counterpointing the symbolic squabbling of the jays at the start and the spreading forest fire through the body of the novel is the rain that is falling at the end. Quenching the life-threatening blaze, the storm offers the prospect of a purging of the old and a renewal of life. "When I went outside," Archer says, "the rain was coming down harder than ever. Water was running in the street, washing the detritus of summer downhill toward the sea." Further, the title of the novel inevitably brings to mind Fyodor Dostoevski's *Notes from the Underground* (1864); by calling attention to that Russian masterpiece and inviting comparison with it, Macdonald leads the reader to see his themes of guilt and suffering in bolder relief.

Critical Context

When it was published in 1971, *The Underground Man* got more critical attention than detective fiction normally receives, including a front-page review by Eudora Welty in *The New York Times Book Review* and a *Newsweek* cover story. With his twenty-second novel (the seventeenth starring Lew Archer), Macdonald finally was given his rightful recognition as successor to Raymond Chandler and Dashiell Hammett in the hard-boiled school and also was accepted as a serious novelist. Yet it is more than a breakthrough novel. *The Underground Man* also is Macdonald's major achievement, the work in which his worldview—including social commentary, particularly on environmental and ecological matters—is given its fullest and most memorable expression. Though all the Lew Archer novels have multiple plots, the several story lines in this one are more skillfully developed and unified than is the case in the previous books. Recurring, too, is the theme of a corrupt society, but Macdonald's portrait here is especially memorable, with Archer's pursuit of the truth revealing the venality behind the facade of propriety.

Thus, echoes of previous Archer novels abound in *The Underground Man*—the primary one being the demonstration that the past usually has the answers to the mysteries of the present. Yet despite the shared similarities of style, tone, theme, setting, and method, it has a distinctive voice and quality and the perfect combination of timeless and timely themes.

Bibliography

Bruccoli, Matthew J. *Ross Macdonald*. San Diego: Harcourt Brace Jovanovich, 1984. Describes the development of Macdonald's popular reputation as a prolific author of detective fiction and his critical reputation as a writer of literary merit. Includes illustrations, an appendix with an abstract of his Ph.D. thesis, notes, a bibliography, and an index.

Schopen, Bernard A. *Ross Macdonald*. Boston: Twayne, 1990. A sound introductory study, with a chapter on Macdonald's biography ("The Myth of One's Life"), on his handling of genre, his development of the Lew Archer character, his mastery of the form of the detective novel, and the maturation of his art culminating in *The Underground Man*. Provides detailed notes and an annotated bibliography.

Sipper, Ralph B., ed. *Ross Macdonald: Inward Journey*. Santa Barbara, Calif.: Cordelia Editions, 1984. This collection of twenty-seven articles includes two by Macdonald, one a transcription of a speech about mystery fiction and the other a letter to a publisher which discusses Raymond Chandler's work in relation to his own. Contains photographs and notes on contributors.

Skinner, Robert E. *The Hard-Boiled Explicator: A Guide to the Study of Dashiell Hammett, Raymond Chandler, and Ross Macdonald*. Metuchen, N.J.: Scarecrow Press, 1985. An indispensable volume for the scholar interested in tracking down unpublished dissertations as well as mainstream criticism. Includes brief introductions to each author, followed by annotated bibliographies of books, articles, and reviews.

South Dakota Review 24 (Spring, 1986). This special issue devoted to Macdonald, including eight articles, an editor's note, photographs, and notes, is a valuable source of criticism.

Speir, Jerry. *Ross Macdonald*. New York: Frederick Ungar, 1978. Serves as a good introduction to Macdonald's work, with a brief biography and a discussion of the individual novels. Includes chapters on his character Lew Archer, on alienation and other themes, on Macdonald's style, and on the scholarly criticism available at the time. Contains a bibliography, notes, and an index.

Wolfe, Peter. *Dreamers Who Live Their Dreams: The World of Ross Macdonald's Novels*. Bowling Green, Ohio: Bowling Green University Press, 1976. This detailed study contains extensive discussions of the novels and a consideration of the ways in which Macdonald's life influenced his writing. Includes notes.

Gerald H. Strauss

UNDERWORLD

Author: Don DeLillo (1936-   )
Type of plot: Postmodernism
Time of plot: The Cold War and immediate post-Cold War eras
Locale: New York City, Phoenix, a reform school in Minnesota, and post-Soviet
    Kazakhstan
First published: 1997

   Principal characters:
      NICK SHAY, a middle-aged waste-management professional of urban,
         working-class origins
      MARIAN SHAY, Nick's wife
      MATT SHAY, Nick's brother
      KLARA SAX, an experimental artist, Nick's first lover
      ALBERT BRONZINI, Klara's first husband and Matt's former chess tutor
      MANX MARTIN, the father of Cotter Martin, whose son caught Bobby
         Thomson's historic 1951 playoff home run
      BRIAN GLASSIC, Nick's coworker, who is having an affair with Marian
      SISTER EDGAR, a nun working with homeless squatters in the lower
         Bronx
      ISMAEL MUÑOZ, the leader of the squatters

The Novel
   Underworld is divided into eleven parts: six narrative sections, a prologue, an epilogue, and three sections narrated from the perspective of Manx Martin. Each section is marked by nonchronological shifts among times and locales, beginning with
the onset of the Cold War and culminating in the post-Cold War 1990's. DeLillo
links the Soviet Union's first detonation of an atomic device, on October 3, 1951,
with the famous Brooklyn Dodgers-New York Giants baseball playoff game that occurred on thesame date. This connection between a sports game and a geopolitically
dramatic weapons test—two "shots heard 'round the world," in the parlance of the
times—becomes the central reference point for the actions, conflicts, and intersec-
tions of characters in the novel.
   The novel is narrated from the points of view of all of its major characters, and
it shifts intermittently between first-person and third-person narration. *Underworld*
begins at the famous Dodgers-Giants playoff. DeLillo's interconnection of both
"shots heard 'round the world" is clear from the outset, because one of the celebrity
spectators attending the game is Federal Bureau of Investigation (FBI) director
J. Edgar Hoover. Hoover hears news from an aide of the atomic test just before Bobby
Thomson comes to bat. Moments later, as outfield fans scuffle for the game-winning
home-run ball, Hoover considers the possibilities of the new age just inaugurated by
the Soviet test. Hoover's historically documented disdain for governmental authority

dominates the narration as streamers fly, crowds pour into the streets, and the United States and the Soviet Union accelerate the Cold War.

Thomson's home-run ball is caught by Cotter Martin, who skipped school that day to attend the game. Cotter's father, Manx Martin, looking for a fast buck to pay surmounting debts, eventually steals the ball from his son and searches for a buyer. The location of the ball never can be fully verified after Manx's theft. From there on, the novel's trajectory is as discontinuous as that of the ball. Each new section of the novel is framed by the unpredictable, fragmented history of where the ball landed in the world of sports-souvenir hawkers. It is revealed early in the narration that Nick paid more than thirty thousand dollars for the ball to a New York collector, Marvin Moser, who spent his life researching the ball's whereabouts. As meticulous as Moser's research is, he admits he cannot account for all of the links in the chain of owners. Thus, even Nick's eventual ownership is in dispute.

The subjective, unverifiable history of the ball becomes a microcosm for the fragmented histories and identities of the persons and nations in *Underworld*. The primary narrative voices of the novel reappear in the epilogue, collapsed into endlessly hyperlinked information on Internet sites. The placement of these voices inside cyberspace but outside of the human cities that have defined them is not dystopian, despite the novel's move away from the human and toward the technological. Nevertheless, the ending is less than comforting. This epilogue, entitled "Das Kapital" after Karl Marx's famous work, dramatizes the overwhelmingly consumerist emphasis of post-Cold War American life. The novel culminates in one final word that could articulate the end of the human struggle of the Cold War and inaugurate something new for the post-Cold War era; this final word is "Peace." Yet peace is unsettling, because the novel traces the rise of what Dwight D. Eisenhower called the "military-industrial complex" and its transformation into something of a consumer- industrial complex. The peace achieved at the end of the novel is uneasy, and it comes at the price of a culture that has absorbed human individuality and choice into consumerist commodities.

The Characters

DeLillo's novel portrays its characters as products of their place and era, instead of independent individuals outside of conflicts of history. Nick Shay's life is central to all events and conflicts in *Underworld*. Young Nick swaggers and speaks a post-World War II Italian-American Bronx vernacular, yet in Arizona, some thirty years later, Nick is almost contrite; his sentences, like the desert landscape itself, are ordered, reflective, sparse. In Kazakhstan, where he confronts Brian Glassic about his affair with Nick's wife, Marian, and where his waste company engages in black-market commerce, Nick's language reverts to his Bronx days. Here, like the dark, cold landscape of this black-market transaction and confrontation with Brian, Nick's actions and words are clipped, aggressive, and grammatically unstructured.

Klara Sax is an experimental artist whose development in the novel from middle-class urban housewife to avant-garde icon is central to the novel's focus on how the Cold War era loosed human possibility at the same time that it sought to constrain it.

In the 1950's, Klara is Albert's dutiful housewife, caring for an apartment and daughter while Albert teaches school and tutors chessplayers after school. Her paintings are a serious hobby, but she does not seek an audience outside of her circle of friends. As American life becomes less structured and less rigid for women in the 1960's, Klara's life, too, opens up. She and Albert divorce; she becomes active in experimental art circles and the antiwar movement. As experimentalism becomes less dangerous and more assimilated in the 1990's, Klara is an aging icon. She is the subject of television documentaries, and she maintains a coterie of young art students who help produce her most stunning work to date, a collection of retired warplanes painted, ornamented, and patterned against the backdrop of the Arizona desert.

Albert Bronzini's character development also mirrors movements and changes in Cold War American culture, yet his changes, unlike Klara's, are framed by decay and neglect. Albert's life is careful and stratified. In the 1950's, he maintained a quiet, bookish existence as a teacher and scholar in his thriving Bronx neighborhood. With his neighborhood becoming increasingly inhospitable at the end of the century, however, Albert spends his final days shuttling back and forth to the apartments of aging neighbors and sitting alone in the park drinking.

Sister Edgar responds to urban decay with obsessive gestures of cleanliness. She washes her hands incessantly and transforms her apartment into a fortress against germs. As a product herself of the Cold War, Sister Edgar associates the threat of germs with Cold War communism. Just as germs exist in infinite multiplicities— Sister Edgar overbleaches her clothes but wonders how she can be sure the bleach bottle itself is clean—so too does her urban world decay in an infinite multiplicity. Ironically, her greatest contact with the outside world is Ismael Muñoz, a squatter to whom she delivers charity food. Muñoz is infected with the AIDS virus, yet he is Sister Edgar's primary contact in her quest to deliver food to the Bronx's most-neglected residents and homeless. In return for money to restock her church's food pantry, Sister Edgar and her assistant, Sister Grace, provide Muñoz with the locations of abandoned cars that he and fellow squatters can strip for parts. Thus, as much as Sister Edgar's world revolves around order and cleanliness, her primary human contacts live in misery, crime, and neglect.

Themes and Meanings

Underworld follows the lives of several main characters attempting to forge peace and order within surrounding threats of conflict and destruction. DeLillo's overriding metaphors of waste and consumption are central to his characters' desire for peace. Nick's company works in waste management; garbage is central to their business, as is consumption, because consumption breeds waste. According to Nick, he and his coworkers are "cosmologists of waste." Indeed, *Underworld* explores waste and rubbish with cosmological seriousness rather than simply literally as garbage. Nick's job is a microcosm in the novel for late-Cold War and post-Cold War American social relations. Prosperity leads to consumption, which leads to waste. In such a culture, political leaders such as Hoover are corrupt; random violence is on the rise; and even the company designated to manage waste conducts black-market deals in nuclear waste. Thus, even those whose job it is to contain waste are blurring the boundaries between consumption (black-market purchasing) and waste (nuclear residue). Although the novel ends with an assertion of "peace," this assertion is always under stress by the possibility that even the imagination has gone to waste in the world of the novel.

In *Underworld*, the city is the center of human contact and the center of social and political relations. As much as cities produce more waste—and less management of waste—than do rural and suburban areas, the novel locates imaginative activity and acts of human compassion in urban areas: the mingling of different races, ethnicities, and social backgrounds after the 1951 playoff game; Bronzini's chess lessons and his caretaking of elderly neighbors; and Nick's richly imaginative Bronx childhood and teenage years. DeLillo takes the reality of urban decay in the 1990's and recasts this decay in terms of the productive possibilities of human imagination. The city, then, becomes the locale of both ruin and millennial hope in the novel.

Critical Context

Like all DeLillo's work, the novel focuses on the heroism and madness that occurs when the individual is placed in both congruity and conflict with the crowd. Like *Libra* (1988), DeLillo's fictionalized treatment of Lee Harvey Oswald and the John F. Kennedy assassination, *Underworld* attempts to assert the individual onto the collective history. In *Underworld*, DeLillo explores how nationalism, war, and peace ultimately trickle down into the private lives and conflicts of ordinary people, and how the lives and conflicts of these people produce a collective history.

As a postmodern novel, *Underworld* blurs the boundary between individuals and multitudes. By asserting that the consistent frame of reference in a novel is fragmented rather than solid, as it otherwise would be in a realist novel, a postmodern novelist aims to portray characters and conflicts in a state of orderly chaos. Moreover, the postmodern novelist aims to enact this chaos in the experience of reading a postmodern novel. The danger in such an approach, especially as manifested in *Underworld*, is that identification with characters and conflicts becomes difficult for readers when the chaos of a novel's subject matter is enacted in the experience of reading. DeLillo's past work demonstrates that he is comfortable in this arena of fragmentation and orderly chaos. In *Underworld*, he keeps the danger of fragmentation in the offing as he explores moments in history that defy the easy rationalizations that a solid, solitary narrator would offer. Thus, solitary action is never fully noble in *Underworld*; those who manage waste also work the black market, and the truly religious, such as Sister Edgar, perceive the world through paranoid eyes.

Bibliography

Begley, Adam. "Don DeLillo: *Americana, Mao II*, and *Underworld.*" *Southwest Review* 82, no. 4 (1997): 478-505. Argues that language is the foundation for DeLillo's explorations of future constructions of the self in relation to collective history. For Begley, DeLillo's careful attention to the role of language in the construction of selfhood makes DeLillo an important voice in twentieth century fiction.

Keesey, Douglas. *Don DeLillo*. New York: Twayne, 1993. Useful introduction to major themes and techniques in DeLillo's work. Includes relevant biographical material and discussions of DeLillo's fiction through 1992.

LeClair, Tom. *In the Loop: Don DeLillo and the Systems Novel*. Urbana: University of Illinois Press, 1987. The first full-length commentary on DeLillo's work. LeClair examines DeLillo's fiction through an interdisciplinary focus that includes the humanities and natural sciences.

Lentricchia, Frank, ed. *Introducing Don DeLillo*. Durham, N.C.: Duke University Press, 1991. Collection of essays by different critics working from a cultural studies approach to DeLillo's fiction.

Nadeau, Robert. "Don DeLillo." *Readings from the New Book on Nature: Physics and Metaphysics in the Modern Novel*. Amherst: University of Massachusetts Press, 1981. Considers DeLillo's fiction in light of recent convergences between science and philosophy.

Tanner, Tony. "Afterthoughts on Don DeLillo's *Underworld*." *Raritan* 17, no. 4 (Spring, 1998): 48-71. Argues that *Underworld*'s major flaw is that the brilliant interconnectedness of characters, themes, and social commentary in DeLillo's previous novels is largely absent in *Underworld*. Tanner asserts that DeLillo mistakenly deemphasizes novelistic treatments of history in favor of random, disconnected prose news items in *Underworld*.

Tony Trigilio

UNHOLY LOVES

Author: Joyce Carol Oates (1938-   )
Type of plot: Stream of consciousness
Time of plot: The 1970's
Locale: Woodslee, New York, 250 miles north of New York City
First published: 1979

> *Principal characters:*
> BRIGIT STOTT, a thirty-eight-year-old writer, the only novelist in the
>   English department of Woodslee University
> ALEXIS KESSLER, a pianist-composer in retreat at Woodslee
> ALBERT ST. DENNIS, the most famous living English poet, in a
>   residency at Woodslee
> OLIVER BYRNE, the dean of humanities
> MARILYN BYRNE, his wife
> WARREN HOCHBERG, the chairman of the English department and
>   author of a book on Dryden
> VIVIAN HOCHBERG, his wife
> LEWIS SEIDEL, who plans to write on St. Dennis
> FAYE SEIDEL, his wife
> GLADYS FETLER, a popular teacher and Shakespeare scholar
> GOWAN VAUGHAN-JONES, the most highly respected critic in the
>   department
> GEORGE HOUSLEY, a Chaucer specialist
> MINA HOUSLEY, his wife
> STANISLAUS CHUNG, a graduate of Oxford and author of a book on
>   Edmund Spenser
> LESLIE CULLENDON, a wheelchair drunk and a James Joyce specialist
> BABS CULLENDON, his wife
> BARRY SWANWON,
> BRAD KEOUGH, and
> JOE CUFF, younger members of the department

The Novel

Comprising five sections, each subdivided into short chapters, *Unholy Loves* moves through an academic year in the lives of the members of the English department at Woodslee University in upstate New York. Each section is introduced by a date on which a social event occurs: September 1, November 5, December 31, March 8, and May 10. At the center of each event is the presence or absence of Albert St. Dennis, famous English poet-in-residence, whom more prestigious universities have failed to attract to their campuses. The action of the novel takes place in the consciousness of the participants in the communal rituals of academia.

In the first section, the reader is introduced to the characters of the novel as they react to St. Dennis and to one another at a party given by the dean of humanities, Oliver Byrne, to welcome their famous guest. Not to be outdone, Lewis Seidel, who hopes to publish an article or book on St. Dennis, hosts a second party, this one after the poet's first public appearance at the university. Seidel is embarrassed when St. Dennis fails to make an appearance. Competition for the attention of St. Dennis is most apparent during the New Year holidays, when it is obvious that those not invited to St. Dennis's New Year's Eve party find themselves at the Housleys', where some of the guests are disturbed at having to settle for second best. In March, a social function at the Wallers in honor of a visiting authority on Russian ecclesiastical history is marked by mordant revelations about failing marriages, ill health, the demise of the love affair between two of the main characters, and, finally, the shocking death of St. Dennis in a fire. A keenly ironic final social event on May 10, a luncheon in honor of the (forced) retirement of Gladys Fetler, a Shakespeare scholar and the department's most popular teacher, concludes the school year.

Around three main characters—St. Dennis, Brigit Stott, and Alexis Kessler—Oates builds a fictional house of mirrors in which all the characters take turns serving as mirrors for themselves and for all the other characters. Occasions for a labyrinthine series of maskings and unmaskings are provided by the social events honoring St. Dennis. Oates weaves long interior monologues with sparse dialogue to reveal each character from many angles. The illusion prevails through much of the novel that no one angle or point of view dominates, yet Oates returns consistently to her three main characters and especially to Stott, subtly moving Stott to the center of things, so that it is her viewpoint with which the reader is finally left. She is the most fully revealed character. Having experienced the total isolation for which Oates's characters have become famous, Stott has not surrendered to it, unlike St. Dennis (for reasons of age) and Kessler (who lives only for his music). In existential acceptance of her condition, she has emerged on the other side of despair. Consequently, she gradually becomes the consciousness through which the author filters the dark personal and professional realities of her own life and of the academic profession.

Like Anton Chekhov's plays, *Unholy Loves* is plotless. What sketchy plot there is consists mostly of the arrival and death of St. Dennis and of the affair of Stott and Kessler that begins and ends with the passing of the school year. Like Chekhov, who uses a cherry orchard as a device for character revelation in his static drama, Oates employs the visiting poet as an echo for the philosophy of her main character and as a structural device by which her characters reflect and refract images of themselves, images that deteriorate progressively, even as they take on a life of their own as monoliths of modern academic types.

The Characters

A novelist of character, Oates distinguishes among her *personae* by the degree to which each is revealed. The three main characters reveal themselves in their full human dimensions. Others, such as the dean of humanities and the department chairman, enjoy only three-quarter profiles. Still others seem only half-drawn, such as Gladys Fetler and Gowan Vaughan-Jones, who are admirable for their personal and professional ethics. The least revealed of the characters are the younger members of the English department, who worry about non-retention and who, consequently, appear as floating Dantean shades in the subterranean psychological regions Oates's characters inhabit.

It is through the mind of Albert St. Dennis that the reader is given first impressions of Woodslee. Nearly seventy-one, he finds himself in America, an alien world, for the first time. Even his deceased wife, Harriet, who flits in and out of his interior monologues, seems quite unable to help him make sense of this strange otherworld. At a welcoming party early in the school year, his dislocation and sense of isolation affect him physically, and he becomes sick on his host's handsome rug. Of the large group assembled for the occasion, only two persons stand out for him: Stott and Kessler, and, at one point, as though in a prophetic gesture, he clasps a hand of each, joining one to the other. His own isolation, however, only grows until rumor has it that he spends much of his time in the small-town library where tea is served by an aging librarian.

For Brigit Stott, the only novelist in Woodslee's English department, St. Dennis presents a possibility "for another of her unholy loves." Recently divorced, she feels her loneliness as a "raging ravenous despair" that has "allowed her to see into the depths of the universe itself, and to find it distinctly inhuman." Having difficulty writing her novel in progress, she recollects a line from Emily Dickinson: "This is the Hour of Lead," the title Oates uses for chapter 4, in which the death of St. Dennis is reported. Realizing early that the aging poet will not be her love, she spends the night (after that party in September) with Kessler, and the two continue a torrid love affair for some months.

Alexis Kessler, a beautiful bisexual man in his twenties (Brigit is thirty-eight), takes on mythic qualities of Apollo. Living for music, he has had some success with ballet compositions in New York and has come to Woodslee "in retreat." He would like to compose music for some of St. Dennis's poems. With his bleached blond hair, his "epicene features," and his controversial ballet in New York, he is simply accepted as a genius, a prodigy, "so handsome and yet so unmanly." He and Stott stir local gossip as they walk along the river arm in arm. When he leaves her for a holiday on a Caribbean island, she returns once more to a serious involvement in her teaching and writing. At the end, he cannot believe that she will not have him back as a lover. He cannot accept her view that their mutual erotic attraction is transient: "But surely, my love, that can't last?" These are his last words and those with which Oates concludes the novel.

Then there are the self-serving and calculating characters of the novel, who are also taken through the same revelatory process as the main characters. Lewis Seidel hopes to capture the favor of St. Dennis to further his plans for "original research" on the poet. One of the "unassailable" members of the English department, he wields power or gives the impression of doing so. In addition, he envies the attention paid

Stott by other males, and he wishes to enjoy her respect and perhaps her more intimate feelings.

Oliver Byrne, the dean of humanities, regards St. Dennis's residency at Woodslee not only as a coup for the university but also as a means of some sort of promotion, if not at Woodslee, then possibly at a school such as Cornell. Academic intrigue reaches caricature proportions in the self-revelations of both Byrne and Seidel. Seidel has a sordid affair with the wife of a young member of the department whose reappointment is in jeopardy, and he himself has developed an illness, as a result of which he spits phlegm with some blood. Byrne's wife, Marilyn, suspicious of her husband's attention to Stott, develops psychological problems that are soon the subject of gossip.

Warren Hochberg, the department chairman and a Dryden scholar, seems to feel threatened by Seidel, who is nearly as powerful as himself. The incongruously named Stanislaus Chung, who specializes in Spenser, was reared as an orphan by American Baptist missionaries in Singapore, attended Oxford, divorced one wife and married another—an American-born Chinese whom he humiliates in public and terrorizes in private. He astonishes the secretaries with filthy obscenities hurled at book salesmen. Still another brilliantly, if briefly, realized character is Leslie Cullendon, who wheels himself into a party already drunk, excusing his bad jokes and stories as a means of bringing cheer to all, frequently at the expense of his harried wife. He is a Joyce scholar.

Like Chaucer's good clerk of Oxenford, Gowan Vaughan-Jones, the department's most respected critic, has a genuine love for his profession. One of the honored few invited to St. Dennis's New Year's Eve party, he wears overcoats too large for him and carries a battered briefcase. The questions that he wishes to ask St. Dennis are genuine and not self-aggrandizing. Gladys Fetler, the popular Shakespeare scholar, who is also genuine in the pursuit of learning, carries off her disappointing forced retirement with the dignity that has characterized her many years at Woodslee.

With their masks on, the older members of the academic community seem unassailable to the younger members. Unmasked, they reveal themselves not only in their vulnerabilities but also in their metamorphoses into degradation (except for Vaughan-Jones and Fetler).

For St. Dennis, Kessler, and Stott, Oates reserves the recognition and acceptance of their conditions, especially Stott, whose powerful vision of herself includes all the other characters. Accepting the existentialist possibility that "magic might depart from every experience," she returns to her writing.

Themes and Meanings

Wondering bitterly how she and Kessler could have loved each other, Stott tries to "still her lover's anguished voice" by reading from Saint Augustine: "To Carthage then I came, where a cauldron of unholy loves sang all about mine ears." Herein lies the novel's main theme and the source of its title. The presence or absence of spirituality in the modern world appropriately coincides with the architectonics of the novel: the poet's presence or absence at the Woodslee gatherings. Quoting George Santayana's definition of masks as "arrested expressions and admirable echoes of feelings once faithful" as her introductory epigraph, Oates early in the novel refers to the few holy and many unholy loves jostling one another in Stott's mind. Stott is destined once more for disappointment in the poet as a possibility for an unholy love and then later in her erotic love for Kessler. Only as she emerges from these loves do her memories of her childhood in Norfolk, Virginia, intrude on her present failures and does she decide to return to a holy love, the fictive re-creation of her conscience through those childhood influences. She wrestles with her creative urges, and these will transform the chaos and the "aloneness" into life, much as the gregariousness at academic parties dispelled her "dark somber joyless thoughts." Novelist Oates writes about the darker depths of the psyche through which fictional novelist Stott must pass before she can once more create. Like her creator, Stott is both a university professor and a novelist.

On the external level of events and social activity, the novel offers a brilliant satiric gallery of academic types. Demanding male egos, mediocre wives, jealousies, backbiting, infidelities—all acquire a ceaseless rhythm of their own and exist not only for satiric purposes but also as an integral part of Oates's gothic vision of life.

As a feminist, Oates reflects the heightened consciousness of the 1970's through Gladys Fetler, who was the only woman in the English department until Stott was hired, primarily as a result of affirmative action pressure.

Critical Context

Oates's tenth novel, *Unholy Loves* contrasts somewhat with her earlier novels in having "struck a cooler note amid the more extreme imaginings," according to a *Times Literary Supplement* reviewer. A balance between the masked and naked world is more consistently maintained here than in the earlier works. In the academic world, as illustrated in the retirement luncheon for Gladys Fetler, the fantasies and the bitter disappointments are absorbed by the warmth of experiences shared. Even the most isolated person participates in the sense of community by his or her very presence. "The myth of the isolated self," Oates has said, "will be the most difficult to destroy." In her stories about academia, dark and satiric though they may appear, isolation and self-destruction are mitigated by the communal sense.

Oates belongs to a select community of writers whose bizarre and savagely cruel world pits the forces of life and those of destruction against each other within an individual, a struggle mirrored in one's social conduct and the external world. Charles Dickens, Fyodor Dostoevski, and Joseph Conrad (and earlier, Sophocles and Shakespeare) lead that community of authors.

Bibliography

Creighton, Joanne V. *Joyce Carol Oates: Novels of the Middle Years*. New York: Twayne, 1992. Creighton presents the first critical study of the novels Oates published between 1977 and 1990, including the mystery novels published under the name of Rosamund Smith. Her critical analysis of *Unholy Loves* is particularly insightful.

Daly, Brenda. *Lavish Self-Divisions: The Novels of Joyce Carol Oates.* Jackson: University of Mississippi Press, 1996. An excellent study that argues that the "father-identified daughters in her early novels have become, in the novels of the 1980s, self-authoring women who seek alliances with their culturally devalued mothers." Offers a perceptive reading of the evolution of feminist elements in Oates's work. Includes a perceptive reading of *Unholy Loves*.

_____. "Marriage as Emancipatory Metaphor: A Woman Wedded to Teaching and Writing in Oates's *Unholy Loves.*" *CRITIQUE: Studies in Contemporary Fiction* 37 (Summer, 1996): 270-288. Daly argues that the novel demonstrates the need for reform of academic authority as well as the ways in which competition within the academic setting prevents growth in the community. She shows how Oates's later novels, *Solstice* and *Marya, A Life*, expand and explore feminist themes within academe.

Johnson, Greg. *Invisible Writer: A Biography of Joyce Carol Oates.* New York: Dutton, 1998. An illuminating look at the novelist once dubbed "the dark lady of American letters." Drawing on Oates's private letters and journals, as well as interviews with family, friends, and colleagues, Johnson offers a definitive study of one of America's most gifted novelists.

Wesley, Marilyn C. *Refusal and Transgression in Joyce Carol Oates' Fiction.* Westport, Conn.: Greenwood Press, 1993. An interesting study spanning the spectrum of Oates's work. Includes a helpful bibliography and index.

Susan Rusinko

THE UNIVERSAL BASEBALL ASSOCIATION, INC., J. HENRY WAUGH, PROP.

Author: Robert Coover (1932-   )
Type of plot: Psychological study
Time of plot: The present and the UBA years LVI and CLVII
Locale: A "major-league" American city, never specified
First published: 1968

Principal characters:
> J. HENRY WAUGH, the inventor and proprietor of the Universal Baseball Association
> HORACE ZIFFERBLATT, his employer and the owner of the accounting firm where Henry works
> LOU ENGEL, Henry's friend and coworker
> DAMON RUTHERFORD, a promising rookie pitcher for the Pioneers
> JOCK CASEY, a rookie pitcher for the Knickerbockers
> SYCAMORE FLYNN, the manager of the Knickerbockers

The Novel

The unsuspecting first-time reader of *The Universal Baseball Association, Inc., J. Henry Waugh, Prop.* will find its first few pages confusing: A character named J. Henry Waugh, greatly excited, seems to be watching not simply an ordinary baseball game but a no-hit game in progress. Henry looks first at the sun, high over the ballpark, then at his watch, but the watch reads almost eleven o'clock, and any American reader knows that major-league baseball is not played in the morning. The confusion intensifies when Henry thinks that it may be a long night—night?—with the sun high over the park? During the seventh-inning stretch, Henry leaves his apartment and goes to the delicatessen downstairs to buy a sandwich. Henry must be watching the game on television, then.

The mystery is resolved soon, though, when it becomes clear that the game is being played only in Henry's mind. The contest is indeed a game, one directed with dice according to a set of rules of Henry's devising, and played by characters existing only in his imagination.

The richly colorful world of the Universal Baseball Association, known only to Henry, contrasts strongly with his humdrum existence as an accountant. Henry is a bachelor with numerous acquaintances but apparently only one friend—another accountant named Lou Engel. Yet there seems a fitness in Henry's attraction to, even fanaticism about, baseball. It is overwhelmingly a game of record keeping: wins and losses, batting averages, earned-run averages, and all the other statistical paraphernalia by which the baseball fan measures out his life and admiration.

Henry prefers the world located in his apartment's kitchen. He has invented not simply a game—he has created an entire eight-team league and played out fifty-five full seasons by the opening of the novel. The number of UBA seasons (always given in Roman numerals in the novel, for example, LVI) has caught up to the fifty-six-year-old Henry's age, a fact which seems significant to him. For only part of his passion is the rolling out of the games themselves. He has recorded each game on a scorecard, maintained all the records and statistics, and even created biographies and personalities for each of the players on each club's twenty-one-man roster. Just as players do in real life, Henry's players grow old and retire, new ones arrive from the "minors" and succeed or fail. Players marry, have children, and go into business or politics after retirement.

After he completes each "season," he records all the information (including prose resumes in a parody of sports-page style) in large record books, labeled the Official Archives; forty volumes line the walls of his kitchen.

As a result of this detailed subcreation, by far the most interesting action of the novel takes place in Henry's mind. As the book opens, Damon Rutherford, son of a Hall-of-Famer and rookie pitcher for one of the clubs, has gone seven innings without giving up a hit. As Henry rolls the dice, his excitement and concentration grow—and Damon does indeed pitch a no-hit game, to Henry's deep delight. His next day at Horace Zifferblatt's accounting firm (although "real" in the world of the story) seems hazy and pale by comparison with the vivid and concrete game. Both Henry and the reader wait impatiently for the evening—and the next game—to come.

When Damon next pitches, he begins again to set his opponents down in order, and Henry is nearly frantic at the thought of two no-hit games back to back. He envisions a new era for the Universal Baseball Association—the "Damon Rutherford Era"—chronicled in the future archives of his league. The turning point arrives, however, when the three dice come up all ones. This roll takes the game out of the ordinary by sending Henry to a special "Stress Chart," according to which unusual events may occur depending on the next roll. On that next roll, each die again comes up showing a single pip, referring Henry to the "Extraordinary Events Chart," consulted perhaps only once a season. A third consecutive roll of 1-1-1 sends Henry to the fateful line: The batter has been killed by a pitched ball, and the batter is Damon Rutherford.

The event has as heavy an impact on Henry as would the death of a son. He becomes depressed, unable to function either in the real or in his imaginary world. He provokes his employer and endangers his job despite the efforts of his friend Lou Engel to help him, and he is frightened by the depth of his involvement in his fantasy world. As the novel moves toward its conclusion, he invites Lou to play the game with him. Perhaps he hopes by sharing the fantasy to reduce it to manageable proportions, to make it simply another game, like chess or Monopoly.

The plan fails. To Lou the UBA is only a game: In a sense, Lou "demythologizes" it. Henry is angered rather than supported by Lou's inability to enter the imaginary world. After a short and sharp argument, Lou departs, and with him departs Henry's last chance for sanity. He is last seen planning for a future that will allow him to do nothing but play his game.

In a moving final chapter, the reader is again in the fiction within a fiction—the

Universal Baseball Association—but a league darkly changed. It is season CLVII: one hundred seasons and thousands of games later. The players are fearfully beginning an annual ritual that re-creates the death of Damon Rutherford, perhaps actually sacrificing a promising young player to the god of the game—a god who sits in a kitchen he no longer notices, compulsively rolling dice.

The Characters

J. Henry Waugh is as tormented a character as one could find in a Russian novel; he stands at the novel's center: Action is seen either through his eyes or within his mind. The people he meets in the "real" world have a certain vitality of their own: his boss Zifferblatt, his friend Lou, Hettie (a B-girl who appears in several scenes). Yet overwhelmingly, the characters of interest are the baseball players. Because the game is constantly on Henry's mind, he tends to see the real world through the filter of his game.

For example, he sees everything in terms of names. While Henry is riding on a bus passing a bus stop, the word "whistlestop" occurs to him, and he has invented a new character, Whistlestop Busby, a second baseman.

The two pivotal baseball players are Damon Rutherford, a young man of great reserve and confidence, and Jock Casey, a rookie like Damon, but one whom fate will cast as a villain rather than as a hero. Henry's hatred for this dice-created phantom grows until, for the first time in the novel, he cheats: He arranges the dice to have Casey killed in retribution. As Henry's grip on reality weakens, it is clear that Jock and Damon are becoming less and less individuals and more and more archetypal figures from myth: Damon, like Baldur in Norse mythology, a dying god, and Casey, the scheming Loki arranging his death.

Themes and Meanings

Coover's novel need not be read as a metaphor for American life or as any comment on society. It is sufficient to see it as the story of a mind succumbing to the real delights of the imagination. J. Henry Waugh has real creative power: What he does differs not at all from what the writer of a novel might do. Henry is talented enough a creator that his audience, even though it is only himself, may justly prefer the world of his dreams to the world of reality: His dreamworld has the color, vigor, energy, and drama—both tragedy and comedy—that Henry's "real" existence lacks. No character in the "real" world is as quirky, as individual, or as full of life as the players of the UBA.

Many of these UBA characters seem to image his own situation in a fragmentary way. A manager the same age as Henry, Sycamore Flynn, has a nightmarish experience: He becomes lost in passages beneath an empty baseball park at night. When, to his relief, he emerges onto the darkened field, he has the feeling that the diamond is peopled with ghosts who are endlessly replaying the game in which Rutherford was killed. What better metaphor for Henry, who is literally losing his way beneath the weight of the baseball fantasy that he has created?

The reader who finds himself wishing (in the middle of a scene in the accounting office) that the novel would return to the playing fields of Henry's imagination can well understand the fascination that the game holds for Henry and can find Henry's ultimate loss of self in the game as a plausible outcome.

Critical Context

Robert Coover's first novel, *The Origin of the Brunists* (1966), was highly enough regarded to win the William Faulkner Foundation First Novel Award in 1966. The critical (and popular) acclaim for *The Universal Baseball Association, Inc., J. Henry Waugh, Prop.* showed that Coover was not a writer with only one story to tell but one who followed his first success with a greater one.

To shorten the novel's title to *The Universal Baseball Association, Inc.*, as is usually done, misplaces its intention: This is a story about J. Henry Waugh, a man who discovers the delights and the dangers of Fancy.

Bibliography

Basbanes, Nicholas, A. "The Traditionalist and the Revolutionary." *Biblio* (September, 1998): 10. An interesting profile of Penelope Fitzgerald and Robert Coover that offers insight into the different ways each approaches writing. Although Basbanes does not directly discuss Coover's novel, the essay does reveal Coover's thoughts on fiction writing, a subject that has a bearing on *The Universal Baseball Association, Inc., J. Henry Waugh, Prop.*

Maltby, Paul. *Dissident Postmodernists: Barthelme, Coover, and Pynchon.* Philadelphia: University of Pennsylvania Press, 1991. An astute comparative analysis of the differences and similarities between the works of these three authors. The discussion of Coover is particularly perceptive. A bibliography is included for further reading.

Miguel-Alfonso, Ricardo. "Mimesis and Self-Consciousness in Robert Coover's *The Universal Baseball Association.*" *CRITIQUE: Studies in Contemporary Fiction* 37 (Winter, 1996): 92-107. Miguel-Alfonso argues, using a baseball motif, that Coover's novel deals with interactions between the various components of fictional writing. He analyzes Coover's control of the story, referentiality, the interplay between writer and reader, and other story elements.

Ott, Bill. Review of *The Universal Baseball Association, Inc., J. Henry Waugh, Prop.*, by Robert Coover. *Booklist* 95 (September 1, 1998): 168. A brief but favorable review which addresses the issue of free will in Coover's novel.

Walter E. Meyers

THE VALLEY

Author: Rolando Hinojosa (1929-   )
Type of plot: Social realism
Time of plot: The 1920's to the 1970's
Locale: The Texas-Mexico border
First published: 1983 (revised from *Estampas del valle y otras obras/ Sketches of the Valley and Other Works*, 1973)

> Principal characters:
> RAFA BUENROSTRO, the autobiographical protagonist of many of the sketches
> DON MANUEL GUZMÁN, a former revolutionary modeled after Hinojosa's father
> JEHÚ MALACRA, the son of Tere Noriega and Roque Malacra, orphaned at an early age
> AUNT CHEDES BRIONES, Jehú Malacra's aunt, who helps to rear the orphaned boy
> DON VÍCTOR, a former revolutionary connected with the circus
> GILBERTO CASTAÑEDA, the husband of Marta Cordero, whose brother, Baldemar, he sees murder Ernesto Tamez
> BALDEMAR CORDERO, Gilberto's friend and brother-in-law
> ERNESTO TAMEZ, a man stabbed to death by Baldemar Cordero

The Novel

This collection of sketches about Rolando Hinojosa's fictional Belken County, situated just north of the Mexican border in Texas, was Hinojosa's first major publication. Originally, it was rendered in Spanish with English translations by Gustávo Valadéz and José Reyna under the title *Estampas del valle y otras obras/Sketches of the Valley and Other Works*. Hinojosa himself translated it under the present title in 1983, adding some material and a set of photographs from his family album. The collection constitutes a novel by some definitions of the term, but it also is the first major segment of Hinojosa's evolving multivolume "Klail City Death Trip" series. Hinojosa focuses on the area around his birthplace, Mercedes, Texas (Klail City in his series). In these sketches, he attempts to capture the ambience of the area and its people.

The Valley lacks the real plot, the dramatic climax, the carefully planned denouement, and the clearly identifiable protagonist found in conventional novels. Nevertheless, it contains pervasive characters, including the frequent narrator, Rafa Buenrostro, the biographical details of whose life closely approximate Hinojosa's. It also presents Jehú Malacra, seen through many eyes at various stages of his development. The last pages of the book, "A Life of Rafa Buenrostro," focus on Rafa.

Three early sketches—a total of twenty-three printed lines—focus on Rafa's early school experience and evoke the sense of separation Mexican American children feel from their Anglo classmates and teachers. The three paragraphs that constitute these sketches are not directly related to one another. Rather, each provides a snapshot of something connected with that early school experience: the teacher, Miss Moy, is described in five lines; a Hispanic girl lies about what she had for breakfast to make herself seem more like her Anglo classmates (eight lines); Rafa punches Hilario Berrago in the mouth during recess (ten lines).

From these school sketches, Hinojosa moves directly to a short vignette about a man from the water company coming to shut off the Ponce family's water supply because they have not paid their bill. The next sketch moves to a neighboring town, Flora, and has no direct connection with what has preceded it.

A six-line sketch follows telling about how in Edgerton the narrator's father had once fired three shots at a man who was trying to knife him. As these sketches unfold, readers, probably at first bewildered at encountering unfamiliar characters in unfamiliar towns, begin to develop a sense of the region about which Hinojosa is writing. The individual sketches may lack plot, yet from them emerge details useful elsewhere throughout this book and the others of the "Klail City Death Trip" series.

One sustained narrative among the sketches focuses on Baldemar (Balde) Cordero's fatal stabbing of Ernesto Tamez in a barroom brawl. Balde's friend, Gilberto (Beto) Castañeda, is married to Balde's sister, Marta. They all live together in Klail City. Beto, witness to the stabbing, gives a deposition recounting what happened. Through it, readers learn the backgrounds of Balde and Beto and of other characters they have previously encountered in the book. A sketch of Beto Castañeda follows.

Some characters in this collection emerge more fully developed in subsequent volumes of the series. Jehú Malacra is a typical example. In this book, readers first meet Jehú's grandfather, an unnamed narrator, and his long-dead great-grandfather, Braulio Tapia. Jehú's father, Roque Malacra, visits the narrator, a widower, requesting his daughter Tere Noriega's hand in marriage.

In fewer than twenty lines, the narrator consents to this request and reflects upon his having visited Braulio Tapia many years before seeking permission to marry Braulio's daughter Matilde, Tere's mother. He also recalls that Braulio's wife, doña Sóstenes, was dead when he approached his prospective father-in-law, as the narrator's wife is dead when Roque approaches him.

In these parallel circumstances, one senses the recurrence of human events that is part of continuance in a county such as Belken. Hinojosa's family lived in the South Texas area from the 1740's and became "accidental" American citizens in 1845, when the boundary between Mexico and the United States was redrawn a few miles south of where they had previously lived as Mexicans. *The Valley* and subsequent volumes follow Jehú Malacra from his birth through his childhood, his war experiences, and his rise as an officer in the local bank and second husband of Becky Escobar, to whom Hinojosa later devotes a full volume, *Becky and Her Friends* (1990).

The Characters

Rafa Buenrostro, the autobiographical narrator of many of the sketches, is a splendid observer. Secure in his identity, he understands the people around him in Hinojosa's Belken County. He also is ambitious and knows something of the world outside Belken's circumscribed boundaries. He has served in the Korean War and is planning to attend the University of Texas at Austin; he also benefits from his position as the youngest son in a family of five. Rafa does more reporting than judging. He appreciates the circumstances of Belken County's Mexican American citizens and understands the lapses and missteps they make.

Jehú Malacra is depicted from birth to young manhood. Losing his parents early, he is reared partly by Aunt Chedes Briones and grows up with his three cousins, Édu, Pepe, and Vicky. Vicky Briones distresses her mother by joining the circus, but her doing so enables Jehú to work with don Víctor in transporting circus props from town to town. Jehú becomes a solid citizen in Hinojosa's later volumes and also develops into a person of some integrity who challenges his boss at the bank. In this volume, readers see Jehú as a circus roustabout and message carrier as he wrestles with the dilemmas people face reaching adulthood.

Emilio Tamez is presented in a brief sketch as someone to whom bad things happen. He lost his right ear in a barroom brawl, but before that, at age eleven, he slipped as he was jumping from wagon to wagon, injuring himself badly enough that he still limps. He can read and write in both Spanish and English, but, according to Hinojosa, he is stupid. He receives considerable abuse.

Ernesto Tamez's relationship to Emilio is unclear. Balde Cordero kills Ernesto in a bar in Klail City. It is evident, however, that Ernesto is related to Emilio, and one character states that Ernesto's family is "an odd bunch."

Balde Cordero stabs Ernesto, but because he is drunk at the time, he does not remember doing so. The implication is that Balde, who is sentenced to fifteen years in prison for murder, is as much a victim as Ernesto.

One sketch entitled "Don Manuel Guzmán" is about Hinojosa's father, who appears in other sketches throughout the book. The father owned three cleaning establishments and part of a bakery. Loyal to the Mexican government, he finally became a policeman in the Mexican district of Klail City and is presented as an ex-revolutionary who matures into a solid citizen. Don Manuel represents a man poised between two cultures, but he is clearly a genuine part of only one of them: He is Mexican to the core.

Braulio Tapia, mentioned briefly in an early sketch bearing his name but relating the story of his son and granddaughter, is presented more fully in a later historical sketch, one of the few that delves into Belken County's history as a part of Mexico. Hinojosa depicts don Braulio, born in 1883, as a revolutionary of the same ilk as don Manuel, who knew Pancho Villa and Álvaro Obregon personally.

Don Víctor is part of the revolution, a Mexican lieutenant colonel married to a Mexican Jew. After she, their son, and their unborn child die of Spanish influenza in 1920, however, the grief-stricken don Víctor ends up in Belken County with the circus. In don Víctor, as in most of his other characters, Hinojosa, providing minimal information, demonstrates how people evolve into what they are.

Themes and Meanings

Hinojosa's main thrust in this first volume of the "Klail City Death Trip" series has to do with establishing the sense of recurrence and continuity that characterizes his fictional (and actual) county in South Texas. The boundary changed in 1845, but the drawing of a line on a map cannot change the hearts, souls, or heritage of a citizenry.

Hinojosa's sketches, if viewed in the light of the full series, also have to do with how people mature into what they eventually become. If his characters are inconsistent, Hinojosa makes no apology, saying merely that people are not consistent as they go through life. Some things about them remain the same, some change. In Hinojosa's eyes, consistency of character is not a valid human trait.

In this volume, as in the others in the series, there is really no dominant character; even in *Becky and Her Friends*, Becky Escobar cannot be called a dominant character in the usual sense. Rather than writing about one or more protagonists, Hinojosa writes about a community of people. Readers meet most of them without being given much background: They just appear on the page engaged in living some small part of their lives.

Some critics disdain this approach, yet it replicates the way people come to know and understand society in real life. People happen upon scenes and draw from them what they can with the information available to them.

Those who judge Hinojosa negatively should remember that when Gertrude Stein replicated actual speech patterns with great accuracy in *Three Lives* (1909), readers accustomed to having authors run interference for them between actual speech and the dialogue of most novels were appalled. Yet in that experimental novel, Stein broke new stylistic ground that led many subsequent authors to reconsider how they would present dialogue in their fiction.

Hinojosa has reassessed the ways human beings derive information from actual occurrences in their lives. In the volumes in his series, he has no misgivings about plunging directly into ongoing action. If one suddenly is plunged into a scene that depicts an event in Flora, Hinojosa does not pause to tell his readers where Flora is or what kind of town it is. He does that elsewhere in the book, but he does not interrupt the ongoing action of his story to provide details without which his readers can still perceive the action.

One cannot deny that an initial reading of a book such as *The Valley* bewilders and confuses readers. Hinojosa, who holds a doctorate in Spanish literature from the University of Illinois and is well schooled in literature, is bent on achieving a depiction that mirrors actual reality. Upon completing this book, readers have a sense of community that few more conventional novels impart.

Critical Context

The 1960's were crucial to Rolando Hinojosa's development as a writer. He completed a five-year stint as a high school teacher and factory laborer in Brownsville,

Texas, and in 1962 began graduate studies at New Mexico Highlands University, receiving the master's degree in 1963. He then moved to the University of Illinois at Urbana for doctoral work.

Hinojosa and his wife arrived in Illinois just before the strident racial uprisings of the 1960's, a period that focused attention upon the problems of blacks. Out of this period grew a hospitable atmosphere for black protest literature and, subsequently, for black literature that had been produced earlier. In this climate, all minority literatures began to be encouraged and reevaluated.

Just before completing the doctorate, Hinojosa took a teaching job at San Antonio's Trinity University, where, fortunately, he came under the influence of Tomás Rivera. Rivera encouraged Hinojosa's writing, urging him to submit a manuscript to the Quinto Sol competition, which Rivera had won in 1970. Hinojosa submitted the original version of *The Valley*, which took the prize in 1972 and resulted in the book's publication the following year.

Bibliography
Akers, John C. "From Translation to Rewriting: Rolando Hinojosa's *The Valley*." *Americas Review* 21 (Spring, 1993): 91-102. Akers analyzes *The Valley*, the English version of his first published fiction *Estampas del valle y otras obras*. He compares this novel with other Spanish works and their English versions, and presents a useful study of the structural, linguistic, and thematic aspects of the English version.
Hinojosa, Rolando. "Chicano Literature: An American Literature in Transition." In *The Identification and Analysis of Chicano Literature*, edited by Francisco Jiménez. New York: Bilingual Press, 1979. Hinojosa contrasts the interest in black writing to that in Hispanic writing. He foresees a developing interest in Chicano literature. His predictions have proved accurate.
_____. "This Writer's Sense of Place." In *The Texas Literary Tradition: Fiction, Folklore, History*, edited by Don Graham, James W. Lee, and William T. Pilkington. Austin: University of Texas Press, 1983. Hinojosa discusses how he transformed the area where he grew up into his fictional county. One senses here the dichotomy he felt as a part of two cultures. Schooled to value his heritage, he could not, however escape Hispanic-Anglo tensions.
Leal, Luis. "History and Memory in *Estampas del valle*." In *The Rolando Hinojosa Reader: Essays Historical and Critical*, edited by José David Saldívar. Houston: Arté Publico Press, 1985. Deals with how Hinojosa structured his memories of childhood to formulate his novel. Also shows how local history infuses Hinojosa's writing.
Saldívar, José D. "Our Southwest: An Interview with Rolando Hinojosa." In *The Rolando Hinojosa Reader: Essays Critical and Historical*, edited by José D. Saldívar. Houston: Arté Publico Press, 1985. In this interview, Hinojosa talks about the evolution of his work. He acknowledges his debt to Tomás Rivera, who encouraged him to offer his work for publication. The piece is valuable in that it traces the progression of Hinojosa's writing.

_____. "Rolando Hinojosa's *Klail City Death Trip*: A Critical Introduction." In *The Rolando Hinojosa Reader: Essays Historical and Critical*, edited by José David Saldívar. Houston: Arté Publico Press, 1985. This essay provides an overall assessment of the "Klail City Death Trip" series and illustrates how Hinojosa conceives of his work. Useful for Hinojosa's comments on local color.

R. Baird Shuman

THE VALLEY OF DECISION

Author: Edith Wharton (1862-1937)
Type of plot: Historical romance
Time of plot: From the mid-1700's until the French Revolution
Locale: Northern Italy, with excursions to Milan, Rome, Florence, and Venice
First published: 1902

> *Principal characters:*
> ODO VALSECCA, the protagonist, an Italian aristocrat who eventually
> becomes the Duke of Pianura
> FULVIA VIVALDI, an ardent liberal idealist who becomes Odo's mistress
> ABATE CANTAPRESTO, Odo's governor
> COUNT LELIO TRESCORRE, the Prime Minister of Pianura
> CARLO GAMBA, an activist in the liberal uprising

The Novel

This two-volume romance chronicles the rise to power of Odo Valsecca during the intellectual and political tumult which preceded the French Revolution. During his childhood and early manhood, Odo comes in close contact with all the major factions—the peasantry, the clergy, the liberal freethinkers, and the nobility—which have a vital stake in maintaining or subverting the antiquated power structure based on rigid class distinctions and superstitious religious traditions. How Odo's actions and ideals are shaped by these forces and the traditions that they represent is the focus of the novel. He comes to the throne with high ideals and expectations and the zeal of a reformer, only to discover that compassion and logic are no match for superstition and self-interest.

As a child reared in extreme poverty by peasants on his mother's estate, Odo experiences at firsthand the brutality of the feudal system. He escapes the drudgery of this life by daydreaming; he feels a "melancholy kinship" with the suffering face of Saint Francis of Assisi painted on the chapel walls.

Once he is seen as a possible heir to his ailing cousin, the duke, Odo is brought to court and indulged in the luxuries of the ruling class. As the years pass, he grows increasingly comfortable with the superficial life of the aristocracy, a life which "made manners the highest morality, and conversation the chief end of man." Although he retains a sense that society needs to be restructured, he is repeatedly drawn into the silken web of sensuality, a world in which "sensation ruled supreme" and "nowhere was the mind arrested by a question or an idea."

Odo's love of beauty, romance, and reform takes on new meaning when he attends a meeting of freethinkers, a group of literati who meet surreptitiously to discuss forbidden economic, philosophical, and religious questions. Here, he believes, are men who lead "a life in dignified contrast to the wasteful and aimless existence of the nobility." Here, too, he meets the beautiful Fulvia Vivaldi, who comes to symbolize for him "his

best aims and deepest failure." Through her, he romanticizes the whole concept of reform and becomes convinced that good intentions will result in social improvements.

When Fulvia is exiled because of her liberal views on church and state, Odo is again
tempted by the sumptuous life of the privileged. As heir-presumptive to the throne, he
is required to travel to the courts of Turin, Milan, Rome, Florence, and Venice. After
various travels, adventures, and political intrigues, Odo is reunited with Fulvia and,
upon the death of his cousin, becomes Duke of Pianura. For social and economic reasons, he marries his cousin's widow and takes Fulvia as his mistress. Together, Odo
and Fulvia attempt to put into practice the liberal principles, espoused by the freethinkers, which would lessen the stranglehold which the nobles and clergy have on the
peasantry.

They encounter resistance from all sides. Most vehement are the peasants, who,
urged on by a manipulative clergy, vigorously protest the reforms which would benefit them. On the day that the duke signs the new constitution guaranteeing greater freedom, he appears in public with Fulvia only to see her shot by an angry mob. After her
death, Odo's desire—whether for reform, revenge, power, or life itself—is gone. He
returns to the reactionary, dictatorial ways of his predecessors. By then, however, the
bloody insurrections in France have spread to Italy. He is forced from the throne. He
leaves Pianura almost willingly, with a brief stop before the picture of Saint Francis,
more of an exile than the frightened nine-year-old boy who began the story.

The Characters

Odo Valsecca is a man divided. His sensitivity, his love of beauty, proves to be both
his most admirable trait and his greatest weakness. He is a sensual idealist who romanticizes his love for liberty in Fulvia. This causes him to underestimate the
passionate intensity of both the reactionaries and the revolutionaries. Although he
has the reader's sympathy, he does not earn his or her complete approval. He is
well-intentioned—and consequently virtually unique in a world in which the lure of
power and appearance are almost irresistible. Yet his early indulgence in the pleasures
at court proves to be his Achilles' heel. He is not so much torn between two worlds as
he is easily diverted from his interest in liberty by luxury. Even after meeting Fulvia,
Odo finds himself, amid the splendor of Venice, wondering "Why should today always be jilted for tomorrow, sensation sacrificed to thought?"

Although he travels widely, experiences life both in a hovel and at court, and comes
in close contact with political opportunists and idealists, Odo's character undergoes
little development. In making Odo's life the focus for the conflicts of a multitude of
political ambitions and ideals in eighteenth century Italy, Wharton makes him too impressionable to be fully convincing. He becomes little more than an emblem for a confused and turbulent age. His high aims and his ultimate failure lack any tragic dimensions.

Odo begins his reign believing "that this new gospel of service was the base on
which all sovereignty must henceforth repose." Yet as his reforms are misinterpreted
or mistrusted and as he loses the support of the peasants as well as the nobles, the lib-

erals as well as the clergy, Odo begins to see himself as "a prisoner of his own folly." He ends by believing that he is simply "acting out the inevitable."

His mistress, Fulvia, is even less fully realized than Odo. From beginning to end she remains an impassioned idealist. From the beginning, her nobility of mind is an inspiration to the vacillating Odo. Yet her life is a too thinly veiled allegory to awaken any deep sympathy in the reader. All of her thoughts and feelings are directed to the service of a single cause. Even her affection for Odo is inextricably interwoven with her desire to see him initiate the reforms which she believes will free mankind from outdated beliefs and superstitions. She becomes, for the reader as well as for Odo, "a formula rather than a woman." Near the end, she becomes increasingly dogmatic and shrill. Odo realizes that "to a spirit like Fulvia's it might become possible to shed blood in the cause of tolerance."

Wharton is much more successful in drawing vivid and memorable portraits of the minor characters. Odo's grossly overweight governor, Abate Cantapresto, groaning under the "double burden of flesh and consequence," is both a ludicrous figure and a shrewd opportunist who misses no chance to ingratiate himself with his superiors or to grow prosperous as Odo's prospects brighten. He instructs his young charge early in the rules for success in an amoral world: The only thing necessary "to complete enjoyment of the fruits of this garden of Eden . . . is discretion."

Count Trescorre, too, advises the youthful Odo to "form no sentimental ties but in his own society or in the world of pleasure." The ambitious count, intelligent and polished, is a vivid portrait of the nobility whose sole passion is power. He is a master of political intrigue, with "the cool aim of the man who never wastes a shot." He carries on an affair with the duchess while making himself indispensable to her husband, the duke. Even though he plots against Odo's rise to power, Trescorre manages to become his prime minister.

The hunchback Carlo Gamba has pledged his life to overthrowing the system which permits—even encourages—the excesses and abuses of the nobility. He is a colorful figure: embittered, sarcastic, and a shrewd political activist. Odo meets him when they are both boys who together explore the castle at Pianura. Gamba, who describes himself as "the servant of your illustrious mother's servants," tells the young Odo, "Call me Brutus . . . for Brutus killed a tyrant." Gamba reluctantly comes to trust Odo once Odo returns to Pianura to become duke. The friendship between those two men of different stations is one of the most intriguing relationships in the novel.

Themes and Meanings

The novel presents a richly detailed account of the political and cultural milieu of eighteenth century Italy and poses several disturbing questions on the nature of society and the danger of reform.

Through Odo's travels, Wharton portrays with vivid, realistic detail the sight and sense of the great cities of Italy as they might have appeared during the period. Indeed, the panoramic description and exquisite detail are much more convincing and arresting than the rather traditional roles of the principal characters. From such careful, yet not labored, descriptive passages of the cities and societies in which poverty and splendor are interwoven, Wharton is able to set the stage for the political unrest which concludes the novel.

Despite good intentions, Odo is unable either to alleviate the suffering of the peasants or to pacify the revolutionaries. He comes to realize that power and principle united do not necessarily result in beneficial conditions for society or for the individual. He finds himself in the position of forcing on his subjects liberties that they neither understand nor desire. Tradition and superstition have a deep hold on the poor, who "would rather starve under a handsome merry king that has the name of being the best billard-player in Europe than go full under [a] solemn reforming Austrian Archduke."

The reformers fare little better at Wharton's hands than the corrupt clergy and nobility. They, too, are blinded by their passions, caught up in a "spirit that was to destroy one world without surviving to create another." Odo eventually comes to believe that they are as misguided as are the rest, deceived by the new rhetoric, "calling instincts ideas and ideas revelations." The quest for liberty carries with it its own paradox and may leave a man more of a prisoner than before. Odo sees his love for Fulvia fade and learns that "the sovereign's power may be a kind of spiritual prison to the man." His finest moment occurs late in the novel when he realizes that "the beauty, the power, the immortality, dwelt not in the idea but in the struggle for it."

The title of the novel is taken from the Book of Joel, an apocalyptic prophesy written, scholars estimate, between 450 and 400 B.C.E. It foretells the plagues, earthquakes, and devastation, when "the sun shall be turned to darkness and the moon into blood," which will precede the Judgment Day. All nations will be called to the "Valley of the Lord's Judgement" and there will be "the roar of multitudes, multitudes in the Valley of Decision."

Critical Context

The Valley of Decision, Wharton's first full-length novel, was preceded by three novellas, a volume of poetry, and a nonfiction volume, *The Decoration of Houses* (1897). The close attention to detail and design in the latter proved to be extremely valuable in her effort to evoke the myriad sights and life-styles of eighteenth century Italy. It is one of only three historical novels of her long career, the others being *The Age of Innocence* (1920) and the posthumously published *The Buccaneers* (1938). In a sense, *The Valley of Decision* might be seen as her first novel of manners, although it is very different from her careful scrutiny of upper-class New York society in her later novels.

The novel is also a harbinger of the social criticism which is an important quality in the later work. Although the characters are rather stock romantic figures, the insight into social conditions is penetrating. Wharton displays a remarkably evenhanded approach in her presentation of diverse segments of society. She demonstrates that the pride and prejudice within a social system run very deep. One reason why Odo's reforms do not succeed is his failure to understand that prejudice and superstition have become "a habit of thought so old that it had become instinctive. . . . To hope to eradicate it was like trying to drain all the blood from a man's body without killing him." Wharton wrote during an age of political and social progressivism. Her first novel is impressive in its balanced view of the evils both of the established order and of reform movements. As in her later novels, she leaves the reader not with answers but with a series of disturbing questions.

Bibliography
Ammons, Elizabeth. *Edith Wharton's Argument with America*. Athens: University of Georgia Press, 1980. Ammons proposes that Wharton's "argument with America" concerns the freedom of women, an argument in which she had a key role during three decades of significant upheaval and change. This engaging book examines the evolution of Wharton's point of view in her novels and discusses the effect of World War I on Wharton. Contains a notes section.
Bell, Millicent, ed. *The Cambridge Companion to Edith Wharton*. Cambridge, England: Cambridge University Press, 1995. Essays on *The Age of Innocence, Summer, The House of Mirth, The Fruit of the Tree*, and *The Valley of Decision*, as well as on Wharton's handling of manners and race. Bell gives a critical history of Wharton's fiction in her introduction. Includes a chronology of Wharton's life and publications and a bibliography.
Bendixen, Alfred, and Annette Zilversmit, eds. *Edith Wharton: New Critical Essays*. New York: Garland, 1992. Studies of *The House of Mirth, The Fruit of the Tree, Summer, The Age of Innocence, Hudson River Bracketed*, and *The Gods Arrive*, as well as on Wharton's treatment of female sexuality, modernism, language, and gothic borrowings. There is an introduction and concluding essay on future directions for criticism. No bibliography.
Benstock, Shari. *No Gifts from Chance: A Biography of Edith Wharton*. New York: Scribner's, 1994. A valuable work by a noted Wharton scholar, this supplements but does not supplant Lewis's biography. Divided into sections on "The Old Order," "Choices," and "Rewards." Includes a chronology of works by Wharton, a bibliography, notes, and index.
Dwight, Eleanor. *Edith Wharton: An Extraordinary Life*. New York: Abrams, 1994. A lively succinct biography, copiously illustrated. Includes detailed notes, chronology, and bibliography.
Gimbel, Wendy. *Edith Wharton: Orphancy and Survival*. New York: Praeger, 1984. Drawing upon psychoanalytic theories and feminist perspectives, Gimbel analyzes the four works that she sees as key to understanding Wharton: *The House of Mirth, Ethan Frome, Summer*, and *The Age of Innocence*. The analyses of these works, with their deeply psychological overtones, are well worth reading.
Lewis, R. W. B. *Edith Wharton: A Biography*. 2 vols. New York: Harper & Row, 1975. An extensive study on Wharton, who Lewis calls "the most renowned writer of fiction in America." Notes that Wharton thoughtfully left extensive records, made available through the Beinecke Library at Yale, on which this biography is based.

Essential reading for serious scholars of Wharton or for those interested in her life and how it shaped her writing.

Lindberg, Gary H. *Edith Wharton and the Novel of Manners*. Charlottesville: University Press of Virginia, 1975. Presents Wharton's style with a keen understanding of the ritualism of the social scenes in her work. Strong analytical criticism with a good grasp of Wharton's use of irony.

Danny Lee Robinson

VEIN OF IRON

Author: Ellen Glasgow (1873-1945)
Type of plot: Family chronicle
Time of plot: 1900-1935
Locale: Ironside and Queenborough, Virginia
First published: 1935

> *Principal characters:*
> ADA FINCASTLE, the protagonist
> JOHN FINCASTLE, Ada's father, America's greatest living philosopher
> GRANDMOTHER FINCASTLE, John's mother
> MEGGIE FINCASTLE, John's unmarried sister
> MARY EVELYN FINCASTLE, Ada's mother
> RALPH MCBRIDE, eventually Ada's husband

The Novel

Ellen Glasgow divides *Vein of Iron* into five parts: "Toward Life," "The Single Heart," "Life's Interlude," "God's Mountain," and "The Dying Age." In the first three parts, Ada Fincastle moves toward union with Ralph McBride. That union is achieved in part 3, though the couple does not marry until Ralph returns from World War I early in part 5. Meanwhile, the family leaves the Manse, their ancestral home in the mountain village of Ironside. She and Ralph begin their married life in metropolitan Queenborough. In part 5, they struggle to return to their beloved home. This return is achieved in the last chapter.

Part 1, "Toward Life," tells, through multiple centers of consciousness, the story of one December day when Ada is ten. The novel begins with Ada's experiences of that day when she expected her father to bring her a doll with real hair. She has saved her money, and she is acutely aware that she will soon be too old to enjoy dolls. Unfortunately, her father is unable to bring her such a doll. Though she is extremely disappointed, she is able, thanks to the strength of the family which understands her and cares for her, to accept the substitute doll.

Other incidents in Ada's life that day, as well as looks into the consciousnesses of her grandmother, aunt, father, and mother, reveal the qualities which sustain Ada through this disappointment and which sustain her and her family through the vicissitudes of their lives. Ada is characterized by imaginative sympathy: She is able to imagine herself inside others and to feel their pain and their moral qualities. She also has a strong will. The qualities of the family which sustain her include her mother's appreciation of beauty and small comforts, her father's intellectual integrity, her aunt's unfailing and uncomplaining service to the material needs of the family, and her grandmother's pride in the family history, a history of pioneer men and women who have overcome great difficulties to live good and happy lives.

The family's life is difficult, largely because John Fincastle has given up a promising career as a Presbyterian minister to write philosophy. He has chosen to approach

God through reason, and as a result, he has been expelled from the ministry. Hence, the family is chronically short of money. They live reasonably well because each family member works so hard to provide the necessities of life. John earns a little money teaching a small school in his home but spends as much of his time as he can on his monumental work of philosophy. His work goes unrecognized in America, though it is appreciated by important European thinkers. John's wife, Mary Evelyn, approves of and defends his choice of life even though it deprives her of many of the comforts to which she was accustomed in her youth, and even though this rough life leads to her premature death. John's sister, Meggie, though she disapproves of John's decision, puts family love above her religious beliefs. Grandmother Fincastle, though she fears that her son is damned for his heresy, loves and cares for him with all of her formidable energy. Despite disagreements and tensions in a family of strong Presbyterian conviction, the essential "vein of iron" holds them together.

Defining this vein of iron is a complex task, for it includes physical strength, the family's sense of its history, a kind of willfulness in favor of what seems right, and an unflagging loyalty to one another and to the family as a whole. It is that quality which no Fincastle will give up. At its center is love. John and Mary Evelyn know what it has cost them for John to write his book, but Mary Evelyn would never have asked John to give it up merely for her comfort. This same sort of love compensates Ada for her disappointment over the doll.

In part 2, "The Single Heart," twenty-year-old Ada suffers the two great losses of her life. First, she is separated from Ralph McBride when he is trapped into marriage with Janet Rowan. This marriage lasts for six years until the discontented Janet finds a wealthier husband. In the meantime, Ada suffers her second great loss when her mother dies. Then, in 1918, just before Ralph goes to war, Ada and Ralph decide to spend his last leave together even though he is still married.

Part 3, "Life's Interlude," records Ada's supreme happiness, as she thinks, when she spends two days with Ralph on Thunder Mountain. She believes that she is wresting this happiness from an uncaring God and a jealous society. Later she sees her act more clearly, but she never regrets it.

In part 4, "God's Mountain," Ada bears Ralph's son while he is serving in Europe, Grandmother Fincastle dies, and the family moves to the large town of Queenborough. Ada's sin is another test of the family's strength, parallel to John's leaving the ministry. Because Ada will not repent, Grandmother seems unable to forgive her, but in fact, Grandmother fears that Ada will be damned. When the child is born, Grandmother comes to Ada's aid, comforting and sustaining her as always, but after the birth of the child, Grandmother quickly declines and dies. Ada feels responsible for the death of her beloved Grandmother. Yet Ada discovers that her Grandmother lives on in her thoughts. She is especially aware of echoing Grandmother's judgments about weak characters and of seeking strength in Grandmother's stories of the strongest of her female ancestors.

Part 5, "The Dying Age," shows the family in Queenborough after the war. Ralph returns to marry Ada, and they prosper in the 1920's. Their home, with John and

Meggie, on Mulberry Street becomes part of a new village. Ralph, however, has been made cynical by the tendency toward self-hatred bred into him by his mother, by his early separation from Ada and his forced marriage to the amoral Janet, and by his experience of senseless carnage in the war. Ada's loving strength supports him, but there is always a tendency to give way to a self-destructive despair. This tendency leads to an automobile accident in which he suffers temporary paralysis. His recovery uses up what the family had saved to return to Ironside and coincides with the beginning of the Great Depression. Ada's strength and the strength and integrity of the Fincastles bring their family closer together as their world crumbles around them. When they reach the end of their resources, and after John has finished his great work, John realizes that he is about to die. To save the family the high cost of burying him in Queenborough, he holds his failing body together long enough to travel to Ironside and to die in front of his home. Enough of his life insurance remains for Ada and Ralph to buy back the old house and to begin again as their ancestors did in this valley.

The Characters

Glasgow's characterizations in *Vein of Iron* are rich and detailed. A special feature of characterization is Glasgow's portrayal of the family's shared consciousness. This consciousness is a shared history which seems to divide into masculine and feminine versions. In the men, there has been a hunger for wisdom and the freedom in which to pursue it. This hunger has appeared in their tradition of dissent which carried them from Scotland, to Ireland, to America, and finally to Ironside. In the women, there has been a steady refusal to surrender to the forces of chaos. They decline to accept defeat by war, disaster, and disease; they draw strength from their past, and they project their family toward life. This sense of a sustaining wholeness in a family determined to continue into the future and dedicated to the pursuit of something beyond life is richly captured and portrayed by Glasgow, especially in part 1. These forces come to a focus in Ada. She makes a whole and happy life in the chaos of "the dying age" because of her sense of belonging to and continuing this way of living which transcends social and political forms.

John is an important foil to Ada. He has chosen to pursue God through reason, but he realizes that God may be pursued just as validly through the emotions. In fact, he recognizes that the central cause of his pursuit is a passion, a hunger to know. In the context of John's scholarship, Ada's search for happiness becomes, also, a search for God. Both find their searches fulfilled repeatedly in various forms in the very process of searching. Both characters repeatedly come to moments in their lives when they are able to affirm that despite much pain, they have been happy and they are happy at the moment.

Themes and Meanings

One main theme of the novel is the clash between a version of Christianity which seems appropriate to the pioneer conquest of a new land, Grandmother's harsh Calvinism, and the kinds of thinking which seem appropriate to sustaining a core of values into the as yet unknown new age. The first half of the novel emphasizes this conflict as Ada tries to find the moral way to be happy in a world where the threats to happiness are no longer the oppressed Indians who carry one off into captivity for ten years, but the amoral woman who carries one's beloved into the captivity of a loveless marriage, the war which carries him off again to an apparently meaningless death, or the spirit of the age which seems to deny the reality of meaning beneath contemporary social chaos.

In Ironside, Ada's problem is finding a good way to pursue what her soul says is happiness. In Queenborough, in the second half of the novel, the problem of sustaining values through a dying age becomes more important. Ada and John observe the "happiness hunters" of Queenborough, a mass of people who seem to think of happiness as something one buys or suddenly receives, rather than as the process of creating and sustaining meaningful human relationships, relationships governed by movement toward some self-transcending goal. While the masses speed along the streets in powerful machines, chasing happiness, the Fincastles make themselves happy day by day out of these basic materials of fidelity and spiritual aspiration. While the masses repeat "I," and never see God, the Fincastles repeat "I/Thou" and, thereby, make God, insofar as "He" is known.

Critical Context

In *The Woman Within* (1954), her autobiography, Glasgow includes *Vein of Iron* with *Barren Ground* (1925), *The Sheltered Life* (1932), and two other novels on the list of works that she thinks are her best. Her second-to-last published novel, *Vein of Iron* was well received both by the critics, who praised it, and by the public which bought many copies.

Critics writing after World War II have disagreed about the novel's quality, some seeing it as a solid, if less impressive return to the themes of *Barren Ground*, others seeing it as declining toward a facile didacticism. Both views are justified to some extent. There are, for example, a few somewhat clumsily contrived conversations and incidents near the end of the novel which seem to be more direct comments on the irrationality of the Depression than contributions to the picture of spiritual chaos in which the Fincastles must reforge their vein of iron. While these weaken the novel, it remains, nevertheless, a strong and moving work, dominated by interesting characters who earn the reader's admiration.

Bibliography

Goodman, Susan. *Ellen Glasgow: A Biography.* Baltimore: The Johns Hopkins University Press, 1998. Supersedes the only previous biography, both in terms of providing new and more reliable information on Glasgow's life and conveying sensitive intepretations of her fiction. Includes notes and bibliography.

Inge, M. Thomas, ed. *Ellen Glasgow: Centennial Essays.* Charlottesville: University Press of Virginia, 1976. Offers ten essays about Glasgow and her work. Six of these were read at the Centennial Symposium honoring Glasgow at Mary Baldwin College and the Richmond Public Library in Virginia in 1973.

McDowell, Frederick P. W. *Ellen Glasgow and the Ironic Art of Fiction*. Madison: University of Wisconsin Press, 1960. The first book analyzing Glasgow's writing. Still useful, offering insights into her writing within the context of her life story.

Raper, Julius Rowan. *From the Sunken Garden: The Fiction of Ellen Glasgow, 1916-1945*. Baton Rouge: Louisiana University Press, 1980. Raper offers criticism of ten of Glasgow's novels, including *One Man in His Time* and *Vein of Iron*, as well as an analysis of some of her short fiction. Also provides a bibliography and an index.

Scura, Dorothy M., ed. *Ellen Glasgow: New Perspectives*. Knoxville: University of Tennessee Press, 1995. Detailed essays on Glasgow's major novels and themes, two essays on her autobiographies, and two essays on her poetry and short stories. Includes a helpful overview in the introduction and a bibliography.

Thiébaux, Marcelle. *Ellen Glasgow*. New York: Frederick Ungar, 1982. Thiébaux offers extensive discussions of Glasgow's works but provides only a short biography which stresses Glasgow's divided personality and the pain that this caused her. Includes a good bibliography.

Terry Heller

VINELAND

Author: Thomas Pynchon (1937-   )
Type of plot: Social realism
Time of plot: The late 1980's
Locale: Northern California
First published: 1989

> *Principal characters:*
> ZOYD WHEELER, a former hippie, a government pensioner and
>   handyman
> PRAIRIE, Zoyd's daughter, who is questing for information about her
>   mother
> FRENESI GATES, Prairie's mother and Zoyd's former wife, a onetime
>   radical who is now an undercover government agent
> BROCK VOND, a government prosecutor who was once Frenesi's lover
>   and is now her controller
> DL CHASTAIN, a onetime friend of Frenesi, Prairie's guide in her quest
> HUB and SASHA GATES, Frenesi's radical parents, who are involved in
>   the film industry
> HECTOR ZUÑIGA, a television-mad drug agent

The Novel

Zoyd Wheeler has been living a quiet life in Vineland, a fictitious town in Northern California, with his daughter Prairie. Zoyd does odd jobs for neighbors, grows marijuana, and collects a government pension for committing a crazy act every year: specifically, for throwing himself through a plate-glass window in a local restaurant in front of television cameras. Prairie works in a local health-food pizza parlor and hangs out with a rock band, Billy Barf and the Vomitones.

Things are changing at the novel's beginning. The site of Zoyd's annual fling is shifted without explanation, and there are rumors of a major government antidrug operation in the area. Various kinds of police and federal troops are seen in Vineland. Hector Zuñiga warns Zoyd that Prairie is in danger, probably from Brock Vond. There are rumors that Vond has lost track of Frenesi, an agent whom he controls, and that he will try to find her by using Prairie. Prairie, on her own, is anxious for more information about her mother; Zoyd and Sasha Gates, Prairie's grandmother, have told her only that Frenesi is underground, hiding from government agents because of her activities in the 1960's.

Prairie, warned by her father that she should leave the area, goes with the band to Southern California, where they are scheduled to play at a Mafia wedding while pretending to be an Italian band. In the powder room, Prairie accidentally draws the attention of DL Chastain, a martial-arts expert who had been close to Frenesi in the turmoil of the 1960's. DL introduces Prairie to the Sisterhood of Kunoichi Attentives, whose files reveal to the young woman the activities in which her mother had been involved as a member of a radical film collective.

DL's life is presented in considerable detail. Daughter of a career Army enlisted man, she had become a student of martial arts with a renowned teacher while her father was stationed in Japan. Her skills, far beyond normal, were sometimes made use of by others in ways she could not always control; at one point, she was programmed to kill Brock Vond but failed. She has taken control of her own life and is now a partner of another master of the martial arts, Takeshi Fumimota, who has his own unusual history.

From the archives at the retreat and from DL, Prairie learns that Frenesi had participated in the rebellion at a small California college, had encountered and been fascinated by Brock Vond, had been seduced by him, and had served as his agent in the murder of a popular professor named Weed. The murder, along with the imminent occupation of the campus of the college by police and federal troops, had brought the rebellion to an end. Frenesi had been spirited away by Vond and sequestered in a secret government camp. Rescued by DL, she had eventually married Zoyd and given birth to Prairie before returning to Vond and becoming an underground government agent.

In the meantime, Frenesi has become wedded to her new life. She has married again to another undercover agent, Flash, and has another child, a son named Justin. She and Flash have been moved from town to town, wherever their services were needed. At the time when Prairie begins her search, however, Frenesi's world is coming apart. The Ronald Reagan Administration has cut off funding for Brock Vond's operation, and Frenesi sets out with Flash and Justin for Vineland.

Prairie also returns to Vineland with DL and Takeshi Fumimota in time for the periodic reunion of Sasha Gates's family; the community feeling of the family helps to dissipate the threat of government intervention. Prairie finally meets her mother, and there is something close to a reconciliation between them. In the end, Brock Vond attempts to kidnap Prairie, who he claims is his daughter; the attempt is frustrated, and he is condemned by higher forces in the government. The raid is called off, the troops and police withdraw from the area, and there is a happy ending, at least temporarily, for Prairie, her friends, and her relatives.

The Characters

Frenesi Gates is among the most fully developed and interesting characters in all of Pynchon's work. She is seen from the point of view of the third-person narrator and also from the perspectives of her mother, Zoyd, Prairie, and DL as well as the Senior Attentive of the Sisterhood. Totally committed to the feminist film collective with which she is associated, daughter of her radical parents in her devotion to social causes, Frenesi is nevertheless fascinated, attracted, and repelled by Brock Vond and by the kind of authoritarian power he represents. At first, she tries to play games with Vond, then she falls in love with him; finally, she is made to face the extent of her own degradation. Over her protests, Vond gets her to transport the gun that will kill Weed, the professor who is at the heart of the student uprising. Once she has done this, she can place no limit on what she will do, and her life working as an agent for Vond is an inevitable next step. Still, as she is seen with Flash and Justin, she has not become a woman without conscience. She misses Prairie and regrets having left her, although she could see no alternative at the time. When the funds dry up and she is cast out of her work by a change in government policy, she instinctively returns to the reunion of her mother's clan. There, she discovers something like mercy and some sort of peace.

The other characters are less original and less developed. Prairie is presented as a typical teenage daughter of hippies, hip herself but self-sufficient and imaginative. When DL takes her to the feminist institute, Prairie takes over a disorganized kitchen and becomes the much-admired chef for the whole organization. When the place is raided, she leaves with DL and Takeshi Fumimota without losing her cool. She wants to find her mother and is shocked by what she learns about Frenesi, but in the end, she neither sentimentalizes nor rejects her mother.

DL Chastain is a superwoman, not only strong physically but also a sensitive guide for Prairie's search. Zoyd is a typical hippie grown older and wiser, caring for Prairie but willing to let her find her own way. Hector Zuñiga is a parody of a drug-enforcement agent, himself helplessly addicted not to drugs but to television. Sasha Gates is a warm woman, politically dedicated to radical causes, caring enough about Prairie to work out an accommodation with Zoyd for the girl's care despite her scorn for Zoyd. Hub Gates is a fine technician, somewhat less political than his wife.

Brock Vond is clearly the villain of the novel. He has used his authority as a kind of roving prosecutor to harass anyone with whom he disagrees, and he deliberately corrupts Frenesi. In the later stages of the action, he is willing to bring all the forces of a repressive government to bear on the entire Vineland community in order to bring Frenesi to heel and to secure Prairie, whom he believes to be his daughter. His failure and destruction at the end are nearly melodramatic, as if, despite all the power it is shown to have in the novel, evil cannot finally win.

Themes and Meanings

Thomas Pynchon's continuing concern with the restrictions placed on the individual by society provides the main intention of *Vineland*: to show the dangers of excessive government control of individual lives and, specifically, to criticize the measures taken during the Reagan years to inhibit independent political activities and the use of drugs such as marijuana, which Pynchon presents as relatively harmless. The police and other enforcement agencies in the novel use powers given to them by recent laws to seize the homes of people suspected of marijuana trafficking: they disrupt lives and ruthlessly invade the privacy of innocents.

Brock Vond is used to give a face and specific qualities to these dangers. His relationship with Frenesi Gates is intended to make clear the extent to which individuals can be corrupted and seduced by uncontrolled power. The fact that Vond is a prosecutor indicates that the law, which ought to be a shield for individuals, is instead being used to intimidate and corrupt them, for no purpose other than to exert control. Vond also makes use of detention camps constructed to house suspect persons in case of a national emergency; for Pynchon, these are no more or less than potential concentration camps.

Nevertheless, *Vineland* is less bleak than Pynchon's other fictions in the suggestions it carries about the possibility of meaningful lives for its characters. Zoyd and Prairie do survive, Frenesi is given a kind of peace, though not necessarily redemption, and the villain is disposed of before he can corrupt Prairie. America toward the end of the century is far from ideal, but it is not entirely a wasteland.

Critical Context

Vineland is the most overtly political of Thomas Pynchon's novels. Themes and ideas from the earlier books are given more direct expression, as if Pynchon had decided that readers and critics were not understanding his principal ideas. The book contains clear-cut distinctions between good and bad characters, and it is the only one of Pynchon's novels to comment directly on the domestic political scene.

At the same time, *Vineland* is, like the earlier novels, varied in its prose styles, making use of wild and sometimes profane humor, original song lyrics, and caustic addresses from the narrator to the characters, among other devices. While it is the first of Pynchon's novels to deal explicitly with supernatural events—including a class of beings called Thanatoids, the shades of people who are dead but not quite gone, and the fact that DL Chastain is invested with superhuman powers—the supernatural has never been entirely excluded from Pynchon's fictional world. If it is less encyclopedic than Pynchon's most famous novel, *Gravity's Rainbow* (1973), *Vineland* is also more accessible.

Bibliography

Bergh, Patricia A. "(De)constructing the Image: Thomas Pynchon's Postmodern Woman" *Journal of Popular Culture* 30 (Spring, 1997): 1-11. Focusing on the character of Frenesi Gates who epitomizes the postmodern woman in Pynchon's novel, Bergh interprets Frenesi's personality through the eyes of Oedipa Maas in *Lot 49* and Prairie Wheeler in *Vineland*. Bergh shows that Pynchon's female characters are shaped by media/visual sources assigned to them by outside sources and that the individual self in Pynchon's works is engulfed and erased by cybernetic technology.

Conner, Marc C. "Postmodern Exhaustion: Thomas Pynchon's *Vineland* and the Aesthetic of the Beautiful." *Studies in American Fiction* 24 (Spring, 1996): 65-85. Conner asserts that Pynchon deals more with the aesthetic of the beautiful in *Vineland* than with the aesthetic of the sublime as in his previous novels. He argues that Pynchon's interest shifts from the accepted concepts of postmodernism to ideas more suited to the ethical problems of the late twentieth century, and offers hope that ethical relations will rejuvenate a world tired of the aesthetics of postmodernism.

Green, Geoffrey, Donald J. Grenier, and Larry McCaffrey, eds. *The Vineland Papers: Critical Takes on Pynchon's Novels.* Normal, Ill.: Dalkey Archive Press, 1994.

A collection of essays that offer a detailed analysis and valuable insight into Pynchon's novel. Useful bibliographical references are included.

Horstman, Joey E. "'Transcendence Through Starvation': Thomas Pynchon's Televisual Style in *Vineland*." *Christianity and Literature* 47 (Spring, 1998): 331-350. Horstman views Pynchon's novel as a postmodern meditation on the nature of television. Although Pynchon criticizes television's role as a major distraction, he also undercuts his criticism by mimicking the technology and so creates a novel that parallels the superficial features of television.

Robberds, Mark. "The New Historicist Creepers of *Vineland*." *CRITIQUE: Studies in Contemporary Fiction* 36 (Summer, 1995): 237-248. Robberds demonstrates that the structure of Pynchon's novel reflects 1960s American cultural history as seen through the eyes of Prairie. In fact, he argues that the whole novel can be taken as a national allegory presenting American society as a culture that has fused and confused television with reality.

Rushdie, Salman. "Still Crazy After All These Years." *The New York Times Book Review* 95 (January 14, 1990): 1, 36-37. The noted novelist highly praises Pynchon's novel, calling attention to its political message and also emphasizing the author's choice of anonymity. Rushdie is most interested in Pynchon's condemnation of political and social conformity and the ways in which governments and other organizations attempt to enforce their views.

John M. Muste

A VISITATION OF SPIRITS

Author: Randall Kenan (1963-   )
Type of plot: Social realism
Time of plot: 1984 and 1985
Locale: Tims Creek, North Carolina
First published: 1989

Principal characters:

HORACE CROSS, a sixteen-year-old high school student who is
struggling against his homosexuality

JAMES MALACHAI GREENE (JIMMY), the principal of Tims Creek
Elementary School and minister of the First Baptist Church of Tims
Creek

EZEKIEL CROSS (ZEKE), the grandfather of Horace, who represents
family and the tradition against which Horace struggles

RUTH DAVIS CROSS, the great-aunt of Horace, a ninety-two-year-old
woman whose feud with the world starts within the Cross family and
extends into elevators and restaurants

GIDEON STONE, a classmate of Horace and his first lover, a young man
who has accepted his own homosexuality

The Novel

Alternating between April, 1984, narratives of Horace's experience with magic and
December, 1985, narratives of a family visit to a dying cousin, *A Visitation of Spirits*
tells the story of a sixteen-year-old African American boy who cannot transform himself away from homosexuality and so cannot continue to face his family and his community.

A Visitation of Spirits is divided into five major sections, each including April,
1984, and December, 1985, narratives. The story is told predominantly from a
limited-omniscient perspective; the center of consciousness shifts within these sections among Horace, Jimmy, Zeke, and Ruth. Three segments entitled "Confession"
(two from Jimmy, one from Horace) break the pattern of alternation, with each of the
confessions showing the two figures wrestling with their own memories.

The 1985 narratives center on Jimmy, Aunt Ruth, and Uncle Zeke driving to see
their cousin Asa, seriously ill in the hospital. These scenes reveal the family at work.
Aunt Ruth and Uncle Zeke argue and accuse each other, with Jimmy trying to act the
peacemaker; he is playing the role of clergyman rather awkwardly because he is first
and foremost a nephew. Their journey takes them to a hospital; once there, Ruth cannot abide the falseness of those who would pray for Asa to live. Their journey home
from the hospital finds them in a restaurant, where a white waitress and Ruth argue.
The struggle between generations as well as between black and white energizes the

scene. No peace within the family results from the meal they share, but a truce of sorts is implicitly declared after their car has broken down and then been fixed.

During the hospital visit, in a scene between Ruth and a young girl who invites her to play video games, the family finds rest and communion. After Ruth plays her first game, her expression is "like a revelation." She and Zeke, who have been arguing relentlessly all day, share a moment of conciliation "as pure and honest as the rain." Jimmy is relieved to have them acting as family.

The other central thread of the novel takes place on the night of April 29 and the morning of April 30, 1984, and is told from Horace's consciousness. Kenan begins with midday on April 29 as Horace cuts a class to sit in the library. There he chooses the exact animal into which he will ritually transform himself that night. The next section shifts to the morning of April 30; Horace is holding a gun on Jimmy at the elementary school grounds. A reader then follows the narrative to fill in the night of April 29 with Horace, a night in which the young man calls forth the demons that possess him and makes a ritual journey to the church, the high school, the theater, and finally the elementary school.

At the church, Horace is baptized into demonology in a sanctuary filled with the spirits he has called forth, some recognizable as townspeople and some misshapen and nightmarish. Horace wants not to be alone as he moves through his night; he continually looks for the demon to shield him and to become him. He always hears the demon's taunting but does as the demon bids. At the high school, he once again sees what appear to be familiar townspeople and misshapen spirits, a mix that figuratively represents Horace's straits: He is one of the inhabitants of Tims Creek, yet he is "misshapen" in his sexual desires and so cannot remain in the world of the townspeople. Making his way from the theater and to the elementary school, Horace (less and less recognizably himself throughout the night) becomes completely spirit as he holds a shotgun on Jimmy and forces him to walk into the woods. Horace's hope that witchcraft would transform him is realized for that brief moment of Otherness, when the demon speaks for Horace to Jimmy. Kenan ends the narration of the morning of April 30 with an intense physical description of Horace's body after he has committed suicide, an unforgettable transformation from life to death. Horace had journeyed to the places in which he sought community and acceptance, in the process finally becoming the demon he judged himself to be.

The Characters

Horace reveals the state of the spurned in the United States. His struggle against himself and his struggle to be accepted result not in acceptance but rather in insanity and death. Horace perceives in his grandfather and great-aunt "an armor one wore to beat the consequences, invisible, but powerful and evident." Horace is, throughout the novel, unable to clothe himself in this armor and so cannot endure. Horace attempts to belong, to join a community, throughout his brief life. As a grade school boy, his friend John Anthony had been his partner in science projects, field trips, sack races, and a love of books, "always books." John Anthony, however, became a sports hero and an auto mechanics student. He becomes popular with the girls, and he grows distant from Horace—the good student—who tries to replace John Anthony with an amorphous academia.

Horace's academic ambitions place him within reach of Gideon Stone, with whom he is assigned to complete a science project, the ultimate result of which is Horace's first homosexual encounter. Unable to accept his own sexual urges, Horace fights against his feelings by joining the track team and beginning to socialize with a group of "white boys" at the high school, boys who have moved to Tims Creek recently. His friendship with those other outcasts from the school is forbidden by his grandfather when Horace comes to the Thanksgiving dinner table with an earring in his newly pierced ear. Horace, no longer the determined student, must watch as Gideon steps into the group and earns a college scholarship. Horace never finds that armor "in the edge of his grandfather's voice, in the stoop of his great-aunt's walk. . . . Integrity. Dignity. Pride." His night of visitation with spirits he spends naked and vulnerable.

James Malachai Greene occupies an uneasy space: He is the religious and intellectual grandson and the redeemer of his mother Rose's sins against the family. Yet his inability to comfort Horace contributes significantly to Horace's suicide. Horace had, at considerable cost to himself, asked the minister if attraction toward men could be all right. The Reverend Jimmy Greene responded that Horace was experiencing adolescent confusion and would change. Horace asked what would happen if he could not change, to which the minister responded that he should pray about it and he would change. After Horace's suicide, the Reverend Greene is left to remember the earlier question and the death scene itself, feeling his failure to help Horace. Continually struggling between others' expectations of him and his own desires, he is, finally, the one called by Horace to be his witness.

Ruth Davis Cross, determined to be self-reliant and resentful of the Cross family wealth and pride, realizes her own culpability in her husband Jethro's alcoholism and flight from responsibility. Ruth outwardly accepted Jethro, playing the role of the good wife. Ruth illustrates further division within the family, feeling the weight of her in-laws' condescension. Her attraction to her husband's cousin Asa makes Ruth feel unworthy, a feeling over which she triumphs as she plays the video game with the child and then declares that snow is coming. Ruth has endured, reared her children, and ultimately accepted her own shortcomings.

Ezekiel Cross tried to rear Horace correctly. Zeke, ironically enough, counseled Horace away from judgment and prejudice against Gideon Stone. Horace had hoped that his grandfather would not allow him to work with a boy from such a disreputable family. Zeke unwittingly placed Horace in irresistible partnership with Gideon, a partnership that Horace cannot continue because of his family and his religious training. Then, when Horace had become friends with several white boys who had recently moved to Tims Creek, Zeke forbade Horace to see the boys, effectively driving him away from his last group of friends. Ezekiel at the close of the narrative remains unaware of Horace's need for acceptance as the key to his suicide. Zeke believes that his own mistake was in not making Horace work in the fields and keep busy.

Gideon Stone is a high school student who stands in contrast to the tormented Horace in accepting and openly admitting his homosexuality. Gideon's family is also the opposite of the Cross family: The Stones make and sell bootleg whiskey, they are not churchgoers, and their home is cluttered and badly needs repair. This "disreputable" family nevertheless values Gideon and supports him. Gideon's speech is consistently clever, demonstrating his ability to deflect the criticisms of other teenagers, again a clear difference from Horace's response to criticism.

Themes and Meanings

The book's central themes are memory and communion. These themes merge in the novel's accounts of hog butchering and tobacco curing, accounts that remind readers of the roots of this novel in people's rituals of survival and community. These rituals are told in the second person, insistent on remembrance and common ritual: "You've seen this [hog killing], haven't you?" "You're familiar with this [tobacco curing], aren't you?" The hog-killing description is entitled "Advent." The parallel between the hog butchered and Horace dead suggests the community's role in Horace's death. Horace as the Christ sacrificed is also suggested in both the title "Advent" and in numerous references to the crucifixion. In a less violent ritual, tobacco curing again draws attention to remembrance: "[I]t is good to remember that people were bound by this strange activity . . . bound by the necessity, the responsibility, the humanity." The repetition and hard work apparent in the task parallel the life of Jimmy Greene as he lives in 1985, rising at five every morning to work on his sermon, always arriving at the elementary school by seven, and leaving school late in the evening. Jimmy Greene and Horace Cross live the rhythms of their respective rituals, yearning for true community and belonging.

Another theme evident in the story of Horace Cross is the powerful need for transformation. Horace seeks through magic to change himself into a hawk with all of its freedom and power, but the magic succeeds only in making him hear and see the spirits and demons that accompany him on his final night. His minister's earlier assurance that he would change is ironically true: Horace has prayed to demons and has changed from a troubled young man to a psychotic young man. His visions lead him to see his own *Doppelgänger* three times, the third time culminating in Horace's shooting his own spirit and seeing the blood flow from the vision of himself. From that moment, Horace as the reader recognizes him is gone, replaced by the one who follows the voice of the demon—a voice that next tells him to shoot himself.

Underlying Kenan's story of Horace Cross and Jimmy Greene is the constant of community. The narrative time sequence itself reinforces the continuity of the family and community, despite Horace's suicide. More than a year and a half after the suicide, the family that mourns Horace continues to visit the sick, cook meals, clean house, and go to work. Jimmy could have followed his own brother's advice and left Tims Creek after his wife died, but he stays within the community, his days following a pattern dictated by his work. Although Kenan leads the reader to feel the loss of Horace intensely, the novel ultimately proves the power of community.

Critical Context

   A Visitation of Spirits was published toward the beginning of a period in the late 1980's and early 1990's which saw a substantial number of books by gay writers and about gay life. Publishers by the end of the 1980's had recognized the intense public interest in the gay community as well as the gay community's book-buying habits. At one level, the novel was guaranteed an audience because of its powerful treatment of a young man's homosexual experience. Once published, the novel earned consistently good reviews, not only for its innovatively structured accounts but also for its strong portrayal of character and rural life.

   The novel explores the landscape of Randall Kenan's own childhood in eastern North Carolina, fleshing out the history of a community whose characters he continued to explore in his collection of short stories, *Let the Dead Bury Their Dead* (1992). In the title story, Kenan tells the history of Tims Creek, founded by runaway and freed slaves, some of whom had been called from their graves by a necromancer who had murdered the oldest son of a white master. Black magic, botany, and homosexuality (all strongly present in the novel) also recur in the collected stories. As compellingly magical as many of Zora Neale Hurston's accounts of Florida, Kenan's works operate within the tradition of African American authors, recalling a slave past and incorporating magic that enables black people to transcend their boundaries, whether those boundaries are imposed by slave owners or by loving grandfathers.

Bibliography

Brophy, Beth. "Books by and About Gays Find a Niche in Big-Time Publishing." *U.S. News and World Report*, April 16, 1990, 42-43. Brophy notes the willingness of publishers to support, even seek, works by homosexuals. The subjects of gay fiction are, she notes, universal themes. Brophy's concise article provides a good start for an examination of publishing and fiction by gays.

Essence. Review of *A Visitation of Spirits*, by Randall Kenan. 20 (September, 1989): 28. A laudatory review that notes main characters, setting, and the tension that moves the plot along.

Hunt, V. "A Conversation with Randall Kenan." *African American Review* 29 (Fall, 1995): 411-420. Kenan offers an interesting overview of his career history, educational background, and writing style. He also mentions those authors who have influenced him the most and briefly discusses *A Visitation of Spirits*.

Kenan, Randall. An interview with Randall Kenan, by Charles H. Rowell. *Callaloo* 21 (Winter, 1998): 133-148. Focuses on the influence that Kenan's extensive traveling has had on his writing. Kenan believes that travel does not afford him an escape from anything. Instead he claims that he always carries his fictional landscape in his head and that his travels have enriched his fiction.

McRuer, Robert. "A Visitation of Difference: Randall Kenan and Black Queer Theory." *Journal of Homosexuality* 26 (August/September, 1993): 221-232. Focusing on the main character of *A Visitation of Spirits*, Kenan's novel considers the question of what cultural work is accomplished when queer desire turns up in such an apparently unlikely and inhospitable place as Tims Creek, North Carolina. McRuer examines how region plays a role in the construction of centers and margins, and argues against always shuffling queer desire "safely" off to the big city.

Nixon, Will. "Better Times for Black Writers." *Publishers Weekly*, February 17, 1989, 35-40. Nixon compiles the divergent views of a number of black writers, Kenan included, who discuss the African American writer's road to publication. Having presented the argument that black women writers have a readier ear at most publishers, Nixon quotes Kenan: "Men don't have Zora Neale Hurston as a buzz word." Nixon briefly chronicles the rise of a black publishing industry, noting the importance of the Harlem Writers Guild.

Publishers Weekly. Review of *A Visitation of Spirits*, by Randall Kenan. May 12, 1989, 283. Discusses briefly the "powerful strain of mysticism" in the novel. The review also notes Kenan's "rare gift for naturalism, capturing the texture of farm life in vivid detail." The one criticism of the novel comments on the "jarring" shifts in time and tone.

Virginia Quarterly Review. Review of *A Visitation of Spirits*, by Randall Kenan. 66 (Winter, 1990): 22. Places Kenan in the company of Trey Ellis, Percival Everett, Don Belton, and Yolanda Barnes as writers depicting the black experience. The review points out that Kenan's novel is one in which "the only bigotry is demonstrated by older blacks." The tightly structured, daring form of the novel earns praise.

Janet Taylor Palmer

WAITING TO EXHALE

Author: Terry McMillan (1951-   )
Type of plot: Social realism
Time of plot: The 1990's
Locale: Denver, Colorado, and Phoenix, Arizona
First published: 1992

>   *Principal characters:*
>   SAVANNAH JACKSON, a thirty-six-year-old African American woman
>   who moves from Denver to Phoenix
>   BERNADINE HARRIS, Savannah's former college roommate, whose
>   husband has left her for a younger white woman
>   ROBIN STOKES, an underwriter for an insurance company
>   GLORIA MATTHEWS, a single parent who owns her own hair salon
>   TARIC, Gloria's son, who is just discovering sex

The Novel

In *Waiting to Exhale*, the four central female characters are members of an organization called Black Women on the Move (BWOM). The problem is that these bright, attractive, and loving women have themselves been on the move too long. They see themselves coming near to middle age fearing that they will not be able to find or sustain a sexual relationship with a black man whom they consider to be eligible. Savannah, with her mind set on a career and upward mobility, has been in three live-in relationships over a period of nine years, and she is holding her breath (waiting to exhale) until the time when she can locate someone whose interests are reasonably close to hers who is faithful, attractive, knowledgeable, and a good lover, attributes evidently extremely scarce among men.

As the novel opens, Savannah is planning a move from Denver, where she holds a well-paying but dead-end job, to Phoenix, where she has accepted a less well-paying job but one that fulfills her creative needs and one that she thinks promises more upward mobility. While in Phoenix, Savannah stays with her college roommate, Bernadine, whose "successful" marriage has just collapsed, her husband having left her for a younger white woman. Bernadine is left to cope with two children, a large house, and considerable stress over money at a time when she should be receiving benefits from her husband's successful career. Not only does he leave her, but he also carefully hides all of his assets so as to try to make a very small settlement and small alimony payments.

Robin, described as flashy and a bit vulgar, has had a series of lovers, all undependable, although she wants to marry and have children. She enmeshes herself in relationships with men who take advantage of her. In her latest such relationship, she foolishly thinks that if she is good enough to her lover, he will eventually propose. Propose he does, but to another woman, with whom he has been having a simultaneous affair.

Gloria, friend to all the women, has a beauty salon and is hairdresser for them all as well. She is successful enough to employ four operators. Gloria's major concern is her son, Taric, who was the result of an indiscretion when she was a senior in college. Her former husband declared himself homosexual and left her and Taric, but he visits every two years, playing an unimportant role in Gloria's life as well as in Taric's.

Through the course of the novel, each woman experiences a kind of coming of age. Gloria finally has a heart attack, brought on by the stress of being without sufficient help at her shop (one of the operators has AIDS), the business of rearing Taric, and overeating. She recovers quickly, however, and finds Martin, a new neighbor, by her bedside, along with Taric and her "sisters," Savannah, Bernadine, and Robin. Martin looks as if he will replace her absent husband and be a father to her son. Bernadine works hard with her lawyer to uncover her former husband's assets and is rewarded with a settlement. She also receives a telephone call from a man she had once dated and whom she thought she would never see again, and with his promised visit she enters a new world. Savannah comes to an acceptance of her circumstances and is comforted with the rewards of her job. In addition, she is able to begin the process of breaking her smoking habit. Robin is pregnant by the man she has been unable to order away, and although she will not have a husband, she will have a child.

The Characters

The events of *Waiting to Exhale* are told in the first person through Savannah and Robin, and in the third person from the viewpoints of Bernadine and Gloria. The shifts in point of view help the reader to discern one character from another, since there is little difference in voice. This technique also serves to separate each woman from the group as a whole. Following each woman in alternating chapters serves to make each one the protagonist of her own subplot and to give the reader a sense of four different stories. Nevertheless, there is sufficient interaction among the four women when they meet and sufficient emotion displayed to consider them as a composite protagonist in a larger whole.

Gloria and Bernadine are the better rounded of the characters, largely because the third-person point of view allows for a wider scope. The two women also experience the most pain and come closest to a happy ending. Through many years of single parenthood, Gloria nurses, sustains, and teaches her son proper behavior, and in the end she is rewarded. Taric, in spite of bad influences all around him, chooses an honorable and reasonable path to a future life, and Gloria's helping hand and friendly demeanor to a neighbor quickly win his support and love. Bernadine reaches the point of near collapse, but through her own determination and hard work, she propels herself to a happy ending.

Savannah and Robin have problems with their parents, and their love and concern for them add dimension to their characters. For the most part, however, the two women suffer as a result of their inability to perceive the worth of people they meet and their willingness to seek sex where they find it. Three times in the novel McMillan reveals the dangers associated with promiscuity, including pregnancy out of wedlock, herpes, and AIDS. Robin's pregnancy at the end of the novel seems more positive than negative, since a child even without a live-in father is a positive value for Robin.

Themes and Meanings

Toward the end of *Waiting to Exhale*, during a celebration of Gloria's birthday, Savannah asks: "Whatever happened to the good old days?" Gloria demands to know what good old days she is talking about, but the question is well put and the answer clear. Men of the "buppie" generation apparently feel no need to court women in the old-fashioned way—no need to commit or to be faithful during a relationship. Women, apparently as open in their sexual needs as men and as willing to participate in sex before commitments are made, are readily available. The problem appears to be that women still seem to need commitment; they still seem to be looking for the good old-fashioned man. Gloria finds such a man in Martin; kindness and admiration lead to love before sex in their relationship. Bernadine too is lucky to find such a man.

It would be a mistake, however, to define Savannah and Robin, and to a lesser extent Bernadine and Gloria, solely in terms of their need for a relationship with a man. They have overcome odds and are doing better than their parents did. They are competing in the real world and making their way themselves. They participate in worthwhile projects and support them with both time and money. They are caring and questioning in a world where human values are not as clearly defined as they once were. Ultimately, *Waiting to Exhale* is an examination of what women of the baby-boom generation—particularly African American women—experience as they carve out new roles and lives for themselves.

Critical Context

Waiting to Exhale is McMillan's third published novel. *Mama*, her first, was published in 1987, and *Disappearing Acts*, her second, was published in 1989. Unlike other black women writers whose works are often lyrical and densely symbolic, McMillan works mainly on the level of social realism, relying on a linear plot line and irony to shape the novels and provide both themes and structure. The novels are set in urban locations, and the female protagonists are lusty, frank, and often profane. They are sometimes married and sometimes have children; the men in their lives are usually violent, alcoholic, or so frustrated by social conditions that they cannot function normally as the women desire. Consequently, the women are left with, for example, the five children that Mildred Peacock has in *Mama* and the need somehow to support them by any means possible. Mildred finds work wherever she can and sex when it offers itself. In *Disappearing Acts*, McMillan deals with another strong black woman, Zora Banks. Banks is a musician who is making her living as a teacher in a junior high school. She has moved from Ohio to New York in an attempt to further her ambitions to be a songwriter and recording artist. Problems arise when she meets Franklin, a high-school dropout and intermittent construction worker. Their love for each other is continually threatened by differences in education, ambition, and job security. Franklin is given to blaming the whole white world for his plight, and, as might be expected, is finally moved to extreme violence against Zora Banks.

Issues raised in *Mama* and *Disappearing Acts* reappear in *Waiting to Exhale*. These continuing concerns include unstable marital relationships, problems of rearing children in hostile environments, inequities in class and education between black men and women, and questions of where, when, and how satisfactory sexual relationships can take place in a time of changing morés and cultural values.

Bibliography
Ellerby, Janet M. "Deposing the Man of the House: Terry McMillan Rewrites the Family." *MELUS* 22 (Summer, 1997): 105-117. Ellerby discusses McMillan's portrayal of African American families living outside white middle-class norms. Ellerby acknowledges that some African American women writers have characterized McMillan's work as pulp fiction, but Ellerby argues that McMillan's novels significantly contribute to exploration of African American families.
Isaacs, Susan. "Chilling Out in Phoenix." *The New York Times Book Review* 97 (May 31, 1992): 12. Isaacs makes the point that the book is enjoyable to read but breaks no new literary ground. Rather, the novel is part of a subgenre that focuses on friendship among women. Isaacs praises the novel for its "wicked wit," "breezy humor," and effective treatment of a group of women who remain friends in good times as well as bad.
Publishers Weekly. Review of *Waiting to Exhale*, by Terry McMillan. 239 (March 23, 1992): 58. Praises the novel for its portrayal of four women bound together in "warm, supportive friendship," its authenticity in characterization, and its broad appeal to a mainstream reading public. Like many of the novel's reviews, this one comments on the profusion of profanities used by the women, which some readers may find disconcerting.
Randolph, Laura B. "Terry McMillan Exhales and Inhales in a Revealing Interview." *Ebony* 48 (May, 1993): 23-26. McMillan talks about the advantages and disadvantages of her success and reveals that her novel is semi-autobiographical in nature.
Sellers, Frances S. Review of *Waiting to Exhale*, by Terry McMillan. *The Washington Post Book World* 22 (May 24, 1992): 11. Sellers comments on the astonishing success of a novel written for and about educated black women, not yuppies but "buppies," who represent a new black middle class, a subject and a commercial market only recently being explored. Generalized "male-bashing" and the characters' preoccupation with artifacts and morés of the pop culture, Sellers says, grow wearisome.
Smith, Wendy. "Terry McMillan." *Publishers Weekly* 239 (May 11, 1992): 50-51. A thoughtful overview of McMillan's career up to the publication of *Waiting to Exhale*. Based largely on an interview with the author, who energetically defends her depictions of African American men.

Mary Rohrberger

WALDEN TWO

Author: B. F. Skinner (1904-1990)
Type of plot: Utopian
Time of plot: Spring, soon after World War II
Locale: Somewhere in the United States
First published: 1948

Principal characters:
PROFESSOR BURRIS, a university psychology teacher and the narrator of the novel
PROFESSOR AUGUSTINE CASTLE, Burris's colleague, a teacher of philosophy
T. E. FRAZIER, the founder of the utopian community named Walden Two
ROGERS, one of Burris's former students, back from World War II
BARBARA MACKLIN, Rogers's fiancée
STEVE JAMNIK, Rogers's war buddy
MARY GROVE, Steve's girlfriend

The Novel

Walden Two is cast mostly in the form of a dialogue—in the tradition of Plato's Socratic dialogues—in which the renowned and controversial behavioral psychologist B. F. Skinner presents his utopian vision of how human society could be reorganized on the basis of "behavioral engineering." As the most famous and influential behaviorist of the twentieth century, Skinner was well qualified to argue that the modification and control of human behavior through "operant conditioning," behavioral modification, and positive reinforcement could create a considerably healthier society.

In this book, his only published attempt at fiction, Skinner describes the visit of six characters to an imaginary utopian community called Walden Two. This community was designed by a behavioral psychologist named T. E. Frazier, who closely resembles Skinner himself. At the end of the book, three members of the group—Steve Jamnik and his fiancée Mary Grove, along with Professor Burris—decide to leave the ordinary world and live in Frazier's Walden Two community.

The book begins with Rogers and his army buddy Steve visiting Burris, Rogers's former college professor, to inquire about the utopian community. Burris, the narrator of the novel, portrays himself as jaded with his teaching career and extremely disenchanted by post-World War II American culture. When Rogers asks Burris about Walden Two, Burris realizes that he and Walden Two's founder, T. E. Frazier, were fellow graduate students, and Burris is able to engineer a visit to the nearby utopian community. The visiting group eventually includes the girlfriends of the two young men and Augustine Castle, an irascible colleague from the university's philosophy department. The rest of the book chronicles the visit of this group to the utopian community and focuses on the conversations that they have there with one another and with Walden Two's founder, Frazier, who gives the group a guided tour while proselytizing for the community's superiority to the outside world.

The most captivating of these conversations occurs in the last third of the book as Frazier (and Skinner) defend themselves from charges of fascism. The issue of the social manipulation and control of human beings seems fairly innocent when Frazier is talking about gardening and tea parties at Walden Two, but when Frazier starts talking about future growth and land acquisition, Castle "seemed to feel that he had found Frazier's weak point at last." Just as with Skinner in real life, Frazier must defend himself against charges of totalitarianism, and this leads Frazier to the issue of free will. Like Skinner, Frazier asserts that human free will is an illusion and that the techniques of behavioral engineering were already being exploited in the real world by insidious and maladroit advertisers, salesmen, politicians, educators, and others. Frazier (and Skinner) believe that the powerful techniques of operant conditioning should be in the hands of enlightened, well-trained, and benevolent scientists who will use the techniques not for competitive advantages but to create a better world.

Novels generally are filled with "incident," events that happen to characters and that propel them into conflicts and resolutions to these conflicts. In this book, there is very little incident. Frazier introduces the community to Burris and his group, arguing mostly with the skeptical Castle about Walden Two's merits, and the members of the group occasionally talk with one another about their evaluation of the utopian community. The main conflict is between Frazier and the skeptical Castle, who disagree over the merits of behavioral modification. The only other conflicts involve whether members of the group will return to the traditional world or choose to stay and live in Walden Two. Steve and his girlfriend Mary struggle briefly with their loyalty to the conventional world and then decide to join the utopian community, while the other couple—Rogers and Barbara—chooses to return to traditional society, despite Rogers's strong attraction to Walden Two. Castle also returns to the traditional world, triumphantly rejecting the Walden Two concept, while Burris makes the novel's most dramatic gesture. In the train station on his return to his university, Burris finally decides to renounce the traditional world and undertakes a three-day, sixty-mile walk back to Frazier's utopian community.

The Characters

Skinner's characters are not complex. They do not develop very much, and they seem to exist simply as a way of convincing the reader that Skinner's vision of a new world order could work in practice as well as in theory.

The ordinary residents of Walden Two, for example, are largely faceless creatures who serve almost as background scenery while Burris and his party take the tour of the facilities. Only slightly more developed are the two couples, Steve and Mary and Rogers and Barbara. Steve and Mary, who struggle briefly but then join the Walden Two community enthusiastically, seem to exist simply to prove that Frazier's arguments and the experience of the Walden Two community would be irresistible to anyone with an open mind. Rogers is also clearly convinced of the utopia's virtues, but he chooses not to join the community because his fiancée Barbara finds the experimental life uninviting. Thus, Rogers takes on the clichéd quality of a tragically misguided romantic lover, while Barbara remains almost as faceless as the regular residents of Walden Two.

More fleshed out as a character is Castle, the skeptical antagonist to Frazier and Frazier's proselytizing speeches. Castle is clearly emotional, stubborn, combative, and inflexible. At times, Castle wavers in his combativeness and seems grudgingly convinced by Frazier's arguments, which helps to make the merits of Walden Two seem more convincing for the reader. At other times, Castle's resistance is portrayed as comically obtuse. In the end, Castle returns triumphantly to the traditional world, and his choice is implicitly portrayed as tragically wrongheaded.

Frazier is the major voice in the book, introducing elements of the utopian community, offering justifications for its design, answering the questions of the group, and countering arguments—mostly from Castle—against the utopian scheme. Frazier is the one character who does display some complexity, portrayed alternately as patiently saintlike and as a borderline megalomaniac who occupies a "throne" on a hillside above Walden Two. From this high vantage point, Frazier observes his creation with a pocket telescope, unashamedly comparing himself to Christ and God the Father. However, the audacity of this characterization is not accompanied by any significant irony or suggestion that Frazier's megalomania is dangerous. Frazier adeptly defends operant conditioning from charges of fascism, and the final lines of the book from Burris, "Frazier was not in his heaven. All was right with the world," serve only to reinforce the idea that this utopian community is safe from totalitarian impulses.

The main character and narrator of *Walden Two* is Professor Burris, whose name clearly recalls "Burrhus," the first name of Skinner himself. Burris expresses mild skepticism over Walden Two and questions Frazier occasionally; more than anything, though, he serves as a moderator for the discussions, setting up Frazier with easy and provocative questions and acting as a buffer between Frazier and the irascible Castle. After much soul-searching, Burris decides to leave his university teaching position in the traditional world and join the Walden Two community, sealing the victory for Frazier's rhetoric.

Themes and Meanings

Like most utopias, *Walden Two* starts with dissatisfaction over its contemporary world and describes an imaginary society to suggest how contemporary problems could be ameliorated. The most general problem that Skinner sees in post-World War II America is that social problems are not attacked with scientific spirit and intelligence. For Skinner, this means quite specifically discarding unmeasurable phenomena as unworthy of serious consideration and substituting a systematic observation of data to discern problems and their solutions. It is in this spirit, for example, that Frazier (and Skinner) dismisses the study of history, which is called a "spurious science" with "no real facts—no real laws."

Thus, early in the novel Frazier reports that the residents of Walden Two have "a constantly experimental attitude toward everything—that's all we need. Solutions to problems of every sort follow almost miraculously."

Many of these problems seem quite mundane, as when Frazier discusses the improved design of afternoon tea service or the washing of cafeteria trays at Walden Two. However, Frazier eventually uncovers other "problems" with his contemporary society that do not immediately strike the reader as in desperate need of radical alteration; when Frazier solves these problems with behavioral technology, Skinner's utopian vision becomes more controversial. For example, Frazier implies that effective child-rearing is a problem in the outside world and reports that the solution at Walden Two is to separate children from their parents at birth, rear the children in carefully controlled communal nurseries, and use operant conditioning to eliminate counterproductive character traits. The caretakers in the nurseries teach self-control in the young by forcing the children to stand five minutes over their supper, without eating, after the youngsters have arrived home tired and hungry from a long walk. Frazier contends that people in the traditional world usually learn self control by accident, which is to say imperfectly.

By the time the tour of Walden Two is ended, Frazier has described and offered solutions for many problems in contemporary American society. Divorce, promiscuity, vocational dissatisfaction, economic hardship, crime—these and many other social ills appear to be cured at Walden Two through behavioral technology, and in the end, half the touring party leaves traditional society to join this better world.

Critical Context

Walden Two, B. F. Skinner's only published novel, was written early in his academic career and represents, as Alan C. Elms asserts, "his first major publication on human behavior." Skinner's career as a behavioral psychologist had begun in the 1930's with laboratory experiments on rats and pigeons. Using positive reinforcement, or rewards for desired behavior, Skinner taught the test animals to push buttons for food and even (with the pigeons) to distinguish colors, dance, and play Ping Pong.

These training sessions took place in a special box, eventually dubbed the "Skinner box," which scrupulously controlled environmental stimuli. Skinner's belief that positive reinforcement could work as effectively on human beings led him in the early 1940's to create a glassed-in crib that served as a training box for children. Designed to create a completely comfortable, supportive, and stimulating environment for early learning, the crib became infamous when Skinner announced in a *Ladies Home Journal* article that he had used it for two and a half years to rear his second daughter, Deborah. The announcement created a national controversy, but in *Walden Two*, Skinner reiterated his belief that children should be reared in communal nurseries for efficient learning rather than in traditional family structures to satisfy conventional values. Though his novel perpetuated his controversial image, millions of new readers surfaced in the early 1960's and made the book the one by which Skinner is most widely recognized.

In later, more academic books such as *Science and Human Behavior* (1953) and *Beyond Freedom and Dignity* (1971), Skinner again argued for the principles behind *Walden Two*. These books created as much controversy as *Walden Two*, but it is Skinner's utopian novel that today remains the clearest and most accessible presentation of his radically behavorist thinking.

Bibliography

Elms, Alan C. "Skinner's Dark Year and *Walden Two.*" *American Psychologist* 36, no. 5 (May, 1981): 470-479. A biographical analysis of Skinner's personal motives for writing *Walden Two*. An indispensable and unique discussion of Skinner's book.

Goldberg, Bruce. "Skinner's Behaviorist Utopia." *The Libertarian Alternative: Essays in Social and Political Philosophy*, edited by Tibor Machan. Chicago: Nelson-Hall, 1974. A philosopher examines the quality of the "reasoning" behind Skinner's ideas in *Walden Two* and finds the reasoning fundamentally flawed.

Krutch, Joseph Wood. *The Measure of Man on Freedom: Human Values, Survival, and the Modern Temper.* Indianapolis: Bobbs-Merrill, 1954. This thorough critique of Skinner's "science of man" finds *Walden Two* an "ignoble utopia."

Roemer, Kenneth M. "Mixing Behavorism and Utopia." *No Place Else: Explorations in Utopian and Dystopian Fiction*, edited by Eric S. Rabkin et al. Carbondale: Southern Illinois University Press, 1983. Analyzes *Walden Two* in the context of utopian literature, evaluates its literary qualities, and glosses many of the book's personal connections with Skinner's life.

Wheeler, Harvey, ed. *Beyond the Punitive Society: Operant Conditioning and Political Aspects.* San Francisco: W. H. Freeman, 1973. Nineteen essays present a critical evaluation of Skinner's ideas and include a response from Skinner to his critics.

Wolfe, Peter. "Walden Two Twenty-Five Years Later: A Retrospective Look." *Studies in the Literary Imagination* 6, no. 2, 11-26. A thorough, balanced, and well-read analysis of Skinner's book.

Terry Nienhuis

THE WALL

Author: John Hersey (1914-1993)
Type of plot: Holocaust novel in diary form
Time of plot: November, 1939, to May, 1943
Locale: Warsaw, primarily in the ghetto sector
First published: 1950

Principal characters:

NOACH LEVINSON, a professional historian and self-appointed archivist of Polish Jewry whose fictive diary constitutes the text of the novel

DOLEK BERSON, an assimilated Polish Jew who gradually changes from a charming drifter to a determined resistance fighter

RACHEL APT, the daughter of a wealthy Warsaw jeweler who compensates for her homely appearance through her heroic character and becomes Dolek's lover after he loses his wife

HALINKA MAZUR (née APT), Rachel's beautiful sister

STEFAN MAZUR, Halinka's husband and a member of the Jewish ghetto police

HENRYK RAPAPORT, a famous leader of the Jewish Socialists and an ardent opponent of Zionist ideology

HIL ZILBERZWEIG, the middle-aged leader of a Zionist youth organization who is induced to make peace with Rapaport through Rachel Apt's mediation

LAZAR SLONIM, a young Socialist who undertakes a hazardous mission to determine the fate of Jews deported from Warsaw

FISCHEL SCHPUNT, the ghetto clown whose antics amuse both the Jews and the Germans

BENLEVI, a distinguished jurist and winner of the Nobel Peace Prize who evades his responsibilities to the Jewish community by leaving Warsaw with a Uruguayan passport

The Novel

John Hersey's intent in writing *The Wall* is to relate the martyrdom of the Jews who lived in Warsaw during World War II in fictional form, and the text of the novel is purported to consist of selections from a very extensive diary originally written in Yiddish that was kept by a historian named Noach Levinson. Even though the diary and the historian are equally fictive, the novel reads very much like an authentic historical chronicle. As published under the title of *The Wall*, the diary begins with the German occupation of the Polish capital in the fall of 1939 and concludes with the razing of the entire ghetto by SS troops as part of the suppression of the revolt that occurred there in the spring of 1943. So assiduous was Levinson in his role of chronicler that the almost daily entries recorded over this period of three and a half years reached a total of more than four million words. This diary, as well as a vast quantity of other documents assembled by Levinson, allegedly was buried within the confines of the ghetto for safety's sake. Even though Levinson is supposed to have died of pneumonia nearly a year after the destruction of the ghetto while hiding out in the "Aryan" sector of Warsaw, he reportedly left detailed directions pertaining to the location of the archive with several trusted individuals who duly recovered it at the war's end.

The fictive archivist Levinson, it should be noted, had a historical counterpart in the person of Emmanuel Ringelblum. As founder of the ghetto archives, this heroic scholar struggled to find and preserve Jewish documents for posterity. While his own writings are far less extensive than those attributed to Levinson by Hersey, the content of Ringelblum's wartime journal, entitled *Notes from the Warsaw Ghetto* (1974), closely parallels the historical events fictionalized in *The Wall*. At the time of the German conquest of Poland, the area of Warsaw that was to become the site of the ghetto was inhabited by 240,000 Jews and 80,000 Gentiles. In the fall of 1940, the Nazis ordered the Gentiles to leave the area, while at the same time some 140,000 Jews from other sectors of Warsaw were compelled to move in. The ghetto was then sealed off by an eight-foot wall, and the death penalty was decreed for any Jew who ventured outside as well as for any Gentile who dared to harbor or assist a person of Jewish ancestry. The number of Jews residing within the ghetto eventually grew to 430,000 as an influx of deportees from different regions of Poland and from other European countries more than replaced those who had died from hunger and disease.

Although the mass extermination of European Jewry actually got under way shortly after the German invasion of the Soviet Union on June 22, 1941, it was not until approximately a year later that the liquidation of the Warsaw ghetto began in earnest. Its inhabitants were told that they were to be resettled in the East, but the journey turned out to be a short one: a trip of some fifty miles to the gas chambers set up in the death camp of Treblinka. As soon as the true nature of the transfer action became known, the disparate political and religious factions within the ghetto banded together and agreed to the formation of a military unit to be known as the Jewish Combat Organization (Z.O.B.). The climax of the unit's armed resistance came when the Z.O.B. opened fire on the Germans and their Ukrainian and Lithuanian auxiliaries as they entered the ghetto on the morning of April 19, 1943. By that time, the total number of inhabitants had dwindled to sixty thousand, but the poorly armed members of the Z.O.B. still managed to thwart the enemy for nearly a month. There was never any hope of victory, except for the spiritual triumph that comes from dying with honor. The last part of *The Wall* itself is devoted to the details of the planning and execution of this act of insurrection and constitutes an eloquent tribute to its heroic grandeur.

The Characters

In the prologue to *The Wall*, the anonymous editor of Levinson's diary states that the version he has prepared for current publication consists of only one-twentieth of the more than four million words to be found in the original notebooks. In order to achieve such a drastic reduction in length, he decided to concentrate on those entries that pertained to the fortunes of a group of individuals belonging to three families, whose respective surnames are Berson, Apt, and Mazur. These families are eventually compelled to live together in a single apartment, owing to the lack of housing within the ghetto. They also take in three other persons as roomers—a rabbi, a former social worker, and Levinson himself. It is ironic that Levinson experiences the joys of family life for the first time as an adult by virtue of this arrangement, and he develops genuine affection for all members of this extended family. For this privilege, Levinson comes close to feeling gratitude toward the Nazis, who have made it all possible.

Because of this newly acquired vantage point, Levinson becomes privy to much intimate information concerning other members of the "family" and is thus able to delineate the varying ways in which these individuals respond to the increasingly brutal conditions of life inside the ghetto with great authority. Levinson witnesses the gradual transformation of Dolek Berson from a man with little purpose in life to a self-sacrificing guardian of the Jewish community. Rachel Apt, on the other hand, is depicted throughout Levinson's diary as constant in her dedication to the welfare of the ghetto's inhabitants. Halinka Apt, perhaps owing to her great beauty, always had a tendency to be more engrossed in personal affairs than her sister, but she grows in stature as the novel progresses until she is almost as heroic a figure as Rachel herself. Their father, Mauritzi Apt, proves himself to be a moral failure and earns the contempt of both his daughters when he engages the services of a plastic surgeon for the sake of replacing the foreskin that was removed at the time he was circumcised as an infant and leaves the ghetto with documents identifying him as a Gentile.

As conditions grow more dire, other individuals find themselves in situations that test their virtue to the utmost. Particularly poignant is the dilemma that confronts Halinka's husband, Stefan Mazur. Having become a member of the Jewish ghetto police, he is obliged to bring four persons to the railroad yard for transfer to Treblinka each day during the period of resettlement. Failure to fulfill his quota will lead to the deportation of his own wife. To save Halinka's life, he tries to get his own parents to volunteer to go to Treblinka. After failing to convince either of them to give their consent, Stefan abducts Berson's ailing wife out of sheer desperation so that he might meet his quota. He himself dies shortly thereafter under somewhat mysterious circumstances amid the confusion caused by a bombing raid on the city of Warsaw by Russian aircraft.

Some entries in *The Wall* pertain to incidents involving characters who are not part of Levinson's "family." In deciding which of these episodes to include, the editor decided to focus on individuals who survived the destruction of the ghetto, since readers are more likely to be interested in the few who survived than in the many who perished. At the end of the novel, a group of forty-three persons, including a Polish guide, makes its way out of the ghetto through the sewers into the "Aryan" sector of Warsaw. Although this hazardous trip is supposed to take no more than seven hours, unforeseen difficulties on the "Aryan" side make it necessary that the group remain in the sewers for an additional twenty-four hours. It is during this delay that Levinson conducts some of his most revealing interviews and is able to clarify many situations that had previously puzzled him. With the sole exception of Dolek Berson, who is inadvertently left behind as the result of the haste with which the Polish rescue party departs from the scene, all who participate in the escape succeed in reaching the safety of a thick forest located just outside the city. As if to emphasize the activist sentiments of the survivors, the editor concludes the volume with the query made by Rachel Apt upon reaching the woods, "Nu, what is the plan for tomorrow?"

Themes and Meanings

Five days after the outbreak of the uprising in the ghetto, Levinson delivers a speech from within a bunker on the great Yiddish writer Isaac Leib Peretz under the auspices of the Jewish Cultural Organization. In the course of this talk, Levinson attempts to formulate a definition of Jewishness that is broad enough to encompass the Hasidic rabbi Baal Shem Tov as well as Albert Einstein. To this end, he cites the words that appear in the conclusion to a volume of essays by Peretz, in which Jews are warned against shutting themselves up in a spiritual ghetto: "Ghetto is impotence. Cultural cross fertilization is the only possibility for human development. Humanity must be the synthesis, the sum, the quintessence of all national cultural forms and philosophies."

Peretz's noble sentiment stands in stark contrast to the narrow nationalism espoused by the ideologues of the Third Reich. As a case in point, one need only consider the definition of a Jew that the Nazis invoked to determine who was to be incarcerated within the ghetto. According to the entry in Levinson's diary dated October 25, 1940, a Jew is officially defined as "any man who has had at least three Jewish grandparents, or two grandparents provided (1) he is active in any Jewish communal organization or (2) he has a Jewish wife." Because this definition is based on racial rather than religious criteria, those Polish Jews who had converted to Christianity also found themselves compelled to live inside the ghetto. Two such Christians of Jewish ancestry whose stories Levinson includes in his diary are a father and son named Jan and Wladislaw Jablonski, respectively. Despite the fact that the son had received an exclusively Roman Catholic upbringing, he quickly comes to accept his new Jewish identity once he takes up residence within the ghetto. His father, whose conversion to Roman Catholicism had been based on sincere conviction, remains steadfast, however, in his adherence to his adopted faith. Irrespective of these differences, both eventually die at the hands of the Germans. The tragic fate of the Jablonskis makes it abundantly clear that the definition of Jewishness is not a matter that Jews can expect to resolve exclusively among themselves.

Critical Context

Even though *The Wall* never succeeded in winning the Pulitzer Prize in fiction, as did Hersey's solitary previous novel entitled *A Bell for Adano* (1944), it still managed to accrue several other major literary awards. Hersey's moral earnestness and thorough research received almost unanimous praise from the critics. Those reviewers who expressed reservations pertaining to the efficacy of the novel found fault chiefly with its journalistic technique. Since similar charges had been leveled against *A Bell for Adano*, Hersey took the trouble of clarifying his views on the function of historical fiction in an article called "The Novel of Contemporary History," which appeared in the November, 1949, issue of *The Atlantic Monthly* a few months before the scheduled publication of *The Wall*. There, he explains, the primary aim of this type of fiction should be to "illuminate" the human beings caught up in historical events rather than the events themselves. In this respect, his purpose in writing *The Wall* was no different from that which motivated him to publish the nonfictional work bearing the title *Hiroshima* (1946).

While *The Wall* and *Hiroshima* are individually regarded as Hersey's finest achievements to date in their respective genres, these books differ greatly in terms of both length and complexity. *Hiroshima* is a short work organized around Hersey's own interviews with six survivors of the atomic holocaust that struck the city on August 6, 1945. *The Wall*, in contrast, is a novel of more than six hundred pages and contains innumerable individual diary entries that are culled from interviews that Levinson allegedly conducted with twenty informants over a period of three and a half years. When all these entries are added to those for which Levinson himself is solely responsible, there are more than fifty characters whose identities the reader needs to remember. This burden might easily have been alleviated had either the author or the publisher taken the trouble to include a dramatis personae to accompany the text of the novel. Despite this obstacle, a close reading of *The Wall* is a richly rewarding experience that few contemporary novels can match in terms of wisdom and compassion.

Bibliography
Fiedler, Leslie. "No! in Thunder." In *The Novel: Modern Essays in Criticism*, edited by Robert Murray Davis. Englewood Cliffs, N.J.: Prentice-Hall, 1969. In discussing authors from his point of view that "art is essentially a moral activity," the controversial Fiedler accuses Hersey of being the author of "The Sentimental Liberal Protest Novel" who fights for "slots on the lists of best sellers" with his "ersatz morality." The essay makes for lively reading at best.
Huse, Nancy L. *The Survival Tales of John Hersey*. New York: Whitston, 1983. An eminently readable and informed study on Hersey that is useful in understanding the scope and development of Hersey as a writer. Explores the relationship between art and moral or political intentions. Includes extensive notes and a bibliography.
Sanders, David. "John Hersey." In *Contemporary Novelists*, edited by James Vinson. New York: St. Martin's Press, 1982. Covers Hersey's work from wartime journalist to novelist. Cites *The Wall* as his greatest novel and considers him the "least biographical of authors." A rather dense study but helpful in quickly establishing themes in Hersey's writings. A chronology and a bibliography are provided.
_____. *John Hersey Revisited*. Boston: Twayne, 1991. A revised edition of Sanders's 1967 study. The first chapter introduces Hersey's career as reporter and novelist, and subsequent chapters discuss his major fiction and nonfiction, including his later stories. Includes chronology, notes, and bibliography.

_____. "John Hersey: War Correspondent into Novelist." In *New Voices in American Studies*, edited by Ray B. Browne, Donald M. Winkelman, and Allen Hayman. West Lafayette, Ind.: Purdue University Press, 1966. A well-known scholar on Hersey, Sanders defends him and insists that he should not be dismissed because of his popularity. Traces Hersey's origins as a war correspondent and the writings that emerged from these experiences. Finally, Sanders settles the dispute as to whether Hersey is a novelist and hails him as a "writer."

Victor Anthony Rudowski

WAR AND REMEMBRANCE

Author: Herman Wouk (1915-   )
Type of plot: Historical chronicle
Time of plot: From 1941 to 1945
Locale: Siena, Italy; Pearl Harbor; Auschwitz, Poland; Manila, the Philippines; London; Singapore; Washington, D.C.; Oak Ridge, Tennessee; Marseilles, France; Burma; Moscow; Leningrad; Stalingrad; El Alemain, Egypt; Corsica; Baden-Baden, Germany; Prague; Imphal, India; and Teheran, Iran
First published: 1978

Principal characters:

> VICTOR (PUG) HENRY, the protagonist, a naval officer and presidential envoy
>
> RHODA HENRY, Pug's estranged wife
>
> WARREN, the Henrys' brilliant son, a naval aviator killed at Midway
>
> BYRON, Warren's younger brother, a submarine officer
>
> MADELINE, the Henrys' only daughter, who has an affair with radio personality Hugh Cleveland but settles down to marry a naval officer working on the atom bomb at Los Alamos
>
> AARON JASTROW, a successful academic and famous writer trapped in Nazi-occupied Europe
>
> NATALIE, Jastrow's niece and Byron's wife, who shares Jastrow's predicament and growing understanding of the Holocaust
>
> ALISTAIR TUDSBURY, a popular British broadcaster and friend of Victor Henry
>
> PAMELA TUDSBURY, Alistair's daughter, who assists her father and who falls in love with Victor Henry
>
> WERNER BECK, a German diplomat and former student of Aaron Jastrow
>
> LESLIE SLOTE, an officer in the foreign service who quits over his government's unwillingness to help the doomed European Jews
>
> ARMIN VON ROON, a German general whose memoirs of Adolf Hitler and of World War II are edited by Victor Henry

The Novel

The action of *War and Remembrance* follows with great fidelity the major events of World War II. The novel begins with the Japanese attack on Pearl Harbor and ends with the dropping of the atom bomb on Hiroshima. All major battles on land and sea are covered. Japanese, American, and German war aims are fully explored and analyzed, including the development of the atom bomb and of the concentration camps. Domestic life in the United States during the war, the acute suffering of the Soviet people during the German invasion, and the collapse of the British Empire in the Far

East all receive significant attention. As a result, the global dimensions of the war become the primary concern of the novel.

War and Remembrance is divided into seven parts that evenly distribute the emphasis that Wouk places on the private lives of his characters and on the public events in which they participate. Part 1, "Where Is Natalie?" shows the United States gearing up for war as Pearl Harbor is bombed and the British are defeated at Singapore. American submarines test their power in the Pacific while events in Europe are governed by the spread of a seemingly invincible Nazi empire. Byron Henry, with the help of others, tries to save his Jewish wife, Natalie, and her uncle, Aaron Jastrow, who are stranded in German-occupied Europe.

Part 2, "Midway," concentrates on an exciting dramatization and analysis of the decisive American victory over the Japanese navy and air force that checked their power in the Pacific. Part 3, "Byron and Natalie," juxtaposes the different fates of the husband and wife as the brash and utterly self-confident Byron locates his wife and son in hiding in Marseilles. Natalie, who has slowly begun to realize that her Jewishness is more important to the Nazis than her American citizenship, refuses to run the risk of escape by a railroad journey, as Byron proposes.

Part 4, "Pug and Rhoda," follows the fortunes of the Henrys' dissolving marriage and of the dissolution of Western civilization. Pug is deeply hurt over his wife's infidelity and is sorely wounded by Warren's gallant death. Reports of concentration camp atrocities are ignored or discounted as governments and their citizens attempt to maintain the fiction that humane values prevail.

Parts 5 ("Pug and Pamela"), 6 ("The Paradise Ghetto"), and 7 ("Leyte Gulf") bring the global war and the private lives of the novel's characters to a climax and resolution. Pug realizes that his marriage cannot be repaired even as the Nazis, clearly having lost the war, continue to murder the Jews and to fight on all fronts. The desperate Japanese attack at Leyte Gulf, the awesome power of the bomb, the gassing of Aaron Jastrow and his cremation in an Auschwitz oven, and Natalie's harrowing survival in the camps point to the author's conclusion: "Either war is finished or we are."

The Characters

At the center of *War and Remembrance* are the characters of Victor Henry and his family. Pug, as his friends call him, is a rather old-fashioned type who respects all the traditional values of marriage and patriotism. These values are challenged, however, when he is attracted to Pamela Tudsbury, a bright woman much younger than his wife, Rhoda. In keeping with his character, rather than thinking only of his personal ambitions, he sacrifices his desire for a command in order to serve as President Franklin Delano Roosevelt's personal emissary to the Soviet Union. As several characters point out, Pug is "incredible" in his devotion to duty and to a personal moral code.

Byron is a close second to his father in demanding that friends, fellow officers, and family obey exacting moral standards. He breaks up his sister Madeline's romance with her married boss, Hugh Cleveland; disapproves of his submarine captain's shooting of Japanese soldiers who are the helpless survivors of a disabled ship; and is cool to his father when he correctly suspects that Pug has had an affair with Pamela.

These upright male Americans seem almost quaint in a world that is overthrowing civilized standards of behavior. Pug and Byron are clearly meant to counterpoint characters such as Aaron Jastrow, who must, to some extent, collaborate with the Nazis to save Natalie's life. A different kind of collaborator, the German diplomat Werner Beck, shrewdly deceives his former teacher, Aaron Jastrow, into believing that he can accept German protection without becoming implicated in the very racial policies that have resulted in the detention of himself and his niece.

In addition to brief but vivid vignettes of historical figures such as President Roosevelt, Harry Hopkins, and Admiral Raymond Spruance (the victor of Midway), several characters serve to fill out both the historical and the cultural background of the war. Alistair Tudsbury is a vivid representative of British bluster and blindness to the country's weak position in the Far East at the outset of the war. Leslie Slote exemplifies the well-meaning but ineffective efforts of a few in the American foreign service to ascertain the truth about the concentration camps and to make it an important consideration in war strategy. Armin von Roon is Wouk's brilliant fictional creation of a German general who expresses the racial biases, if not the fanaticism, of Adolf Hitler's Germany. Excerpts from his memoirs, which Victor Henry translates and upon which he comments, constitute a fascinating way of critiquing American character and war plans.

Themes and Meanings

One of the principal themes of the novel is how unprepared America was, militarily and morally, to fight a global war, and how it astonished the world with its ability to acquire the means to defeat all its foes. President Roosevelt is credited with the political greatness that ensured cooperation among the allies and solid support for the war at home. While not endorsing Armin von Roon's portrait of Roosevelt as the evil genius of the war who knew how to keep the Soviets fighting while America minimized its losses, Wouk does see the president as practicing realpolitik by giving the Soviets, through the policy of Lend-Lease, virtually all the material that they requested; by not challenging their territorial claims; and by restraining Prime Minister Winston Churchill's opposition to Soviet leader Joseph Stalin.

The Nazi extermination of the Jews and the dropping of the bomb on Hiroshima are not equated in moral terms, but Wouk clearly identifies these two events as shattering traditional views of the world. The systematic, bureaucratic, and industrialized killing of a people, is, in his words, a "new fact" about human nature that the world will forever have to reckon with. Similarly "new" in a terrible way is the atom bomb, "the new light [that] seared more than sixty thousand people to cinders." Although more people died in conventional bombing raids over Dresden and Tokyo, the concentration of such force in a single bomb inevitably ended not only World War II but also the thought of any survivable global conflict in the future.

Critical Context

A sequel to *The Winds of War* (1971), *War and Remembrance* has met with mixed critical response. On one hand, reviewers extol Wouk's sure grasp of military and political history and the exciting manner in which he presents the major theaters of war, particularly Midway. The characterization of Armin von Roon, the fictional German general, has been singled out for particularly high praise, revealing as it does an extraordinary ability to get within the mind of a character who is utterly alien to American ways of thought. On the other hand, Victor Henry has been called a "prig" who is all too perfect, always in the right place at the right time, and most of the other fictional characters have been dubbed stereotypes with little depth or color.

It is true that Wouk runs the danger of stereotyping by presenting rather ordinary characters such as Pug's wife, Rhoda. Compared to the exciting historical events that Wouk dramatizes so crisply, her affairs seem dull and prosaic. Yet she seems a valid marker of precisely those areas of American life that were largely untouched by a war that did not take place on American soil. It is easy for characters such as Rhoda to maintain their illusions, to ask "What's WRONG with illusions?" Indeed, von Roon has this typical kind of obliviousness in mind when he speaks of Americans lacking "the European sense of the past, and writers of broad culture."

More troubling for reviewers, however, is Wouk's honoring of American history. Unlike Norman Mailer's *The Naked and the Dead* (1948), which explores the incipient roots of Fascism in the American mentality, or Joseph Heller's *Catch-22* (1961), which exposes the absurdity of war, *War and Remembrance* argues that the war was worth fighting, that nothing short of a global conflict could have preserved genuine American values. Wouk concedes various American faults—anti-Semitism, individual acts of atrocity, the conflicting feelings over the dropping of the Hiroshima bomb, and so on—but he steadfastly maintains that "there were differences" between America and its opponents. The Nazis, after all, pursued an ideology that mandated the Holocaust—even at the expense of German armies that could have been supplied by the very trains that were diverted to transport Jews to concentration camps.

Wouk writes, in other words, as a veteran of the war who unabashedly identifies not only with the fighting men but also with the flawed political system that survived the war. While his novel is critical of several wartime decisions—especially of Roosevelt's unwillingness to help the Jews—it is also historically accurate in demonstrating how difficult it would have been to broaden public awareness of the Holocaust.

Unlike many other American novels, *War and Remembrance* does not project the bitterness of the postwar world back onto the war itself. In Wouk's view, the war was a time when civilization itself seemed to be held in the balance, when America and its allies were facing what Aaron Jastrow calls "the problem of senseless evil." Many sound explanations of German and Japanese war aims are given in the novel, but, as Jastrow concludes in a lecture on the Book of Job to a group of Jews bound for Auschwitz, there is a "missing piece" of the universe that Job cannot understand, that human beings have not fathomed. Jastrow insists, however, that human beings—such as Job—are the answer, in the sense that only human beings can put the question of "senseless evil" to themselves. Toward the end of *War and Remembrance*, Jastrow's journal and von Roon's memoirs become more and more closely intertwined, leaving the reader with the clash of profoundly different sensibilities, political and theological antinomies that account for a world at war with itself.

Bibliography

Gerard, Philip. "The Great American War Novels." *World & I* 10 (June, 1995): 54-63. Gerard notes that World War II was "the last public event that defined a generation of novelists." In this essay, he looks at the works of many of them, including Wouk's *The Caine Mutiny*. Although Gerard does not address *War and Remembrance* directly, his comments can be extended to Wouk's other war novels.

Mazzeno, Laurence W. *Herman Wouk*. New York: Twayne, 1994. A collection of critical essays that explores various aspects of the works of Herman Wouk. Includes an index and bibliographical references for further reading.

Shapiro, Edward S. "The Jew as Patriot: Herman Wouk and American Jewish Identity." *American Jewish History* 84 (December, 1996): 333-351. Shapiro explores similarities between American identity and Jewish identity in the works of Herman Wouk, which portray the Jew as the defender of American institutions and values. Shapiro also notes that Wouk viewed the history of the American West and Israel's struggle for independence as analogous.

Shatzky, Joel, and Michael Taub, eds. *Contemporary Jewish-American Novelists: A Bio-Critical Sourcebook*. Westport, Conn.: Greenwood Press, 1997. The entry on Wouk's life includes major works and themes, an overview of his critical reception, and a bibliography of primary and secondary sources.

Carl Rollyson

THE WAR BETWEEN THE TATES

Author: Alison Lurie (1926-　　)
Type of plot: Social satire
Time of plot: 1969-1970
Locale: Upstate New York and New York City
First published: 1974

> *Principal characters:*
> BRIAN TATE, a professor of political science
> ERICA TATE, Brian's wife
> WENDY GAHAGHAN, a graduate student with whom Brian has an affair
> DANIELLE ZIMMERN, Erica's best friend, a French instructor at Brian's
>   university and a divorcee
> ZED, a 1960's dropout, the proprietor of the Krishna Bookshop, and a
>   longtime admirer of Erica

The Novel

The war between the Tates is fought on two fronts simultaneously. The less-destructive engagements are the skirmishes between two generations—Brian and Erica Tate and their two, young, teenage children, Jeffrey and Matilda. The once adorable Muffy and Jeffo have become coarse and insolent, "awful lodgers—lodgers who paid no rent, whose lease could not be terminated." Their wickedness takes the usual forms: a preoccupation with loud music, a sulky intransigence when faced with any request from their parents, and flamboyant impulses in dress and grooming.

Yet as these generational conflicts work themselves out—a land mine here, a mortar burst there—armed combat of the deadliest kind is being waged in the marital trenches between Brian and Erica. The battle is set off by an old tactic: the ambush of a middle-aged man by a much younger woman. Brian, a professor of political science at Corinth University, is working hard on a scholarly book when Wendy Gahaghan, a slightly soiled flower child, insistently presents herself to him as a romantic sacrifice to what she perceives as his genius and goodness. Once their affair is in full flush, Erica is quick to find out. The Tates at first effect a nervous truce, but Erica's dramatic discovery that Wendy is pregnant leads to Brian's banishment to an apartment. The pregnancy is aborted, but the hostilities continue.

During her separation, Erica leans on her friend Danielle Zimmern, already divorced from her English-professor husband and thoroughly embittered by her own marital wars. Yet when Danielle meets Bernie Kotelchuk, a congenial veterinarian, she relents somewhat, and she provides Erica with a useful model of sexual generosity.

Kotelchuk, hearty and masculine, is contrasted with Sanford Finkelstein, who goes simply by Zed. Erica had known Zed years before at Harvard, and she is delighted to find him running the Krishna Bookshop in Corinth, drawn there apparently by his unexpressed feeling for Erica. Zed is a gaunt, balding guru to Wendy and many of her friends. His passivity and yearning attract Erica's sympathy, leading her to an offering of herself to Zed that ends comically but sadly.

While Danielle is enjoying her new lover, Bernie, and Erica is experimenting with Zed, Brian is savoring the mixed pleasures of life with Wendy and her militant, doping student cohorts in the struggle for women's liberation on the Corinth campus. The dissidents focus their anger on Don Dibble, a conservative professor of political science whom Brian dislikes intensely. In a facetious moment, Brian suggests that the agitators take Dibble hostage in his office and is appalled when they do exactly that. The interlude ends quickly with Brian's absurd rescue of the hapless Dibble by means of a rope that Brian smuggles into Dibble's office and then hangs out of his window. In a comic conclusion, Brian is beaten for his treachery by the irate girls whom he has deceived.

Brian's next blow is his discovery that Wendy is pregnant again, but this time there is a complication: The father may be—probably is—a Pakistani graduate student in engineering. The force of Wendy's obsession with Brian is now spent, and the frazzled Brian is ready to give her up when she announces she is leaving for a "far-out commune" in Northern California. The pregnant Wendy departs with a new friend, Ralph, who she says "really digs kids" and "wants to work out a total relationship." Zed leaves Corinth at about the same time, and the battle-scarred Tates are left to their own devices. The war ends with a promising settlement in sight and the hope that, though the Tates may not live happily ever after, they will perhaps comfort each other in their joint struggle to be honest, decent people.

The Characters

Brian Tate, forty-six years old, holds an endowed chair in his department and has written two scholarly studies and a textbook, but "he is a dissatisfied and disappointed man." With a long line of accomplished ancestors, he has felt the need to be successful but has not attained the deanship that he covets. All of his worldly efforts have been colored by his awareness of being only five feet five—and "all his adult life Brian had behaved so as to compensate for, even confute, the sign set on him by fate." He has become, in fact, a dull man, a man whose self-discipline has led him to a dead end. Although his conjugal life has not always been perhaps as complete as his fancies have led him to dream, he has enjoyed a contented married life and has never exploited his students sexually. He has had his invitations and turned them down, scorning the weakness of colleagues who have fallen. "He loved Erica, and he had serious work to do."

So although it is hard to admire Brian Tate, it is easy to sympathize with him in his misery. He certainly gets little profound satisfaction from his misalliance with Wendy. A middle-aged student of George Kennan and American foreign policy cannot be expected to find a gratifying way of life in the company of young rebels passing around joints and cliches about the establishment. He is at the end of the novel a chastened man, "embarrassed and ashamed of his behavior over the past year."

For Erica Tate, the discovery of Brian's affair is a crushing shock. Erica has always expected Brian to be a great man in his field, interpreting his solemnity and humorlessness as evidence of high seriousness. Even as time runs out and the greatness fails to materialize, she remains Brian's devoted helpmate. Besides her husband, she has the sacred Children to whom to devote her life. She is a traditionalist, basically conservative in her social, sexual, and cultural values, attitudes, and styles. Facing up to the transmogrification of dear Muffy and Jeffo into teenagers is difficult enough, and Brian's infidelity leaves her reeling.

It is typical of Erica that she treats Wendy with great kindness when she turns up sick and pregnant at Erica's door. When she renews her old friendship with Zed, she offers him herself. She fulfills herself in nurturing others: The great man she marries, the children, pregnant mistresses, and forlorn Zen dropouts—all elicit her care and mothering.

Erica's fastidiousness contrasts with her friend Danielle's open earthiness and hearty tolerance of the world and its imperfections. The two women complement each other well: "Women age like wild apples, Erica read once. Most, fallen under the tree and ungathered, gradually soften and bulge and go brown and rotten; and that is what will happen to Danielle. Others hang on to the branch, where they wither and shrink and freeze as winter comes on. That is how it will be with her."

Little needs to be said about Wendy. Full of earnest goodwill but heedless, prey to the appeal of every radical slogan, warm but shallow, compassionate but often rancorous and lacking in charity, she and her friends left a lot of clutter behind them in the 1960's for other people to pick up, but their energy and idealism often worked for the good. Wendy herself is no leader, but she swells the rout led by shriller voices. In her intellectual shiftlessness she will find it hard to set a stable course, but she does not know this. Her innocence is implausible but beguiling: "I know there've been some bad vibes, but I've got my head together now, and everything's going to work out."

Themes and Meanings

Lurie is a gentle satirist. Her characters thrash around comically in the snares that they set for themselves, but though they are often weak, they are never vicious. They invite sympathy and do not provoke contempt. The Tates' domestic situation is a commentary on American middle-class life: the middle-aged husband struggling as his dreams begin to fade and elude him; the wife coping with suddenly obnoxious teenagers, thinking about a part-time job, and watching her neck for wrinkles; the children who flame out in unpredictable ways under the pressures of adolescence. In the end, things turn out as well for the Tates and Wendy as most people could hope for, given life's predicaments. Lurie seems to be saying that, although existence may not be a divine comedy, much of it is still comic, and, given any luck at all, it can be at least tolerable if people are considerate and understanding.

The Tates' domestic drama is played out against a background of late 1960's social changes. Of special concern to Brian and Erica is the encroachment of Glenview Heights, a raw, new subdivision, on the pastoral landscape they had sought out when they moved to Corinth. Ranch houses, featuring carports that "bulge with motorboats and skimobiles," loom up to block off their sunsets, and Erica identifies the vulgarization of her surroundings with the distressing changes in Jeffrey and Matilda; "natural beauty and innocence are being swallowed up in ugly artificial growth, while she watches helplessly."

The War Between the Tates ends with one of the classic defining scenes of the late 1960's and early 1970's—a peace march. As the procession advances down the main street of Collegetown, it attracts what Brian views as "freakish, violent, and socially disruptive elements": a guerrilla theater group, a WHEN contingent, a Gay Power delegation, and a rabble of Maoists. The march culminates in a great brawl, choreographed to a score of police sirens. Everyone will rise the next day a little older, a little more scarred, and—with luck—a little wiser, and the ranch homes will continue displacing the oak trees. As Erica muses, "Everything and everyone is in flux now, confused, disintegrating in time and space."

Critical Context

The War Between the Tates, Lurie's fifth novel, is generally regarded as her best. Among her earlier novels, the best known is *The Nowhere City* (1965), an Easterner's satiric look at life in Southern California. She followed *The War Between the Tates* with *Only Children* (1979) and *Foreign Affairs* (1984), which was awarded the Pulitzer Prize in fiction. As befits a novelist of manners, she has also published a wide-ranging study of dress, *The Language of Clothes* (1981).

In *The War Between the Tates*, all of Lurie's strengths as a novelist are readily apparent. She writes sharp, convincing dialogue and moves her narrative with well-conceived scenes. All of her technical ability serves a broad, generous vision of the human situation; her intelligent grasp of what prompts her characters to behave as they do is matched by her charity toward them. Although she is sensitive to women's concerns, she does not write mainly to dramatize women's problems and could not be called a feminist, nor does she make of the novel a vehicle for political propaganda.

Bibliography

Costa, Richard H. *Alison Lurie*. New York: Twayne, 1992. Costa provides a critical and interpretive study of Lurie with a close reading of her major works, which includes a chapter devoted to *The War Between the Tates*, a solid bibliography, and complete notes and references.

Newman, Judie. "Alison Lurie: A Bibliography, 1945-1989." *Bulletin of Bibliography* 49 (June, 1992): 109-114. A useful bibliography of Lurie's writings.

Pearlman, Mickey. "A Bibliography of Writings About Alison Lurie." In *American Women Writing Fiction: Identity, Family, Space*, edited by Mickey Pearlman. Lexington: University Press of Kentucky, 1989. A listing of secondary writings on Lurie's works and career.

_____. "A Bibliography of Writings by Alison Lurie." In *American Women Writing Fiction: Identity, Family, Space*, edited by Mickey Pearlman. Lexington: University Press of Kentucky, 1989. A listing of writings by Lurie.

Frank Day

THE WAR OF THE END OF THE WORLD

Author: Mario Vargas Llosa (1936-   )
Type of plot: Historical chronicle
Time of plot: The late 1890's
Locale: Brazil, primarily the backlands
First published: La guerra del fin del mundo, 1981 (English translation, 1984)

> *Principal characters:*
> THE COUNSELOR, an apocalyptic prophet and Lord of Canudos
> GALILEO GALL, a revolutionary and a phrenologist
> EPAMINODAS GONCALVES, the head of the Progressivist Party
> BARON DE CANABRAVA, the head of the Bahia Autonomist Party
> RUFINO, a tracker and guide
> THE NEARSIGHTED JOURNALIST, whose mission is to explain Canudos
> JUREMA, Rufino's wife, Gall's victim, and the Journalist's lover

The Novel

Using the epoch-making historical work of Euclides da Cunha, *Os sertões* (1902; *Rebellion in the Backlands*, 1944), Vargas Llosa re-creates the turbulent events of late nineteenth century Brazil in a novel of revolution that has a clear relationship to the continuing history of revolt in Latin America as exemplified in the Maoist *el sendero luminoso* of his native Peru. As he elaborates the facts and biases of Cunha's "Bible of Brazilian Nationality," he follows the career of the millenarian preacher Antonio Conselhiero, his sectarian community at Canudos in the backlands of northern Brazil, the military campaigns to destroy the anti-Republican stronghold of the Counselor's followers, and the political intrigues of the monarchists and Republicans in a newly independent Brazil. When he departs from Cunha's social history, he carefully maintains a fidelity to the historical details and backgrounds against which his characters act.

Like much late twentieth century fiction, the novel is, in part, a work about writing. The efforts of the unnamed Nearsighted Journalist, likely modeled on Cunha himself, to whom the novel is dedicated, to explore, record, and explain the facts and hypotheses of a revolt doomed to failure, are central to the plot. The Journalist is, himself, caught up in the campaign against Canudos and becomes a questionable eyewitness to the events (he lost his eyeglasses there). As the Journalist encounters each of the figures whose exploits and intentions he will later seek to note, classify, and explain, so Vargas Llosa develops his own story by notation, classification, and explanation. At one point in the process of conducting his research into the revolt, its antecedents and consequences, the Journalist exclaims that Canudos is filled with stories; the telling of those stories becomes his obsession and the telling of the Journalist's story is a major portion of the novelist's objective.

This work combines these many stories into a version of history that merges imagination with fact and provides a complete fiction that clearly embroiders the facts yet also rests upon the facts of the siege of Canudos. The story of the Counselor, for example, is a fully articulated exercise in hagiography which includes such standard elements as a mysterious birth, a period of childhood isolation, a time of itinerancy that includes wanderings in deserted places, the gathering of a band of unlikely followers, the performance of good works for the poor and oppressed, the function of preaching, the foundation of a community of believers, and martyrdom at the hands of the established political force. This overarching fictionalization of the Counselor's life contains overtly biblical dimensions as well as elements common to many aspects of the *Acta Sanctorum*, with the difference that Vargas Llosa's clear-eyed reconstruction of history eschews a pietistical viewpoint usually associated with hagiography. The novel also works on a political level, pitting the ostensibly hapless band of Canudos against the inexorable military machine of the Brazilian Republic. In this phase of the narration Vargas Llosa creates an unrelieved and intensely stark chronicle of the dehumanizing aspects of military campaigns and warfare. From the first pitched battle in which the republic suffers ignominious defeat to the virtual extermination of the sect, the novel explores the effects of the politics of confrontation upon all who engage in it and does so by using the vehicle of fiction to comment on the meanings of historical events.

The stories of the many characters intersect in the apocalyptic battle of the siege of Canudos which pits the fanatic band that follows the Counselor's anti-Republican teachings against the military strength of the Brazilian Republic. This climactic "war of the end of the world" represents, for those few survivors who followed the Counselor, the triumph of the Antichrist as embodied by the republic and its trappings, the census, the metric system, civil marriage, and the separation of church and state.

The Characters

One of the novel's indisputable strengths lies precisely in the telling of the many stories of Canudos through a highly artistic rendition of characters. Vargas Llosa works through an accumulation of physical detail, psychological description, and expert dialogue to create memorable, individualized, and well-articulated characters who both create history and bear its burden. The Counselor is both a realistically portrayed and a mysteriously evoked presence throughout the work. He gathers into his New Jerusalem at Canudos the poor, halt, deformed, mad, and fallen as well as a considerable group of sometime bandits and outlaws; the figurative lions lie down with the lambs in a unity of peace that is quickly galvanized into a church militant. At times, the Counselor appears to be John the Baptist preaching conversion in the wilderness; at times he appears to be a reincarnation of Jesus of Nazareth who has come to bring fire and the sword.

In the tradition of those whom he has called "God-supplanters," such as Henry Fielding, Honoré de Balzac, James Joyce, and William Faulkner, Vargas Llosa not only re-creates reality but also competes with it. His rich characterizations of the Counselor and the Journalist are replicated in a variety of lesser characters such as his soldiers, bandits, adventurers, circus performers, and clerics whom he imbues with a protoliberationist theology so that they would be quite at home in late twentieth century Brazil. One of the many successful creations in the work is the adventurer Galileo Gall, a red-headed Scot with a penchant for phrenology, Marxist thought, and the spread of international revolution. Gall turns up in Brazil after several revolutionary escapades in Europe just in time to participate in the Counselor's revolt. The naïve Gall plays into the hands of the head of the Progressivist Republican Party and editor of the *Journal de Noticias*, the diabolical Epaminodas Goncalves. Goncalves tricks Gall into smuggling guns to Canudos, arranges for his ambush, and plans to expose him as a British agent serving the monarchial and imperial interest of Queen Victoria, who is in league with the deposed Emperor of Brazil, the Bahia Autonomist Party, and the Baron de Canabrava (the owner of the land at Canudos). Gall's bizarre activities, outlandish appearance, incoherent revolutionary speeches, unwitting role in the destruction of Canudos, and uncanny escapes from certain death combine to make him one of contemporary fiction's more interesting picaresque characters.

One of the novel's true protagonists (along with the Journalist) and its unexpected heroine is Jurema. She alone can provide details of her own experience and indignities to the Journalist, can provide him with information about his own bewildering time at the siege of Canudos, can finally explain the circumstances of Gall's exploits, and can thus help the Journalist forge the links between Gall and Goncalves and between Goncalves and the Baron de Canabrava, whose unspoken and uneasy alliance rests upon the secret of the guns of Canudos. Just as the novel works to explore a segment of Brazilian history forgotten or unknown outside Latin America, so Vargas Llosa explores, in the character of Jurema, conventions about Latin American women and the ways in which Jurema transcends them. The wife of Rufino, a tracker and guide, she saves Gall's life in the ambush that Goncalves had planned; she then becomes Gall's sexual victim and later his comforter, companion, and fellow traveler on the way to Canudos. After she has been violated by Gall, she seems to have little choice except to travel with him, tend his wounds, and wait for Rufino to find and kill her. On her journey to Canudos, however, her fatalism and passivity change, and she becomes, of necessity, increasingly assertive and resourceful at saving her own life, as well as Gall's and the Journalist's. This last act of saving the Journalist's life eventually causes her to become the heroine of the Journalist's life and of his numerous stories of Canudos.

Other characters are the subjects of extreme authorial irony. The reformed criminal, Abbot Joao, and the odd Little Blessed One aim at high spiritual goals but have little notion of what they mean or how to attain them. Still other characters become caricatures, such as the lion of Natuba, a bearded lady, and a dwarf. In all, the characters range from hundreds of "extras" to fully developed multifunctional protagonists in this drama of Brazilian life in the late nineteenth century.

Themes and Meanings

The principal theme of the novel is a theme implicit in most serious historical fictions, the attempt to explain, to make sense of a series of historical events and, in so doing, to assess their meanings for the present. In this sense, the novel works as a metafiction as the author writes of an author who writes of the actions and written reports of actions of the revolt in the backlands. Two other equally forceful themes borrowed from the epic tradition are concerned with the metaphors of life as journey and life as warfare. Vargas Llosa also manipulates the traditional themes of fiction, love, honor, revenge, adventure, idealism, the education of naive characters, lost innocence, trial by experience, and the effects that a rapidly changing social context has upon individuals caught up in those changes. In the treatment of all these themes, Vargas Llosa relentlessly seeks the meaning of events and actions, the individual meaning for each of his characters, the larger meaning for the Brazilian Republic in the aftermath of Canudos, and the meanings that the lessons of history hold for the present.

Frequently, Vargas Llosa introduces themes and, through the magical interaction of characters, allows them to play themselves out without authorial comment. Thus, for example, the love theme not only is particularized in the romantic love of the Journalist for Jurema but also extends to such varied aspects of love as that between Rufino and Jurema (a relationship of power and control), between Gall and Jurema (again, a power relationship), the love of the Counselor for his followers, the love of God, and the love of country: All these loves are motivating factors for the characters and work together to illustrate the potentially destructive force of love as a ruling passion. So, too, the theme of messianism that is at the very core of the work plays itself out in the actions of Counselor and his followers on one side and in the lives of Brazilian politicians and generals on the other. Messianism, itself an exaggeration, possibly a necessary one, draws to itself both adherents and disbelievers who must engage one another militantly until only one party can emerge. It is worth recalling that while Vargas Llosa chronicles the events of some generations ago, the chronicle itself may be viewed as parable for contemporary Latin America where the lines of a new messianism are clearly drawn between those intent upon carrying out one sort of ideological revolution in a practical, political, and military forum and those who would cling to and support an equally powerful ideological base: In the novel's terms, this is a clash between the oppressed Christian commune and the forces of an implacable democratic republic; in contemporary terms it is a clash between Marxist thought and capitalist thought. One key to viewing the novel as an allegory of current events is the character Galileo Gall, who is intent on spreading the international revolution of Marxism in the backlands of Brazil but who is indeed mistaken in thinking that Canudos is part of that revolution. So, too, the modern reader may wonder whether any of the ideologies at war with one another take into account the individuals who must suffer and die for them.

Critical Context

In *The War of the End of the World*, Vargas Llosa continues a probe of Latin American history, life, and culture that has occupied his works for more than a quarter of a century. Long recognized as one of the more important writers in Latin America, his works include volumes of plays, literary criticism, and nonfiction. He has steadily gained in reputation as a remarkable novelist of international stature for such earlier achievements as *Conversación en la catedral* (1969; *Conversation in the Cathedral,* 1975), *La ciudad y los perros* (1963; *The Time of the Hero,* 1966), *La casa verde* (1965; *The Green House,* 1968), and *La tía Julia y el escribidor* (1977; *Aunt Julia and the Scriptwriter,* 1982).

The War of the End of the World, like Vargas Llosa's earlier novels, presents a vision of Latin American life and culture that has, in the last half of the twentieth century, provoked considerable interest in the English-speaking world, particularly in the North American discovery of *el boom latinoamericano* of the 1960's and 1970's, a literary renaissance in which Vargas Llosa is a major force.

Bibliography
Booker, M. Keith. *Vargas Llosa Among the Postmodernists.* Gainesville: University Press of Florida, 1994. A thorough examination of Vargas Llosa's works from a postmodern point of view. Includes an essay on *The War of the End of the World.*
Castro-Klarén, Sara. "Mario Vargas Llosa." In *Latin American Writers,* edited by Carlos A. Solé and Maria I. Abreau. Vol. 3. New York: Charles Scribner's Sons, 1989. Offers a comprehensive and critical discussion of Vargas Llosa's life and works. Provides a selected bibliography for further reading.
Gerdes, Dick. "Mario Vargas Llosa." In *Spanish American Authors: The Twentieth Century,* edited by Angel Flores. New York: H. W. Wilson, 1992. Profiles Vargas Llosa and includes an extensive bibliography of works by and about the author.
Kristal, Efrain. *Temptation of the Word: The Novels of Mario Vargas Llosa.* Nashville, Tenn.: Vanderbilt University Press, 1998. A collection of perceptive essays on Vargas Llosa's novels written from the 1960's through the 1980's. A helpful bibliography for further reading is also included.

John J. Conlon

WARTIME LIES

Author: Louis Begley (1933-   )
Type of plot: War
Time of plot: 1933-1945
Locale: Poland
First published: 1991

> *Principal characters:*
> MACIEK, the narrator and central figure in the story
> TANIA, Maciek's aunt, guardian, and guide in their escape from the Nazis
> GRANDFATHER, Tania's father; stubborn and defiant, he eludes capture throughout the occupation but is finally exposed and shot by the Germans
> REINHARD, a former German soldier; he becomes Tania's lover and helps her and her family hide from the Nazis until he is betrayed by a Jewish partisan

The Novel

Wartime Lies recounts the experiences of Maciek and his aunt Tania during World War II. Polish Jews, they elude capture by the Nazis by posing as Aryans, but in their journey through cities and villages, cellars and rented rooms, they witness horrific scenes of German brutality that scar Maciek for life.

Maciek, now a man in his fifties, recollects his childhood in Poland, beginning in 1933. Through his eyes, readers see everything. The only child of a Jewish physician in the small town of T., he leads a pampered life. His mother dies in childbirth, so his aunt Tania moves in to oversee his upbringing. Frail and nervous, he is also stubborn, but his beautiful nanny, Zosia, can coax good behavior from him. Even his grandfather helps by teaching him to drive a carriage and throw a jackknife. In 1941, the persecution by the Nazis begins. Jews are forced out of their homes, beaten, and deported or shot in the streets. Maciek and his family must move to an apartment, and Zosia must leave, too, for Aryans are not allowed to work for Jews. The retreating Russians take Maciek's father to Russia for the duration of the war. Crowded into a single apartment with the grandparents and another family, Tania and Maciek share the same bed, as they will for the remainder of the war. Toilet facilities and running water vanish; curfews and armbands with yellow stars appear. At the German supply depot where she finds work, Tania meets Reinhard, a German who falls in love with her and helps her and her family hide when her job no longer protects them.

Reinhard is betrayed, and the Gestapo comes for him. Rather than fall into their hands, he shoots the grandmother, who is hiding in his apartment, then himself. Receiving the news from a friend, Tania flees with Maciek to Warsaw, where they pose as mother and child and where they find Grandfather, who is also hiding from the Ger-

mans. To avoid suspicion, Maciek receives religious instructions and first communion. On one of their outings, gunfire forces Tania and Maciek into a cellar. The Germans come, gathering Poles and marching them to the trains bound for Auschwitz. At
the station, Tania boldly accosts a German captain, insisting that she is an officer's
wife and must board a train going to her home, which lies in a direction away from
Auschwitz. The officer, impressed by her educated and confident manner, helps her
onto a train bound for the Polish countryside.

The narration leaps forward two months. Tania and Maciek live with a family of
farmers. Tania helps harvest potatoes and beets, while Maciek tends the cows. Harvest
done, Tania becomes a traveling agent for Komar, a dealer in homemade vodka.
Nowak, another vodka dealer, is attracted to her and helps find her father, now living
in a nearby village. She goes to find him but arrives too late; he has been shot by the
Germans. When she spurns Nowak's advances, he threatens to expose her as a Jew.
Again, she and Maciek flee, taking shelter in another small town. Finally, the guns fall
silent and friendly Russian troops arrive, bringing an end to the war.

The narrative leaps forward again. Maciek's father has returned, and Maciek,
well-fed, well-clothed, has a new name and new Aryan identity. The persecution of
Jews has not stopped, however, so deception continues to be a way of life. Eventually,
all those he knew as a child will go away, including his beloved Tania. Maciek himself
will no longer exist, buried in the wartime lies.

The Characters

Some characters are vividly drawn, such as Zosia, whose amber hair and high spirits charm the child Maciek, whereas others are little more than names. The officious
and curious individuals in the boarding houses where Tania and Maciek stay remind
one of the ever-present danger of exposure. The peasants introduce Maciek and Tania
to hard life on a farm. Though each character plays key roles in Maciek's journey,
most of the characters have a ghostly quality as they pass in and out of the narrator's
memory.

Maciek is the narrator and one of the novel's two principal characters. When the
novel opens, he is in his fifties, reads the classics, and avoids discussing the Holocaust
with others. Privately, he pores over accounts of the torture of political prisoners, calling himself a "voyeur of evil." In his narration, he shows little emotion, whether he is
describing an erotic experience with Zosia or horrific scenes of war. The flatness of
his emotional range suggests that the trauma of his childhood has so benumbed him
that he is incapable of feeling strong emotion.

Tania is Maciek's maternal aunt. When the Nazis arrive in Poland, her principal aim
is to save her nephew from the Germans. Beautiful, headstrong, well educated, and
highly intelligent, she becomes increasingly heroic as danger mounts, sometimes using her considerable sexual appeal to win favors from those, such as Reinhard, who
can help her evade capture. Her every move, word, and thought is carefully contrived,
and her humanity extends even to caring for the elderly and sick. Though chance plays
a large part in her success in saving Maciek, her extraordinary ingenuity and courage

tip the balance. Maciek expresses a passionate love for his aunt, and many of their nights together in bed are tender, affectionate, and erotic. His brief, unemotional announcement at the end, "One day soon, Tania will leave," leaves a hollow place in the heart.

Grandfather is a country gentleman who is an important figure in Maciek's years before the German occupation, taking the child on outings and teaching him the pleasures of good food and Polish liquor. Tall, mustached, always attired in black, he is the picture of the worldly, wealthy gentleman in prewar Poland. He is also brave and defiant, like his favorite daughter, Tania, and like her he evades capture by posing as an Aryan. Near the end of the war, he is recognized as a Jew and shot.

Reinhard is a former German soldier who has lost an arm in a factory accident and works for the Nazis in Poland. His bravery in helping the partisans, especially Tania and her family, sets him apart from other Germans and Polish non-Jews. His extreme sacrifice stands in stark contrast to those who rob, betray, and persecute Jews. When the Gestapo close in, he saves Maciek's grandmother from capture by shooting her, then shoots himself.

Themes and Meanings

In *Wartime Lies*, Begley focuses on the relation of truth and falsehood. Deception is a means of survival with tortuous consequences. As a child, Maciek learns to tell lies with such commitment that they become the truth of his existence. Ironically, this way of surviving depends on the eradication of his true identity. To distance himself from the emotional impact of his earlier experiences, and yet to understand it, the adult Maciek turns to literature, where he finds that civil expression can overlie the horror of his past and mitigate the mental turmoil it has caused. Literature also raises questions concerning pity, heroism, and justice, which lie at the heart of his childhood memories. Tania has taught him that the Germans cannot bear to feel pity, just as Dante in the *Inferno* has no patience with it. Yet the adult Maciek, seeing parallels between Dante's damned and the Jews of Poland, feels that the innocent and frightened deserve pity. Without the capacity to feel pity, one becomes like the Germans, barbaric. Dante admires the defiant ones among the damned, but those who endure in silence also deserve admiration, Maciek believes. Dante's inferno reminds him of the cellars, the suffering, the darkness of the cities lit by fires. He sees Poland's inferno as a metaphor of the relationship between man and God, but he cannot see justice in Jewish persecution.

Though this is a tale of great suffering and loss, detachment prevails throughout the narrative and suggests that within the narrator lies an emotional void that cannot be filled by any new emotions. His survival has depended on detaching himself emotionally from not only the truth but also from his own suffering and that of others. His new name, identity, and life underscore the discontinuity with which he is left and the irony of his triumph. Because Tania succeeds in saving Maciek and herself, this is a tale of triumph, but too many Jews have perished for Maciek to feel anything but guilt and self-loathing. The memories that continue to haunt him suggest a psychological devastation that will be with him always, and the questions concerning justice, pity, and heroism will remain unanswered.

Critical Context

Wartime Lies, Begley's first novel, shares a long tradition of firsthand accounts of the Holocaust, the most famous being Anne Frank's *The Diary of a Young Girl* (1947). The list continues to grow and contains both true and fictionalized accounts of the Holocaust. Begley chose to fictionalize his experiences because, he said, fiction gives him greater freedom in capturing the truthfulness of his emotions. It also gives him a way to dramatize philosophical and moral issues of his experience. Creating a fictional character such as Maciek also enables Begley to create a personal history whose design is consistent with the meaning of his story. Giving events a fictional structure allows him to bring together the development of character and theme, as he does in the novel's climactic scene at the train station, where Tania achieves a psychological triumph over German brutality and turns the plot away from death in Auschwitz and toward safety in the village. Her heroism, predicated on masterful deception, is given a shape and drama that real life seldom, if ever, offers. Begley needs the novelist's artful deception to give meaning to this scene.

In interviews, Begley has implied that historical truth would have taken him away from his purpose, which, readers may infer, was to portray a man who survived horrific times but, in doing so, lost his true self. This theme is also found in Begley's second novel, *The Man Who Was Late* (1993), in which the protagonist, Ben, develops the theme of self-loathing introduced in *Wartime Lies*. Begley's third novel, *As Max Saw It* (1994), returns to themes such as defiance, guilt, innocence, and suffering. All three novels are evidence that Begley remains haunted by the issues inherent in his childhood experiences. His fiction enables him to examine their philosophical nature while dramatizing their psychological effects.

Bibliography

Buck, Joan Juliet. "An Occupied Gentleman." *Vanity Fair* 56, no. 2 (February, 1993): 72-82. Buck places *Wartime Lies* in the context of Begley's personal life. Although the essay does not offer literary analysis, it helps explain the genesis of *Wartime Lies* and its relation to Begley's second novel, *The Man Who Was Late*.

Dresden, Sem. *Persecution, Extermination, Literature*, translated by Henry G. Schogt. Toronto: University of Toronto Press, 1991. Dresden's study of Holocaust literature clarifies the tradition of which *Wartime Lies* is a part. Of special interest is a discussion of the differences between writing about the Holocaust fictionally or factually. Though written before Begley's novel appeared, Dresden's book provides insight into *Wartime Lies*.

Horowitz, Sara R. *Voicing the Void: Muteness and Memory in Holocaust Fiction*. Albany: State University of New York Press, 1997. Horowitz examines a wide range of Holocaust fiction, including *Wartime Lies*. She studies the relation of muteness to the lies that Maciek tells and to the disappearing identities that result from those lies. A superb view of the psychological effects of the Holocaust on the fiction that expresses them.

Mendelsohn, Jane. "Fiction in Review." *The Yale Review* 83, no. 1 (January, 1995): 108-120. Mendelsohn notes parallels between all three of Begley's novels, devoting most of her attention to *Wartime Lies*.

Steinberg, Sybil, ed. *Writing for Your Life Number 2*. Wainscott, N.Y.: Pushcart, 1995. The profile of Begley discusses his three novels and his interest in "the strange power of words."

Bernard E. Morris

THE WATERWORKS

Author: E. L. Doctorow (1931-   )
Type of plot: Postmodern
Time of plot: 1871
Locale: New York City
First published: 1994

Principal characters:
> MCILVAINE, the narrator, who edits a newspaper
> MARTIN PEMBERTON, a reporter searching for his dead father
> AUGUSTUS PEMBERTON, his father, a war profiteer and slave trader
> SARAH PEMBERTON, Augustus's second wife
> EMILY TISDALE, Martin Pemberton's fiancée
> EDMUND DONNE, the only honest police official in New York
> WREDE SARTORIUS, a brilliant physician who conducts unethical
>   experiments
> EUSTACE SIMMONS, the aide to Augustus Pemberton
> HARRY WHEELWRIGHT, an artist friend of Martin Pemberton

The Novel

The Waterworks is twenty-eight chapters of disjointed recollection in which McIlvaine, an elderly former news editor, recalls from some indeterminate time in the future incidents of 1871 in New York: his search for a missing freelance book reviewer, Martin Pemberton, and Martin's tycoon father, Augustus Pemberton. First, the cynical Martin announces that he has seen his supposedly dead father in a horse-drawn omnibus with other stupefied old men. When Martin is missing, McIlvaine summons Edmund Donne, one of the only honest policemen in the New York run by William "Boss" Tweed and his ring of corruption. Donne and McIlvaine question Martin's artist friend Harry Wheelwright. One night, Harry and Martin go to Woodlawn cemetery and hire some men to dig up the body of Augustus. In the coffin, they find the body of a boy. Donne and Sarah Pemberton, Augustus's wife, engage in a romance, and Sarah learns that Augustus deliberately disinherited her and her young son Noah by liquidating all of his assets before he died.

Sifting evidence, Donne finds an orphanage in which no graft passed hands. Eustace Simmons, Augustus's right-hand man in his slave-trading business, is the director, and Dr. Sartorius, who signed Augustus's death certificate, is the attending physician. Donne surrounds the orphanage, rifles through the building, and finds the emaciated Martin Pemberton in a hidden cell. Martin, however, is traumatized and cannot talk. Continuing his investigation, McIlvaine finds six elderly men who died rich but left their families in poverty. The names of the same men are on a list found in Eustace Simmons's log in the orphanage. Martin regains his speech and tells his story.

After finding that Augustus was not in his grave, Martin had been abducted to Sartorius's elaborate hideaway, where Martin found his father alive amid the elderly clientele, kept in a state of semiconscious lethargy. Martin, who was allowed to roam free in Sartorius's hideaway provided he not try to leave or interfere, was at first stunned by Sartorius's scientific brilliance and his innovative experiments. Yet soon he realized that Sartorius was keeping alive these terminally ill old men by transfusing them with blood and glandular matter from young homeless children. Sartorius was sapping the lives of young children to prolong that of the elderly. The whole project was being bankrolled by the fortunes of the old tycoons.

Donne finally traces the old men's trust fund to the Waterworks, a reservoir inside which Sartorius has set up his laboratory. Donne captures Sartorius and goes to Ravenwood, the old Pemberton estate, where he finds the dead Augustus on the grounds. He also finds the body of Eustace Simmons clutching a chest with a fortune in it.

Sartorius is declared insane and locked away amid screeching and howling madmen; eventually, his head is crushed by one of the inmates, and he is buried in a potter's field. For a moment, the novel seems to come to a traditional ending, as the recovered Martin Pemberton is married to Emily Tisdale and Donne is wedded to Sarah Pemberton in simple and touching ceremonies. As McIlvaine walks away from Donne's wedding, though, he sees the city frozen in time on a Sunday when the wheels of industry and business are still.

The Characters

The characters are not built on psychological depth but are of the stock types that people the gothic mystery genre. However, Doctorow goes beyond mere stereotypes to add the ambiguity of a postmodern mystery. McIlvaine, the editor of *The Telegram*, is the narrator, and he is absorbed in the narration of the story. His work is his life, and the freelance reporters who work for him make up his only family. He is a confirmed bachelor whose one marriage prospect died of heart failure. He is also an elderly man recollecting the one story on which he never got his "exclusive." This sets up an ironic distance in the narrative, as McIlvaine claims that memory distorts and notes that his tale might arise out of his own insanity, though he tries to assure the reader that he is thought of as sane. Though he tries to maintain the detachment of a reporter, he finds himself involved in the tale he is telling. Yet McIlvaine is only one of the novel's alienated heroes.

Martin Pemberton, who wears a great Union Army coat, sees the objects of the Civil War only as modes of fashion. He is a cynical, acerbic young man who writes scathing reviews of potboilers and reports on the fashion of the wealthy ladies whom he detests. He wrote a scathing exposé of his father's underhanded business practices that led to his being disinherited. His shaky engagement presents only a glimmer of a close attachment. His quest for his dead father reveals only his ambivalent feelings.

Edmund Donne fulfills the role of the detective in a sort of Sherlock Holmes/Doctor Watson combination with McIlvaine. Like McIlvaine, Donne too is a middle-aged bachelor who is absorbed in his work. He is one of the few honest policeman in a corrupt system. He knows the city thoroughly, cares for his informers, and sifts through paperwork for the key clues. Only after the novel comes to a close do Martin and Donne get married, leaving their family lives outside the realm of the novel.

The villains are as detached as the heroes. The novel centers on Dr. Wrede Sartorius, a brilliant physician from Germany who became involved as a doctor in the Civil War. He improved the techniques of surgery so that he could amputate limbs in a matter of seconds, and he modernized post-operative treatments. Yet Sartorius did not aid his patients out of a sense of mercy; rather, he engaged in a Faustian quest for new knowledge. Sartorius is a loner who has no love for his patients and treats his colleagues with disdain. He is a man without a conscience who is driven by intellect. He gathers rich old men and gives them prolonged life in a diminished state. Although his revolutionary methods of blood transfusion and brain-wave measurement become standard medical practice, he is not interested in cures; rather, he sees science as the new God. He too is a man who has dedicated himself to his work and has no relatives to claim him.

Another alienated villain is Eustace Simmons, the pock-marked right-hand man to Augustus Pemberton in his illegal slave trade and other underhanded activities. Simmons makes the easy move from working for Augustus to working for Sartorius. He is the perfect organization man, running the mechanisms of the underworld. After his death, no one is there to claim his body. In the background are two other figures. Augustus Pemberton is the tycoon profiteer who sells shoddy goods to the army and engages in the illegal slave trade. Like a modern magnate, he is more interested in buying and selling businesses than in running one. In a last-ditch effort to sustain his life, he disinherits his wife and young son. A last shadowy figure in the book who never makes a direct appearance is the corpulent racketeer Boss Tweed, who through his system of graft and corruption runs the city of New York, from the mayor to the lowliest police officer.

Themes and Meanings

The story shows on one level the incredible abuse of power. Rich tycoons live in luxury while homeless children are driven to fight for the right to sell newspapers or into prostitution. Labor disputes end in riots. The metaphor for the last abuse of power is when the blood is being taken from poor homeless children to sustain the lives of rich old men, who become true vampires preying on the poor to the last.

Another theme is the abuse of science. In alliance with government and wealth, science has run amuck. Sartorius may arise out of the laboratory of Frankenstein, but it is no mistake that he is heading in the direction of Joseph Mengele and the cold-blooded scientific experiments of the Nazi death camps. Certainly, Doctorow is pointing out that science without any ethical principles is a dangerous force that can take humanity anywhere, from environmental destruction to nuclear holocaust.

In the midst of the elaborate story, Doctorow paints a picture of New York City in 1871. He takes readers through the gaslight, into horse-drawn traffic and the smell of dung, and shows them tramps scavenging for garbage at the dock, vagrant children in tatters warming themselves over a steam grate, and the mob at the exchange. From the rich society lady describing her ensemble to the fights in seamy waterfront taverns, Doctorow wants to paint a picture of the city Edith Wharton left out of her novels. McIlvaine lives in the soul of the city that seems to create itself, where one day there is a mansion in a field and the next a row of houses with street traffic.

Another theme is embodied in the postmodern ambiguity and fragmentation of the narrative. The narrator uses ellipses and dashes to show his hesitation in getting the story down. Characters are not met directly but are embedded in the accounts of other characters. The narrator also uses flash-forwards to take the reader ahead of the story, and he questions his own power of getting all the details straight. The fragmentation and piecing together of characters' lives from newspaper accounts to documents to witnesses gives a shadowy grasp on characters and adds to the ambiguity of the story.

Critical Context

E. L. Doctorow, who was named "Edgar" after Edgar Allan Poe, has called *The Waterworks* his "Poe story." Certainly, the novel has elements of Poe in its combined interest in science and detection, its detective-story format, its fascination with the crossover between life and death, and its narrator who defends his sanity. The dead man who will not stay dead and the ghastly exhumation scene in the eerie night mist are also reminiscent of Poe. Yet there is also the Nathaniel Hawthorne theme of the scientist who tries to conquer the forces of nature and puts the love of science before the love of humanity. There is also a glimpse of Herman Melville's innocent narrators, trying to search out the truth behind the pasteboard mask of life.

The Waterworks, like other novels by Doctorow, takes place in New York City. Together with *The Waterworks*, Doctorow's *Ragtime* (1975), *Billy Bathgate* (1989), and *The Book of Daniel* (1971) explore the panorama of a hundred years of New York. Like his other novels, *The Waterworks* focuses on a historical figure; as J. P. Morgan appears in *Ragtime* and Dutch Schultz in *Billy Bathgate*, Boss Tweed looms over *The Waterworks*. Also as in his other novels, Doctorow uses the framework of a popular genre to create a novel of ideas. He used the Western in *Welcome to Hard Times* (1960) and the gangster story in *Billy Bathgate*; in *The Waterworks*, he uses mystery detection with an element of science fiction. In *The Waterworks*, Doctorow once again raises history to the level of myth.

Bibliography

Baker, John F. "E. L. Doctorow." *Publishers Weekly* 241, no. 26 (June 27, 1994): 51. Doctorow discusses the influences on writing *The Waterworks* and his techniques in writing the novel.

Doctorow, E. L. Interview by Donna Seaman. *Booklist* 91, no. 3 (October 1, 1994): 238. Doctorow discusses the influences and themes in *The Waterworks* as well as its connections to his other works.

"Doctorow's City." *The New Yorker* 70, no. 19 (June 27, 1994): 41. Review that discusses the uses of New York in *The Waterworks* and other novels. Also recounts Doctorow's views on writing a historical novel.

Goodman, Walter. "*The Waterworks*." *The New Leader* 77, no. 6 (June 6, 1994): 35. A review article that focuses on the genre elements in *The Waterworks* as well as its relationship to other Doctorow novels. Also discusses the narrative technique and possible influences from British literature.

Solotaroff, Ted. "*The Waterworks*." *The Nation* 258, no. 22 (June 6, 1994): 784. A review article that discusses the influences of Poe and Melville on *The Waterworks* and gives an in-depth analysis of the novel's characterization and themes.

Paul Rosefeldt

THE WAVE

Author: Evelyn Scott (Elsie Dunn; 1893-1963)
Type of plot: Historical chronicle
Time of plot: From April 11, 1861, to May 24, 1865
Locale: All sections of the United States touched by the Civil War; also Portugal
   and Germany
First published: 1929

> *Principal characters:*
> JEFFERSON DAVIS, President of the Confederate States of America
> EDWIN GEORGE, a merchant and Union spy from Tennessee
> EUGENIA GILBERT, the sister-in-law of Edwin George and a Union spy
>   from Virginia
> ULYSSES S. GRANT, Union general
> ROBERT E. LEE, Confederate general
> ABRAHAM LINCOLN, President of the United States of America

The Novel

Beginning on April 12, 1861, with the firing on Fort Sumter by Confederate forces, and ending with the parade of victorious Union troops in Washington, D.C., on May 24, 1865, the action of Evelyn Scott's *The Wave* conforms externally to the events of the American Civil War. On its simplest level, the book is a fictional account of that war; Scott's real emphasis, however, is on the effect of the war on the hundreds of characters which crowd her novel. The key to her method, and to the thematic point of *The Wave*, is the book's epigraph, a statement discussing the relationship between the movement of a wave and an object riding the water. The point of the epigraph is that unless affected by wind or current, a floating object remains relatively stationary. Scott's characters are like the objects riding the wave—largely unaware of the meaning of events beyond their personal dimensions and certainly unable to see the Civil War from the viewpoint of history.

Scott divides *The Wave* into twenty numbered chapters and subdivides each of these into a number of episodes, each having its own focal character and moment of tension or conflict. The novel achieves its effects, therefore, by juxtaposition of characters and actions. In the first half of the book, the episodes in a particular chapter are used to show a conflict between the mechanistic force of the war itself and the actions, presumably free, of various persons in both the North and the South. Dickie Ross, in the first chapter, rows across Charleston Harbor in anticipation of the firing on Fort Sumter; a man called Percy gets caught up in a mob protesting Abraham Lincoln's movement of troops through Baltimore; a little boy, Henry Clay, observes the squabbling between his Yankee mother and his Rebel aunt when his father joins the Confederate army; a Northern soldier, Franklin Rutherford, experiences the battle of Manassas; and elderly Mrs. Witherspoon, a Confederate mother, is informed of the death of one son and the wounding of the other in the same battle. Not one of these individuals is aware of the pattern of events catching him up; each believes that he acts freely and according to his own will. The reader of *The Wave*, however, is aware of the ways in which these characters are victims of external events.

The center of the book, by implication the turning point of the action, is the battle of Gettysburg. From this point, the characters are increasingly aware of a lack of freedom; they struggle unsuccessfully against the circumstances imposed by history, and the more intelligent among them are disillusioned or admit to selfish motives. Silas, a former slave and member of Colonel Shaw's regiment from Massachusetts, is rejected by white Union soldiers with whom he is held prisoner in a barn; like Samson, he pulls the building down on them. Edwin George and Eugenia Gilbert, each spying for the Union and assuming the other is a Confederate sympathizer, disguise sexual attraction and financial interest under the mask of patriotism. Abraham Lincoln, Jefferson Davis, Robert E. Lee, and Ulysses S. Grant, the actual figures from history playing the largest roles in *The Wave*, also acknowledge the discrepancy between public and private selves. Glimpsed in church in Richmond before abandoning the city to troops under Grant, Davis appears to embody an aristocrat's commitment to the Southern cause. In bed during his flight from Union troops, Davis nurses wounded pride and admits to himself that he sees events only in terms of his ambition to will a new nation into being. Seated at Ford's Theatre before he is shot by John Wilkes Booth, Lincoln thinks that it benefits him that the public considers him to be a great man. In his own estimation, he is "selfish, self-obsessed, and self-centered," as are the rest of the characters in the novel. For great man or small, the range of action is limited by history; the difference is that the great man recognizes this limitation and can use it, at times, to his advantage.

The Characters

There are three sorts of characters in *The Wave*: the few great figures of history, such as Davis, Lincoln, Lee, and Grant; the many ordinary men and women caught up in the history of the period in which they live; and the mechanism Scott calls war, which involves all these characters in the action.

Least aware of their status as victims of circumstances are people such as Fanny May, a woman recovering from childbirth and the death of her baby, who drives out to watch the fighting near Richmond in the hope of seeing her husband, Philip. The armies in conflict are faint figures on the horizon, and Fanny May is unable to see them clearly because of the crowd of observers—a neat demonstration of Scott's point that, for ordinary people, the surface of life gets in the way of vision. The great man, by contrast, stands apart from the crowd; he is able to see beyond the appearance of things. During the campaign in the wilderness, Grant sees that his capacity of action depends upon public perception of his ability: "The hint of a divergence between someone's opinion of him and his own idea of himself was enough to throw him into a panic." Lee has a similar insight shortly before the surrender at Appomattox; mixing with the young officers of his staff, he feels a certain constraint and attributes it to the fact that they do not know, as he does, "that strength, even for the strong, has its limitations." Lee, Grant, Lincoln, and Davis know their limitations within the larger sweep of events. They have a sense of time approximating Scott's own, and unlike more ordinary people, they recognize their helplessness before the wave of history. In defeat, Davis, the coldest and most willful of them, wishes to "be as a stone, clean and unfeeling." He aspires to be forgotten by history rather than remembered for his failure.

Scott's treatment of Davis, Grant, Lee, and Lincoln does not break ground; it does not go beyond the accounts of these men provided by reliable historians and biographers. Scott is not partisan, however, and *The Wave* does not argue for the justice of either the Southern or the Northern cause. The nonhistorical characters are not stereotypes constructed to illustrate a political thesis. Within the limitations of Scott's episodic method of construction, they are varied, rounded, and psychologically complex.

Themes and Meanings

While the novel is not intended to carry the weight of a defense of the antebellum South, *The Wave* is constructed to demonstrate the concept of history implied by the book's epigraph and by the repeated use of the wave motif in the text. This notion that people are helpless before the force of history, even if they can see its limitation of their free will, controls the development of the novel. It is a factor limiting the book's appeal, yet it frees Scott to order the materials of Civil War history, about which she did considerable research, into a coherent structure. The historical determinism central to *The Wave* is present, in less insistent forms, in *Migrations: An Arabesque in Histories* (1927) and *A Calendar of Sin: American Melodramas* (1931); together, the three novels constitute a history of the United States from approximately 1850 to 1914. The trilogy is also an account of the effects of social change on fictionalized members of Scott's family.

Critical Context

Published to critical praise from Joseph Wood Krutch, Carl Van Doren, and Clifton Fadiman, *The Wave* was the only best-seller among Scott's novels. It may even claim the distinction of encouraging Southern writers such as Stark Young and Margaret Mitchell to turn to the writing of novels about the Civil War. While Young's *So Red the Rose* (1934) and Mitchell's *Gone with the Wind* (1936) were more successful commercially, they were flawed by sentimentality. *The Wave*, indeed the whole trilogy of which it is a part, stands in marked contrast to the works of these writers because of its technical experimentation. Only William Faulkner, in *Absalom, Absalom!* (1936), stands superior to Scott as a prose stylist detailing the Civil War in fiction.

Only in terms of the care with which it is structured and in its pervasive irony is this novel typical of Scott's fiction. In an earlier trilogy, comprising the novels *The Narrow House* (1921), *Narcissus* (1922), and *The Golden Door* (1925), she explored the psychological effects of unhappy marriages on three generations of the Farley family. A feminist as well as a writer, Scott had run off to Brazil in 1913 with a married man, treating this experience in her impressionistic autobiography *Escapade* (1923); the problems facing the female artist are also central to the novels *Eva Gay: A Romantic Novel* (1933), *Bread and a Sword* (1937), and *The Shadow of the Hawk* (1941).

Bibliography
Bach, Peggy. "A Serious Damn: William Faulkner and Evelyn Scott." *The Southern Literary Journal* 28 (Fall, 1995): 128-143. Bach compares the challenges that both William Faulkner and Scott faced as writers. Both transcended the restrictions of southern traditions, were subjected to unfair criticism by the critics, and were condemned by Freudians who attributed the characters' opinions to the authors. Although biographers downplay the assistance the novelists extended to each other, Bach argues that they actually helped each other gain recognition.
Callard, D. A. *Pretty Good for a Woman: The Enigmas of Evelyn Scott.* New York: Norton, 1985. A definitive biography that offers keen insight into the social challenges Scott faced as a female writer. Discusses some of her works and includes a bibliography for further reading.
White, Mary Wheeling. *Fighting the Current: The Life and Work of Evelyn Scott.* Baton Rouge: Louisiana State University Press, 1998. A well-researched biography of Scott that profiles one of the most creative minds among American modernists. Although not a critical work, White's book does offer insight into the influences that shaped Scott's work, including *The Wave.*

Robert C. Petersen

THE WAY WEST

Author: A. B. Guthrie, Jr. (1901-1991)
Type of plot: Historical realism
Time of plot: 1845
Locale: Independence, Missouri, and the overland trail to Oregon
First published: 1949

Principal characters:
LIJE EVANS, a Missouri farmer and later a wagon-train leader
REBECCA EVANS, his wife
BROWNIE EVANS, their son, a boy on the edge of manhood
DICK SUMMERS, a former mountain man, pilot of the wagon train
MERCY MCBEE, the pretty daughter of the poor white Henry McBee
IRVINE TADLOCK, the organizer and first leader of the wagon train

The Novel

The Way West is an account of a wagon-train journey from Independence, Missouri, to Oregon in 1845. On a superficial level, it is a realistic story of a group of pioneers who complete their arduous venture without major disaster. Although one family turns back, a man and a boy die, and a dissident group swings south to California, the pioneers reach their Oregon destination, ready to begin a new life.

A second plot line in the novel traces the development of a social structure, suggesting that the wagon-train organization finally shaped will be the basis for a new kind of society that is to be formed in the new settlements. In Independence, Missouri, Irvine Tadlock organizes the wagon train and makes sure that he is elected leader of it. His insistence on authority, discipline, and order, however, comes to be resented by the pioneers, both because he lacks real knowledge of the frontier and because the wilderness demands a flexibility and an independence of thought that Tadlock does not have. The turning point of this plot line comes midway in the novel, when Tadlock is deposed and Lije Evans is made the new leader. Although Evans is not sure of his own abilities, he proves himself to be the kind of leader needed in the new country.

The third level of action in *The Way West* is psychological. As the wagon train moves through the spring and summer months, facing external dangers and internal dissension, Guthrie penetrates the minds of several characters, revealing the doubts and dreams which set them on the trail to Oregon and tracing their responses to the challenges of the journey and to the wilderness through which they pass. Appropriately, at the end of the novel, Guthrie focuses on the characters who have responded best to the experience of the trail: Dick Summers, who has reaffirmed his love of life in the wilderness; Lije Evans, who has proven himself as a leader of men in the new land; Rebecca, who has cheerfully endured the hardships of the journey and compassionately accepted her new daughter-in-law; Brownie Evans, now a man, not a boy; and Mercy McBee Evans, now a woman and a loving wife, not a romantic girl.

The Characters

In every settled society, there are men slow to words and action, men whose real capacities are not evident to themselves or to those around them. Yet when that society is threatened by disaster or challenged by change, such men, gifted with common sense, a feeling for fair play, and the willingness to take counsel with others before making the necessary decisions, may become the new leaders of the society. Such a man is Lije Evans. Beginning his journey to Oregon with no very high opinion of himself, he finds himself speaking for the right and the sensible, defending the camp dogs against the malicious, and insisting that the train delay when a man sickens with camp fever. After his election as the new wagon-train leader, he has to prove himself to himself; he arrives in Oregon as a leader of society and a builder of the nation.

The first leader of the wagon train, Irvine Tadlock, is the kind of loud-mouthed, selfish, ambitious man, followed by hirelings, who is familiar to readers of Western novels. The antithesis of Tadlock is the former mountain man Dick Summers, wise, experienced, and brave but not foolish. Having just lost his wife when the novel begins, Summers willingly signs on as pilot for the wagon train, and he is conscientious and effective. His world, however, is that of the wilderness, and he is more at home in his memories of Indian squaws and solitary campfires than in the world of the settlers.

Brownie Evans and Mercy McBee, the young lovers of the novel, could have been stock characters. Mercy, however, is a complex person. The unhappy daughter of vicious and filthy parents, she is ready for escape, and therefore she is easily seduced by a man with manners. Her courage when she finds herself pregnant and rejected, her practical honesty in admitting her situation to Brownie, who loves her, and her willingness to go on with her life make her a sympathetic and interesting character. In his response to her, Brownie, the young man who has been learning about the wilderness from Dick Summers, becomes a person of depth and compassion. (It is disappointing to meet him as a narrow-minded, bad-tempered adult in *These Thousand Hills*, published in 1956.)

Mercy's seducer, Curtis Mack, is rather sketchily drawn as a sexually frustrated man whose anger further alienates his wife, impels him to random murder, and produces spasms of guilt that are intensified by his affair with Mercy. His wife, Amanda Mack, is one of the women in the train who cannot accept their situation. Despite her very real love for Curtis, she dislikes sex and fears pregnancy so much that she turns from him and from life itself. Although Judith Fairman does not reject her husband, she finds it difficult to accept the death of her son from a snakebite, the son whose delicate health had impelled the family to undertake the move West to higher, less malarial country. Like Amanda Mack, Judith Fairman distances herself from life. These women are contrasted to Rebecca Evans, the wife who leaves her flower beds and her loved cabin in Missouri because she has sensed Lije's need for a challenge, who nightly makes a home beside the wagon, who counsels and encourages Lije and the other pioneers, and who reveals her capacity for cheerful, realistic adjustment to life at every halt along the trail.

Themes and Meanings

The Way West explores the effect of the wilderness experience on people from a settled society with an authority structure and codified behavior. Because it detaches people from that authority structure, forcing them to form a new society, with new priorities, and because it places them in the midst of a vast natural environment that knows no codes, inhabited by Indians who have different values from those of white people, the wilderness experience presents a challenge to every individual's character and enables them to make choices as to their own future and that of their society. Not every member of the wagon train is aware of the challenge or of the possibility of choices. Many cling to their old convictions and their cherished inhibitions until survival forces a change. Many move through the wilderness without ever truly perceiving it. Those who do respond to it, accept the challenge, and make choices based on their own revised value systems, reach a higher level of life.

The theme of the wilderness challenge necessarily involves the relationship of humans to nature. Guthrie has been much praised, and occasionally attacked, for his lyric descriptions of nature. He is responsive to the beauty of the West, but that beauty is rooted in the sublime: the towering mountains, the tumbling rivers, the deafening thunder, the singing wind, all seemingly designed to give people second thoughts about their importance in the great plan of creation. It is ironic that though Guthrie's sympathetic characters respond strongly to the grandeur of nature, they are all involved in destroying that which they love: The beavers, the buffalo, the plains, the forests, and the Indians dwindle, alter, or vanish when these lovers of the wilderness try to tame it. In later books of his Western series, Guthrie questions whether the kinship to nature of the best pioneers can be preserved in concern for the environment among their children and grandchildren.

Also related to the theme of challenge presented by the wilderness is the inadequacy of the religion which the settlers carry into the wilderness, as reflected in petty moralizing and staunch but inflexible beliefs that cannot stand the test of experience. If such limited views persist in the new settlements, Guthrie implies, the wilderness experience will have failed to produce better individuals and a better society.

Critical Context

The Way West was A. B. Guthrie's second major novel, following *The Big Sky* (1947), which had firmly established him as a writer of realistic Western novels having a thematic and psychological depth rarely found in the genre. Although many critics preferred *The Big Sky* because it re-creates the era of the mountain men rather than the familiar period of the wagon trains, it was *The Way West* that won for Guthrie the Pulitzer Prize in 1950. The later novels in his Western series have been less praised than the first two works, perhaps because as the American West gradually lost its epic scope, the novels themselves necessarily have become smaller in vision.

In his treatment of the conflict between civilization and the wilderness, Guthrie can be compared to Joseph Conrad, with whom he shares an ambivalence toward the primitive, recognizing its appeal but admitting its dangers, both physical and moral.

Among American writers, Guthrie is often compared to James Fenimore Cooper, who shared Guthrie's fascination with the wilderness, his love of untamed nature, and his tragic awareness that those who love the wilderness are the same people who join in taming and destroying it.

The incidents in Guthrie's novels can be found in dozens of other Western novels. Many other Western novels, however, are merely adventure stories in which the good defeat the bad. Guthrie, who wrote the screenplay for the classic film *Shane* (1953), in his novels creates complex characters who make choices which are not easy and who, like Shane, must pay a price for every moral triumph. For that reason, A. B. Guthrie, Jr., is one of the most important Western novelists.

Bibliography
Chatterton, Wayne. "A. B. Guthrie, Jr." In *A Literary History of the American West*. Western Literature Association. Fort Worth, Tex.: Texas Christian University Press, 1987. Chatterton gives an overview of Guthrie's career.
Erisman, Fred. "Coming of Age in Montana: The Legacy of A. B. Guthrie, Jr." *Montana: The Magazine of Western History* 43 (Summer, 1993): 69-74. Erisman evaluates Guthrie's legacy and contributions to the literature of the West.
Ford, Thomas W. *A. B. Guthrie, Jr.* Boston: Twayne, 1981. Ford provides a critical and interpretive study of Guthrie with a close reading of his major works, a solid bibliography, and complete notes and references.
Guthrie, A. B. *The Blue Hen's Chick: An Autobiography*. New York: McGraw-Hill, 1963. Reprint. Lincoln: University of Nebraska Press, 1993. Guthrie's autobiography illuminates the themes of his novels and the autobiographical direction his later fiction would take.
Kich, Martin. *Western American Novelists*. Vol. 1. New York: Garland, 1995. Part of a multi-volume annotated bibliography of prominent Western writers of the 1930's and 1940's, including A. B. Guthrie. Primary and secondary resources, including first reviews of Guthrie's novels, are included.
Petersen, David. "A. B. Guthrie: A Remembrance." In *Updating the Literary West*. Western Literature Association. Fort Worth, Tex.: Texas Christian University Press, 1997. An overview of Guthrie's life and career.

Rosemary M. Canfield Reisman

THE WEDDING

Author: Mary Helen Ponce (1938-   )
Type of plot: Comic realism
Time of plot: The 1950's
Locale: Taconos, a fictional town in Southern California
First published: 1989

> *Principal characters:*
> BLANCA MUÑOZ, a young Mexican American woman who marries
>   Sammy-the-Cricket Lopez
> SAMMY-THE-CRICKET LOPEZ, leader of the Tacones gang
> LUCY MATACOCHIS, Blanca's best friend, a bossy authority on the ways
>   of the characters' world
> TUDI, a Tacones gang member who wishes for a peaceful life
> SALLY, a friend of Blanca who likes Tudi
> FATHER RANGER, the unconsciously hypocritical parish priest

The Novel

 The Wedding fictionally re-creates a small-town barrio (neighborhood) near Los Angeles in the 1950's and traces events surrounding the wedding of Blanca Muñoz and Sammy-the-Cricket Lopez. Ironically contrasting a young woman's romantic dreams with her world's reality, the novel portrays working-class Mexican Americans' ability to live spirited lives on the fringes of society.

 The Wedding's two parts, told by an omniscient narrator, focus mainly on Blanca. The first part ranges from the characters' childhood to just before the wedding. The second part narrates the traditional events of the barrio wedding day.

 The novel begins when the eighteen-year-old Blanca and the twenty-two-year-old Cricket start dating. Both are junior-high-school dropouts with menial jobs; Blanca plucks turkeys, and Cricket collects garbage. Blanca, living at home, helps her mother with expenses. She and her girlfriends fantasize about romance and excitement— specifically, an ideal man with a steady job and a "cool" car. Unglamorous and inexperienced, Blanca lacks criteria for judging men. She finds Sammy-the-Cricket impressive because in fights he knocks his opponents senseless. Cricket is a *pachuco*, one of the 1950's Mexican American youth who wore tailored, baggy "zoot suits" and often were involved in street gangs. Leader of Los Tacones, the neighborhood gang, Cricket had earned his nickname by stomping a member of the rival Planchados gang after beating him up.

 On their first date, Blanca and Cricket see *Gone with the Wind*, a film Blanca has seen ten times, at the drive-in with their friends Tudi and Sally. Tudi, driving his own car, refuses Cricket's urging to ram a car of Planchados who are peacefully leaving the drive-in. During the courtship, Cricket gets Blanca pregnant. Her condition apparently prompts Cricket's offhand suggestion that they marry; however, since the narrative does not mention the couple's intimacies, Blanca's pregnancy becomes obvious only at the wedding dance.

As Blanca plans the wedding, her life's reality intrudes upon her romantic hopes. Blanca wants to be the first in her family to marry ceremonially and thus make her family respectable. Blanca also confronts Cricket's silent, obsessive will to dominate. Cricket sees a wedding as a means of increasing his own social status. Realizing he will not contribute toward expenses, even an overnight honeymoon, Blanca works overtime at turkey-plucking to earn extra money. Traveling by bus to Los Angeles, she buys her wedding dress at a bridal store that sells refurbished factory seconds to Mexican American brides. She selects a *Gone with the Wind*-style gown that allows her to see herself as a real bride and trendsetter, the first bride in Taconos to wear a "colonial" wedding dress. The marked-down veil, adorned with *azares* (wax orange blossoms traditionally worn by Mexican American brides), symbolizes Blanca's yearnings for the wedding and her future.

The wedding day occurs against Blanca's ambivalence: excitement at the day's events, irritation with her expanding body, regret at surrendering her independence and her future paychecks to Cricket, and anticipation of her wifely status. During the morning wedding mass, said by Father Ranger, misfortunes undercut romance. Cricket, hung over from partying with his friends, wears his "boppers" (dark glasses), and Blanca must hold him upright. The junior bridesmaid throws up on the hand-embroidered kneeling cushions. Neither bride nor groom receives the sacrament of communion because Cricket, in a screaming fit, had refused to prepare by going to confession.

After the mass, the high-spirited events proceed ceremonially. The wedding party cruises the streets in the Tacones' cars festooned with paper flowers. After the wedding breakfast at maid-of-honor Lucy's, the cars parade into Los Angeles to have the wedding pictures taken. The afternoon reception features a meal provided with dignity by Blanca's mother and the neighborhood women. The Tacones speculate about the possibility that the Planchados might crash the evening's dance. The prevailing opinion among the young people is that only dances with fights are any good.

The wedding dance presents a panorama of guests and wedding participants who are hoping that something will happen. Blanca, recognizing Cricket's ugly egotism, feels unwell but eager for the splendid occasion. She revels in dancing, especially fast numbers. Cricket, threatened by Blanca's skill, sulks because his inept dancing endangers his reputation. As the celebration heightens, Blanca starts to miscarry. When the Planchados arrive, a melee of fighting and dancing ensues. Two ambulances are required: one for the groom and the Planchados leader, and one for the miscarrying bride, who insists that Cricket will change and is worth keeping. Blanca enters the hospital emergency room talking about her beautiful wedding.

The Characters

Blanca Muñoz, the main character, engages the reader's affection despite her narrow vision. Developed through narrative rather than omniscient analysis, she is portrayed as young and fun-loving. She is typical of her poor Mexican American community in that she does not really look ahead to her lack of expectations or her bleak future. She yearns for the good life of love, excitement, and possessions, as these values filter into her lower-class Mexican American town through films, music, and merchandising. In the passivity and remoteness that her man, Cricket, expects of her and in the wifely role she expects to assume, she further typifies difficulties confronting Mexican American women of the 1950's. Blanca plans her wedding to give her life excitement and meaning.

Sammy-the-Cricket Lopez, Blanca's boyfriend and leader of the Tacones gang, provides a vivid example of misplaced values among Taconos's blue-collar males and of the dead-end status that mainstream society assigns uneducated Mexican American men. A *pachuco*, he spends weekends on streetcorners dressed in his zoot suit, preoccupied with egotistical *machismo* (exaggerated masculinity) and waiting for something to happen. With fine irony, his clothes function as the chief image of his leadership. Instead of financially helping his indulgent mother, he works only to buy his tailor-made wardrobe, a habit that does not augur well for Blanca's future paychecks. Though his viciousness as a fighter redeems him in the eyes of some of Taconos's young people, his leadership is negative and local. His failure at transactions with Blanca and with the larger community reveals him as a marginalized personality who can deal with life only through the gestures of frustration.

Father Ranger, the parish priest, quickly loses the reader's respect. He regards his assignment to the Taconos church as an opportunity to indulge his own interests. He recognizes the community's problems and the irrelevance of some of the church's teaching. His apathy makes him emblematic of an institution that could empower its members but instead is part of the problem.

Lucy Matacochis, Blanca's best friend, serves as a tough, quick-witted, abrasive foil to Blanca. Giving the reader a clear-eyed view, she sees Cricket's meanness and advises Blanca not to stay with him. Though she leads a self-involved, rough young life and works in her aunt's bar, she knows how to look out for herself. She presents a flawed but positive image of a Mexican American woman trying to protect her body and her future.

Tudi, Cricket's driver and errand-runner, serves as a foil to Cricket. Recognizing that the rival gangs work amicably side by side during the week, he wishes for peace in the young people's lives. Though decent, Tudi is both literally and metaphorically toothless. Dominated by Cricket and turning to him for guidance in crises, Tudi helps to cause trouble.

Sally, who is sketchily developed as one of Blanca's numerous girlfriends, provides an example of the unselfish values inherent in the community. Gentle and giving, she appreciates Tudi's decency and dislikes Cricket's bullying egotism.

The women of "los turkeys," Blanca's coworkers, serve as a chorus. Advising Blanca and celebrating her mating, they exemplify a vigorous life force.

Themes and Meanings

With humor and sympathy, *The Wedding* treats themes important to Latinos, women, and a multicultural society. The novel is a coming-of-age story that tells of a teenage girl's maturing as a woman. Developing this universal theme, the novel strikingly dramatizes adolescent girls' preoccupations with their physical appearance, their future as women, and men. Since Blanca succeeds within her frame of reference, the novel also dramatizes the reality that many women face quite limited possibilities.

Ponce establishes the themes of *The Wedding* mainly through the Mexican American cultural context. One way she establishes background is through names, the meanings of which may be ironic—"Blanca" and "Taconos," for example. Ponce also ironically develops the novel's cultural themes. She celebrates Blanca's great event while depicting the flaws of Blanca's and the community's frame of reference. In the larger arena, the straightforward narrative reveals the real poverty of the Taconos community. The characters have no myths, superstitions, or dreams to guide them. On the outskirts of "Los," as the young people call Los Angeles, they are cut off from the imaginative past of their Latino heritage. The young men have only posturing *machismo*; the women, scraps of stories and current misinformation about contraception and abortion.

The narrative implies a related social and historical theme: that mainstream institutions have stunted Mexican American minorities by colonizing (isolating and dominating) them to keep them out of the way. The setting of the 1950's, a period of relative complacence and prosperity for American society, creates a backdrop for this concept. Ponce exemplifies the young people's wish to join the mainstream in the fact that they speak their own barrio English rather than Spanish. The schools should provide linguistic and cultural transitions to the larger society; however, they include Blanca and the other Mexican Americans only halfheartedly, with the result that all the young people drop out by the eighth grade. The church, which could provide continuity with a spiritual past and strength to reestablish cultural identity, continues its rituals without seriously engaging the lives of the people in its charge. Blamed for not having skills, the characters have access only to dangerous or physically unpleasant jobs. The novel suggests that though the young people are fascinated by Los Angeles, they have learned to be wary of contact with the larger world and prefer to stay in their neighborhood.

Ponce proposes that, lacking expectations, deprived communities find ways to keep themselves alive. Taconos creates a high-spirited life in events themselves, in spectacle, not in the meaning behind events. Weddings, fights, whatever happens is important. The gangs, which trade insults and punches rather than bullets or knifings, tangle more from boredom and the wish to create action than from hostility. Each event of the wedding day—the mass, the breakfast, the parading cars, the reception, the dance—is as important to the participants as ritual, though none is endowed with overarching meaning. Dramatizing the reasons for the physical and inner poverty of the barrio and its women, Ponce respectfully acknowledges their vitality. Capturing the details of the characters' lives, Ponce's humor affirms serious issues.

Critical Context

Focusing on Mexican American women, *The Wedding* enlarges the themes of Ponce's volume of short stories *Taking Control* (1987). Ironic narratives of sometimes unrecognized failure, these stories depict women attempting to live out their own standards in relation to their Latino culture. Ponce participates in the vigor of Latina fiction writing in the late 1980's, years when Latina writers reflected on their identity in relation to the United States' literary mainstream, to mainstream feminism, and to their own heritage.

Ponce's straightforward narrative, focusing on the characters' actions and conscious lives, distinguishes her method from the dream-sequence and stream-of-consciousness techniques of Latina authors writing in English such as Lucha Corpi in *Delia's Song* (1989) and Cristina Garcia in *Dreaming in Cuban* (1992). Like a number of Latina writers, Ponce takes risks with the English language. Using Spanish phonetic spellings for words in conversations, Ponce veils meaning momentarily and thus reveals the characters' cultural difference. Though she narrates with sometimes broad comicality in *The Wedding*, Ponce's use of humor links her with an aspect of Latina writing that is beginning to receive critical attention.

The Wedding treats the special bicultural reality of Latina women at the same time that it connects with the feminist mainstream. An obvious but important focus of the novel is female subjectivity (woman as the subject of events and of her own life).

The novel also expresses the feminist interest in perceptions of the female body. Constantly evoking the body, its dampness, its smells, and its visceral reactions, Ponce "writes the body." The young women's inscribing their faces and nails with vivid 1950's cosmetics proclaims their sexuality, the color they wish their lives to have, and their outsider status. In her 1990 essay "The Color Red," Ponce observed that in the 1950's, lower-class Mexican Americans wore bright colors that Mexican Americans wanting an "American" look regarded as too vivid.

Through constant references to Blanca's uncomfortable flesh, the novel emphasizes the basic physical level of reality that women in the community occupy. In its silences, the novel also encompasses the concept of women's secret knowledge—about Blanca's intimacy with Cricket, her pregnancy, and her most private emotions.

Bibliography

Gonzalez, Ray. "Hoyt Street: An Autobiography." *The Nation* 256 (June 7, 1993): 772-774. Gonzalez presents a reading list of modern Chicano writing, briefly commenting on a number of books, including Ponce's autobiography *Hoyt Street*. Although his article does not specifically mention *The Wedding*, it offers a useful perspective of the body of Ponce's work in relation to other Chicano authors.

Hernández, Guillermo. "Satire: An Introduction." In *Chicano Satire: A Study in Literary Culture*. Austin: University of Texas Press, 1991. Hernández examines *pachucos* as historical and literary figures. Originally often seen as comical, this urban counterculture gradually became seen as threatening. Hernández discusses the *pachucos'* trademark "zoot suit" as a distortion of mainstream culture's business suit.

McCracken, Ellen. "Subculture, Parody, and the Carnivalesque: A Bakhtinian Reading of Mary Helen Ponce's *The Wedding*." *MELUS* 23 (Spring, 1998): 117. McCracken argues that Ponce's novel has earned a place in the late twentieth century canon of novels written by Mexican American women even though it does not fit the mold of critically popular work of the 1990's. She maintains that since the critics have lauded the exotic nature, rich language, and magic realism of Sandra Cisneros, Julia Alvarez, and others, they should also appreciate the humorous insider's perspective of Pachuco culture offered by Ponce.

Magnarelli, Sharon. "Taking Control." *Hispania* 71 (December, 1988): 844-845. A review of Ponce's 1987 volume of short stories. Magnarelli focuses on the characters' ironic inability to "take control," a theme Ponce reinforces in *The Wedding*. Magnarelli discusses the characters' "paradoxical combination of insight and blindness," a paradox underlying Blanca's character.

Vallejos, Tomás. "Social Insights." *American Book Review* 11 (January, 1990): 13. Vallejos explores sexism in Chicano culture and associates the structure of Ponce's novel—thirteen chapters in part 1 and nine in part 2—with an Aztec prophecy of thirteen time periods of heaven followed by nine periods of hell. He notes that the novel sets the "heavenly" illustrations of the traditional Chicano wedding against the "hellish" reality of the Chicano working class.

Vásquez, Mary S. Review of *The Wedding*, by Mary Helen Ponce. *Hispania* 73 (December, 1990): 1005-1007. Vásquez focuses on Ponce's skill with dialect and on the wedding, which as spectacle fulfills Blanca's dreams. She comments that the "poignant tension between too much and too little" informs the second half of the novel.

Barbara G. Bartholomew

WEEDS

Author: Edith Summers Kelley (1884-1956)
Type of plot: Naturalism
Time of plot: Early twentieth century, from approximately 1910 to the 1940's
Locale: Rural Kentucky
First published: 1923

Principal characters:

JUDITH PIPPINGER BLACKFORD, the protagonist, a vivacious woman, the daughter and then the wife of a sharecropper and the mother of three children

JERRY BLACKFORD, her sharecropper husband

LIZZIE MAY PIPPINGER POOLER, her older sister, the "ideal" wife, mother, and rural homemaker

DAN POOLER, Lizzie May's sharecropper husband

LUELLA PIPPINGER, Lizzie May's less attractive fraternal twin

LUKE and HAT WOLF, a crude sharecropping couple, Judith and Jerry's closest neighbors

THE REVIVALIST, a charismatic, fiery-eyed traveling preacher, Judith's lover for a few months.

JABEZ MOORHOUSE, an idiosyncratic loner, Judith's "double" who is twenty years her senior, the Thoreau of the tobacco fields

The Novel

Much of *Weeds* is filtered through the experience and perception of Judith Pippinger, an unusually alive and exuberant offspring of impoverished, backwoods Kentucky, the product of inbreeding, malnutrition, geographical isolation, and poverty, a dark red rose blooming "against the drabness of the dooryard, now bare with summer draught. . . . Gorgeously it flaunted on its distorted stem." The novel follows her from young, eccentric girlhood, when she is a dark-haired, unruly sprite among pale, long-faced, listless children, to young adulthood, to middle age and old age.

As a young girl, she follows her father around, helping with the outdoor chores—the milking, the cleaning of the pigsty, and the feeding of the chickens—rather than be trapped indoors helping her mother and sisters cook, clean, sew, mend, and tend to the needs of the male children. At a young age, she finds solace in the beauty of nature, the colors of the sky, the shapes of the hills. The book is structured chronologically, tracing Judith's coming-of-age, while it also rigorously follows the cycle of seasons, just as the seasons dictate the fortunes of the sharecroppers.

When Judith is twelve years old, her mother dies of a cold. Attended by her older sisters in their starched and patched aprons, the piercing winds of February blowing through the chinks in the two-room shack, Annie Pippinger leaves her husband and five children, the cupboards bare except for cornmeal and a bit of sowbelly, the apples and potatoes gone with her. "The mouse-like little woman was claiming more attention now than she had ever done in all the forty-odd years of her drab existence." Dismally, the family carries on, but as spring follows winter, the family manages, seasons pass, and Lizzie May, Luella, and Judith come of courting age. First Lizzie May, who is pretty in a bleak, blonde, pinched way, is selected. Then it is Judith's turn. A young man named Jerry Blackford courts her by meeting her while she gathers the calves at nightfall, stealing her away from a young buck in his father's horse and buggy. "It was all that easy for Jerry. It was a speedy, simple, natural courting, like the coming together of two young wild things in the woods. Jerry, who was of a practical turn of mind, immediately began to plan for their future."

Judith slowly transforms from "the on'y woman . . . that's got a man's ways," to a young wife, to a mother of one, then two, then three. Now she, too, has an uninsulated, two-room shack of her own, heated in the dead of winter by the fire of a potbellied stove. At first, Judith helps Jerry in the tobacco fields, planting and then laboriously topping the plants, then stripping and bundling, from four in the morning to seven at night. After the babies come, she is relegated to the inside, doing the housework and the child rearing that she is temperamentally unsuited to do. Slowly, her life encircles and enslaves her. She lives in a gray tedium, alienated from her husband and from the other sharecroppers' wives, who find compensation and even joy in their impoverished, dismal lives: Lizzie May in her rag rugs and her clean children, Hat Wolf in her catalog finery and her *The Homemaker's Companion*. Jabez Moorhouse, Judith's spiritual double, a man able to appreciate the sound of a fiddle, the healing quality of nature, and the sight, smell, and feel of the land, has known her all her life. He says to her, a woman grown old at thirty after three babies, an attempted abortion, a miscarriage, a short-lived affair, the death of more loved ones, failed crops, low tobacco prices, and pervasive poverty: "It makes me feel bad, Judy, to see you go like all the rest of us, you that growed up so strong an' handsome, so full o' life an' spirits. I've watched you sence you was a baby growin' like a pink rosebud, an' then blossomin', so beautiful to see. And now. . . ."

After their baby, Annie, survives the flu which has taken the lives of many others, Judith reconciles with her husband, from whom she has been emotionally estranged, and with her narrow life: "She was through with struggle and question, since for her nothing could ever come of them but discord. . . . She would go on for her allotted time bearing and nursing. . . . And when her time of child bearing was over she would go back to the field, like the other women. . . ." Yet on the last pages of the novel, which seemed to be ending in reconciliation and accommodation, Judith hears of Jabez's death and "what light and color had remained for her in life faded out. . . ." Her soul mate gone, she is left, the "natural" woman, bound to her husband and children, tied to the land that they will never own and the meager cycle of existence wrested from it. Thus, the novel ends with the fire in her soul extinguished.

The Characters

Judith Pippinger Blackford is a prototype of the working-class heroine later used by Agnes Smedley in *Daughter of Earth* (1929) and Harriette Arnow in *The Doll-*

maker (1954). She is a fully realized character caught in constricting circumstances, portrayed, for the most part, neither sentimentally nor heroically. She can be likened, to a great extent, to the protagonist in Richard Wright's *Black Boy* (1945). She is interesting not only in her love of the outdoors and her affinity for "man's work," but also in her forthright sexuality. She is sexually intimate with Jerry before they are married. "Accident was kind to them and did not thrust upon them with untimely speed the physical results of the sweet intimacy that they enjoyed." In like manner, when she finds herself strongly attracted to a traveling revivalist, she risks scandal and ostracism and has an affair with him. Unlike Emma Bovary, she realizes that he is not a permanent solution to her dreary existence, awakens from "the dream," and ends it.

Without the author laying the blame on her husband, Judith is depicted as becoming cynical with her role as sharecropper's wife and a mother; her affections harden toward her family. So disenchanted does she become with her lot in life that she wonders if her daughter's life is worth saving. "She would live only to endure, to be patient, to work, to suffer; and at last, when she had gone through all these things, to die without ever having lived and without knowing that she had never lived." When her daughter survives the flu, she attempts to come to terms with her life, to accept it without chafing, but when her spiritual double, Jabez Moorhouse, dies, she realizes that this "peaceful resignation" is also a dream dissipated at the question: "Whatcha got for supper, Judy?" At the novel's end, she is Sisyphus rolling the rock to the top of the mountain, knowing it will roll back down, over and over again. Unlike Albert Camus's Sisyphus, however, she is not ennobled by this consciousness of her condition; she cannot embrace the rock.

Her husband, Jerry Blackford, is portrayed sympathetically. A healthy, robust, well-meaning young man, he strives to make enough money from the unpredictable tobacco crop to buy his own land, the only way out of the poverty cycle of the tenant farmer. Like the other sharecroppers, he is unable to get ahead. After one particularly backbreaking season, during which he is detained two weeks by flu from getting the tobacco to market, the prices drop drastically and the harvest is a failure. "Suddenly he dropped to the floor beside her, and with his arms across her knees and his face laid upon his arms, broke into dry, convulsive sobs, harrowing to hear."

Jerry is characterized by Judith's sister Lizzie May as being a "good husband," hardworking and not hard drinking. Marriage separates him from Judith rather than uniting them, but he seems too tired from his physical labor to notice and later is helpless to change it. He is an oblivious Sisyphus; like Judith, he is prematurely aged by hard work, malnutrition, and disappointment, but he continues to hope for the best. Unlike Judith or Jabez Moorhouse, he does not glimpse nor does he yearn for another dimension to his life.

Jabez Moorhouse is a farmer-philosopher-bon vivant. Though twenty years her senior, he shares with Judith a common aesthetic: a love of beauty, a hunger for life, and a tangible sensuality that those around them lack. He also perceives that his life as a sharecropper is a dead end: "I cud a made a preacher . . . or a congressman or a jedge or learnt to play the fiddle good if I'd only had a chanct. But all my life I hain't done nothin' but dig in dirt. An' all the rest o' my life I'm going to keep right on a-diggin' in dirt." To Judith one day he confesses: "You an' me together, Judy, might a made sumpin out of our lives, anyway got in a little play along with the grind." Jabez seems closest to Camus's happy Sisyphus, the man conscious of his plight who is able, finally, to embrace it.

Hat and Luke Wolf and Lizzie May and Dan Pooler as couples serve as foils to Judith and Jerry Blackford. Early in the novel, neither of these couples seems to possess the "natural" love and affinity for each other that Judith and Jerry do, but later in the novel, their marriages prove to be stronger than the Blackfords'. Though both Dan and Luke are drunkards when they have the money, and though Luke is unspeakably stingy with the horsey, hardworking Hat, both couples are basically content with their lot as rural tenant farmers. They share a mutual complacency, one that Judith cannot share with Jerry. As the years roll by, this gap is widened. No amount of housekeeping, rug weaving, or reading of *The Homemaker's Companion* can mask for Judith the fruitlessness of her existence. The satisfaction that Lizzie May experiences from keeping her home and children neat and clean, from the dirt floors covered with rag rugs, the windows curtained with a bit of store-brought frill, is not Judith's. Nor does she, like Hat, endlessly complain of her lot, ferreting pennies away from her husband to send away for bits of dress material.

Luella Pippinger, Lizzie May's fraternal twin and Judith's older sister, is the resident spinster. For women in rural Kentucky, "spinsterhood" is an institution, the only alternative to marriage. Lightly sketched, docile to the point of near invisibility, she also serves as a foil to Judith and her plight.

The revivalist is never named. He is a dark-eyed force awakening and arousing Judith's passion. She tires of him, finding him hypocritical and weak. Refreshingly, though she shares the fate of both Hester Prynne in *The Scarlet Letter* and Emma Bovary in *Madame Bovary*, she is not branded for life as is Hester, nor is she suicidal at the end of her romantic liaison as is Emma; it is Judith who tires of the relationship; it is Judith who severs it.

Themes and Meanings

The theme of *Weeds* is one that is common to naturalistic novels: Environment, to a large degree, determines people's fate; it forms them and, in some instances, crushes them. Some characters, such as Jabez Moorhouse and Judith Pippinger, are able to understand the limitations imposed on them by environment; they are able to transcend for brief moments their crippling circumstances. Even these "conscious" characters, however, ultimately remain as trapped as their unseeing brethren.

Kelley writes in the same vein as Theodore Dreiser, Hamlin Garland, and William Dean Howells. She accurately and painstakingly re-creates the milieu of the poor white Southerners, breathing life into her characters, major and minor, male and female, landowners and tenant farmers. For this reason, *Weeds* can also be characterized as a regional novel, one that renders a way of life that is unknown to most. Her naturalistic approach is anchored to the land, the weather, the planting, the harvesting, the slop jars, the cornmeal cakes, the hog's belly, the thirty-mile trips to the nearest town, the revival meetings, the funerals, and the dances. Without tedium, yet without gloss, she realizes the life and the people of the region, always individualizing and differentiating, without cataloging and generalizing.

By emphasizing the effect of the social environment on the individual, Kelley is primarily a sociological novelist, but she is also a political writer. Without advancing any solutions, she is indirectly critical of the economic system which enslaves the tenant farmer: the landowners, the tobacco companies, the store owners, all of whom have more power over the destiny of the poor farmer than does the farmer himself. Not only does he have no real control, but also he is rendered virtually helpless to change his economic and social status. Thus, a large segment of the population is at the mercy of a much wealthier, smaller section, an indirect indictment of the capitalist system as it operates in the rural South. These farmers are trapped in their way of life, but to a large extent, it is a human-made trap.

Weeds can also be described as a "lost" feminist novel. Judith is definitely a strong, female character at odds with her role as housewife and mother. Kelley chronicles Judith's slow entrapment, beginning with her first pregnancy. She shows her stultifying life: the hard work, the isolation, the repetition, and most important, her lack of choice. Her biological imprisonment, caused by pregnancy after pregnancy, and the financial and emotional burden placed upon the family's already strained circumstances are made clear. Though both Judith and Jerry are bound by their economic circumstances, Judith directly suffers the consequences of her sexual passion; she tries to remedy this by sleeping on a separate cot, but in doing this, both are isolated from human intimacy. Thus, the harshness and the bleakness of their lives is exacerbated, and this form of control over her destiny only increases the bitterness of her life. When she becomes pregnant a fourth time from the liaison with the traveling preacher, she contemplates a homemade abortion. Her attempt fails, but mercifully she later miscarries.

One of the themes of *Weeds* concerns people's relationship to nature. The natural person is exemplified by Jabez Moorhouse, and to a certain extent, by Judith Blackford. They retain their close relationship to the natural world; they are susceptible to its beauty and its call. This quality separates them from the bulk of the community, who live under the thumb of nature but who are not in tune with the natural people within themselves.

Critical Context

Though *Weeds* was favorably reviewed in 1923 (Sinclair Lewis, an old friend and former fiancé being one of the reviewers), it never became popular. The book was revived in 1972 through the efforts of Matthew J. Bruccoli in his Lost American Fiction series under the auspices of the University of Southern Illinois at Carbondale; Kelley's selected papers are in a collection there, while her letters to Sinclair Lewis and Upton Sinclair are in collections of the Lilly Library at the University of Indiana.

The reissuing of her novel brought her more critical attention, especially from the aspect of regionalism and feminism, but the novel has never become popular. Her second novel, *The Devil's Hand*, about life in California's Imperial Valley as seen through the eyes of two female protagonists, was written between 1925 and 1929. It was finally published in 1974, eighteen years after her death.

Her first novel garnered more critical acclaim than the second; neither was widely read. Nevertheless, *Weeds* has been called by many "a little masterpiece" of its type, a sensitively rendered and fully realized portrait of poor Southern life.

Both books are loosely autobiographical. Kelley was born in Ontario, Canada, and earned an honors degree in languages at the University of Toronto. She migrated to New York in 1905 and worked on Funk and Wagnall's *Standard Dictionary*. In 1906, she became Upton Sinclair's secretary and lived in Helicon Hall, a Socialist commune in Englewood, New Jersey. There she met and became engaged to Sinclair Lewis; though she married another man, they remained friends. After divorcing Alan Updengraff, she and her two children lived with sculptor Claude Fred Kelley, whose last name she assumed. From 1914 to 1945, they lived as tenant tobacco farmers in Kentucky, boardinghouse managers in New Jersey, and chicken farmers in California. Though both she and her husband were educated, they lived the life she describes in *Weeds*. They tried to make their living from the land while pursuing their art. The theme of human alienation from nature came naturally to Kelley, as did her portrayal of a woman and mother whose artistic soul is all but smothered by the harsh economic realities of her life.

Bibliography

Bradbury, John M. *Renaissance in the South: A Critical History of the Literature, 1920-1960*. Chapel Hill: University of North Carolina Press, 1963. Bradbury presents a survey of the times and the context in which Kelley produced her novel.

Cook, Sylvia J. *From Tobacco Road to Route 66: The Southern Poor White in Fiction*. Chapel Hill: University of North Carolina Press, 1976. Cook explores the theme of white Southern poverty in novels including *Weeds*.

Goodman, Charlotte. "Edith Summers Kelley." In *The Oxford Companion to Women's Writing in the United States*, edited by Cathy N. Davidson and Linda Wagner-Martin. New York: Oxford University Press, 1995. Goodman furnishes a biographical sketch of Kelley, a discussion of *Weeds* as a female *Bildungsroman*, and a brief bibliography for further study.

_____. "Widening Perspectives, Narrowing Possibilities: The Trapped Woman in Edith Summers Kelley's *Weeds*." In *Regionalism and the Female Imagination*, edited by Emily Toth. New York: Human Sciences Press, 1985. An analysis of Judith, the novel's central character who must face the limitations imposed by poverty and gender.

Irvin, Helen. *Women in Kentucky*. Lexington: University Press of Kentucky, 1979. Includes an analysis of *Weeds*.

Sandra Christenson

WHAT I'M GOING TO DO, I THINK

Author: Larry Woiwode (1941-   )
Type of plot: Psychological realism
Time of plot: 1964
Locale: Madison and Milwaukee, Wisconsin; Pyramid Bluffs, Michigan (littoral northwestern Michigan); and Chicago, Illinois
First published: 1969

Principal characters:

> CHRISTOFER (CHRIS) VAN EENANAM, the protagonist, a Wisconsin-born, twenty-three-year-old graduate student in mathematics, possessing animal good looks, who is physically fit but spiritually and psychologically anguished
>
> ELLEN SIDONE ANNE STROHE VAN EENANAM, a twenty-one-year-old graduate of the University of Wisconsin, with blonde hair and blue-green eyes, Chris's wife (pregnant before marriage), who is much disturbed by the allegedly accidental death of her parents and by her propagandistic upbringing by her grandparents
>
> ALOYSIUS JAMES STROHE, Ellen's wealthy, spry, shrewd, and devious grandfather, a former brewmaster and now the owner of his own brewery (producing Auld Meister beer)
>
> GRANDMA STROHE, Aloysius's wife, thin, prim, old-fashioned, and manipulative, an almost fanatical Christian Scientist
>
> ORIN CLAUSEN, a farmer and the closest neighbor to the Strohes' lakeside lodge, who is late-middle-aged, hardworking, stingy, sparing of speech, set in his ways, coarse, and prejudiced against Catholics
>
> ANNA CLAUSEN, Orin's widowed sister-in-law, a zealous Lutheran, a partner in the farm work and finances, covertly generous and sympathetic; she is quiet, lonely, and acrimonious toward Orin

The Novel

Because the author's emphasis is mainly on what happens within his characters, particularly within Chris and Ellen, the external action is compact, told partly through flashbacks and cyclical repetition of certain facts or incidents. Toward the end of his undergraduate days in Madison, Wisconsin, while at a party, Chris meets Ellen, whom he finds intelligent, disturbed, withdrawn, and deeply affecting. Beginning turbulently and evoking mixed feelings, the relationship continues for three years, including a one-year hiatus, which Ellen spends on her own in New York, partially influenced by her grandparents' disapproval of Chris, whom they have met in the couple's inspection visit at the Strohes' labyrinthine seventeen-room villa in Milwaukee. At the end of this period, moved by what is still a mixture of not altogether consistent deep feelings and by Ellen's premarital pregnancy, the couple decide to wed, call several churches in Madison, and finally convince a sympathetic young Presbyterian minister (who is not told about Ellen's as yet undetectable condition) to perform a quick ceremony.

After a second, even more disastrous visit at Ellen's grandparents' place to break the matrimonial news, the couple honeymoon at the Strohes' lodge in Michigan, on the shore of Lake Michigan. Most of the novel takes place there, as the couple continue to grapple with their innermost feelings and beliefs, each other, their new marital state, and their impending parenthood (including thoughts of abortion). Along with working hard to repair and restore the lodge and its grounds, the couple also explore their environs and learn about their closest neighbors, the Clausens—especially through Orin's inconsiderate treatment of Chris in the extended, nightmarish account of the hay baling on the Clausens' farm.

Toward the end of their stay at the lodge, while outside pursuing their separate activities, separately but simultaneously Chris and Ellen have a vision or premonition that they will have a son who dies at birth. In a brief one-page "coda," this event is verified, the child's death symbolizing the couple's troubled beginnings and mixed feelings about the pregnancy, Chris's ever-increasing psychological and spiritual anguish from lack of certainty about self and values, and his identity-suicide (revealed in the coda) in having given up the study of mathematics (a true aspiring of his spirit to attain the Ph.D.) to settle for an accounting job (earthbound and pedestrian).

The concluding epilogue recounts the couple's return to the lodge seven years later, in 1971, for a month-long vacation, focusing on Chris's flirtation with suicide by drowning in the lake; a tense moment when Chris seems to contemplate shooting Ellen's ailing old dog, Winston, to end the latter's misery; and the final emptying of his omnipresent .22 caliber rifle into a discarded plastic milk container—with one last, enigmatic shot fired out into the lake, probably symbolizing Chris's frustrated outreach for attainment of self-knowledge, certainty, and self-satisfaction.

The Characters

Not only is this novel focused on the internal action of its characters (their thoughts, feelings, motivations) more than on external action, but it also is further focused or delimited to a small group of characters. This economy contrasts with many modern works of fiction that teem with individuals, including Woiwode's own second novel, *Beyond the Bedroom Wall: A Family Album* (1975), which introduces sixty-three characters by the end of the second of forty-four chapters. On the other hand, beyond the six principal characters of *What I'm Going to Do, I Think*, there are only a dozen or so more characters mentioned (some treated for only a few sentences) in its 309 pages.

This intentional narrowing of focus helps convey the intensity of the main characters' inner lives as well as the contraction of their world. Chris and Ellen are continually doubting, thinking, worrying, and feeling about who they are, what they should believe, and what they should do next. Besides occasional forays into the world of nature at the lodge, their world is circumscribed—limited to each other (and to concern about the unborn child) and, too often, unfortunately, to themselves as individuals. The overwhelming atmosphere of the novel is one of unhappy isolation and solipsism.

At the same time, Woiwode vividly depicts characters by using exterior detail, though almost always in order to reveal personality. Ellen moves with a "sad sashay" (Chris's repeated phrase) when sorrowful, suggesting her self-absorption and obliviousness to the outside world; Grandma Strohe habitually holds her elbows tight at her sides, suggesting her strictness and belief in self-containment; Grandfather Strohe's appearance ("a stocky, heavy-jawed German with bright, bulging eyes and square patches of bristly eyebrows . . . totally bald") suggests his combative nature, as does the meaning of his first name (literally, "famous in war"). The coarseness of personality and manner produced by rural or farm life is caught by the author's description of Hank Olsen's physiognomy ("a stocky, middle-aged wrestler-type, with small eyes, a broad nose with nostrils the size of dimes") and of Orin Clausen's actions (such as downing a whole thirty-two-ounce can of cherry juice and then, a little later, publicly urinating against the side of the barn).

The symbolism that so pervades the novel and its characterization, along with psychological analysis, is epitomized in the protagonist's name; the oddity of his surname (though not its meaning) is explicitly referred to three times in the book. The significance of his first name (literally, "bearing Christ") is strongly hinted in Woiwode's *Beyond the Bedroom Wall* by the Neumiller family patriarch's giving his son the middle name Christopher because the latter was born on Christmas Day. Cristofer's anxieties in *What I'm Going to Do, I Think* stem in part from the lapse of his Catholicism, with no certain core of beliefs and feelings and models of conduct to substitute in its place. Too often, because he is so ironically far from his namesake, he does harm to himself and Ellen.

Chris's surname seems to be compounded from *een* ("one") and *naam* ("name") in Dutch—Chris twice, with a mixture of pride and embarrassed self-consciousness, mentions the tracing of his lineage back to a scribe of Peter Stuyvesant in Old New York. Ironically inverse to the unity or harmony embodied in his surname, Chris suffers from inconsistency and division. Though mostly discarding his Catholicism, he yearns for belief; though loving Ellen, at times he feels hatred or estrangement instead; though worried about finding his true self, he is always adolescently role-playing or disguising in Ellen's presence, further multiplying false identities; though he has a destructive urge (seen frequently in his actions and alluded to in one of Ellen's censures), he constructively and creatively restores much of the lodge; though ashamed of his rural parents and background, he prides himself on all his rural savvy (wherefrom many of his pragmatically constructive skills are derived); though tormented by, and tormenting Ellen for, Ellen's year in New York (and her two brief affairs), Chris, on his bus trip from graduate school to his new wife's hometown, makes sexual advances to a young coed, unconsummated only because of his drunken passing out.

Themes and Meanings

The novel's unusual title, echoed three times in the novel proper and once in the epilogue, abstracts the main themes: the nature of right conduct (what to do), self-identity (I'm), the impact of past on present—or present on future (going to do), and self-knowledge as well as belief (I think). The first use of this signature phrase—Chris's recollection of his father's response to the three serious accidents that Chris suffered one summer: "What I'm going to do, I think, is get a new kid"—conveys the other key theme: the generation gap, or relationship of parents and children.

How these themes are expressed is intimated by one of the novel's three epigraphs, from canto 5 of Dante's *Inferno* (the Italian could be translated, "and I fell as a dead body might fall"). It alerts the reader not only to the novel's moral dimension (Chris and Ellen's premarital carnal relations have had consequences that Dante understands and condemns in canto 5) but also to the novel's comprehensive symbolism, a second shared feature of the novel with Dante's work. Indeed, this symbolism is so widespread that the book borders on the classification of symbolism or allegory for its plot. A sampling of such symbols, in roughly chronological order, would begin with the recurrence of the number three (or multiples of three) in the book, also reminiscent of Dante's *The Divine Comedy*. The novel has thirteen chapters (perhaps signifying misfortune for the main characters), each divided into three subchapters, making thirty-nine sections, while the main flashbacks are handled in the second and third subchapters of the first three chapters. All these, plus some seventeen or more other occurrences of the number three, recall the Trinity (connoting religious belief, or unity amid diversity) and Chris's aspiration for a Ph.D. in mathematics. In a nightmare, stream-of-consciousness sequence, the awakening Chris thinks "*Every even number is the sum of two primes*. Peace! Peace!" which relates to the threes (a prime number—as is thirteen; it also represents the numeric total of Chris, Ellen, and the unborn baby) and the couple, or two (Chris and Ellen, an even number) that need to be harmonized from the separate individuals, or ones.

Some further symbols, by no means all, include the wreck in the lake (the mystery in life that Chris would like to resolve, the wreck of his relationship with Ellen); the island named Manitou in the lake (the Indian version of religion and belief); Ellen's ring, which Chris wears even before marriage but loses while diving to the wreck (the loss of the couple's ringlike unity); the labyrinthine villa of the Strohes, where Chris is judged (linking the grandfather with the devious Minos of myth, as well as the judge in Dante's *Inferno*); Chris's rifle (the destruction entwined with the drive toward complete certainty, without acceptance on faith of some mystery in life); Ellen's lifelong interest in birds (her desire to escape from the burdens of her parents' death and grandparents' injurious upbringing); the drawer filled with keys through which Anna Clausen searches to find a replacement for Chris and Ellen's lost one (sympathy by the couple, shown in a never-taken visit to the lonely Anna, would have held the key to their own salvation); Chris's spraining his ankle when coming down from his leap for joy after the wedding (the blend in life of enjoyment and sorrowful consequences); the game of Bridge-It that Chris and Ellen repeatedly play at the lodge (union is needed in their real-life relationship); Indians encountered in Pyramid Bluffs (failure of harmony among men—among races or peoples; remnants of past acts in the present); the Petoskey stones on the beach (layers of the past, or interrelationships of diverse parts in a whole); the unnamed boy seen by the couple on the beach (what could have been a happy life for the couple had their child lived); and the apple that Chris finds on his trail in the epilogue (the sorrow and travail that follow exclusion from Edenic happiness possible for the couple at the opening of the novel).

Critical Context

What I'm Going to Do, I Think received the prestigious William Faulkner Award at the time of its publication, appeared on the best-seller list, and was translated into a number of languages. Woiwode's second novel, the massive *Beyond the Bedroom Wall*, was also a critically acclaimed best-seller. His third novel, *Poppa John* (1981), failed commercially and received generally negative reviews; in time, however, that estimate may be revised. Woiwode has published many short stories, most of which have been excerpts from novels in progress; several of his stories have been included in collections of the year's best. He has also published a volume of poetry, *Even Tide* (1977).

There is a particularly close connection between Woiwode's first two novels. In many ways, the second novel carries on or elaborates motifs and concerns of the first: religion and especially Catholicism (as well as anti-Catholicism), the presence of the supernatural in visions or premonitions, parentage or parents and children (many more successes or near-successes occur in the second novel, in contrast to the failures in the first), the importance and influence of the past, and sensitivity to the natural environment (especially of the northern Midwest). Moreover, even particular incidents or characters are echoed or recognizably transmuted (indeed, a sly allusion to the first novel's title is woven into chapter 8 of the second). For example, the horror of the stillbirth at the end of the first book is paralleled by Alpha Neumiller's reaction to a preserved fetus used in a carnival sideshow in the second; Orin Clausen's coarseness in urinating against the side of his barn is paralleled by Ed Jones's writing his name in the dust with his stream (an apt symbol equating physical coarseness with his identity) while urinating out the backdoor of his house.

Unquestionably, Woiwode is important as a regional novelist focusing on the North Dakota, Wisconsin, and Illinois Midwest, and also as a writer among whose main interests are the role of religion (particularly Catholicism) and belief in twentieth century America.

Bibliography

Nelson, Shirley. "Stewards of the Imagination: Ron Hansen, Larry Woiwode, and Sue Miller." *Christian Century* 112 (January 25, 1995): 82-85. Nelson interviews Hansen, Woiwode, and Miller, focusing on the role of religion in their works, as well as readers' reactions to their novels.
Scheick, William J. "Memory in Larry Woiwode's Novels." *North Dakota Quarterly*

53, no. 3 (1985): 29-40. Scheick discusses the importance of memory in three of Woiwode's novels, *What I'm Going to Do, I Think* (1969), *Beyond the Bedroom Wall* (1975), and *Poppa John* (1981). He identifies two types of memories, those that make a character feel guilt and long for death and those that develop a sense of connection to one's family. The ability to order these allows Woiwode's characters to achieve a balance between them.

Woiwode, Larry. "Homeplace, Heaven or Hell." *Renascence* 44 (1991): 3-16. Woiwode discusses the problem of being considered merely a regional writer because he writes about the Midwest. He says that all writers must write about some place, and only geographical chauvinism makes one place better than another. The author also asserts that the main duty of a Christian writer is to write the truth, which means to write about a place in precise detail.

_____. "Where the Buffalo Roam: An Interview with Larry Woiwode." Interview by Rick Watson. *North Dakota Quarterly* 63 (Fall, 1996): 154-166. A revealing interview about Woiwode's homecoming and the effect it has had on his writing.

Norman Prinsky

WHAT MAKES SAMMY RUN?

Author: Budd Schulberg (1914-   )
Type of plot: Black humor
Time of plot: The 1930's
Locale: New York City and Hollywood
First published: 1941

Principal characters:

SAMMY GLICK (née SHMELKA GLICKSTEIN), a dynamic and ambitious
   young man
AL MANHEIM, an intelligent writer fascinated by Glick
KIT SARGENT, a talented and wise screenwriter
JULIAN BLUMBERG, a talented but unassertive writer
SIDNEY FINEMAN, an older and respected Hollywood producer
LAURETTE HARRINGTON, a rich and beautiful woman who becomes
   Sammy's wife

The Novel

What Makes Sammy Run? tells of the rise to riches and fame of Shmelka Glickstein, who when he was five years old began to change his name to Sammy Glick. The
action spans the 1930's, moving from New York to Hollywood (and briefly back to
New York again). The title not only names the novel's central character but also asks
the novel's major question: What makes Sammy do what he does?

Sammy's tale, which is told by a newspaperman named Al Manheim, proceeds
chronologically, with flashbacks when other characters tell Manheim their Sammy
stories. Manheim marks very clearly the stages of Sammy's development. At first
Sammy, aged about seventeen, is only a copy boy at the *New York Record*. Not only
does he run his errands faster than anyone else, but he also angles to improve himself;
he learns points of grammar from Manheim. Sammy is confident, aggressive, ambitious, opportunistic, and attuned to the moment. He bides his time until he gets a col-
umn of his own—about the new medium, radio.

Sammy's next stage comes when an unassuming writer named Julian Blumberg
brings him a script to review. Sammy, who is not creative or even a writer, sees the
script's potential. Sammy telephones a leading Hollywood agent and sells the story
for five thousand dollars. Sammy is thus off to Hollywood, abandoning Blumberg and
a naïve girlfriend, and after a few months, Manheim follows him.

Sammy is now a young screenwriter striving to get ahead. When he shows
Manheim around, he dresses in a California casual style and drives a yellow Cadillac
roadster. He seduces some women with promises of jobs in the movies, though he also
is the lover of Kit Sargent, a talented screenwriter. Sammy shows Manheim how he
gets ahead by improvising the beginning of a screen treatment for a South Seas movie.

In a flashback, Manheim learns how he also butters up studio heads by doing political jobs for them.

Sammy's next stage is more ominous. He lures Blumberg to Hollywood, then treats him shamefully once again. When Manheim confronts him, Sammy seems like a gangster, and he dismisses Manheim's appeal to Jewish solidarity with contempt.

Sammy wants to be among Hollywood's highest-paid writers. To get to the top, he must write a successful play, so Sammy does just that. Manheim realizes that the play is an artful pilfering of *The Front Page* (a hit play by Ben Hecht and Charles MacArthur). As a playwright, Sammy is more authoritative and seems to show, as he manipulates people, broader cultural horizons than before.

Sammy's next stage takes place as screenwriters try to organize a union. Sammy aligns himself with the highest-paid writers, a group that double-crosses the lower-paid writers and breaks the union. Both Blumberg and Manheim lose their jobs. Sammy in turn double-crosses one of the double-crossers and becomes a producer.

Manheim retreats to New York, but when Sammy calls, Manheim returns to Hollywood to discover the end of Sammy's story. Sammy takes over as head of World-Wide Pictures by elbowing out Sidney Fineman, an illustrious but fading film pioneer. All he needs is the approval of Harrington, the moneyed chairman of the board. At a lavish party given at his new mansion, Sammy gets Harrington's blessing, but he becomes obsessed with Harrington's daughter, the aristocratic Laurette. They are married. Within hours after the wedding, Laurette is unfaithful and lets him know she will be unfaithful in the future. Sammy cannot get rid of her, for her father owns his company. Sammy is trapped, yet he rallies and faces his unhappy future. Manheim thinks that justice has been done: Sammy's life will be eaten away as by a disease.

The Characters

In *What Makes Sammy Run?* Schulberg appears to have invented a new stock character: Sammy Glick. Perhaps growing up in poverty in a New York City ghetto has made him a man without a conscience: totally self-centered, young, pushy, ruthless, conniving, smart, immoral, possessed of extraordinary energy, and determined to succeed. He is incapable of friendship or love; he uses men to further his career, and he uses women and discards them. What he lacks in ability (he can only feed on other's ideas), he makes up in a kind of secondary creativity. He can take someone else's stories, elaborate upon them, and sell them.

The novel's other character's are also stock characters, but more familiar kinds. The narrator of the novel, Al Manheim, is Sammy's foil. He is intelligent, literate, and moral, a man who believes in social and family ties. The reader knows he is reliable, for he was educated at Wesleyan and is a son of a rabbi from a small New England town. He thus combines traditional Jewish moral authority with the New England virtues of honesty and plain-speaking. Like most readers, he hates what Sammy does, but his hatred alternates with fascination.

Almost all of the other characters are also American Jews. Although Julian Blumberg is a talented writer, he is woefully unassertive. He is a good man; he has a good wife. He exists to be duped, used, and discarded by the likes of Sammy. Sidney Fineman is another such character. Although he once made memorable films, he is uneasy with the present emphasis on money over art—an easy prey to Sammy's wiles.

Kit Sargent, who is probably not Jewish, is talented, witty, and wise, and she possesses a subtle beauty very different from that of the usual Hollywood starlet. She shares Manheim's function: They form a chorus to point out Sammy's evil deeds and to direct the reader's reactions. Their slowly developing friendship and love underlines Sammy's heartlessness. In contrast, Laurette Harrington represents Sammy's ultimate dream: elegance, money, sex, and class. Of the other women in the novel, Billie Rand is the most notable, the loose woman with a heart of gold.

Schulberg develops these characters economically, mainly though smart and funny dialogue. Their persons and actions are described only briefly, except for Sammy's aging face and his wardrobe. Schulberg focuses his symbolism on Sammy. His wonderful, fashionable shoes call attention to his running, an action that the title and the early chapters emphasize. Sammy's force is communicated in metaphors drawn from machines, mainly automobiles, though he also resembles a little animal such as a ferret or a rabbit.

Though each of the novel's stock characters plays a role in presenting Sammy and in asking the title's question, some of them are more fully developed. Billie's friendliness and her distaste for Sammy are memorable. Kit and Manheim are complex enough to engage a reader's attention, and Schulberg has created Sammy himself with enough attention to his childhood years and with enough real magnetism (and even charm) to make some readers feel at times a kind of affection for him.

Themes and Meanings

Many of the novel's values are the commonplace ones associated with Manheim and Kit: friendship, honesty, fidelity, love and wholesome sex, social responsibility. Schulberg adds praise of union activities (the writers' guild is a good thing) and eloquently extols the dignity and joy of good work in the film industry.

Because films can be good, it is important to try to understand those people in the industry who misuse their authority. Manheim and Kit ask over and over again what it is that makes Sammy run. What makes people like Sammy do what they do, without any regard for other human beings? Schulberg himself, in a 1952 introduction, advances the theory that Sammy is typical of second-generation immigrant children, driven to succeed in a country to which their parents could not adapt. In the novel itself, Kit uses popular psychology to generalize that Sammy simply expresses his anarchic id, unfettered by the ego and superego that restrain the rest of us.

The novel itself provides another psychological explanation when Manheim unearths the facts of Sammy's childhood. His betrayal of the screenwriters' guild can be explained by his father's losing his job because he was loyal to the union. Sammy's ruthlessness is a reaction to his brother's virtue; his contempt for women stems from his ugly introduction to sex. Sammy feels no bond with his fellow Jews because of the anti-Semitic violence he suffered as a child. His family's dire poverty causes him to pursue money at all cost. To make money, to escape from the ghetto—these motivations make Sammy understandable.

Schulberg, through Manheim, offers another answer as well, an answer that becomes an underlying theme. In the novel's concluding sentences (and in the ending of his introduction), Schulberg emphasizes that Sammy's world mirrors American society as a whole. In its immoral pursuit of wealth, its push and hurry, and its selfishness and corruption, the United States is propelled by a profit-driven capitalism in which only the Sammys can succeed. Sammy's life is thus an update, parody, and denial of the career of that great American success, Horatio Alger.

Critical Context

Upon publication, *What Makes Sammy Run?* was an immediate though controversial success, much like Sammy himself. Though Schulberg presents a great range of Jewish characters, from Sammy to the saintly Blumberg, *What Makes Sammy Run?* was called anti-Semitic by many.

The novel grew out of Schulberg's political convictions and his experience growing up in Hollywood and later working as a screenwriter himself. His fable dramatized many of the social and political issues of his day, giving Sammy's story a politically left-of-center reading that was not so strident as to offend many readers. In addition, readers were both fascinated and repelled by its central character and by the Hollywood background: the infighting, intrigues, and sexual escapades of that city's glamorous people. The book raises serious issues as well. Its treatment of sex was frank for its day. It deals sympathetically and openly with the problems that immigrants experienced in adjusting to American life.

This was Schulberg's first novel. He went on to write other successful works that show many of the same concerns. His novel *The Harder They Fall* (1947) was about corruption in professional boxing. His story and screenplay for *On the Waterfront*, which dramatized corruption at the docks, won an Academy Award in 1954. His 1950 novel *The Disenchanted* drew upon the life of his acquaintance F. Scott Fitzgerald, a man who could be seen as defeated by Hollywood, a clear contrast to the successful Sammy Glick.

Echoes of Fitzgerald's *The Great Gatsby* (1925) are heard in some descriptions of Sammy Glick. The greatest stylistic emphasis on *What Makes Sammy Run?* may be the slapstick, smart-talking comedies that Hollywood was turning out during Schulberg's early years as a screenwriter.

Bibliography

Hartung, Philip T. Review in *Commonweal*, June 6, 1941, 163. A typical contemporary reaction to the novel's indecency and immorality: Hartung remarks that some communities may ban it; that the novel seems anti-Semitic; and that Hollywood insiders say it is accurate.

Schulberg, Budd. Introduction to *What Makes Sammy Run?* New York: Random

House, 1952. The Modern Library edition. The author makes revealing comments about his novel's genesis and themes.

_____. *Moving Pictures: Memories of a Hollywood Prince.* New York: Stein and Day, 1981. Schulberg describes growing up in Hollywood.

Winchell, Mark Royden. "Fantasy Seen: Hollywood Fiction Since West." In *Los Angeles in Fiction: A Collection of Original Essays*, edited by David Fine. Albuquerque: University of New Mexico Press, 1984. A good discussion of authors who created the negative antimyth of Hollywood. Schulberg's novel is compared unfavorably to Fitzgerald's *The Last Tycoon* (1941). The fictional Fineman is based on the real Irving Thalberg.

George Soule

WHAT'S BRED IN THE BONE

Author: Robertson Davies (1913-1995)
Type of plot: Bildungsroman
Time of plot: The 1910's to the 1980's
Locale: Blairlogie, Ontario; Oxford University; and Lower Bavaria
First published: 1985

> *Principal characters:*
> FRANCIS CORNISH, a spy, art expert, artist, and reclusive art collector
> ZADOK HOYLE, an undertaker and bootlegger
> ISMAY GLASSON, Francis's cousin and, briefly, unfaithful wife
> MARY-BENEDETTA (MARY-BEN) MCRORY, Francis's aunt
> TANCRED SARACENI, an art restorer
> THE LESSER ZADKIEL, the angel of biography
> THE DAIMON MAIMAS, Francis's personal demon
> RUTH NIBSMITH, Francis's fellow spy and true love

The Novel

The plot of *What's Bred in the Bone* is set in motion by the confession of a frustrated biographer, Simon Darcourt, that he is unable to get at the truth of the life of Francis Cornish. What follows is a biography as no human chronicler could ever tell it, presented by the Lesser Zadkiel, the angel of biography, and the Daimon Maimas, whose function lies somewhere between being Francis's guardian angel and his indwelling spirit.

Darcourt lays out the central mystery of the novel when he reveals his concern that Francis may have faked some pictures that have become quite famous as having been painted by the old masters. Arthur, a conservative banker, hovers on the verge of canceling the biography altogether, while Darcourt frets that the work may be unwritable due to lack of evidence.

Davies follows his belief (made clear in his earlier novels) that childhood holds the keys to a life. In the case of Francis Cornish, much of his future is shaped by events that take place well prior to his conception. His mother, Mary-Jacobin (or Mary-Jim) McRory, becomes pregnant by a temporary staff worker at a swank hotel during her London debutante season. Frantic, the family arranges a marriage of convenience to Major Francis Cornish, a rather stiff, impoverished, but ambitious suitor. Further, the women of the family try, unsuccessfully, to induce an abortion. Their efforts only succeed in producing some monstrous birth defects in the child, subsequently known as Francis I. Officially said to be dead in early childhood, he is actually kept in an upper-story room and known to the malicious townspeople as the Looner. Francis eventually becomes aware of his brother's existence through his association with the local undertaker and McRory bootlegger Zadok Hoyle, who turns out to be the Looner's biological father.

Francis, a solitary child by nature, is further isolated by his family's wealth in working class Blairlogie. He turns to art, aided by three sources: his great aunt Mary-Ben's collection of art reprints, a learn-to-draw book by Harry Furniss, and his intimacy with the human body through his association with Zadok. He continues his studies in art at the University of Toronto and Oxford University. There, three fateful meetings take place. He encounters, and later marries, his cousin, the faithless Ismay Glasson, who ultimately deserts him for a quixotic leftist and a disastrous stint in the Spanish Civil War. He also makes the acquaintance of Tancred Saraceni, master art restorer, smuggler, and secret anti-Nazi, with whom he will work during the war years and after. Finally, he is recruited (largely through his father's intelligence work) by "Uncle" Jack Copplestone, who becomes his spymaster.

When, after Oxford, Francis goes to Schloss Düsterstein, he serves two masters: Saraceni, who is restoring old paintings and smuggling as many out of Nazi hands as he can, and British Intelligence, for which he counts the number of railway cars bearing their human cargo to the nearby concentration camp. He succeeds at both endeavors, owing to his talents for art and secrecy. In Bavaria, he also meets his one true love, Ruth Nibsmith, who turns out also to be a spy for British Intelligence and who is eventually killed in the bombing of London. While with Saraceni, he also achieves his two greatest achievements: the exposure of an alleged Old Master as a forgery in very public circumstances, and his two mature paintings in the Old Master style. One is a portrait of F. X. Bouchard (the dwarf tailor of Blairlogie, who is driven to suicide by the cruelty of the locals) as a court jester, while the other, "The Marriage at Cana," draws on everyone and everything that has been important to his life. These works, while acclaimed, are both his apotheosis and his retirement, since to produce any more would risk public disclosure.

In his final three decades, Francis becomes a recluse, a miser, and a hoarder, rather than a collector, of art. His one relationship, with the would-be art impresario Aylwin Ross, has homosexual, although probably unconsummated, overtones. That friendship ends disastrously when Francis, sensing he is being used, refuses to rescue Ross from a grandiose plan gone awry and the younger man commits suicide.

His last years are telescoped into a very few pages, for the focus of the novel is on how a young man develops into a true artist, however briefly. The novel then pulls back away from the death of Francis, to a final discussion between the two minor immortals, and then to a conversation Arthur has with Maria in which he decides to authorize Darcourt's still-problematic biography.

The Characters

One could reasonably argue that there is only one character in *What's Bred in the Bone*: Francis Cornish himself. Indeed, Francis is the only character whose presentation is rounded and complex. Others, Zadok Hoyle or Tancred Saraceni, for example, may occupy the stage long enough to achieve a degree of complexity, but in general, the personages of the novel flit across the story only briefly, leaving a single imprint. Francis, on the other hand, is as fully achieved as a novelist can make a man—tender, tough-minded, generous, stingy, gullible, devious, wide-eyed, cynical, creative, critical, emotionally stunted, and open-hearted in various degrees and at various times. Although Francis is difficult for other people in the novel to read, he is a richly complex psyche for those, the two immortals and the reader, capable of looking deeply into him. Such an approach makes sense in a novel whose form is overtly that of a biography. As in actual biographies, secondary characters come in for comparatively scant development, while the main figure occupies virtually every paragraph.

The characters of the novel, aside from Francis, function as plot devices, that is, as comparatively static, even symbolic figures against which the main character can react and develop. In keeping with the author's symbolic imagination and his interest in the psychology theories of C. G. Jung, many of the characters are archetypal figures, psychological types illustrative of the various enabling or crippling forces the one complete mind—Francis himself—in the novel might encounter. Ismay Glasson, though the protagonist would cast her as Guinevere, is the false heroine, the temptress and betrayer. Similarly, Saraceni, accused by some of having the power of the evil eye, represents the magus figure, the wizard who acts as father and mentor, to the young artist. It may be true that he shares that role, or inherits it, from Zadok Hoyle, whose introductory anatomy lessons are accompanied by moral lessons and the smell of embalming fluid. Aunt Mary-Ben, the maimed spinster, is the crone who sets Francis on his path. As in traditional romance, the true love-interest, Ruth Nibsmith, at first appears as the quiet, not inevitably attractive woman—not quite the loathely lady subsequently revealed as the princess, but certainly a variant on that paradigm. Each character fulfills a symbolic role that corresponds to functions out of the quest romance from the medieval literature Francis loves, as well as being Jungian psychological archetypes.

At the same time, all these characters behave in perfectly straightforward modern fashion, so that they make sense for the reader who interprets literally, the reader for whom, in Ezra Pound's phrase, "a hawk is simply a hawk." The combination of plausible, realistic behavior and archetypal significance on the part of the characters is a standard Davies touch.

Themes and Meanings

The novel's chief theme is the meaning of life, or more precisely, the meaning of a life. The outward manifestations of the life of Francis Cornish are very quiet indeed. His main accomplishments scarcely register on the public record, and certainly not as attributable to him. The nature of his clandestine activities, whether espionage or art faking, do not lend themselves to public recognition. At the same time, his accomplishments are great, in their way. "The Marriage at Cana" finds acclaim as a masterpiece. Similarly, his spying, in its small way, assists a winning war effort. Finally, his art collection and philanthropy provide the cornerstones for a national gallery. Yet this greatness lacks the usual measures of success or happiness: friendships, family, progeny, recognition. Davies suggests that Francis is no less great for all that.

A major theme explored here is the influence of early factors in shaping a life. The proverb that provides the title, "What's bred in the bone will not out of the flesh," also provides an issue Davies wants to explore. He therefore devotes disproportionate space to Francis's youthful experiences, scarcely any to his final years.

The novel also explores what it means to be a Canadian in the twentieth century. Francis is a child during World War I, an adult during World War II. Throughout the period, Canada remained a minion of Great Britain. Only in the postwar era, during the time of Francis's art collecting and philanthropy, did Canada begin to come into its own as a country. His life, then, in all its missteps and successes, mirrors the modern life of his own country.

Finally, Davies asks questions about art and fashion. In particular, he wonders why one must work in the mode of one's own time. Francis proves to be the greatest Old Master of his century. Yet he lives in the age of cubism and abstract expressionism, and to work in the style of another age will be seen as derivative. When Davies has his characters assert that modern painting cannot fully articulate the subtleties of life, he clearly is speaking also of modern fiction, which he feels can never approach the fullness of Charles Dickens, Henry Fielding, or Jane Austen.

Critical Context

This novel constitutes the second part of the loosely connected Cornish Trilogy, Davies's third trilogy (after the Salterton and Deptford trilogies). While Darcourt and Maria play considerably greater roles in the opening novel, *The Rebel Angels* (1981), the reader needs no knowledge of that earlier work to understand this one, nor does the third, *The Lyre of Orpheus* (1988), rely on the second. As with his earlier trilogies, this one revolves around a loosely constituted set of characters, and around a much tighter set of themes and concerns.

As with all his work, the issue of Canadian identity occupies a good deal of space, as do problems of artistic temperament and mode. These questions are to a large extent autobiographical. Like his main character, Davies moved between provincial Ontario and England, where he attended Oxford and worked as assistant to Sir Tyrone Guthrie at London's Old Vic theatre. Unlike Francis, Davies made his reputation by returning to Canada, where he was editor of the Peterborough Examiner newspaper for twenty years, the first Master of Massey College of the University of Toronto, and an important playwright while he emerged as one of Canada's greatest novelists. Like Francis, however, his artistic inclinations were not at all those of his moment. His novels tend toward the size and scope of those of the Victorian masters of the form; indeed, it is not extravagant to call his novels Dickensian, minus the sentimentalism, which Davies despised. While metafictional elements creep into this novel through the introduction of Zadkiel and Maimas, they also function to justify a nineteenth century-style intrusive omniscience that contemporary novelists typically shy away from or use ironically.

What's Bred in the Bone, then, presents an interesting mix of traditional and modern elements. Traditional romance, Victorian narration, Jungian psychology, tarot and astrology, social analysis, and metafiction swirl together in a brew that proved highly popular with the reading public and the critical establishment.

Bibliography

Bradham, Jo Allen. "Affirming the Artistic Past: The Witness of *What's Bred in the Bone*." *Critique: Studies in Contemporary Fiction* 32 (Fall, 1990): 27-38. A study of the artistic and aesthetic preoccupations of the novel.

Cude, Wilfred. "Robertson Davies and the Not-So-Comic Realities of Art Fraud." *The Antigonish Review* 80 (Winter, 1990): 67-78. Examination of issues of art fraud raised by the novel.

Diamond-Nigh, Lynne. *Robertson Davies: Life, Work, and Criticism*. Toronto: York Press, 1997. Brief biography and critical overview.

Dopp, Jamie. "Metanarrative as Inoculation in *What's Bred in the Bone*." *English Studies in Canada* 21 (March, 1995): 77-94. A critique of the novel's conservatism, which the author says is hidden behind the work's apparent metafictional tendencies.

Grant, Judith Skelton. *Robertson Davies: Man of Myth*. Toronto: Penguin, 1994. The first full-length biography of Davies. Includes backgrounds and critically useful information on the novel.

Spettigue, D. O. "Keeping the Good Wine Until Now." *Queen's Quarterly* 93 (Spring, 1986): 123-124. A review of the novel and an overview of Davies's fiction to date.

Thomas C. Foster

WHEAT THAT SPRINGETH GREEN

Author: J. F. Powers (1917-   )
Type of plot: Philosophical realism
Time of plot: The 1940's to the 1980's
Locale: The American Midwest
First published: 1988

> *Principal characters:*
>> FATHER JOE HACKETT, a Roman Catholic priest who struggles to find a spiritual life within the confines of the church
>> FATHER WILLIAM STOCK, a money-oriented priest who is pastor of St. Francis and Clare's, the church that the young Joe Hackett attends
>> FATHER BILL SCHMIDT, a curate at Joe Hackett's church who moderates his early radicalism and becomes a hardworking parish priest
>> FATHER LEFTY BEEMAN, a priest who has trouble attending to the business and pastoral affairs of a parish
>> MONSIGNOR TOOHEY, a brusque administrator of the archdiocese who is the boyhood and clerical enemy of Joe Hackett

The Novel

Wheat That Springeth Green traces the spiritual development of a Roman Catholic priest, Father Joe Hackett, from an adolescent display of the outward manifestations of saintliness at the seminary, through a middle period in which he sinks deeper into the ways of the world, to a final and sudden transformation in which he achieves a true and unassuming spirituality.

The novel is divided into three sections. The first section covers the main character's youth, his time in the seminary, and his early years as a curate in a parish. The early years of Joe Hackett are ordinary, with little to suggest any deep yearning for a religious life. He says that he plans to be either "a businessman or a priest." He is the only child of parents who own a local coal company, so business is a natural career for him. He also seems to be attracted to the life of a priest, however, since it appeals to his idealism and desire to help the poor. His youthful days end with a similar division in his career choices; he experiences a sexual initiation but then confesses that sin. Joe will not overcome this division between the body and the soul until the end of the novel.

At the seminary, Joe has a yearning for a fuller spiritual life, in contrast to both the majority of students and the faculty. This desire, however, is more a matter of pride than holiness. Joe seems to equate spirituality with wearing a hair shirt; he wears the hair shirt even after the rector has asked him not to. As a result, he becomes isolated and is in conflict with nearly everyone in the seminary. Ironically, when Joe becomes a priest in a parish, he finds that the pastor, Father Van Slagg, spends all of his time in the church pursuing the spiritual life that Joe has desired so fervently. As a result, Joe is forced to deal with the everyday events of the parish; he has no time for prayer or contemplation. He then spends five years at Archdiocesan Charities working as an administrator. He has more time for prayer but little desire to engage in contemplation. He moves further from a spiritual life with each office he holds.

In the next section, Joe is a pastor of his boyhood parish, St. Francis and Clare's, and he has abandoned all desires for a fuller spiritual life. He drinks and eats too much. He is portrayed as watching baseball on television with a drink in his hand, and he is never seen praying in the church. He is, instead, engaged in parish projects such as building a rectory or searching for the proper bed to purchase for his new assistant priest. When that assistant, Bill Schmidt, takes up his position, he is contrasted with Joe Hackett; Bill has some of the same spiritual pretensions that Joe had in his younger days. When the young curate and his friends discuss problems in the church, Joe takes the conservative position he scorned at the seminary. Bill and his friends make Joe uncomfortable; this helps to prod him out of the passivity and comfort into which he has fallen. There are other assaults on his role as a priest; he gets telephone calls from an unidentified parishioner calling his saintliness into question. This unidentified voice is providential, since it challenges Joe to alter his worldly life and stirs him from his spiritual sloth.

A deeper conflict develops in Joe's parish when the archbishop of the diocese sends out a high monetary assessment to all parishes. Joe has prided himself on not turning the pulpit into a money-making operation as his former pastor, Father Stock, did. He decides not to appeal to his parishioners but to badger delinquent parishioners to pay their share. The search for the necessary funds exhausts both Joe and Bill, but his conflict is providentially resolved when Father Stock dies and leaves Joe a legacy of ten thousand dollars. Joe uses the legacy to meet the assessment of the archbishop. It also enables him to spare his parishioners. Joe's determination not to turn the church into an institution that is more concerned with money than the Gospel suggests that Joe still has a desire for a fuller spiritual life. The title of the novel is from a song that describes the emergence of green wheat after it has been buried for many days in the dark earth; Joe Hackett is about to emerge from his spiritual slumber.

A change in Joe comes about in the last section of the book. He takes a vacation and visits a religious house of the Blue Friars, where he refuses both food and liquor, a clear indication that he is changing his life. He spends the rest of his vacation working at a Catholic Worker house for derelicts in Montreal, a pastoral activity that Joe never considered in his role as a parish priest and pastor. In the last episode of the book, there is a surprise party for Joe, and it is revealed that he is leaving the parish to become a Catholic Worker. He is abandoning his life of ease and his obsession with material things. He discovers a true spiritual life as he ends his life of ease and accepts the "cross" that is the lot of those who follow Christ.

The Characters

Joe Hackett is the protagonist of the novel; the point of view is limited omniscient, and everything is filtered through his consciousness. He is a man and a priest with many faults. His early attempts at spirituality come more from pride than love of God. He wears a hair shirt to show his saintliness, but it is merely an outward sign. He is closer to the Pharisees of the New Testament than to Christ. He soon discovers that he has no time to develop his spiritual side; he must spend all of his time attending to the business of the parish. When he becomes a pastor, all spiritual thoughts seem to vanish. His life as a pastor is marked by visits to the liquor store and by watching television with a drink, and his pride has been replaced by an acceptance of worldly things. His one heroic moment is ironically linked to the world; he prevents a robbery at his local liquor store. There is, however, a yearning in Joe for a fuller and truly spiritual life, which he finds at the end of the novel.

Bill Schmidt is Joe's curate, and he begins as a typical young priest who wishes to overturn all the rules and practices of the church. His rebellion is a mirror image of the earlier stance of Joe, and he helps Joe to see himself more fully. In addition, Bill acts as a goad to challenge Joe's life of ease. Bill's friendship with a dropout from the seminary creates conflict between him and Joe, but Bill gradually changes as he sees the irresponsibility of his earlier views, and he begins to work selflessly in the parish. In a sense, he is acting like the true pastor of the church, as the unidentified caller keeps reminding Joe.

Father Felix is a monk who comes to St. Francis and Clare's every Sunday to say Mass. He loves the life of the monastery. In contrast to Joe, he has little need for material things. He also is not as conservative as Joe is in church matters, as he displays some sympathy for Bill and his friends, especially their anger at the stress the church places on money and business matters. He is used as an ironic foil to Joe, although he is comically represented in the abstruse sermons he delivers, which are filled with allusions to the medieval world and seem to produce unexpected results.

Father Lefty Beeman is another comic character. He is an incompetent priest who has twice been appointed as a pastor and has twice failed. He is interested in the politics of the church, although he always seems to be wrong about new developments and appointments. He is, perhaps, Joe's closest friend, and he repeatedly joins him for drinks. At the end of the novel, he is given another chance at becoming a pastor as he takes over St. Francis and Clare's.

Father William Stock is the antagonist in the novel. He spends all of his time raising funds for the church. Every sermon is a demand for money, and he is called "Dollar Bill" by his exasperated parishioners. He changes at the end of his life, however, sending Joe a note admitting his guilt and giving him a legacy to right the wrong.

Monsignor Toohey is an amusing character who manages to enrage everyone in the novel with his irritating style as a diocesan administrator. He is a boyhood enemy of Joe Hackett who continues to plague him in the priesthood.

Themes and Meanings

Wheat That Springeth Green has many themes. The first deals with the dual roles of a Catholic priest. A priest is supposed to spend his life in prayer and contemplation in order to be brought closer to God. Yet he also has to involve himself in fund-raising, building, supervising a school, and seeing to the administration of a parish if the church is to be sustained. Paradoxically, it is harder for a man who has supposedly dedicated his life to God to find time to speak with God; a priest has to serve both God and Mammon. Neither Father Van Slagg's life of prayer nor Father Stock's worldliness resolves the dilemma. Joe Hackett does not seem able to find a way out of this dilemma, and his interaction with people inside and outside the church is deficient in spirituality. It is only when Joe truly gives himself to others by working at a Catholic Workers home for derelicts that he discovers a spiritual role within the world. He is then called on to make sacrifices and give up his ease and desire for the things of the world.

Powers also examines the contrast between true and false spirituality. False spirituality is portrayed as relying on outward signs such as the hair shirt. It calls attention to the person performing self-conscious rites and isolates a person from others. Powers shows these practices as pretentious and unfulfilling. True spirituality consists of unassuming deeds rather than public displays of sanctity. When Joe accepts the "cross" at the end of the novel, he does so in a quiet and selfless manner. A true spiritual life seems to be defined as not merely removing oneself from the world but in giving oneself to those in need within the world. When Joe is ministering to derelicts in Montreal, he is on the true path. He is told to "keep it up," a sure indication that he has finally found his true vocation.

Finally, Powers explores the Roman Catholic Church as a historical institution. He shows the problems and difficulties the church has in adapting to challenges by young priests for changes and the continuing need for expanding facilities in the burgeoning suburbs. Powers documents the problems some priests have with alcohol in this novel and in his earlier fiction. Joe Hackett makes so many visits to the liquor store that it becomes an ironic motif in itself. The structure of the novel suggests that there is a built-in division that all parish priests must face. As secular priests, their mission is to be among the people they serve. Yet how can they be within the world and not surrender to it? *Wheat That Springeth Green* acknowledges this problem and suggests that it cannot be successfully resolved by abandoning parish work. Priests must live a life dedicated to helping those in need and rejecting the comforts and snares of the world. That life of caring necessarily involves living simply as a priest instead of as a businessman or administrator.

Critical Context

Wheat That Springeth Green is J. F. Powers's second novel, and it continues his investigation of the life of the American priest. The earlier collections of short stories, *Prince of Darkness and Other Stories* (1947) and *The Presence of Grace* (1956), dealt with the problems of the Catholic priesthood. In stories such as "The Valiant Woman," Powers suggests that salvation is an outgrowth of daily annoyances and problems. A life of calm and ease is not, to Powers, a Christian life; the worldly priest at the end of "The Prince of Darkness" is given a letter informing him that Christ gives people "not peace but a sword." For Powers, the enemy is not Satan but the spiritual sloth that a life of ease creates. The fuller portrait of an American priest in *Morte d'Urban* (1962) is very similar to that in *Wheat That Springeth Green*. Both characters are captured by the wiles of the world but reverse their course suddenly at the end of the novel. Father Urban becomes the saintly leader of his community of priests, and Joe Hackett joins the Catholic Workers. Powers's vision is essentially comic both in its representation of the absurdities that come with the priestly life and with his optimistic resolution of the spiritual struggle of those priests. Divine providence is still there to redirect his wayward priests who have lost their way on the path to Christ.

Bibliography
The Atlantic. Review of *Wheat That Springeth Green*, by J. F. Powers. 262 (January, 1988): 15. A brief, unsigned review of the novel that stresses Powers's elegant writing and humor.
Clark, Walter H., Jr. "A Richter Scale Can Be Handy." *Commonweal* 115 (November 4, 1988): 592-594. Includes a discussion of the theological implications of the novel. Clark sees the spiritual change within Joe, and he credits Bill Schmidt with helping to bring about that change.
Iannone, Carol. "The Second Coming of J. F. Powers." *Commentary* 87, no. 1 (1989): 62-64. This essay presents a brief overview of Powers's work and a fuller discussion of *Wheat That Springeth Green*. Iannone criticizes what she sees as the sudden and unconvincing ending of the novel.
Long, J. V. "Clerical Character(s): Rereading J. F. Powers." *Commonweal* 125 (May 8, 1998): 11-13. This article first presents an overview of the Catholic themes in Powers's writing and then offers character analyses of Father Urban Roche in *Morte D'Urban* and Father Joe Hackett in *Wheat That Springeth Green*. An appreciative assessment of a writer whose "work reminds us that grace is never as remote as the devil would have us believe."
Moynihan, Julian. "Waiting for God in Inglenook." *The New York Review of Books* (December 8, 1988): 51-52. Moynihan stresses the balance of joy and sorrow in the novel, and he points out the effectiveness of the comic scenes.
Sullivan, W. "J. F. Powers and His Priestly Company." *Sewanee Review* 98 (Fall, 1990): 712-714. Sullivan's essay addresses the curiosity that people have about the lives of priests, an attitude that Powers deals with in his novels. The perception that the lives of priests are similar yet dissimilar to the lives of ordinary people is discussed and the character of Joe Hackett is examined in the light of this perception.

James Sullivan

WHITE BUTTERFLY

Author: Walter Mosley (1952-   )
Type of plot: Detective and mystery
Time of plot: 1956
Locale: Los Angeles, California
First published: 1992

> *Principal characters:*
> EZEKIEL "EASY" RAWLINS, a clandestine property owner and part-time
>   detective
> REGINA RAWLINS, Easy's wife, a nurse who is troubled by Easy's
>   apparently ill-gotten wealth
> EDNA, the Rawlins' infant daughter
> JESUS, Easy's adopted son, a Mexican American rescued by Easy in an
>   earlier novel
> RAYMOND "MOUSE" ALEXANDER, Easy's best but most dangerous
>   friend
> QUINTEN NAYLOR, the black policeman who originally tries to get Easy
>   involved with the investigation
> MOFASS, the front man for Easy's business operations
> ROBIN GARNETT, the first white victim in the series of murders Easy is
>   asked to investigate

The Novel

White Butterfly takes place in 1956. Ezekiel "Easy" Rawlins, the hero of Walter Mosley's previous two detective novels, is now married to a beautiful black nurse named Regina. Easy and Regina are rearing two children, their infant daughter, Edna, and Jesus, a young Mexican American boy rescued by Easy in an earlier adventure. This life is not idyllic, however. Easy has not told Regina about his secret business holdings or the detective work he does on the side for friends and the police. There are also other instances of miscommunication between the two that cloud the future of their marriage.

The situation worsens when Easy is approached first by black policeman Quinten Naylor and then by a slew of high city officials for help in tracing a serial murderer loose in Watts. This final burst of attention is brought about by the first white victim, Robin Garnett. Up until this time, the victims had been black prostitutes and exotic dancers. The white victim, however, was a college student from a respectable family. Like the other victims, her body was partly burned and mutilated. Easy resents the sudden concern of the white officials, apathetic when the victims were black. He is nevertheless coerced into helping when the police threaten to pin the crimes on Easy's best friend, Mouse.

Easy goes to work, frequenting bars and asking questions that lead him to a suspect and to a disturbing revelation. The white coed led a double life, coming down to Watts to work as a stripper/prostitute known as "the White Butterfly." When Easy reports this to the police, he is told to abandon this line of inquiry, partly because the girl's father is a former district attorney. Curiosity gets the better of Easy, and he goes to speak to the girl's mother, who is understandably upset. The police chastise Easy and penalize him by arresting Mouse. Easy talks the police into releasing Mouse, and the two of them track the suspect, a black man, to San Francisco. They locate him just in time to witness his death in a bar fight, one set up by the local police. They also learn that San Francisco has had a chain of similar serial murders about which the black population was never informed. The suspect's death becomes the final step in a scandalous coverup.

Frustrated, Easy returns to Los Angeles, where he learns that Robin Garnett supposedly had a baby. When he attempts to put the girl's parents in touch with the woman keeping the baby, he is arrested for extortion. Easy reveals that Robin was killed by her father, Vernor Garnett, in order to avoid embarrassment over his daughter's conduct. Garnett's connections to law enforcement officials had given him knowledge of the serial murders, and he had tried to pass his daughter's murder off as another in the series.

Amid all this, Easy decides to be more open with Regina, but it is too late. Regina has run off with another man, taking Edna with her. Easy is left heartbroken, turning to the bottle until Mouse and Jesus bring him back from the brink of self-destruction.

A side plot involves Mofass, the man who manages Easy's business holdings. Mofass gets himself into trouble with white developers from whom he received a bribe. Although Easy will not bail Mofass out of trouble, the two work together to get the upper hand over the white businessmen. Although Easy's marriage fails, he is able to solidify his finances and, therefore, his independence.

The Characters

Easy Rawlins is in many ways the typical private investigator of hard-boiled detective fiction. He works essentially for his own ends and is a free agent. He has a strong desire to uncover truth, even if he is the only one who ever possesses it, and to bring about justice, even when it is inconsistent with the law. A healthy dose of compassion, as exhibited by his love for his adopted son, Jesus, makes Easy a particularly well-drawn model of the hard-boiled detective as pioneered by major figures such as Dashiell Hammett's Sam Spade, Raymond Chandler's Phillip Marlowe, and Ross MacDonald's Lew Archer. In short, Easy is a crusader for justice and truth in an unjust and illusory world.

Easy is not flawless. He drinks too much and is susceptible to certain male impulses. Easy is also complex. His character combines cynicism, based on his knowledge of the ways of the world, with idealism, based on his belief in a better world with which his conduct is in accord. Easy's racial identity is also crucial to understanding his character. Whereas other private eyes are alienated philosophically from an unjust world, Easy himself is a member of an oppressed race. Part of the challenge he faces involves dealing with white powerholders from a position of socially imposed inferiority. Easy manages to triumph despite this obstacle, solving mysteries and keeping the authorities off his back. He also struggles to keep an even keel in his personal life.

Mouse represents a different model of accommodation to American racism. Put simply, Mouse is a killer. Easy, too, could kill when he served in the armed forces during World War II, but he has scruples and hesitates to use violence. Mouse has a hair-trigger personality, particularly when he perceives a threat to his manhood. As such, he is adept at dealing with the heavy-handed white developers in *White Butterfly*. In the two previous Easy Rawlins novels, it was Mouse who killed the primary villain, in the nick of time to save Easy. This suggests a complementary relationship between Easy and Mouse. Without Easy, Mouse's violence would be random and ultimately self-destructive; without Mouse, Easy would have been dead well before the events in *White Butterfly* ever took place.

Quinten Naylor represents a third model of accommodation to racial inequality and injustice. Educated and decidedly "East Coast" in his demeanor, Naylor deals with the racial obstacles facing him by achieving a position of authority. Unlike Easy, Naylor has to stay within the law, even when the law is unjust. On the other hand, Naylor is treated as an equal by most of his fellow police detectives and, within certain narrow limits, is able to reduce the severity of police brutality and other injustices suffered disproportionately by African Americans. Naylor works from within the system to make small but significant dents in American racism.

Mofass, Easy's front man, is consumed by greed. His response to racial subordination is to use his wits to accumulate wealth through any means available. Unfortunately, Mofass somehow always manages to outsmart himself, suggesting that greed is ultimately self-destructive.

Regina, Easy's wife, plays a small but important role in the novel. Because of the inner turmoil experienced by Easy as he deals with racial oppression, he finds it difficult to open up to Regina. They miscommunicate in tragic ways and ultimately break up. Although the theme is not overtly elaborated, Easy's marriage to Regina is a hidden casualty of racism, as is the general relationship between black men and women in American literature and life.

Robin and Vernor Garnett are also, in a manner of speaking, victims of racism. Robin is drawn to Watts by the forbidden fruit of black sexuality. Vernor Garnett is driven to murder by the disgrace of interracial relationships even as recently as the 1950's.

Themes and Meanings

White Butterfly is a hard-boiled detective novel that explores important racial themes. The hard-boiled genre features a lean style of language, suspense, fast-paced action, and psychological as well as social realism. As Raymond Chandler pointed out in his essay "The Simple Art of Murder," hard-boiled detective literature differs from the more "civilized" British detective story in its focus on the "mean streets" of America's cities and real motives behind human behavior. Rather than unraveling puzzling crimes (for example, locked door mysteries), hard-boiled writers explore the puzzle of the human heart.

The detective in hard-boiled literature is usually a lonely "knight," full of human flaws yet somehow devoted to truth and justice, so devoted that he or she is willing to risk life and limb for a small payment or no payment at all. Unlike police officers, hard-boiled detectives are not limited by their bureaucratic position or by the law; they do face other limits. They usually end up coping with the world's injustices rather than bringing about complete reform.

Easy Rawlins is just such a loner. Despite his personal flaws, he takes risks and bends rules to make the world a little better. He also has a hunger to know the truth, though he is willing to lie if it serves his purposes. What distinguishes Mosley's work is that the social realism he deals with involves the issue of race. The theme of color in Mosley's title is notable and alludes to Duke Ellington's song "Black Butterfly."

Following such prominent authors as Richard Wright, Ralph Ellison, and Chester Himes, Mosley explores the problems of black identity in a hostile homeland, police brutality (as well as more subtle forms of discrimination), and the depth of black alienation. Perhaps most poignant is his treatment of violence as a theme. Mosley's Easy Rawlins hesitates to use violence except in self-defense. On the other hand, Easy is aided by his friend Mouse's willingness, even eagerness, to use violence. This collaboration between Easy and Mouse speaks directly to the dilemma faced by black Americans as they struggle for the appropriate means to obtain justice.

Mosley's examination of race in America also has a historical dimension. Mosley's first three novels are part of a projected eight-book series chronicling the history of Watts (and the United States) from 1948 to the early 1990's.

Critical Context

White Butterfly is Walter Mosley's third novel, following *Devil in a Blue Dress* (1990) and *A Red Death* (1991). All three books feature Easy Rawlins and Mouse, and all three have been commercially and critically successful. Part of Mosley's success can be attributed to the existence of a ready market for variations within the hard-boiled detective genre.

This genre is associated most often with early pioneers Dashiell Hammett, Raymond Chandler, and Ross MacDonald, but by the time Mosley started writing there were dozens of successful authors working within the genre. In addition, the previously white, male realm of the private investigator had given way to a diverse group, including a number of female detectives as well as an occasional African American, such as Jackson F. Burke's Sam Kelly, Ken Davis's Carver Bascombe, and Ed Lacy's Toussaint Moore.

Mosley has established himself as something more than a detective writer, however. He has used the form of the traditional hard-boiled detective story to explore important racial themes. Mosley has notable predecessors in this respect. Hammett explored the issue of race briefly in his short story "Nightshade" (anthologized in 1944), and Harry Whittingham's 1961 novel *Journey into Violence* explores southern racism in a political context. Mosley's closest precursor is Chester Himes. Himes's first novel, *If He Hollers, Let Him Go*, takes place in Los Angeles and uses a hard-boiled prose style to explore the issues of racial justice and black alienation. Himes's novel ends with the main character, Bob Jones, about to enter the Army in 1943; Mosley's Easy Rawlins starts his tales just after serving in the war.

Bibliography
Geherin, David. *The American Private Eye: The Image in Fiction*. New York: Frederick Ungar, 1985. Geherin examines some of the more prominent fictional private eyes, discussing development and common attributes. Features a chapter on the "compassionate" private eyes, among whom Easy Rawlins would certainly be numbered.
Hitchens, Christopher. "The Tribes of Walter Mosley." *Vanity Fair* 56 (February, 1993): 46-50. Using the favorable comments of newly elected president Bill Clinton as a springboard, this interview features Mosley's assessment of his mixed (black and Jewish) cultural roots.
Hughes, Carl M. *The Negro Novelist: A Discussion of the Writings of American Negro Novelists, 1940-1950*. Freeport, N.Y.: Books for Libraries Press, 1967. Looking at authors such as Ralph Ellison, Chester Himes, and Richard Wright, this book reveals deep-seated themes explored by an earlier generation of pioneering black writers. Despite Mosley's identity as a detective novelist, his work clearly harks back to these themes.
Lomax, Sara M. "Double Agent Easy Rawlins: The Development of a Cultural Detective." *American Visions* 7 (April/May, 1992): 32-34. Provides some details on Mosley's life and career. Also makes a preliminary attempt to fit his work into the tradition of black literature.
Mason, Theodore O., Jr. "Walter Mosley's Easy Rawlins: The Detective and Afro-American Fiction." *Kenyon Review* 14 (Fall, 1992): 173-183. Discusses Mosley's first novel, *Devil in a Blue Dress*, in the light of the African American novelistic tradition. Cites several modern critics as providing a solid foundation for reading Mosley's and other African American detective fiction.
Mosley, Walter. "A Message Louder than a Billion Pleas." *Los Angeles Times*, May 5, 1992, p. B7. In this brief commentary article, Mosley discusses the Rodney King episode and subsequent uprising in Watts. Mosley asks readers to consider the videotape excerpts of King's beating by police in the light of the oral history of black Americans. Mosley's projected series of novels will look specifically at the Watts riots of the 1960's and 1990's.
Puckrein, Gary A. Review of *White Butterfly*. *American Visions* 8 (February/March, 1993): 34. A favorable review of Mosley's novel. Puckrein notes that "cleverly woven throughout the story is a discussion of black male/female relations, a topic that too few black male novelists explore in any depth."
Williams, John. Review of *White Butterfly*. *New Statesman & Society* 6 (September 3, 1993): 41. Criticizes the plot as "functional and little more," but praises the novel

for "a powerful, if not always likeable, new installment in the most impressive series of crime novels since Ross McDonald."

Young, Mary. "Walter Mosely, Detective Fiction and Black Culture." *Journal of Popular Culture* 32 (Summer, 1998): 141. Focuses on the characters of Easy Rawlins and "Mouse" Navrochet. Young argues that Mosley created two heroic characters based on traditional black culture because he wished to adapt the genre of detective novels to continue African American cultural traditions.

Ira Smolensky

WHITE FANG

Author: Jack London (1876-1916)
Type of plot: Allegory
Time of plot: Circa 1900
Locale: The Klondike and San Francisco
First published: 1906

Principal characters:
    BILL, a frontiersman
    HENRY, a frontiersman
    ONE-EYE, an older, experienced wolf, the father of White Fang
    KICHE, a wolf-dog hybrid, the mother of White Fang,
    WHITE FANG, a wolf-dog hybrid
    GRAY BEAVER, a Native American, White Fang's first master
    BEAUTY SMITH, a cook and dishwasher, White Fang's second master
    CHEROKEE, an English bulldog, White Fang's nemesis
    WEEDON SCOTT, a mining engineer, White Fang's third and last master

The Novel

White Fang is told in six parts. In the first, two frontiersmen, Bill and Henry, have a running battle with a wolfpack. In the second, the perspective shifts to the wolves, especially One-Eye and Kiche, whose mating produces White Fang. The perspective shifts for the last time to White Fang himself. The last four parts consist first of White Fang living with his mother in the wild and then his life under three very different human masters.

Jack London uses the omniscient third-person narrator throughout the book. In the first part, Henry and Bill are driving a dogsled containing the corpse of an English lord whose body they are taking back to civilization. They discover that they are being followed by a pack of wolves. A she-wolf lures the sled dogs one at a time outside their camp at night, and the wolves kill and eat them. For some reason, Henry and Bill have only one rifle and three bullets. Bill wastes those bullets in a futile pursuit of the wolves, which kill and eat him. Henry stays alive by keeping a fire going. Finally, another dogsled team traveling in the opposite direction rescues him.

The perspective then changes to the she-wolf. She and the pack search for food while at the same time three males show an interest in her. The first is a large gray wolf who is leader of the pack, the second an old wolf without his right eye, and the third a three-year-old male. The gray wolf and the old wolf, called One-Eye, team up to kill the young one, then the old one attacks the gray wolf from behind and kills him. This gives One-Eye the right to mate with the she-wolf. Eventually, the she-wolf finds a cave and gives birth to a litter of cubs.

The she-wolf tends her young while One-Eye hunts for food. However, she has to hunt herself when a lynx kills One-Eye. Only one male in the litter survives. One day while the she-wolf is hunting, the cub leaves the cave. He blunders into a ptarmigan nest and eats all the young. When the mother ptarmigan returns, the cub has his first battle and retreats. Then he discovers that he cannot walk on water and almost drowns in a nearby stream. After reaching a river bank, the cub encounters a weasel, which would have killed him had not the she-wolf returned. After that first day, the cub regularly ventures outside and gains experience in killing and avoiding being killed.

One day, he and his mother encounter a hunting party of Native Americans. One of the Native Americans, Gray Beaver, recognizes the she-wolf and calls her "Kiche." A wolf-dog hybrid, she had run away a year previously but now was ready to return to domesticity. The cub, named White Fang by his captors, stays with her. Gray Beaver tames White Fang and becomes his master. Gray Beaver sells Kiche to another Native American who takes Kiche away from the village. White Fang is now alone with the humans and the camp dogs.

The next summer, Gray Beaver travels to Fort Yukon to sell furs. He takes White Fang along with him and trades the dog for whiskey. White Fang's new master is Beauty Smith, so called because of the ugliness of his face. He enjoys beating White Fang and keeps him in a pen. Smith makes money on White Fang by having him fight other dogs to the death. The wolf defeats all comers until Smith matches him against an English bulldog named Cherokee. White Fang finally meets a dog who can best him. The bulldog is about to kill White Fang when a stranger stops the fight.

The stranger is Weedon Scott, a mining engineer from California who finds the dogfights appalling. He takes White Fang away from Smith and treats the wolf with kindness. This is a new experience for White Fang, and he responds positively. When Scott returns home to California, he takes White Fang with him. The wolf establishes a place for himself in Scott's home, especially when he kills an escaped convict intent on killing Scott's father. White Fang mates with a sheepdog, and the story ends with the birth of their offspring.

The Characters

London did not have the benefit of twentieth century studies of wolf behavior in nature and of instances in which a wolf has bonded with a human. Instead, he relied on his own imagination and the highly inaccurate conjectures of nineteenth century naturalists. Therefore, the reader can accept only the characters of White Fang and the other wolves on the allegorical level. The human characters function more as types than individuals, especially the three masters of White Fang. His character is the only one that London allows to grow.

White Fang is born in the wild. The best part of the book occurs when he ventures out of the cave and into the wild. White Fang grows up hating other dogs and wolves and regards all creatures in terms of whether they are his prey or he is their prey. Eventually, his last master redeems White Fang by love and domesticates him.

Kiche was born in captivity and escaped into the wild but ultimately returns to her human masters. The high point of her life occurs when the three male wolves fight to the death to determine who will mate with her. Eventually, Kiche becomes indifferent to White Fang, her son, and raises another litter of cubs.

One-Eye got his name because he lost his right eye in a battle years before the events described in the novel. He is intelligent, brave, and dedicated; most important, One-Eye is a survivor. He dies only because he is trying to feed his family.

Cherokee is a highly developed product of civilization. He is a dog bred for one function only, killing other dogs. Only Weedon Scott's intervention stops him from killing White Fang. This serves to demonstrate the ultimate superiority of civilization over nature.

Gray Beaver represents humanity that lives in primitive civilization. He demonstrates his superiority over White Fang by training him to obey humans. Unfortunately, when he encounters an allegedly higher civilization, he degenerates into a drunkard. London's racism, very common among his contemporaries, portrays this as the natural order of things rather than as the corruption of an innocent. The power of the white man, even the worst kind such as Beauty Smith, overwhelms Gray Beaver.

Beauty Smith is a cowardly sadist who takes pleasure in beating White Fang and in watching White Fang kill other dogs. His status in society before acquiring White Fang is the lowly position of cook and dishwasher. He uses White Fang to advance his position in society by appealing to the baser emotions of other men.

Weedon Scott is a civilized person of intelligence and good character. The son of a judge, he is a member of the upper middle class. The dogfight disgusts him, so he takes White Fang away from Smith and treats the wolf with kindness. London clearly implies that when White Fang accepts him as his master, he is moving up in the hierarchy of human beings.

Bill and Henry are almost caricatures. The reader has to question whether they would have survived for long in the wilderness, considering thier poor judgment in taking so few arms and so little ammunition on their trek. Of course, Bill does die as a result of his own stupidity and impulsiveness.

Themes and Meanings

London considered *White Fang* to be the companion piece to his more famous work *The Call of the Wild* (1903). The latter story describes the transformation of a domestic dog into a wild one. The former, on the other hand, shows a wild wolf-dog hybrid becoming a domestic dog, which London considered to be progress. *White Fang* is partly an autobiographical allegory based on London's conversion from teenage hoodlum to married, middle-class writer. White Fang's puppyhood parallels London's childhood. Because he is three-quarters wolf, White Fang is different from the other dogs both in the Native American camp and in civilization. Likewise, London was an outcast because of his illegitimacy. His biological father refused to marry his mother, and he was born out of wedlock. Both White Fang and the young London regarded themselves as surrounded by enemies and reacted with violence and aggression. They both had mothers who became indifferent to them. Kiche raises another litter; London's mother was obsessed with astrology and get-rich-quick schemes.

On another plane, the story is an allegory of humanity's progression from nature to civilization. Love and discipline change a wild wolf into a domestic dog. By implication, such values can also transform society from one that lives by a disguised law of "eat or be eaten" to one founded on humane values.

At the same time, White Fang moves up the hierarchy by killing. Beauty Smith values him for his ability to kill other dogs. Scott's family finally accepts White Fang when he kills an escaped convict who threatens to kill Scott's father. The implication is that the metamorphosis of both the individual and society will require violence at some point.

Critical Context

White Fang, London's fifth novel, and was a best-seller. It is one of his many stories set in the Klondike, where London lived from 1897 to 1898. He went there in search of gold and was part of the last gold rush in North American history.

The years of London's life, 1876 to 1916, were roughly the period in which America changed from a predominantly agricultural nation to an industrial one. London wrote the novel during the administration of Theodore Roosevelt, who rigorously enforced antitrust laws to break up business monopolies such as U.S. Steel and Standard Oil. These monopolies had justified themselves by arguing that competition in business was like competition in nature in which the natural law was, in Herbert Spencer's words, a matter of "survival of the fittest." Spencer was a strong influence on London, who based his view of nature on Spencer's ideas and on his own experience in the Klondike and as a sailor.

At the same time, there was a strong labor and socialist movement in reaction to the poverty of the working people. London wrote essays and gave speeches for the movement. Karl Marx was another strong influence on London, especially in emphasizing the transition of society from capitalism to socialism through violence. However, London's devotion to the labor movement was always superficial; he was more interested in destroying the old society than in building a new one. His attitude was more nihilistic than humanitarian.

Friedrich Nietzsche also influenced London's writing of *White Fang* with the idea of the superman (although in this instance it is a "superdog") and of the worship of power. White Fang is strong enough to defeat almost all dogs in one-to-one combat. He is also intelligent enough to perceive that humans have more power than animals and that whites have more power than Native Americans. Here again, London's racism, which was an embarrassment to his socialist colleagues, shows itself.

Bibliography

Day, A. Grove. *Jack London in the South Seas*. New York: Four Wings Press, 1971. Illustrated account of London's abortive 1907 voyage around the world on his private yacht, the *Snark*. The trip permanently damaged his health.

Hedrick, Joan D. *Solitary Comrade: Jack London and His Work*. Chapel Hill: University of North Carolina Press, 1982. Psychological-sociological analysis of London's writings.

O'Connor, Richard. *Jack London: A Biography.* Boston: Little, Brown, 1964. A good introduction to London's life and works.

Stasz, Clarice. *American Dreamers: Charmian and Jack London.* New York: St. Martin's Press, 1988. A biography of London and his second wife, with more emphasis on Charmian than other biographies.

Watson, Charles N. *The Novels of Jack London: A Reappraisal.* Madison: University of Wisconsin Press, 1983. An overview of London's novels and novellas, with an emphasis on Herman Melville's influence. Watson devotes one chapter exclusively to *White Fang.*

Tom Feller

WHITE NOISE

Author: Don DeLillo (1936-   )
Type of plot: Philosophical realism
Time of plot: The 1980's
Locale: Blacksmith, a fictional college town in the United States
First published: 1985

Principal characters:

JACK GLADNEY, a college professor specializing in studies of Adolf
    Hitler
BABETTE GLADNEY, Jack's neurotic wife
STEFFIE GLADNEY, their nine-year-old daughter, obsessed with health
HEINRICH GLADNEY, Jack's son by a previous marriage, whom Babette
    fears will become a mass murderer
MURRAY JAY SISKIND, Jack's friend, an Elvis Presley specialist
ALPHONSE STOMPANATO, the head of the popular culture department
WILLIE MINK, Babette's drug supplier and seducer

The Novel

At once hilarious and horrifying, Don DeLillo's *White Noise* dramatizes a contemporary American family's attempt to deal with the mundane conflicts of day-to-day life while grappling with the larger philosophical issues of love, death, and the possibility of happiness in an uncertain world. The novel is divided into three sections. All incidents, images, and exchanges among characters in the first section, "Waves and Radiation," culminate thematically in the second section, "The Airborne Toxic Event." The third section, "Dylarama," chronicles not only the direct effects of the "event" but also the indirect but even more profound changes in the way the characters subsequently see themselves and their world.

The novel's first-person narrator is Jack Gladney, a college professor specializing in studies of Adolf Hitler. Many of the other characters are also in some sense observers of contemporary culture: Murray Jay Siskind, an Elvis Presley specialist; Jack's other colleagues in the popular culture department; his son Heinrich, who translates technical information to his father and the reader; and his daughter Steffie, whose obsession with health has made her into an expert in drugs and medical matters. The bulk of the novel is less a sequence of important events than a series of dialogues concerning various interests and obsessions.

Immediately after the opening chapter, with its description of incoming college students—luggage, stereos, tennis rackets, and other equipment in tow—Jack goes home and discusses with his wife Babette what he has just witnessed. In the middle of the discussion, Babette remarks that she can hardly imagine people with such material wealth being concerned with death. The comment seems irrelevant to the subject at hand, and neither she nor Jack pursues it. DeLillo has subtly introduced a theme that will grow larger over the course of the novel, that of death, and how one can live in full knowledge of its inevitability.

The remainder of part 1 follows much the same pattern, with Jack and someone else discussing a phenomenon that at first may seem only mildly interesting (the ominously beautiful sunsets, some strange pills of Babette's that Jack discovers) but that involve associations that acquire greater power through repetition (the environment, conspiracies of one kind or another, and, always, death).

The action begins to accelerate in part 2, in which a train derailment unleashes a noxious drifting cloud. The fact that no one knows much with certainty about the cloud—or if "they" know, they are not telling—adds to Jack's and his family's anxiety. Eventually, they leave their home and join a caravan of refugees fleeing the toxic event zone. Jack is briefly exposed to the cloud. The family finally is quarantined alongside hundreds of others in a large barracks. Nine days later they are allowed to return home.

In part 3, Jack and his family must deal with the physical and emotional effects of the toxic event. For Jack, the most tangible effect is a "nebulous mass" discovered during an X-ray examination. The mass may mean nothing or it may mean, eventually, death. Jack is equally worried about Babette after he finds a cache of Dylar tablets. He learns that the drug is designed to treat a peculiar neurosis, the excessive fear of death. After confronting Babette, Jack also finds that she has been "purchasing" the experimental drug by having sex with the sleazy Willie Mink. Jack confronts Willie, then shoots him, but not fatally.

The novel ends, appropriately, with very little resolved. Mink is in the hospital but apparently thinks he has shot himself. Babette still fears death, as does Jack, and the sunsets are still ominously glorious.

The Characters

One of the principal philosophical conclusions of *White Noise* is that people act less than they are acted upon, as victims of forces beyond their control or knowing. Appropriately, Jack, the central character, does very little in the novel. His one dramatic action is to shoot Willie Mink, but this has no more practical effect on the direction of the novel than the tossing of a pebble has on the course of a river. Jack sees, listens, thinks, and comments, but there is little that he can do. Mostly, he thinks about death and chaos in reference to himself, his family, and ultimately American society.

Babette broadens and intensifies the emotional impact of themes that Jack, early in the novel, considers mostly in the abstract. When it is discovered that the apparently normal Babette has been taking drugs (at the expense of giving herself to the contemptible Willie Mink), for example, Jack realizes that her fears are symptomatic of life in modern America.

Similarly, their nine-year-old daughter Steffie's precocious knowledge of pharmaceuticals and health matters indicates her to be a budding Babette. At some point in the future she will become obsessed with death, if she is not already.

Her half-brother Heinrich serves a similar, although more complex, function. Like Steffie, he is precociously aware of the intricacies of modern technological society, his field of expertise being science and the media. Whereas Steffie is vigilant in protecting herself and her parents against potential harm, Heinrich is fascinated with and more a product of his culture. In one funny and disturbing scene, Heinrich and his father argue for three pages whether it is raining. Heinrich refuses to acknowledge what his senses clearly tell him because the radio weather report said that it would not rain until later in the day.

Murray Jay Siskind is involved in none of the major scenes in the novel, but he provides the reader, through his conversations with Jack, with insights into popular American culture. The scene in which Jack and Murray simultaneously lecture to a class on the lives of Hitler and Elvis, for example, is a comic and thought-provoking masterpiece.

Lecherous, amoral, rodent-like Willie Mink is modern society sunk to its sleazy, wretched low. He serves as a marker of the depths of American culture and morals.

Because contemporary culture is so vividly and convincingly rendered, DeLillo's characters impress the reader with their individual realities. Their most important function, however, is to represent certain thematic positions or reactions to various aspects of modern society. They are less actors than voices in a symposium on life and death in America.

Themes and Meanings

In *White Noise*, the characters themselves announce the themes—death, the nature of reality, government conspiracies, the possibility of happiness in contemporary America—and then analyze them through their thoughts and especially through their conversations throughout the novel. *White Noise* is, therefore, as much a symposium or colloquy as it is a traditional realistic novel.

The various themes and conflicts in the novel can be summed up in one question: Why are modern people so unhappy? No character in the novel suffers from hunger or poverty. The novel begins and ends, in fact, in a context of material comfort and plenitude. The opening scene of parents helping their sons and daughters unload their belongings in preparation for the first days of college makes Jack uneasy and leads Babette to think of death. The last scene takes place in a supermarket with shelves laden with items that the characters certainly have the wherewithal to purchase; because the shelves have recently been rearranged, however, the shoppers are unsettled to the point of neurosis and desperation.

One problem with American life may be that people mistakenly believe that their problems are idiosyncratically modern and American. They try to invent new remedies, such as psychoanalysis, space-age drugs, and self-indulgent material goods, for afflictions that are not new at all. *White Noise* is replete with imagery connecting the present and the past. The black cloud issuing from the train derailment, for example, reminds Jack of a Norwegian death ship. Jack, his family, and the others fleeing the cloud are not, he realizes, much different from refugees of ages past. Jack is not the only one to make such a connection. His son Heinrich laments or enthuses (it is not always possible to tell with Heinrich) that they seem to have been plunged back into the Stone Age. Later, a fellow refugee complains that they have all been quarantined like lepers in the Middle Ages.

Jack and the others concern themselves with death, love, infidelity, the fear of the unknown, and the question of what is knowable. These are problems and issues that have plagued humanity since Adam met Eve. If the problems seem worse today, it is not because the issues have changed—death is death, after all—but because people seem to have convinced themselves that the afflictions of the human heart, body, and spirit can be addressed and assuaged by modern technology.

The characters in *White Noise* are surrounded by things that consume their time, energy, and hope but ultimately do no good. Television and radio bombard them with information that is of no real value. The computers that supposedly have transformed the world cannot save it from regressing to the Stone Age. Babette's Dylar may be a wonder drug, but it does not save her from fear of death. If modern people are more unhappy than their predecessors, it is because disillusionment—with themselves and with the sparkling edifice of modernity—has been added to the age-old infirmities of humanity.

Critical Context

Although once almost a cult figure in contemporary American fiction, by the 1980's Don DeLillo had carved out that most desirable of literary niches for himself, as both a best-selling novelist and an award-winning darling of critics. This position was cemented in 1985 with the publication of *White Noise*, a best-seller and winner of the American Book Award.

DeLillo has built his reputation on a series of novels remarkable for their variety of subject matter within a consistency of theme. *Ratner's Star* (1976) is a science-fiction novel, *The Names* (1982) is a novel of political intrigue, and *Libra* (1988) is a historical novel dramatizing and offering a theory of the assassination of John F. Kennedy. Not all are as funny as *White Noise* often is, but in all of them DeLillo shows himself to be a witty writer who can vividly invoke a cast of colorful characters beset by paranoia and the catastrophes of modern life.

DeLillo's style is distinctive and his themes are consistent, so that one can identify a DeLillo novel after reading only a few paragraphs, despite the variety of subject matter. DeLillo nevertheless does not work apart from and outside literary tradition. His like-minded contemporaries and literary antecedents are more obvious than obscure.

The contemporary writer with whom DeLillo is most obviously aligned is Thomas Pynchon, who, in novels such as *Gravity's Rainbow* (1973), dramatizes humanity's precarious existence in a technological nightmare-world where conspiracy abounds.

Both DeLillo and Pynchon are inheritors of two recent literary movements, the Beat school and the "black humor" movement. The Beat writers—Jack Kerouac and Williams S. Burroughs prominent among the novelists and Allen Ginsberg most famous among the poets—lent their manic voices in the 1950's and 1960's to an outcry against a materialistic, soulless American plutocracy. DeLillo's Jack Gladney would surely share their sentiments. The black humor or absurdist writers—among them Joseph Heller and Eugène Ionesco—offered less a specifically political and American agenda than a philosophical stance toward humanity and its condition: Life is absurd, and in the face of it all one can do, most often, is to laugh hysterically. All of these writers belong to the rich tradition of satirists who look unflinchingly at people and their pretentions, communicating their horror and humor to the reader.

Bibliography
Aaron, Daniel. "How to Read Don DeLillo." *South Atlantic Quarterly* 89 (Spring, 1990): 305-319. Aaron provides a general survey of the salient elements in DeLillo's fiction. He addresses various themes and concerns under such headings as "catastrophe" and "conspiracy." *White Noise* figures prominently in his examples.
Bonca, Cornel. "Don DeLillo's *White Noise*: The Natural of the Species." *College Literature* 23 (June, 1996): 25-44. Bonca examines *White Noise* as one of a few postmodern novels that has the ability to reach students and encourage them to explore the effects of mass media and the idea of death. Bonca describes his experiences teaching the *White Noise* and discusses recent critical work on the novel.
Caton, Lou. "Romanticism and the Postmodern Novel: Three Scenes from DeLillo's *White Noise*." *English Language Notes* 35 (September, 1997): 38-48. Caton examines the novel's depiction of romantic attitudes despite the critical view of the novel as skeptical about an orderly universe. Catton asserts that *White Noise* questions the notion that people have never been confronted with the philosophical crises that they face at the end of the twentieth century.
DeCurtis, Anthony. "'An Outsider in This Society': An Interview with Don DeLillo." *South Atlantic Quarterly* 89 (Spring, 1990): 281-304. Especially important and interesting because DeLillo is generally so reluctant to speak or write about himself. Most of the interview focuses on *Libra*, then recently published. The last several pages, however, largely concern *White Noise*.
Edmunson, Mark. "Not Flat, Not Round, Not There: Don DeLillo's Novel Characters." *Yale Review* 83 (April, 1995): 107-124. Discusses how DeLillo's characters reflect the modern self and challenge Freudian notions. Edmundson analyzes this method in several of DeLillo's books, including *White Noise*.
Goodheart, Eugene. "Some Speculations on Don DeLillo and the Cinematic Real." *South Atlantic Quarterly* 89 (Spring, 1990): 355-368. Goodheart notes that DeLillo characteristically puts the "existence of the self into question." This old theme is made fresh by the use of cinematic techniques that make the characters, even in their own eyes, two-dimensional. *White Noise* is discussed at length.
Keesey, Douglas. *Don DeLillo*. New York: Twayne, 1993. A thorough introductory study of DeLillo that covers DeLillo's major works and includes a chapter devoted to *White Noise*.

King, Noel. "Reading *White Noise*: Floating Remarks." *The Critical Quarterly* 33 (Autumn, 1991): 66-83. King begins with a theoretical discussion of the term "postmodern." He concludes that *White Noise* is at once a "quite traditional novel" and a meditation of the postmodern. The novel shows modern times as an age of "distorted communication and information."

LeClair, Tom. *In the Loop: Don DeLillo and the Systems Novel*. Urbana: University of Illinois Press, 1997. LeClair asserts that DeLillo should be acknowledged as one of America's leading novelists. In this study, LeClair examines eight of DeLillo's novels in detail from the perspective of systems theory.

Lentricchia, Frank, ed. *Introducing Don DeLillo*. Durham, N.C.: Duke University Press, 1991. A collection of critical essays which are a solid overview of DeLillo's art, and the social and intellectual context of his writings.

_____, ed. *New Essays on "White Noise."* New York: Cambridge University Press, 1991. This collection of essays provides an overview of DeLillo and his novel.

McClure, John A. "Postmodern Romance: Don DeLillo and the Age of Conspiracy." *South Atlantic Quarterly* 89 (Spring, 1990): 337-353. McClure addresses the concept of the conspiracy, prevalent in DeLillo's fiction. Historical currents are the stuff of romance; DeLillo's modern heroes locate romance in espionage and conspiracy. McClure discusses DeLillo in a context of such writers as Joseph Conrad, E. M. Forster, and Graham Greene.

Peyser, Thomas. "Globalization in America: The Case of Don DeLillo's *White Noise*." *CLIO* 25 (Spring, 1996): 255-271. Although *White Noise* is often seen as "obstinately domestic," Peyser argues that DeLillo presents a disturbing vision of a globalized America whose cultural and territorial boundaries exist in theory only.

Saltzman, Arthur. "The Figure in the Static: *White Noise*." *Modern Fiction Studies* 40 (Winter, 1994): 807-826. An analysis of DeLillo's technique of flooding the main characters with information and cultural debris without compromising plot.

Dennis Vannatta

A WIDOW FOR ONE YEAR

Author: John Irving (1942-   )
Type of plot: Character study
Time of plot: The late 1950's to 1995
Locale: Long Island, New York, and Amsterdam
First published: 1998

> *Principal characters:*
> TED COLE, an admired writer and illustrator of children's books
> MARION COLE, Ted's beautiful wife, who disappears and becomes a
>   mystery writer
> RUTH COLE, Ted and Marion's daughter, who becomes a successful
>   novelist
> EDDIE O'HARE, an unsuccessful novelist who as a young man worked
>   for the Cole family
> HANNAH GRANT, Ruth's best friend, her total opposite in character

The Novel

A Widow for One Year focuses on writers as it tells a sprawling story that covers nearly forty years. The novel introduces numerous characters, each one well drawn and memorable, and effectively relates a variety of events, often in a comic manner. Yet its main narrative thrust lies in the way writers develop, the private and public lives they lead, the methods they employ, the reasons they write, the material they use, and the success they gain. Told in the omnisicient third person, the novel opens in 1958 when sixteen-year-old Eddie O'Hare enters the dysfunctional Cole household on Long Island as an assistant to Ted Cole, a much-admired writer and illustrator of children's books. His distraught wife Marion, a strikingly beautiful woman, continues to grieve over the deaths in an automobile accident of their two teenaged sons. The parents, who were in the back seat of the car, escaped the crash physically unhurt but emotionally devastated. Weary of his wife's obsessive behavior, Ted handles his anguish with alcohol and womanizing. Their four-year-old daughter Ruth lives in an overprotected and sometimes chaotic environment amid memories of her dead brothers, whose pictures line the walls of the house. As the summer passes, Eddie and Marion engage in a tempestuous sexual affair, which affects Eddie for the rest of his life and provides Marion with an opportunity to escape both her cruel, philandering husband and her daughter, whom she is afraid to love lest she too might be lost. At summer's end, Eddie returns to his exclusive private school, where his father is an English teacher. Marion vanishes, taking all of the boys' pictures with her. Ted, who continues to drink and chase women, hires a faithful couple to run the household and to help rear little Ruth. These events cover about one-third of the novel and foreshadow what will happen in the future.

Once the fateful summer's events have been told in stunning detail, the narrative moves forward to find Ruth and Eddie as adults. They meet again in New York in a perfectly executed and highly comic scene when bumbling, insecure Eddie introduces a confident Ruth, who is reading from her new novel. While Eddie has published several novels, mainly rehashings of his long-ago affair with Marion, he has enjoyed little success and makes his living primarily through appearances at writers' workshops. On the other hand, Ruth has published fiction that has drawn a wide circle of admirers and turned her into a cult figure, which becomes evident at the reading, where Ruth stars and Eddie stumbles.

The two writers renew their acquaintance, and a circle of friends develops. All sophisticated New Yorkers, the group includes Ruth's alter ego, the sexually charged Hannah Grant, who believes that Ruth writes mainly about her, and Ruth's editor, who later becomes her first husband. The rest of the narrative falls unevenly between Eddie and Ruth, with Ruth receiving the major share of the attention. In one particularly intriguing sequence, Ruth goes to Amsterdam on a book tour and while there carries out research for her new novel in the city's famous brothel district, where she witnesses a prostitute's murder. Because no incident, no detail in the complex narrative structure is irrelevant or goes unused, this experience leads Ruth into yet another adventure and finally into a second marriage. The death of her first husband and her subsequent year-long widowhood lends the novel its title, which is further amplified by the mysterious widow who haunts Ruth.

As the 537-page novel concludes, the major characters find the peace and security and love for which they have been searching—either through their lives or through their fiction. Even Marion, who has become a mystery writer in Canada, reappears, much to the delight of the aging Eddie and the once-deserted child Ruth, who has at last found her mother.

The Characters

John Irving's characters always emerge as distinctive individuals. They are stronger than the sometimes weak and meandering plot, which gains its momentum from their personalities and actions. Thus action more than description defines the characters in *A Widow for One Year*. In fact, physical details are scarce, and the reader may find it difficult to picture the characters. The theme also emanates from the characters, who in this novel either reveal what it is like to be a writer or to be a writer's friend or relative—and what it is like to engage in a search for love in one form or another. When Ruth is asked where she gets the ideas for her novels, she replies that her books do not have ideas, that she has no ideas, but that she begins with the characters, and from them the ideas flow. So it is with Irving's fiction.

Ruth, whose childhood had been such a nightmare and whose sexuality was suppressed, discovers and reveals herself through the fiction she creates. Appearing stubborn and willful at times, self-centered and self-absorbed at other points, she does prevail as the artist who is determined to get at the truth of life—both in her writing and in her own experience. Irrevocably affected by his teenage affair with an older woman, Eddie behaves consistently throughout, showing a lack of confidence and an inability to handle his life in a mature fashion. That he fails as a novelist results in large part from his stunted emotional growth. Yet he remains a likable character, even though Irving treats him more or less comically as an adult. Contradictions distinguish the character of Ted Cole, a failed novelist who delights children with his books but seduces their mothers. While Marion Cole is absent from most of the novel, her memory lingers over the narrative: a temperamental, volatile, passionate, selfish woman. It is possible to imagine how she behaved during her long absence, so that when she reappears her character is re-established easily.

The narrative introduces a number of colorful supporting characters. There are the wronged women whom Ted has seduced and discarded. There is Eddy's father, who borders on a cliché representation of the pretentious English teacher at an exclusive boys' school but who manages to retain his humanity in spite of these encumbrances. While Irving depicts all manner of human folly through his characters' behavior, he avoids undercutting or ridiculing them. For example, the crude, ribald, sexual predator Hannah Grant is overwrought, but she ultimately evolves into a somewhat sympathetic and understandable personage. While Irving appears to tolerate her excesses, she is often just plain tiresome and offensive to the reader.

Irving's method of characterization relies on exaggeration, odd behavior, and well-defined actions. The characters develop incrementally, never revealing themselves fully at first but becoming whole as the outrageous plot, which they determine, unravels.

Themes and Meanings

While the novel is primarily about writing stories, it develops a broader theme through this sustained metaphor. To a degree, the theme that the writers attempt to get across in their imaginary books—one actually called *A Widow for One Year*—turns into the major theme of the real *A Widow for One Year*: love in its many forms.

The love of children is illustrated through Marion and Ted's grief over their lost sons and the fear of losing their remaining child. This relationship is further developed through the way Ruth guards and values her own child. Casual sexual relations and genuine feeling between two people are set in opposition throughout the novel. Hannah's reckless sexual behavior and Ted's excessive philandering contrast dramatically with Ruth's and Eddie's quests for fulfillment. The passages in Amsterdam's brothels chronicle a depraved side of sexual encounters, where love no longer matters but is replaced by money and, in some instances, brutality. Friendship emerges as another form of love, which Irving explores and extends in the novel. Although he has been accused of sentimentality in his fiction, the way he handles human relationships does not actually border on the sentimental—unless a desire to attain love in its varied guises does indeed constitute an excess of sentiment. When *A Widow for One Year* ends, the major characters have found the elusive security and peace for which they have been searching and which love assures. Even sex-hungry Hannah begins to re-examine her views.

That Irving mixes comedy and tragedy sometimes makes it difficult to take him seriously. On one hand, he writes remarkable scenes that border on burlesque, such as the literary reading where a befuddled Eddy ineptly introduces Ruth and the stage-hand ogles her breasts while she reads from her feminist novel. He satirizes American society in exquisite tones—such as the snobbery inherent in private schools or the pre-tentiousness in an area such as the Hamptons on Long Island. In contrast, though, Irving's retelling of the accident that claimed the two boys' lives is a haunting episode, as is the murder of the prostitute in Amsterdam. Yet this melding of comedy and trag-edy represents life faultlessly.

Critical Context

Irving has said that his favorite novelist is Charles Dickens. Irving's past novels and *A Widow for One Year* could well qualify him as an American Dickens: a writer who loves rich and at times seemingly irrelevant details, who tells his story in a forthright manner and depends on coincidence in plotting, who masters both comedy and trag-edy—which he mixes audaciously, and who develops quirky characters whose ac-tions carry the story. To a degree, Irving's fictional technique marks him as an old-fashioned writer. That may well be the reason that his work continues to enjoy popular success, especially in a time when so many novelists are bent on experimenta-tion and obscurity. Irving never crosses the border of conventional fiction; nor does he fall into ambiguity and abstractions. Ruth Cole says that her novel is not about any-thing, that it is just a good story. While it is possible to draw thematic implications from Irving's novels, they are also first and foremost good stories. This quality is un-doubtedly the reason for the continuing popularity of Irving's most widely admired novel, *The World According to Garp* (1978), as well as the broad reception of the nov-els that followed, which show a tremendous variety in settings, characters, and situa-tions.

The quest on which Irving always sends his characters—that of fulfillment, secu-rity, peacefulness within a turbulent world, the attainment of love—remains a familiar one, a quest with which readers can identify. That the characters, once they have struggled and experienced setbacks and faced all manner of odds, do in the end dis-cover a sense of oneness with others always rings true. Readers understand and appre-ciate this timeless discovery.

Bibliography

Harter, Carol C., and James R. Thompson. *John Irving*. Boston: Twayne, 1986. Al-though the study covers Irving's fiction only through *The Cider House Rules* (1985), it remains a clear and forthright introduction to his work. The authors focus in part on the reasons for the popular appeal of the novels.

McWilliam, Candia. "Love, Grief, and Breasts." *The New Statesman* 127 (May 22, 1998): 55. McWilliam complains that the women in *A Widow for One Year* behave too much like men, condemns the "unfunny comedy" and "slapstick" humor, and dislikes the obsession with sex and body parts. She admits that the novel's theme is "patently prompted by love" but asserts that the book fails in its execution of so powerful a theme.

Pritchard, William H. "No Ideas! It's a Novel!" *The New York Times Book Review* 147 (May 24, 1998): 7. This review of *A Widow for One Year* stresses Irving's kinship to Charles Dickens, explores the comic touch, praises the book's readability, and places the new novel in the context of Irving's earlier work.

Van Gelder, Lindsy. "Yupward Mobility." *The Nation* 266 (May 11, 1998): 52-54. Van Gelder calls Irving the "American Balzac, or perhaps our Dickens." She praises him for his brisk storytelling, for believable and memorable characters in spite of their "collection of tics," and for caring "about the smallest aches of the human heart." She concludes that Irving has captured "the whole yuppie Zeitgeist": the search for commitment, meaning, and success.

Wymard, Eleanor B. "'A New Version of the Midas Touch': *Daniel Martin* and *The World According to Garp.*" *Modern Fiction Studies* 27 (Summer, 1981): 284-286. This comparative study of John Fowles's and Irving's novels focuses on their similarity as old-fashioned fictions, on the comic elements, and on the way they depict characters clashing with the demands of modern life.

Robert L. Ross

THE WILLIAMSBURG TRILOGY

Author: Daniel Fuchs (1909-1993)
Type of plot: Surrealism
Time of plot: The 1930's
Locale: Primarily the Williamsburg area of Brooklyn, New York
First published: Summer in Williamsburg, 1934; *Homage to Blenholt,* 1936; *Low Company,* 1937 (First published together as *Three Novels: Summer in Williamsburg, Homage to Blenholt, Low Company,* 1961; published as *The Williamsburg Trilogy: Summer in Williamsburg, Homage to Blenholt, Low Company,* 1972)

> *Principal characters:*
> *Summer in Williamsburg*
> PHILIP HAYMAN, a senior at New York City College
> MR. HAYMAN, Philip's father
> SAM LINCK, one of Philip's neighbors
> UNCLE PAPRAVEL, Philip's uncle
>
> *Homage to Blenholt*
> MAX BALKAN, a dreamer
> MANDEL MUNVES, an amateur etymologist
> COBLENZ, a gambler
> RITA, Max's sister
> RUTH, Max's girlfriend
> MR. BALKAN and
> MRS. BALKAN, Max's parents
>
> *Low Company*
> LOUIE SPITZBERGEN, a soda shop owner
> MOE KARTY, a gambler
> SHUBUNKA, the owner of a string of houses of prostitution
> ARTHUR, a dishwasher

The Novels

The *Williamsburg Trilogy* consists of three separate novels, *Summer in Williamsburg, Homage to Blenholt,* and *Low Company.* Each has a separate plot and group of characters. All are set for the most part in and around the Williamsburg section of Brooklyn. The first two involve mainly characters who live on Ripple Street in Williamsburg. The third is set primarily in Neptune Beach, a seaside resort based, critics say, on either Brighton Beach or Coney Island. *Summer in Williamsburg* consists of a series of vignettes focussing on different characters whose lives weave together, often simply by virtue of their living in the same area. Although Philip Hayman, the book's central character, has no contact with Sam Linck, Linck's tempestuous relationship with his wife and mother and adulterous relationship with

Marge figure prominently. Still, Philip and Linck live in the same building, where Sam's mother is landlady.

The novel traces Philip's growing awareness of Williamsburg as part of the lives of the people who live there. The book begins with the suicide of one of Philip's neighbors and includes the suicide of the man's wife and her murder of their children; the attempted suicide of Philip's friend, Cohen, a dreamer and bungler; and Cohen's death in a fire in the tenement in which they live. It also traces the rise of Philip's Uncle Papravel, of whom Philip's father disapproves and for whom Philip's brother Harry works. Papravel's thugs intimidate Morand, owner of the Silver Eagle Bus Line, to get him to shut his Williamsburg office. Papravel works for Rubin, president of the Empire Bus Line, who wants a monopoly on the lucrative summer business between Williamsburg and the Catskill Mountains. Papravel puts Morand out of business and becomes president of the Silver Eagle Line, with Rubin as his vice president.

Homage to Blenholt traces Max Balkan's growth from jobless dreamer immersed in get-rich schemes involving no work on his part to person determined to get a job, help his parents financially, and marry his girlfriend Ruth. Mandel Munves, an unemployed amateur etymologist, proposes to Rita, Max's sister, and comes up with what seems the impossible idea of running a delicatessen with Max. As a result of a gift of three hundred dollars from Coblenz to Max's mother out of his gambling winnings, the dream may come true.

The book's title comes from Max's determination to attend the funeral of Blenholt, the commissioner of sewers. Max venerates Blenholt, a petty criminal. Max never met Blenholt but is determined to attend the funeral. Coblenz and Munves, who promised to go, desert Max, so he goes with Ruth, who never wanted to go. During the funeral procession and memorial service, Max makes a fool of himself, and Ruth flees. Late in the novel, one of his get-rich schemes seems about to bear fruit. He suggests that a group of onion growers bottle onion juice. A group representative meets with Max and tells him that they have been bottling it for years. Instead of returning with hundreds of dollars, Max returns with a bag of onions.

In *Low Company*, Shubunka runs a string of whorehouses in Neptune Beach. When a syndicate gives him part of a day to get out of town or be killed, he argues that he too is human and deserves to be treated with dignity. He tries to hire thugs to oppose the syndicate, but none will work for him. He tries unsuccessfully to bribe some hoodlums who work for the syndicate. After two thugs beat him and he realizes he is in real danger, he tries to hide at Herbert Lurie's apartment but thinks the syndicate has followed him there. He is last seen fleeing for his life.

Spitzbergen owns Ann's, a soda shop in Neptune Beach, but he also owns some apartment houses and rents them to Shubunka. When the syndicate takes over, their men tell Spitzbergen that he now does business with them, and he reluctantly agrees. He immediately abandons Shubunka in spite of the years of their relationship. He does not want to get mixed up with the syndicate but feels that he has no choice.

Moe Karty was a successful accountant. He is now a gambler who thinks he has a sure system for making a fortune on the races but cannot find anyone to back him. He stole money from his wife's brothers, and they demand its immediate return. Her brother Harry beats Karty, and they threaten him with greater pain. Karty convinces Arthur, Spitzbergen's dishwasher, to steal twenty dollars from Ann's cash register. With the money, Karty takes Arthur to the races and loses. Later that day, Karty begs Spitzbergen for money. When Spitzbergen says no, Karty loses his temper and beats Spitzbergen to death.

The Characters

Different characters people each of the works in the trilogy. In *Summer in Williamsburg*, many of the characters, such as Philip, Cohen, Sam Linck, Harry, Papravel, Mr. Hayman, and Mrs. Hayman, are fully realized individuals. Even many of the minor characters, including Mrs. Linck (Sam's mother), Anna Linck (Sam's wife), Marge (Sam's girlfriend), Miller (a miser), and Morand, come to life. In his attempts to understand Williamsburg, Philip grows. Sam, however, remains static, taking up with Marge again and again, even after she gets into a fight with Mrs. Linck and Anna, makes anti-Semitic remarks, and gets some of her friends to beat Sam, and after Anna catches Marge and Sam together. Cohen changes moods rapidly but never grows. Morand finally becomes an attractive figure when Papravel breaks his spirit. Papravel, however, is a ruthless gangster who stands by his men, even when one of them kills a state trooper. He singlemindedly pursues his goals, destroying anyone getting in his way. His brother-in-law, Philip's father, always is concerned with leading a moral life. Mrs. Hayman constantly helps others and ministers to the needs of her family. Philip ultimately decides that he admires his father tremendously and that the life of someone like Papravel is not for him.

The characters in *Homage to Blenholt* are closer to being types. Max is a dreamer, so caught up in his schemes that he does not recognize that people suffer because of him. Munves is so absorbed by his small etymological discoveries that he does not notice the problems in the world around him.

Coblenz suffers from toothache, gets drunk, breaks things in his apartment, wins money, and gives it to Mrs. Balkan, telling her to take it, for he does not need it, and adds, "I was just thinking of jumping off the roof." Mrs. Balkan insists, "It's only for lend." As soon as Coblenz leaves the Balkan apartment, however, he regrets having given away the money. Max, Munves, and Coblenz have been classified as *schlemiels*, a Yiddish term for bunglers and habitual victims.

None of the characters in *Low Company* is honest or even concerned with honesty. All are self-centered and, with the possible exceptions of Arthur and Shubunka, willing to hurt others without hesitation in pursuit of their own goals. Karty is the worst. He has no sense of responsibility for the money he stole from his brothers-in-law. He gets furious when people refuse to lend him money, so much so that he beats Spitzbergen to death when he finally refuses. He has no qualms about getting Arthur to steal money from Spitzbergen's cash register.

Themes and Meanings

 Summer in Williamsburg is basically a serious novel about the relationship between environment and character. The book traces the way Williamsburg, a poor neighborhood, acts upon its inhabitants, mostly first and second generation Jewish immigrants. It explores the degradation of the children and the admiration of success, no matter how achieved. It also shows admiration for those like Philip's father, who lead moral lives in spite of temptations to do otherwise. *Homage to Blenholt* is a comic novel about the serious need to accept adult responsibilities. It treats the need to relinquish dreams and live in the often-unpleasant real world. Max's father used to be a Yiddish tragedian but now earns money carrying sandwich boards advertising Madame Clara's hair salon. At the end of the novel, Max's father feels sad when he recognizes that his son "would grow old and ageing [sic], die, but actually Max was dead already for now he would live for bread alone," and Mr. Balkan knows he has "witnessed the exact point at which his son had changed from youth to resigned age." In Max, Mr. Balkan sees his own change from Yiddish actor to sandwich-board carrier and feels sorrow for his son. *Low Company* explores the seamier side of humanity. Full of unlikable characters, it portrays human beings as greedy, insignificant creatures unconcerned about one another. Each is concerned ultimately with his or her own pleasures, not caring what happens to others. In this novel, humankind is not a pleasant thing. Even nature participates in the viciousness. The rain interferes with Spitzbergen's business at least as much as the human hoodlums do. Only after Spitzbergen dies does the weather become beautiful, and then people ironically flock to Neptune Beach.

Critical Context

 The Williamsburg Trilogy was at first largely ignored. According to Fuchs, *Summer in Williamsburg* and *Homage to Blenholt* each sold only four hundred copies, and *Low Company* sold only twelve hundred. Only after the three novels were published did Fuchs conceive of them as a trilogy. In 1961, they were reissued under one cover; Fuchs then began to get critical recognition. When Fuchs later went to Hollywood to write movie scripts, one of the movies he wrote was *The Gangster* (1947), based on *Low Company*.

 Fuchs is sometimes compared to Nathanael West, especially in *Day of the Locust* (1939), West's chronicle of Hollywood in the 1930's, in which West focuses on the difference between humanity's possibilities and humanity's actualities. In style, too, the trilogy is compared to West's work, since both tend to be surrealistic, especially *Low Company*, with its nightmarish vision.

 Fuchs's novels focus on relatively poor, secularized Jews living in New York City. Thus, they resemble works like Michael Gold's *Jews Without Money* (1930) and Henry Roth's *Call It Sleep* (1934), although Fuchs apparently shares none of the left-wing political concerns of Roth and Gold. Yet like Roth's and Gold's works, the trilogy has been labeled basically as a work of the Great Depression.

Bibliography
Fiedler, Leslie A. *To the Gentiles.* New York: Stein and Day, 1972. A brief, largely negative treatment of Fuchs in the context of Jewish American literature. Fiedler, though, praises *Homage to Blenholt.*
Guttmann, Allen. *The Jewish Writer in America: Assimilation and the Crisis of Identity.* New York: Oxford University Press, 1971. Briefly examines the trilogy in the context of other Jewish American works that treat the generational conflict as the children of immigrants become more and more Americanized.
Klein, Marcus. *Foreigners: The Making of American Literature, 1900-1940.* Chicago: University of Chicago Press, 1981. Gives sensitive, perceptive readings of all works in the trilogy. Places them in the context of the contributions of "foreigners" to building a distinctively American literature.
Miller, Gabriel. *Daniel Fuchs.* Boston: Twayne, 1979. A book-length introduction to Fuchs's life and writing. Contains careful readings of each book in the trilogy.
Sherman, Bernard. *The Invention of the Jew: Jewish-American Education Novels (1916-1964).* New York: Thomas Yoseloff, 1969. Treats surreal aspects of *Summer in Williamsburg.*

Richard Tuerk

WIND FROM AN ENEMY SKY

Author: D'Arcy McNickle (1904-1977)
Type of plot: Historical realism
Time of plot: The first half of the twentieth century
Locale: Western Montana, in the area near Flathead Lake and St. Ignatius
First published: 1978

Principal characters:
BULL, the leader of the Little Elk Indian tribe
HENRY JIM, Bull's elder brother, who adopts the ways of whites
ANTOINE, Bull's grandson, recently returned from a government school in Oregon
TWO SLEEPS, a holy man, a seer adopted by the tribe
POCK FACE, Bull's nephew, who kills a white man
LOUIS, Pock Face's father
THEOBALD, Pock Face's mild-mannered cousin, son of Basil
TOBY RAFFERTY, the superintendent of the government agency that oversees the Little Elk Indians
DOC EDWARDS, a government physician
JIM COOKE, Adam Pell's nephew, who is murdered by Pock Face
ADAM PELL, the builder of a dam on Little Elk land
THE BOY, a Native American intermediary

The Novel

In *Wind from an Enemy Sky*, D'Arcy McNickle, a member of the Confederated Salish and Kutenai tribes of the Flathead Indian Reservation, born and educated in Montana, writes of the difficult period in American history during which the United States government attempted to subdue Native Americans peacefully. McNickle, a government employee for most of his life, presents a balanced view of what occurred during this period in one small Native American enclave in the Flathead Lake-St. Ignatius area of Montana.

On the surface, McNickle presents the story of a Native American extended family that includes Pock Face, who, carrying his grandfather's rifle, steals furtively into a canyon where white developers have built a dam on tribal land. The Little Elk Indians equate the damming of their river with its murder. The dam has an immediate negative impact upon fishing and farming on their tribal lands.

As Pock Face and Theobald, his cousin, approach the dam, they spy a white man walking across its surface. Pock Face fires one shot. Jim Cooke, ironically on his last day of work before going east to marry, dies instantly.

The remainder of the story revolves around the government's efforts to mete out justice to the murderer. This surface story, however, provides the justification for a compelling subtext that illustrates the difficulties involved when one well-established culture attempts to impose itself upon another. *Wind from an Enemy Sky*, maintaining throughout an objective view of two disparate cultures, proffers a poignant political and social statement about culture and values in multi-ethnic settings.

Readers will feel empathy for members of the two major societies depicted in the novel, even though these societies remain at loggerheads and are divided within themselves. Toby Rafferty, the government agent in charge of the Little Elk Reservation, and Doc Edwards, the agency physician, have compassion for the Native Americans with whom they work.

Rafferty, for example, demonstrates trust and sensitivity toward Bull and his followers, releasing them from custody on their own recognizance after the murder to attend the final hours of Henry Jim's life. Doc Edwards, who treats Henry Jim as death nears, employs the tactics and technology of white medicine, yet he never loses sight of the faith and reliance that Henry Jim and his kinspeople repose in tribal ways of treating illness.

Despite this, the crucial and undeniable fact is that the whites who represent the dominant culture are unabashedly out to annihilate the Native American culture. The whites deal as kindly as they can with their Native American charges, but they shamelessly try to homogenize them into mainstream American life.

The whites' most effective tactic is forcibly to wrest Native American children from their families, shipping them to government schools. There, officials take the children's native clothes and burn them, then cut their hair and delouse them—all great affronts to Indian culture. The younger the children, the better their chance of acculturation.

Bull's grandson is snatched from his family while Bull is hunting one day. The boy is sent to a government school in Oregon, some thousand miles from his home, there to be stripped of his identity. He is assigned the new name of Antoine Brown; he learns how to pray and eat and be civil. He is told to forget his home and his people. Meanwhile, his mother, Celeste, devastated at being robbed of her only child, becomes a raving lunatic and soon dies. Only then is the boy permitted to return to Montana and his family.

McNickle never suggests that whites are motivated by evil intentions, yet their intentions are so greatly in conflict with Native American custom that they pose an insuperable barrier between the cultures. The dam that the white power structure has imposed upon the Indians symbolizes the incursions the dominant society makes upon tribal lands and traditions, much as the dam does in Thomas King's *Green Grass, Running Water* (1993).

Whites such as Adam Pell and Toby Rafferty champion Native Americans, but in doing so, they alienate the very people they champion. Whites, for example, become restive when Indians sing at crucial times when the whites need to talk with them. They cannot understand why Indians frequently answer questions allegorically, through tale-telling rather than directly.

On the other hand, both Rafferty and Doc Edwards know that when they enter an Indian abode, they should not initiate the conversation. They are on someone else's turf, and, following Native American tradition, they allow their host to speak before they attempt utterance, no matter how pressing their business.

McNickle depicts Native Americans as passive, unfailingly loyal, intelligent, and, to whites, enigmatic. They handle problems in their own ways. They consider whites noisy and aggressive, often commenting that agitated whites shout. The Indians counter with neither loudness nor aggression.

The Characters

Bull, the son of Enemy Horse, is the patriarch of his tribe. He is used to represent stalwart Native Americans who dare to resist acculturation and maintain traditional values. He lives in a changing world, but he clings tenaciously to his heritage. Although he seeks accord with the whites officially representing the dominant culture, he refuses to knuckle under to them. He is a thorn in the flesh of those who think that a good Native American is one who forsakes tribal traditions and enters the mainstream of American life.

Henry Jim, Bull's elder brother, has joined the white world. He cooperates with government officials. He has built a wooden house in which his daughter-in-law, a member of a tribe to the south, has gone so far as to cover the floors and windows with cloth—much to the dismay of his Native American relatives, most of whom will not enter his house, preferring to stay outside on their horses when they need to see him. Henry Jim has fenced his land as the whites do. He cannot, however, shake his Native American roots. As death approaches, he moves from his house into a tepee outside it, reverting to his tribal customs as his life runs out.

Two Sleeps, not originally a member of the tribe, appeared in the tribal village one day, beaten, exhausted, and hungry. The elders were about to expel him when he collapsed. Of necessity, they ministered to him. He then shared with them a vision that he had about a herd of buffalo he sensed was grazing nearby. When this vision proved to have substance and the Indians had killed enough buffalo to feed themselves for the foreseeable future, they accepted Two Sleeps as their holy man, their seer. They took him into their community and venerated him, by that act reflecting their mystical orientation.

Antoine represents the Native American who, although snatched from his culture, refuses to forget it and ultimately returns to it. He is, basically, a moderate young man in whom one sees some of the charisma that characterizes Bull, his grandfather, whom he might one day succeed.

Pock Face, on the other hand, is an angry youth who has bolted from the government school. He is outraged that the dominant society is robbing his people of the very resources they need to survive. The symbol of this theft is the dam Adam Pell has built on tribal land to collect the river water that Pock Face's tribe, living downstream from the dam, requires for its sustenance. Pock Face, in his own view, commits a moral act of vengeance by randomly killing Jim Cooke.

Toby Rafferty wants genuinely to help the Native Americans whose welfare and control are his official responsibility. He represents the well-meaning "new-settlement-house humanist," as McNickle calls him. His intentions are indisputably excellent, but they are building blocks that pave the road to hell.

Doc Edwards, Rafferty's close friend, is the official physician of the Little Elk Agency and has refused advantageous transfers because he believes in what he is doing. He is sensitive to his Native American charges but is never able to surmount the barriers that separate the two cultures.

Adam Pell, the builder of the dam, considers himself a true champion of Native Americans, both in the United States and in Peru. He has a utopian vision of what technological progress can mean to the Little Elk, but he cannot communicate this vision to them, nor has he sought their counsel in developing it.

Themes and Meanings

Wind from an Enemy Sky is concerned largely with the inability of the Native American and dominant societies in the United States to communicate productively with each other. As McNickle presents it, Native American society is deeply suspicious of the dominant society that has, through the years, oppressed it. Promises made have seldom been promises kept. The suspicions that keep Indians from interacting productively with government agencies are spawned not by paranoia but rather by extensive bitter experience.

The dam the government built has diverted a river on which the Indians depend. The waters that the dam captures will nourish the fields of white homesteaders, to whom the government has sold Indian lands at $1.25 an acre. The Native Americans look upon these land sales as forms of robbery. Added to this justifiable charge is the charge that white officials have kidnapped Indian children and sent them to distant government schools against their will.

Among the most pervasive and impressive symbols in this novel is that of the Feather Boy medicine bundle. This sacred artifact is taken by a reservation clergyman, Stephen Welles, and given to Adam Pell's museum in exchange for a stipend the museum bestows upon Welles's church. Welles mendaciously assures Pell that the medicine bundle was given to the museum with the full knowledge and consent of the tribe.

As Henry Jim lies dying, he calls for the return of the medicine bundle, which is thought to possess spiritual properties. Toby Rafferty writes to Adam Pell asking for its return and explaining its importance to the Little Elk. Pell and his staff search the museum's storerooms for this contribution, carefully cataloged, then placed in long-term storage.

To Pell's distress, the medicine bundle, when found, has irreparably deteriorated. Pell decides to visit the reservation and to make amends to the tribe by parting with a solid-gold Inca statue he had obtained with great difficulty and at considerable expense after years of searching. His motives are perfectly acceptable by the standards of his society, but his reparations are incredibly insulting to the Native Americans with whom he is trying to reach an accord. They view his demeanor and his proposal, quite correctly, as outrageously condescending.

To make matters worse, the Indians, ever modest, are to be given a statue of a nude figure. Pell's gesture is insensitive in the extreme, but not intentionally so. Rafferty, better attuned to Native American sensitivities than Pell, attempts to dissuade him from telling the Indians that their sacred medicine bundle has been lost. Yet Pell, honest and forthright, tells the Indians of the loss and of the generous indemnity he proposes making to compensate them, simultaneously robbing them unwittingly of their hope and demeaning their heritage.

Pell's disclosure leads an outraged Louis, in a tribal meeting with government officials, to grab Bull's rifle. Bull leaps up, wrests the rifle from Louis, and shoots Pell dead. He then fires the rifle at Rafferty and kills him. At this point, The Boy, a Native American intermediary between his people and government officials, does what he has to do: He aims his pistol at Bull and shoots him dead.

Thematically, McNickle suggests by these acts the inevitability of tragedy in dealings between Native Americans and representatives of the dominant society. He also demonstrates how some Native Americans—Henry Jim and The Boy, for example—move into the white world or attempt to straddle the two worlds, placing them in impossible positions. For Henry Jim, it is impossible to shake the Native American heritage, which the dying man finally embraces again.

Critical Context

D'Arcy McNickle's novel was produced at a time when ethnic sensitivity and multiculturalism were gaining considerable prominence in literature. As part of Harper and Row's Native American Publishing Program, *Wind from an Enemy Sky* was published along with books by such other Native American writers as Heyemeyohsts Storm, James Welch, Adolf Hungry Wolf, Duane Niatum, Simon Ortiz, and Nas' Naga.

Other Native American novelists were also making headway in the 1970's. N. Scott Momaday's *The Way to Rainy Mountain* (1976) appeared two years before McNickle's novel. In 1978, the same year the *Wind from an Enemy Sky* was issued, the University of Minnesota Press published one of Gerald Vizenor's earliest books, *Indians and Whites in the New Fur Trade*. As early as 1936, McNickle himself had published *The Surrounded*, which was widely considered the finest Native American novel prior to World War II. McNickle's *Runner in the Sun: A Story of Indian Maize* appeared in 1954, followed in 1973 by *Native American Tribalism*, published by the Oxford University Press.

A decade before *Wind from an Enemy Sky*, a flood of African American writing spawned a renewed interest in minority literatures. Native American, Chicano, feminist, and gay and lesbian literature began to share with African American literature the prominence that the social upheavals of the 1960's had generated. The trend would continue in succeeding years, as the works of minority writers became accepted parts of the academic canon. As an early pioneer of the Native American novel, D'Arcy McNickle has benefited from this reappraisal, receiving belated recognition as an important voice in American fiction.

Bibliography
Larson, Charles R. "Books in English in the Third World." *World Literature Today* 53 (Spring, 1979): 247. Larson calls *The Surrounded* "the most significant novel by an American Indian written before World War II." He then discusses the forty-year lapse between that book and *Wind from an Enemy Sky*, which he sees as concerning "conflicting loyalties *within* the Indian community."
Owens, Louis, "The 'Map of the Mind': D'Arcy McNickle and the American Indian Novel." *Western American Literature* 19 (Winter, 1985): 275-283. Owens discusses *The Surrounded* and *Wind from an Enemy Sky*, focusing on the problems of communication between the white and Indian worlds.
Parker, Dorothy. *Singing an Indian Song: A Biography of D'Arcy McNickle*. Lincoln: University of Nebraska Press, 1992. Details McNickle's early years at a boarding school and his lengthy career as an agent for the Bureau of Indian Affairs. Provides information crucial to the interpretation of his fiction.
Purdy, John L. *The Legacy of D'Arcy McNickle: Writer, Historian, Activist*. Norman: University of Oklahoma Press, 1996. Presents a thorough, annotated bibliography of McNickle's published articles, as well as book reviews of his works. Devotes a chapter to *Wind from an Enemy Sky*.
_____. *Word Ways: The Novels of D'Arcy McNickle*. Tucson: University of Arizona Press, 1990. A thorough critical discussion of McNickle's fiction. Purdy focuses on McNickle's use of Native American oral tradition to enhance the written conventions of the novel.
Ruppert, James. *D'Arcy McNickle*. Boise, Idaho: Boise State University, 1988. An entry in the Western Writers Series that gives a good overview of McNickle's life and work.
Vest, Jay Hansford C. "Feather Boy's Promise: Sacred Geography and Environmental Ethics in D'Arcy McNickle's *Wind from an Enemy Sky*." *American Indian Quarterly* 17 (Winter, 1993): 45-68. Focuses on the Little Elk tribe's medicine bundle and its relationship to the Native American environmental ethic. Sees *Wind from an Enemy Sky* as a trickster narrative.

R. Baird Shuman

THE WINDS OF WAR

Author: Herman Wouk (1915-   )
Type of plot: Historical romance
Time of plot: From 1939 to 1941, beginning shortly before Adolf Hitler's invasion
of Poland and ending with the Japanese attack on Pearl Harbor
Locale: Washington, D.C., England, Germany, Czechoslovakia, the Soviet Union,
Italy, and other major sites of World War II
First published: 1971

Principal characters:
> VICTOR (PUG) HENRY, the central figure, a career naval officer and
> reluctant emissary of President Franklin Delano Roosevelt
> RHODA HENRY, his wife
> WARREN, the Henrys' elder son, also a naval officer
> BYRON (BRINY), the Henrys' younger son who becomes a submariner
> MADELINE, the Henrys' daughter, a broadcasting assistant
> NATALIE JASTROW, eventually the wife of Byron
> PAMELA TUDSBURY, Victor's mistress

The Novel
The action of the novel projects the lives of the principal characters against the
events leading to American entry into World War II. Victor Henry and his family are
"tumbleweeds," blown around the globe by the "winds of war." Victor is an ambitious
and frustrated naval captain who stumbles into favor with President Franklin Delano
Roosevelt through a fluke prediction. As a result, Victor becomes Roosevelt's untitled
emissary to various nations and in the process meets most of the world's leading figures: Joseph Stalin, Winston Churchill, Benito Mussolini, and the archvillain Adolf
Hitler. His family members and close friends, in like manner, whirl about the globe in
pursuit of adventure, love, and identity.

Despite the uneasy peace negotiated at Munich in 1937, Europe is openly preparing
for war in 1939. Hitler dominates the headlines, and the question is not whether he
will provoke war but where: He already has Czechoslovakia, but he clearly wants to
invade Poland, France, and the largest target of all, the Soviet Union. As a military
man, Victor Henry is clearly involved, but when his sons follow him into naval service, the events of the war become events in each character's personal life. Byron
falls in love with Natalie Jastrow, whose Jewish ancestry is as much an issue with his
own family as it is with the Fascist leaders of Europe. Her uncle, Aaron Jastrow, affords a further complication when he first refuses, and then desperately tries, to leave
Mussolini's Italy. As Victor's new and unplanned intelligence career sends him dash-
ing off to all the major nations, the separation from his wife, Rhoda, leads to extramarital affairs for both him and Rhoda. Meanwhile, Byron and his sister Madeline take
advantage of this turmoil to rebel: Byron, by marrying Natalie; Madeline, by going

to work for a famous but lecherous news commentator, Hugh Cleveland. Despite everyone's avowed desire for peace, the threat of war has brought excitement into their lives.

Victor Henry's translation of the (fictitious) writings of the German General Armin von Roon, called *World Empire Lost*, offers astute but biased views of world events. Similarly, the occasional appearance of real-life figures, especially President Roosevelt, provides a strong historical thread to the subplots involving the various main characters. Most of the action focuses on the European front, though the novel ends with the dramatic shift of world attention to the Pacific. Although the progress of world events is well known, the fate of the characters remains more or less in suspense.

The novel's conclusion does not attempt to answer the great twofold puzzle of the attack on Pearl Harbor: why Japan perpetrated, and how the United States could have allowed, such a devastating surprise. There is no attempt of any consequence to view the war from Japan's perspective, though von Roon's "book" and several other characters offer a broad range of German viewpoints. Because the novel is the first part of a two-volume sequence, the fates of the principal characters are necessarily left unresolved; the book ends as the United States officially enters the war.

The Characters

Victor Henry does not come off as a wholly sympathetic or even heroic figure. Rather, like many of the "heroes" of *The Caine Mutiny* (1951), Victor is a flawed man with professional integrity and a knack for being in the right place at the critical time. Roosevelt praises his eye for detail, and no one questions his dedication as an officer. Yet he himself admits that he has been a mediocre husband and, to his daughter Madeline especially, a rather poor and distant father. Despite his long service record and strength of character, he has no really close personal friends in the navy. His son Warren is very much of the same mold: tough, loyal, athletic, "navy" head to toe. The potential black sheep of the family, Byron, possesses as much physical courage as the other Henry men, and more personal courage, as shown by his marrying a Jewess and his impertinence toward superior officers. The women are more complex, but only Madeline transcends the stereotype of 1940's women: devoted to a man, preferably one's husband, and resigned to a "woman's place." Her relationship with Hugh Cleveland defies convention more than does Byron's sometimes trivial rebelliousness.

Victor Henry's loyalty to flag and navy contrasts with his often wandering eye and occasionally wandering heart. The younger women of the novel interest him more than his still attractive wife. His fascination with the darkly beautiful Natalie eventually leads to his grudging approval of Byron's marriage.

The central women of the novel, along with Byron Henry, possess a loyalty and depth of character perhaps beyond those of the more conventional men. Natalie Jastrow risks her own and her baby's safety to help her eccentric uncle, Madeline overlooks Hugh Cleveland's obnoxious private personality to help him utilize his public talents, and both Pamela and Rhoda set aside propriety for the sake of love. Although, as a member of the family, Warren Henry is "important," he seems rather wooden compared to his flamboyant younger brother, the daring women, and even his complex, brooding father.

Thus the novel appeals to both men and women. The conventions of the time and no doubt the author's own inclinations emphasize love rather than sex, but the treatment is more realistic than romantic. The personal cowardice of Byron's rival, Ambassador Leslie Slote, and the backbiting of some of Victor Henry's rivals put the main figures in a better light, for they at least have substance and strength.

Themes and Meanings

Victor Henry frequently expresses the central theme of the novel; he talks of how the war has "scattered" the family, perhaps beyond any hope of full regrouping, and describes the main characters themselves as "tumbleweeds" blown about by the growing "winds of war." As various events move the characters around the globe, there is a tone reminiscent of Johann Wolfgang von Goethe's line comparing the soul of man to the water, and the destiny of man to the wind. None of the main characters has the political power or personal strength to resist the push of historical events; only Hitler and Roosevelt seem to be the "world historical" figures of German philosophy who can shape events rather than be controlled by them.

The focus of the novel on Germany raises the problem of anti-Semitism. This issue receives extra attention because of the role of Aaron Jastrow, Natalie's famous uncle, who has written a book entitled *A Jew's Jesus*. Several confrontations between American officials and the Nazis show that the United States officially deplored anti-Semitism, even in the face of diplomacy, threats, and bribes. On the other hand, the social conventions are less enlightened, though gradually the Henry family accepts Natalie, and Victor writes Roosevelt a memo deploring the wholesale slaughter of Russian Jews by Nazis. A cab driver expresses an all-too-popular sentiment when he vows that Roosevelt will not sacrifice American lives "to save the Jews," but Roosevelt himself never speaks in such terms.

On the stage of international politics, Victor Henry seems, like millions, to be struggling for identity. Shorter than his wife, obviously insignificant beside such great men as Roosevelt and Churchill, Victor finds significance in his navy career and above all in the physical symbol of his heart's desire: a battleship, under his command. Yet the closer he comes to his goal, the less meaning it has; the airplane is superseding the battleship as the key to military power. Although the war divides his family and almost destroys his marriage, he grows to a new awareness of how undependable such worldly things as battleships and presidential favors can be and how indispensable ordinary human relationships are. At the end, both he and Rhoda are happier with their role as grandparents than with their extramarital conquests or their dinners at the White House and at Hermann Göring's castle.

As several figures note, World War II represents a change in the old world order. Britain is becoming a paper tiger, France is even more impotent, and the new giants are the United States and the Soviet Union. For all his madness, Hitler was one of the few prophets to see that unless someone—presumably the Germans under his leadership—took immediate action, the world would be divided up by these two upstart superpowers. Though the novel disparages the rantings of German philosophy about "world history," it is itself an illustration of the process of world struggle, change, and cold, hard political reality.

Critical Context

The *Winds of War* invites immediate comparison with Wouk's most famous novel, *The Caine Mutiny*, for which he won the Pulitzer Prize in 1952. Critics naturally contrast staid and dependable Victor Henry with the unstable, incompetent Captain Queeg. Yet a more apt comparison is that made by Timothy Foote, between *The Winds of War* and Leo Tolstoy's *War and Peace* (1865-1869). Like *War and Peace*, and unlike Wouk's earlier "navy" novel, *The Winds of War* presents a vast panorama that ultimately spans the globe. Wouk himself acknowledges that he had always intended to write a "big" novel after his own navy career in World War II, and he was tempted to expand *The Caine Mutiny* before cutting it back to its limited scope.

Wouk's novels run against the trend of experimental novels and, with their middle-class, patriotic values, are not high in critical esteem. *The Winds of War* was his first real blockbuster since the 1950's; he had turned away from fiction to write a personal account, *This Is My God* (1959, 1973), and his subsequent novels, *Youngblood Hawke* (1962) and *Don't Stop the Carnival* (1965), were on a lesser scale. He had been carrying the idea for *The Winds of War* for twenty-five years before the novel's publication. The reading public, always his kindest critic, received *The Winds of War* with considerable enthusiasm, though it did not become a household word until 1983, when it was made into a highly celebrated television miniseries.

The critics, who almost universally deplored the pedestrian mediocrity of *Marjorie Morningstar* (1955) and *Youngblood Hawke*, recognized that in *The Winds of War* Wouk had demonstrated an astute analysis of military strategy and depth of historical detail. They also noted, however, that the characters were not wholly believable, and Victor Henry was simply too blandly patriotic and, at bottom, unattractive.

The Winds of War set the scene for its sequel, *War and Remembrance*, which followed in 1978 and, like its predecessor, quickly became a best-seller. Together, these two profound historical romances, as Wouk calls them, represent sixteen years of research and writing; they constitute an enduring contribution to the literature of World War II.

Bibliography

Gerard, Philip. "The Great American War Novels." *World & I* 10 (June, 1995): 54-63. Gerard notes that World War II was "the last public event that defined a generation of novelists. . . ." In this essay, he looks at the works of many of them, including Wouk's *The Caine Mutiny*. Although Gerard does not address *The Winds of War* directly, his comments can be extended to Wouk's other war novels.

Mazzeno, Laurence W. *Herman Wouk*. New York: Twayne, 1994. A collection of critical essays that explores various aspects of the works of Herman Wouk. Includes an index and bibliographical references for further reading.

Shapiro, Edward S. "The Jew as Patriot: Herman Wouk and American Jewish Identity." *American Jewish History* 84 (December, 1996): 333-351. Shapiro explores similarities between American identity and Jewish identity in the works of Herman Wouk, which portray the Jew as the defender of American institutions and values. Shapiro also notes that Wouk viewed the history of the American West and Israel's struggle for independence as being analogous.

Shatzky, Joel, and Michael Taub, eds. *Contemporary Jewish-American Novelists: A Bio-Critical Sourcebook*. Westport, Conn.: Greenwood Press, 1997. Includes an entry on Wouk's life, major works, and themes, with an overview of his critical reception and a bibliography of primary and secondary sources.

Jim Crawford

THE WINNERS

Author: Julio Cortázar (1914-1984)
Type of plot: Satire
Time of plot: The 1950's
Locale: Buenos Aires and a cruise ship along the coast of Argentina
First published: Los premios, 1960 (English translation, 1965)

Principal characters:
> GABRIEL MEDRANO, a dentist, cynical intellectual, womanizer, and freethinker who is dissatisfied with life
> CARLOS LÓPEZ, a bohemian high school teacher of Spanish
> PERSIO, a proofreader, an absentminded, offbeat philosopher, literate visionary, and would-be writer
> FELIPE TREJO, a high school student dealing with his emerging sexuality
> PAULA LAVALLE, an attractive redhead, courted by López, companion to, although not emotionally involved with, Raúl Costa
> RAÚL COSTA, an architect who is liberal, homosexual, and attracted to Felipe Trejo

The Novel

The novel is divided into four chapters, entitled "Prologue," "Day One," "Day Two," and "Epilogue." In the opening section, eighteen people, representing a broad spectrum of Buenos Aires society, are gathered in the Café London. They are the winners, with their invited guests, of a mysterious lottery whose prize is an ocean cruise with a secret itinerary. They are greeted courteously but evasively by an inspector from the "Ministry of Cultural Affairs" who tells them about certain "technical problems" that have complicated the arrangements. They are taken to the *Malcolm*, a freighter of uncertain nationality, where they discover that the whole after portion of the ship is barred to them. The prohibition, at first unexplained, is later implausibly blamed on an outbreak of "Typhus 224." The only contact with the other part of the ship is provided by the waiters, a bartender, a single officer who represents the invisible captain, a doctor, and a few uncommunicative seamen who speak an unrecognizable language.

On the first day at sea, the motley group of passengers becomes acquainted, developing attractions and enmities, social and sexual, but the mysterious prohibition becomes the focus of a major division into two groups, sometimes referred to as "the group of the damned" and "the peace party." The latter are the partisans of the establishment who accept without question whatever explanations are offered by the representatives of Magenta Lines. The former band, composed of the more unconventional, socially critical thinkers, rejects the explanations, suspecting something much more sinister, and makes plans to confront the forces of evil directly.

On the following day, the determination of the rebellious party to act in the face of what it sees as at least official high-handedness leads to two attempts to cross the barrier—both of which result in violence. Felipe, anxious to prove his manhood, tries to exploit the interest shown in him by one of the sailors named Orf and is raped by him, while a direct armed assault designed to reach the telegraph leads to the death of Medrano at the hands of the crew.

In the epilogue, which narrates events that take place on the morning of the third day, the inspector arrives by seaplane to offer the passengers air transportation back to Buenos Aires on condition that they sign a document ratifying an official version of the incident, absolving the shipping line and the ministry of responsibility. All must agree to sign or they will all be endlessly delayed. The defenders of authority declare themselves immediately ready to sign and beg to be allowed to continue their cruise. The rebels refuse to sign, but the reader is left with the clear impression that their defiance will not lead to action.

The novel is narrated in short scenes relying heavily on dialogue provided by a third-person narrator clearly more interested in the rebels. The constant silly pretentiousness of the conversations of the conservative party contrasts with the sympathetic, although frequently ironic presentation of the deliberations of the rebels. Felipe's battle with his emerging sexuality, for example, is treated with sensitivity and in detail. The reader's sympathy is enlisted on the side of the nonconformists in the most obvious way; for example, the official version of Medrano's disappearance flatly contradicts the narrated events.

Interspersed throughout the narrative scenes are passages in italics which convey the meditations of Persio on the nature of perception and the relationship between experience and imagination. These sections employ an avant-garde, associative, modernist style that contrasts with the rather conventional language of the remainder of the novel, which relies for much of its effect on the slightly parodic imitation of a range of Argentine voices.

The novel is basically comic, not only in the sense that there is a great deal of humor in the satiric treatment of the snobbish and intellectually arteriosclerotic and much wry humor in the portrayal of the thinkers, but also in the sense that even the culminating violent events are treated completely without sentiment, without any sense of tragedy.

The Characters

There are eighteen passengers on the boat, all slightly caricatured representatives of a variety of social backgrounds, ranging from the top end of the working class to the low end of the power elite. The tough guy Atilio Presutti (nicknamed Pelusa), whose brother is a popular tango singer, is accompanied by his girlfriend, Nelly, and their two cliché-spouting socially ambitious mothers. At the other end of the scale, Don Galo Porriño, a wealthy merchant of Gallic descent, travels in a wheelchair with his chauffeur in constant attendance. López and Doctor Restelli teach at the same school, although they represent quite different social and political points of view:

Restelli is a reactionary dandy who quickly allies himself with the peace party, while López is a bohemian leftist who drinks beer with his students and joins the ranks of the malcontents. Felipe Trejo, one of the less popular students at the same school, has invited his nasty, spoiled little sister along as well as his unctuously snobbish parents. Claudia Lewbaum, divorced from a neurologist, and her son Jorge have invited the absentminded and slightly crazy intellectual Persio to accompany them because they fear for his health. The two other couples are so unalike that they seem deliberately contrasted. Lucio and Nora, desperately but conventionally and even grotesquely in love, have recently eloped and are worried about the reaction of her respectable parents. Paula and Raúl share a platonic but genuine friendship.

Several of the male members of the radical group are roughly of the age and political views of Cortázar. At least two of them—Medrano, the intellectual haunted by the temptation of political involvement, and Persio, avant-garde aesthete and literary theorist—may be seen as expressing central concerns of the author. Yet none of the characters escapes the generally ironic tone of the narrative or the invariably parodic tone of the dialogue.

It is impossible to avoid the impression that the narrowness of vision of a whole society is being suggested. The situation of the passengers, manipulated by arbitrary and remote authority, leads some to attempt to find answers, while most are quite content to accept what they are told. Even those who actively seek the truth compromise in the end, however, and their efforts and sufferings are seen to be empty.

Themes and Meanings

The novel must be read, in part, as an allegory of the political situation in the Argentina that Cortázar had left in 1951. This shipload of fools at the mercy of an authority that is perceived as sinister and arbitrary, with its bureaucratic nonsensicalities, is a microcosm of Argentina. As is usual in Cortázar's work, however, it is not so much the political situation itself that concerns him as it is the uncritical, even unheeding, acquiescence of the average person, who, confronted with such a situation, does nothing. It is the impact of the oppressive regime on people whose lives are ruled by received opinion and cultural conventions that fascinates Cortázar. Yet complacency in the face of abuses of power and the dilemma of the contemplative mind confronted with the violence of the world are common enough problems to make the book more than a political allegory of a particular situation or moment.

Through the meditations of Persio, the reader is led to contemplate another of Cortázar's major themes, the relationship between art and reality, between artistic contemplation and political involvement. While *The Winners* is not as clearly an "antinovel" as *Rayuela* (1963; *Hopscotch*, 1966), it foreshadows it in its ironic treatment of the themes of the European literary tradition (Orf as Orpheus at the gates of the underworld, for example) and particularly in the experiments in nonlinear narrative that comprise the passages in italics.

As in much of Cortázar's fiction, the central characters are involved in a quest for personal fulfillment. The need to enter the forbidden zone of the ship assumes symbolic significance. The leaders of the party of the damned suffer in varying degrees from a sense of incompleteness, which they seek, unsuccessfully, to remedy by their action. As everywhere in Cortázar's world, this sense of alienation is felt both in its intensely personal aspect and in relation to the social context. The need to discover personal integrity involves the encounter with the other, with otherness. The group's quest for the truth about the mysteries of the after end of the ship parallels Felipe's more personal adventure in self-discovery, but both lead to a loss of innocence which is too painful to be openly admitted. As Felipe returns to Buenos Aires, concocting stories of wild shipboard romances with which to regale his friends, the others bluster unconvincingly about their intention to make their discoveries of official abuses public.

Critical Context

The Spanish edition of *The Winners* was Cortázar's first novel, published in Buenos Aires in 1960, but it did not appear in English until after the appearance of the very successful *Hopscotch*. Although it is not as great a novel as *Hopscotch*, it is a witty and intriguing treatment of the themes of the later novels and is particularly relevant to the study of Cortázar's development as a novelist. It treats for the first time the major themes of Cortázar's long fiction and shows him struggling with the question of form as well. The sections in which the narrator expresses Persio's meditations in a radically experimental style are perhaps not convincingly integrated into the body of the narrative. On the other hand, Cortázar's gift for imitating voices and for recording in a way that always rings true the variety, richness, and frequent silliness of human consciousness is already well developed in this work.

The Winners may be seen as an early contribution to the body of Latin American literature that began to invade the North American and European literary consciousness in the 1960's. Written, like many other books of the period, by an exile from a country in political turmoil, it reacts boldly but ironically, with humor and without ideology, creatively and wittily in such a way that the whole world can identify with its central dilemmas.

Bibliography

Alazraki, Jaime, and Ivar Ivask, eds. *The Final Island: The Fiction of Julio Cortázar.* Norman: University of Oklahoma Press, 1978. Perhaps the finest collection of criticism on Cortázar, a representative sampling of his best critics covering all the important aspects of his fictional output.

Boldy, Steven. *The Novels of Julio Cortázar.* Cambridge, England: Cambridge University Press, 1980. The introduction provides a helpful biographical sketch linked to the major developments in Cortázar's writing. Boldy concentrates on four Cortázar novels: *The Winners, Hopscotch, 62: A Model Kit,* and *A Manual for Manuel.* Includes notes, bibliography, and index.

Guibert, Rita. *Seven Voices: Seven Latin American Writers Talk to Rita Guibert.* New York: Knopf, 1973. Includes an important interview with Cortázar, who discusses both his politics (his strenuous objection to U.S. interference in Latin America) and many of his fictional works.

Harss, Luis, and Barbara Dohmann. *Into the Mainstream: Conversations with Latin-American Writers*. New York: Harper & Row, 1967. Includes an English translation of an important interview in Spanish.

Hernandez del Castillo, Ana. *Keats, Poe, and the Shaping of Cortázar's Mythopoesis*. Amsterdam: J. Benjamin, 1981. This is a part of the Purdue University Monographs in Romance Languages, volume 8. Cortázar praised this study for its rigor and insight.

Peavler, Terry L. *Julio Cortázar*. Boston: Twayne, 1990. Peavler begins with an overview of Cortázar's life and career and his short stories of the fantastic, the mysterious, the psychological, and the realistic. Only one chapter is devoted exclusively to his novels. Includes chronology, notes, annotated bibliography, and index.

Stavans, Ilan. *Julio Cortázar: A Study of the Short Fiction*. New York: Twayne, 1996. See especially the chapters on the influence of Jorge Luis Borges on Cortázar's fiction, his use of the fantastic, and his reliance on popular culture. Stavans also has a section on Cortázar's role as writer and his interpretation of developments in Latin American literature. Includes chronology and bibliography.

Yovanovich, Gordana. *Julio Cortázar's Character Mosaic: Reading the Longer Fiction*. Toronto: University of Toronto Press, 1991. Three chapters focus on Cortázar's four major novels and his fluctuating presentations of characters as narrators, symbols, and other figures of language. Includes notes and bibliography.

John H. Turner

WINTER IN THE BLOOD

Author: James Welch (1940-   )
Type of plot: Psychological realism
Time of plot: The early 1970's
Locale: Northern Montana
First published: 1974

> *Principal characters:*
>> THE NARRATOR, a young Blackfeet man struggling to put the deaths of
>> his father and brother behind him
>> TERESA, the narrator's mother, a practical, hardened woman, a survivor
>> THE OLD WOMAN, Teresa's mother, one of the few remaining links to
>> the narrator's ancestry
>> YELLOW CALF, a blind elder, either mystical or insane
>> FIRST RAISE, the narrator's father, who, like his son, was a wanderer
>> MOSE, the narrator's brother

The Novel

Winter in the Blood intertwines the narrator's tale of passage from a boy to a man with the mysterious story of his grandmother's role in the Blackfeet tribe's tragic past. The book consists of four sections of varied lengths and a brief epilogue.

Winter in the Blood begins as the narrator returns home from a drunken escapade to find that Agnes, the woman with whom he has been living, is gone and has stolen his gun and electric razor. Attempting to forget about the woman and his things, the narrator helps his mother and Lame Bull with the ranch chores. Lame Bull marries Teresa, making him an owner of the ranch, a role into which he throws himself with relish.

Teresa's marriage triggers the narrator's memory of his father and brother's deaths. He talks with Teresa about First Raise and is disturbed by the fact that she remembers their life together much differently than he does. Teresa further uproots her son by telling him that there is no work for him on the ranch now that Lame Bull is in charge. When Agnes is spotted in Malta, the narrator decides to go after her. As his thoughts return to Agnes, he makes the reader aware of his grandmother's reasons for hating the young woman. Once the youngest wife of a Blackfeet chief, the grandmother hates Crees for what she believes to be their treachery. Crees had scouted for the cavalry, the Long Knives, who chased the Blackfeet from their home at the base of the mountains. The narrator repeats his grandmother's story of a winter of starvation and the death of her husband. She was cast out by the tribe in mourning for their chief. The narrator believes his grandmother when she says that the women of the tribe envied her beauty. He also believes the rumor that a half-breed drifter with whom his grandmother settled down wasn't his real grandfather.

The narrator temporarily sets aside his grandmother's story and catches a ride to Dodson, a nearby town with a bus stop. The narrator travels on to Malta, where he is quickly caught up in a series of bewildering events. He helps Agnes's brother roll a drunken white, meets an Easterner running from a mysterious past, and falls into bed with a barmaid.

Back home briefly at the beginning of part 2, the narrator visits Yellow Calf and is drawn to the blind old man who claims to understand the calls of animals. On the road again, checking out a report of Agnes in Havre, the narrator runs into the Easterner, who is running from the Federal Bureau of Investigation (FBI), and agrees to drive him across the Canadian border. Before the two can set out, the narrator's companion is apprehended, and the narrator is punched in a bar by Agnes's brother. Tired "of town, of walking home hung over, beaten up, or both," he hitches a ride back to the ranch in part 3. His grandmother has died. The narrator and Lame Bull dig the woman's grave. He is reminded of hacking First Raise's grave out of the frozen earth and remembers the time he and his brother ran their father's cattle, the day Mose was struck on the highway and killed.

In part 4, the narrator returns to Yellow Calf's shack. Yellow Calf knows the truth about the narrator's grandmother. The Blackfeet thought that the woman, the newest member of the tribe, had brought them "bad medicine," that she had been responsible for their devastation. The narrator wonders how his grandmother avoided starvation in the abandoned tepees on the edge of camp. Yellow Calf does not say so, but the narrator is convinced that the old man hunted to feed his grandmother, kept her alive, and had a child with her. Yellow Calf is his real grandfather.

On the way home from Yellow Calf's shack, the narrator discovers a cow stuck up to her chest in mud. It is the same wild-eyed animal that started the panic of his father's cattle on the day that Mose was killed trying to stop the herd from running across the highway. Roping the cow to his saddle horn, the narrator mounts his horse, Bird, and attempts to pull the beast out of the muck. When Bird loses his footing and falls, throwing the narrator to his back, the cow slips down the bank of the slough in which she had been stuck. Lying unable to move, listening to the two animals' final cries, the narrator experiences a feeling of pleasant calm as he is soaked by a summer rain.

The old woman's lonely burial is related in the epilogue. Teresa moans as Lame Bull utters a vague memorial. The book concludes with the image of the narrator throwing his grandmother's tobacco pouch into her grave.

The Characters

The narrator seems hopeless. The reader must decide whether it is bad luck or bad judgment that plagues him. A recurring symbol of his frustration is his belief that the river has no fish in it, a conviction he holds in spite of the many locals and tourists who insist that they catch fish in the river all the time.

That the narrator continues both to fish and to believe that the river is barren is a paradox that perfectly combines the senses of perseverance and of doom that characterize him. The combination is useful, however, in the pursuit of his grandmother's tragic story. For uncovering the act of kindness Yellow Calf had performed, the narrator is rewarded with the truth about his heritage.

Teresa is both a caring and a callous mother. She killed Amos, the duck who won the family's heart by surviving a grisly accident, but served him for a special Christmas dinner. She reinforces the notion that even sources of nurturing, such as the land and one's precious memories, can be brutal. Her marriage contributes to a feeling evoked throughout the book that the glory of the past can never be fully recovered. In place of the dramatic and powerful First Raise, Teresa has the unremarkable Lame Bull. The union of Teresa and Lame Bull, however, shows the narrator that personal tragedy can be overcome, that life goes on.

The old woman, like her grandson, is never called by name. This shared emptiness links the narrator and his grandmother. The old woman's incessant rocking is echoed by the narrator's wanderings to and from town and back and forth between the past and the present. Instead of contributing to the erosion of the narrator's identity, the old woman's death enriches her grandson's understanding of family history. His grief takes the form of curiosity strong enough to uncover a truth that restores his pride. The tobacco pouch in the narrator's hands as he stands over his grandmother's grave is a sign of the increased compassion for and understanding of the old woman.

Yellow Calf draws from the narrator an optimism, a faith, that the young man rarely exhibits. The narrator is skeptical concerning the elder man's professed ability to understand the calls of wild animals, but he is tender in Yellow Calf's presence. When the narrator understands that the old man is his grandfather, he speaks with more pride than at any other time in the novel, and he is never more at ease with the memory of his father than when recalling that First Raise had brought him to Yellow Calf as a boy. Yellow Calf's goodness partially redeems the narrator's own sense of worth.

First Raise and Mose represent a time when the narrator felt less alone in the world. His memories of a breakfast cooked by First Raise and a trail ride with Mose are richly detailed, suggesting the reverence with which the narrator preserves them. First Raise and Mose also illustrate the difficult relationship to whites that has influenced the narrator's coming of age. First Raise played the clown for white people in the bars in Dodson; Mose and the narrator grew up idolizing the white cowboy in Western films. Through these associations, the book reminds the reader that the politics of race are at work.

Themes and Meanings

Winter in the Blood is a psychological self-portrait, the record of its first-person narrator's attempts to comprehend and endure tragic loss. The other characters who populate the world of the novel become foils for the exploration of one individual's mental life and the cultural legacy this existence reflects.

Several times the narrator speaks of creating distance between himself and his psychological demons. He is aware that he must heal himself, but he almost always undertakes disastrously wrong courses of treatment. He attempts to stem the grief that has flooded through him since the deaths of his father and brother by escaping his boyhood home for towns and bars. His appetites are dangerous tools. Drinking leads inevitably to fighting or to debilitating sexual encounters, or both, and leaves the narrator in the bruised, defeated state in which the reader first encounters him. His self-destructive personal life does not keep him from thinking of his dead father and brother. As the young Blackfeet man begins to tell his tragic stories, the reader has the sense that the narrator's excursions into memory are as unstoppable as his forays into town.

Further complicating the situation is the issue of the narrator's faulty memory. Teresa remembers events differently from her son, and her versions make it hard for the narrator to revere First Raise, to think of his father as a hero. He has known his grandmother's story for so long that he does not realize that he is not sure how it ends. The narrator's memory, like a historical record, is always under construction and subject to change. His search for the very tales he is telling emerges as a major theme of the book.

The mental act of storytelling comes to depend on the physical activity by which the details of the stories are accumulated, as if the narrator's restless wandering literally shakes loose the memories of First Raise and Mose. The culmination of this idea is the narrator's incredible attempt to pull the wild-eyed cow from the mud, much as he has succeeded in pulling his grandmother's secret from Yellow Calf. That his final test is physical, a question of his strength alone against the elements, is a poignant reminder that, despite making nourishing connections with his past, the narrator will never permanently shake the sense of isolation that plagues him.

In addition to the theme of personal loss and recovery, the novel discusses the idea of cultural dislocation. The impact of Western expansion on the Blackfeet tribe is represented by the grandmother's story of the winter of starvation. The same forced relocation that separated the tribe from its traditional home separated the narrator from his cultural roots. Through Yellow Calf, the narrator is able to reconnect with his tribe, and the novel is able to join the personal and cultural narratives. Yellow Calf emerges both as a Native American hero and as the narrator's real grandfather. Yellow Calf lends a proud aspect to a past that the narrator had formerly viewed only as a source of shame.

Critical Context

In *Winter in the Blood*, James Welch introduces the themes and techniques he would continue to develop in later works. The novel begins the project of establishing through literary means the identity of the Native American. Welch was born in Browning, Montana, a small town that serves as the headquarters of the Blackfeet reservation. He attended high schools on both the Blackfeet and Fort Belknap reservations in Montana. He is the author of a book of poems, *Riding the Earthboy Forty* (1971), that evokes life on the reservation, and he was at one time a professor of Indian studies at the University of Washington; his efforts toward cultural preservation have thus been varied and significant. The themes and techniques of his first novel reflect this concern. The narrator is able to understand that his true pursuit is not of his appetites but his heritage. His boyhood heroes had been the white cowboy actors who rode and roped on the big screen. This ironic confession demonstrates the scarcity in Western arts of representations of Native Americans, a lack that Welch himself seeks to fill.

The first-person narrative of self-discovery and the elaborate time sequence of the novel are techniques that illuminate the theme of cultural reconstruction. The plot switches between three time frames: the present, the narrator's youth, and the youth of his grandmother. As the narrator reexamines his own past, he realizes that the history of his people is a forgotten but nevertheless important part of his consciousness. Welch's later works *The Death of Jim Loney* (1979), *Fools Crow* (1986), and *The Indian Lawyer* (1990) are perhaps more ambitious in scope, but the impetus for these works is located in the pathos, comedy, and celebration that has attracted the attention of scores of critics to *Winter in the Blood*.

Bibliography
Armstrong, Meg. "'Buried in Fine White Ash': Violence and the Reimagination of Ceremonial Bodies in *Winter in the Blood* and *Bearheart*." *The American Indian Quarterly* 21 (Spring, 1997): 265-298. Armstrong explores the themes of power, transformation, and identity in James Welch's *Winter in the Blood* and Gerald Vizenor's *Bearheart*. She argues that the texts must be read with the understanding of ceremony and the body in order to wholly appreciate American Indian literature.
Ballard, Charles G. "The Theme of the Helping Hand in *Winter in the Blood*." *MELUS* 17 (Spring, 1991): 63-74. Ballard discusses Welch's combination of Blackfeet Indian mythic imagery with Western literary techniques in Welch's novel. The image of the helping hand emerges as the wanderer learns from the people he meets during his journey and also from the Indian wisdom of his grandparents.
Davis, Jack L. "Restoration of Indian Identity in *Winter in the Blood*." In *James Welch*, edited by Ron McFarland. Lewiston, Idaho: Confluence Press, 1986. Davis sets Welch's tale of a rediscovered Native American identity against the historical backdrop of "the military conquest of American Indians." The critic argues that, as a work of imagination, the novel challenges and expands the historical and anthropological assumptions by which the Native American condition is generally understood.
Eisenstein, Paul. "Finding Lost Generations: Recovering Omitted History in *Winter in the Blood*." *MELUS* 19 (Fall, 1994): 3-18. Eisenstein explores the similarity in style between Welch's novel and Ernest Hemingway's works, particularly *In Our Time*. He focuses on the literary strategies of omission that both authors have in common: while Hemingway omitted for revision, Welch uses omission as a literary device.
Gish, Robert. "Mystery and Mock Intrigue in James Welch's *Winter in the Blood*." In *James Welch*, edited by Ron McFarland. Lewiston, Idaho: Confluence Press, 1986. Gish is concerned with the technical achievements of the novel. He articulates the relationship between content and form, focusing on the combined presence of tragedy and comedy.

Ruoff, A. LaVonne. "Alienation and the Female Principle in *Winter in the Blood.*" In *James Welch*, edited by Ron McFarland. Lewiston, Idaho: Confluence Press, 1986. Ruoff examines all aspects of femininity in the novel, even the relationship between the wild-eyed cow and her calf. She supplements her discussion with fascinating research into Cree, Gros Ventres, and Blackfeet tribal customs.

Sands, Kathleen M. "Alienation and Broken Narrative in *Winter in the Blood.*" *American Indian Quarterly* 4 (May, 1978): 97-105. Sands is a prominent critic of Welch and other Native American writers. She discusses the relationship between theme and structure in the novel, arguing that the concept of alienation is underscored by the narrator's attempt to locate himself within the novel's several time frames.

Nick David Smart

THE WITCHES OF EASTWICK

Author: John Updike (1932-   )
Type of plot: Philosophical
Time of plot: The late 1960's
Locale: Eastwick, Rhode Island
First published: 1984

Principal characters:
ALEXANDRA SPOFFORD, a sculptress who controls storms
JANE SMART, a cellist who sometimes flies
SUKIE ROUGEMONT, a reporter who casts love spells
DARRYL VAN HORNE, a crass yet charismatic inventor and newest
    Eastwick resident
CLYDE GABRIEL, the boozy editor of the *Eastwick Word*
FELICIA GABRIEL, a self-righteous crusader for decency
JENNY GABRIEL, Clyde and Felicia's daughter, who returns to Eastwick
CHRIS GABRIEL, Jenny's dull brother

The Novel

Set in a typical small New England town, *The Witches of Eastwick* offers a witty, ir-reverent, and pointed glimpse of small-town people and values, but with a twist. The three main characters are witches, and amid local gossip, scandal, and sorcery, they seek the perfect relationship by any means.

The Witches of Eastwick is divided into three chapters. These sections ("The Co-ven," "Malefica," and "Guilt") respectively introduce the players and the situation, re-solve the various conflicts that arise, and detail the aftermath. The story is related by an unseen, omniscient narrator who is a town resident.

The story begins as the three principal characters, Alexandra Spofford, Jane Smart, and Sukie Rougemont—all divorced, and whose former husbands are literally gather-ing dust on shelves in their homes—prepare to meet at Sukie's for one of their weekly "Thursdays." At such rendezvous, the three relax with a few drinks, gossip about the latest affairs they are having with various tired Eastwick husbands, and practice witchcraft.

During the first section of the novel, the narrator details the minutiae of life in Eastwick; however, the focus remains largely on the three witches, the various tricks and pranks they play (at times outright nasty), and their own boredom-generated af-fairs. The reader becomes acquainted with Alexandra's deep, earthy rootedness and power; with Jane's cranky, precise nature and passion for music; and with Sukie's good-natured, inquisitive sensuality.

Darryl Van Horne makes his appearance at a community concert. Ostensibly, he has come to Eastwick to further his aim of inventing a solar-energy-collecting paint, but little is actually known of Darryl. The town is enthusiastic about his plans to renovate an old property that has been a tax drain on the community for some time. His near-grotesque appearance and "New York vulgar" manner repulse some, including the more sensitive Alexandra, but his brash and outspoken coarseness charms others, especially Jane. Immediately, it is clear that Darryl is interested in the three witches, and shortly, through appeals to each of their secret desires, he has managed to coax all of them into visiting the old Lenox mansion, which he is lavishly remodeling to suit his hedonistic purposes.

Soon, Darryl and the three witches are frequent companions at his home. There, sometimes on his dome tennis court (where tennis balls undergo startling transformations), but especially within the environs of his decadently lavish "playroom," which includes a mammoth teakwood Jacuzzi, the four cavort sensuously, waited upon by Darryl's servant, Fidel.

Meanwhile, changes are taking place within the community. Ed Parsley, the young Unitarian minister, lately Sukie's lover, runs off to join the peace movement. (He is later killed while making a bomb.) Prim Brenda Parsley, Ed's wife, finding a hidden assertiveness within herself, takes over the church's ministry. Felicia Gabriel, the shrewish moral crusader, begins to find an odd assortment of feathers, thumbtacks, and insects issuing from her mouth. Clyde Gabriel, Sukie's boss and the editor of the *Eastwick Word*, consumed by alcohol-induced guilt and in constant misery brought on by his wife's nagging, kills her with a fireplace poker, then hangs himself. This event brings Clyde and Felicia's children, Jenny and Chris, back to Eastwick. Soon, the two youths begin to take part in the regular festivities at the old mansion.

Things begin to sour among the Eastwick fivesome of Darryl, Alexandra, Jane, Sukie, and Jenny as jealousies start to surface. Alexandra, Jane, and Sukie all nurture fantasies concerning an eventual life together with Darryl, but he surprises and ultimately alienates the three by his announcement of marriage to the young Jenny. Stung by this seeming rejection, the witches conjure a spell aimed at avenging themselves upon Darryl and his smug new bride. Jenny becomes increasingly ill, and though Sukie and, especially, Alexandra have remorseful thoughts about their deed, they do nothing about it.

At the story's end, power begins slowly to shift among the female residents of Eastwick. In the aftermath of Jenny's long sickness and eventual death, Alexandra, Jane, and Sukie drift apart as a new coven forms from newer residents. The narrator reveals how the three eventually go on to form new lives away from Eastwick, but the memory of their presence seems to linger ethereally among the quaint byways of the small community.

The Characters

It is clear from the detailed opening that Alexandra, in her late thirties, is the driving force behind the small coven and the focus for the author's principal characterization. She seems to derive her power from the earthly elements, and her command of elemental forces is demonstrated by her control of a summer storm and by her "bubbies": small clay statuettes that she sells at local boutiques. Yet Alexandra can also be moody and vain. As well as storms, her momentary whims can cause death. She alternately engages the reader's empathy and awe with her earth-mother characteristics and engenders fear when, for example, she impulsively wills the death of a squirrel marauding in her garden. Through her own self-doubts, Alexandra demonstrates the shifting concerns of power, love, and sexuality being examined in the story.

Jane Smart, also in her late thirties, is a cellist, and that facet becomes the primary focus for her characterization. Jane is willful, hostile, and gifted; she is impatient with much save the passion for her music. Wildly decadent given the proper motivation, Jane demonstrates the self-indulgent ego that cares for little except personal gratification. It is through Jane that the reader begins to understand how power corrupts.

Sukie Rougemont, in her early thirties, is a reporter for the *Eastwick Word*. The reader cannot help but see Sukie in a favorable light. Alexandra's constant comments about Sukie's "monkeyish" curiosity and energetic, girlish demeanor add to this impression. Sukie is shown to be sympathetic and caring, but her outward manner of exuberance and sympathy may mask a certain cunning and calculation that can be chilling. Her seeming good nature may belie a sense of powerlessness and guilt that fuel a jealousy that ultimately becomes destructive.

Darryl Van Horne, though not specifically referred to as such, is a demonic manifestation. From his arrival out of nowhere to his orgies at the Lenox mansion, Darryl epitomizes those things the reader will consider crude, obnoxious, and vulgar; however, Darryl is also strongly charismatic. His tastes are eclectic. The furnishings of his home reflect a desire to acquire objects of art but also reveal an insensitive nature that disregards enduring artistic merit. He furnishes his home opulently only in relation to his own need for gratification. Therefore, his playroom, the scene of wild bacchanals, is minutely appointed to service every physical pleasure or desire, while the rest of his house is a scattering of furniture and uncrated objects.

Jenny Gabriel returns to Eastwick lost and unsure of herself. Confronted with the gruesome deaths of her parents, she and her ineffectual brother Chris are befriended by Darryl and the three witches. Soon, Jenny's seemingly shy nature is conquered, and she joins in the frequent debauches. Finally, she consents to Darryl's marriage proposal. Yet Jenny may not be the total innocent she at first seems. She is quick to recognize the essential power struggle between herself and the witches, and she seeks to consolidate her own position by becoming Darryl's wife. Her effort proves her undoing, however, for the witches perceive a threat and act to preserve their own sense of family, which Jenny has usurped.

Themes and Meanings

As with many stories, this novel can be read from different perspectives. On one level, it posits the possibility of instant wish gratification and questions the moral implications of such a proposition: Would such power corrupt? and to what degree? What is the nature of such corruption? How much pleasure is too much? On another level, the novel is a somewhat bawdy romp filled with satiric pokes and jabs at small-town Americana.

It is through the everyday lives of the principal characters that these themes are explored, as well as others concerning religion, gender, and morality. The narrator guides the reader through Alexandra's middle-aged doubts about herself and her consequent use of witchcraft to prop up her unexciting life. Chiefly through Alexandra, readers come to know how daily annoyances can be taken care of with a murmured spell, or a thought. Readers also see, however, the darker side to such power, as when Alexandra's petulance causes the elderly Mrs. Lovecraft to break her hip. In the same way, Jane's passion for the cello becomes an obsession under the tutelage of the devilish Darryl. In the end, her instrument lies in splinters, testament and analogy to her own shattered ambitions. Sukie's caring, free-spirited innocence also undergoes a transformation, and she changes from the buoyant confidante of Alexandra into a vengeful witch.

Darryl might be thought of as both focus and source for the witches' powers, yet he never demonstrates any supernatural abilities himself, nor is he suggested to be otherworldly in any but superficial ways. He seems wholly unsurprised and comfortable with whatever the three women do. Darryl seems to feed the witches' needs while at the same time feeding upon their lavish attentions. He is largely seen as a passive receptor, and Updike may thus be suggesting that evil and corruption are fed more by human needs than from outside sources.

The story examines the consequences of unchecked power and may be asking the reader to consider the issue of moral behavior. What if, with a nod of the head, one could bypass the normal social checks and balances and, for example, get rid of the neighbor's annoying dog? Could anyone be counted upon to exercise control with such power? In *The Witches of Eastwick*, the three witches constantly circumvent such controls. Besides being alternately amusing, thrilling, and lascivious, the novel gently brings such considerations to the reader's attention.

Critical Context

The Witches of Eastwick can be seen as something of a departure for John Updike, yet the book is also a continuation of themes expressed in his earlier fiction. The work's mythological nature does have at least one precedent in Updike's third novel, *The Centaur* (1963), but aside from that, the novel reveals Updike's continuing regard for detailing the smallest aspects of daily life with meticulous care. His preoccupation with what goes on behind closed doors and his penchant for scrutinizing dreary existence have struck some critics as obsessive; still, Updike's skill at portrayal cannot be denied, even by his harshest detractors.

To many critics, the writing in *The Witches of Eastwick* is generally thought to be as good as that in some of Updike's best efforts, including *The Poorhouse Fair* (1959), *Of the Farm* (1965), *Couples* (1968), and the Pulitzer Prize-winning *Rabbit Is Rich* (1981), which immediately preceded *The Witches of Eastwick*. Yet some critics have also blasted Updike's novel for being pretentious, mean-spirited, and overly indulgent. As well, *The Witches of Eastwick* has been thought by some to demonstrate an essential dislike for women.

Since the period of his earliest works, critical focus has shifted from a concern with Updike's lush, detailed style to a consideration of his themes, which, some say, he treats in a shallow and inconsequential manner. Much of the severest criticism might be summed up by the charge that Updike writes very well about nothing much. Updike has countered by claiming that such critics are looking only for ever-increasing thrills. He suggests that the normal and the real are profound in their own respects.

Bibliography
Bloom, Harold, ed. *John Updike.* New York: Chelsea House, 1987. In his introduction, Bloom commends the artful style of *The Witches of Eastwick*, focusing especially on the characterizations of the three witches. To Bloom, this is more than a satiric novel; it reaches into horror for its powerful effect. Though Bloom praises the novel's concluding passages, he suggests a stylistic flaw in them as well.
Campbell, Jeff H. *Updike's Novels: Thorns Spell a Word.* Wichita Falls, Tex.: Midwestern State University Press, 1987. Chapter 5 contrasts Updike's *Marry Me: A Romance* (1976), *Couples*, and *The Witches of Eastwick*. Campbell focuses first on the sociological aspects of these novels, and especially on the deterioration of marriage. With regard to *The Witches of Eastwick*, Campbell discusses themes of feminism, the demythologizing of Satan, and the balancing of self between the internal and external worlds.
Newman, Judie. *John Updike.* New York: St. Martin's Press, 1988. Newman suggests that *The Witches of Eastwick* questions the relationship between imaginative power and political power. Her analysis thoroughly investigates the story's major characters, and she concludes by demonstrating how the novel might be read as commentary on the Vietnam War.
Schiff, James A. *John Updike Revisited.* Boston: Twayne, 1998. Schiff's highly readable overview of Updike's prose works provides commentary on his best-selling books, as well as his lesser known works. A chapter is devoted to a critical treatment of *Couples* and *The Witches of Eastwick*, which Schiff groups together under the heading "Marriage Novels."
Verduin, Kathleen. "Sex, Nature, and Dualism in *The Witches of Eastwick.*" *Modern Language Quarterly* 46 (September, 1985): 293-315. Verduin considers the heated controversy Updike's work generated among feminists and demonstrates how the author highlights the complicity between women and nature in the novel, especially through the vehicle of witchcraft. A scholarly treatment of women's shifting roles in society as revealed by Updike's various characterizations of women.
Welsh, J. M. "Bewitched and Bewildered Over 'Eastwick.'" *Literature and Film Quarterly* 15, no. 3 (1987): 152-154. Contrasts Updike's novel with the 1987 film version. Though Welsh regards the novel as superior, he sees the ending as weak. He concludes that the film has plenty of popular appeal but little connection with the apparent concerns of the novel's author.

George Thomas Novotny

WOMAN ON THE EDGE OF TIME

Author: Marge Piercy (1936-   )
Type of plot: Utopian realism
Time of plot: The 1970's and the year 2137
Locale: New York City and environs, and Mattapoisett, Massachusetts
First published: 1976

> *Principal characters:*
> CONSUELO (CONNIE) RAMOS, a thirty-seven-year-old inmate of a
>   mental institution
> LUCIENTE, a plant geneticist and time traveler from the year 2137
> DOLLY, Connie's favorite niece, a prostitute
> GERALDO, Dolly's pimp
> LUIS, Connie's brother, who operates a plant nursery in New Jersey
> SYBIL, Connie's friend and a fellow inmate
> BEE, Luciente's friend, who becomes Connie's lover during a trip to the
>   future
> JACKRABBIT, Luciente's friend, an artist of the future

The Novel

   Woman on the Edge of Time is a jeremiad, a lament for and a tirade against the plight of woman in the twentieth century. Connie Ramos is a thirty-seven-year-old Chicana, impoverished and without the support of friends or family, who is imprisoned in a mental institution for an alleged outburst of violent behavior. Trapped by a lifetime of deprivation and powerlessness, she is labeled mad, drugged, held captive, and stripped of all personal dignity. The specific degradations of her life in Bellevue Hospital, in Rockover State Psychiatric Institute, and finally in the New York Neuro-Psychiatric Institute are the culmination of and a metaphor for the harsh realities of the life of a middle-aged minority woman alone in contemporary urban society. The evils which plague her life are the evils which plague her society: cruelty, physical violence, the debasement of women, the abuse of children, private rage, and public indifference to human suffering. Connie's story is a polemic about the hell that women endure in a world where biology is destiny.

   The madhouse that is Connie's personal prison and the madhouse that is her society are escaped only in her intermittent mind excursions into the future. Through the agency of Luciente, a time traveler from the year 2137, she leaves her confinement and enters the twenty-second century. In her first trip to the idyllic society of Mattapoisett, Massachusetts, she discovers that women are no longer responsible for childbearing and child rearing. Luciente explains that this is the result of what she calls women's revolution: "As long as we were biologically enchained, we'd never be equal. And males never would be humanized to be loving and tender." In Mattapoisett, embryos are grown in community brooders, and after delivery the care of each child is assumed by three people who together elect to parent that child until puberty.

Because in 2137 females have been released from biological motherhood, gender has become relatively insignificant. All may parent yet lead full personal, professional, political, and social lives. Each being is essentially androgynous, both male and female. This radical change in gender definition is reflected in language. The pronouns "he" and "she," "him" and "her," "his" and "hers" have been replaced by a common pronoun, "per." Piercy quickly establishes a theme that is central to her politics and to her art—that freedom for women must entail freedom from childbirth. Yet this is only the most radical social transformation. Luciente thinks of the twentieth century as "The Age of Greed and Waste." In per time, 2137, materialism has been eradicated; cultural riches are shared by everyone, and urban centers such as New York have been dismantled and replaced by small, self-sufficient, self-governing communities. The device of Connie's time travel compels both her and the reader to look at two planes of existence juxtaposed: a present hell for women and a potential paradise for all.

Connie's incarceration is interrupted often by subsequent visits to Mattapoisett, which introduce her to educational methods, work patterns, social customs, eating habits, sexual mores, governmental structures, and therapy techniques—all sharply contrasting with those in Connie's world. The Utopian society of Mattapoisett is the novelist's teaching device, intended to help Connie to "intersee," to perceive the dynamics of her own world and conceive of other possibilities. Luciente's world constitutes an implied critique of contemporary society and a vision of its potential for improvement directed at readers too. Connie's brief explorations of futures other than Luciente's offer oblique warnings of the disastrous results of persisting in current directions. Although rather mechanical in its exposition, the dialectic between Connie's present and Luciente's future is the central purpose of the novel.

The Characters

Connie's powerlessness equals the feminine condition in this world. She is an institutionalized woman, literally and figuratively. Piercy graphically depicts the horrors of Connie's life in mental institutions. She shows the isolation; the sluggish nightmare world of strong tranquilizers; the neglect and disdain of the staff and doctors; the malign bureaucracy; the lack of hygiene, good food, clothing, privacy, and contact with the outside world. The horror increases when Connie is among the patients forced to participate in an experiment in which electrodes are to be surgically implanted in her brain to suppress violent behavior. Yet the ghastliness of her situation is felt far more intensely than the strength of her personality. The character of Connie is the central weakness of the novel: In both worlds, she is a spectator. As a character, she certainly arouses sympathy, but not strong identification and caring. Connie is the author's self-conscious political construct, an emblem of victimization of all women more than a fully realized and engrossing fictional being.

Connie seems a puppet in a political allegory because this is a thesis novel. Thesis overpowers characterization. The thesis is simply summarized, though not simply realized in life. Woman must go to war with her society, battle the many forces that hold her captive, and win freedom, if not for herself, for future generations. This is not, however, the archetypal war of the sexes. This is a fiercer war, the war of the individual against all society. Woman wars alone. Men are pimps, abortionists, psychiatrists who callously declare patients paranoid schizophrenics and experiment on them with the same indifference used to dissect chimpanzees. Piercy's male characters are a catalog of various forms of abuse of women. Only Connie's first husband, Martin, and her blind black lover, Claud, are presented as human, but both are dead, fellow victims of societal blight.

Are the characters of the future more vital? Not really. Luciente is no messiah. Luciente resembles Connie, as if Connie's alter ego were displaced in time. The guided tours of Mattapoisett are reminiscent of walking through a blissed-out commune of the 1960's. All the androgynies of this future, including Luciente, are pacific and self-satisfied stick figures. Like most residents of more perfect fictional worlds, they are devoted to telling others smugly how they eradicated the ills of society and how happy they are. The author has endowed their constant holidaying and displays of affection for one another with little more life than the recreation room at Rockover.

Themes and Meanings

Battling the oppression of women in twentieth century society has long been Piercy's personal and literary preoccupation. Her many novels and volumes of poetry dwell on woman's worthy nature and her benighted existence. The anger and the radical negations of the status quo of a committed feminist are obvious in her bleak portrait of Connie's life and in her explications of a new social order. Connie's life is a compendium of the personal and public oppressions of a minority woman. Hers is a life of poverty, conditioned dependence on males, responsibility for childbearing and child rearing, lack of education, demeaning employment, and political alienation. She is trained to passivity and accommodation, deprived of feelings of self-worth, then indicted as mad when her grief and rage break through her sex-typed behavior. These things exist, and they must cease, but the ways of saying so have become a bit predictable. Unfortunately for this novel, there are few surprises in liberation dogma.

If the present is the villain of this novel, the future is the hero. In the brave new world of 2137, men and women are equal—in fact, they are almost indistinguishable. The environment is protected, human responsibilities accepted, and personal freedoms respected. Laudable as such changes are, this future is nevertheless disturbing. It feels like a revival of the past, a synthetic primitivism with Tom Swift technology. Piercy's version of future language is stilted, repetitive, and distracting. It sounds like the flat, clipped communications that teenagers use to establish their collective independence. The general tone of the novel is the tone of most quarrels with society—rhetorical exhortation and incitation. Piercy's issues are so broad, however, her condemnations so pervasive, her expectations so elusive, how is one to respond? No matter how impassioned the sentiments, her audience may feel manipulated, not motivated.

In the dialectic of present and future, an important question is left unanswered. How did this new future come to be? The reader is given no clue. The conclusion suggests that the reformations may have been initiated by individual and/or collective declarations of war on society. Luciente closes her last encounter with Connie by declaring, "Power is violence. When did it get destroyed peacefully? We all fight when we're back to the wall." The implication is that, for Connie, violence is the only sane response to an insane world. Poisoning people with weed killer, however, does not seem like a viable mode of social transformation.

Critical Context

Marge Piercy is one of America's most political writers. The seriousness of her convictions and the intensity of her commitment to change in the lives of women are apparent in all of her works. *Woman on the Edge of Time* may be her most direct response to questions about what kinds of changes she seeks. In this novel, she both outlines the problems that she sees and explicates the transformations that she envisions. Frequently, reviewers have remarked that this is really two novels, a realistic fiction and a Utopian fantasy, and each might be more effective if presented separately. On the contrary, the dialectic between present and future is essential to her thesis, to her investigation of humanity's potential for change.

The change in Connie appears startling. In the last chapter, she tells a fellow inmate, "I was not born and raised to fight battles, but to be modest and gentle and still." Soon after making this statement, she addresses herself in the mirror and articulates her new perception of herself and of the world: "I murdered them dead. Because *they* are the violence-prone. Theirs is the money and the power, theirs the poisons that slow the mind and dull the heart. Theirs are the powers of life and death. I killed them. Because it is war." Although Piercy devotes much energy to making Connie's sanity convincing, the narrative continuum of her life experience, her time-travel experience, and her declaration of war at the conclusion may mislead some into believing that her story is indeed the raving of a madwoman. Such a reading of the character would undercut the entire novel, making it little more than a case study. The novel is propaganda for a visionary alternate social order, a potential Utopia. Believe Connie sane, and her violence is contained in her passivity as the future is contained in the present. In Piercy's schema, present and future, like violence and passivity, are not contraries; they are a single vital process. Dialectic is seeing one truth in two ways.

Seeing the world for what it is and seeing its potential are not enough to produce change. In Piercy's radical ideology, action must follow. Freedom can be won only by women fully at war with this world, martyring themselves so that their daughters might live lives of greater range and humanity than theirs. Yet seeing is the necessary first step, and seeing is what Piercy demands here.

Bibliography

Adams, Alice. "Out of the Womb: The Future of the Uterine Metaphor." *Feminist Studies* 19 (Summer, 1993): 269-289. Adams explores the evolution of the uterine metaphor in relation to the debate among feminists concerning natural and artificial methods of childbirth. In her analysis of Piercy's novel, Adams compares Piercy's alternative family structure with real-life alternatives and addresses the concept of the womb as a separate entity from the mother.

Afnan, Elham. "Chaos and Utopia: Social Transformations in *Woman on the Edge of Time*." *Extrapolation* 37 (Winter, 1996): 330-340. Perceiving Piercy's novel as a classic work in feminist utopian writing, Afnan asserts that the chaos theory is a central theme in the novel, the concept of nonlinearity being its most significant aspect. Afnan also explores the process of social change through the selection of either utopia or dystopia.

Booker, M. Keith. "Woman on the Edge of a Genre: The Feminist Dystopias of Marge Piercy." *Science Fiction Studies* 21 (November, 1994): 337-350. Booker explores the political commitment that informs Piercy's *Woman on the Edge of Time* and *He, She, It*. He asserts that her feminist stance is rather unusual in a tradition that has been dominated by a masculine agenda and shows how both books reinforce their feminist political statements through literary techniques.

Levitas, Ruth. "We: The Problem in Identity, Solidarity, and Difference." *History of the Human Sciences* 8 (August, 1995): 89-105. Examines Y. Zamyatin's *We* and Piercy's *Woman on the Edge of Time* to show how the use of the word "we" is gendered and therefore reflective of society's repression of women. Concludes that both utopian works show that language reflects social conditions, and that achieving equality, while taking into account differences, is dependent on social perceptions.

Rudy, Cathy. "Ethics, Reproduction, Utopia: Gender and Childbearing in *Woman on the Edge of Time* and *The Left Hand of Darkness*." *NWSA Journal* 9 (Spring, 1997): 22-38. Rudy focuses on the feminist debate concerning new reproductive technologies and their relationship to male power and control over the bodies of women. Rudy asserts that Piercy's and Ursula Le Guin's novels strengthen women's position in their struggle to control their own reproductive rights.

Virginia Crane

THE WOMAN WHO OWNED THE SHADOWS

Author: Paula Gunn Allen (1939-   )
Type of plot: Psychological realism
Time of plot: The 1970's
Locale: Albuquerque, New Mexico; San Francisco, California; and Oregon
First published: 1983

Principal characters:
EPHANIE ATENCIO, a half-breed Pueblo Indian from Guadalupe
ELENA, a childhood friend of Ephanie
STEPHEN, a cousin and lifelong friend of Ephanie
TERESA, a white friend of Ephanie who calls herself a witch
THOMAS YOSHURI, a Nisei man whom Ephanie marries
AGNES ATENCIO, Ephanie's daughter
BEN ATENCIO, Ephanie's son

The Novel

In her novel *The Woman Who Owned the Shadows*, Paula Gunn Allen employs Laguna women's traditions to trace one woman's search for psychic balance. The novel is divided into four parts, each preceded by a prologue. These prologues tell the traditionally oral stories of Thinking Woman, also known as Spider Woman or the Grandmother, and of her two sister goddesses whom she sang into being, Uretsete and Naotsete. The bodies of the four parts are sectioned into short vignettes that follow middle-aged protagonist Ephanie Atencio as she struggles to gain a sense of self and purpose. Allen parallels Ephanie's own experiences to the goddess stories and in doing so establishes the acceptance of traditional woman lore as the key to a woman's individual spiritual harmony.

Told in stream-of-consciousness style, the novel begins with Ephanie, recently abandoned by her husband, in a state of mental turmoil. She vaguely hears Stephen's attempts to aid her in grasping reality, yet she feels suffocated by him and longs for him to understand her and to let her be herself. With Elena, Ephanie had been who she wanted to be; as children, the two seemingly had complete understanding of each other, seeing themselves as Snow White and Rose Red, as two halves of a whole. Ephanie recounts their separation and the final words of betrayal spoken by Elena that separated them forever. Ephanie connects this memory to her present need for a friend, someone who will accept her as Stephen does not. After Stephen makes love to her, she realizes that something is "out of time, off-pace." She flees Albuquerque, leaving her children with her mother.

Settling in San Francisco, Ephanie sends for her children. The three experience city life and attend the local powwows, looking for acceptance into that community as something connected to and yet different from their home. Ephanie is discontented, however. Going to the Indian Center less and less, she rationalizes her withdrawal by claiming a desire to see "how the other half lives." She spends more time with the non-Indian friends she has made at her group therapy session, particularly Teresa. Ephanie and Teresa grow close, though Ephanie is always troubled by feelings of disconnectedness and isolation. She meets Thomas Yoshuri, who claims to "need" Ephanie. In desperation, hoping to find care for her children and a reason for her own existence, Ephanie agrees to marry Thomas despite Teresa's warnings and her own misgivings.

The marriage predictably fails, and Ephanie, now pregnant, runs off to Oregon, where she gives birth to twin boys. Thomas joins her for the birth and stays with her until, not long afterward, Tommy dies of crib death. Part 2 ends with their final separation and divorce.

In part 3, again alone and now also experiencing guilt about her young child's death, Ephanie yearns even more desperately to be understood. She recalls the stories of disrespect shown toward Iyatiku and searches for the meaning in her dreams of the strange *katsina*, messenger between the spirits and the people. She visits Guadalupe with Teresa, but this trip only stirs up the mysterious disquiet within her. During their return to California, Ephanie and Teresa stay in Colorado with some friends of Teresa who are full of statistics about the injustices wielded against indigenous people. Ephanie resents her people being seen as romanticized victims by those who blame anyone but themselves. She retraces the shunning of her family by her own community because of her grandmother's marriage to a white man. Connecting all of this, Ephanie is again overwhelmed and angered by lack of understanding. Possessed with the desire to do something, to take power in any way possible, Ephanie hangs herself, instantaneously regrets her action, and cuts herself free with the knife propitiously stuck in her pocket.

In the final section of the novel, Ephanie madly searches, though for what she is not sure, through books and her own writing. Eventually she discovers the key to her own enlightenment. More stories of the goddesses come to her; through these and stories of her family's life, she begins to see pain. Ephanie's struggles, her stories, and her writings intertwine, forming circles that she prays will lead her to understanding. She is certain that if she could understand, people, beasts, and the earth would be healed.

Finally, she unleashes the memory of her childhood fall from an apple tree and how, overpowered by the anger and guilt of her fall, she stifled the energy and freedom of her spirit. A spirit woman comes to her and tells her the stories of the goddesses of her people. Through this oral telling, Ephanie understands the combinations and recombinations that form the whole of reality. She puts the fragments of herself back together and sings with the surrounding shadows that have taken the shapes of women, women singing and stepping in balance and harmony.

The Characters

The characters in *The Woman Who Owned the Shadows* serve largely as focal points for Ephanie as she examines her own pain and strives to take control of her life. The members of Ephanie's family, namely her mother and grandmother and her children, are not developed characters. The short explanations of the love Ephanie's grandmother held for her tribal ways, despite being shunned, in addition to her mother's own feelings of isolation, provide the necessary background for Allen's development of Ephanie as a woman divided from both mortal women and the goddess women in her life. Similarly, Elena's character is not developed to any significant degree, but instead the childhood friend's apparent betrayal of Ephanie confirms Ephanie's blame of external forces and people for her own internal isolation.

In the same manner, the two men in Ephanie's life provide stimulus for further examination of her internal dilemmas. Stephen is presented as a ghostly character. He is introduced during Ephanie's initial mental desperation, the most disorienting and fragmented passage in the novel. That he is continually rejected by Ephanie, though he seems to be a consistently loyal friend, hints at the (eventually revealed) underlying mystery in Ephanie's unhappiness.

Thomas, too, is only sketchily drawn. He is rejected by society because of his Japanese heritage, yet he is also deprived by that same society of his Japanese culture. His unhappiness parallels Ephanie's isolation. Neither can separate from his or her respective heritage and join white American society; neither can experience the life that ancestral culture offers. Thomas shows no interest in attending to Ephanie's needs in any way, remains self-consumed and unconnected to his short-term wife, and thus leaves Ephanie still searching for understanding.

Teresa is both generous and good-hearted, though Ephanie is repeatedly disheartened by her impression that Teresa, too, fails to understand her. Teresa's virtues, patience and tolerance, are exhibited by her efforts to convince Ephanie to accept the Colorado women, despite their insulting presumptions, based on their good intentions and their attempts to understand unfamiliar cultures. The rift that comes between the two women is temporary. Teresa will benefit from Ephanie's final awakening—the spirit woman who comes to Ephanie tells her that she must now "Give it [her newfound knowledge] to your sister, Teresa. The one who waits. She is ready to know."

Ephanie's gradual awakening to and synthesis of the traditional stories, her family stories, and her own experiences is the heart of the novel. Allen fastidiously renders Ephanie's initial depth of confusion and distress, attributing it to her divided and warring sense of self. The novel commences with Ephanie's utter lack of comprehension of the time or place in which she exists. She looks inside herself, but she is bewildered by her external and internal senses. She is unaware of her inner division even though she expresses it from the very start, referring to her name as "half of this and half of that." Allen sets up Ephanie's fragmentation of self and then moves her continually toward a realization of that disunity and the ultimate "re-membering" of the parts.

Themes and Meanings

The discovery of self through the acceptance of tribal traditions is a central theme of Allen's novel. The frequency of tribal stories appearing in the main text increases from the beginning of the novel to the end, just as Ephanie's comprehension of the connections between her life and the stories of the goddess women of her Guadalupe people increases. Her path toward self-discovery is established once she performs her own rite of exorcism and begins sweeping away the alien gods in her life, namely Thomas at this point. Spider, the goddess Grandmother, becomes increasingly more powerful in her consciousness. Ephanie attempts suicide only to discover in herself a fierce will to live; her life-affirming self wins over her destructive self. Her understanding deepens. She sees the blooming apple tree of light as the tree in her own childhood, and she sees Sky Woman, who in her "arrogance and brightness" had taken a fall, as herself, who had experienced her own childhood fall. She discovers that the stories exist to fit into life, that all along the stories were tied to the suppressed stories of her own existence.

Although at the beginning of the novel she was disoriented, by the end of the novel Ephanie unifies herself and realizes the tribal notion of time as inner harmony. She understands the combinations and recombinations that had so puzzled her. The visualization of reality as a coherent whole—a web of interwoven events, humans, and spirits—connects Ephanie to her people, tribal reality, and ritual ways.

The last prologue tells of how Spider will seduce the uninitiated into her cave and never free them if they do not have "the special protection that only knowledge can give." Ephanie reaches understanding and learns the knowledge that is necessary for the "initiated." She overcomes the absence of ritual teaching in her childhood and discovers, through the tribal narratives she integrates with her own life, the element of ritual tradition within herself. The experiences and stories of the past become a timeless part of the current moment, in which ritual past is the nurturing life force of the present.

Critical Context

Allen, who describes herself as of mixed Laguna Pueblo, Sioux, and Lebanese American heritage, is a scholar, a professor, and a poet. *The Woman Who Owned the Shadows*, her first novel, was published by the feminist press Spinsters/Aunt Lute and is Allen's testament to the empowerment and direction that tradition offers to the individual. In the work, she examines how Native Americans can incorporate their tribal beliefs into twentieth century America. The layering of tribal stories within the main plot, as well as fundamental reliance on a tribal notion belief of the interconnectedness of reality, firmly establishes *The Woman Who Owned the Shadows* in the genre of tribal literature. She follows in a tradition of Native American writers who operate on tribal sensibilities, such as N. Scott Momaday and Leslie Marmon Silko. The novel, additionally, makes a zealous feminist statement emphasizing the matriarchal line of power through knowledge and female spirits.

In 1986, Allen's feminist critical study on woman lore in Native American traditions, entitled *The Sacred Hoop: Recovering the Feminine in American Indian Traditions*, was published. In that work, she discusses both the feminine and feminist aspects of tribal traditions and history as well as current Native American literature and critical studies. Within the book, she critiques her own novel and the works of a number of well-established Native American writers. Her discussion of tribal literature skillfully illuminates the complexities inherent in describing an art form rooted in a particular culture. Allen explores the assumptions underlying literary criticism and the writing of literature, examining concepts such as ceremonial time as compared to Western industrial time and the use of myth and dream vision in Native American literature.

Allen has written two major volumes of poetry, *Shadow Country* (1982) and *Wyrds* (1987), in addition to many chapbooks of poetry. She edited a collection of critical essays entitled *Studies in American Indian Literature* (1983) and a collection of Native American women's myths entitled *Grandmothers of the Light* (1991). Additionally, a portion of Allen's work entitled *Raven's Road* appeared in a 1986 collection of works in progress by Native American writers.

Bibliography

Allen, Paula Gunn. "Who Is Your Mother? Red Roots of White Feminism." *Sinister Wisdom* 25 (1984): 34-36. This article, in which Allen discusses what she calls "gynarchial societies," illuminates Allen's vision of a holistic female-centered society. She explains the similarities between Native American female-centered traditions and the peace-seeking radical movements of the West. Allen suggests that it is vital for feminists and society in general to turn toward this tradition to heal a warring existence.

_____. "Whose Dream Is This Anyway? Paula Gunn Allen: Generation, Regeneration, and Continuance." In *The Sacred Hoop: Recovering the Feminine in American Indian Traditions*. Boston: Beacon Press, 1986. Allen describes the Keres supreme being Grandmother Spider and shows how her novel reflects the relationship between woman lore and the events in an individual's life. She also discusses time and structure, suggesting that the four geographic locations in the novel parallel the four female life phases in Keres cosmology. Finally, in this short but useful discussion, Allen explains her attempt to emulate the oral tradition and her belief that traditional rituals are life-affirming in whatever form they are presented.

Keating, Analouise. *Women Reading Women: Self-Invention in Paula Gunn Allen, Gloria Anzaldua, and Audre Lorde*. Philadelphia: Temple University Press, 1996. Provides an excellent overview of feminist literature written by women of minority cultures. The essay on Paula Gunn Allen focuses on Native American origin myths that emphasize the "mother" aspect of creation. A useful lens through which to view *The Woman Who Owned the Shadows*.

Lang, Nancy H. "Through Landscape Toward Story/Through Story Toward Landscape: A Study of Four Native American Women Poets." *Dissertation Abstracts International* 52 (September, 1991): 918A. Although Lang does not discuss *The Woman Who Owned the Shadows*, she does examine Allen's poetry in regard to its emphasis on land and the significance land holds in tribal tradition. Intended for academic readers.

Scanlon, Jennifer, ed. *Significant Contemporary American Feminists: A Biographical Source Book*. Westport, Conn.: Greenwood Press, 1999. The book highlights fifty feminists of the late twentieth century, including Paula Gunn Allen. The entry offers valuable insight into her life, education, work, and accomplishments. Although the entry does not extensively analyze specific novels, it does provide useful information on themes, characters, and other aspects of Allen's work.

Van Dyke, Annette. "The Journey Back to Female Roots: A Laguna Pueblo Model." In *Lesbian Texts and Contexts*, edited by Karla Jay and Joanne Glasgow. New York: New York University Press, 1990. Van Dyke discusses the basic Pueblo belief system, establishing an understanding of this culture as vital to the understanding of Allen's novel. The chapter is easily accessible to most readers and thoroughly explores *The Woman Who Owned the Shadows* as a "ritual handbook" that reclaims "woman-ness" and the importance of female self-affirmation. Van Dyke additionally analyzes how Allen leads the reader through the same healing process as experienced by her protagonist, Ephanie.

Tiffany Elizabeth Thraves

WOMEN AND MEN

Author: Joseph McElroy (1930-   )
Type of plot: Science fiction
Time of plot: The 1970's and the future
Locale: New York City, New Mexico, and outer space
First published: 1987

Principal characters:
   JAMES MAYN, a science journalist
   GRACE KIMBALL, a New Age feminist
   THE HERMIT-INVENTOR OF NEW YORK
   FOLEY, a prison inmate
   RAY SPENCE, a suspected murderer
   LUISA, a Chilean diva
   LARRY SHEARSON, a mathematics student
   MARGARET, Mayn's grandmother

The Novel

   Women and Men is divided into eight major chapters, five of which are called "Breathers," with twenty-three sub-chapters. Set in New York and New Mexico, the novel also traverses a universe populated by angelic and earthy creatures, through whom the author discusses the flux and flow of relationships between the sexes against the backdrop of supertechnology. In addition, Joseph McElroy plays with the elasticity of time in an ongoing "dialogue" about the difficulty of human memory to retrieve the past.

   The novel opens with a woman giving birth to a child with the aid of her husband. Neither parent is identified, and it is only later that the possibility arises this anonymous child may be the central character or his mother. It may even be the unidentified reader. The book is narrated in turn by James Mayn, a middle-aged science journalist, an "Interrogator" reminiscent of a South American torturer, and New Age feminist Grace Kimball, among others. While Kimball and Mayn are tenants in the same New York apartment building, they never actually meet. Instead, they share what seem to be only tangential common concerns and friendships. Kimball runs a "Body Self" workshop in which a miscellany of women participate in elaborate acts of mutual masturbation. In one scene, the sex guru projects separate slides of male and female genitalia to point out the real lack of visual difference between the two. Grace plays the role of sex goddess for women, urging them to liberate themselves from stifling marriages. With an ability to abandon herself to her own sexuality, Grace has accurate insights into the unhappiness of other women. For example, she can discern the ambiguous feelings Clara, a Chilean woman, has concerning her husband. Occasionally, the narrative follows the interior conversation of a member of the Body Self Workshop as she gives herself over to the experience of being naked and vulnerable with other women.

Mayn's search is primarily twofold: He yearns for an answer to the riddle of why his headstrong mother, Sarah, committed suicide, and he is equally compelled to come to terms with the impossibility of true intimacy. As he attempts to glue the fragments of his past together, Mayn envisions a future where a couple—a man and a woman—are jettisoned into space and intertwine to become one man/woman. In his mind, this melding of genders represents the perfect union.

There are substantial passages in which Mayn's grandmother, Margaret, recalls an Indian myth about a princess of Choor and her relationship with a Navajo prince. References to Choor and the Anasazi people bring the story back to the Southwest, as McElroy tells of black mesas, sweeping vistas, and of a people more securely rooted in American history and the soil than, presumably, white Americans are capable of being. It is through this densely layered spiritual epic that Mayn comes closer to suturing the wound caused by his mother's untimely death.

The effects of his divorce are painfully palpable and continue to resonate for Mayn as he courts a young female journalist. During sex, Mayn cannot stop thinking of his former wife. He contemplates transformation into a sea lion, a monster, and a worm "digesting Earth" as he attempts sexual intimacy. Instead of a postcoital conversation of a sensual nature, the girl and Mayn discuss Chilean politics and space travel. For a brief moment, the girl becomes Mayn's former wife, although it is left open as to whether Mayn has confused the two women or one actually becomes the other.

The shorter chapters, which stand alone as separate narratives from the much more involved "Breather" sections, concern the lives of such characters as intuitive twelve-year-old Davey (in a chapter entitled "the future"), whose parents are going through a divorce. During an evening he spends with his mother at a restaurant, an armed man terrorizes and robs the customers. In another chapter, a retarded African American messenger makes his way through the streets of Manhattan like a strangely compelling angel. His journey offers a highly detailed vision of storefronts, people walking, and the fits and starts of city traffic. There is also a Chilean opera singer who, in an effort to lose weight, ingests a tapeworm that proceeds to eat away at her insides.

The novel ends in New York, as the Navajo prince simply vanishes into the crates containing the as-yet unassembled Statue of Liberty. Thus, McElroy joins New York at one of its earlier stages of becoming a powerful city with New Mexico as it represents the last great open frontier of America.

The Characters

While the majority of the characters are more like disembodied voices, the two who stand out most recognizably are James Mayn and Grace Kimball. Mayn's character is closest to what one might imagine as that of the author's: thoughtful, able to be in the moment and then quite removed, and relentlessly observant of his fellow creatures, as though such attention to nuance might make a lasting connection between himself and another human being. His heart aches for a remembered time when his family lived happily together, and Mayn also grapples with the wrenching loss of his mother, Sarah. These losses appear to tear Mayn from his moorings, as his psyche travels through space. Beyond the obsessive involvement with his own personal anguish, Mayn's sphere of compassion extends to those who suffered under the Salvador Allende regime in Chile. Given the frequently elliptical style in which McElroy writes, the novel suggests a dipping into and out of Mayn's consciousness as he repeatedly confronts the limitations of his own humanness.

With her Body Self workshop, which completely excludes men and focuses on supporting only women in their quest for sexual fulfillment and independence, Grace Kimball might appear to hate men, but this is not true. She anguishes over breaking up her lover's marriage and in particular over how Marv, her lover's husband, will cope with the split. Kimball exuberantly embraces her body's ability to produce pleasure. A 1970's feminist, Kimball does not necessarily advocate a world devoid of men; rather, she is on a mission to help women awaken the power within themselves to be sensual beings. If this awakening contributes to the deterioration of a marriage, perhaps the marriage was built on an unsteady foundation.

Although the character of Davey, the prepubescent boy whose parents are soon to part, is relatively minor, he is clearly drawn and handled with a special tenderness. He loves his mother, Ann, perhaps with greater devotion as he senses her sadness. Other characters such as the Hermit-Inventor of New York and the Interrogator represent aspects of the human experience rather than individuated people. The reason that Kimball and Mayn never meet may be because they, too, are halves of a whole, the yin and yang of humanity.

Themes and Meanings

Women and Men deconstructs traditional narrative structure through a variety of techniques. McElroy employs inner monologues in which characters battle with their own consciousness, ruminate on past events, and speculate about a sometimes foreboding future as it is impacted by technological and scientific advancements. The issue of such advancements is at the heart of the novel, at times a direct threat to intimacy, at times a challenge to communication and self-comprehension. Murkily defined "voices" repeat throughout the narrative, while others surface only once as they function in a point-counterpoint manner to spin long missives about many issues including nuclear war, space travel, urban and rural American life, and the joys and dilemmas of men and women.

While *Women and Men* concerns itself with the intangibility of closeness and the personal fragmentation of life in cities, the book ultimately manages to offer an optimistic, although enormously complex, portrait of modern life as history impinges on and molds the present. In James Mayn, one finds a man unable to dream and haunted by a failed marriage. With a mind as troubled as it is able to absorb and process vast amounts of information (so much so that the effect is overwhelming), Mayn travels back and forth from the future to the present and so into the past. Time itself is a malleable element, fixed or pliant as it is imagined to be.

Critical Context

A decade in the making, *Women and Men* is McElroy's sixth novel, and one that some critics believe brought the themes of his earlier novels together. The book was criticized as an indulgent piece of work, in part due to its massive length of more than a thousand pages and its intentional subversion of traditional story structure. McElroy was elsewhere praised for his Proustian passion for detail, his devotion to the authenticity of human thought, and his ability to interweave a complex of both universal and profoundly personal matters into a single book. The novel has been compared to James Joyce's *Ulysses* (1922) and Thomas Pynchon's *Gravity's Rainbow* (1973) because it shares a similar deconstructionist, postmodern approach and a tendency toward extended reveries. McElroy's fascination with science and technology does not fall into sarcastic elitism or blind awe. *Women and Men* reflects a keen eye and a tenacious determination to push the reader's intellectual prowess and commitment to the process of reading. McElroy's earlier novels, *Smuggler's Bible* (1966) and *Hind's Kidnapping: A Pastoral on Familiar Airs* (1969) rely more openly on a recognizable realism, while *Ancient History: A Paraphrase* (1971), his third novel, marks a commencement of the fragmentation and reconstitution of the narrative. Nevertheless, despite the obvious theme of a father-son relationship, *Smuggler's Bible* uses an unusual geometric structure. It is a system of connectedness between people, places, events, and methods of communication that identifies McElroy's work as both unique and in the tradition of such writers as Pynchon and Joyce.

Ancient History: A Paraphrase is narrated by Cy, Dom's best friend, who in the course of trying to make sense of Dom's suicide becomes a kind of social scientist as he goes back into Dom's past to find answers. McElroy's next two novels, *Lookout Cartridge* (1974) and *Plus* (1977), both share concerns about power— psychic, physical, and verbal. *Plus* plays with such images as a brain orbiting Earth; *Women and Men* occasionally has a mobile home, split in half so the interior is in full view, orbiting the Earth close enough to see every detail. What is especially strange in the latter image is that the humans who observe this "wide load" seem barely ruffled by the sight. Such displacement of familiar sights is a hallmark of McElroy's writing.

In addition to his novels, McElroy has written numerous short stories, essays, and book reviews. He is regarded as a master of the postindustrial age, one who challenges the reader's intellect in unexpected ways.

Bibliography

Karl, Frederick R. *American Fictions: 1940-1980.* New York: Harper & Row, 1983. Well-crafted criticism on McElroy's first five novels.

Kuehl, John. *Alternative Worlds: A Study of Postmodern Antirealistic American Fiction.* New York: New York University Press, 1989. An excellent overview of postmodern fiction, including an introduction that suggests that this movement is an outgrowth of such early Transcendentalists as Ralph Waldo Emerson and Nathaniel Hawthorne.

LeClair, Thomas. "Reformulation: Joseph McElroy's *Women and Men.*" In *The Art of*

Excess: Mastery in Contemporary American Fiction. Urbana: University of Illinois Press, 1989. A critical comparison of Joseph McElroy, Thomas Pinchon, Roland Barth and other postmodernist writers that brings together issues of ecology, cybernetics, and anthropology in recent American literature.

Porush, David. "The Imp in the Machine: Joseph McElroy's *Plus.*" In *The Soft Machine: Cybernetic Fiction.* New York: Methuen, 1985. An interesting discussion of McElroy's fifth novel.

The Review of Contemporary Fiction, Spring, 1990. Special Issue. A comprehensive collection of essays, an interview, and bibliography of McElroy's body of work.

Nika Hoffman

THE WOMEN'S ROOM

Author: Marilyn French (1929-   )
Type of plot: Social criticism
Time of plot: The 1950's and the 1960's
Locale: A New Jersey suburb and Cambridge, Massachusetts
First published: 1977

> *Principal characters:*
> MIRA, the narrator and protagonist, a housewife and later a Harvard
>   graduate student
> NORM, her husband, a doctor
> ADELE,
> SAMANTHA, and
> MARTHA, Mira's friends during her years of marriage
> VAL,
> CLARISSA,
> ISOLDE, and
> KYLA, Mira's friends in Cambridge
> BEN, Mira's lover during her Cambridge years

The Novel

The Women's Room follows Mira through her repressive childhood and marriage, through her devastating divorce, and finally through her years as an English graduate student as she, for the first time, acquires control over her own life. As a child, Mira is restricted by her parents' attempts to mold her into a young lady. Her mother declares that legs should be crossed only at the ankles and that girls do not engage in rough play. Even though Mira is young, she imagines that the edicts are "strangling her, stifling her."

As a college student, Mira's fear of pregnancy and of the consequent loss of freedom develops into a fear of sex. Thus she avoids intimate relationships. Her openmindedness and her independence, however, are taken by her male colleagues as signs of sexual permissiveness. After a night of drinking and dancing, she is almost raped by a group of her friends. The experience confirms that a woman can never be as free as a man but must always be on guard. Angry that she needs protection and angry that men think they have a right to her body, she withdraws into herself.

When she meets Norm through family friends, she is impressed with his acceptance of her attitude toward sex. Sensing that as long as she is single she will be a target for aggressive male behavior, she accepts his offer of marriage for the protection it will provide. At her wedding, however, she weeps over the loss of her freedom, and indeed her married life becomes more restricted. She forgoes her college education to support Norm while he attends medical school. She accepts a low-paying, unchallenging job because he will not allow her to commute to New York City, where the better jobs and corresponding higher wages are. She is reliant upon her friends to take her grocery shopping because he will not teach her how to drive. Finally, when she becomes pregnant, she is truly tied to the house.

Married life for Mira is a constant round of finishing household chores and of caring for her two sons. Norm is absent frequently, his time spent at the hospital or at his mother's house, where he is undisturbed by the noise of his children. If not for the other neighborhood women, young mothers like Mira, her life would be unbearable. These women frequently get together in the afternoon while their children play in the backyard or are at school. They give "support and affection and legitimacy to each other." They joke about their lives, which are often filled with undefined rage and frustration, but they never challenge "the men's right to demand and control."

When Mira married, she unintentionally exchanged her parents for a husband. Without protest, she now accepts her husband's dictates on child rearing, on the selection of their friends, and on where they live. Always, Norm makes her feel inferior, that her work does not matter, that she in fact does not matter.

As Norm's practice becomes established, they move to an elegant house. Mira continues to devote her life to polishing and cleaning, organizing her activities on index cards so that nothing is missed. She tries to fit the image of wife and mother portrayed on television and in magazines, but she is not satisfied, believing that her husband and her sons have rewarding lives while she functions as their maid.

When Norm, after fifteen years of marriage, announces that he wants a divorce, Mira crumbles. Again she relies on the support of other women, who listen to her and even bandage her wrists after her suicide attempt. Following the advice of one of her female friends, she returns to college and completes her undergraduate degree. When she is accepted as a graduate student at Harvard University, she moves to Cambridge and, at the age of thirty-eight, begins anew.

Alone and an outsider, Mira is at first miserable, until she meets a group of sympathetic and caring women. Like Mira, these women (Isolde, Kyla, Clarissa, and Val) have had to fight against male domination to acquire an identity. With their help, Mira creates a new life out of the ruins of her marriage. In the process, her relationship with her sons becomes freer, more honest, and closer. In time, when Mira is ready to enter into another relationship with a man, she meets Ben, and the two become lovers.

They respect each other's careers: Ben seems to realize the importance of her studies, and she encourages him in writing a book based on his African experiences. They have a satisfying sexual relationship, and for a time Mira is completely happy. Yet the idyllic existence cannot last. Ben is offered an important position in Africa, and without consulting her he assumes that she will accompany him. He expects her to give up her dream of teaching, move to Africa, and have his child. Mira realizes that he has discounted her, her goals, and her ideas in much the same way that Norm, years earlier, had discounted her. She refuses to leave Cambridge, thereby ending their relationship.

The novel concludes with Mira living alone and teaching at a junior college, because the job market is such that there are no positions at a university available for a forty-year-old woman, even with a degree from Harvard. To occupy a long, dull summer, she embarks on a project of writing about the women that she has known; the novel *The Women's Room* is the result.

The Characters

French has populated her novel with many female characters whose experiences are similar; all the women's stories concern male domination and corresponding female powerlessness. Mira, the protagonist and the narrator, tries to fit in with what is expected of her, but her intelligence and sensitivity rebel at the role of wife and mother that she has accepted. Her frustration results from the fact that her work is rendered valueless by her husband and, in a larger sense, by society, and therefore she herself has no worth. Her story is repeated throughout the novel in the lives of her friends both in the New Jersey suburbs and in Cambridge.

There is Adele, a Catholic with five children and pregnant with the sixth, who at thirty is haggard. She has put her husband through law school and now envies his elegance and his evenings with his clients and law partners. When he is at home, he is as demanding as one of her children, waiting for her to serve his martini and expecting his discarded tie to be picked up.

There is Samantha, whose husband loses his job and refuses to accept employment other than in sales, so Samantha becomes a typist. Her meager check barely covers the essentials for the family of four and cannot cover her husband's debts. Eventually they divorce, but she is still responsible for his bills. She and her children move to a cheap apartment and spend a few months on welfare, but through her hard work, they survive.

There is Lily, who, because of her inability to fit the mold of the good housekeeper and wife, is committed to a mental institution. There is Martha, who is laughed at when she considers going to law school. The women struggle to keep their lives together, but the price is high: suicide, excessive drinking, nervous breakdowns, and ulcers.

When Mira moves to Cambridge, she is once more fortunate to find supportive women. Again, however, the same pattern of frustration caused by male oppression is repeated.

Isolde, Kyla, Clarissa, and Val establish an identity apart from the men in their lives, but they are scarred and, in the case of Val, destroyed. Val, strong, honest, and clear-sighted, is the backbone of the group, but her life is shattered when her daughter Chris, a student at the University of Chicago, is raped. Because of the crime and Chris's subsequent treatment at the police station and later at the courthouse, Val realizes that she cannot prevent her daughter from becoming a victim in the male-dominated society. Therefore, Val refuses to collaborate with the enemy and joins the "lunatic fringe" of militant feminists. Eventually she is gunned down when she and five other women attempt to engineer a female prisoner's escape.

The male characters in the novel are shallow and one-dimensional. They all treat women as inferior and do not take seriously their concerns. Norm, Mira's husband, wants a wife to complement his lifestyle, to provide a finishing touch. Ben also comes to see Mira merely as an extension of his interests.

Themes and Meanings

The novel's central focus is on the powerlessness of women in twentieth century industrial society. Women have relinquished control over their own lives: "They give men the power to determine their identities, their value, to accept or reject them. They have no selves." This male authority exists partly because women do not challenge it. Chris does not fight her attacker, and Mira accepts Norm's decrees. Male domination is also sustained through socialization, as shown in Mira's childhood, and through institutions such as marriage, the law, and the Catholic Church. As Val argues, "The institutions get us all in the end. Nobody escapes."

The novel suggests that women, in order to develop their own identities, must eschew relationships with men and rely instead on the support of other women. The novel does not, however, deny important elements in women's experience. Child rearing, cooking, and decorating are valuable female activities. In addition, women's efforts to create harmony in the family and in the community are lauded.

Critical Context

French based her best-selling first novel on her own experiences. The author of critical studies of James Joyce and William Shakespeare, she is familiar with the academic world, like Mira receiving a degree from Harvard and teaching English in colleges. In addition, she has two children and went through a difficult divorce.

French uses the characters in *The Women's Room* to illustrate her views about society. She wants to destroy the false fairy-tale image, derived from magazines and television, that many women accept concerning their marriages, their lovers, and their lives. She believes that by exposing the causes of oppression in women's lives, she can bring society closer to a more humane and just ideal, and she chooses fiction as a vehicle for her ideas because it is a most effective medium. The power of the book to speak to women is undeniable. Many women who, like Mira, grew up in the mid-twentieth century, have identified strongly with the characters and have testified that French has spoken the truth about their own lives.

The book has been praised more for its political impact than for its qualities as fiction. As fiction, it is flawed. The plot is unstructured and repetitious. Characters appear and disappear. Furthermore, no male character is clearly defined. The sections that focus on the problems of contemporary society and on possible alternatives are didactic. The novel's undeniable contribution lies in the fact that it gives powerful voice to the grievances of many women.

Bibliography

Brown, Ellen. "Between the Medusa and the Abyss: Reading Jane Eyre, Reading Myself." In *The Intimate Critique: Autobiographical Literary Criticism*, edited by Diane P. Freedman, Olivia Frey, and Frances Murphy-Zauhar. Durham: Duke University Press, 1993. Various essays explore the feminist approach and biographical connections in French's work.

Current Biography. "Marilyn French." 53 (September, 1992): 10-14. Offers biographical background on French, as well a brief critiques of some of her works. Describes *The Women's Room* as a dramatization of a woman's search for herself in a society dominated by males.

French, Marilyn. "The Great Chain." In *The World of George Sand.* New York: Greenwood, 1991. French does not specifically address issues in any of her novels; however, she examines the treatment of women in relationship to political ideologies portrayed in books of the past. Offers interesting insight into French's feminist philosophy.

_____. *Season in Hell: A Memoir.* New York: Random House, 1998. A moving account of French's battle against esophageal cancer. Although this work does not address any of French's works, it does offer insight into her tenacious character.

Sweeney, Susan Elizabeth. "*The Madonna, The Women's Room,* and *The Scarlet Letter.*" *College English* 57 (1995): 410-425. Relates the treatment of women in these well-known novels to the theories of Sigmund Freud.

Barbara Wiedemann

THE WONDERFUL WIZARD OF OZ

Author: L. Frank Baum (1856-1919)
Type of plot: Fantasy
Time of plot: The early 1900's
Locale: Rural Kansas and the imaginary land of Oz
First published: 1900, as *The Wonderful Wizard of Oz*; retitled *The Wizard of Oz*, 1902

Principal characters:
> DOROTHY, a young girl growing up on a farm on the Kansas prairie
> TOTO, Dorothy's dog
> UNCLE HENRY, Dorothy's uncle
> AUNT EM, Dorothy's aunt
> THE SCARECROW, a living scarecrow Dorothy meets in Oz
> THE TIN WOODMAN, a wood-chopper made entirely of tin
> THE COWARDLY LION, a lion befriended by Dorothy in Oz
> THE WICKED WITCH OF THE EAST, an evil witch accidentally killed by Dorothy
> THE WICKED WITCH OF THE WEST, an evil witch who pursues Dorothy
> THE WIZARD OF OZ, a circus balloonist who passes himself off as a wizard after landing in Oz
> GLINDA, the Good Witch of the South

The Novel

The *Wonderful Wizard of Oz* consists of twenty-four chapters that tell the story of Dorothy's arrival in Oz and her adventures in that magical country. An omniscient narrator tells the story in simple language. It begins on a Kansas farm where Dorothy, an orphan, lives in a one-room house with her grim, hardworking uncle and aunt. A tornado appears and Dorothy, her uncle, and aunt run for a cellar under the house. When Toto, Dorothy's dog, jumps out of her arms, Dorothy runs to get the gog, and she and her pet are carried away by the winds. Dorothy falls asleep as the house whirls through the air.

When she awakens and goes outside her house, she finds she is in a strange and beautiful country inhabited by small, strangely dressed people known as the Munchkins. Dorothy's house has fallen on the Wicked Witch of the East, ruler of the Munchkins. Dorothy is awarded the Witch's silver shoes, which have some magical power unknown to the Munchkins or to the Good Witch of the North, who has come to meet Dorothy. The Good Witch tells Dorothy to go to the Emerald City, ruled by the Wizard of Oz, in the hope that the Wizard may be able to help the little girl return home.

On her way to the Wizard's city, Dorothy acquires three unusual companions: a scarecrow who complains of having no brains, a woodman made entirely of tin who complains of having no heart, and a lion who complains of having no courage. Dorothy suggests to each of them that the accompany her to see if the Wizard can help them.

After a number of adventures, Dorothy, Toto, and the three odd friends reach the Emerald City, where all of the houses seem to be made of green marble and studded with emeralds. They make their requests of the wizard, who goes by the name of Oz. The wizard refuses to grant their requests until they kill the Wicked Witch of the West, who rules the western people known as the Winkies.

The adventurers travel to the west, and the Witch sends wolves, crows, bees, and her frightened Winkie subjects against them. Dorothy and her friends manage to defeat all of these adversaries, but the Witch finally uses a magic golden cap to send Winged Monkeys to destroy the Tin Woodman and the Scarecrow and carry Dorothy and the lion to the witch as slaves. After Dorothy becomes a servant in the witch's castle, the witch manages to grab one of the little girl's magic silver shoes. In anger, Dorothy throws water on the witch and, as it happens, this melts the old woman. The grateful Winkies then find and repair the Tin Woodman and the Scarecrow, and the lion is set free from his prison.

After using the witch's magic golden cap to have the Winged Monkeys fly them back to the Emerald City, Dorothy and her friends discover that the magnificent wizard is only a former ventriloquist and circus balloonist who happened to land in Oz. However, after some thought, he is able to meet the requests of Dorothy's companions by giving the Scarecrow brains made of bran and pins, the Tin Woodman a silk heart stuffed with sawdust, and the lion a drink claimed to give courage. After three days, the wizard offers to fly Dorothy back to Kansas with him in his old balloon. Unfortunately, Toto jumps after a kitten at the last moment, Dorothy runs after him, and the wizard and his balloon float away without her.

Dorothy calls upon the Winged Monkeys, but they are unable to cross the desert that surrounds Oz. Therefore, Dorothy and her friends leave Oz to travel to the southern country of the Quadlings, where Glinda the Good Witch of the South rules, in the hope that Glinda can help Dorothy return home. After still more adventures, they reach Glinda, who tells Dorothy, in exchange for the golden cap, that the silver shoes will carry her anywhere she wishes to go if she only knocks the heels together three times. Dorothy does so and is flown back to Kansas, losing the silver shoes over the desert on the way.

The Characters

Baum's characters are simple, but also sympathetic. Dorothy, the heroine, is a straightforward little girl who shows courage and perseverance. Dorothy is a poor orphan, a type of character recurring in children's literature. In the drawings by the original illustrator of the book, W. W. Denslow, Dorothy seems to be very young, perhaps only five or six years of age, although she frequently seems to behave as a much older child would. Baum also gives little hint to her appearance. Letting readers construct their own images of the child heroine may have been intentional, because it made Dorothy an "Everychild," a representative of children in general.

Baum's great success with his other characters was the creation of individuals who are at once impossible and entirely believable. The Scarecrow, the Tin Woodman, and the Cowardly Lion have won the sympathy of generations of readers. Part of this success may be the result of the depths of personality that the author was able to convey by giving these fantastic creatures human qualities of self-contradiction. The Scarecrow complains that he has no brains, but he shows himself to be the most thoughtful of Dorothy's companions, and his quest for intelligence demonstrates that this is what he values. Similarly, the Tin Woodman places the highest importance on feeling, and shows a continual concern with emotion as he seeks a heart. The Cowardly Lion is a coward in his own eyes, but he accompanies the others through dangerous adventures and sometimes protects the group with his fierce roar. These three characters embody the classical human virtues of intelligence, caring, and courage, but their self-doubts keep them from being reduced to mere symbols of these qualities.

At the end of the story, all the characters achieve self-realization by accomplishing their goals. Dorothy does eventually manage to return home, having found that she had actually had the power to do so all along. The Scarecrow also apparently had his goal, his intelligence, within his grasp all along, since all the Wizard needs to do is to mix bran and pins and needles in the straw man's head to convince the Scarecrow of his intellectual powers. The Woodman and the Lion, respectively, require only a silk heart and a drink to arouse confidence in their capacities for love and bravery.

Themes and Meanings

Although Baum intended his story as an entertainment for children, it also contains a good deal of social satire offered with a gently mocking sense of humor. The gap between appearance and reality is a persistent theme in *The Wonderful Wizard of Oz* and in many of Baum's other books. The centerpiece of the book is the journey to the Emerald City, home of the great Wizard who can grant all wishes. Once the main characters reach the city, though, they find that it is all an illusion and that the Wizard himself is a fraud. They themselves are capable of all the real magic.

The strange landscape and the absurd events and creatures are primarily intended for entertainment, but they also convey a sense of the wondrous and magical parts of life. Readers can see the book, then, as a good-natured rebellion of imagination against the tyranny of calculating rationality. The similarities that some may see between this book and intellectual movements such as surrealism owe much to this rebellion.

Critical Context

L. Frank Baum had struggled through a number of careers, working as a newspaperman and department-store buyer among other jobs, before achieving a modest success as a writer of children's verse and stories. *The Wonderful Wizard of Oz*, though, was the book that established his reputation. It became an immediate best-seller, outselling all other children's books during the 1900 Christmas season. In 1902, a musical version of the story was staged at the Grand Opera House in Chicago to enormous popular acclaim. There were a number of efforts to put the story in film, but none of these met with much success until the Hollywood film company Metro-Goldwyn-Mayer staged it in 1939, with Judy Garland as Dorothy, Ray Bolger as the Scarecrow, Jack Haley as the Tin Woodman, and Bert Lahr as the Cowardly Lion. The 1939 film continues to run on television regularly and is probably more familiar to the public than the original book version.

After *The Wonderful Wizard of Oz*, Baum attempted to repeat his success with other attempts at fairy stories and fantasies. His readers, however, wanted more stories about Oz. Baum responded by producing fourteen more Oz books. None of these received the popular or critical recognition given to the first, but they did create dedicated readers who eagerly awaited each new volume. The demand was so great that even after Baum's death, a new "Royal Historian of Oz," Ruth Plumly Thompson, was chosen by the publisher of the Oz books, Reilly and Lee. Beginning in 1921, Thompson published a book about the magical land of Oz every year for nineteen years. Others, in the years following Thompson, have attempted to follow in Baum's footsteps with other tales about Oz.

In the years before Baum's writing became popular, interest in the fairy tale as a literary form had increased greatly. The Brothers Grimm and Hans Christian Andersen had brought the fairy tales of continental Europe to written form. In Victorian England, Andrew Lang assembled collections of fairy tales from England and other countries. Major English literary figures, such as John Ruskin and Oscar Wilde, also tried their hands at fairy stories. Lewis Carroll's works were received by a public willing to appreciate fantasy.

Literary critics have argued that the popularity of the fairy tale was a reaction against an increasingly industrialized society. America, however, was rapidly industrializing in the late nineteenth and early twentieth centuries and it had few fantasy writers to match those of England. Baum, then, may be considered one of the first American masters of the fairy tale and the fantasy.

With its appealing characters, its dreamlike adventures, and its well-constructed story, *The Wonderful Wizard of Oz* is one of those rare books that can offer pleasure to both children and adults. Although it never becomes shallow moralism or mere allegory, it always conveys hints that its characters and events are somehow metaphors for features of the world of its readers.

Bibliography

Carpenter, Angelica Shirley, and Jean Shirley. *L. Frank Baum: Royal Historian of Oz*. Minneapolis: Lerner Publications, 1992. A detailed account of Baum's career and writings. Includes numerous maps and illustrations. Also contains plot summaries of most of Baum's books.

Hearn, Michael Patrick. Introduction to *The Annotated Wizard of Oz*, by L. Frank Baum. New York: Clarkson N. Potter, 1973. This sets Baum's best-known work in the context of his life and work.

Riley, Michael O. *Oz and Beyond: The Fantasy World of L. Frank Baum*. Lawrence:

University of Kansas Press, 1997. A comprehensive analysis of Baum's development as a fantasy writer. It considers the influence of Baum's childhood and adult experiences on his writing and looks at how his works reflect his philosophical and social views.

Carl L. Bankston III

THE WORKS OF LOVE

Author: Wright Morris (1910-1998)
Type of plot: Regional romance
Time of plot: From the 1880's to the 1930's
Locale: Nebraska, California, and Chicago
First published: 1952

Principal characters:
WILL JENNINGS BRADY, the protagonist, a chicken farmer and egg
    entrepreneur
ETHEL CZERNY BASSETT, his first wife
WILL BRADY, JR., his adopted son
GERTRUDE LONG, his second wife
T. P. LUCKETT, a booster who inspires Will to make something of
    himself

The Novel

    Set for the most part in the desolate plains and dusty small towns of eastern Ne-
braska, *The Works of Love* traces the history of a naive man and his difficulties in feeling at home with his fellow man.

    Orphaned at an early age, Will Brady has no option but to take the world as he finds
it. His lack of culture and education indicate that he has no means of understanding
the world. He has, however, no inclination to understand it. He gets to know his limitations and frustrations as an intermittent series of pangs occasioned by nocturnal
glimpses of the lights on railroad semaphores and by a desire for female companionship. His formative experiences of life and love are obtained in his sojourn in
Calloway, Nebraska, where he works at the Merchant's Hotel and on his nights off
visits Opal Mason, a lonesome whore.

    As a result of one of these visits, Will's life becomes more complicated. Feeling
that he should be married and having Opal reject him, he finds himself associated with
one of her young colleagues, Mickey Ahearne. Nothing comes immediately of this association. Mickey is pregnant and already engaged; the second time Will sees her, she
is leaving town with her fiance. The complication arises when Will receives, by rail, a
picnic basket containing an infant and a note saying, "My name is Willy Brady." Yet,
strange as this event is, neither Will nor anyone else in Calloway thinks very much
about it.

    This episode establishes the manner in which all further incidents in the novel are
perceived by the characters. Will is impressed by the way T. P. Luckett, a frequent
guest at the Merchant's Hotel, extols the virtues of Nebraska as a land of opportunity.
He also falls for Luckett's groundless and inflated estimation of Will's acumen. As a
result, Will enters the egg business, supplying the products of his chicken farm to rail-

road companies. The business succeeds magnificently and without discernible effort. Not even a devastating outbreak of chicken disease seriously impedes its progress. Yet, despite its large profits, the only satisfaction it contains for Will is the release in him of a sympathetic, intuitive feeling for the shape, weight, and color of eggs.

Similarly, when the owner of the hotel dies, Will, without exactly knowing why, finds himself marrying the widow Ethel Bassett. The marriage is a disaster, socially and sexually, and ends with Ethel leaving him. This initiates Will into a hitherto unknown degree of loneliness. Yet this unfortunate turn of events does not stir Will to take decisive action. Rather, finding himself obliged to be in Omaha frequently on business, he drifts into a relationship with a cigar-counter clerk named Gertrude Long in a city hotel.

Thanks to his business success, Will is able to provide his new bride, Gertrude, with a lavish lifestyle. The culminating expression of his wealth is a mansion on the prairie. The house, however, is never properly habitable because of Will's ignorance in such matters. Gertrude becomes an unhappy recluse in it, pining for the nickelodeons and busy streets of Omaha. Her longings are shared by Will, Jr., so that the domestic arrangement seems to consist of father and two children.

Eventually, Gertrude runs away. On her return, Will attempts to rehabilitate their relationship by means of a trip to California. In the course of the vacation, however, Will discovers that Gertrude is an alcoholic. The relationship ends, but Will is given help in enduring his loss by means of a quasi-religious experience. An anonymous, bearded old man tells him: "There's no need for great lovers in heaven. Pity is the great lover, and the great lovers are all on earth."

The novel's concluding section seems to reveal the force of the old man's statement. Here Will is shown living within the confines of his own pathos. By this time, he is in Chicago. He spends his days sampling his neighborhood's social mix. In this "wasteland," experience is given its ultimate enactment as a blend of worldly inconsequentiality and ineffable desire. As at the end of T. S. Eliot's *The Waste Land*, human voices awaken Will Brady and he drowns—in a sewage canal, dressed as Santa Claus.

The Characters

In effect, there is only one character in *The Works of Love*, the protagonist. Although Gertrude's fate is of concern to him, and the future of Will, Jr., a source of worry, neither these two nor any other character establishes a fully developed reality independent of Will Brady's within the confines of the novel. The minor characters with whom Will is intimately connected obviously have an impact on his circumstances and on the various directions of his life. Still, they do not succeed in altering his nature or in influencing the manner in which he perceives life. On the contrary, they seem to dull his vision of the world.

In contrast, Will frequently encounters characters in the course of supposedly predictable social transactions who illuminate or reinforce the nature of his own experience. The anonymous man in California who speaks to Will of love and pity is a case in point. Similarly, there is Mr. Lockwood, a former college track star and current sporting-goods salesman, who carries clippings of his former triumphs in his wallet. He is an illustration in passing of a man who, like Will, is condemned to the narrowness of his own nature. "Some writer of books might even say that these clippings poisoned him"—just as the author of *The Works of Love* implies that Will Brady, having spent so much time at sea, metaphorically speaking, drowns at last in his own confusion.

The author's decision to concentrate on Will exclusively is stated baldly at the novel's outset. "Will Jennings Brady is there by himself. That might be his story. The man who was more or less by himself." Will combines a sense of the singular and of the bereft: "a man who neither smoked, drank, gambled, nor swore. A man who headed no cause, fought in no wars, and passed his life unaware of the great public issues." He is a man whose life consists solely of his own history.

The question certainly does arise, as the author says: "Why trouble with such a man at all?" The answer appears to be precisely because of his singularity. Will appears to be socialized. He marries, engages in business, and mixes successfully with most levels of society. Yet his evident normality deepens his strangeness, a strangeness of which Will is aware but about which he can do nothing.

The novel's most sustained treatment of Will's sense of his strangeness arises out of an attempt that he makes to understand his adopted son. In order to do so, he reads some boys' books, including Jules Verne's *Journey to the Moon*. Having completed the book, Will muses

> that he did even stranger things than the men in books. It was one thing to go to the moon, like this foreigner, a writer of books, but did this man know the man or woman across the street? . . . Could he explain why there were grass stains on the man's pants? That might be stranger, that might be harder to see, than the dark side of the moon.

The Works of Love is dedicated to two writers, Loren Eisley and, in memoriam, Sherwood Anderson. Mention of the second of these names is especially illuminating. It suggests that Will Brady may be seen as one of Anderson's "grotesques," a term Anderson uses to describe the emotionally deformed provincials in that outstanding classic of American regional fiction, *Winesburg, Ohio*.

Themes and Meanings

A main theme of the novel is contained in one of its epigraphs, which quotes D. H. Lawrence: "We cannot bear connection. That is our malady." This deficiency is certainly borne out in the consistent lack of fulfillment in Will Brady's personal relationships.

The statement also seems to apply in a more extended sense. Will is a successful entrepreneur. His business career embodies the realization of the American Dream, financially considered at least. Yet this achievement does not give Will a sense of identity with the society that facilitated it. In fact, he seems at the end more painfully devoid of social and cultural attachments than he was as a raw youth in Calloway, and as though to emphasize this lack, the novel's style becomes noticeably more tentative:

Words such as "somehow" and "perhaps," and rhetorical questions, occur with increasing frequency.

The novel's main emphasis, however, is less cultural and material than it is spiritual. Adrift in Chicago, Will is less able than ever to deny the otherness of others. Still, his very openness to otherness does not help to prevent him from succumbing to it, and he is in no position to understand it, as the following series of questions indicates:

> Was it any wonder that men wrote books about other things? that they traveled to the moon, so to speak, to get away from themselves? Were they all nearer to the moon . . . and such strange places than they were to their neighbors, or the woman there in the house?

It may be that "the world needed . . . a traveler who would stay right there in the bedroom, or open the door and walk slowly about his own house."

Will's fleeting perception of this need is, in effect, a poignant reminder of his incapacity to satisfy it. His tragedy is to embody a vision of the works of love—love's generosity, naïveté, resilience—which he can neither control nor comprehend.

Critical Context

Wright Morris is a highly respected author, the recipient of numerous prestigious awards as well as significant critical attention, yet his work seems not to have earned for him a large public. Despite its many virtues, most notably its emphasis on spirit and vision, his work is often seen as nebulous and lacking in drama. Perhaps his stature may always be overshadowed by the generation immediately preceding his own, the generation of Ernest Hemingway and F. Scott Fitzgerald.

The Works of Love is one of the author's more admired works. Even here, however, the protagonist's passivity and simpleness tend to make him a case history whose experiences confirm both the author's view of the individual's invincible loneliness and his belief that a redemptive ethic arises out of the negotiation of that loneliness. Not the least dubious aspect of this belief is its vagueness. The fact that the ethic cannot be socially mediated, as *The Works of Love* demonstrates, somewhat limits its credibility. In addition, since Will Brady is the ethic's exemplar, he must also be a victim of loneliness.

Nevertheless, the author's commitment to such concerns makes him at least as worthy of serious attention as some of the better-known but more callow members of his generation. This novel is also an excellent introduction to Wright Morris's Nebraska, further accounts of which can be found in *The Home Place* (1948) and *The Field of Vision* (1956). As the author himself has remarked: "*The Works of Love* is . . . the linchpin in my novels concerned with the plains." In his fidelity to spirit, and also to place, be it ever so humble, Wright Morris has added to one of the most distinguished genres of American imaginative prose.

Bibliography

Crump, Gail B. *The Novels of Wright Morris*. Lincoln: University of Nebraska Press, 1978. Crump explores Morris's novels and provides an overview and analysis.

Knoll, Robert. *Conversations with Wright Morris: Critical Views and Responses.* Lincoln: University of Nebraska Press, 1977. A collection of essays and interviews with Morris.

Madden, David. *Wright Morris.* New York: Twayne, 1965. Madden provides a critical and interpretive study of Morris with a close reading of his major works, a solid bibliography, and complete notes and references. Useful for Morris's work through the early 1960s. An expanded version in the Twayne Authors series by Joseph J. Wydeven was published in 1998.

Morris, Wright. "Wright Morris and the American Century." Interview by James Hamilton. *Poets & Writers Magazine* 25 (November-December, 1997): 23-31. Morris comments on his career and his writing and photography over a period of fifty years. He discusses creative imagination and the influence of the American nation on his writing.

_____. "Wright Morris: The Art of Fiction CXXV." *Paris Review* 33 (Fall, 1991): 52-94. Interview by Olga Carlisle and Jodie Ireland. A lengthy interview with Morris on various aspects of his life and career.

_____. *Writing My Life: An Autobiography.* Santa Rosa, Calif.: Black Sparrow Press, 1993. Morris reflects on his life and career as a photographer, essayist, novelist, and critic.

Wydeven, Joseph J. *Wright Morris Revisited.* New York: Twayne, 1998. The first complete examination of the work of Wright Morris as a novelist and a photographer. Wydeven includes a portfolio of photographs by Morris along with a detailed analysis of the novels, criticism, and memoir that Morris produced. Wydeven focuses on Morris's principal theme of the American Dream and the promise of the American West.

George O'Brien

THE WORLD ACCORDING TO GARP

Author: John Irving (1942-   )
Type of plot: Comic picaresque
Time of plot: 1942 through the early 1970's
Locale: Boston; Steering, a fictional New Hampshire preparatory school; Vienna, Austria; and New York City
First published: 1978

Principal characters:

    T. S. GARP, the protagonist, an author

    JENNY FIELDS, Garp's mother, a nurse and later an author

    HELEN HOLM, Garp's wife, a professor of English

    ERNIE HOLM, Helen's father, a wrestling coach at Steering

    DEAN BODGER, of Steering School, a friend to Garp and Jenny

    STEWART PERCY (FAT STEW), an incompetent Steering history instructor

    CUSHMAN (CUSHIE) PERCY, Stewart's daughter

    TINCH, Garp's English mentor

    CHARLOTTE, a Vienna prostitute

    HARRISON FLETCHER, Helen's colleague, later her lover

    ALICE FLETCHER, Harrison's wife, later Garp's mistress

    MICHAEL MILTON, Helen's graduate student, later her lover

    ROBERTA MULDOON, a transsexual and a former football player

    ELLEN JAMES, the namesake of the "Ellen Jamesians," a radical feminist group

The Novel

Jenny Fields, a generous but unconventional woman, decides that she wants, more than anything, a child of her own; still, she does not want a husband. She has a child by an Air Force technical sergeant named Garp, who, as a ball-turret gunner, has sustained brain damage. Since Sergeant Garp had lost all mental function, Jenny plans the insemination entirely on her own, and since she has never learned the man's first name but wishes to memorialize him through the child, she calls the boy "T. S.," the flyer's rank.

This outrageous and absurdly dark humor characterizes nearly all the novel's many episodes. Young Garp inherits his father's considerable libido as well as his mother's scrupulous honesty. His experiences at Steering, where Jenny later works as school nurse, teach him more about life than any of the courses that he takes. Like Jenny, Garp reads avidly, but he finds balance in this intellectual activity by wrestling on the Steering team. Through his wrestling, Garp meets Helen Holm, the coach's daughter, a strikingly beautiful, supremely intellectual girl who will eventually become his wife. The purity of Garp's feelings for Helen contrasts with his lust for "Cushie," Cushman Percy, the daughter of an incompetent history instructor at Steering.

Unlike Helen, Garp is not intellectually inclined and does not wish to be. He is a mediocre student and, with the unconventional Jenny's support, never applies for college. Instead, accompanied by his mother, Garp pursues experience rather than theory through a year's residence in Vienna. This sojourn provides a chance for Garp to write his first published work while Jenny produces her successful and sensational autobiography, *The Sexual Suspect*. Vienna challenges Garp's libido, and he becomes involved with Charlotte, a prostitute who also mothers him. He visits Charlotte when she is dying and discovers his love for her is deeper than his lust ever was.

Vienna also supplies the scene of Garp's novella, called *The Pension Grillparzer*. This tale-within-a-tale appears complete and deals with the recurring fear of death and of being forgotten. Garp names it for the Viennese author Franz Grillparzer, a writer whose work Garp believes did not deserve to outlive the nineteenth century.

The last half of *The World According to Garp* concerns his marriage to Helen Holm and the birth of their children Duncan and Walt, as well as Garp's continuing struggle for recognition as a writer. Garp's higher love for his family continues to be at odds with his lust. There are encounters with a degenerate mother (Mrs. Ralph), seduction of babysitters, and liaisons with Alice Fletcher, all against a background of personal unhappiness, professional frustration, and violent death. Indeed, the accident that kills Walt would not have happened had it not been for the lack of a moral sense which had come to characterize the married life of Garp and Helen.

Even Walt's death (as well as Jenny's assassination) appear against a background of grim humor. Garp does achieve popular, but not artistic, success as a writer, and, despite his own violent death, victory over the "Under Toad," the sinister force which destroys the human spirit.

The Characters

As is appropriate for a modern picaresque, this novel presents numerous characters. They appear, disappear, and, when least expected, reappear. Even the minor characters are unconventional, and all in some way give definition to Garp and his family. In short, they populate the writer's world. Usually, they illustrate one or more of the four motifs in Garp's life: writing, wrestling, sex, and death.

Often the manner in which a character will die accompanies that character's first appearance. For example, Tinch, Garp's English mentor at Steering, tells his pupil that he is himself rotting on the inside, though Irving reports that "Old Stench," as the boys call him, will actually freeze to death some years later. This minor character actually brings the novel to its second major phase, for it is Tinch who suggests Garp's trip to Vienna, the city which becomes so important in his formation as a writer.

Similarly, Garp's unconsummated sexual experience with Cushie occurs on the muddy banks of Steering River. The riverbank also provides Garp's first encounter with the "Under Toad": "An awful *slorp*ing noise pursued him through the mud flats, as if beneath the mud some mouth was gasping to suck him in."

Symmetry also occurs in the relationships between characters. When Garp consummates his relationship with Cushie, it occurs in a bed of the Steering Infirmary, recalling Garp's own conception in a patient's bed at Mercy Hospital. In the same vein, Charlotte, the Vienna whore, resembles her city; her outward glamour merely conceals corruption. Like Tinch, she is dying within. The implication is that there is no hope for meaningful vision, no possibility of real transcendence.

Then Garp marries Helen, and hope emerges from sordidness, though only temporarily. He increasingly doubts his ability as a writer, becomes a "house husband," and worries about the welfare of Duncan and Walt, this despite his philandering with babysitters and the *ménage à quatre* with the Fletchers. His writing becomes increasingly autobiographical, and as it does, it becomes less-genuine art.

Irving's inclusion of complete examples of Garp's writing not only satisfies a requirement of picaresque; it also allows the reader to trace the changing nature of Garp's style. Walt dies, Duncan loses an eye, and Garp breaks his jaw in a bizarre automobile accident which occurs in part as a result of Helen's affair with Michael Milton, one of her graduate students. This accident, which also causes the sexual mutilation of Michael Milton, is more violent than any other episode in the novel; indeed, it is among the most violent scenes in contemporary fiction.

Garp becomes like Marcus Aurelius, the Roman emperor who sensed the pull of death and obscurity yet felt powerless to fight against it. Garp's wired jaw makes him resemble an "Ellen Jamesian," one of a group of radical feminists who have cut out their tongues to protest a child's rape. Garp is, therefore, a writer without a voice, in actuality and in his fiction. *The World According to Bensenhaver*, the novel which he writes at this time, is so sensationally autobiographical that it ensures his financial security, but it ruins him as an artist. Still, the birth of his daughter Jenny, his befriending of the orphaned Ellen James, his purchase of the old Steering mansion, and his return to Steering as wrestling coach give him happiness and allow him to transcend the horrors of his life.

Jenny Fields, Garp's mother, seems more firmly in control of her life. She is always certain of what she wants from life and almost always obtains it. Helen, though she has more formal education than any of the novel's principals, experiences the same sorts of difficulties as does her husband. She too discovers happiness in curtailed ambition within the confines of her family and the books she loves.

Themes and Meanings

The World According to Garp is a sprawling, episodic novel, with the colorful, sometimes roguish, but endearing illegitimate son of Jenny Fields as its hero. It is also a *Bildungsroman*, a novel about the formation of a writer, Irving's portrait of the artist. Its episodes point toward attempts to triumph over the "Under Toad" of death and obscurity. Garp at first seeks to accomplish this through his fiction but comes to the conclusion that writing an immortal novel is not the only way to find meaning in life. In this, Garp adapts Aurelian stoicism to his own needs, recognizing the necessity of rising above one's own pain to live in closer harmony with nature. Jenny knows this instinctively; her son learns it through bitter experience.

The Pension Grillparzer obliquely introduces the "Under Toad" theme through

Duna, the trained bear which eventually becomes clawless, toothless, and unwanted. Vienna, the place of Aurelius's death, is a city without hope or the possibility of regaining its former eminence. It is a city of the old, the corrupt, and it mirrors Garp's own early life.

Critical Context

Garp is Irving's masterwork, reflecting the author's wide reading and worldview. It follows the protagonist from conception to death, a technique used in Laurence Sterne's *Tristram Shandy* (1759-1767). Its outrageous tone matches Sterne's, and several of the episodes, such as Michael Milton's mutilation, resemble scenes in *Tristram Shandy*. T. S., Garp's "name," seems a literary joke to identify Irving's hero with his fictional predecessor.

Other life-death references are more explicit. Irving quotes Randall Jarrell's "The Death of the Ball Turret Gunner," a poem which notes the fetal position of the most vulnerable man aboard a B-17, the "Flying Fortress" of World War II. The reference is explicitly to Garp's father, but it implicitly refers to human vulnerability to death. The poem and the reference imply the link between life and death as well as the cyclical view of history espoused by Aurelius.

Irving rejects the strongly autobiographical associations in *The World According to Garp*. He has Garp maintain that the autobiographical approach to literature is the least worthwhile. Still, Irving was born in New Hampshire, in 1942 (as was Garp), attended Exeter (Steering?), wrestled while there, and lived for a year in Vienna. This merely implies that a similarity exists between Garp's frustrations and fears and those of his creator.

Kurt Vonnegut, Jr., was Irving's mentor, and Irving believes that effective storytelling is the measure of a novelist's success. Irving admires Charles Dickens and deplores the self-reflective novel which obscures rather than clarifies.

Bibliography

Campbell, Josie. *John Irving: A Critical Companion.* Westport, Conn.: Greenwood Press, 1998. Offers a brief biography of Irving's life, as well as an overview of his fiction. Devotes an entire chapter to *The World According to Garp*, which includes discussion of plot and character development, thematic issues, and a new critical approach to the novel.

Irving, John. "*Garp* Revisited." *Saturday Night* 113 (May, 1998): 71-73. An interesting look back by Irving at his own book twenty years after he wrote it. He comments on the details of the plot, addresses the question of whether it contains biographical elements, and reveals how he felt as his 12-year-old son read the work in progress before its publication.

_____. An Interview with John Irving, by Suzanne Herel. *Mother Jones* 22 (May/June, 1997): 64-66. Irving discusses his views on religion, censorship, literature, abortion, and wrestling. His thoughts on these topics illuminate the tone and philosophy of his writings.

McKay, Kim. "Double Discourses in John Irving's *The World According to Garp*." *Twentieth Century Literature* 38 (Winter, 1992): 457-475. McKay observes that Irving's novel fuses the roles of the biographer and fiction writer into the character of the narrator in the tradition of the *Bildungsroman* genre. She also notes that the conflicts in Garp's life are presented as conflicts of memory against imagination. Wilson, Raymond, J. "The Postmodern Novel: The Example of John Irving's *The World According to Garp*." *CRITIQUE: Studies in Contemporary Fiction* 34 (Fall, 1992): 49-62. Wilson argues that Irving's book displays several narrative strategies that are typical of the postmodern novel. Its form recapitulates the history of the twentieth century novel; bizarre events are sometimes favored over realistic ones; in the final third of the novel, the characters lose depth; and, finally, the novel draws attention to the process of its own writing.

Robert J. Forman

WORLD'S FAIR

Author: E. L. Doctorow (1931-   )
Type of plot: Autobiographical
Time of plot: The early 1930's to 1940
Locale: New York City, mostly in the Bronx
First published: 1985

Principal characters:

EDGAR ALTSCHULER, the protagonist, younger son of a Jewish family living in the Bronx

DONALD ALTSCHULER, Edgar's brother, who becomes a musician and signal corpsman

DAVE ALTSCHULER, Edgar's father, a failing businessman and a freethinker

ROSE ALTSCHULER, Edgar's mother, who is both practical and religious

MEG, a classmate to whom Edgar is devoted

The Novel

World's Fair begins with the earliest memories of Edgar Altschuler and concludes when he is nine years old with two visits to the World's Fair in Flushing Meadows, New York. Edgar is the first-person narrator of thirty-one chapters, but his retrospective point of view merges the naïve impressions of a child with the more perceptive reflections of an adult. Four brief sections narrated by Rose, two sections narrated by Donald, and one section narrated by Edgar's Aunt Frances supplement Edgar's egocentric version of the family history. By making the street address and first names of the fictional Altschulers coincide with the actual address and names of his own family, Doctorow suggests that Edgar's story of growing up is a thinly disguised account of his own boyhood.

Presented as a memoir, this novel has a loose, episodic plot. First, Rose establishes a foundation for Edgar's narrative with brief comments about her parents' emigration from Russia and her own birth on the Lower East Side. Then Edgar describes his horror upon awaking in a urine-soaked crib and the subsequent comfort of being dried and transported to his parents' warm bed. Amid such scenes of parental protection, Edgar also recalls episodes fraught with fear and mystery. A car almost kills his dog Pinky, and thugs from nearby Italian and Irish neighborhoods draw swastikas on the family's garage doors.

As Edgar's horizons expand, he observes tensions in the extended family during Sunday visits to Dave's parents and at a Seder meal. He also overhears his parents argue about Dave's business mistakes, his gambling, and his alleged infidelities. On a trip to Far Rockaway beach, Edgar discovers discarded condoms, but no one will clarify for him their mysterious purpose. Edgar's grandmother becomes senile and warns of cholera epidemics and attacks by the Cossacks. If these threats are exaggerated,

Nazi atrocities in Europe (discussed by adults in hushed tones or in a language foreign to Edgar) are all too real. Later, Edgar discovers his grandmother dead in her own bed, and this death motivates Rose's transition from secular to observant Jew.

At school, Edgar must mediate between two extremes of his personality—docile, attentive student in the classroom and hyperactive hellion on the playground. Throughout such trials, Donald is usually a patient and trustworthy guide. Nevertheless, Donald cannot protect his younger brother from terrible hints of mortality—the near drowning of a classmate, a fatal automobile accident that spills over onto the school playground, the crash of the Hindenburg. For several weeks Edgar is himself near death when his appendix bursts and he suffers peritonitis.

After Dave's business fails and Donald leaves home to train as a civilian signal corpsman, the remaining Altschulers move to a much smaller apartment. In spite of the family's financial reverses, Edgar does realize his dream of visiting the World's Fair. He goes first as the guest of Meg, a classmate who has been the object of his affection since first grade. Meg's mother is a kind but unconventional woman who works in the Fair's Amusement Zone. Here she must wrestle with Oscar the Amorous Octopus and allow him to remove her bathing suit. After watching this underwater burlesque, Edgar is both shocked and gratified that he has finally learned some crucial secret of life. Edgar goes to the fair a second time as a winner of an essay contest in which he describes the typical American boy. Accompanied this time by his family, Edgar visits several exhibits displaying a utopian vision of the future, but he notices peeling paint and other signs of decay in pavilions that will soon be demolished. He is impressed by the time capsule at the fair, and his final act in the novel is to bury his own capsule in Claremont Park. As emblems of his nine years of life, he includes such items as a Tom Mix decoder badge, his handwritten biography of Franklin Roosevelt, a harmonica, a book on self-taught ventriloquism, and one of his mother's torn stockings.

The Characters

Since Edgar is the first-person narrator for most of this novel, he naturally becomes the most fully developed character. This point of view permits full revelation of Edgar's thoughts and feelings, but it constrains and sometimes distorts the presentation of other characters. As a child Edgar, acts only within a small realm, and his knowledge is sorely limited. Thus, his narrative cannot easily follow other family members into the larger world and interpret their actions soundly. In one of the seven sections of the novel not seen through Edgar's eyes, Donald observes, "It's only natural that we remember things differently." Those sections narrated by Donald, Rose, and Aunt Frances do correct and amplify Edgar's story, but they are not long enough (only twenty-eight pages) to provide full development of other characters.

Edgar's central role as narrator is entirely appropriate, however, for a novel focusing on growth from infancy to the brink of adolescence. At the age of nine, Edgar does not complete his rite of passage into maturity, but he has encountered episodes of senseless violence, sudden death, mature sexuality, and the fallibility of adult protectors. Such experiences bring partial but painful knowledge, and Edgar gradually develops from naïve preschooler to more perceptive student of life. Even if he remains somewhat callow, his responses thus far predict further progress in maturation and illumination.

Throughout much of the novel, Donald is the stock big-brother protector and adviser. He is a good athlete, conscientious student, and responsible part-time worker in his father's music store. When Donald gets a summer job as a musician at a resort hotel and becomes involved with girls, his story becomes more intriguing, but readers learn of these experiences away from home only through one letter and the sketchy report of a neighbor who visited the hotel. Later, Donald flunks out of college, but the reasons and his reactions are not fully explained because they are largely tangential to Edgar's story.

Dave and Rose display conflicting traits. While he is impulsive, impractical, and irreligious, she is disciplined, orderly, and active in the sisterhood of the synagogue. Edgar reports frequent disagreements between the two, but, like Edgar, the reader never gets confirmation of many allegations. The four sections narrated by Rose all come early in the book (when the mother is naturally the most important character in a small child's life). Later, her unhappiness is apparent but never closely examined.

Meg and, especially, her mother Norma offer startling contrasts to Edgar's staid and respectable world. The daughter of an exotic dancer, Meg is quiet but self-assured. She arouses Edgar's juvenile affection and becomes his closest confidante. Norma provokes Rose's disapproval. Her behavior sometimes surprises Edgar, but it always reflects kindness and simple wisdom.

Themes and Meanings

As an uncompleted initiation story, *World's Fair* portrays a boy's tentative journey toward maturity. In displaying Edgar's growing sensitivity to language and skill as a writer, Doctorow also provides a portrait of the artist as a small boy. Edgar's two trips to the fair serve to focus and develop these two intertwined themes.

Edgar first visits the fair as the companion of two sexually alluring females. He affirms his nascent manhood by protecting Meg and bravely riding the parachute jump with her. Later, he asserts his independence and maturity by leaving Meg behind and watching her mother's nude performance. In this voyeuristic episode, his sexual initiation is vicarious but still decisive.

Early in the narrative, when his mother uses a strange idiom, Edgar displays a keen interest in and love of words. Appropriately, then, his second trip to the World's Fair results from his success as a budding literary artist. By describing the typical American boy in an essay contest, Edgar wins tickets to the fair for his entire family. Edgar's essay displays his emerging skill as a writer but also his ability to blend and harmonize disparate components of life. Using his own childhood experiences as raw materials, he synthesizes uniquely ethnic elements with more generic traits of boyhood to produce a creative definition. At the fair, Edgar further displays the powers of observation and discrimination necessary for the artist. The magnificence of fair exhibits still awes him, but he now assumes a dual perspective and also notes shabbiness and deterioration. Perhaps he already suspects that the utopian promises of the fair, staged amid the horrors of world war, will never be realized.

In burying his personal time capsule, Edgar may be putting away childish things as he enters a new stage in life. At the same time some specific items in the capsule are emblems of his continuing struggle toward personal and artistic maturity. The decoder badge, for example, symbolizes his persistent efforts to probe and decipher the mysterious conversations, objects, and events surrounding him. The book on ventriloquism focuses on a skill similar to that of the literary artist. Just as the ventriloquist animates a lifeless dummy by projecting his or her speech, the creative writer must invent fictional characters and give them authentic voices.

Critical Context

Winner of the National Book Award in 1986, *World's Fair* is Doctorow's sixth novel. Most of his novels, such as *Ragtime* (1975) and *The Waterworks* (1994), recreate earlier historical periods and use actual or fictional events from the past to make social and political commentary. In *Welcome to Hard Times* (1960), for example, nineteenth century settlers on the Western frontier cannot escape evils of the East embodied in the Bad Man from Bodie. *The Book of Daniel* (1971) questions the workings of the American legal system by focusing on the trial and punishment of two characters much like Ethel and Julius Rosenberg.

World's Fair is one of several Doctorow novels set in Depression-era America. In *Loon Lake* (1980) a poor drifter falls into the strange world of an eccentric millionaire and emerges as that tycoon's corrupt adopted son. The events of *Billy Bathgate* (1989), chronicling Billy's apprenticeship to the gangster Dutch Schultz, are much more overtly criminal.

Doctorow has acknowledged autobiographical elements in *World's Fair* and labelled it an "illusion of a memoir." As such, it deftly maintains a dual focus. It is a rich documentary of life in a Bronx community during the 1930's, with occasional glances outward at America's economic disruption and Nazi tyranny in Europe. At the same time, it is a highly individual account of personal and artistic development. The novel offers a detailed picture of another era, intriguing glimpses of Doctorow's life and thought, and a timeless story of tentative initiation.

Bibliography

Fowler, Douglas. *Understanding E. L. Doctorow.* Columbia: University of South Carolina Press, 1992. A useful introduction to Doctorow's themes and techniques.

Harter, Carol C., and James R. Thompson. *E. L. Doctorow.* Boston: Twayne, 1990. Straightforward biocritical survey of Doctorow's work, with useful bibliography and chronology.

Levine, Paul. *E. L. Doctorow.* New York: Methuen, 1985. Concise analysis of Doctorow's short stories and the five novels prior to *World's Fair*, with particular emphasis on his revision of history.

Morris, Christopher D. *Models of Misrepresentation: On the Fiction of E. L. Doctorow.* Jackson: University Press of Mississippi, 1991. A theoretical study of the problems of fictional representation based on ideas of Paul de Man, Jacques Derrida, and J. Hillis Miller. Suggested for more advanced students.

Parks, John G. *E. L. Doctorow.* New York: Continuum, 1991. Perceptive commentary on Doctorow's novels and the play *Drinks Before Dinner* (1979), with particular attention to important social and political forces in American history.

Albert E. Wilhelm

THE WRECKAGE OF AGATHON

Author: John Gardner (1933-1982)
Type of plot: Philosophical pseudohistory
Time of plot: The sixth century B.C.E.
Locale: Sparta, ancient Greece
First published: 1970

Principal characters:
>AGATHON, an Athenian seer imprisoned for suspected instigation of the
>   Helot rebellion against the Spartan tyrant Lykourgos
>DEMODOKOS, the youthful Helot disciple, called Peeker by Agathon,
>   who is imprisoned to serve the aged seer
>TUKA, Agathon's wife, who returned to Athens to avoid involvement in
>   the self-destruction or wreckage wrought by her husband
>IONA, the mistress of Agathon and a leader of the Helot rebellion
>DORKIS, a friend of Agathon and the husband of Iona, martyred for his
>   role in the rebellion

The Novel

The action of the novel encompasses Agathon's imprisonment for his presumed involvement in the rebellion of the Helots against the Spartan tyrant Lykourgos, his escape at the hands of the Helot rebels, and his subsequent death from plague in the Helot headquarters, a commandeered tomb turned infirmary. An epilogue to the life and action of the novel is provided when Peeker is sent by the Helots to Athens to give Tuka the scrolls that both he and Agathon produced during their imprisonment, the scrolls that comprise the content of the novel.

The form of the novel is autobiographical. Chapters from the feverish mind of Agathon are interlaced with chapters detailing the apprentice observations of the seer-in-progress, Peeker. These interlaced chapters treat the historical context for both men's lives as well as observations on the present action. Through the minds of these imprisoned scribes, the reader comes to know the life and loves of Agathon and the impact of the culminating wreckage of that experience on Peeker.

While Agathon is the focus of the novel and its dominant spokesman, it is Peeker who is its heart. The novel is a *Bildungsroman*, a novel chronicling the coming of age of Peeker. Moving from youthful embarrassment at the nonconformist whom he is destined to follow through dutiful response to one in such obvious need, Peeker grows in the nature of compassion and reaches maturity in recognition that genius always has its flaws. He emerges as an emblem of hope when he offers redemptive acceptance to Tuka at the novel's conclusion.

Peeker exists as a necessary complement to Agathon in the novel. He is destined to carry on the tradition of the thinker. His character is the growing, changing reality that completes the cycle of decay and wreckage seen in Agathon. That his chapters begin and end the novel is no accident. His is the role of interpreter, a role that he resists and is inadequate to perform, yet he is imprisoned in the form of seer and finds it to be the natural expression of his soul.

As the novel develops, Peeker grows in his ability to write, his understanding of the information he hears and the experience he perceives, and his ability to act on behalf of another person. By the time he reaches Athens, he has found the maturity to be at ease in the home of Agathon's widow and children. A true seer now, he embodies compassion, insight, and hope.

The Characters

Both fool and troublemaker, Agathon is characterized as a human wreck by Peeker at the beginning of the novel. Little more than a drunken derelict, the old man is filthy in both mind and body, a man who dines on garbage and entertains himself by making lurid suggestions to those who pass him by. Yet Peeker acknowledges him to be a man who is curiously compelling in personality, a man capable of inspiring discipleship and gathering listeners.

While Peeker cannot at first define the positive worth of the man he follows, the reader, privy to the obsessively filled prison parchments, hears with Peeker the stories in which the seer records his early education with Konan under Klinias, his childhood-friendship-turned-lifelong-love for Tuka, and his various assignations with Thayla, Iona, and countless others whose paths he crossed. As the stories unfold, the gap between the external personage of Agathon and the internal reality of the man narrows. With Peeker, the reader balances the weaknesses of the life with the brilliance of mind that enables the thinker to compare the compassionate justice of Solon with the stifling legality of Lykourgos and to see that all systems are finite.

What the reader learns about Agathon from his autobiographical chapters must be filtered through the sophisticated consciousness of a man accustomed to designing roles to be played to accomplish certain desired results. He cannot be trusted to portray himself or others as they actually are; rather, he portrays experience as he wishes it to be perceived. Peeker, on the other hand, writes his chapters out of the guileless innocence of youth. Much of the charm of his characterization comes from revelations that he does not know he has made. He believes that he must decide whether he will become a seer; the reader knows that he has already made that decision, that it is a part of the very fabric of his existence. He believes himself to hate Agathon and all that he has become; the reader realizes that he loves the man, that the seer has become the father he has never known.

Tuka and Iona, the two major loves of Agathon's life, represent the tension between emotion and idea in the novel. Tuka the artist is limited to an emotional response to life. She perceives all of reality from her heart and no amount of talking, of expressing ideas can fill the emotional vacuum in her being. If she does not feel reality, that reality does not exist in her consciousness. Tuka is unable to accept Agathon's logical explanation that she is his major and lasting love, despite his relationship with Iona. His separation of emotion and idea simply increases the emotional vacuum in her being.

That Agathon might be able to separate love and the idea of love is, to Tuka, part of the wreckage, the outward expression of moral distortion. Her emotional being at its extreme forces rejection of Agathon. She fears that the only way she can avoid becoming a part of the wreckage is to withdraw, to remove her family to Athens.

Iona is ruled almost entirely by her head rather than her heart. When she gives herself to a love relationship, she participates in the idea of love rather than the emotion of love. Hers is an ideological movement to some greater reality. She is motivated and compelled by what her head dictates. The possibility of writing for her is the extension or the external image of this precondition to idea that is similar to the possibility of the harp as an external image of Tuka's emotional reality. Because Iona is ruled by the preeminence of the realm of ideas, she has the natural instincts of the revolutionary. In her extreme, she gravitates to fanatical devotion to a singular idea. This single-minded preoccupation causes her to forfeit all emotion and thus live beyond the seer's love. The wreckage of the novel is partly realized in Agathon's inability to find satisfactory resolution of these two feminine roles or the larger reality they represent in his life.

Just as Tuka and Iona are used to express one line of tension in the novel, so Dorkis is contrasted with Agathon to present another line. While Agathon is the man of complexity, the man unable to act because his multidimensional worldview negates the distinctive value of the individual act, Dorkis is the man of simplicity, the man who can act with dignity and even heroism because his singular worldview clarifies and dignifies the individual action. Agathon is awed by the beauty of this simplicity, but he innately doubts its truth. Dorkis dies a heroic death, according to Agathon, because he accepts the reality of evil. Such acceptance can come, however, only when evil is seen as an isolated reality distinguished from all other realities. Since Agathon can never divorce a single reality from all reality, he is destined to find escape in playing the fool.

Themes and Meanings

While the novel treats the nature of justice, the meaning of truth, and the limitations of humanity, it is the centrality of suffering that is the major preoccupation, the superstructure that provides a single dominant configuration for these themes. Agathon's life is defined by the suffering that he has caused for Tuka, the suffering that he could not prevent Thalia from experiencing, the suffering imposed on the community by the insensitive laws handed down by Lykourgos, and the heroic response of Dorkis to senseless execution. Unable to heal wounds, he assumes the ludicrous role of the sufferer who refuses to free himself. The prison rats he courts and accepts as his rightful community return his favors with the insidious germ of ultimate suffering. The plague in the final analysis becomes simply a symbol of the wreckage that life has already produced.

Suffering is identified in the novel as evil, as a result of the finite quality of humans, and as the inescapable reality of life. People inflict suffering on themselves and on those they both love and hate. They cannot avoid such complicity. When they try to act in love, they invariably cause the one loved to suffer, yet withdrawal only compounds the problem.

The novel suggests that suffering may be the only reliable truth people can trust. It is certainly authentic in its impact on people and in its motivation for response. It can be neither denied nor escaped. While each character must face his or her own suffering, it is Agathon's suffering that is most clearly chronicled in the autobiographical development of the novel. The objective correlative for his suffering is the ever-present prison company of the rats. All of Agathon's efforts to domesticate them in fantasy and fact fail to stay their progress. They eat away at his numbed consciousness until the rage of the fever and weakness they bring finds response.

Peeker, on the other hand, has the youthful physical resources to distance himself from the rats, to knock them away when they begin to nibble. Yet Peeker must watch their progress with his mentor. Watching and waiting brings its own suffering for him and, more important, brings him the lessons of suffering: tolerance, patience, understanding, and wisdom.

Critical Context

The Wreckage of Agathon is Gardner's second published novel. Its publication, four years after *The Resurrection* (1966), marked his acceptance as a serious writer of fiction and in a sense paved the way for the publication of *Grendel* (1971) and *The Sunlight Dialogues* (1972), the two books generally considered to be the cornerstones of Gardner's reputation as a writer of fiction. Because early readers and critics did not understand the carefully layered construction of his work or appreciate his heavy use of philosophical thought, *The Sunlight Dialogues*, completed more than a year before *The Wreckage of Agathon*, was rejected by three publishing houses before 1970.

As Gardner's reputation continues to grow, so does the critical appreciation for the artistry of *The Wreckage of Agathon*. Early reviewers were struck by correspondences between the book and contemporary unrest, but they were somewhat impatient with the heavy reliance on philosophical argument. Current appreciation of the work rests on the depth of thought and the universal quality produced by the body of philosophical argument that the book carries.

Bibliography

Butts, Leonard. *The Novels of John Gardner: Making Life Art as a Moral Process.* Baton Rouge: Louisiana State University Press, 1988. Butts draws his argument from Gardner himself, specifically *On Moral Fiction* (that art is a moral process) and discusses the ten novels in pairs, focusing on the main characters as either artists or artist figures who to varying degrees succeed or fail in transforming themselves into Gardner's "true artist." As Butts defines it, moral fiction is not didactic but instead a matter of aesthetic wholeness.

Chavkin, Allan, ed. *Conversations with John Gardner.* Jackson: University Press of Mississippi, 1990. Reprints nineteen of the most important interviews (the majority from the crucial *On Moral Fiction* period) and adds one never before published interview. Chavkin's introduction, which focuses on Gardner as he appears in these and his other numerous interviews, is especially noteworthy. The chronology updates the one in Howell (below).

Cowart, David. *Arches and Light: The Fiction of John Gardner.* Carbondale: Southern Illinois University Press, 1983. Discusses the published novels through *Mickelson's Ghosts*, the two story collections, and the tales for children. As good as Cowart's intelligent and certainly readable chapters are, they suffer (as does so much Gardner criticism) insofar as they are concerned with validating Gardner's position on moral fiction as a valid alternative to existential despair.

Henderson, Jeff. *John Gardner: A Study of the Short Fiction.* Boston: Twayne, 1990. Part 1 concentrates on Gardner's short fiction, including his stories for children; part 2 contains excerpts from essays and letters in which Gardner defines his role as a writer; and part 3 provides excerpts from important Gardner critics. Includes chronology and bibliography.

_____, ed. *Thor's Hammer: Essays on John Gardner.* Conway: University of Central Arkansas Press, 1985. Presents fifteen original essays of varying quality, including three on *Grendel*. The most important are John M. Howell's biographical essay, Robert A. Morace's on Gardner and his reviewers, Gregory Morris's discussion of Gardner and "plagiarism," Samuel Coale's on dreams, Leonard Butts's on *Mickelsson's Ghosts*, and Charles Johnson's "A Phenomenology of *On Moral Fiction.*"

Howell, John M. *John Gardner: A Bibliographical Profile.* Carbondale: Southern Illinois University Press, 1980. Howell's detailed chronology and enumerative listing of works by Gardner (down to separate editions, printings, issues, and translations), as well as the afterword written by Gardner, make this an indispensable work for any Gardner student.

McWilliams, Dean. *John Gardner.* Boston: Twayne, 1990. McWilliams includes little biographical material, does not try to be at all comprehensive, yet has an interesting and certainly original thesis: that Gardner's fiction may be more fruitfully approached via Mikhail Bakhtin's theory of dialogism than via *On Moral Fiction.* Unfortunately, the chapters (on the novels and *Jason and Medeia*) tend to be rather introductory in approach and only rarely dialogical in focus.

Morace, Robert A. *John Gardner: An Annotated Secondary Bibliography.* New York: Garland, 1984. An especially thorough annotated listing of all known items (reviews, articles, significant mentions) about Gardner through 1983. The annotations of speeches and interviews are especially full (a particularly useful fact given the number of interviews and speeches the loquacious as well as prolific Gardner gave). A concluding section updates Howell's *John Gardner: A Bibliographical Profile.*

Morace, Robert A., and Kathryn VanSpanckeren, eds. *John Gardner: Critical Perspectives.* Carbondale: Southern Illinois University Press, 1982. This first critical book on Gardner's work covers the full range of his literary endeavors, from his dissertation novel "The Old Men" through his then most recent fictions, "Vlemk,

The Box Painter" and *Freddy's Book*, with separate essays on his "epic poem" *Jason and Medeia*; *The King's Indian: Stories and Tales*; his children's stories; libretti; pastoral novels; use of sources, parody, and embedding; and theory of moral fiction. The volume concludes with Gardner's afterword.

Morris, Gregory L. *A World of Order and Light: The Fiction of John Gardner.* Athens: University of Georgia Press, 1984. Like Butts and Cowart, Morris works well within the moral fiction framework which Gardner himself established. Unlike Cowart, however, Morris emphasizes moral art as a process by which order is discovered rather than (as Cowart contends) made. More specifically the novels (including Gardner's dissertation novel "The Old Men") and two collections of short fiction are discussed in terms of Gardner's "luminous vision" and "magical landscapes."

Rosanne Osborne

YELLOW BACK RADIO BROKE-DOWN

Author: Ishmael Reed (1938-   )
Type of plot: Comic epic
Time of plot: 1801-1809, during the presidency of Thomas Jefferson
Locale: Yellow Back Radio, a town in the Old West, and Washington, D.C.
First published: 1969

Principal characters:
    THE LOOP GAROO KID, a black circus cowboy
    DRAG GIBSON, his antagonist, a powerful rancher
    MUSTACHE SAL, Kid's former mistress, Drag's new wife
    CHIEF SHOWCASE, an American Indian, Drag's lackey
    FIELD MARSHALL THEDA DOOMPUSSY BLACKWELL, an army general
    PETE THE PEEK, CONGRESSMAN, Theda's lover and cohort
    POPE INNOCENT, an old friend and adversary of the Loop Garoo Kid

The Novel

    Yellow Back Radio Broke-Down begins in the epic manner, establishing the epic stature of the hero, the Loop Garoo Kid, and previewing the main line of the action. The novel is cosmic in scope. Loop has existed at least since the ancient Egyptian civilization and will still be around to play the Las Vegas casinos in the twentieth century. He appears now as a black circus cowboy, traveling in the early nineteenth century on the American frontier, in the company of a dancing bear, a juggler, a barker, and a HooDoo woman, Zozo Labrique. Within the larger time frame, Loop is the cosmic jester, the human spirit, the principle of liberation. Drag Gibson, his primary antagonist, is the principle of evil, or tyranny. In this localized story, Loop is a HooDoo version of the Western hero, using African magic instead of a Colt .45. Drag (whose name refers to a cowhand rounding up stragglers in a cattle drive) is a rancher with the ambition to control the town of Yellow Back Radio and then extend his influence beyond to Video Junction and the power structure in the East. The media metaphor identifies the conflict; Drag's control of the media would give him control of America. *Yellow Back Radio Broke-Down* is an updated parody of the Western dime novel, a comic epic of the Old West.
    Whether by chance or by fate, Loop and the traveling circus enter Yellow Back Radio precisely when it is in need of a hero. They are greeted by the mysterious murder of their advance man and the presence of only children on the streets. Having revolted against an oppressive older generation, the children now control the town, but the helpless leading citizens have gone to Drag for help. This is the moment for which Drag has waited. He sends his cowhands to massacre the troupe and the children (in a classic wagon-train attack). The only survivors of the bloody battle are Loop, who escapes into the desert, and two of the children, who head out in search of the Seven Cities of Cibola, the technological paradise of the future. Before dying, Zozo passes

on to Loop her magic charms; then, trapped in the desert by a band of social-realist badmen, Loop has the promise of even more charms from Chief Showcase, who rescues him in a futuristic flying machine, a helicopter. Loop soon settles in a mountain cave, practicing HooDoo rituals that will combat the evil influence of Drag. His first act is to take over the town of Video Junction by placing a charm on the radio waves. In action modeled on the Theban story of Dionysus and Pentheus, Loop destroys the men of the town and sends the women and children into the mountains, smoking, drinking, and riding nude on goats. Like Dionysus, Loop has control of the people's minds and begins his revenge against the Pentheus of the story. He performs a Hoo-Doo ceremony to gain the necessary spiritual power.

Then follows a series of magical events that portend Drag's demise, one as dismembering as that of Pentheus. Loop's incantations cause Drag's skin to itch. He sends a nightmare to Drag's green horse (Germanic hordes descending on Rome) in order to enervate and steal it. (The horse was among Drag's lovers.) He places his brand on Mustache Sal, his own former lover and now Drag's mail-order bride, to use her in his stratagems. She begins a plot to poison her husband and take over his ranch. One sees her out in the mountains mixing a witch's brew. Loop appears at Drag's wedding to issue a prophecy about Drag's fate and appears simultaneously at two other locations, broadcasting HooDoo from the Yellow Back Radio Station and stampeding Drag's cattle. Loop later appears in the Yellow Back saloon to perform two symbolic acts: Using his whip, he first strips the marshal of his star and then the Protestant preacher of his crucifix. When Drag hires the famous killer John Wesley Hardin to kill Loop, the white python of the HooDoo mysteries squeezes Hardin to death. When this ploy fails, Drag calls upon the Pope, who, he thinks, will help him defeat Loop. Meanwhile Chief Showcase has notified Field Marshall Theda Doompussy Blackwell and Pete the Peek, Congressman, that now is the time to attack Drag and win over the West. Through the Pope's wisdom, Drag locates Loop, arrests him, and prepares to execute him by guillotine. When the Pope visits Loop in jail it is clear that they are old friends and adversaries. The Pope insists that Loop return to Heaven to pacify a former lover. Loop, an immortal force that the Pope cannot compel to obey, determines to stay on Earth and lead the forces of disorder. Loop, in fact, expects to suffer a martyrdom rivaling that of Christ; at the last moment, however, the two children arrive in a Chicken Delight truck to announce the discovery of paradise, and immediately afterward the United States Army, headed by Theda, arrives in taxis to surround the people of Yellow Back. The soldiers kill Drag's cowhands with ray guns; Drag, in a duel with Theda, falls backward in a drunken stupor into the pit of carnivorous swine; Amazons descend from the mountains to kill Theda and his soldiers, and Loop escapes the gallows unscathed. All the survivors of Yellow Back follow the children to the future earthly paradise, while the Amazons choose to return to the forest, now liberated from the threat of American institutions, and Loop on his green horse leaps into the sea to catch up to the Pope's ship returning to Rome. This task on Earth completed, Loop apparently returns to join the cosmic forces.

The Characters

In a novel such as this, a melange of comic epic, fantasy, myth, parody, and *roman à thèse*, one should not expect, as Reed warns the reader in an early episode, any verisimilitude that would make possible the usual development of character. Reed clearly debunks conventional attitudes toward the novel form. The characters are either comic exaggerations or parodies. Loop, the protagonist, in a mad and improbable fashion, follows the path of the epic hero. Like Satan in John Milton's *Paradise Lost* (1667, 1674) he is the antagonist of the prevailing order, but, unlike Satan, he does not gradually degenerate into a reprehensible creature. Instead he is, as William Blake considered Satan, the real hero of the story. His name is a pun on the French word for werewolf, *loup-garou* (a term brought by French settlers to Louisiana, where it is used in folklore to refer to a human being who has been transformed into an animal), and while he resembles Odysseus, Aeneas, Wyatt Earp, and other frontier heroes, he is perhaps closest to the fabulous creature out of African, American Indian, and other folklores—the Trickster. He spends much of the novel in his mountain cave (his underworld) performing demonic mysteries. He whispers fantasies into the ears of the populace, is seemingly everywhere at once thwarting the plans of the enemy, eventually suffers imprisonment and imminent martyrdom, but magically escapes as forces converge to destroy his executioners and establish a new society. His final leap off the mountain into the ocean (from where on the American continent might this be?) is superhuman. Such a comic treatment hardly allows for subtle character delineation, but the creation of such a character is not a mere tour de force—though such an exercise might not be abhorrent to Reed. Reed's aethestic breaks out of the common mold in revolutionary fashion to shock the audience into new perceptions—or, as he might say, back into the old repressed perceptions. What is more important to Reed than individualized qualities is the full expression of one's spiritual energies. Africa represents that fullness en masse; Loop Garoo, the black circus wizard, the cosmic jester, represents it in the individual.

Reed builds his other characters in similar outrageous fashion. Chief Showcase, the last Indian in the West, holds out a promise of survival for his culture. Significantly, he plays the role of an Uncle Tom (similar to that of Uncle Robin in *Flight to Canada*, 1976); the trusted and naïve lackey of Drag Gibson, he in fact works behind the scenes to ensure Drag's defeat. After Mustache Sal is seduced and sexually fulfilled by Chief Showcase, she changes his name to Chief Feelgood the Hawk in a Woman's Valley. Reed would regard this as a healthy attitude toward the American Indian. It certainly cuts through artificial conventions and returns sexuality to a natural state. Mustache Sal herself is symbolic of female sexuality, at once an explosion of natural energy and a threat to the male ego. She had in the past betrayed Loop Garoo, and during the course of the story she copulates with every man she encounters, before and after she is the bride of Drag Gibson. Her immediate goal is to poison Drag and take over his empire. Only Loop, who brands her with a bat-shaped iron, and Chief Showcase, in an all-night sexual bout, are able to subdue her. Presumably that is really what she wants. The three main evil characters are hardly subtle in their ambition to control the country. Drag is the hard-nosed, earthy, inhuman breeder of cruelty; Pete the Peek, Congressman, and Field Marshall Theda, the greedy, greasy, perverted homosexuals, are ineffectual masterminds of Eastern orthodoxy in American politics. They are highly exaggerated parodies of what Reed thinks of American institutions and the people who control them. They are, according to the Amazons who destroy them, "biological accidents." In such a fantasy world of good and evil, character is less important than high jinks and shocking exposé.

Themes and Meanings

In the eternal conflict between the forces of order and the forces of anarchy, Reed clearly stands on the side of the latter. Hence he would prefer to use such terms as "oppression," "tyranny," "ignorance," "intolerance," and "incomprehension" to describe the defenders of the status quo, and "progress," "change," "freedom," "creativity," "imagination," "fantasy," and "peace" to identify those who defy traditional restrictions. Reed attacks Protestantism as a restrictive religious movement, morally, sexually, and aesthetically; the federal government as an avowed enemy of Jeffersonian democracy, which Reed uses as a symbol of the ideal state; and capitalists such as cattle baron Drag Gibson as absolute despots. Among the oppressed are the younger generation, artistic geniuses, the alienated individualist, Indians, and African Americans. These are people who have no political or economic power but, if they can attune themselves, have access to the secret forces of life, represented in the novel as HooDoo.

The Christian religion suffers blasphemous abuse from Reed. Judas is Loop's personal Loa because he put his finger on the devil. Christianity has been the enemy of black people for two thousand years. When the Pope comes to draw Loop away from Earth to the restrictive confines of Heaven, Loop explains that Christianity is only part of the total cosmic scene and Jesus only one of God's sons. Buddha is another, and Loop a third. The Western world not only has neglected the cosmic jester but also has identified him with the devil. When this Dionysian force is denied, the legitimized powers appear as the only good. The Pope himself admits that he is in his present position because he won the power struggle. He gives credit to the African religion and calls Africa the subconscious of the Earth, the birthplace of humanity. He admits the long-kept secret that Egyptian civilization was black. He recognizes HooDoo as the syncretic and creative version of African Ju Ju that developed in America. While Drag contemptuously calls it Mumbo Jumbo (the title of another novel by Reed), the Pope knows its powers. With them, Loop destroys evil in the United States and allows Amazons to return to their natural religion and children to walk into an open future. Only then does he rejoin the Pope.

Just as important to Reed as the secrets of religion are the means of communicating them. In a sense, the medium is the message. Yellow Back Radio and Video Junction are the Main Streets of modern America. The talk-show host controls the minds of the citizens. When Loop, through HooDoo charms, changes the radio waves, he changes the message—he introduces fantasy into the culture. Early in the novel, Loop announces Reed's aesthetic theory. Threatened with extinction by the social-realist gang while suffering in the desert wilderness, he counters their insistence on verisimilitude, character development, and social purpose with the theory that art should be open: It can be "a vaudeville show, the six-o'clock news, the mumblings of wild men saddled by demons." That may be the best description of an Ishmael Reed novel, but the "mumblings" are those of a sorcerer: Poems are curses. Loop appeals to the ancient practice of cave dwellers drawing pictures of the animals they intend to kill. Art captures the spirit of the enemy and manipulates it. It is HooDoo ritual, the artist a ceremonial priest. When Chief Showcase delivers a poem damning the Anglo-Saxon culture that annihilated the Indian tribes, his audience perceives it as the harmless cry of a "dear child of nature," but for Reed it is a curse and plays its role in destroying the enemy. What is more, art is not only poems and novels. Reed has Loop claim that all human experience should be considered art, including the black experience in America; it is "*as beautiful as anything that happened anywhere else in the world.*" With art, as with religion, politics, and economics, Reed advocates complete openness and freedom of the human spirit.

Critical Context

In this, his second published novel, Reed explored themes upon which he was to elaborate, from different angles, in later novels. In particular, he is intent upon placing Christianity within the larger perspective of history—especially that of the Third World of African culture. Whereas religion receives major attention, Reed makes it clear that art is its natural vehicle. The relation of art to religion became the theme of *Mumbo Jumbo* (1972) and *Flight to Canada*. As in other novels, Reed shows past and present to be inseparable. Dionysus, the Germanic sacking of Rome, HooDoo magic, Amazonian fervor, Old West massacres, and the military-industrial complex explain one another. The forces of evil and good are always melodramatically presented, but here, as a consequence of the form, the ending is not only happy but idyllic. It is a parody of the Western dime novel, where the hero must ride off victoriously into the sunset. In subsequent works the prospects are more somber, and the cyclical view of history, only suggested in *Yellow Back Radio Broke-Down*, is more prominent. The forces of evil are only temporarily overcome, or they are very much alive, and the protagonist is only beginning to find his way to combating them. The sober realism of the novelist, Raven Quickskill, at the end of *Flight to Canada* is characteristic. As with other contemporary black novelists, such as Alice Walker and Toni Morrison, nobility, pride, and hope balance out the harsh realities of racial oppression.

Bibliography

Dick, Bruce, ed. *The Critical Response to Ishmael Reed*. Westport, Conn.: Greenwood Press, 1999. Focusing on Reed's nine published novels, this volume features a wide range of critical opinion concerning Reed's writings, including *Yellow-Back Radio Broke-Down*. A detailed introduction surveys the response to Reed's works, a chronology lists the major events in his life and career, and a bibliography suggests books for further reading.

Lindroth, James. "Images of Subversion: Ishmael Reed and the Hoodoo Trickster." *African American Review* 30 (Summer, 1996): 185-196. Lindroth demonstrates how Reed transforms the traditional hoodoo trickster into a subversive character in order to satirize and criticize negative aspects of modern society such as racial discrimination. He uses the Loop Garoo Kid in *Yellow-Back Radio Broke-Down* as one example among others found in Reed's works.

McGee, Patrick. *Ishmael Reed and the Ends of Race.* New York: St. Martin's Press, 1997. McGee examines Reed's fiction from the point of view of gender and race theory. He asserts that Reed's novels should be understood as critiques of racial ideology, and he examines Reed's fiction as a response to the disparities of postmodern and postcolonial history.

Singh, Amritjit, and Bruce Dick, eds. *Conversations with Ishmael Reed.* Jackson: University Press of Mississippi, 1995. A series of interviews with Reed that cover his life, career, and reasons for writing. Reed discusses several of his works in detail.

Weixlmann, Joe. "African American Deconstruction of the Novel in the Work of Ishmael Reed and Clarence Major." *MELUS* 17 (Winter, 1991): 57-79. Weixlmann discusses novels by Clarence Major and Reed. He asserts that both authors' novels have "given new freedom, direction, and shape to black cultural reality" and have subverted the Western concepts and traditions that have served to define the novel well into modern times.

Thomas Banks

A YELLOW RAFT IN BLUE WATER

Author: Michael Dorris (1945-1997)
Type of plot: Family
Time of plot: The 1960's to the 1980's
Locale: Montana and Washington
First published: 1987

Principal characters:
RAYONA, the fifteen-year-old daughter of a Native American mother
and a black father
CHRISTINE, Rayona's mother, a woman in her forties, who must come
to some accommodation with her impending death and her often
chaotic life
AUNT IDA, the supposed mother of Christine and of Lee
DAYTON NICKLES, Lee's closest friend
EVELYN and SKY, a married couple who befriend Rayona
FATHER HURLBURT, a Catholic missionary
FATHER TOM NOVAK, Father Hurlburt's assistant
ELGIN, Rayona's father

The Novel

A Yellow Raft in Blue Water explores relationships among four generations of a Native American family. The novel is organized into three sections, each narrated by a
woman of the family: the first section by Rayona, a girl of fifteen; the second, by
Christine, her mother; and the third by Aunt Ida, generally supposed to be Christine's
mother. Moving backward through the three generations, the book gradually illuminates the origins of the tensions still poignantly felt by the characters.

Structurally, and perhaps thematically, Christine is at the center. She is terminally
ill, but neither Elgin, the estranged husband with whom she still shares occasional
brief reconciliations, nor Rayona, their daughter, is willing to acknowledge this truth.
After all, Rayona tells herself, her mother has been a regular customer of the Indian
Health Service in Seattle. And Elgin has other things on his mind: He has decided to
put his relationship with another woman on a permanent footing. Leaving the hospital, Christine, accompanied by Rayona, points her battered car toward the Native
American reservation in Montana where she grew up and which she left more than
twenty years before.

As Rayona sees it, when they arrive at the reservation, Christine dumps her daughter on the doorstep of the woman who has always insisted on being called Aunt Ida,
even by her daughter Christine. Where Christine has gone, Rayona does not know, but
life with Aunt Ida is intolerable. When Father Tom suggests that Rayona accompany
him to a "Teens for Christ" convention, Rayona is unenthusiastic, but at least it might

make a change. Along the way, some abortive sexual fumbling occurs, and the embarrassed Father Tom, who was the instigator, is relieved when Rayona decides she will go back to Seattle rather than return to the reservation.

Rayona never makes it to Seattle. She finds work at Bearpaw Lake State Park and enjoys something that vaguely resembles a family life with Evelyn, a superficially hard-bitten but fundamentally generous woman, and Sky, her faded hippie husband. Attending a rodeo with Evelyn and Sky, Rayona enjoys a surprising triumph. Riding in place of her cousin Foxy Cree, who is too drunk to perform, Rayona wins an award and discovers a talent. The horse, it turns out, belongs to Dayton Nickles, an old friend of Christine's brother Lee, who was a great rider. Dayton brings Rayona back to the reservation and to Christine.

In Christine's view, she has not abandoned Rayona. Accepting the inevitability of her death, Christine hoped to place Rayona under the care of Aunt Ida, who is, after all, the girl's grandmother. In the face of Aunt Ida's cold greeting, Christine fled because she no longer had the strength to fight, and because she did not want Rayona to see her mother brought low.

Christine explains none of this to Rayona; she has never been one to explain herself. Yet it is part of her narrative, as is the story of her relationship with her brother Lee. The relationship was intense enough to make Christine jealous of Dayton, Lee's best friend. Spurred by this jealousy, she goads Lee, whom the reservation regards as symbolizing the hope of the future, into enlisting in the military, thus pointing him in the direction of his death. Christine left the reservation even before Lee did, and it was on the day that Dayton's letter informed her of her brother's death that she met Elgin.

It is, ironically, to Dayton that a dying Christine turns for support after leaving Rayona at Aunt Ida's. Dayton left the reservation himself, but he has returned after serving time in jail on a charge of having sexually molested a teenaged boy. Dayton makes Christine welcome, and it is he who reunites Christine and Rayona.

Aunt Ida's narrative brings the novel to its conclusion. If Ida has always insisted that Christine call her Aunt Ida, that is because she is not Christine's mother. Christine's biological mother is Clara, the sister of Aunt Ida's mother; Christine's father is Lecon, Aunt Ida's father. The relationship had developed when Clara had come to nurse her ailing sister. Scandal was avoided by a ruse that created the impression that the child's mother was the fifteen-year-old Ida, while the father was unknown.

Ida reared Christine, but always in the fear that Clara might reclaim her daughter at any time. This fear, in turn, created in Ida a fear of the pain that might arise for both Ida and Christine should Christine come to depend on Ida's love.

It was different with Lee. Lee was truly Ida's. His father was Willard Pretty Dog, a disfigured veteran of World War II, but not even Willard knows this. No one can take Lee away; Ida can love him openly. This, and not the preference for the male child that Christine had supposed, explains the difference in Ida's treatment of the two.

Only Father Hurlburt, the priest who becomes Ida's most trusted friend, knows the truth in all this. He is with Ida as the novel ends. It is the day on which Christine, still an adolescent, loses her faith, a faith she will recover as she approaches death. In the dark, Father Hurlburt cannot see what Ida is doing. He is a loyal friend and a good man, but, as a man with cut hair, he does not recognize the rhythm of braiding.

The Characters

Three powerful women, each representing a different generation, dominate the novel. Each of these women—Rayona, the fifteen-year-old girl; Christine, her mother; and Aunt Ida, supposedly Christine's mother—also functions as the narrator of one of the novel's three parts. It is, then, above all through their own voices and through the thoughts, feelings, and perceptions expressed in those voices that readers come to know the characters. In Rayona, readers recognize the adolescent's uncertainties about her own identity and her place in the world. For Rayona, these anxieties are intensified by her mixed racial heritage and by the instabilities of her family life. It is no wonder that she is tempted to borrow an identity when she reads the letter the solid, middle-class De Marcos have written to their daughter Ellen. Yet it is no surprise that Rayona is able to leave this bourgeois fantasy behind, as her experience at the rodeo and her reconciliation with the mother whose illness Rayona can now accept allow her to come to terms with who she herself is.

Christine speaks on the run. Staying in one place, physically or emotionally, has never been her strongest trait. She went through a series of boys and men on the reservation, which she left years ago. She has never settled in a single place. She thought that in her relationship with Elgin she was settling on a single man, but when Elgin began to wander, it was not in Christine's nature to stand still. Now she is in a hurry. She has, she knows, only a short time to live, and she must get her life into whatever kind of shape it can now assume. Her return to the reservation allows her to reestablish some degree of continuity with her past. She faces the destructive consequence of her past jealousy and, in doing so, becomes open to friendship with Dayton. Yet she is still concerned for the future: What will become of Rayona?

The third member of this trio is Ida. Like Rayona and Christine, Ida faced a crisis in her midteens, and the consequences of that crisis are felt by the two younger women. The obligation of caring for Christine and the fear of losing her have to a considerable degree determined the face Ida presents to the world, even to those closest to her. Fear kept Ida from identifying the father of Lee, her natural son; what if the father one day decided to claim the son? When, in the first two parts of the novel, readers see Ida through the eyes of Rayona and Christine, she seems distant, forbidding, and unwelcoming. It is only when she is finally allowed to speak for herself that she is revealed as a woman of powerful feelings, capable of moral heroism.

Each woman tells in her narrative more than she will ever tell either of the others. Christine will die in the belief that Aunt Ida is her mother and that Ida has never allowed her daughter to call her by her proper name, Mama.

Themes and Meanings

A Yellow Raft in Blue Water might be read as a meditation on family, on the mysteries of self and community, on the search for identity as individual and as member of the larger group, and on the pursuit of independence in the light of the reality of inter-dependence.

The main characters of the novel, Rayona, Christine, and Ida, while deeply in-volved with one another, remain in important ways isolated. They touch one another at a multitude of levels, but they communicate with one another only indirectly and, it sometimes seems, haphazardly. Family relationships have been distorted by the fam-ily secret that Ida carries, but family remains at the heart of the story.

The characters derive some of their identity from their complex relationship to the Native American community, but after Lee's death, the interaction of Ida and of Christine, who has moved off the reservation, with the community at large becomes limited. Moreover, Christine has married a black man, and Rayona, of mixed racial heritage, fantasizes an identity on the basis of a letter sent to someone else, a daughter of the white middle class.

As Catholics, the three women are also members of a faith community. Dorris hardly offers an idealized portrait of the church (the priests, for example, are depicted as vessels of clay), and the book implies no necessary affirmation on the author's part of religion in general or of Catholicism in particular. Yet two of the novel's three parts close with Christine's spiritual crisis, her loss of faith, suggesting that the char-acter's Catholic identity, however complicated and ambiguous, is not to be taken lightly.

What complicates the characters' relation to the community as much as anything is the pursuit of independence. Both Christine and Rayona set out on their own; each is motivated, at least in part, by a desire to reject the mother who has, it seems, rejected her. Yet each character will learn the truth of interdependence, and if this is a novel of setting out, it is even more strongly a novel of return. Rayona returns to Christine. Christine returns to the reservation, to the church, to Ida. Dayton Nickles is a pivotal figure. He is instrumental in Rayona's return, and he gives Christine the shelter and support she needs; yet the women also bring the gift of warmth and caring to a lonely man. It is perhaps as a gesture toward the theme of interdependence, with its sugges-tions of interaction and interweaving, that Dorris ends the novel with the image of two friends, Ida and Father Hurlburt, the Catholic priest who is also part Indian, sharing a concern for Christine, while Ida braids her hair, twisting, tying, blending.

Critical Context

An anthropologist by profession, Michael Dorris made his debut as a novelist with *A Yellow Raft in Blue Water.* Dorris's wife, Louise Erdrich, is also a novelist; her *The Beet Queen* had been published in 1986 to critical acclaim. The two commonly worked in close collaboration; a later novel, *The Crown of Columbus*, was in fact signed by both. Their normal procedure, however, was to attribute authorship to who-ever wrote the first draft. The other partner then functioned as an editor, offering com-ments and suggesting revisions. The book might go through several drafts and was not finished until both partners agreed on every word. Although the arrangement was un-usual, the result was an impressive body of work.

Both husband and wife were part Indian, and as *A Yellow Raft in Blue Water* illustrates, the Native American experience was for them an important subject. The characters in their works are a long way from the stereotypical Indian—howling, breechclouted savage or faithful Tonto—of American popular culture, and certainly a novel such as *A Yellow Raft in Blue Water* serves an important corrective function. Yet if Dorris rejected the old stereotypes, it was far from his intention to substitute for them the puppets of any ideology. Rather, he let readers see his characters in all of their troubled humanity, and he showed their world in all of its everyday reality.

Bibliography
Broyard, Anatole. "Eccentricity Was All They Could Afford." *The New York Times Book Review*, June 7, 1987, 7. Broyard observes that in *A Yellow Raft in Blue Water* Dorris describes a dying culture. The reviewer also notes that there is not much conventional plot but that the book's women are beautifully realized, and that the real movement of the novel lies in the way the three versions of their story comment on and harmonize with one another.
Chavkin, Allan, and Nancy Feyl Chavkin. *Conversations with Louise Erdrich and Michael Dorris*. Jackson: University Press of Mississippi, 1994. A gathering of interviews with Dorris and his wife that have appeared in various sources since the late 1980's. The interviews also cast light on the values—literary, ethical, spiritual—that inform the couple's work. Indispensable to any serious study of either writer.
Cowart, David. "'The Rhythm of Three Strands': Cultural Braiding in Dorris's *A Yellow Raft in Blue Water*." *The Journal of the Association for the Studies of American Indian Literature* 8 (Spring, 1996): 1-12. Explores the symbolism of the braid in Dorris's novel as portrayed in the joining together of the lives of Ida, Christine, and Rayona through the common cultural bond they share.
Kakutani, Michiko. "Multiple Perspectives." *The New York Times*, May 9, 1987, p. B13. Kakutani notes the similarity in narrative method between this novel and *The Beet Queen* and comments that a strength of Dorris's novel is its depiction of elusive states of mind through tiny details. Kakutani's observation that the men in the novel are either sex objects or cads seems surprisingly off the mark.
Lesser, Wendy. "Braided Lives Under Big Sky." *The Washington Post Book Week*, May 31, 1987, 5. Dorris's style is seen as a matter of pressing down on the prosaic until it yields its own poetry in a sharp observation of reality. The mundane, through cumulative effect, becomes the marvelous. Dorris, Lesser comments, also creates a number of good minor characters.
MacCurtain, Austin. "In Free Fall." *The Times Literary Supplement*, March 11, 1988, 276. MacCurtain observes that the device of multiple narrators gives density and richness of texture to the story. Its themes emerge without an omniscient authorial voice. Yet the high literary polish of the narratives may distort the terms in which such people see themselves and tell their stories.
Morris, Adalaide. "First Persons Plural in Contemporary Feminist Fiction." *Tulsa Studies in Women's Literature* 11 (Spring, 1992): 11-29. Focusing on Dorris's *A*

Yellow Raft in Blue Water, as well as Joan Chase's *During the Reign of the Queen of Persia* (1983) and Lynne Sharon Schwartz's *Disturbances in the Field* (1983), Morris explores the attempts of the authors to combine two philosophies in order to create a feminist political alliance that crosses generations, race, class, age, and sexual preference.

W. P. Kenney

YONNONDIO
From the Thirties

Author: Tillie Olsen (1913-   )
Type of plot: Proletarian realism
Time of plot: The early 1920's
Locale: A Wyoming mining town, a South Dakota farm, and Omaha, Nebraska
First published: 1974

> *Principal characters:*
> MAZIE HOLBROOK, a six-and-a-half-year-old girl at the opening of the
>   novel
> ANNA HOLBROOK, her mother
> JIM HOLBROOK, her father, an itinerant miner, farmer, and general
>   laborer

The Novel

The plot of this short novel is simple and incomplete. Jim and Anna Holbrook and their growing family move from a small Wyoming mining town to a farm in South Dakota and finally to Omaha, Nebraska, always in search of work and the elusive realization of their dreams for a settled and secure life. Their quest is frustrated at every turn by the power of circumstance: by bad weather and worse luck and by the social and economic forces that are beyond their control in the West of the 1920's. In Wyoming, a drunken miner tries to throw Mazie down a mine shaft to appease the fierce gods he believes inhabit that dark place—and falls in himself instead. In South Dakota, they cannot work hard enough to make their small tenant farm profitable. In Omaha, after months of working in sewers for subsistence wages, Jim finally gets work in a meat-packing house—and Anna has a miscarriage and nearly dies. The novel breaks off abruptly at this point, where Tillie Olsen stopped writing it in 1937. She had planned to follow the lives of Mazie and her brother Will into the 1930's and to show the influence of these early years as the two became adults in the struggles of the Depression. When she rediscovered and reassembled the manuscript in the early 1970's, however, she decided to add "no rewriting, no new writing," as she explains in a note at the end. The novel is thus a brilliant fragment, evocative but finally incomplete.

Like many other proletarian novels of the 1930's, *Yonnondio* describes the migration or flight from farm and town to the city, as families searched and scratched to earn a living in the midst of drought and farm crises in the South and Midwest in the years before the stock market crash of 1929. From the sound of the "iron throat" mine whistle calling men to work—or warning families of accident and death—at the opening of the novel, to the putrid smells of the slaughterhouses of Omaha in a heat wave at the end, this is the story of a working-class family struggling against the social and economic hardships of life in 1920's America. It is the other side of the Horatio Alger myth, the underbelly of the American Dream. Like Upton Sinclair's *The Jungle* (1906) and John Steinbeck's *The Grapes of Wrath* (1939), *Yonnondio* is about survival in "the other America" for the disenfranchised. Predictably, the novel has some of the best descriptions of work to be found in twentieth century American fiction, not only in the sections detailing Jim's jobs in the packing house but also in longer passages describing Anna's daily life as mother and housewife.

The novel is fragmentary and unfinished in narrative style as well. There is little of the smooth narrative flow of popular fiction here; instead, Olsen jumps from incident to incident, from one character's perception to another's, often with little or no transition or explanation. The perspective is also rather blurry: Much of the novel is narrated through the consciousness of the young Mazie, but other sections are rendered from the point of view of her mother. (The first perspective reminds one of the narrative techniques in Henry Roth's *Call It Sleep* of 1934, one of the best proletarian novels to come out of the 1930's; the second anticipates the powerful prose style of Olsen's own 1961 collection of stories, *Tell Me a Riddle*, and in particular of the title story.) Finally, there are also narrative inserts in the novel where Olsen provides a broader perspective or looks at other characters in ways the Holbrooks could not see them. Like John Dos Passos's *U.S.A.* (1937-1938), another Depression novel with which *Yonnondio* shares much, Olsen's short work mixes several narrative voices and experiments with both style and structure. Had the novel been completed or rewritten in the 1970's, undoubtedly some of its rough spots would have been sanded down; as it is, the novel has the texture of an unfinished, experimental proletarian work written in the 1930's—which is exactly what it is.

The Characters

The novel's three main characters are Jim, Anna, and Mazie; the other Holbrook children play a secondary role, and various neighbors and co-workers form a third level of characterization. The central character is probably Mazie, for much of the action of the novel is filtered through her consciousness and she is clearly the persona of the adult author. The thematic center of the book, however, is Anna Holbrook, the courageous, suffering mother who is trying to wrestle dignity out of her family's struggle to survive in this world, and the main protagonist is Jim, whose search for work propels the action of the novel but whose weaknesses also contribute to its tragedy. (It is Jim's demands for sexual relations with his pregnant wife that lead to the final miscarriage.) Jim is not a bad man; like the rest of the Holbrook family and like their neighbors in various Western homes, he is merely a victim of the crushing socioeconomic circumstances that existed in pre-Depression America.

Mazie's mind is poetic, and it permeates the novel. She is a sensitive child (often with thoughts too adult for her own good), and her voice lifts the novel above the sordid level of its drama. Similarly, the actions of Anna to hold this family together in spite of inordinate difficulties raise this domestic tragedy above the level of much fiction of the 1930's. At the end of the novel, and in spite of her weakened condition, Anna is taking in laundry to earn money for her children's education, and she and the children wander the outskirts of Omaha in search of the spring dandelions she can use as greens on her meager supper table. She is a valiant, remarkable woman who reminds the reader of the protagonist of Harriette Arnow's *The Dollmaker* (1954) and of a number of women in contemporary feminist fiction.

Themes and Meanings

The themes in such a short and simple work are quite near the surface. Like so much of the fiction of the 1930's, and in particular the social realist fiction influenced by the generally leftist critical ideas at work in that decade, *Yonnondio* focuses on the conflict between a working-class family and the overwhelming social and economic forces arrayed against them. Like the Joads in Steinbeck's classic proletarian novel at the end of the decade, the Holbrooks are asking only to be allowed to live and work. "But there is more—" another character says: "to rebel against what will not let life be." Olsen presents a family facing the hardships of poverty in America; in the rest of this unfinished novel, she would have shown the children fighting against that poverty and injustice in the 1930's. Olsen is no propagandist in *Yonnondio* (although her prose, especially in the early pages, can be didactic), but she reveals that the Holbrooks' condition hardly results from their own actions or inactions. These people are clearly the victims of a capitalist system that, at the least, exploits its workers for profit without concern for their safety, and, at its worst, poisons even the social and domestic relations among them. Yet the focus in *Yonnondio* is on the Holbrook family, not on the larger society, and rarely in 1930's fiction were relationships among family members rendered with such graphic clarity.

The strong presence of Anna Holbrook and the emergent character of her young daughter Mazie (who, like the protagonist of *Call It Sleep*, will grow up to write this novel), are positive counterpoints to the oppressive social conditions in the novel. In spite of all the poverty and suffering, in spite of the brutalization of individual workers and whole families, something in the human spirit endures. In Olsen's lyric prose there is both an indictment of a system that can brutalize people in this way and an optimism that a character such as Mazie Holbrook will survive.

Critical Context

Fragmentary and incomplete though it is, *Yonnondio* is still one of the more important novels to emerge (even if forty years late) from the 1930's. In some ways, the novel is as important for what it represents as for what it does or fails to do. On one hand, it is a proletarian novel that fulfills the reader's best expectations for that abused genre. In the early 1970's, in the middle of a revival of both popular and critical interest in the literature of the 1930's, *Yonnondio* unexpectedly appeared to confirm what certain critics and scholars had been arguing since at least the Cold War: that the proletarian novel had qualities of sensibility and commitment rare in American fiction and deserved better treatment at the hands of historians. A number of proletarian novels have in fact been reprinted since Olsen's book proving this thesis, including several others by women: Fielding Burke's *Call Home the Heart* (1932, reissued 1983), for example, and Josephine Herbst's Trexler trilogy: *Pity Is Not Enough* (1933), *The Executioner Waits* (1934, reissued 1977 and 1985), and *Rope of Gold* (1939, reissued 1979 and 1984).

These last works introduce a second major critical revival of the past few decades, the rediscovery of a neglected American literary canon, particularly the work of women and other literary minorities. *Yonnondio* represents still another novel in a long and growing list of recently rediscovered works by women writers, from Rebecca Harding Davis's *Life in the Iron Mills* (1861, reissued 1972), for which Tillie Olsen wrote a long and intelligent afterword, through Agnes Smedley's *Daughter of Earth* (1929, reissued 1973), to Meridel Le Sueur's *Ripening* (1982), a collection of essays and stories by a woman who, like Olsen, was also a radical journalist during the Depression. Granted that *Yonnondio* is not a reprint, Tillie Olsen was for a long time a forgotten American writer, and, as she has made clear in the essays collected in *Silences* (1978), the domestic circumstances of a woman writer's life often explain a great deal about her productivity, as in the publishing history of *Yonnondio*.

Thus, *Yonnondio* not only is a brilliant fragment from the 1930's—a flash of feminist and proletarian consciousness from the Depression—but also is reminiscent of other works from the 1930's and from other decades, works by women and by other underrepresented literary constituencies in the American canon that are still in the process of being recovered. In her depiction of Anna Holbrook, a character in the mold of Ma Joad and Gertie Nevels (of *The Dollmaker*), Tillie Olsen has shaped a new American heroine, a woman who, in the struggle to bring dignity to her family, adds stature to American literature.

Bibliography

Dawahare, Anthony. "'That Joyous Certainty': History and Utopia in Tillie Olsen's Depression-Era Literature." *Twentieth Century Literature* 44 (Fall, 1998): 261. An analysis of Olsen's literary works of the 1930's. Explores how the labor movement and events such as the hunger marches, Bonus March, rent strikes, and other expressions of working-class rebellion influenced Olsen's major work of the 1930's, *Yonnondio*. Maintains that Olsen depicts the functioning of the working-class family as an index of the level of exploitation and the value of a society.

Faulkner, Mara. *Protest and Possibility in the Writing of Tillie Olsen.* Charlottesville, University Press of Virginia, 1993. Focuses on four major themes in Olsen's writings: motherhood, relationships between men and women, community, and language. Faulkner examines *Yonnondio* as well as many of Olsen's lesser-known writings.

Jameson, Elizabeth. "Written, They Reappear: Rereading *Yonnondio*." *Frontiers* 18 (September-December, 1997): 141-145. Jameson's personal evaluation of the novel. She discusses the book's major themes, examines its class and gender relationships, and relates the lessons she learned from her initial reading and reexamination of Olsen's novel. She sees the novel as encouraging women to seek new opportunities and to define their identity through the novel's emphasis on family.

Finally, the book underscores the importance of collective action and interdependence.

Nelson, Kay H., and Nancy Huse, eds. *The Critical Responses to Tillie Olsen.* Westport, Conn.: Greenwood Press, 1994. Nelson and Huse's volume presents a comprehensive view of Olsen's life and works over the past sixty years and examines the social contexts of her writings. An illuminating review of *Yonnondio: From the Thirties* by Scott Turow, a chronology of Olsen's life, and an extensive bibliography are especially helpful in understanding Olsen's novel in relationship to her other works.

Orr, Elaine N. "On the Side of Mother: *Yonnondio* and *Call it Sleep.*" *Studies in American Fiction* 21 (Autumn, 1993): 209-214. Compares *Yonnondio* (1936) with Henry Roth's *Call It Sleep* (1934) by examining motherhood from the perspective of daughter and son. While Olsen portrays the daughter as physically and mentally close to the mother, Roth's portrayal of the son emphasizes the son's obsession with his mother. He otherwise lacks empathy; thus, the mother in *Call It Sleep* has no voice in the text.

_____. *Tillie Olsen and a Feminist Spiritual Vision.* Jackson: University Press of Mississippi, 1987. Orr examines the religious and feminist aspects of Olsen's writing.

Orr, Lisa. "'People Who Might Have Been You': Agency and the Damaged Self in Tillie Olsen's *Yonnondio.*" *Women's Studies Quarterly* 23 (Spring-Summer, 1995): 219-228. A discussion of Olsen's exploration of the interdependence between the individual and society in *Yonnondio*. Points out that Olsen emphasizes that the self can change social structures and also explores the guilt that working-class people experience when they succeed and rise above their origins.

Pearlman, Mickey, and Abby P. Werlock. *Tillie Olsen.* Boston: Twayne, 1991. An extremely useful scholarly book-length study of Olsen's work. Contains analysis of *Yonnondio*, her short stories, and her nonfiction work. Contains detailed annotated notes as well as a comprehensive bibliography.

David Peck

YOU MUST REMEMBER THIS

Author: Joyce Carol Oates (1938-   )
Type of plot: Family
Time of plot: 1946-1956
Locale: Port Oriskany, New York, a fictitious city
First published: 1987

Principal characters:
    ENID MARIA STEVICK, a delicate and scholarly adolescent girl who has
        an obsessive affair with her half-uncle Felix
    FELIX STEVICK, a former prizefighter, now trading in real estate, whose
        passionate affair with his young niece is the central action of the
        novel
    WARREN STEVICK, Enid's brother, a Korean War veteran, now a peace
        activist
    LYLE STEVICK, the bookish, anxious father of Enid and Warren,
        half-brother of Felix

The Novel
    You Must Remember This is a chronicle of the Stevick family from 1946 to 1956.
The primary movement in the novel involves the love affair between Enid Maria
Stevick and her half-uncle Felix. The novel also deals with many other love relationships of Stevick family members.
    The novel begins with a shocking description of Enid's attempt to commit suicide
by ingesting an overdose of aspirin. The story then moves back to an earlier time in the
family history, the time that led to the suicide attempt. Enid's preoccupation with
death as a child is clear as she looks at a picture of a boy who tried to escape from a
Nazi death camp. Oates describes the poverty of the Stevick family and the neighborhood in which they live, an area in which the air is polluted by chemicals from nearby
factories. There is an emphasis on sex and violence in their lives.
    The first and only time that Enid sees her Uncle Felix box occurs when Lyle Stevick
takes his children to a boxing match. Enid is the youngest child of the Stevick family
in attendance. Although she is shocked and almost overwhelmed by the blood and violence of what she sees and wonders why people would want to hurt each other like
that, she is impressed at seeing her uncle in a new way. Felix seems a person that Enid
does not know, and she wonders if he would know her.
    One senses the sexual undercurrent between Enid and Felix from the beginning. On
the beach near the summer cottage of Geraldine and Neal O'Banan, the sister and
brother-in-law of Enid, Felix offers to give fourteen-year-old Enid a boxing lesson.
The "boxing lesson" becomes more sexual in nature as it continues. Felix is snake-
quick in his movements, which leave Enid frustrated because she cannot return his
blows. After a while, Enid springs at her uncle in a frenzy, and Felix sees that he has

gone too far. Love and hate are often closely connected in the relationship of Felix and Enid.

The day after the boxing lesson, Felix offers to take Enid for a drive. They visit the vast old Hotel Rideau, which Felix has purchased. Felix and Enid begin to play a game of hide and seek, which ends with the drunken Felix attacking his niece.

Felix apologizes the next day, but his attack awakens in Enid her latent adolescent passion for her uncle. Felix realizes immediately that he has made a terrible mistake. Since Enid is the daughter of his half-brother Lyle, the attraction is even incestuous. Felix pleads with Enid to keep silent and to forget his attack on her. Enid's passion has been aroused, however, and she will not end her affair with her uncle. When Felix tries to end their relationship, Enid, in a romantic gesture, attempts suicide by carefully ingesting forty-seven aspirin tablets. Partly from guilt and fear and partly because Enid's strong will to die attracts him, Felix recommences their surreptitious love affair after Enid leaves the hospital. The intense feelings of the lovers contrast sharply with the drab, conventional world of the other Stevick family members.

The furtive romance of Enid and Felix goes on, in motels far enough from Port Oriskany that no one will identify them. Felix gives drinks of vodka and wine to his niece to "loosen her up." Their clandestine affair continues, with Felix at first being careful not to make any mistakes during their encounters. Oates details the blood, pain, violence, and anger that accompany Enid's loss of virginity in this love-hate relationship.

Felix is out of town often, involved in real-estate transactions. Enid continues attending high school, developing a circle of friends. Felix sees Enid occasionally, but a traumatic experience for him occurs when he glimpses Enid outside her school at lunch time with a circle of friends, male as well as female. Possessively, jealously, he carries her away from her school, and they make love in his car. In his jealousy and passion, Felix fails to take precautions, and Enid finds herself pregnant. Felix arranges for her to have an abortion. The blood, pain, resentment, and guilt that Catholic Enid feels at her abortion are convincingly described.

Felix loses his youth in the course of the novel as Enid loses her attraction for death. The novel ends as the former lovers go their separate ways. Felix is hospitalized after being severely beaten by the father of Jo-Jo Pearl, the young man, now deceased, for whom Felix was a mentor in boxing. After Felix recovers, he telephones Enid to say that he is going to be married and will move away from Port Oriskany. Enid also will leave Port Oriskany, to study music at the Wescott School in Rochester,

The Characters

Enid Stevick, the central character in *You Must Remember This*, is another of Oates's intelligent, talented young scholar heroines. Enid is by turns cold and fragile; like Connie in the story "Where Are You Going, Where Have You Been?," Enid has two sides to her personality. There is Enid Stevick, shy, intelligent, Roman Catholic, a model student, always receiving high grades. The other side of Enid is "Angel-face," the daring, conniving, sensual side. "Angel-face," with the encouragement of some older girls, is a shoplifter, and, repeating "Why not?" about the affair, propels Enid into the passionate but destructive relationship with her handsome young Uncle Felix.

Felix Stevick is the most vibrant character in the novel. He is an extremely attractive former prizefighter. Felix is an outsider, troubled by his illegitimate birth and the suicide of his father. Felix exercises an instinct for self-destructive violence. This impulse to self-destructive behavior in Felix is what attracts him to Enid after her attempted suicide and leads him to continue their obsessive, incestuous affair. Felix is attractive but lonely and alienated, seeing himself an outsider except in the prizefight ring or in his lover's arms.

Warren Stevick is the brother of Enid, the only male in a family of three sisters. He served in the Korean War and was seriously wounded. During his struggle to survive, Warren had an epiphany. Always helpful and considerate of others, he realized that his mission in the future must be to help others. In his idealistic political journey, he becomes a pacifist, then serves on an unsuccessful Adlai Stevenson presidential campaign, and finally works for Children's Aid in a Philadelphia slum neighborhood. In his contacts with his favorite sister, Enid, he makes perceptive statements applying to the central themes of the book.

Lyle Stevick is the bookish head of the Stevick family, father to Enid, Warren, and their two sisters. Lyle has a dead-end job as the owner of a secondhand furniture store. He worries about government corruption and fears enemy bombs; his main obsession is building a backyard bomb shelter. His worries typify, although in a ludicrous fashion, the worries of many people in the late 1940's and early 1950's.

Themes and Meanings

The main focus of this work is on love in its many forms. In addition to the love affair that gives momentum to the action, many other sorts of love are depicted in this novel, especially familial love and romantic love. The author's main point is that love does not carry with it any particular knowledge. As Warren Stevick writes to his sister Enid, "The people I have loved most in my lifetime (including you) I haven't known at all." It is only when Oates's characters are away from family and lovers, with people who do not know them or have not known them for very long, that they find themselves.

The primary impetus for the author was the recollection of the decade 1946 to 1956; she focuses on selected areas of American life during that decade. The novel is suffused with the romance, nostalgia, and, to the author, innocence of that epoch. Oates gives the reader a sense of the era by mentioning well-known film stars, politicians, popular singers, and television personalities. Arthur Godfrey, Jack Benny, Marilyn Monroe, and Dinah Shore are all named to give a sense of the times, as are major political events: nationwide, the Joseph McCarthy hearings and the Stevenson campaign; worldwide, the Korean War and the fear-inducing spread of Communism.

This novel, Oates's seventeenth, centers on the passionate love-hate relationship between Enid and Felix. Here love resembles lust in its purely physical, unthinking nature. The lovers do not know each other completely. Enid does not know much about the career of Felix as a boxer, about his mother, about his relationship to his father (who had committed suicide), or about the source of the money that Felix seems to have in abundance. Felix is similar to Jay Gatsby in that mysteries surround him. He is often restless and becomes angry if Enid questions him too much about his life.

Felix thinks he knows his teenage niece well, especially after they commence their affair, but he learns that there is an element of calculation as well as sensuality in her nature. The half-joking "boxing lesson" that Felix offers Enid turns serious as Enid springs at him in an erotic fury. The next day, the drunken Felix attacks Enid. He apologizes for his behavior and pleads with Enid to keep silent, by this time realizing that he had been manipulated into consummating a drunken pass he regretted immediately. The romantic gesture of Enid's attempted suicide is another conniving attempt on her part to continue their mutually destructive, incestuous relationship. Felix recognizes and is attracted to a willpower as strong as his own. The violent nature of their hopeless, destructive love is best symbolized by the shocking and detailed description of the abortion Enid has to undergo toward the end of the novel.

Love relationships unaccompanied by knowledge are evident in two other cases in the novel. Both love affairs involve men of the Stevick family, whose thoughts Oates paints convincingly. One sees romantic love in the story of Warren and Hannah, and one sees the return of familial love after the mysterious incident between Lyle Stevick and Elvira French. In each case, the mysterious nature of love, particularly the extent to which people may be lovers physically and still not know each other, is affirmed.

Critical Context

You Must Remember This preserves lower-class American life as it existed in the United States in the 1950's. Oates describes vividly and in detail the New York State setting of her childhood. The author writes that, in her mind, she traverses Port Oriskany's streets and ponders its buildings, houses, vacant lots, and, most of all, the canal that runs through it as it did through her birthplace, Lockport, New York. The canal, in Enid's fevered imagination, as in Oates's own, seems an object of utter beauty.

The novel is perhaps the most personal of the author's novels. Oates once wrote that the contours of Enid Stevick's soul very much resemble her own. The novel is also the history of an era the author loved. It focuses on certain selected aspects of American life, most notably politics (the antipodes of the Red Scare and the early pioneering antinuclear arms movement represented by Warren Stevick). In addition to politics, Oates evokes remembrances of popular culture in the 1950's, primarily music and Hollywood films. She includes the names of popular songs with suggestive and evocative titles such as "Stormy Weather" and "These Foolish Things." She mentions the names of film and television stars. She identifies the cars people drove (Felix is always driving a shiny new car) and remembers the professional prizefighting that vast numbers of Americans watched weekly on television and the great champions who were in their prime in that era. Oates knows much about boxing; in 1987, she published a nonfiction book, *On Boxing*, which showed her expertise in that area.

Enid is of a background similar to that of the author. Oates was a teenager in the 1950's, as Enid is. Even in stature, the slim frame of Enid resembles the build of the author. Yet except in its setting and in a few of its specific incidents, the novel is not autobiographical. The setting, the fictitious city of Port Oriskany, New York, is an amalgam of two cities: Buffalo, the first large city in the experience of the author, and Lockport, the city of her birth and the home of her paternal grandmother. Oates attended sixth grade and all of junior high school in Lockport, and the city consequently is suffused with the extravagant dreams of early adolescence, such as the dreams of Enid Stevick. Adolescent dreams tie in with the working title of the novel, "The Green Island." The greenness suffusing the novel is the greenness of nostalgia, of romance, of innocence.

In this novel, Oates turned back to the realistic novel after a quartet of experimental novels, including mystery, a romance, and a tale of Gothic horror. One sees the influence of Emily Dickinson in Enid's preoccupation with death and of D. H. Lawrence in the description of the passionate love between Felix and Enid. The irrational nature of intense feeling is beautifully depicted here. As Warren Stevick tells Enid near the end of the novel, love carries with it no knowledge.

Bibliography
Creighton, Joanne V. *Joyce Carol Oates: Novels of the Middle Years*. New York: Twayne, 1992. Creighton presents the first critical study of the novels Oates published between 1977 and 1990, including the mystery novels published under the name of Rosamund Smith. She offers an insightful analysis of *You Must Remember This*.
Daly, Brenda. *Lavish Self-Divisions: The Novels of Joyce Carol Oates*. Jackson: University Press of Mississippi, 1996. An excellent study that argues that the "father-identified daughters in her early novels have become, in the novels of the 1980s, self-authoring women who seek alliances with their culturally devalued mothers." Offers a perceptive reading of the evolution of feminist elements in Oates's work.
Johnson, Greg. *Invisible Writer: A Biography of Joyce Carol Oates*. New York: Dutton, 1998. An illuminating look at the novelist once dubbed "the dark lady of American letters." Drawing on Oates's private letters and journals, as well as interviews with family, friends, and colleagues, Johnson offers a definitive study of one of America's most gifted novelists. Includes a careful reading of *You Must Remember This*.
Milazzo, Lee, ed. *Conversations with Joyce Carol Oates*. Jackson: University Press of Mississippi, 1989. Part of the Literary Conversation series, this volume has seventeen pages containing references to *You Must Remember This*. The author also responds to the frequent criticism of the violence in her writing. Essential for a student of Oates, especially of *You Must Remember This*, the book contains an introduction, bibliography, chronology, and index.
Updike, John. "What You Deserve Is What You Get." *The New Yorker* 63 (Decem-

ber 28, 1987): 119-123. This thoughtful, insightful essay by one of Oates's most well-respected contemporaries offers perceptive comments, both positive and otherwise, about the novel, which he calls "exceedingly fine."

Wesley, Marilyn C. *Refusal and Transgression in Joyce Carol Oates's Fiction.* Westport, Conn.: Greenwood Press, 1993. An interesting study spanning the spectrum of Oates's work. Includes a helpful bibliography and index.

Linda Silverstein Gordon

THE YOUNG LIONS

Author: Irwin Shaw (1913-1984)
Type of plot: Realistic war novel
Time of plot: From New Year's Eve, 1937, to spring, 1945
Locale: The Bavarian Alps, New York City, North Africa, England, France, and Germany
First published: 1948

Principal characters:

CHRISTIAN DIESTL, a former ski instructor and a sergeant in the German army

MICHAEL WHITACRE, a successful New York playwright enlisted in the United States Army

NOAH ACKERMAN, a social worker drafted into the United States Army soon after his marriage

LIEUTENANT HARDENBURG, a German officer

GRETCHEN HARDENBURG, his wife

LAURA WHITACRE, Michael's wife, a beautiful actress

HOPE PLOWMAN, Noah's wife

JOHNNY BURNECKER, Noah's best friend in the platoon

LIEUTENANT GREEN and

COLONEL COLCLOUGH, American officers

The Novel

The Young Lions tells the stories of three soldiers, one German and two American, in World War II. Though they are continents apart when the novel begins (Christian Diestl is in Austria, Michael Whitacre is in New York, and Noah Ackerman is in Santa Monica), the tide of events brings their lives together briefly and fatally along a forest path in Germany.

The book's almost seven hundred pages recount the progress of its three protagonists. Their lives are presented chronologically, kept parallel in time as the narrative focuses first on one protagonist, then on another. Paying little attention to the broad sweep of the war, the novel concentrates on the personal dramas and the small combats that determine each man's fate. Christian, Michael, and Noah live out destinies shaped by their conscious decisions as well as by unconscious impulses and by the accidents or coincidences of environment. Though the particulars of their experiences differ, these three soldiers learn the common, bitter truth of combat: "You can't let them send you any place where you don't have friends to protect you."

Christian's career follows the victories and the defeats of the German army in Western Europe. He participates in the easy conquest of France and in the early success of the Afrika Corps; he savors the intoxicating spoils (women and food) of victory. When Nazi fortunes turn at the battle of El Alamein, Christian learns the brutal lessons of survival during a series of retreats. First in North Africa, then in Italy, at Normandy Beach, and finally along the Rhine, Christian fights to live despite Allied troops, German army stupidity, and the dictates of conscience. Considering going underground at the war's end, Christian plans one last ambush of two American soldiers walking unsuspectingly through a wood.

One of them is Michael Whitacre. Hating Fascism and having enjoyed the good life (marriage to a beautiful woman, financial success, a career writing for Broadway and Hollywood), Michael patriotically enlists in the infantry when the war begins. At boot camp he finds platoon life petty and squalid; quickly, he uses well-connected friends to transfer to a noncombat unit. From this safe vantage, Michael observes the war until he is run down by a truck as he drunkenly seeks shelter during an air raid. Waiting for reassignment, he meets a soldier from his boot camp platoon. Impressed by the man's attitude toward the war, Michael decides to accompany him to the front lines.

This soldier, the other American for whom Christian lies in wait, is Noah Ackerman. The frail son of an itinerant Jewish salesman, Noah lived miserably before the war: "Noah's life had been wandering and disordered. Often he had been deserted, . . . left for long periods with vague, distant relatives, or, lonely and persecuted, in shabby military schools." Then he meets Hope Plowman. She helps transform him into a poetic, passionate lover who triumphantly confronts the prejudice of her Protestant parents toward a Jewish prospective son-in-law.

Drafted into the army, Noah faces the rigors of training as well as the anti-Semitism of his platoon. He fights the ten biggest men in the company, losing nine contests physically but winning all of them psychologically. Hardened in will and body, Noah proves a brave soldier during the Normandy invasion. Wounded and evacuated, he successfully schemes to return to his platoon, where his buddies await him.

The chance encounter of three soldiers in the forest is the novel's brief, intense climax. Christian fires, killing Noah and wounding Michael. Stalking his attacker skillfully, the anguished Michael wounds Christian with a grenade and then shoots the helpless, taunting German. Michael carries his comrade back to his friends in the platoon.

The Characters

The central characters of *The Young Lions*, it has been charged, are not real characters but the embodiments of ideas. Critics and reviewers tend to find too little individualization and too much symbolism in the personalities and the actions of Christian, Michael, and Noah. Shaw's characters, it appears, are propaganda figures rather than rounded characters.

Christian, for example, seems a stereotypical Nazi soldier. There is nothing German about him except his army uniform; whatever might be the influences of geography, culture, and history upon German character are ignored. Instead, readers follow Christian's moral deterioration as he lives out the consequences of Nazi philosophy. Having heard that Germans are a master race who can rightly rule by force over inferior races, Christian loses all moral scruples as the novel progresses. His actions become increasingly savage: In the struggle to survive, nothing human can be allowed to have value. From callous attacks on enemy soldiers, Christian proceeds to abandoning his own men ruthlessly, to murdering innocent civilians, to betraying a wartime friend to fanatic SS troops. Christian follows out the ultimate logic of his worldview: If Nazism allows the strong to use the weak as they see fit, then the strong may sacrifice even Nazis to stay alive. In his most inhuman act, Christian disguises himself as an inmate during a concentration camp riot and stabs a German officer to death in a successful ploy to hide his identity.

Michael Whitacre likewise appears to embody a social class rather than to exist as an individual. Michael is the typical prewar liberal whose heart is in the right place—he despises the Fascism sweeping Europe—and who speaks enthusiastically of democracy. When Michael comes face to face, however, with fellow Americans who are uneducated, prejudiced, and unthinking, he recants his patriotic gesture of enlisting and seeks to protect himself in a more privileged detachment. Yet even as he flees active service, he experiences the archetypal guilt of the liberal for acting in a way that he knows is weak. It is not surprising that Michael comes to the conclusion that "five years after the war is over, we're all liable to look back with regret at every bullet that missed us."

Noah, who emerges as the novel's most admirable character, seems weakened by being constructed as such an obvious underdog. He is Jewish, an obvious sociological counterpoint to the Christian Germans who begin to carry out genocide and to the German Christian who shoots him. Noah suffers the most physically of any protagonist, but his spirit grows more courageous and undaunted the more he suffers. Noah seemingly represents the democratic hope that out of the furnace of combat, good men find their mettle hardened like iron and ordinary men are transmuted into heroes. Michael clearly owes his spiritual redemption (imaged in his killing of Christian) to Noah's example.

A similar weakness appears in the minor characters. Rather than being created as individuals, they are created in repetitive clusters around the central characters. Christian, Michael, and Noah stand in relief against the background of a superior officer, a lover (or lovers), and soldiers of their own rank. The comparisons and contrasts among these clustering groups appear obvious and predictable.

Around Christian cluster Lieutenant Hardenburg, Hardenburg's wife, Gretchen, and the soldier Brandt. Hardenburg is a walking mouthpiece, rationalizing the brutality and enjoying the savagery of war. His wife, Gretchen, who seduces Christian and leads him into depravity, is as ruthless in the bedroom as her husband is on the battlefield. Brandt, a war photographer, sees human suffering only as a propaganda device. Christian absorbs their values readily and acts them out upon others.

Around Michael cluster Colonel Colclough, Michael's wife, Laura, and soldiers such as Private Keane. Colclough cares as little for his men as does Hardenburg, but out of stupidity rather than arrogance; Laura is no more faithful to Michael than Gretchen is to Hardenburg, but Laura has the civility to divorce her husband. Private Keane smirks at Michael's military incompetence on several occasions: Without Michael's personal and social advantages, he shows himself the better soldier.

The best cluster, unsurprisingly, groups around the heroic Noah. His superior is Lieutenant Green: Like Noah, Green is physically frail and intimidated by more robust men. Yet Green proves unflappable in battle, capable of leading when officers such as Colclough go catatonic with fear. Noah's wife, Hope Plowman, alone of all the women in the novel, is a faithful lover; she inspires her man with noble sentiments about love, family, and honor. Most of the men in Noah's platoon come to respect him, but none more than Johnny Burnecker. A simple Iowa farm boy, Johnny becomes Noah's psychological brother. Johnny lived humbly before the war, and Noah wants to live with him and like him after the war: one with the earth, partaking of the cycle of birth, harvest, and rebirth.

Although the symbolism of the main characters and the schematic arrangement of minor characters is obvious upon reflection, it is not obvious during a first reading. Shaw is a fine storyteller who gives his characters strong dramatic as well as thematic functions. Shaw, a playwright and short-story writer before he turned novelist, skillfully creates scenes by dramatic confrontation or by descriptive force. Each chapter, by describing a major event in the career of one protagonist, contributes toward the movement of the novel. Yet many of those individual events are more compelling than the novel as a whole.

Sometimes the compelling force comes from the dramatic interaction of the characters. The chapters that recount Noah's confrontation with anti-Semitism and Michael's flight from suspicion during boot camp are among the best in the novel. At other times, the compelling force comes from tension-filled narratives. The chapters describing Lieutenant Hardenburg's ambush of a British patrol and the siege of Noah's platoon at a Normandy farmhouse are action-filled, suspenseful descriptions that could stand as separate short stories.

Shaw's characterization may be defended in another way. Common sense and psychological theories concur that all human beings are shaped by sociological, historical, and political forces to some extent. Given that a war is a sociological, historical, and political event, Shaw's creation of characters to represent—at least partially—abstract forces is reasonable. That he employs them skillfully for literary purposes is clear from the narrative and dramatic power of the book. In the light of these successful uses, many readers may not care that Shaw did not create memorable, three-dimensional characters.

Themes and Meanings

The biblical passage from which Shaw draws his title suggests the most important themes of the work: "Behold, I am against thee, saith the Lord of hosts, and I will burn her chariots in the smoke, and the sword shall devour thy young lions: and I will cut off thy prey from the earth, and the voice of thy messengers shall no more be heard."

Shaw's novel portrays a world, abandoned by Divine Providence, where war is nothing more than senseless destruction. Not only does the world, in the constant battle between light and dark, lack divine guidance, but it also lacks the guidance of wise statesmen. Shaw does not explicitly state these themes, but God and presidents are conspicuous by their absence. The novel remains so firmly focused on the loves, hates, hopes, and fears of the soldier's microcosm that the characters live and die with no comfort from abstractions or slogans about Good overcoming Evil, about Democracy surpassing Fascism, about God and Truth proving to be on Our Side. For soldiers there is only the fact of combat, and their only hope—political or physical—is expressed in the wretched vision which Michael has: "The exiles, living in mud and fear of death, had, in one way at least, found a better home than those from which they had been driven, a blood-spattered Utopia, now on the fringe of German soil, where no man was rich and none poor, a shellburst democracy, where all living was a community enterprise."

Many parts of the novel gruesomely depict death in battle and may be read as clear antiwar statements. Yet Shaw suggests that out of slaughter may come a fragment of knowledge that could save the world. Noah is shot as he is exclaiming, "The human beings are going to be running the world!" Though warfare is horrible, even the man sickened by slaughter can draw a distinction between those who must be fought because they reject Noah's simple hope and those who fight in order to make that hope a reality. The novel possesses a tragic sense that even good men cannot reform the world without shedding blood.

Critical Context

After the war, literary critics expected much of the novel in general and much of Shaw in particular. Hope was high that World War II would produce the novel that summed up the American experience as Ernest Hemingway's *The Sun Also Rises* (1926) had epitomized America's World War I. Hope was high for Shaw, especially since his prewar plays and wartime stories tackled the issues of a national struggle.

Inevitably such high hopes could not be met. As a genre, novels of American involvement in World War II have generated little critical enthusiasm. Something always seemed lacking: The novels (such as *The Caine Mutiny*, 1951) that are positive about the war are lamented as jingoistic and naïve; those (such as *Catch-22*, 1961) that are negative about the war parrot fashionable nihilism. A war novel may be a book that can never be considered apart from its political implications and therefore will never please every critic. General readers respond more favorably to war novels: For twenty years after the war, fictions about World War II constantly made best-seller lists.

Shaw's novels after *The Young Lions* continued to draw similar reactions. Brisk sales and favorable reviews confirmed his ability to produce interesting narratives with large, intricate casts of characters, but his works have not received serious critical attention. Shaw's fiction is limited in its ability to deal with subtle ideas; for the most part, he contented himself with reflecting popular worldviews rather than with shaping a vision of his own. Shaw himself countered that critics have yet to appreciate an ironic vein that underlies his work.

Bibliography
Giles, James R. *Irwin Shaw*. Boston: Twayne, 1983. Giles provides a critical and interpretive study of Shaw with a close reading of his major works, a solid bibliography, and complete notes and references.
Magill, Frank N., ed. *Cyclopedia of World Authors*. 3d ed. 5 vols. Pasadena, Calif.: Salem Press, 1997. For an overview of Shaw's short and long works, drama, screenplays, and nonfiction, consult the entry on Irwin Shaw in this set.
Shnayerson, Michael. *Irwin Shaw: A Biography*. New York: Putnam, 1989. Shnayerson reconstructs Shaw's life from his days as a playwright through his career as a screenwriter and novelist. Shnayerson's biography offers insights into Shaw's personality and his times.

Robert M. Otten

YOUR BLUES AIN'T LIKE MINE

Author: Bebe Moore Campbell (1950-   )
Type of plot: Historical realism
Time of plot: The 1950's to the 1980's
Locale: Hopewell, Mississippi
First published: 1992

> *Principal characters:*
> FLOYD COX, a bigoted, poor white man convicted of killing Armstrong
>   Todd
> LILY COX, Floyd's wife
> LESTER COX, Floyd's father
> JOHN EARL COX, Floyd's brother
> ARMSTRONG TODD, a fifteen-year-old black man killed for speaking to
>   Lily Cox
> IDA LONG, a mixed-race woman who knows Lily
> ODESSA DANIELS, Armstrong's grandmother
> DELOTHA TODD, Armstrong's mother
> WYDELL TODD, Armstrong's father
> CLAYTON PINOCHET, a white newspaper editor
> STONEWALL PINOCHET, Clayton's father, a pillar of Hopewell

The Novel

Set in the town of Hopewell in the Mississippi Delta, *Your Blues Ain't Like Mine* is the story of the lynching of a black man by a family of whites. The novel traces the story of the lynching and the subsequent effect on different members of both the town and Armstrong Todd's family.

Your Blues Ain't Like Mine is divided into fifty-one chapters. The story is told by an omniscient narrator, but from several different points of view: those of the Cox family, the family of Armstrong Todd, and the Pinochet family.

The novel opens in the home of Lily and Floyd Cox, poor whites in the segregated town of Hopewell. Floyd owns a pool hall and juke joint frequented by blacks. While at the pool hall, Armstrong Todd, a black teenager from Chicago who has been sent to live with his grandmother Odessa, speaks French to Lily. This seemingly minor incident causes a violent reaction on the part of Floyd's family, who encourage him to teach Armstrong a lesson about how he should behave in the presence of his supposed betters. The anger accelerates to the point that Floyd, Lester, and John Earl drive to the Quarters, the black neighborhood, and murder Armstrong in his grandmother's backyard.

Lily is not at all comfortable with the murder that has taken place, but she is bullied into not protesting by her abusive husband and his domineering family, which is governed by the bigotry of their past as poor whites in the Deep South. The family decides to lie if they are confronted about the murder. They reason that the death of a "nigger" will not make any difference to the local authorities. The move for desegregation is taking hold, however, as is the Civil Rights movement. The local authorities believe that they must at least have some pretense of a trial if they are going to avoid more bloodshed.

Caught in the middle of the racial tension is Clayton Pinochet, the editor of the *Hopewell Telegram* and member of one of the most prominent families in Hopewell. It is expected that he will adhere to the old Southern values. Clayton, however, is part of the generation that begins to question the separation between blacks and whites. He had employed Armstrong at the newspaper and found him to be a bright young man with whom he enjoyed talking. In addition, Clayton has for many years had a black mistress, Marguerite. His father, Stonewall Pinochet, cannot understand his son's seeming affection for blacks and constantly admonishes him for not conforming to the bigoted ways of the old guard.

Delotha Todd, Armstrong's mother, comes to Hopewell from Chicago when Armstrong is murdered; she too struggles with Southern ways. When she goes to the train station to arrange for her son's body to be taken to Chicago, she finds that, since he is black, his coffin will have to go in the livestock car. In addition, the white town leaders want to prevent Armstrong's body from leaving Hopewell, because they fear that the newspapers in Chicago might print stories that would cause bad publicity. Delotha must sneak the body out of town in a truck in the middle of the night.

As the novel progresses, the lives of all those involved in Armstrong's murder change. Lily and Floyd find that, because of the changing attitudes toward blacks, they are ostracized by the rest of the town. Their attitudes, as well as those of the upper-class whites, have started to become old-fashioned, if not obsolete.

Delotha and Wydell, estranged before Armstrong's murder, are drawn back together. They open a combination barbershop and women's hairdressing salon in Chicago and become successful. They also have three more children, two daughters and a son to whom Delotha is obsessively attached; she often calls him by his dead brother's name. Yet their grief for Armstrong does not leave them. Wydell returns to drinking, and Delotha becomes more and more depressed. Finally, they lose their business. In addition, Wydell, Jr., gets in trouble at school, causes problems at home, and finally ends up in a gang. He is saved in the end by his father, who has enough gumption to know that only he can save his son.

In Hopewell, the town grows and changes as the story progresses from the early days of the Civil Rights movement to the mid-1980's. Clayton Pinochet decides that he must follow his conscience, and he begins tutorial classes for blacks. His resolution is tested fully, however, when he learns that Ida Long, a black woman who has been his friend and whose son he has tutored, is actually his half-sister. Ida must also come to terms with being the daughter of Stonewall Pinochet. She comes into her own when she tells Clayton that she wants her share of the estate and that she wants everyone to know the identity of her father. Clayton is caught between the old and new worlds. When he is asked to take his father's place among the Honorable Men of Hopewell, he decides that he is not, in his father's eyes, an honorable man. In order to be honorable in his own eyes, he leaves his past behind and tells Ida that they will work out a settlement. The novel ends with Wydell and his son returning to Hopewell in search of the peace that they both desire.

The Characters

Armstrong Todd, a fifteen-year-old African American from Chicago, is portrayed as someone caught in the wrong place at the wrong time. He is accustomed to the more accepting North and tests the limits of acceptance in the South when he speaks French to Lily Cox. Tragically, he finds that the South is not ready to accept a black man who is educated and has the presumption to show that he is educated. Armstrong is portrayed as an intelligent young man with a promising future; however, there is a daring streak in him which is eager to challenge the established order. It is this streak that causes him to offend Floyd Cox and that eventually causes his death.

Floyd Cox, an uneducated white man, is painted as an almost stereotypical bigoted white Southern male. He and his family are poor, and Floyd and his wife Lily are the poorest of the entire family. He and Lily both dream of a better life, but Floyd is caught by both economic conditions and his own attitude. Like his peers, he believes that if it were not for blacks, he would be better off economically. When Armstrong speaks French to his wife, the act is all the provocation Floyd needs. His manhood has been threatened, and he reports the incident to his father and brother. They goad him into teaching Armstrong a lesson. Floyd really does not want to provoke a fight; he is content to exaggerate his previous confrontation. Yet he goes along with Lester and John Earl, showing his basic inability to make major decisions for himself. The need to fit in and go along with the established order is too strong for him.

Lily Cox, Floyd's wife, does not agree with Floyd's actions. In fact, Lily really does not understand segregation, partially because she has a secret friend. She and Ida Long share an affection for watching the trains at the station. They enjoy each other's company, and Lily is at a loss to understand why they should not be friends.

Clayton Pinochet is the editor of the *Hopewell Telegram*. He is ashamed of his father's bigotry; in fact, Clayton actually prefers the company of blacks to that of whites, a fact that disturbs Stonewall Pinochet. Throughout the novel, Clayton must battle his internal conflict and his domineering father.

Wydell Todd, Armstrong's father, had left Delotha and become a drunk. He finds out that his son has been murdered and returns to Delotha. They find that they now have common ground and decide to try to make their lives work. Ironically, Wydell is originally seen as an alcoholic who is unable to do anything for himself. After his son's death, he becomes the strong member of the marriage. He gets his barber's license, and it is he who encourages Delotha to try to leave the past behind. Ultimately, it is also Wydell who must try to save their son, Wydell, Jr., from gangs and street life.

Delotha Todd, Armstrong's mother, sent Armstrong to be with Odessa, her mother. She thought he would be better off in Hopewell than in Chicago. Although she and Wydell do become financially successful, she is never able to put her grief over Armstrong in perspective.

Ida Long, a light-skinned black woman, is Lily's friend at the train station. Ida has had to live with the fact that she does not know who her father is and has always been told by her peers that she does not have a father. After her stepfather dies, she goes through his papers and finds that she is the daughter of Stonewall Pinochet, one of the most blatant bigots in Hopewell. Ironically, she and Clayton are good friends, and she must decide what to do. She emerges as a strong, determined woman when she tells Clayton that she wants not only a share of the estate but also recognition that she does have a father.

Themes and Meanings

The major issue confronted in the novel is change and its effects. Some of the changes are brought about by the shock that the murder of Armstrong Todd causes. Other changes are brought about by the shifting views of society. All the changes are painful for the people involved. Armstrong Todd's family must somehow manage the grief that is brought about not only by his death but also by the way he died. The Cox family must somehow try to justify their decision to commit murder and must realize that society's shifting values make their act no longer acceptable. Stonewall Pinochet and his contemporaries must watch their world, which is based on the idea that whites are better than blacks, start to crumble. Clayton Pinochet, caught in the middle of the changes, must somehow try to make sense of the fact that, even though he is from one of the aristocratic families, he really does prefer the company of blacks.

Campbell's main point is that any change is difficult. A person's social standing does not matter; when the values of a society start to change, all people find that their place in society shifts, and this shift can cause friction.

The murder of Armstrong Todd was based on the 1955 murder of Emmett Till, a fourteen-year-old who was lynched for speaking to a white woman in a Mississippi town. Campbell fictionalizes the incident and then carries the story past the bare details by examining the effects this event would have on three distinct groups of people.

Campbell presents the themes to the reader by telling the stories of three very different groups of people—the Todds, the Pinochets, and the Coxes. Each group must learn to manage the changes that occur. It is interesting to see how the lives of the characters overlap and, as the novel progresses and the times change, begin to merge.

Critical Context

Your Blues Ain't Like Mine is Bebe Moore Campbell's first novel; she had previously written short stories and two nonfiction books. Her first nonfiction work, *Successful Women, Angry Men*, was published in 1986. She published her memoir, *Sweet Summer: Growing up with and Without My Dad*, in 1989.

Campbell, a longtime journalist, has contributed to *Savvy, Essence, Lear's*, and many other publications; the bulk of her work is concerned with social issues. In 1980, she received a literary grant from the National Endowment for the Arts. She has also been a regular contributor to National Public Radio broadcasts.

Bibliography
Campbell, Bebe Moore. "Growing Up Black." *Seventeen* 49 (December, 1990): 102-105. In this article, Campbell interweaves interviews with three young black women with information about what it is like to grow up black in the United States in the 1990's. She discusses societal stereotypes and bigotry. The article is an illuminating look at how young black women see themselves within society.

_____. "I Hope I Can Teach a Little Bit: An Interview with Bebe Moore Campbell." *Southwest Review* 81 (Spring, 1996): 195-213. Campbell discusses major African American writers, as well as her views on race relations in the United States; the support African Americans offer each other through the cohesive black community; and the unrealistic standard of beauty that American society forces upon women—white or black.

Essence. "Graceful Passages." 21 (May, 1990): 130-136. In this article, several authors discuss the changes in their lives and the world in the past twenty years; Campbell discusses the influence of the blues on her life. She also talks about the importance of inspiration to her writing.

Graeber, Laurel. "It's About Childhood." *New York Times Book Review*, September 20, 1993, 13. Graeber asserts that Campbell's novel portrays the roots of racism as springing from dysfunctional families. Campbell also believes the problem is further exacerbated by the fact that African Americans blame their failings on the effects of white domination.

Langstaff, Peggy. "Getting to the Novel: How and Why Some Experienced Nonfiction Writers Made the Transition to Storytelling." *Publishers Weekly* 239 (November 16, 1992): 35-37. Campbell discusses her previous attempts at writing fiction and outlines her nonfiction publishing career.

Publishers Weekly. Review of *Your Blues Ain't Like Mine.* 23 (June 22, 1992): 44. Praises the novel for the varied details drawn from modern life that "add to the rich, textured background," as well as the "masterfully drawn and sympathetic characters that a less able hand might have rendered in stereotypes. . . ."

Time. Review of *Your Blues Ain't Like Mine.* 140 (November 9, 1992): 89. This brief review praises Campbell's first novel for its "clean, elegant prose" and its realistic portrayal of the crime of racism for "which everyone pays."

U.S. News and World Report. "Working Wives, Threatened Husbands." 102 (February 23, 1987): 46. Contains valuable information on Campbell's views concerning the dynamics of two-career marriages. Provides the reader with some understanding of the relationships of the characters in *Your Blues Ain't Like Mine.*

Victoria E. McLure

ZERO

Author: Ignácio de Loyola Brandão (1936-   )
Type of plot: Sociopolitical surrealism
Time of plot: The late 1960's
Locale: A large city in Latin America
First published: 1974 (English translation, 1983)

>   Principal characters:
>   JOSÉ GONÇALVES, the protagonist, a vagabond worker at odd jobs
>   turned assassin and subversive
>   ROSA, his wife
>   ATTILA, his friend and fellow subversive
>   GÊ, the terrorist leader

The Novel

   Zero was written in Brazil in the late 1960's, during the first years of the repressive military regime which took power in 1964. The setting of *Zero* as a "Latindian American country, tomorrow," stated on the introductory page, is a thin disguise for Loyola Brandão's contemporary Brazil. Certain dates, historical names, geographical references, and institutional acronyms link the novel to that country, although many of the events and the atmosphere could fit several other Latin American countries ruled by authoritarian military regimes. Finished in 1969, *Zero* was too controversial for Brazilian publishers in the early 1970's, despite the author's previous respected and successful publications, and was first published in Rome in Italian in 1974. The following year, during the beginning of the regime's political opening, it was published in Brazil to the acclaim of critics and a public thirsty for a literary treatment of the country's dark period, during which censorship was in effect.

   The salient characteristic of *Zero*, as a novel, is unconventionality. It is an extensive prose narrative containing a degree of character and plot development and thus may be deemed a novel. Its unconstrained language, its bizarre characters and episodes, and especially its chaotic structure, however, clearly set it apart from the norm. Yet this unconventionality is the critical element for the author's creation of a critical, surrealist portrait of the times in his homeland.

   Zero is a series of titled, disjointed narrative units, lists, drawings, and graphs, the majority of which sketchily relate major events in the characters' lives, but many of which serve to convey social, political, and philosophical commentary linked to the plot only as a backdrop to reinforce tone and atmosphere. The plot revolves around José Gonçalves's evolution from vagabond to subversive. At the outset of the work, the reader sees José doing the first of his odd—both diverse and strange—jobs, killing rats in a run-down film theater. Later, he writes slogans for Coca-Cola bottle caps and books acts for a national freak show that makes up an entire neighborhood. Finally, he carries out robberies and assassinations for Gê, the leader of the subversive "Commons." Other significant events in his life are his residence in an abandoned book warehouse, where he reads and gains political consciousness; his courtship of and marriage to Rosa, whose dubious background causes him anguish; his murder of individuals whom he believes are doing him wrong; and his arrest, torture, and subsequent escape.

Plot development is secondary to tone and atmosphere, and the reader is required to piece it together from frequent but disjointed and transitionless glimpses that are intercalated among other, unrelated but equally chaotic observations and commentaries made by the narrator. These latter elements include statistics on Latin American countries, mini-subplots on exploited individuals, a labeled drawing of a malnourished man, ludicrous Orwellian government pronouncements, plentiful ironic footnotes and "Free Associations," and even strings of nonsense syllables. Attention is focused naturalistically on torture, pain, sexual acts, deformities, and the like through detailed listings.

The chaotic nature of the novel's structure is underscored by the deliberate breaking of convention in punctuation and spelling, seen, for example, in the placement of commas between verbs and their objects and the phonetic rather than normative spelling of many words. The novel's emphasis on the base and the ugly is heightened by frequently coarse and brutal language almost devoid of any lyric quality.

The Characters

None of the characters is fully developed. Indeed, they all seem to be caricatures drawn by a literary expressionist. There are virtually no physical descriptions, only sketchy background information, and little sense of balance in them as real persons. They speak, act, and react in exaggerated, often implausible ways, as people appearing in dreams and nightmares. Many characters come on the scene, provide some significant insight into the work's meaning, then disappear for the rest of the novel.

The character of José Gonçalves, the protagonist, is drawn by his actions and words. The reader is told little of his background, there is no introspection, and what other characters say about him centers on his outward behavior. Even the third-person narrator, who is not omniscient, relates only what José does and says. Nevertheless, the reader can follow a basic evolution of the protagonist's character. José becomes aware of the depravity of his occupation as rat killer, gains political consciousness and a general awareness of the world around him through reading, marries, seeks a house and a better job, and begins an individual revolt through acts of robbery and murder. Although he eventually joins the Commons, the violence he commits in conjunction with this radical group essentially continues his personal revolt and is not motivated politically. Thus, he is largely a pathetic character who does not grow in his human dimension but, as a victim of his times and environment, ends up contributing to the general despair of society.

Rosa is the object of José's love, fear, and rage. Her role is more that of a foil for José than that of a character in her own right. His courtship of her makes him confront the scorn of others (who tell him that she is an immoral woman). With her, he vents his sexual energy and his incipient revolt and violence. For her, he seeks a general improvement in his life, during which he encounters inanity and frustration. Her death at the hands of government torturers seals his fate with that of the Commons. Rosa, though enigmatic, is loving and suffering, while José is violent and aggressive.

Attila, a nickname reflecting his violence when he is drunk, is the closest thing to a friend that José has. Besides drinking, he smokes marijuana and chases women. Although the reader does not see what leads him to join the Commons with José, his rowdy character allows him to fit well into their terrorist activities. He serves as a sounding board for José, allowing him to express some of his anger.

Gê is portrayed as a dedicated, cool-headed professional revolutionary along the lines of Che Guevara; their similarity is enhanced by the phonetic similarity of their first names. For him, everything has its role as seen from the perspective of Marxist dialectics, and he attempts to recruit José by appealing to his potential role. Since José is not ready to embrace this concept, Gê simply directs his rage and uses his bravery and skill with a gun as means to further the revolutionary end.

Various other characters populate the pages of *Zero* in brief portraits that reinforce more general themes and motifs. Carlos Lopes, for example, appears several times throughout the novel in a sort of story-within-the-story, to underscore the absurdity and inhumanity of the sociopolitical system. Seeking medical aid for his ill child at a public hospital, he is sent from window to window over some two years' time in a futile search for the proper functionary. Finally, with his dead, mummified child in his arms, he is arrested for not having updated a certain form. Toward the end of the novel, Carlos Lopes is linked to the larger plot as the reader sees him among Gê's men. Another character briefly portrayed is Crato, a man of so great a resolve that he withstands the most horrendous torture, including witnessing the torture and murder of his family. Such secondary characters generally serve as poignant examples of the injustice inherent in the sociopolitical order, the major theme of the novel.

Themes and Meanings

Zero's chaotic structure, brutal language, pathetic characterization, and bizarre plot all point up the major theme of the novel—that the society it depicts is chaotic, brutal, pathetic, and bizarre. The novel portrays the regime's baleful effects on that society in its devastation of the individual, whether through malnourishment, torture, constant fear, or violent death. The tragedy inherent in this sociopolitical order is underscored by the constant depiction of abnormal behavior and physical deformities, to the point, in fact, that they become the commonplace and the expected. An instance of biting irony comes when José recognizes that a healthy, well-adjusted, normal man who applies for a position in the freak show is indeed the greatest freak of all because of his very wholesomeness.

The specific targets of the author's criticism are the military rulers' moral hypocrisy, indiscriminate brutality, and paranoia, which subsequently effect the fabric of society, shaping it to the regime's mold. There is no philosophical commentary on the absurdity of the human condition in general or the alienation and dehumanization of people in modern society. The macabre, the absurd, and the grotesque in *Zero* are a clamor of protest against conditions in a specific place and time—conditions in which a few people are responsible for the suffering of many.

Critical Context

Zero is the best known of Loyola Brandão's works. It continues the themes and attitude of his previous novel, *Bebel que a Cidade Comeu* (1968), but evinces an evolution into a more audacious, experimental creation. Some subsequent works—the novel *Dentes ao sol: Ou, A destruiçao da catedral* (1976) and the stories of *Cadeiras proibidas* (1979), for example—also have certain parallels in theme and perspective but are much more conventional in structure, language, and development of characters and plot.

Zero represents a significant landmark in modern Brazilian prose fiction, with its bold structure, contumacious tone, and unrelenting indictment of the military regime. Numerous other Brazilian novels have rendered a critical portrayal of life under this repressive regime with similar themes, techniques, and tone, notably Ivan Angelo's *A festa* (1976), Carlos Heitor Cony's *Pessach: A travessia* (1967), and Roberto Drummond's *Sangue de Coca-Cola* (1983), but *Zero* stands out as the most innovative and powerful of the literary protests of those dark times.

Bibliography

Krabbenhoft, Kenneth. "Ignacio de Loyola Brandão and the Fiction of Cognitive Estrangement." *Luso-Braizilian Review* 24 (Summer, 1987): 35-45. A discussion of the theme of metamorphoses in Loyola Brandão's works.

Ronald M. Harmon

ZUCKERMAN BOUND

Author: Philip Roth (1933-   )
Type of plot: Comic realism
Time of plot: 1965-1976
Locale: Newark, the Berkshires, New York City, Miami Beach, Chicago, and Prague
First published: 1985: *The Ghost Writer*, 1979; *Zuckerman Unbound*, 1981; *The Anatomy Lesson*, 1983; "Epilogue: The Prague Orgy," 1985

Principal characters:

NATHAN ZUCKERMAN, the protagonist, a controversial Jewish American novelist and short-story writer

VICTOR (DOC) and

SELMA ZUCKERMAN, his parents

LEOPOLD WAPTER, a prominent Newark Jewish leader, judge, and severe critic of Nathan's early fiction

E. I. LONOFF, a reclusive older Jewish American writer whose work and life Nathan admired as a young man

HOPE LONOFF, his long-suffering wife of thirty-five years

AMY BELLETTE, a mysterious young refugee and survivor of the concentration camps whom Nathan meets at the Lonoffs'

ALVIN PEPLER, a Newarker who once achieved fame on a quiz show

CAESARA O'SHEA,

GLORIA GALANTER,

DIANA RUTHERFORD,

JENNY, and

JAGA, Nathan's mistresses

MILTON APPEL, a prominent Jewish intellectual who writes a scathing critique of Zuckerman's work

ZDENEK SISOVSKY, an exiled Prague writer whom Zuckerman meets in New York

OLGA SISOVSKY, Zdenek's estranged wife, whom Zuckerman goes to Prague to meet

GILBERT CARNOVSKY, Nathan's most infamous fictional creation

The Novels

The trilogy and epilogue gathered together in *Zuckerman Bound* trace twenty years in the literary and personal life of Nathan Zuckerman. His story begins in *The Ghost Writer*, narrated by Zuckerman in 1976, which recounts events of twenty years earlier. At odds with his father and pillars of his community such as Judge Leopold Wapter over the content of his first stories, which present unflattering portraits of Jewish characters, Nathan visits the isolated Berkshire home of E. I. Lonoff, "the most famous literary ascetic in America," to submit himself for candidacy as a spiritual son.

During the winter evening and morning he spends at Lonoff's, he gets the validation that he is seeking—Lonoff toasts "a wonderful new writer" and declares that Nathan has "the most compelling voice I've encountered in years." He also gets, however, a lesson he had not anticipated: about just how much the religion of art to which he has dedicated himself demands of its acolytes and of those close to them.

For if Nathan's dedication to his art has begun to alienate him from his loving family, Lonoff's single-minded dedication to his parables of "terminal restraint," to a life made up of "turning sentences around," has already cut him off from those nearest to him, especially his wife, Hope. While Nathan is visiting, her frustration and unhappiness explode, destroying his illusions that a writer's life will be a serene and ordered idyll.

The proximate cause of Hope's outburst and the means of escape from their isolation that both the older and the younger writer briefly imagine is a young woman named Amy Bellette. A refugee from Europe, a survivor of the camps with a shadowy past, she is a former student of Lonoff who has taken on the task of arranging his manuscripts. To Lonoff, she offers the possibility of starting over—a possibility finally as inconceivable to him as it would be to one of his characters, whose impulses are extinguished by "the ruling triumvirate of Sanity, Responsibility, and Self-Respect." To Nathan, who imagines that she is actually Anne Frank, spared from the Holocaust to become his wife, she is a way of silencing his critics by allowing him to demonstrate his Sanity, Responsibility, and Self-Respect. For both Lonoff and Zuckerman, however, Amy is finally only a fantasy of escape. Each is left to face the consequences of his vocation without her help.

In *Zuckerman Unbound*, set in 1969, those consequences multiply for Nathan with dizzying and hilarious effects. As the novel begins, he has recently published his fourth book, *Carnovsky*, a no-holds-barred account of growing up Jewish in Newark. Wilder than anything the serious young writer has written before, it quickly becomes a *succès de scandale* that disrupts his entire life. His youthful ambitions for artistic fame are fulfilled, but fame in contemporary America turns out to be a bit more than he bargained for.

His picture is on the cover of *Life* magazine; people stop him on the street to advise him about how to invest his money and to ask him about "his" sexual exploits; his mail is almost evenly divided between propositions and letters comparing him to Joseph Goebbels; a rock singer he has never met leaves the audience of *The Tonight Show* doubled over with laughter by describing her experience with his sexual proclivities; his name is linked in gossip columns with other women he has never met; a jet-setting film star he *has* met, Caesara O'Shea, leaves him for Fidel Castro; and when he turns on his television set, he finds a panel of psychiatrists analyzing his castration complex.

In Florida, his mother is being inundated with telephone calls from the press asking what "Mrs. Carnovsky" is really like, while, back in New York, Nathan is getting calls from a mysterious kidnapper with a social conscience who is demanding fifty thousand dollars for *not* kidnapping her. Also, a nonstop talker and whiner named Alvin

Pepler—who may or may not be the kidnapper manqué—keeps popping up to regale his "fellow Newarker" with tales of the Gentile plot which knocked him off of the quiz show *Smart Money* in the 1950's, and of the Broadway musical about his life that he is trying to get produced.

Nathan is not amused. At least one Nathan is not. His agent can tell him to relax and enjoy his brief moment of media stardom, but careful, responsible, respectable Nathan will not disappear after all these years so that impulsive, irresponsible, libidinous Nathan can let go. Especially since, while all of this is happening as a result of his having let loose in his fiction, all the ties that have bound, but also anchored, his life are also falling away. His third marriage, to a woman as serious and sensible as a part of him is, is on the rocks because he finds married life—like his earlier fiction—"stultifying." His father, whose life was totally dedicated to duty and responsibility, dies in a Miami Beach nursing home cursing him. The Jewish Newark he knew and wrote about is gone. On the novel's last page he is left unbound and unmoored, adrift.

The Anatomy Lesson takes place during the Watergate summer of 1973, four years after the success-debacle of *Carnovsky*. Nathan's mother has recently died, and her funeral has severed his last ties with his family and his brother, Henry. Following her funeral, he finds himself unable to write, flat on his back with crippling and unexplained pain in his neck and shoulders, suddenly going bald, and enraged by a devastating attack on his work by the prominent New York intellectual Milton Appel. The cause of his pain is unknown—it may be physical, it may be psychosomatic—but that does not make it any less real or debilitating. Freed of the constraints of family and wives, he finds himself immobilized. Living in New York, he is as alone as E. I. Lonoff ever was in the remote Berkshires. Unable to move, he is visited regularly by four women who minister to his medical and sexual needs. Jenny is a sensitive artist; Diana is a witty and worldly student; Gloria, his lawyer's wife, is a lusty and lascivious diversion; Jaga is a Polish émigré who works in the salon he visits to ease his pain (and his baldness).

In frustration and desperation with his pain and the dead end he has met as a writer—he "had lost his subject. His health, his hair, and subject. Just as well he couldn't find a posture for writing"—he concocts a scheme to start over. Inspired by alcohol and the painkilling Percodans he begins to swallow like jelly beans, he decides to give up writing altogether and go to medical school at the University of Chicago.

In the novel's final third, he completely loses control. Using Appel's name, he pretends to be the notorious publisher of the pornographic magazine *Lickety Split*. Spewing anger and obscenity, he lands in Chicago, harangues an old friend who is a doctor at the university's Billings Hospital, and manages to wind up in the hospital himself with his jaw broken and wired shut. Trying to escape his blocked career as a writer, he ends lying in bed with a pad and pencil his only means of communication.

In "Epilogue: The Prague Orgy," Zuckerman confronts the consequences of art in another culture: Eastern Europe. The time is 1976, and Nathan has abandoned his desperate quest for another life and another career. Through Zdenek Sisovsky, a Czech émigré writer (and his companion Eva Kalinova, a Czech émigré actress renowned in Prague for her portrayals of Anne Frank and Anton Chekhov's heroines), he is drawn out of his obsession with his own life long enough to begin to put that life into some perspective.

In his own country, Sisovsky explains, "I can at least be a Czech—but I cannot be a writer. While in the West, I can be a writer, but not a Czech." Like Zuckerman, he is both unbound and bereft of a subject. When Sisovsky describes the Yiddish stories that his Jewish father once wrote—"Not only a Jew, but like you, a Jew writing about Jews; like you, Semite-obsessed all his life"—and explains that his estranged wife, Olga, has the stories in Prague, Zuckerman finds himself off to Czechoslovakia on a secret mission of literary and cultural retrieval.

His Prague guide, Bolotka, invites him to visit the regular Tuesday night orgy hosted by the film director Klenek. ("You like orgies," he says, since *Carnovsky*'s reputation has clearly preceded Nathan, "you come with me. Since the Russians, the best orgies in Europe are in Czechoslovakia.") In fact, the orgy is rather tame. At Klenek's, though, Nathan does meet Olga, who offers to marry and return to the United States with him. Instead, he convinces her to hand over Sisovsky's father's stories. Shortly afterward he is picked up by the Prague secret police, hustled to the airport, and expelled from the country. The stories are confiscated by the authorities, and the guard who checks his passport utters the trilogy's last words. "Zuckerman the Zionist agent," he says to the writer whose career has been a painful struggle to escape the bonds of ethnic solidarity. "An honor to have entertained you here, sir. Now back to the little world around the corner."

The Characters

Nathan Zuckerman is clearly Philip Roth's alter ego, and the major events in Zuckerman's career—a Newark youth, study at the University of Chicago, early stories that elicited high praise from literary critics and outrage from Jewish leaders, several serious and stylistically restrained novels focused on Jamesian moral dilemmas, then a notorious and sexually explicit novel of growing up Jewish that made its author a public figure in 1969, and later an interest in Franz Kafka, a visit to Prague, and ties with "Writers from the Other Europe"—certainly reflect those in Roth's.

Yet autobiography is finally not the point. In Zuckerman, Roth found the perfect vehicle for exploring the conflicts that have plagued all of his characters since *Goodbye, Columbus* (1959). Those conflicts—between conformity and rebellion, ethnic solidarity and personal identity, public image and private desires, ethical and artistic ideals and mundane realities—underlie each part of the trilogy and determine its overall movement.

Nathan is as complex a character as Roth has ever created, and his complexity lies in both his emotional reaction to these conflicts and his being able to see, even sympathize with, opposing attitudes. Nathan's father, Doc Zuckerman, for example, is presented with an unfailing sympathy that is almost totally alien to the satiric spirit of much of Roth's early work. Even Nathan's most severe critics—Judge Wapter and

Milton Appel—are allowed to make their cases as best they can. His mother, Selma, is heartrending in her simplicity and love for the son whose principles she cannot understand.

The trilogy is full of "doubles," of characters strikingly similar to and yet significantly different from Nathan. Thus, the ways that Lonoff and Amy, Alvin Pepler, Milton Appel, and Zdenek Sisovsky speak for and against Nathan and his attitudes are fundamental to the book's method of characterization. For example, Amy-Anne's career as a writer-turned-public-icon in Nathan's fantasy mirrors many of the same conflicts about "what is good for the Jews" and the media's treatment of works of art with which Nathan also struggles. Alvin Pepler—a creation of comic genius, absolutely unforgettable—is Nathan's secret sharer, his own dark impulses rampant and incarnate. Sisovsky's "doubt" about his vocation and anger at his "critics" reflect Nathan's, as does his devotion to Kafka. Lonoff seems at first to be the embodiment of every young writer's ideal view of the artist. Even Lonoff, however, cannot escape the turbulence, the burdens of fame, the struggle both to live a life and to invent lives that Nathan is forced to confront during his own career.

The most unforgettable and audacious invention in *Zuckerman Bound* is Amy-Anne. To introduce Nathan's fantasy in a way that makes the reader accept it, to reinvent Anne Frank and yet not violate the outline of her life, to motivate Nathan's fantasy and then cause it to collapse—all of this exhibits a mastery of his materials and a willingness to take big risks by which Roth's readers cannot avoid being awed.

Roth's critics have been harsh in their comments about his characterization of women, observing that none of his female characters is as interesting or as fully realized as Nathan. This is partially true—although Amy-Anne, Hope Lonoff, Mrs. Zuckerman, and Jenny are certainly memorable and capable of arousing the reader's sympathy—but it is also largely irrelevant. Nathan—his obsessions, conflicts, consciousness—is the subject of *Zuckerman Bound*. To *him*, everyone else is less interesting than his relationship with them—and this is part of the point and part of his problem.

Themes and Meanings

From the beginning, Roth has been preoccupied with the useful and useless fictions people seem compelled to invent to get along. Sometimes seriously, sometimes hilariously, he has chronicled the wounds of the casualties strewn over the battlefield separating men's and women's actual and ideal selves—the battlefield where their fictions turn on them; where they are torn apart by the struggle between who they are, what they feel, and who they are *supposed* to be, what they are *supposed* to feel.

Beginning with *My Life as a Man* (1975), Roth has pursued his explorations of this struggle in the context of conflicts between life and art. In "Salad Days," the first part of *My Life as a Man*, he introduced the character of Nathan Zuckerman. There, Nathan was a pampered Jewish son and a precocious undergraduate English major with literary ambitions, whose story ended with a warning that "he would begin to pay . . . for the contradictions: the stinging tongue and the tender hide, the spiritual aspirations and the lewd desires, the softy boyish needs and the manly, magisterial ambitions." In "Courting Disaster (or Serious in the Fifties)," the second part of *My Life as a Man*, he was a University of Chicago graduate student and instructor so enamored of the challenging moral complexities of the Great Books, so caught up in his own contradictory impulses that he managed to trap himself into one of the most disastrous marriages in contemporary American fiction. In the final part of *My Life as a Man*, "My True Story," Roth introduced another alter ego, Peter Tarnopol, the "author" of the two Zuckerman stories. Through Tarnopol's true story—and the relationships between it and his "useful fictions"—Roth investigated the relationship between autobiography and fiction in a revealing and provocative new way.

In *The Professor of Desire* (1977), the emphasis shifts, but the relationship between the lives invented by writers (Chekhov, Kafka, Robert Musil) and the life the protagonist and title character is trying to live is at the heart of his struggles. In *A Philip Roth Reader* (1980), which Roth himself edited, this ongoing theme is summed up in the title for one group of his selections: "Literature Got Me into This and Literature Is Gonna Have to Get Me Out."

The problem is that in the lives of Roth's characters, literature invariably does the former and inevitably fails to do the latter. For the early and later versions of Nathan Zuckerman (as for Peter Tarnopol and David Kepesh, the protagonist of *The Professor of Desire*), the order and moral seriousness of art are as much temptation as vocation. Trying to live by fiction, each discovers that the world's disorder is not subject to the artist's control, that moral seriousness is easier to carry off in art than in life. Paradoxically, while their own lives and choices are shaped by books, Roth's protagonists—modernists all—reject the pleas of those who tell them that images in books matter, that what they write may have real consequences for real people, including themselves.

Roth has described the subject of *Zuckerman Bound* as "the moral consequences of the literary career of Nathan Zuckerman," or "the unintended consequences of art." The consequences vary—for Zuckerman, for his family and his community, for E. I. and Hope Lonoff, for Zdenek and Olga Sisovsky—but in *Zuckerman Bound*, there are consequences that theories of "art for art's sake" refuse to recognize. In this *Bildungsroman*, spanning twenty years, Nathan learns the hard way that this is true. This point is underlined by the fact that *The Ghost Writer* is narrated by Nathan in 1976—*after* he has returned from Prague.

Critical Context

Roth's style, his approach to his persistent themes, has developed during the course of his career, and during each phase of that development he has engaged himself with the works of other writers. The Jamesian realism of his first novel (*Letting Go*, 1962) and the Dreiserian/Flaubertian realism of his second (*When She Was Good*, 1967) were followed by black comic extravaganzas (*Portnoy's Complaint*, 1969), as close to Lenny Bruce as to Kafka, and then by a style (in *The Professor of Desire*) best described as Chekhovian. Less exuberant, less hysterical, more measured than that of his raucous comedies, this style has allowed the voices of Kepesh and Zuckerman to be, by turns, thoughtful and flippant, sympathetic and self-conscious, nostalgic and ironic, compassionate and satiric. Indeed, *Zuckerman Bound* is distinguished by a sense of the unexplainable mysteries of living and writing, a tenderness and a maturity that will come as a surprise to those who have only read his earlier work. His voice is now inimitable, able to shift from high comedy to deadly seriousness in the space of a comma. His control is such that he can remind his readers of Henry James, Kafka, Lenny Bruce, and Chekhov in the same work while remaining, without question, Philip Roth.

The Ghost Writer has been widely hailed as Roth's masterpiece. A sensitive, deeply moving, exquisitely crafted portrait of the artist as a young man, it deserves a prominent place on the ever-lengthening list of important contemporary American novels in which the writer's subject is a writer and his subjects. Like Saul Bellow's *Humboldt's Gift* (1975), it is a memoir that describes the impact of an older Jewish American writer's life and work on a younger writer. Like William Styron's *Sophie's Choice* (1979), it treats a young writer's relationships with his father, with his abandoned roots, with a young woman who escaped the Holocaust, and with the participants in a doomed love affair. Like Bernard Malamud's *Dubin's Lives* (1979), its underlying theme concerns the contradictions between a writer's dedication to the life of his art and his dedication to living itself.

Zuckerman Unbound is a hilarious tour de force, with a surprisingly touching subtext. *The Anatomy Lesson* is a book full of anger, excess, and rue. "Epilogue: The Prague Orgy" is a complex and many-layered coda.

Roth first visited Prague in the mid-1970's and shortly afterward began to edit a series of works issued by Penguin Books under the general title "Writers from the Other Europe." His comment that, for writers there, "nothing is allowed and everything matters" while, in the West, "everything is allowed and nothing matters" is the kernel from which *Zuckerman Bound* grew. In the process of growing, however, it changed, so that the trilogy and epilogue are an exploration and assertion of the various ways in which fiction *does* matter—both here and there.

Bibliography

Cooper, Alan. *Philip Roth and the Jews*. Albany: State University of New York Press, 1996. Cooper explores the spectrum of Roth's writing, including his early works, the "post-Portnoy seventies," and the Zuckerman novels. An excellent overall critical view.

Gentry, Marshall B. "Ventriloquists' Conversations: The Struggle for Gender Dialogue in E. L. Doctorow and Philip Roth." *Contemporary Literature* 34 (Fall, 1993): 512-537. Gentry contends that both Doctorow and Roth are different from other Jewish authors because of their incorporation of feminist thought into traditionally patriarchal Jewish literature. He notes that their reconciliation of feminism and Judaism could alienate them from both groups, but commends their attempt nonetheless.

Greenberg, Robert M. "Transgression in the Fiction of Philip Roth." *Twentieth Century Literature* 43 (Winter, 1997): 487-506. Greenberg argues that the theme of transgression pervades Roth's novels, and he demonstrates how this idea of infraction allows the author to penetrate places where he feels socially and psychologically excluded. An intriguing assessment of Roth's work.

Halio, Jay L. *Philip Roth Revisited.* New York: Twayne, 1992. Halio offers a brief biographical sketch of Roth, as well as in-depth discussions of his works. Includes a chapter entitled "Comic Bildungsroman: *Zuckerman Bound.*" Also includes helpful notes and a selected bibliography for further reading.

Halkin, Hillel. "How to Read Philip Roth." *Commentary* 97 (February, 1994): 43-48. Offering critical analyses of several of Roth's books, Halkin explores Roth's personal view of Jewishness, as well as other biographical elements in his works.

Podhoretz, Norman. "The Adventure of Philip Roth." *Commentary* 106 (October, 1998): 25-36. Podhoretz discusses the Jewish motifs in Roth's writing and compares Roth's work to that of other Jewish authors, including Saul Bellow and Herman Wouk. He also voices his disappointment concerning Roth's preoccupation with growing old as expressed in his later novels.

Bernard F. Rodgers, Jr.

MASTERPLOTS II

AMERICAN FICTION SERIES, REVISED EDITION

GEOGRAPHICAL AND ETHNIC INDEX

African American

TITLE INDEX

AUTHOR INDEX